2°   0°   2°   4°

Y

Biarritz
Aire
Orthez
Toulouse
R. Garrone
nterrabia
Pasajes
stian
Bayonne
St Jean de Luz
oza
Vic Bigorre
St. Pé
Tarbes
St Jean Pied de Port
Sorauren
Roncesvalles P
P y r e n e e s
Pamplona
NAVARRE
Sanguessa
Andorra
Figueras
Rosas
G. of Rosas
42°
Gerona
Tudela
Ebro
Monzon
Manresa
Hostalrich
Zaragoza
Lerida
Cervera
Barcelona
Calatayud
Maria
Mequinenza
Pia de Cabra
Molins de Rey
Belchite
Valls
Almonacid
Alcaniz
Tortosa
Tarragona
Cuenca
40°
B A L E A R I C   I S L A N D S
Minorca
Requena
Valencia
Morjaca
Cabera
Jucar
Iviza
Almanza
Denia
Villena
Yecla
Formentera
Castalla
S E A
Alicante
38°
Murcia
Cartagena

PENINSULAR
1808 - 1814

Scale

0   50   100 Miles

—— Principal Roads

36°

M E D I T E R R A N E A N

N A V A R R O

V A L E N C I A

C A T A L O N I A

E

viosa

ra

iciosa

URCIA

A

2°   Meridan 0° of Greenwich   2°   4°

WELLINGTON

By the same Author

THE DUKE OF WELLINGTON, 1819.
From a painting by James Ward R.A., in the author's possession.

WELLINGTON

BY

PHILIP GUEDALLA

"I have been much exposed to authors"
—WELLINGTON to MRS. NORTON

THE LITERARY GUILD

NEW YORK

1931

TO

JOHN FORTESCUE

GRATEFULLY

¶ *The authorities, published and unpublished, on which the text is founded are fully cited in the notes grouped at the end of the volume. References to these notes (of which more than 1,500 have been necessary) appear in the margin of the text; and it is hoped that this system provides the necessary aids to scholarship without defacing the narrative page with footnotes or interrupting sentences with small, imprisoned numerals.*

PREFACE

*H*OW *many English streets, squares, monuments, and licensed premises bear the name of Wellington? His title has become one of the commonplaces of urban, and even Imperial, topography. He has his thoroughfares and schools and clubs and institutions; obelisks and open spaces still take their names from him, though he has vanished from the bootmaker's. Yet his memory, in spite of all these verbal honorifics, seems a trifle faded. He cast so large a shadow once; all Europe was his province, and no public act was quite complete until the Duke approved. There was no other Duke; how could there be?*

But he survives to later memory as little more than the instrument of a single victory and the gruff hero of a dozen anecdotes; and one is left reflecting on the contraction of that vast achievement to so meagre a residue. It was inevitable, perhaps, that his Indian career should be forgotten, since silence is posterity's one repartee to Anglo-Indian reminiscences. But seven years of patient and brilliantly successful warfare in the Peninsula, by which the British expeditionary force was brought from a beach in Portugal to the recovery of Spain and a victorious invasion of Napoleonic France, are less easily mislaid. Yet such a steady march to victory was, perhaps a shade inimical to his chances of lasting popularity in England. For a kindly nation seems to prefer its heroes slightly unsuccessful; its mind dwells more readily upon a last stand or a forlorn hope than upon the unchivalrous details of a crushing victory; and if it is to be allowed to choose, its favourite event will always be after the pattern of Rorke's Drift, its chosen hero in the manner of Sir John Moore. Judged by these sentimental tests, Wellington's career in Spain was far too successful to be really appealing. A second factor intervened to wither his Peninsular laurels, since British tradition is predominantly maritime and loves to murmur, with Admiral Mahan, that "those far-distant, storm-beaten ships, upon which the Grand Army never looked, stood between it and the dominion of the world." It is profoundly flattering to an island race to view sea-power as the deus ex machina *of war; and the Blue Water view of history is so picturesque. Besides, it substitutes for adoration the sprightlier figure of Nelson who, though victorious, at least atoned for his success by falling in the hour of victory. But it is hardly just to those British soldiers whose efforts actually won the war, which sea-power alone was important to win.*

And Waterloo? That, surely, cannot have been forgotten. Hardly; though a century of French assertion, combined with a steadily increasing Napoleonic cult, seems to have imposed the odd belief that Waterloo was lost by the Emperor rather than won by Wellington. His years of peace slide still more easily towards oblivion, since a generation with peace-treaties of its own is scarcely impressed by authors of earlier peace-treaties; though it might well spare a glance for a system which effectually silenced the guns of Europe for half a century and for a soldier who inspired such universal trust that the whole problem of Reparations was left by common consent in his hands.

His subsequent career in politics has done more, perhaps, than any other influence to efface his memory, since it provoked the Whigs. By a peculiar division of labour British history, quite considerable parts of which have been made by Tories, has been very largely written by Whigs; and Whig historians are a little apt to dispose summarily of Tory reputations. Viewed by such eyes, the Duke became a stiff-necked conqueror trailing an unwelcome scabbard into civilian assemblies. It was even feared that his faith in democracy was imperfect, that he did not trust the people. Why should he? Half his life had been devoted to a war against the French Revolution; and it was hardly likely that he would find revolution any more congenial because it happened to be English. Crowds had no sanctity for him—he had seen far too many—and the purely arithmetical basis of democracy failed to impress the Duke. Shocked by this revelation, the Nineteenth Century tended to belittle his entire achievement. Perhaps the Twentieth may feel inclined to number it among his merits.

At any rate, his portrait richly deserves to hang in the great gallery of English prose. But it is not there yet, though it is nearly eighty years since the Duke died. Stevenson, who was once to paint it for a series of Andrew Lang's, fingered the brushes for a little while. Many hands have sketched his long career (and I am indebted to almost all of them); but when Waterloo is passed, they nearly always falter, and the story dies away in a desultory stream of anecdote. I have tried to follow its whole course; and when novelists devote a quarter of a million words to the records of persons who did nothing in particular, I make no apology for requiring three-quarters of that quantity to describe the Duke of Wellington. Indeed, his career might even entitle him to the full ration customary for the portrayal of a thoughtful bank-clerk or an introspective commercial traveller. But in this case brevity has a real value, since his reputation seems to lie buried under the immense cairn of printed matter which posterity has raised in his honour. His correspondence has been printed in thirty-four volumes; and those 20,000 pages are the foundation of this book. I have done my best to supplement them by exploring the vast literature of his age and by using a mass of unpublished MS. material. The richest treasury of documents is, of course, at Apsley House; and the generosity of the Duke of Wellington in giving me full access to the papers has been of inestimable value. For the rest, the magnitude of the undertaking has laid me under so many obligations for unpublished material, illustrations, and other assistance that I am forced to tabulate my acknowledgments.

Duke of Wellington, K.G.	*Apsley House Papers and portraits*
Earl Beauchamp, K.G.	*Walmer MSS.*
Earl Camden	*Camden Papers*
Earl of Longford	*Wellington-Pakenham letter*
Viscountess Gough	*Pakenham information*
Lord Gerald Wellesley	*Mornington-Fortescue letters*
Miss Lowry Cole	*Lowry Cole Papers*
F. M. Guedalla, Esq.	*Wellington-Flint correspondence*
C. Hamilton, Esq.	*Hamwood Papers*

ix

C. A. Oliver, Esq.	Wellesley-Gordon correspondence
Thomas U. Sadleir, Esq.	Irish researches and information
M. G. de la Villebiot	Angers information
Office of Arms	Mornington Declaration
Dublin Castle	

But though my thanks are tabulated, my gratitude is not.

One further source of information has been explored, since places are frequently as informing as documents. I have, therefore, so far as possible, studied the Duke's career on the spot. Whilst I make no pretence to supplement the military historians, numerous journeys to Spain and Portugal have familiarised me with the Peninsula; and I have made detailed studies of the ground at Salamanca, Talavera, Burgos, San Sebastian, and the lines of Torres Vedras. I have visited such points of minor interest as the Duke's school at Angers, and the scenes of his early life in Ireland. The kindness of the Duke of Wellington enabled me to conduct the greater part of my documentary researches in my subject's own library at Apsley House; and I am indebted to the Marchioness Douro for a sight of Stratfield Saye and to Earl Beauchamp for a thorough exploration of Walmer Castle. But I cannot conclude my thanks without particular acknowledgment of the sustained and various assistance which I have received from Lord Gerald Wellesley, who has made many of these expeditions possible, taken part in some of them, furnished unpublished documents, and given every aid to my undertaking.

The writing of this book, though it is founded upon much earlier reading and travel, was begun in 1928; and since that date it has extinguished all other interests (and almost all other occupations) for me. I feel bound to thank all who have borne with me during that time—and one dear person in particular.

P. G.

1931

CONTENTS

ILLUSTRATIONS

The Education of Arthur Wesley

La gloire des grands hommes se doit mesurer aux moyens qu'ils ont ens pour l'acquérir—La Rochefoucauld.

I

CASTES mark their children deeply; and as a caste, the English
gentry resident in Ireland were pronounced. Every conquest leaves
a caste behind it, since conquerors are always apt to perpetuate their
victory in superior social pretensions. Had not the Romans been the
noblemen of Europe? Even a Norman raid became an aristocracy in
England; and in Ireland the Anglo-Norman conquest left a similar
deposit. Such castes are frequently absorbed, assimilated by their subject
populations. But where race combines with religious differences and
recurrent insurrection to keep the two apart, the schism is absolute and
the conquerors remain an alien caste. Such castes, where they survive,
are aristocratic by necessity, since their *hauteur* is less a mannerism than
the sole condition of their survival. For without a sinful pride the conqueror will vanish, merged in his subject population—the Norman turned
Englishman, the Anglo-Irish a mere Irishman, and the Anglo-Indian
"gone native." But while their pride remains, the little garrisons live on.

Generations of secluded life amongst an alien and subject population
breeds aristocrats. For the perpetual proximity of inferiors is a rare school
of high demeanour. Anglo-Irish magnates knew themselves observed by
long, resentful rows of Irish eyes; and what conqueror could condescend
before such an audience? The silent watchers made and kept them
prouder than ever; and in the last half of the Eighteenth Century the
Anglo-Irish magnate was indisputably *grand seigneur*. The visitor from
England might stare at occasional crudities—at oxen roasted whole, at
fourteen meat dishes for dinner, at a host who sat before his claret half
the day and all night long, lord of "vast but unproductive" acres, dispensing in a mansion "spacious but dilapidated" hospitality that was
"lavish but inelegant." The Irish *ton*, perhaps, was sometimes a shade
barbaric. There was an awkward contrast between the Duke of Leinster's
guests at Carton and the little houses of Maynooth huddled at its gates,
while behind the big façade the house-party breakfasted to the sound of
French horns off chocolate and honey and an immense table of "hot

3

bread—cold bread—brown bread—white bread—green bread, and all coloured breads and cakes." A chasm yawned between the classes, as it yawned between Versailles and France. But safe on the hither side the gentry lived their lordly lives, drank claret, toasted the "glorious, pious, and immortal memory," ran races, and matched fighting-cocks. Their very differences wore an aristocratic colour, since they adored the point of honour; and Dublin duellists met behind Lucas's Coffee-house near the Castle with more than contemporary gusto. Even their rivalries were lordly. As their rents rode ever higher on the mounting tide of Irish population, they scattered their argosies (and mortgaged their remotest prospects) in the lordliest game of all. For they built as recklessly as kings. The trim Palladian façades rose gracefully in every Irish county; tall windows looked down innumerable avenues of trees towards the ornamental water; obelisks defined the prospect; and Grecian temples ornamented the demesne with hints of the antique. Outbuilding neighbours afforded even richer sport than horse-racing; and a light-hearted gentry built with an increasing fervour, since rents could never fall while tenants swarmed in every cabin. Besides, borrowing was always easy; and the cheerful landlords sat before their wine in the new glories of their mansions, an aristocracy indeed.

They bore themselves, besides, with the immense patrician dignity that comes from superposition on a foundation of slavery. For the native Irish, even in the last years of the Eighteenth Century, were not far removed from slavery. The lash, the penal laws, the casual assault arouse misgivings in the onlooker. Misgivings turn to suspicion, when an English visitor notes that "a landlord in Ireland can scarcely invent an order which a servant, labourer, or cotter dares to refuse to execute. . . . Disrespect, or anything tending towards sauciness, he may punish with his cane or his horse-whip with the most perfect security. . . . Knocking down is spoken of in the country in a way that makes an Englishman stare." Suspicion deepens, as the same eye observes the strings of little Irish cars along the winding Irish roads "whipped into a ditch by a gentleman's footman, to make way for his carriage"; the "spalpeen broker," shipping his gangs of barefooted mountaineers to work in English fields, confirms it. It met the observant eye of Arthur Young a few years later—"Speaking a language that is despised, professing a religion

4

that is abhorred, and being disarmed, the poor find themselves in many cases slaves even in the bosom of written liberty." And when a Lord-Lieutenant writes that "the poor people in Ireland are used worse than negroes by their lords and masters, and their deputies of deputies of deputies," the whole unpleasing truth appears.

For the nearest social parallel to rural Ireland was to be found three thousand miles away in the cotton-fields of Carolina. There, too, a little caste lived on its acres. The grace of Southern manners on the white-pillared porches of Colonial mansions matches the ease of Irish country-houses. There is the same profusion, the same improvidence against the same background of slavery. The same defects recur. Even the fighting-men and gamesters of the Irish countryside, who "kept miserable packs of half-starved hounds, wandered about from fair to fair and from race to race in laced coats, gambling, fighting, drinking, swearing, ravishing, and sporting, parading everywhere their contempt for honest labour," are reproduced in every unprepossessing detail on Mississippi levées. Ireland, it seems, had Southern wastrels as well as Southern charm. For who can fail to recognise the meaner types of Southern life in "the class of little country gentlemen, . . . bucks, your fellows with round hats edged with gold, who hunt in the day, get drunk in the evening, and fight the next morning"? Small wonder, then, that a mild critic finds the Irish upper classes "exposed to all the characteristic vices of slaveholders, for they formed a dominant caste, ruling over a population who were deprived of all civil rights and reduced to a condition of virtual slavery. They were separated from their tenants by privilege, by race, by religion, by the memory of inexpiable wrongs." The fires of religious persecution had burned low, since persecution connotes an enthusiastic faith; and enthusiasm was the last defect of an Irish Churchman in 1769. For a thoughtful Deist could hardly be expected to derive unlimited satisfaction from the spectacle of his brother-Deist at the stake. But though persecution had almost vanished, its legacy of social inequality remained. There were still serfs and, not less deeply caste-marked, "Protestant Bashaws." Slavery survived, and the vast dignity that marks slaveholders. For such a caste does not part lightly with the lordly faith that some are born to rule and some to serve. Elsewhere the same soil put out the stiff blossoms of Washington and Lee; and something, perhaps, of that unbending quality in war and statesmanship which grows in cotton-fields was latent in Ireland's Virginian gentry.

But though their aristocracy was real enough, the temptation (always strong) to view eighteenth-century life as a protracted costume play is nowhere stronger than in Ireland. Not that it was a genteel comedy of wigs and patches, devised by stage costumiers and laboriously played with carefully flirted handkerchiefs and dutifully taken snuff. The Dublin round—*ridotto*, dinner, dance, Italian opera, charity concert, Drawing-room—was natural enough. For one lived as other people lived in 1769, when all life in its more elegant forms had a faint air of *bal travesti*. But if the whole prevailing air was slightly unreal, still greater unreality hung on the air of Dublin, until it almost seemed a masquerade. Indeed, it was—a light-hearted masquerade where pleasant, slightly insignificant persons wore the impressive costumes of great officers of state. It was a little parody of England—Court, judges, bishops, Lords, and Commons—played out upon the stage of Dublin and watched with scared indifference by rows of Irish eyes. The stage was crowded; Lord Chancellors elbowed Masters of the Rolls; Privy Councillors nodded on every side to major-generals; bishops abounded; and there was a glorious profusion of Hereditary High Treasurers, Chief Barons, Remembrancers, and every known variety of public dignitary, with functions and without. The *rôles* were awe-inspiring; but the maskers often seem a shade inadequate under their dominoes. For lawyers, whose merits might reasonably have escaped detection in the Temple or Lincoln's Inn, appear in ermine on the Irish bench; and estimable clergymen, designed at best to fill a quiet canonry, inhabit vast episcopal palaces and preach to hushed cathedrals. It was the Irish masquerade, a delectable charade in which a little group of English families played at the government of Ireland upon a high and lighted stage in Dublin.

Dublin, in the spring weather of 1769, was never more Dublin. Somewhere beyond the hard, blue waters of St. George's Channel the Irish packets found a city where the ordered elegance of pagan ornament proclaimed the Eighteenth Century. For it was eighteenth-century indeed. Grilles, cornices, and porticoes attested it. Flambeaux announced the fact with iron tracery; door after door insisted blandly with a delicious fan-light and a pair of elegant pilasters; it echoed from painted walls where

6

the discreet festoons wandered from urn to urn; unnumbered chandeliers nodded assent with every gleaming prism; and where ceilings were an exquisite blend of stucco and mythology, marble deities reclined in bas-relief on innumerable mantelpieces. Murmuring (in heroic couplets) the last enchantment of the Eighteenth Century, Dublin sat decorously true to type beside its river. Other capitals might falter in their allegiance. In London the steady pulse of the century, shaken dangerously by the dis-ordered tramp of Mr. Wilkes' supporters, wavered a little; it throbbed faintlier now in Paris under an ageing king; and, ingenious Mr. Towns-hend aiding with a tax on tea, tempers rose in Boston to a most inelegant pitch. Perhaps the Eighteenth Century might not last for ever. Boston rioters and Middlesex electors almost seemed to suggest a doubt. But could it ever end in Dublin? Dimly conceivable elsewhere, the notion there became wholly unthinkable. Every doorway seemed to deny it; each modish column barred the way; and carved divinities looked down in bland denial, refused the extravagant surmise with every attribute held in their marble hands or poured from their cornucopiæ and, the wild thought dismissed, resumed their allegories. So Flora's altar smoked again with stony clouds of incense, Ceres renewed her sheaves, and Endymion his slumbers. Behind the porticoes of Dublin it would always be the Eighteenth Century. For the stamp of its century was unmistak-ably on Dublin.

And on its people, too. It was not easy to be born in Dublin, where every wall exhaled it, and escape the Eighteenth Century. Had not Mr. Walpole informed Pitt's sister Anne a few years since that "all the spirit or wit or poetry on which we subsist comes from Dublin"? At the Castle on spring nights in 1769 loyal ladies dropped their curtseys to Lord Townshend by Viceregal candlelight, while their lords said hard things about him in the Irish House of Commons with a watchful eye upon the pension list. Perhaps the face of politics was slightly un-prepossessing. Even Mr. Walpole had enquired a trifle acidly, "Pray, sir, how does virtue sell in Ireland now?" Placemen filled places, pensioners drew pensions, and in a dim perspective beyond Dublin landlords col-lected rent. Something, perhaps, was stirring on those shadowy hills where flitting figures burned outbuildings, houghed cattle, or cropped Protestant ears, as the Irish pipes wailed out *The Lad with the White*

7

Cockade. Rebellious Whiteboys were matched by Oakboys no less outrageous and even by Steelboys, while distracted soldiers shot impartially at either. But Dublin went on as usual. Ladies poured tea in Sackville Street; their lords fingered decanters; and Signora Cotilloni, fresh from her triumphs in "a neighbouring kingdom," begged leave of the *Dublin*   14 *Mercury* to acquaint the nobility and gentry of her arrival and of her intention to open a Dancing Academy, and even to perfect her female pupils "in all the necessary manœuvres of coquetry, to manage the eyes to advantage, to smile a man into hopes or frown him into uncertainty, to deny favours without offending, and grant them with grace," the whole concluding with the loyal (and not untimely) sentiment, *Honi soit qui mal y pense.*

That week Lord Mornington, lately removed from Grafton Street, was with his countess at their new town house. They were in treaty with Lord Antrim for the lease; but the house seemed to be theirs   15 already. Built in the latest mode, it stood in Merrion Street, and the two stately flambeaux were not unworthy to enlighten guests in search   16 of Mornington House. Their ceilings were a graceful medley. Urns, shells, and garlands graced the new dining-room, where convivial Irish gentlemen might finger convivial Irish glass, while the ceiling in the drawing-room was a more womanish affair of birds and flower-baskets. But these new glories failed to engage Lady Mornington, since she lay upstairs in the big bedroom at the back. It looked across a little garden to the open space of Merrion Square. A harassed doctor called; the apothecary from Dawson Street brought round a soothing draught; and then a child—her sixth—was born on May Day, 1769. They called him   17 Arthur, and the Dublin round was undisturbed. Fine gentlemen fought duels; coaches went up and down the street; ladies stepped out of chairs; wits rhymed; and the long tide crept slowly round the bay from Dalkey to the hill of Howth.

II

THE happy father was an earl. He was, besides, Professor of Music at Trinity College, Dublin. For he was an earl of parts. Earldom itself, indeed, was something of a novelty, since it was barely nine years old. Lord Mornington was a Wesley of Dangan, son of the first Lord Mornington who, born a Colley of Castle Carbury, had inherited both name and fortune from his cousin, Garrett Wesley, whose mother had been a Colley. The name of Wesley accompanied the money; and the same generous impulse had once suggested to the wealthier Wesleys a frustrated interest in Charles Wesley, then passing through Oxford on the long road to Methodism. The Colleys, emerging from the English Midlands in the later Middle Ages, had retained their English purity through three centuries of life in Ireland. No single Irish name adorns their pedigree; and when Richard Colley, as his cousin's heir, assumed in 1728 the no less English name of Wesley, they were still Anglo-Irish squires.

The Wesley fortune eased affairs. There was an ampler air; the family was moved to the big house at Dangan, and its new master entered the Irish House of Commons for the adjacent and well-disciplined borough of Trim. He planned improvements in the grounds, planted considerably, and dwelt upon the pleasing theme of ornamental water. There were to be canals that ships might ride on, lakes with islands in them, and a sufficiency of temples. It was an easy, cheerful home where everyone assembled in the hall for breakfast, shuttlecock, a little dancing, draughts, and family prayers, or strolled about the grounds and visited the temples. Apollo, Neptune, and Diana each received due honour in their shrines, and the company paraded gravely, bearing white staffs inscribed with their "Parnassus names" and complaining slightly that it made them look "like the sheriff's men at the assizes." For hospitality at Dangan extended even to the supply of classical allusions, and lady visitors were gratified by the *rôles* allotted them in Mr. Wesley's mythological charades. A delighted guest informed her correspondent that she was "nothing less

9

than Madam Venus," whilst one belle united in her lovely person all   3
three Graces, and their host was a trifle apt to nominate three rival
goddesses and to reserve for the master of the house the arch *rôle* of
Paris. He had an organ in the hall, and there was always a good deal
of music. They often breakfasted to the harpsichord, to say nothing of
a simultaneous game of shuttlecock. For bewildered guests found the
Wesleys equal to the contrasted charms of drinking chocolate, the battledore, and counterpoint in the big hall at Dangan, all at once and without apparent interference with the enjoyment of either. Their picnics were
invariably to music. Even on a little run from Dublin they hesitated to
rely upon the unaided powers of "cold fowl, lamb, pigeon pye, Dutch   4
beef, tongue, cockells, sallad, much variety of liquors, and the finest
syllabub that ever was tasted." But the Muses were invoked, a lady
placed at the harpsichord jangled a little, and afterwards Mr. Wesley's
violin kept time to his daughters' dancing. For, as a courtly ear observed,
he "played well (for a gentleman) on the violin." Sometimes, indeed,   5
they essayed the grander pleasures of a water-concert on the canal at   6
Dangan where, their flag hoisted on "a very pretty boat," they rowed
harmoniously between the listening fields of Meath.

So, music and the classics aiding, the years passed pleasantly. An heir
appeared; Mr. Wesley, presently ennobled as Lord Mornington, passed
to the Irish House of Lords; the big house was burnt and sumptuously   7
rebuilt. Mythology reigned in the grounds; the temples multiplied, and
seats for exhausted worshippers graced every alley; obelisks abounded;
and each sacred grove displayed the gracious gleam of statuary. Presently
a visiting godmother found a small Garrett Wesley, whose one desire
was to celebrate her arrival with an artillery salute. For he was governor
of a tiny fort, as well as lord high admiral of a considerable fleet that
rode on the canal, comprising the yawl *Fanny* and the barge *Pretty Betty*,   8
the whole commanded by the flagship *Caroline*, a model of the King's
yacht, carrying a battery of guns and a complement of two, destined
originally for presentation to a royal duke and acquired by some happy
accident for Dangan. But when the honour of a salvo was declined
politely, his instinct for military courtesies was satisfied by hoisting all
his flags at once.

The boy was musical. Indeed, one feels that unless he had been, life   8 at Dangan with an organ in the hall and the harpsichord at breakfast would have been unbearable. But while the first Lord Mornington played well (for a gentleman), his heir stood in no need of such genteel allowances. For he approached proficiency of a more plebeian order. In fine, he was a prodigy. Almost from birth the infant marvel intimated his enjoyment of his father's performances by beating time; and as the air changed pace, awed onlookers saw the tiny hands alter their beat. Nor did his growth belie the promise of these talented gesticulations. The dawn of taste even preceded speech. For when a guest essayed to take the violin from his father, the infant interposed; and the transfer could only be effected while the small, indignant hands were held. But the visitor proving to be no less than the celebrated Dubourg, the fastidious infant, having once heard that virtuoso, was with difficulty persuaded to permit the noble amateur to resume his instrument. Indeed, when Dubourg was in the house, the child, with rare (if scarcely pious) discernment, would never let his father play. At nine he scraped a bow himself, rendering *Christ Church Bells* and *Sing one, two, three, come follow me,* and shortly afterwards played second violin in Corelli's Sonatas, an experience to which connoisseurs attributed that lifelong steadiness in time which never, it was said, deserted him. Then, pricked by the emulation which stirs musicians to their greatest efforts, he turned composer. For a local clergyman, having won considerable applause with a country dance of his own composition, Master Wesley responded with a minuet marred by a slight excess of fifths, and shortly afterwards achieved a duet for French horns and an *Andante.* His gifts survived the discouragements incidental to membership of a large and cheerful family, since his sisters drove him continually from the harpsichord in a sisterly opinion that he spoiled the instrument. But he played by stealth; and when an organ was installed in the chapel at Dangan, he startled the family by playing an impromtu fugue at the organ-maker's. His studies progressed; and though he lacked formal instruction, compositions flowed from his pen with such happy consequences that when he consulted Rosengrave and Geminiani, those masters modestly replied that they could not be of the least service to one who had already mastered the science.

The gentle youth grew up; and his godmother found him at thirteen

"a most extraordinary boy," almost unnaturally good at lessons and play-   7
ing the violin at sight. His varied accomplishments extended to ship-
building and fortification as well as music; and their diversity was
almost equal to her own somewhat injudiciously assorted passions for
conchology, gossip, fossils, and every form of petrifaction. For she was
no less than Mrs. Delany. At twenty-two he stepped sedately into the
family borough, and uneventfully represented Trim in the Irish House of
Commons. In the next year his father died, and he succeeded to the title.
The exacting dowager found him a trifle lacking in "the punctilios of
good breeding." Perhaps a nobleman required a thought more polish   9
than the organ and Trinity College, Dublin, had power to impart; and
when he chose a wife, her disapproval grew more pointed. His first choice
was admirable. Lady Louisa Lenox was a duke's daughter; and all was   10
smiles, until Mr. Conolly, of Castletown, offered his ampler means. The
rival, as a loyal godmother confessed, had "double his fortune (and
perhaps about half his merit)." But even dukes are human; and Lord
Mornington was blandly informed that "the young lady had an insurmountable dislike to him." The wounded lover reeled; for the ducal
alliance was not without its savour. But his wounds were promptly
assuaged by Miss Hill, of Belvoir. Her father, though he had once
kept a bank in Dublin, was younger brother to a viscount. Perhaps
his manners were a shade excessive, since he was always apt to give   11
a slightly unconvincing rendering of the fine gentleman. But, manners
apart, he was agreeable, "with a *little pepper* in his composition," which   12
might enliven the mild Wesley stock. The bride was turned sixteen, a
fine young woman in Mrs. Delany's estimation, although "rather a little
clumsy, but with fine complexion, teeth, and nails, with a great deal
of modesty and good-humour." These charms prevailing, the young
Lord Mornington paid his addresses. Mr. Hill was gallantly informed   13
that the eager bridegroom asked no fortune, was even prepared to
make a settlement himself; if the bride had any fortune, he chivalrously
"desired it might be laid out in jewels for her." So all was smiles again.
The clothes were bought; the settlements were drawing up; and Lord
Mornington was seen at the play in Dublin, looking a little solemn.

They were a happy pair, though his exacting godmother still had
her moments of uncertainty as to how far her qualities would remedy

14 his defects. He was "a very good young man on the whole," if slightly lacking in punctilio; but Anne Mornington herself lacked finish, although she made shell flowers. (Yet even then she seemed wanting in distinction; for when she furnished Mrs. Delany with a shell or so for her endless decorations, they were nothing rare.) Unclouded by these mysterious defects, their life opened happily enough. They lived at Dangan or in Grafton Street. An heir was born in Dublin, and a grate-

15 ful press recorded "the great joy of that noble family." King George II died; and the new reign brought Mornington a step in the Irish peerage. A pleasing fancy traces his earldom to the new sovereign's interest in music; but it had a likelier connection with the exigencies of Irish government, since the fountain of honour played steadily upon obliging Dublin legislators, and the next dozen years enriched the Irish nobility with thirty-three barons, sixteen viscounts, and twenty-four earls.

The new Earl of Mornington had his own interests. For the Muses followed him to Dublin, where he initiated a Musical Academy and supported burlesque productions in opposition to the Italian burletta of a rival theatre. It was an age of musical refinement, when Irishmen

16 proudly recorded that "the god of music had taken a large stride from

17 the Continent over England to this island . . . and it has been observed that Corelli is a name in more mouths than many of our Lord-Lieutenants." Respectful instrumentalists played Handel to listening cathedrals; and when Lord Mornington essayed a charity concert, an orchestra of noblemen and gentlemen obeyed his *bâton*. A Lord-Lieutenant's daughter sang; there was a peer among the flutes; a noble clergyman bowed diligently above his 'cello. The Italian taste prevailed; and one vocalist recalled to a disgusted ear Mingotti's "trills and squalls." But these ardours did not check Mornington's melodious pen, which ran mostly to Church music, with strong predilection for full harmony and the minor third, but had its lighter moments. For he could even stoop to

18 glees, and grateful glee-singers rendering *Here in cool grot* and *Come, fairest nymph* acknowledged a noble author. *'Twas you, Sir*, was his work as well, to say nothing of *By greenwood tree* and *Gently hear me, charming maid*. Small wonder, then, that Trinity College conferred a Doctorate of Music and even advanced the earl to be professor. For music had quite

vanquished his earlier leanings towards naval architecture and the principles of Vauban.

Meanwhile his family increased. They had named the heir Richard
after the first Lord Mornington; and the happy infant bore the title of
Viscount Wellesley, a prouder, mediæval form of Wesley. The second
was called Arthur after her father; but he did not survive, and the first
Arthur Wesley died in childhood. Then came a third son, named William, followed by a short-lived Francis, and a daughter, whom they
christened Anne after Lady Mornington. The sixth child, born at the
new house in Merrion Street, was a boy. They called him Arthur, too.
So he got her father's name and perhaps (who knows?) something of
her father's pepper.

III

LIFE opened for the child in Dublin; and as they brought him down the big staircase lit by its one tall, pillared window for his first outing in Merrion Street, the bland, unhurried days followed each other. Not that the times were bland. It was a wild decade, that opened (in Mr. Walpole's pained enumeration) with "no Government, no police, London and Middlesex distracted, the Colonies in rebellion, Ireland ready to be so, and France arrogant, and on the point of being hostile." Crowds had an ugly tendency to roar *God save great Wilkes our king*, and public men were in a flutter—"Lord Bute accused of all and dying in a panic; George Grenville wanting to make rage desperate; Lord Rockingham, the Duke of Portland, and the Cavendishes thinking we have no enemies but Lord Bute and Dyson, and that four mutes and an epigram can set everything to rights; the Duke of Grafton like an apprentice, thinking the world should be postponed to a whore and a horse-race; and the Bedfords not caring what disgraces we undergo, while each of them has £3,000 a year and three thousand bottles of claret and champagne." That summer— Arthur Wesley's first—London was alarmed by a terrific *revenant*. For at St. James's men heard the blind tapping of a familiar crutch across the palace floor, looked nervously behind them, and saw the tormented eyes under the peak of a great wig which were all that remained of Chatham. The old man had come to Court again, "himself" (as Mr. Walpole tittered "*in propriâ personâ*, and not in a strait-waistcoat"; and his sovereign's eyes protruded more than ever, as that imperial nose descended with tremendous deference to meet those ailing knees. Overseas the angry quaver of Mr. Samuel Adams's voice hung on the air of Boston; lion and unicorn still ramped cosily upon the State House; but who could say how long they would remain with an angry voice insisting that taxation was slavery, that Rome was never better than when it had no king, that thirty thousand men with bayonets and knapsacks would infallibly spring from the soil of Massachusetts. It was a flurried age, when Mr. Walpole feared the worst and England lived uneasily under the mosaic

15

ministry of Burke's inimitable apologue; and in the wings Lord North was waiting for his turn.

But these discontents scarcely reached Mornington House. Burke wrote a pamphlet; and Lord Mornington composed a glee. The angry *Junius* strained the limits of invective; and that gentle nobleman made a mild addition to the English hymnal. Mobs roared; and he was seen, a little puffy now, bending a dark, shaven chin above deft fingers at the key-board. As America flamed into civil war, his peaceful *bâton* waved imperturbably above the busy violins of Dublin gentlemen at a charity concert. His calm was perfect—almost, it would seem, too perfect for his countess, since Mr. Walpole breathed to Lady Ossory a wicked "history of Lady Mornington," asking with finished malice "where should bawds and bishops pay court but to youthful hypocrisy! Could her Ladyship apprehend a cold reception where Lord Pembroke is a Lord of the Bedchamber?" Once, indeed, his calm was interrupted, when a Dublin footpad named Murphy stopped his sedan-chair, let off a pistol, and removed his   3 lordship's gold watch with all his money. But the rogue was apprehended and left to dangle in a halter on the mound at the corner of St. Stephen's Green.

Sometimes they breathed the calmer air of Dangan; and from the big windows of his country home the small Arthur Wesley saw Meath roll-   4 ing gently into the distance. They sent him to the little school at Trim just down the road, where his brother Wellesley had displayed his early promise. That promise was, indeed, their pride. For Richard, their eldest, was exceptionally gifted; the other children lived in awe, and a loyal family prepared to applaud the rise of Richard Wellesley. He rose, whilst Arthur played at home with William and Anne, to Harrow. But Harrow failed to hold the aspiring youth for more than eighteen months, since a school riot, occasioned by the appointment of an Etonian headmaster, claimed him. Marked by these prejudices as a born Etonian, he was removed and sent to Eton. His faculties reviving in that nobler air, he became a prodigious Latinist and a considerable Grecian. They were all in England now; for the family (increased by the addition of a small Gerald, a still smaller Henry, and a tiny Mary Elizabeth) had let the Dublin house and moved to Knightsbridge. Lord Mornington was heard   5 at the harpsichord one night at Lady Stamford's, where a distinguished amateur played first violin and a lady vocalist rendered *Dové sei* so sweetly that one grateful member of her audience "slept better than for many nights before."

Transplanted from his native island, the small Arthur Wesley studied the rudiments at Brown's seminary (later dignified as Oxford House Academy) in King's Road, Chelsea; and the splendid Richard passed on to Christ Church. That was the year that British armies laboured heavily through Carolina, while the mature intelligence of Lord George Germaine was busy organising defeat at the War Office. King George's guns thudded without conspicuous success in almost every hemisphere. The fires of victory burned low, and every tent was full of disappointed paladins. Gage was at home forgetting Bunker's Hill; Burgoyne was back in Hertford Street explaining Saratoga; and Howe was polishing his *Narrative*. Even the fleet, at war with France and Spain and heavily outnumbered, rode insecurely; and for a summer week of madness the mob ran wild for "No Popery" and Lord George Gordon, while the dull glare of burning houses glowed on the London sky. Small wonder that the harassed North begged to resign; but his inexorable sovereign pointed implacably to duty and the unique (though sadly underrated) perfection of the British constitution.

Like his afflicted country, Lord Mornington was not without his troubles. For the subsequent finances of infant prodigies are often far from cheering. His married life had opened with the rich prospect of eight or ten thousand pounds a year. But twenty years devoted to the Muses (at what cost the Muses only knew) had darkened the financial prospect. Few orchestras enrich their patrons; Musical Academies are rarely remunerative; and his man of affairs in Dublin surveyed a mournful landscape. For his later airs were pitched, like so many of his youthful compositions, in a minor key. Their migration to London, though hardly well-conceived as a measure of economy, had been in the nature of a retreat. They were rather stinted now, "not able to appear in any degree as we ought," though he still kept his coach. But lodgings in Knightsbridge were a sad decline for the noble *maestro*; and at the prospect of a continued effort to live on £1,800 a year Lord Mornington grew positively rebellious. There was so much to be provided—Richard's allowance, and the six younger children's education, to say nothing of the costly array of masters requisite if Anne's accomplishments were to be perfected with due elegance. One estate was already deeply mortgaged; but his dreams in Knightsbridge were haunted by an unpleasant sum of £16,000 that had to be raised somehow. Richard, of course, might join with him to raise it. But would he? After all, that eminent young man would shortly come of age; and he might not consent. Then, was it altogether wise to remove his property from his own power? For he had dismal recollections of too trusting parents sadly ill-treated by their unnatural offspring. It was a depressing problem, for which the hopeful earl found a solution in an ingenious scheme for raising £3,000 a year, rising in a yet more hopeful postscript to the cheering theme of lottery tickets—"If you will send me ten numbers I shall take two and give each of my Children and my Lady one, but don't let these numbers run all in order, but different thousands if possible." Such expedients are not unfamiliar in the after-lives of patrons of the arts.

Nor was the brilliant Richard, trailing a nobleman's gold tassel from his cap at Christ Church, untouched by these melancholy concerns. His allowance was a family problem, since their touching faith persisted that he was "likely to make a figure in the world from his great abilities," and such prospects plainly called for at least four hundred pounds a year. But graver themes engaged him in the very moment of his triumph as Chancellor's prizeman for 1780 with a Latin ode on Captain Cook. His father was unwell, and a prudent counsellor in Dublin reviewed the unpleasing prospect. There was the mortgage, and the debts, and the eternal £16,000 that had to be raised somehow. If the earl recovered, he would really have to live at Dangan. If not, his heir must sell the Dublin house and travel. His adviser, having lived abroad himself and been twice to Italy, grew almost eloquent on travel. The sapient Richard was, he felt, unlikely to indulge in "any of the fashionable vices and follies wch ruin so many young Men," but touched with a nobler aspiration "to bring home a knowledge of the different Constitutions & Policy of the several States he visits," a sober programme, with the additional advantage of being vastly cheaper. For his adviser added with justice that "the flowers of travelling may be gathered at a moderate expense, they ornament Character. The weeds are costly, they poison the mind & are a canker in the future." In fine, when he succeeded, the young gentleman would

be well advised to economise abroad. His choice came all too soon. For
Lord Mornington died in May, 1781, and the Madrigal Society lost their
most zealous member. Music apart, he had always been a shade inadequate: Mrs. Delany had foreseen as much. And if she had foreseen his
sons, what else could she expect? For fame reserves no niche for the
father of the Gracchi.

So Richard became an earl at twenty, and Arthur at twelve had lost
his father. They buried him with seemly state, and more than eighty
pounds of Richard's inheritance vanished in the pious outlay—fourteen
mutes with black gloves and truncheons; cloaks and crape hat-bands for
the little party of eight mourners; and black gloves for the Knightsbridge
landlady, to say nothing of a stupendous canopy (the undertaker's pride),
nodding with sable plumes, and hired for the sad occasion. Two coaches
followed him; and for once a Wesley outing lacked its music. Something
of him, perhaps, lived on in Arthur's violin. For the small boy played;
and if he remembered anything of his father, it was the pleasant, slightly
ineffectual figure conjured up for him three-quarters of a century later by
the Muse of *Jeames de la Pluche:*

> His father praps he sees,
>   Most musicle of Lords,
> A-playing madriggles and glees
>   Upon the Arpsicords.

IV

T**H E** little family bore their bereavement. Now there were only eight of them—Lady Mornington, the fine young woman of Mrs. Delany's distant recollection, a dowager at thirty-nine; the incomparable Richard; William, just turned eighteen; and Arthur, a boy of twelve, with two small brothers and a pair of sisters. The young earl came down from Oxford and assumed his mournful post as head of the family. Mournful in more ways than one, since family finance in 1781 was uninviting. A thoughtful cousin had, it is true, reduced their burdens by leaving an estate in Queen's County to William (together with the name of Pole). But something must be done for his mother, to say nothing of five children all waiting for expensive educations and his own career. Besides, there were the debts. It was all highly disagreeable for a rising man. He came of age in June, and the next month he was in Dublin raising mortgages on the Meath lands. But the further programme of an inexpensive Continental tour failed to attract him, since foreign spas afford few opportunities for statesmanship, and Richard was resolved to be a statesman. Taking his seat at the long table of the Irish House of Lords, he quickly shewed that mild temper of rebelliousness which is the surest path to office. But the family were not sacrificed to this brilliant opening. For that very year two of his brothers went to Eton.

The autumn mists of 1781 crept up from a Virginian river, and the British guns were flagging behind the crumbling works of Yorktown, when Arthur Wesley went to boarding-school. The trap closed on Cornwallis three thousand miles away, as the two small brothers stared round at Eton. For there were two of them. He took Gerald with him; and this pair of Daniels (though one of them was only nine) kept one another in countenance among the lions of their new abode. Lions, indeed, abounded. For Eton, in the spasmodic reign of Jonathan Davies, was a marked advance upon Brown's academy at Chelsea. Numbers alone were terrifying, since three hundred boys were quite enough to alarm two newcomers from Knightsbridge. Had not the formidable Chatham confessed

20

that "he scarce observed a boy who was not cowed for life at Eton; that a public school might suit a boy of turbulent forward disposition, but would not do where there was any gentleness"? But, turbulent or not, the two small Wesleys survived this stern initiation. Lower boys were scarcely disturbed by their vociferous headmaster. That slightly indecorous figure was almost as remote as royalty itself, which was always riding past the Long Walk with empty, staring eyes, or buttonholing stray promenaders on the terrace with his "Well, well, my boy, when were you last flogged, eh, eh?" or, more searchingly, "What's your name? who's your tutor? who's your dame?" concluding the invariable reassurance of, "*Very* good tutor, *very* good dame" from royal lips. The two small brothers were largely untroubled by these high matters. But the long ritual of lessons, "absence," chapels without number, and still more lessons, all to be performed under three hundred pairs of watching eyes, was quite sufficiently alarming.

3   They boarded at Naylor's, played in the muddy garden of the Manor House, and shared rooms with strangers. Decorum did not always reign, since Arthur fought a battle—his very first—with a schoolfellow named Smith, provoked by being stoned while bathing, for whom fate reserved the still more mournful destiny of being brother to a wit (even a thrashing from Arthur Wesley may well have been more palatable than a life-long course of Sydney's brightest sayings); and there were schoolboy jokes about the maids, who slept in a room just off the kitchen, termed,

4   with exaggerated courtesy that stayed in Arthur's memory for forty years, the "Virgins' bower." Far more sedate was their scholastic progress. Not theirs the lofty destinies of Richard, whose declamations had drawn tears from royal eyes and compliments from Garrick; no statesmen, lured by their promise, drove down from London to enlist their gifts. For they were not, were very far from being their unnaturally gifted school-fellow George Canning; and no Mr. Fox stopped at their door. Early promise was the last thing about them. Breasting the slope to-

5   gether, they had advanced within the year to "Upper Greek," where they toyed with Ovid, Terence, and the Vulgate. By the next Easter they were both deep in the recesses of the Fourth Form, sustained upon a sober diet in which, though Ovid still predominated, there were nutritious

6   extras in the way of Cæsar, Æsop, and Greek Testament. It was de-

pressing to observe how close his younger brother trod to Arthur's heels; for if Wesley *ma.* sat fifty-third out of seventy-nine, Wesley *mi.* came fifty-fourth, the hounds of spring keeping assiduous company with winter's traces. The fact was not without its consequence for Wesley *ma.*, since he was shortly afterwards withdrawn from Eton. School bills were heavy, and Richard was moving up into the costlier arena of British politics. Besides, there was a third brother now in the abysses of the Lower Remove; and with Wesley *minimus* to pay for, the ant-like pace at which Wesley *ma.* scaled Parnassus scarcely rewarded outlay. So early in 1784 his brief rearguard action with the classics ended.

Its effects remain slightly mysterious. For the classical attainments, with which Eton equipped her sons for public life, were not for him. He once prescribed his rules of public speaking—"One is, I never speak about what I know nothing, and the other, I never quote Latin"—a wise   7 abstention, since his quantities were always uncertain. Did not the nation's hero, in the full robes of Oxford Chancellor, once alarm the Sheldonian Theatre with a *Jacobus* whose second syllable was short, hastily atoned for by a *Carolus* whose second (and still more fatal) syllable was long? Yet, however impervious to Ovid, no Etonian could possibly escape a sense of the indisputable truths of revealed religion, since these were publicly rehearsed with impressive and even wearisome regularity. What else he learned is more obscure. Scarcely, it seems, a genius for friendship. Nor was he formed upon the playing-fields. Indeed, the playing-fields were hardly formed themselves. Cricket and fives were practised; but the remaining catalogue of Eton games varies between the infantile and   8 the purely occult. It is not easy to believe that hoops and hop-scotch developed valuable qualities; few statesmen owe their eminence to early marbles; nor do the martial virtues thrive upon a simple diet of peg-top and battledore. The civic lessons of Bally Cally, Conquering lobs, and Hunt the dark lanthorn must remain enigmatic; but the heartening presence of Puss-in-the-corner may be felt to indicate that the stern reign of pure athletics was still far distant. Nor was Arthur's own recollection less unheroic. For revisiting the place in later years, he stared into Naylor's (then Ragueneau's) garden, and enquired affectionately for a broad,   4 black ditch he used to leap over, adding that in his own belief he owed his spirit of enterprise to the tricks he used to play there. The tribute may be found unsatisfying by athletic purists and a shade disappointing even to Etonians, since their playing-fields appear only in the attenuated form of a ditch in a dame's garden. But, such as it was, he paid it.

The next instalment of his education took him abroad. For, taste coinciding with finance, his mother chose to travel; and Arthur travelled with her. Not that they travelled far. For their brief journey ended in a town with which he was to have a fuller acquaintance, since they lay at Brussels. The cheerful, slightly equivocal little capital of the Austrian Netherlands lived uneventful days in 1784, only slightly complicated by the unlikely spectacle of a reforming Kaiser. For the solemn Joseph II, who ranked among the best-travelled men in Europe (since he had visited almost all his own dominions), suffered from the fatal illusion that he was a man of his times and—yet more fatal impulse—resolved to move with them. But the times, at any rate in Belgium, were sadly immobile; for the best intentions of Teutonic persons are often wasted upon Belgium, and his most progressive gestures were coldly received by a community that was still obstinately mediæval. To this accompaniment Lady Mornington and Arthur took up their residence in Brussels. It lasted for a year —the year that saw the last of Dr. Johnson and the first of Palmerston, that heard Mr. Pitt denouncing Mr. Fox above the lively uproar of the Westminster election, that saw the *Tragic Muse* begun and the *Decline and Fall* nearly ended. Arthur, perhaps, fell something short of her ideal. The retreat from Eton had not been altogether to his credit. And then he was fifteen. Few boys, whatever their moral excellence, are seen to the best advantage at fifteen: an excess of limb scarcely lends charm to an unaccustomed gruffness. Small wonder, then, that Lady Mornington vowed to God she did not know what she should do with her awkward son Arthur. Really, with Richard winning golden opinions in Parliament, William in the Irish House of Commons, Gerald destined for the Church, and Henry still too young to think about, Arthur's future began to be something of a problem. Meanwhile, it could do him no harm to learn a little French, if only with a Belgian accent.

French, it appears, was almost all he learned at Brussels. Their obliging landlord dispensed vague draughts of learning. But a fellow-pupil remembered Arthur Wesley mainly for his devotion to the violin. For the Muse was easier to woo in foreign lodgings than at Eton. So the world glided into 1785; and he played on, as the slow days went by in Brussels. Ste. Gudule struck the hours; the light slanted from the west across the uneventful fields by Hougoumont; and in a Brussels room an awkward boy was playing on the violin.

That year his education moved him on once more. Lady Mornington went home to England. But two years of Eton and twelve months of casual tutoring in Brussels being judged insufficient, he must go somewhere to be "finished"; and since his range included little in the way of manly accomplishments, he was consigned to Angers, where the fifth of a dynasty of riding-masters presided over a celebrated academy. It stood behind a noble grille of iron-work—such iron-work as Marie Antoinette, the Queen, passed through each time her coach rumbled discreetly off to Trianon and turned into the tiny drive before her tiny palace. But at Angers the shapely modern work was gracefully disposed under the very hulk of the Middle Ages, where King René's castle lay—striped, blackened, and truncated—like a grounded leviathan. The tall Academy behind the grille was modern too—trim angles of white stone, a rounded hall, and at the back a flight of stately little steps descending from the tall façade, where art had carved a sheaf of palettes, French horns, and books, contrasted decorously opposite a panoply of arms, such armour, baldricks, and cuirasses as classical hero never wore. Its educational resources consisted mainly of a riding-school. But the curriculum included dancing lessons, together with a course in fencing. This happy blend was customary in such establishments, when dancing was apt to start at dawn, followed by riding, fencing, and a little grammar, with mathematics in the afternoon and a final dancing class to close the happy day. It was an age of elegance, when *haute école* and foils were felt to lack something if unaccompanied by Terpsichore. These studies, vaguely military in intention, were often followed by young gentlemen in search of a more general finish; and for about a year, his destiny being still uncertain, Arthur pursued them, walking the streets of Angers, seeing King Louis' soldiers in their white, or pounding round the riding-school in strict accordance with the rules of horsemanship. But the niceties of *haute école*, even when expounded with hereditary fervour by M. de Pignerolle, were scarcely more attractive than construing Ovid; and his attention often wandered. It was far pleasanter to pass the time

playing with his dog or dining with the local gentry. He was often at
the Duc de Brissac's, where the wine was poor and there was not much
to eat, although their host had been an ornament of Versailles, under
Louis XV. The old nobleman kept open house, though Pignerolle's cadets
were a little apt to make themselves unpleasant to injudicious guests.

He saw a good deal of the French. There was one of them who had
a brother in the Church named Talleyrand; and one day at the Duc de
Praslin's table he met an Abbé Sieyès, full of vague politics designed for
the new Assembly of Notables and preparing to astound the world with
his conundrum, *Qu'est-ce que le Tiers État?* He even retained a dim
(and, most likely, unfounded) recollection of meeting Chateaubriand,
then a wild-eyed subaltern in the King's army. But his most congenial
world was a small English set known, by the pleasing Continental practice of promiscuous ennoblement, as the *groupe des lords*. For more than
one young gentleman of quality was sent to Angers, and among them
a real lord or so. One pair, who lived in lodgings in the town and kept
a famous cook, saw a good deal of Arthur. It was a cheerful world, where
Pignerolle's cadets tried their very hardest to be manly, lose money at
the tables, run into debt, and pick really grown-up quarrels (*bourgeois*
French parents were mildly shocked by the establishment, because *"elle
n'était remplie que de seigneurs Français ou Anglais, et . . . l'on ne con-
naissait pas de pays, où le libertinage, le jeu, le ton querelleur soient
poussés plus loin que dans cette ville"*), although their manliest efforts
were occasionally contradicted by the school confectioner's advertise-
ments of sweets.

Arthur, staring up in the big round bastions of the castle or watching
the gaitered infantry go stiffly by in their three-cornered hats, was seventeen. He had been two years abroad; and it was time for him to find a
calling. They found one for him, since his mother had announced without enthusiasm that he was "food for powder and nothing more." Richard
must use his influence and try to get him a commission. The rising man
(he was in the ministry now, one of Mr. Pitt's Junior Lords of the Treasury) approached the Lord-Lieutenant; and that potentate was presently
informed of "a younger brother of mine, whom you were so kind as to
take into your consideration for a commission in the army. He is here at
this moment, and perfectly idle. It is a matter of indifference to me

what commission he gets, provided he gets it soon." Dangan was mort- 14
gaged, and there was not much to spare for the support of younger
brothers. But Richard's nonchalance was less uncritical than might appear, since there was at least one variety of commission which he felt
to be unsuitable for Arthur. For he declined the artillery, feeling perhaps 15
that Arthur's birth (no less than Arthur's education) unfitted him for
service in the learned arm. Such scruples were not universal. Watched by
another family, another widow's son born the same summer and educated at another French academy was with his battery already. The
pinched young subaltern, just seventeen and newly-joined, was deep in
his gunnery. The guns attracted him; he even found a charm in mortars;
and the frayed uniform grew dirtier than ever on the shadeless polygon
of Valence. But then Lieutenant Bonaparte was not a Wesley, was not
quite (as Arthur afterwards observed) a gentleman. Such ardours are
not for Etonians. For Arthur's reading eschewed Rousseau; less ardent,
he composed no novelettes of passion; and at no moment of his life was
he capable of five perusals of *Werther*. More equable, he waited for the
Lord-Lieutenant, through the good offices of Richard, to do something
for him. And in due course he did. For on March 7, 1787, Arthur Wesley
received the King's commission as Ensign in the Seventy-third. It was a
Highland regiment; and, better still, it was in India, where there was
not the slightest need for him to join it.

V

H E W A S gazetted Ensign just in time for his eighteenth birthday.
It was the year of Mr. Pitt's *Entente Cordiale* and Hastings' impeachment. Mr. Burke was tuning up the deeper notes of his invective;
Boswell was writing hard; and Mr. Gibbon, busy with his final volume,
enjoyed the prospect of his lake. The century seemed at high noon,
though the shadows fell a little longer as the sun, that decorously gilded
sun, declined towards its last decade. Its melody was fuller than ever.
Don Giovanni was heard that year, and Gluck's melodious shepherd
mourned his Eurydice. Boucher was gone; but Fragonard still scattered
rose-leaves. Countesses simpered for Gainsborough, and the cloaked Venetian maskers looked their most mysterious for Guardi. But they were all
simpler (if a thought sweeter) now. For the sad tale of *Paul et Virginie*
left no dry eyes that season, and the Queen of France was watching
duchesses milk cows under the trees at Trianon, when Arthur Wesley
first put on the red coat he was to wear, with impressive variations, halfway into the next century.

He had a calling now, though scarcely a profession, since he could
hardly live upon an Ensign's pay; and their main anxiety was to find
means of preventing him from following his unit to the East upon a
pittance. Not that he shared their hesitations. The calling seemed to interest him and, as he said in later years, he "was not so young as not
to know that since I had undertaken a profession I had better try to
understand it." His curiosity, which Latin elegiacs had singularly failed
to stir, began to move; and in a laudable pursuit of knowledge he had a
Highland private weighed in full marching-order. But the family curtailed these barrack-yard experiments. For something better must be
found for Arthur than bare regimental prospects; and hope gleamed,
as usual, from Dublin Castle. That autumn there was a new Lord-Lieutenant, and Lady Mornington promptly asked him to do something for
her boy. His reply was more than charming. For the obliging man made
him an aide-de-camp the very instant that he had his own appointment.

27

Meanwhile, there was his leave to be arranged, his small belongings to be purchased, and (had he not been an Ensign for eight months?) something in the way of promotion. Advancement came to him through an ingenious series of exchanges rather than from any vulgar exercises in the barrack square. For the younger brother of a rising man found military life less arduous than a lonely gunner at Valence; and, after flickering uncertainly through the Ninth Foot, by Christmas he was a Lieutenant in the Seventy-sixth.

There was so much to be contrived for him, and his mother worked her very hardest. Now she was prouder of him. For Angers had done wonders for her awkward son. He had not learnt to dance for nothing, and the Duc de Praslin's table was a rare school of manners. Besides, the awkward age was over. He was eighteen; Eton was all forgiven now; and the grace acquired in French provincial *châteaux* quite effaced any shortcomings in his Latinity. So it was all written off to her two inseparable friends in Wales, and the "Dear Ladies" at Llangollen learned at becoming length from Lady Mornington how extremely obliging the Lord-Lieutenant had been, and how "there are so many little things to settle for *Arthur* who is just got into the army and is to go to Ireland   2 in the capacity of Aid De Camp to Lord Buckingham, and must be set out a little for that, in short *I must* do *every thing* for him and when you see him you will think him worthy of it as he really is a very charming young man, never did I see such a change for the better in any body he is wonderfully lucky, in six months he has got two steps in the army and appointed Aid De Camp to Lord Buckingham which is ten shillings a day." Her pride in him was almost breathless; and there was still much to be arranged. For his new regiment had been raised for service in India; and if Dublin Castle was to see its latest aide-de-camp, he must exchange again. So she was busier than ever on his account (with the added torment of an intolerable bout of toothache)—"I have so much to get settled for Arthur, that I am sure it will not be done in the time.   3 The King has given him leave to go to Ireland only upon condition of making an exchange into another regiment, as the one he is in is destined for the East Indies, and it cannot go without its full compliment of officers; this will cost some money and take some time to effect it; but at all events he will be a gainer." She seemed to grudge him nothing now; and it was all safely engineered at last. For in the first weeks of 1788 he got his transfer to the Forty-first; and, the laborious penury of foreign service thoughtfully eluded, the new aide-de-camp was packed off to Dublin. On the road he stopped to pay a call. For as they drove through Wales, he looked in upon the Ladies at Llangollen and earned the commendation of his mother's friends—"Lady Dungannon and Arthur Wesley arrived. A charming young man. Handsome, fashioned tall, and elegant. He stayed till two, then proceeded to Ireland."

So he was back in Ireland, his formal education ended. It had been a strange affair. Two years of Latin elegiacs, followed by two years of—what? Of French, of *haute école*, of ballroom deportment, of dinner at the Praslins'. Yet he had managed somehow to profit by it, though the virtues that won his mother's unexpected praise were rather social than military. His seat upon a horse was secure, if unattractive; his French was fluent, though he mastered it rather by vigorous assault than by more insidious methods (someone remarked in later years that he spoke French as he fought them—*bravement*); and in some mysterious way he had acquired a habit of private reading. But Dublin was unfriendly to studious habits, and Dublin resumed him—the cheerful, rather factious Dublin of 1788, where Lord Buckingham kept his Court and Mr. Grattan made his speeches. Chariots turned out of Dame Street, passed the Castle sentries, and set down before the Lord-Lieutenant's door; and lights shewed in windows, where gentlemen were losing money at the tables or Dublin hostesses received. The aide-de-camp was seen at parties—not always to his advantage. For somebody refused an invitation to a picnic until she was assured that "that mischievous boy" would not be there; and one heartless beauty, upon whom his company had palled, went home alone and left him stranded to get back as best he could with the musicians. The bright Vice-regal world enveloped him and, Dublin completing what Angers had begun, he learned to point a toe and turn a compliment. He played as well and naturally lost; and, these diversions straining a yearly stipend of £172 9s. 3d., he was occasionally left to stare disconsolately at the Liffey from his windows on Lower Ormond Quay. But his landlord, a sympathetic bootmaker, relieved the young gentleman's more pressing needs on loan, and was rewarded by full repayment and a place. Not all his rescuers were so fortunate. For a friend of his agent's brother, who advanced £100 to Lieutenant Wesley in 1789, was repaid by Major-General Sir Arthur Wellesley in 1806.   9

He had his duties too. For aides-de-camp were expected to ride out with the Lord-Lieutenant or to take their turn at Vice-regal ceremonies among the gilded pillars of St. Patrick's Hall; nor was it quite without significance that when Lieutenant Wesley first saw the world, he saw it from behind a throne. Besides, his brother Mornington, busy with his own career at Westminster, was always giving him estate business to do. So he had quite enough to think about in Dublin—his debts, his duties, and his violin; for he still played. He had a change of uniform as well, though without promotion. But it was a convenience for him to get a regiment that was stationed in Ireland. Since no acute professional interests attached him to the infantry, a fresh exchange transferred him to the cavalry; and he was now Lieutenant Wesley of the Twelfth Dragoons. Within the month a mob went roaring against the Bastille, and the first heads were bobbing through the Paris streets on the first pikes. Mr. Fox was in ecstasies; but Dublin (and the Eighteenth Century) went on. The ladies danced; their masters dined; the aides-de-camp rode out as usual, though Arthur's sister Anne enquired in some agitation of the Ladies of Llangollen, "A'n't you sorry for poor dear France, I   10 shall never see Paris again"; and as the echoes died away, Lieutenant Wesley was putting on his new cavalry uniform.

A graver initiation waited, since he was nearly of age. Richard, the rising man in London, marshalled his forces. His brother William sat for their Irish borough. The post was not exacting; and, with Arthur growing up, William might very well be transferred to Westminster, while the young Castle aide-de-camp relieved him in the Irish House of Commons. So an English seat was found for William, and Arthur at twenty stood on the edge of Irish politics. Irish politics in 1790 were full of an uneasy stir. For there was positively an Irish question. Perhaps it had been answered at Bunker's Hill. Had not Mr. Flood announced that "a voice from America had shouted to liberty"? Napper Tandy   11 might even be the voice of the people (which France was now so busy proclaiming to be divine); and conceivably the truth might be with that ecstatic commentator who had recently distilled an apocalyptic national-   12 ism from the Book of Revelation and heartened the Lord-Lieutenant in well-doing by the coincidence between the harps, the sea of glass, the linen robes of Holy Writ and Ireland's coat of arms and leading manufactures. But borough-owners were largely untroubled by these lofty problems. For Castle politics in the age of Lord Chancellor Fitzgibbon were mercifully simple, consisting mainly in the humbler arts by which majorities are managed. Trim, represented by a Castle aide-de-camp, would be a unit in the Crown's majority; but before he could perform these simple evolutions, Arthur must qualify to represent it. First he became a Freemason, being initiated into Lodge 494, of Trim, co. Meath. Then he ran his first political errand. It was a matter of some delicacy that brought him into Trim one March day in 1790. For the Corporation, it seemed, was about to confer its freedom upon Mr. Grattan, a proceeding that could scarcely be congenial to the Castle. The family was bound to oppose it; and before an audience of eighty Lieutenant Wesley made his first recorded public speech. According to his own report, he "got up and said that the only reason given why Mr. Grattan should get the freedom of the corporation was his respectability, that really if we were to admit every man because one or two people said he was respectable, the whole community would belong to the corporation, that *he* could never be of any use to us and never would attend, and that I would certainly object, however great my respect for him." This was sensible enough. Then the orator grew more ingenious: "I said I should always vote for three sorts of people, those who were made to repel a party striving to turn the old family interest out of the borough," for a lawyer who might be serviceable upon election business, and for local residents. The meeting adjourned. But the young emissary was not inactive during the adjournment, since "I told my friends that it was a question of party, that they must stick by me"; and under this strenuous leadership the opposition carried the previous question in triumph. On the same eventful day he announced his candidature, and was promptly button-holed by an elderly voter, who declined to promise until he knew what Lord Mornington proposed to do about a bond for £70. This was extremely awkward; and the candidate, with rare discretion, "said I would have nothing to do with it, as in case of a General Election such a transaction would entirely vitiate my return." The simple appetites of eighteenth-century electors stirred on every hand; but the youthful politician, though considerably embarrassed, was not unskilful: "I was in the most difficult situation I ever experienced, and only got out of it by sticking up manfully to what I first said. I must say that, although I was plagued with requests of all kinds and totally unable and disinclined to make any promise . . . they behaved as handsomely as people could do. . . . They are all fine fellows."

Such was his first engagement. It ended in a modest triumph and a gratified despatch to Richard. But politics, it seemed, drew him as little as soldiering, since a postscript added that, "I am still of the same opinion with regard to your going abroad, and hope you will accept my offer to accompany you." Richard, however, stayed in England; and Arthur's duty called, however faintly, in Ireland. For, his regiment apart, the assault on Trim was promptly followed up; the Irish Parliament dissolved that spring; and Arthur was returned in 1790 for the family borough. There was some fear of a petition; for malice had been heard to whisper that the young gentleman was not quite of age when Trim elected him. These apprehensions kept him busy. He left his regiment in June, and posted to Dublin for grave consultations with the Lord 14 Chancellor and the Attorney-General. But his constituency was not neglected, since that summer he subscribed five guineas to the local races. The House met in July, and the petition was set down for hearing. But 15 the petitioners failed to proceed; and, all apprehensions set at rest, Lieu- 16 tenant Wesley was beyond dispute Member of Parliament for Trim.

If contact with the Trim electors was an imperfect education in democracy, the Irish House of Commons was unlikely to impress its new recruit with the virtues of Parliamentary government. Two-thirds of 17 that assembly owed their election to less than a hundred borough-owners; one-third were in receipt of salaries or pensions from the Crown; their collective appetites absorbed almost one-eighth of the Irish revenue; and it was not surprising that they rarely deviated from an inveterate conviction that the King's government must be carried on. Such was the first assembly in which Arthur Wesley learned to legislate.

Not that he legislated with any undue fervour. The rafters rang with the eloquence of Mr. Grattan; and he served modestly on a committee. Dublin repeated the latest sally of Sir Boyle Roche; and the Castle aide- 18 de-camp was inconspicuously jobbing supporters into small places. His zeal enriched the public service with a deputy barrack-master, whilst another suppliant was safely lodged in the Lottery. But as the voices rose and fell behind the portico on College Green, Arthur Wesley's never vied with the solemn note of Sir Hercules Langrishe; and for two years after his election he remained discreetly mute, a boyish-looking figure with a high colour, a red coat, and a large pair of epaulettes, sitting among the silent cohorts genially termed by Wolfe Tone "the common prostitutes of the Treasury Bench." He was a Captain now, promoted in 1791 to command a company in the Fifty-eighth Foot on the Irish establishment, and regimental duty sometimes took him as far as Cork; though he soon turned cavalryman again, exchanging into the Eighteenth Light Dragoons in the next year. But he was mostly to be found in Dublin, on duty at the Castle, or strolling to the House of Commons from his rooms in Grafton Street, or else at Dangan deep in new tenancies, ejectments, renewals, and all the fierce joys of estate management. That noble property was a sad trial to them now. There was the mortgage interest to be found. And for what? The big iron gates were always waiting, their tracery etched on the ragged skies of Meath; and the long drive still led down the hill and over the bridge across the ornamental water. But they never seemed to go there. No organ-music woke the hall; the still canal heard no more water-concerts; and the garden gods waited forlornly in their temples. Besides, the intrepid Richard needed cash for his assault on Westminster. His ties with Ireland were always of the slightest (did he not live to resent his own Irish marquessate as a "double-gilt potato"?), and he had turned his back on Dublin. There was the seat at Trim, of course; a vote on College Green was not without its uses; and it would be as well for them to keep their hold on Castle favours through the family borough. But Arthur could look after that. There was no need for Dangan, though. Richard had never cared for it. What did a rising man in London want with a mortgaged Irish mansion? Mr. Pitt could surely see his worth without that to set him off. His discreetly orthodox opinions on the Regency question were even approved by Majesty itself, now happily restored to reason; and when Windsor smiled, Dangan was surely far behind him. So before 1792 was out, the place was for sale.

While Richard spread his wings in London for these impressive

flights, obedient Arthur stayed behind in Ireland. His brother's deputy
(and Irish patriots found hard things to say of "the petty pilfering,   25
jobbing, corrupting tricks of every deputy of a deputy of an English
minister"), he cultivated Meath electors, subscribed ten guineas to the   26
Corporation plate, and earned Mornington's slightly condescending praises
for his management of Trim, "where by his excellent judgment, amia-   27
ble manners, admirable temper, and firmness he has entirely restored the
interest of my family." Versed in these unobtrusive arts, he even made
a maiden speech, rising to second the Address one January day in 1793.
It was a fluttered world, in which the French—wild-eyed and shouting
unfamiliar songs—threatened by turns to conquer Holland and behead
their king, and an exuberant Minister of Marine promised his countrymen
the added joys of a descent on England with the pleasing objects of
depositing fifty thousand caps of liberty, planting its sacred tree, and
holding out fraternal hands to the groaning subjects of King George.
Small wonder, then, that Captain Wesley, seconding the Address on
College Green, hazarded the blameless sentiment that "at a time when   28
opinions were spreading throughout Europe inimical to kingly government it behoved us, in a particular manner, to lay before our gracious
Sovereign our determination to support and maintain the constitution,"
with more (but not much more) to the same effect. Taking a wider survey he "reprobated, in very severe terms, the conduct of the French towards their king, and their invasion of the territories of foreign princes,
and their irruption into the Austrian Netherlands." Then, returning
homewards, he particularly approved a faintly liberal allusion to the
Catholic question in the Speech from the Throne—"He had no doubt
of the loyalty of the Catholics of this country, and he trusted that when
the question would be brought forward, respecting that description of
men, that we would lay aside all animosities, and act with moderation
and dignity, and not with the fury and violence of partizans." It was a
theme on which fuller reflection brought him worse counsel.

But Catholic Emancipation in 1793 was, by a queer inversion, the
policy of sound reactionaries. Pitt was propitious; Burke could not forget
that he was an Irishman; Popery itself grew daily more congenial to all
who ranged themselves with Catholic allies against the godless excesses
of Paris; and even the Castle gave a sulky acquiescence. Its drilled ma-

jority, sometimes a little out of step, obediently passed a Catholic Relief
Bill, which conferred the franchise and removed the major disabilities,
excepting the exclusion of Catholics from Parliament. That must be
maintained; for who would lay an impious finger on the palladium of
Protestant ascendancy? Not Arthur Wesley, since he was positively
chosen as the Castle spokesman to resist the bold amendment. It was
his second speech in Parliament; and since his first the whole world
was changed. For a king's head had fallen in Paris, and England was
at war. The fact, though he might not suspect it, concerned him intimately. It concerned, indeed, his whole generation and Anglo-Irish
younger sons more than most. For the bland decorum of the Eighteenth
Century was sharply interrupted by a new age, which the fantastic calendar of Paris did well to date from the Year One. Elegance went out of
fashion; and young gentlemen who trailed a graceful scabbard after the
Lord-Lieutenant were a thought behind the mode. A stir was in the
air, as Europe drifted into its long duel with the Revolution; and the
war, of which a Castle aide-de-camp watched the opening from Dublin,
came closer to him until, a little grey about the temples, he observed its
final scene from the saddle above Hougomont.

But as the drums began to sound in February, 1793, he was speaking
in the Irish House of Commons. This time he managed to abstain from
general reflections. His tone, though unsympathetic to the full Catholic
claims, was reasonable. For having voted for the Catholic franchise, he
"had no objection to giving the Roman Catholics the benefits of the
constitution." But there were plainly limits; and a Parliament of Papists
seemed to exceed them. When both sides were satisfied with a more
gradual measure, the cautious young gentleman declined to "agitate a
question which may disturb both." Not that he was a Protestant alarmist.
His common-sense scouted the orthodox dismay at visions of enfran-
chised Papists voting solidly behind their priests—"Have not Roman
Catholics, like Protestants, various interests and various passions by
which they are swayed? The influence of their landlords—their good or
bad opinion of the candidates—their own interests—and a thousand other
motives? It appeared to him that they would not vote in a body, or as
had been supposed, if the bill should pass in its present form; but if the
motion of the honourable gentleman should be adopted, then indeed

they would undoubtedly unite in support of Roman Catholic candidates."
This was a fair sample of moderate opinion from a young gentleman on
the Castle list whose brother wished to stand well with Mr. Pitt. In
that judicious mood much might have been done for Ireland. But it
was the year 1793; and it is the fate of Irish hopes to be dashed by
European wars.

The world was stirring around him. But his interests seemed all to
lie in Ireland. His seat in Parliament, his place at Court kept him in
Dublin; affairs occasionally called him to Dangan; and regimental duty
took him no farther than an Irish barrack. There were other interests
as well. For Lord Longford had a sister; Kitty Pakenham had a pair
of bright eyes; and Captain Wesley often called at Rutland Square. Vows
were exchanged; but what are vows without a competence? Longford,
considering his sister's prospects on a Captain's pay, was stern. Plainly the
couple could not marry. But Arthur might find out a way—there was
no need for him always to be a Captain. Richard must manage something for him. So that spring he wrote to Richard; the purchase money   31
was advanced; and before April was out, he was a Major in the Thirty-
third. But it was not enough to be a Major. If Kitty was to be achieved,
he must rise in his profession. Cards had betrayed him more than once;   32
and card-playing was promptly forsworn. He had a deeper passion,
though, which seemed to stand between him and promotion. For music
(was he not his father's son?) absorbed his leisure; and a violin was
often in his hand. Music had brought his father almost to poverty, and
a little grimly he resolved to break the charm. Besides, it would never do
for a promising young officer to indulge in secret orgies of the violin.
To say the least, it was not martial. Brass, perhaps; or even wood-wind
(Frederick the Great had played the flute); but scarcely strings. His
head, if it was ever to wear laurels, must be filled with drill-ground
evolutions, not with the adorable intricacies of counterpoint or the sweet
wail of strings. So one day in that eventful summer of 1793 he burned   33
his fiddle. He never touched another, though the taste lived on in him.
For dinner-parties years away were carried off from Apsley House to   34
hear the Ancient Concerts; their host's preference was understood to
lie with Handel, and even with Corelli, though the severity of the
programme was somewhat mitigated by his invariable seat upon a special

sofa between two handsome women. He could still take pleasure in a
lady's touch upon the harp, and was assiduous at the Opera, when Jenny
Lind was singing; his wrist, although he only used it now for carrying
the Sword of State upright in the House of Lords, remained supple as a
35   violinist's; and once in later years, when Madame Lieven played some
waltzes on the pianoforte, he supported her (an executant once more)
upon the triangle. There was always a thin strain of music in him. But
the charm was broken now. His father's fate had warned him; and
when Major Wesley, in hopes of Kitty Pakenham, resolved to be a soldier,
the flames licked a broken violin in Dublin. Perhaps an artist died. He
never cared to have it spoken of.

VI

THAT summer, as the Queen of France sat waiting in her prison, the storm broke. It had climbed slowly up the sky; and as it climbed, the light died out of Europe. There was a hush, and the familiar sounds came plainly over the still air—the tap of heels, the rustle of polite society, the scratch of rhyming pens, the buzz of coffee-houses, and even the level voice of Mr. Pitt assuring the hopeful Commons that "unquestionably there never was a time in the history of this country, when, from the situation of Europe, we might more reasonably expect fifteen years of peace than at the present moment." His hope died on the silence, and the dainty world began to lose its colours. For a cloud had swung across the sun, and a long shadow seemed to fall across the trim parterres. Even Mr. Pitt could see it now. "The war," he observed, with a singular change of heart, "is not only unavoidable, but, under the circumstances of the case, absolutely necessary to the existence of Great Britain and Europe." The skies were leaden; and Burke raved in the gathering gloom, while Gibbon with grave elaboration begged leave to agree with him—"I admire his eloquence, I adore his chivalry, and I can almost excuse his reverence for church establishments." The century, the eternal Eighteenth Century, had turned to bay; and all its children —positive, polite, and sceptical—took up their places for the conflict. For the storm broke that summer; and the thunder which had muttered above Paris rolled halfway round the world. There was a sudden gleam of bayonets; and Europe marched, as the French rallied round the great voice of Danton. But before the stiff battalions of the Monarchies could reach their stations, France dashed to meet them, breaking like surf along the frontiers. Austrians pounded the northern fortresses; the Prussians barely held along the Rhine; Spain moved deliberately in the sunshine of the Pyrenees; and half the west was up in the King's name, while Britons resolved with loud huzzas to—

> stand by the Church, and the King, and the Laws;
> The old Lion still has his teeth and his claws;

38

Let Britain still rule in the midst of her waves,
And chastise all those foes who dare call her sons slaves.
Derrydown.

The surf rose higher now; a wilder melody hung on the air above its charges. But the seventh wave was still delayed. Perhaps it lurked among the shallows, where a lean captain of artillery trailed dustily along a road near Avignon in charge of sixteen gunners and two guns. It was his first command. For Captain Bonaparte was an apprentice, the long form of Carnot sprawled in the dust of office floors across his maps to shift the candles with his armies, and the heads were falling fast in Paris, when Major Wesley took to soldiering.

But soldiering in such a season meant rather more than the punctual performance of regimental duties in Irish barrack squares. It was not quite enough for him to jingle spurs in Dublin corridors behind the Lord-Lieutenant; and that summer he was writing once again to Richard, desiring him "to ask Mr. Pitt to desire Lord Westmorland to send me as Major to one of the flank corps. If they are to go abroad, they will be obliged to take officers from the line, and they may as well take me as anybody else. . . . I think it both dangerous and improper to remove any part of the army from this country at present, but if any part of it is to be moved, I should like to go with it, and have no chance of seeing service except with the flank corps, as the regiment I have got into as Major is the last for service." He must see service, if he was to rise in his profession. But his application, if it was ever made, was disregarded —fortunately, perhaps, since the flank companies despatched that year from Ireland went off to die of yellow fever in Martinique. So Arthur Wesley eluded the crowded cemetery at Fort Royal, to say nothing of the more dreadful fate that waits upon returned heroes of Colonial warfare. For their conversation, a just object of alarm, abounded in the tedium of concealed enemies and cocoa trees—"Here stood the enemy . . . and here, my love, are my fellows: there the cocoa trees. . . ." How the delicious Harriette learned to dread that opening in later years. But whatever else Miss Wilson had cause to fear from Arthur, it was never that.

The Thirty-third still kept the peace in Ireland; and the assiduous Major drilled his men, as the world reeled through the stupendous calendar of '93. His century, with all that Arthur Wesley lived for—Dublin

39

Castle, Dangan, and the King's uniform—was assailed that year. *93 est*
la guerre de l'Europe contre la France et de la France contre Paris. . . .
De là l'immensité de cette minute épouvantable, 93, plus grande que tout
le reste du siècle. He missed the rhapsody, perhaps, but caught a little
of the uproar. For his countrymen were shouting Dibdin's chorus:

> Thus in famed Ninety-three   9
> Britons all shall agree,
> While with one heart and voice in loud chorus they sing,
> To improve *"Ça ira"* into *"God Save the King!"*

That summer, as the armies swayed along the frontier, Paris raved. There
was a fever of eloquence, a rash of tricolour cockades, a frenzy of citizenship. Voices rose shriller now on the still air above the stifling city;
the big knife clanked down at briefer intervals in the great square beyond the Tuileries; and France, beside herself, shewed the pale face of
the Terror like a Medusa's head to the oncoming battalions of the invasion. Marat died in those hot weeks and Charlotte Corday; and a young
man stood muttering, as the cart went by, that it were beautiful to die
with her. But Arthur Wesley was still drilling redcoats in the soft Irish
sunshine. He went to England in the autumn. For Dangan had found
a purchaser at last; and when Richard signed away the big square house,
Arthur witnessed his signature. They had no ornamental water now;   10
the garden gods knew other owners; and the family, their castle gone,
depended solely upon Richard and his soaring prospects. That day the
guns were opening above Toulon, watched by a "short, taciturn, olive-   11
complexioned young man, not unknown to us, by name Buonaparte,"
ranking now as Lieutenant-Colonel.

Arthur was soon promoted too; and as the gunfire echoed round the
hills behind Toulon, Lieutenant-Colonel Wesley went back to Ireland
to command the Thirty-third. (From Ensign to Lieutenant-Colonel in less
than seven years was creditable going—more creditable, perhaps, to
influence and army-brokers than to military science. But there was little
need for a Lieutenant-Colonel to blush at twenty-four, when Kitty
Pakenham's brother was a Major at seventeen, and Cotton had a regi-   12
ment at twenty-one and Lowry Cole at twenty-two.) As the leaves fell,
the crisis deepened. Disordered tides of war raced round the coasts of
Europe; a Paris court-room heard the unpleasant voice of Fouquier-

Tinville denounce a hunted woman, grey-haired at thirty-eight, as a Messalina, a Medicis, a Merovingian tyrant; the French infantry went roaring up the slope through the October mist at Wattignies; in Paris the knife fell and rose again and fell; and Arthur Wesley still sat on in Dublin, busy with regimental accounts. Late in the year, though, there was a vague hint of active service. For the strategy of British ministers is normally composed of a vast number of divergent gestures; and finding their commitments in Flanders, Provence, and the West Indies palpably insufficient for an army of 20,000 men, they gaily contemplated a descent on Normandy. A force was fitting out at Portsmouth for the French coast, and there was a notion that the Thirty-third would sail with it. Sudden departures are no less disturbing to gentlemen of honour than to their creditors, and Arthur made careful dispositions to discharge his Dublin debts, his income being assigned to an obliging tradesman who undertook to pay them off. But Moira's expedition started down-Channel on its aimless cruise without the Thirty-third; and as the year went out, Colonel Wesley was left standing in the wings, still waiting for his cue.

Dublin retained him, as a fresh year opened and the echoes of a world at war floated across St. George's Channel. They were still there in February. Spring came, the dreadful spring of '94, when Revolution, thirsting still and gorged with its enemies, turned unnaturally upon its own children. The Girondins had gone already, gone singing down the narrow street that ended in the waiting crowd, the planks, the angular machine. He was in Cork, still striking regimental balances the month a big, square-shouldered form came up against the evening sky in Paris and stared across a packed and silent square muttering, "Danton, no weakness." May found him there as well, still signing army forms. But the next month they got their orders; and Colonel Wesley prepared to take his first battalion on his first active service. It fell, by the symmetry of fate, in Belgium.

The skein of war was slightly tangled. Rarely without complexity for Allies and always apt to yield its richest tangles to Austrian fingers, it bore extensive witness to the welter of cross-purposes which was the Allied substitute for strategy. Soldiers of European standing did their solemn best to conduct a war as wars should be conducted. Having learnt

41

their profession fighting against or under Frederick the Great, they took measures admirably calculated to outmanœuvre a Prussian army of 1760. But the delicate precision of their military minuet somehow failed of its effect upon the coarser fibre of French *Demi brigades* in 1793. Fashions, perhaps, were changing; and at Hondschoote the prim tactics of the Eighteenth Century met the untutored onslaught of the Nineteenth with all the *gaucherie* of last year's fashions at a dress-parade. Besides, there was the Revolution. It appeared to affect them in the oddest manner, so that troops, which by every rule were off the board, insisted upon scrambling to the attack without a vestige of formation, shouting the most unusual songs. It was all highly disconcerting. Military science was almost wasted on such adversaries. For armies threatened with complete (if theoretical) disaster by the loss of a strategical point failed from sheer ignorance to notice it, and pressed obstinately forward. The best military minds had learnt to play at war as other men at chess; but chess is rarely satisfactory with an opponent who declines to learn the rules and is more than a little apt to spill the board. So the stiff *Kaiserlicks* tramped dutifully in all directions, and nothing came of it. White-coated infantry faced with cerise, with mauve, with green, with every colour in the Imperial spectrum moved in strict obedience to orders; gunners in grey tilted their big tricornes and served little guns; preposterously hatted units threw pontoon bridges across slow-flowing Flemish rivers; while, furred and frogged, hussars of every shade—Kaiser in blue, Barco in blue and green, Wurmser in green and scarlet—jingled off, watched by respectful villagers, or dismounting stiffly from red saddle-cloths with the big Hapsburg cipher trailed their long scabbards over the Flemish cobblestones. It was a brave display; but nothing came of it. For the skein of war was tangled. Wound by the Emperor, the King of Prussia, the *Reich*, King George, the Cabinet, the Duke of York, and half the *Almanach de Gotha*, it abounded in sudden turns that led nowhere, and was generously involved with every knot of European policy. (Few campaigns are less rewarding than those directed by Foreign Office strategy.) For in '94 the crusading march of outraged Europe upon Paris had degenerated sadly. Checked at Mauberge the year before, it declined after Tourcoing to a precarious defensive strung awkwardly along the Belgian frontier. France gathered strength in front of them,

42

and the invaders halted in a mood of dull bewilderment, resolved apparently to await its impact in the impressive posture of a sanitary cordon. But the dispositions convenient to frontier-guards in dealing with infected persons will not usually avail to check a nation in arms.

Somewhere towards the right of this depressed array a British contingent, shaken at Tourcoing and more than a little jaded by the endless series of aimless withdrawals and attacks that were not followed up, stood waiting in the Flanders plain. Waiting, indeed, appeared to be their leading occupation. For, apart from one major (and distinctly unsatisfying) engagement and a few dashing encounters, their derisive countrymen had summarised their operations with tolerable accuracy:

> The rare old Duke of York,
> He had ten thousand men;
> He marched 'em up to the top of the hill,
> And he marched 'em down again.

The Duke, indeed, was young; his command was in the neighbourhood of thirty thousand; and there were no hills in sight. But, these facts conceded, there was little fault to find with the disrespectful *précis* of their position and prospects. Vaguely alarmed, the Cabinet sent reinforcements. For Ostend was palpably in danger. It has been observed that Belgian ports hold a peculiar power of fascinating English statesmen; and their heads are sadly affected by names which, in the case of Queen Mary, were harmlessly engraved upon the heart. Ostend, like Antwerp, had the fatal charm. So the Thirty-third were moved at last: they sailed from Cork in the first week of June; and after nineteen days at sea Colonel Wesley landed his regiment at Ostend.

He was on active service now. Had not an elderly Colonel of the Guards warned him of its approaching trials—"You little know what you are going to meet with. You will often have no dinner at all. I mean," the horrified Guardsman had added, "literally no dinner, and not merely roughing it on a beefsteak or a bottle of port wine." The forecast was correct. For the Duke's army lacked almost everything. There was even a shortage of generals; and their exiguous supplies reached the dejected redcoats through the intermittent activities of the new Waggon Train, known (from their origins and tunic) as the "Newgate Blues." Once more a British army swore terribly in Flanders.

For it was a continuation of Marlborough's wars conducted with much of Marlborough's equipment and lacking only Marlborough to complete the resemblance. But Arthur Wesley and the rest of Moira's reinforcements were still among the sand-hills of Ostend. The Colonel found himself commanding a brigade of three battalions; and when Moira marched away to join the main Allied army, Wesley's brigade was left as rearguard "to settle matters at Ostend" (the French, including a young Colonel named Murat, were getting near) "and then to come on as quick as I could." Ostend was promptly evacuated; and preferring a short sea voyage to a dangerous flank-march in face of an advancing enemy, he re-embarked his men, put them on shore again at Antwerp, and reached the Duke of York's position before the leading files of Moira's force which had come overland. So his first minor operation comprised a deft retreat and a neat use of the ubiquity conferred by sea-power on British expeditionary forces.

There was an agonised succession of Allied conferences, while the line still held uneasily in front of Brussels. They met at Braine-l'Alleud; they met again, by a felicitous choice, at Waterloo. But with Austrians to line it, that position was scarcely at its best. The French tide was running strongly across Belgium; and finally each Ally went his way. For the last strand of Allied strategy had almost parted. The Austrians trailed off towards the east, while the Duke of York, receding slowly northwards, still undertook to keep the French out of Holland by the united efforts of the Dutch, his own little army, and a few German troops in British pay. Then the retreat began. There was a small affair at Boxtel in Dutch Brabant one September day, when Arthur Wesley took his battalion into action under the eye of Abercromby. The Thirty-third were competently handled, holding their fire in face of the on-coming French until their Colonel ordered a volley. The old General (whose bushy eyebrows gave one, as someone said, "the idea of a very good-natured lion") called a few days later to convey "the Duke of York's thanks and his to the Thirty-third for their good conduct on the 15th." But these laurels failed to dazzle him, since the same letter which conveyed the news to Richard announced that he would be back in Ireland before the winter was out. There was the usual trouble with their Irish tenants; and as he lay in front of Nijmegen, Arthur's mind

44

was full of small practical expedients of estate-management in Ireland. Not that his eye, as it turned homewards, was blurred by sentiment; for as he offered slightly contradictory counsels, he added tartly, "This is Irish language, but not less true for that country of scoundrels."

The winter deepened round them, and the retreat went on through the dreary landscape and grotesque nomenclature of the Netherlands. They stood along the Waal; and Arthur, whose health was none too good, lived in a perpetual rearguard action. Now he commanded a brigade, and acted in virtual independence—"I was on the Waal, I think, from October to January, and during all that time I only saw once one General from the headquarters." But the young Brigadier, haunted by thoughts of leave, commanded without especial gusto. Hope gleamed a little, as the French hung on the edge of winter-quarters—"I think it impossible for any troops (even the French) to keep the field in this severe weather. As soon as their intentions are decided I intend to go to England." The French, alas! were ignorant of these refinements, and frankly disinclined to treat campaigning as a seasonal occupation. Besides, the season, however unpleasant, was particularly propitious for their offensive, since the frost eliminated water-lines which must otherwise have served as strong defences. So the war flickered along his outposts through the black nights of a Dutch winter—"We turn out once, sometimes twice every night; the officers and men are harassed to death. . . . I have not had my clothes off my back for a long time, and generally spend the greater part of the night upon the bank of the river." By day the enemy were entertaining enough, "perpetually chattering with our officers and soldiers," and ready to oblige on request with lively performances of the *Carmagnole*. But as he watched the ice-packs grinding in the Waal or wrote out his endless regimental accounts, he still thought of leave—"I intend to go to England in a few days, that is to say, if the French remain quiet, and if the regiment is relieved from the advanced post upon the river Waal, where it has been for above six weeks." The French, however, with republican discourtesy resumed the offensive; and in the last week of the year the Thirty-third cleared a Dutch village with the bayonet.

The year went out on his discomfort, on a winter land of freezing polders and ice-bound canals, on a ragged army straining precariously to

defend a country which had not the least wish to be defended. For the
Dutch found the French invasion more congenial than their Allied
champions. The countryside was frankly hostile, and there were even
dark suspicions of the Dutch army. Arthur was once instructed to escort
a Dutch officer through his lines for a secret interview with Pichegru.   15
Watched by the Colonel, two muffled figures met on the ice; and shortly
afterwards (it seemed a little sinister) the French were in Utrecht. The
Dutch defences broke in all directions; there was a brief resistance in
front of Arnhem, when the Thirty-third performed once more; then
the retreat went miserably on in the short winter days. With the French
in the Dutch ports and solemn Dutchmen dancing round trees of liberty in Amsterdam, there was no way to England for the retreating army
except across the frozen heaths that lay between the Zuider Zee and the
North German ports; and their line of march slanted towards the east.
It lay across an endless plain of white under the dark winter sky. Trying at first, the retreat soon deepened into tragedy. For the army was
practically unclothed; a few units had great-coats purchased by public
subscription over a year before, and the remainder owed the small
comfort of a flannel waistcoat to the private charity of officers.

An arduous winter on the long road from Antwerp to the north of Holland had left them in rags; and as the iron frost gripped these pitiable
scarecrows, they died along the frozen tracks. The last semblances of discipline almost vanished in its grip; for having no supplies they looted, and
having no enemy to fight they fought one another. All the torments of   29
1812 were let loose upon them in one dreadful week of January, 1795.
The white plain lay behind them now; but it was marked with broken
waggons, with frozen pack-horses, with silent heaps that had been marching yesterday, even with women. The worst was over then. They reached
the Ems at last; and a rueful General reported to the Duke of York,
"Your army is destroyed; the officers, their carriages, and a large train
are safe, but the men are destroyed. . . ." Life was easier now; discipline
returned, and Brigade Orders began to abound in prohibitions of pro-   30
miscuous shooting of all edible forms of game. A Hanoverian unit (Jägers
in more than name) having found someone's deer quite irresistible, the
sporting instincts of the British were restrained by a threat of court-
martial for any soldier "detected in using his firelock except when on

Duty." The winter turned to spring, and they dragged their way to the quaysides of Bremen. A period of endless embarkation returns set in. But Colonel Wesley, his duty in the field once done, eluded the confusion. They reached the port in March; and before the month was out, he was in London. His regiment was still abroad. Transports slid up the German river to fetch them home; and one Monday morning (it was April 13, 1795) the remnants of the Thirty-third were marched on board. The long campaign was ended.

Ended for Arthur Wesley also. Another chapter of his education closed, he was in England. It had been arduous—more arduous than the old Guardsman's forecast. But it had been instructive too. He said of it in later years that he had "learnt what one ought not to do, and that is always something." Few campaigns, indeed, were more admirably designed to perform the functions of the awful warning. The least attentive mind could hardly miss its lessons. It has been frequently observed that British armies are at their finest in retreat. But the higher command seemed almost over-anxious to display these qualities. Arthur himself was most unfavourably impressed by the limpness of headquarters, which left regimental officers in virtual independence—"We had letters from England, and I declare that those letters told us more of what was passing at headquarters than we learned from the headquarters themselves. . . . The real reason why I succeeded in my own campaigns is because I was always on the spot—I saw everything, and did everything myself." Not so the Duke of York and his headquarters. Besides, what they did was almost certain to be wrong—"There was a fellow called Hammerstein, who was considered the chief authority in the army for tactics, but was quite an impostor; in fact, no one knew anything of the management of an army, though many of the regiments were excellent." But, excellent or not, authority left them to freeze and frequently to starve; for it had yet to dawn upon the martial mind that orders on the day of battle are of far less importance than regular meals upon the intervening days. The lesson was not lost on Arthur. Nor, perhaps, the disastrous consequences of indiscipline upon retreating troops, or the effect of a judicious volley from British infantry in line upon the scrambling columns of the French. It was a dozen years before he saw their blue uniforms again, and the interval taught him the art of war. But he had learnt some of it in Holland through that dreary winter.

VII

R ETURNED, but not conspicuously laurelled, the Colonel of the Thirty-third resumed the problem of his own career. The years were passing (he was twenty-six that spring), and so much remained to be achieved—promotion, Kitty Pakenham, even a competence. For the most devoted younger brother could hardly be expected to live for ever upon Richard's prospects; and, these apart, Arthur had really not much more to live on. Five hundred pounds a year, perhaps, comprised the total of a Lieutenant-Colonel's pay with the allowances of a Castle aide-de-camp. One could not cut a figure in the world on five hundred pounds a year. Indeed, it was distinctly doubtful if that income would suffice to meet the cost of past appearances. For Dublin and his creditors were waiting, and the returning warrior faced the bleakest of financial prospects.

He faced it with resource; for Irish patronage was always a resource to those with friends at Dublin Castle. There was no need for him to go to Dublin, though. The new Lord-Lieutenant was in London; and Arthur promptly waited on Lord Camden with a modest intimation that he should take some opportunity of stating the claims which he conceived himself to have upon the Government of Ireland. But Pitt's latest Lord-Lieutenant had more to think about than a remunerative place for Colonel Wesley. There was the rest of Ireland to be considered; and Ireland in 1795 stood in need of full consideration. For whilst Arthur Wesley had been countermarching on by-roads in Holland, Lord Fitz-william had been countermarching with no less vigour upon Catholic Emancipation. Camden was to succeed that unhappy strategist; the whole country was in a lively uproar; and with all his problems still unsolved the new Lord-Lieutenant went off a little grimly to take up his residence in Dublin. The faithful aide-de-camp, still close to the Viceregal ear, followed his chief and paced the Castle yard again. Dublin had draw-backs for him, too. His tradesmen lived in Dublin; but a trifle of four-teen pounds to settle with a clothier was not to be thought of—was, in fact, suspended until the hero of Assaye, returning as a Major-General, paid the account twelve years away.

The spring of 1795 grew bright above these cares. He lived in quarters now more advantageously than in his former lodgings. Catholics, United Irishmen, Defenders, Peep of Day Boys all pressed on Camden; but none pressed so hard as Arthur Wesley. The Thirty-third, returned from Germany, were peacefully encamped in Essex. But their determined Colonel traced his parallels and laid his mines, as he besieged the Lord-Lieutenant. That dignitary was evidently disinclined to be taken by storm; the March reconnaissance in London had shown that. So Arthur settled down in Dublin to a siege *en règle*. All April he was in the trenches. He spoke discreetly to His Excellency "upon a certain object of mine in this Country"; he spoke of it again; he wrote a note enclosing—here he unmasked his batteries—a letter from Lord Mornington in Richard's most majestic manner. That nobleman informed the Lord-Lieutenant, as one earl to another, of his happiness at news of Camden's civility to Arthur— "You may easily believe how happy this account has made me, and how strongly I feel these proofs of your friendship for me." (A helping hand to Arthur was, it seemed, a mere form of courtesy to Richard.) But more might yet be done—"My Brother tells me, that the situation of Secretary at War . . . is likely to be opened soon"—and what more suitable to Arthur, more gratifying to Richard, or more convenient to the public service? The note concluded with a scornful word or so on "His *ci-devant* Excellency," Fitzwilliam, and the sage reflection (familiar to belligerents in need of consolation) that the French "are very nearly exhausted even by their victories."

This bold attack encountered an insurmountable defence from the besieged Lord-Lieutenant, which wrung from Arthur the slightly rueful admission that "I see the manner in which the Military Offices are filled, and I don't wish to ask for that which I know you can't give me." Plainly his next assault must take another road. But before the storming-party left his trenches, he prepared their way with slightly touching ingenuity. He was still in Parliament; and if only he could be of service to the Castle, perhaps the Castle might be less impregnable. His chance arrived one night in May, when angry gentlemen denounced a former Lord-Lieutenant for the high misdemeanour of denuding Ireland of

49

troops. The voices rose; Lord Westmorland was sadly trounced; and
when Curran had dealt scornfully with "6,000 clowns, without shoes,
and with ribbands in their hats," Grattan rose to a *crescendo*. Soaring
at once into his loftiest manner, he spoke boldly of impeachment, of a
Lord-Lieutenant convicted of the very act for which King James had
been deposed—"How can we otherwise dispose of him? here are the
laws which contain the covenant, and here are the army returns which   5
contain the breach of it—can we connive with Lord Westmorland, and
combine and confederate with him against the law—against the Revolution—against the Declaration of Rights—against . . . ." His lightnings
played about the absent peer; and the official answer—that recruits had
been raised to fill the gaps created by withdrawals—sped dancing like
a dead leaf down the gale of his eloquence. "The new levies . . . . the
suggestion of an evasion, not of a defence, it is the suggestion of a trick
—of an impostorship—of a fraud; it is not a bad defence, but a scandalous
prevarication—a sort of clerk-like dexterity—but so clumsy, so miserable,
and so glaring—that it does not keep within the letter of the act, whose
object it professes to defraud, and of whose provisions it professes to
cheat the public." His closing sentence dropped a challenge—"It is a
striking circumstance, that in a debate where the conduct of Lord Westmorland towards the Irish army has been so publicly and so loudly
arraigned, no one veteran of the army, nor any old officer, has ventured
to defend him." The challenge confidently made by Grattan was promptly
accepted. For Colonel Wesley rose to follow him. He had not spoken for
two years; and even then he spoke without *éclat*. But the intrepid Colonel
was prepared to follow Grattan in debate: men have earned medals for
acts of lesser heroism. Not that he failed in the encounter. For as he
spoke, the chilling voice of common sense fell on the listening chamber.
"What did the act require? 12,000 men for the national defence: Were   6
they or were they not in the country? It was admitted that the public
service demanded troops to send abroad, and an addition was therefore
made to the establishment by parliament. Was it the new levies just
recruited that were to be sent abroad to meet an enemy, or the disciplined
soldiers? The question answered itself, and justified sending the old
regiments out of the Kingdom, and retaining new corps." That cleared
Lord Westmorland; but he remained upon his legs a moment longer

to deal faithfully with a previous speaker who had described the new recruits as ragamuffins. "He congratulated that hon. baronet on his military sagacity, who would send ragamuffins upon foreign service; but he assured the hon. baronet that however he might treat the new levies with contempt, they were not objects of contempt to the enemies of their country." It was an adequate performance; and few acts in his military career were more courageous than the prompt reply to Grattan's challenge.

The House rose in the first week of June; and he went off to Trim to think about his own affairs. They owned no castle now, and Arthur had a bachelor's refuge—rectangular refuge of a bachelor growing slightly rectangular himself—among the trees at Fosterstown. The Lord-Lieutenant must be stormed again; and this time he launched a fresh assault against another face of the Viceregal fortress. His tone was not so lofty now:

> "I assure you nothing but the circumstances under which I labour would induce me to trouble Your Excellency's Government at any time and the Offices to which Lord Mornington has desired me to look are those at the Revenue and Treasury Boards and considering the persons who are at present at these Boards, and those it is said are forthwith to be appointed to them, I hope I shall not be supposed to place myself too high in desiring to be taken into consideration upon the first vacancy at either of them. If Your Excellency and Mr. Pelham are of opinion that the Offices at those Boards are too high for me, of course you will say so; and as I am convinced that no man is so bad a judge of the justice of a claim as he who makes it. . . .
>
> "You will perhaps be surprised at my desiring a civil instead of a military Office. It certainly is a departure from the line which I prefer; but I see the manner in which the military Offices are filled, and I don't wish to ask you for that which I know you can't give me. Although the necessities under which I labour from different circumstances have nothing to do with the question whether I have a claim to the Offices I have mentioned, I again repeat that nothing but them should induce me to trouble Your Excellency's Gov't at any time."

Always his wretched circumstances. They haunted him that year. It was June now; and as he sat waiting for the Lord-Lieutenant's answer in his little house at Trim, he faced a cheerless outlook. After all, a place in the Irish Revenue would mean security; and he might even sell the King's commission for the price of a home with Kitty Pakenham. For there had been little in his Dutch campaign to kindle military ardour. Strange that the summer, which saw Arthur Wesley contemplate civilian life, witnessed the stranger spectacle in Paris of General Bonaparte applying for transfer to the Turkish army.

But Arthur's manœuvre failed completely; and as the summer turned to autumn, he launched his last attack supported by his invariably heavy gun, Lord Mornington. The Lord-Lieutenant was informed discreetly that the incumbent of an Irish post would shortly be resigning; that there was "the best reason in the world why he should"; that someone in England would have a grievance if he did not; that, in fine, a vacancy might be expected in the eligible place of Surveyor-General of the Ordnance for Ireland; and that Arthur "should prefer to have that office to any of those which I mentioned in my letter to you." He would not for the world have pressure put on the incumbent to resign. For one thing, he was an uncle of Kitty Pakenham. Besides, place-hunting has its etiquette: one does not forcibly create the vacancy that one desires to fill. But Camden, still obdurate, resisted every assault. Foiled by the long defence, Arthur drew off his forces and, resigned at last to military life, raised the long siege of Dublin Castle: sieges would never be his *forte*.

That autumn he was with the Thirty-third once more. They were in England still, waiting for the tangential strategy of Mr. Pitt to dispose of them. The regiment lay near Southampton under orders for the West Indies; and their Colonel wrote to inform the Lord-Lieutenant that he proposed to go with them. The Earl, relieved from his besieging aide-de-camp, was distinctly gratified. He was, as courtesy required, "very sorry we are likely to lose you next winter," but could not but "approve of your determination to accompany your reg't to the West Indies, as I am convinced that a profession once embraced should not be given up. I shall be very glad if I can make some arrangement satisfactory to you against you come back, but if a vacancy should happen in the Revenue Board I fear the Speaker's son must have the first." That written, he turned again to a distracted Ireland, and Arthur went about his regimental duties. He was not well that autumn, seemed slightly feverish, and consulted a physician. His Dutch winter might well have left its

COLONEL HON. A. WESLEY, 1795
From a painting by John Hoppner, R.A., at Apsley House.
By permission of the Duke of Wellington, K.G.

mark. Besides, a touch of fever was the right preparation for a soldier's grave in St. Domingo. So he lived once again in the shadow of Miss Harriette Wilson's dreaded cocoa trees. They were ordered to Barbados first, and then to capture the Dutch islands; for the Cabinet, having singularly failed to rescue Holland, had resolved upon the more prudent course of rescuing the Dutch colonies. Meanwhile they waited near Southampton, as autumn turned to winter and the Channel grew daily less inviting. They sailed at last; and as the fleet of transports with the tall ships of their convoy swept with all sails set past Weymouth one November day, men crowded to the shore to watch. But the November day was followed by a November night. A gale went screaming over Portland; and in the morning seven wrecks were grimly aligned along the wind-whipped Chesil Beach. The rest put back to Portsmouth, sailed once more in the first week of December, and more venturesome than ever tempted the Channel in the teeth of a midwinter gale. It blew for seven weeks, blew one of them clean past Gibraltar to the Spanish coast, scattered a hundred into the unknown until they dropped weeks later, one by one, into West Indian harbours, and blew thirty—Arthur's amongst their number—back to the sheltering Solent after seven vivid weeks of crowded maritime adventure. So the Thirty-third saw England once again; and their Colonel completed an unpleasant spell of duty, which had comprised one storm at sea and seven weeks of gale. But few gales have ever done more useful service. For it spared him a campaign in the West Indies and (most likely) the West Indian grave that generally followed. "It's very hard," as the redoubtable *Major Monsoon* informed *Charles O'Malley*, "to leave the West Indies if once you've been quartered there," since "what with the seductions of the coffee plantations, the sugar-canes, the monsoons, the brown skins, the rainy season, and the yellow fever, most of us settled there."

The voice of duty called, though not quite so raucously, in the first weeks of 1796. Restored to their unwilling country, the storm-tossed regiment reposed at Poole. They passed the winter there in the deep calm of Wessex. Meanwhile, their destinies were altered; for Whitehall, which had proposed them for the Western hemisphere, consigned them to the Eastern. Now they were under orders for India and sailed in April. But

their Colonel was not well enough to go with them. He was still convalescent in Dublin. There was so much to be arranged before he could
leave Ireland—a paper to be written for his successor on the management   13
of Trim electors, his post as aide-de-camp to be resigned, his brother's
interests, estate affairs, to say nothing of his own. These dismal occupations filled the spring days in Dublin, as a ragged army swept through
the passes into Italy and the names of Bonaparte's first victories—Lodi,
Montenotte, Mondovi—were sounded upon silver trumpets. But Colonel
Wesley, getting back his health, went patiently about his business. He
was full Colonel now. The Castle was still vaguely benevolent, assured
him of its continued sympathy, and murmured something indistinct about   14
a future prospect of the Revenue Board, adding to Richard that it felt
"so much the propriety and spirit of Col. Wesley's conduct in going to
the E. Indies that I should be very happy to relieve his mind from the   15
embarrassment it feels on account of some pecuniary arrangements which
he was obliged to leave unsettled when he left England. He mentioned
these circumstances to me"—and His Excellency, it seems, had vanished
in a haze of insubstantial promises of profitable places. So Ireland slipped
behind him, rattling miserably down towards the melancholy rapids of
'98 in a froth of violence, night drilling, and informers, with the fatal
miasma of rebellion "creeping" (in Grattan's words) "like a mist at the   16
heels of the countryman."

In June he was in London, lodging at 3 Savile Row, and wafted on
his way by the good wishes of an agent, who could not quite suppress
an anxious hope that he would leave express instructions to Lord Morn-   17
ington to pay, should the worst happen, £955, 4s. 8d. of outstanding
bills. He did his final shopping at a bookseller's in Bond Street; and before the month was out, he was at Portsmouth waiting for a wind. The
Thirty-third had sailed in April; but a fast cruiser should overhaul them   13
before they passed the Cape. And so, his trunks packed, his lot decided
now, he waited on the Hard. Among his baggage a large corded trunk
contained the last additions to his library. Now, men will frequently
buy books with the simple object of display, but rarely when the books
are to be their sole companions in distant countries. Such libraries are
more revealing. Arthur's was newly bought from Mr. Faulder, the
bookseller in Bond Street, whose corner shop became that very year the

18 background of Gillray's agreeable record of Lord Sandwich's encounter with a more than usually bouncing barrow-wench. The bookseller's account survives with its particulars of solemn quartos, of barely sprightlier octavos, of Oriental phrase-books and forbidding pamphlets, down to the corded trunk itself:—

HONBLE. COL. WESTLEY

June 6, 1796.   B*ot* of R. Faulder.

	£	s.	d.
Crawfurd's Sketches of the Hindoos		6	6
Dow's History of Hindostan. 3 vol. 8ᵛᵒ	1	1	
Verelst's Bengal. 4°		7	6
Vansittart's Narrative. 3 vol.		18	
Bolt's India Affairs. 3 vol.	1	11	6
Scrafton's Reflections on Bengal		3	
Holwell's Historical Events with other Tracts		6	
Cambridge's War in India		6	
Dirom's Campaigns. 4°	1	1	
Monro's Narrative	1	1	
Mackenzie's Campaigns. 2 v.	2	2	
Fullarton's Account of India. 8°		6	
Scott's History of the Dekkan. 2 vol.	2	2	
Analysis of British India. 3 v.		18	
Plans for the Government of India. 4°	1	1	
Hastings' Memoirs of Bengal		3	6
History of Hyder Ali Khan. 2 v.		5	
Rennel's Map and Memoir	2	2	
D'Herbelot, Biblotheque Orientale	1	18	
Richardson's Persian Dict*y*. 2 vol.	12	12	
Hadley's Persian Grammar		7	6
Moises Persian Interpreter. 4°		16	
Halhead's Bengal Gram.	1	1	
Account of the Siege of Mangalore		6	
Jones' Hist. de Nadir Shah		18	
Fraser's History of Kati Jehan		3	6
Volney's Egypt. 2 vol.		16	
Savary's Egypt and Greece. 3 vol.	1	1	
Cæsar's Commentaries		4	6
Plutarch's Lives. 6 vol.	2	2	
Locke's Works. 9 vol.	4	4	
Paley's Works. 5 vol. gilt	5	5	6
Blackstone's Commentaries. 4 vol.	1	16	
Smith's Wealth of Nations. 3 vol.	5	5	
Ainsworth's Dictionary. 8°		10	6
Tableau de l'Histoire Moderne. 3 tom.		10	6

55

	£	s.	d.
Bolingbroke's Works. 4 vol.		3	3
Swift's Works. 24 vol.		2	10
Voyage de Bernier. 2 tom.		5	
Russell's Laws of the India Company	2	2	
" Hist. of the India Company		5	
Trunk, Cord, &c.	1	11	6
	£58	2	6

His programme of reading was severe, but salutary. For nearly half his acquisitions were palpably designed to equip him for the East with a substantial grasp of its history, language, and administration. His purchases were strong upon the late wars with Tippoo; excepting Cæsar, all his new military works were purely Indian; nor was current Indian controversy disdained. It was plain from these elaborate researches that Colonel Wesley destined himself for a long stay in India, since officers in quest of quick promotion and the first passage home scarcely require such full documentation. Dublin was fading from his vision now. As Richard wrote of him in the next year, "If Arthur has good luck, he will be called to act on a greater stage than dear Dublin." His stage, it seemed, was India; and the bookseller's bill shewed that he meant to learn his part. It was his chance in life—the very first that had come his way. For Dublin Castle had been little more for its anxious aide-de-camp than an expensive pastime; and military reputations were scarcely to be made in Holland. But India was different. Richard, a student of Indian affairs, could see that "the Station is so highly advantageous to him, that I could not advise him to decline it." For India might make something of him— and he of India. At any rate, he meant to try. So much was plain from the forbidding volumes in his trunk.

The rest were no less arduous—Cæsar to be attempted with a Latin dictionary and vague memories of Eton afternoons; Plutarch (in English); the foundations of belief to be explored with Locke and Paley, the mysteries of commerce with Adam Smith, of law with Blackstone, and of Toryism with Bolingbroke. One item only amongst his new purchases was for recreation—a set of Swift. Arthur, it seemed, was just a shade sardonic in his tastes. Besides, what amateur of Irish politics could fail to savour Swift? There was a link between them, too; for

Laracor, the little church near Dangan, had been a living of the Dean's as well as Wesley property. So Swift, in twenty-four small volumes, was packed in Arthur Wesley's trunk for India.

20 He had other books, of course. His London purchases did not compose the whole of Colonel Wesley's library, though they formed almost half of it; since a later list survives in his own writing, which includes his recent acquisitions together with books that manifestly came from his rooms in Dublin:—

LIST OF BOOKS

No. 1

Vols.

2 Richardson's Persian Dictionary
2 Herbelot's Bibliotheque Orientale
3 Reports Secret & Select Committees
1 Harleian Miscellany
15 Œuvres du Roi de Prusse
2 Volney's travels

Vols.

1 Howell's Events
24 Swift's works
13 Hume's History of England
8 Smollett's Continuation
9 Woman of Pleasure
10 Faublas

No. 2

Vols.

4 Blackstone's Commentaries
1 Verelst India Affairs
3 Bolt's India Affairs
3 Orme's Indostan
2 Edward's West Indies
1 Petit Neptune François
9 Locke's works
5 Paley's works
1 Graves' regulations
3 Smith's Wealth of Nations

Vols.

7 Raynal's Histoire des Indes
1 Hastings' Trial
1 Account of the Siege of Mangalore
1 War in Asia
1 Walpole's Answer to Bolingbroke
3 British India Analysed
1 Moore's Narrative of Little's Detachment
1 Sketches of the Hindoos

No. 3

Vols.

1 Manufactures and Commerce of Bengal
1 Dirom's Narrative last campaign
1 Plans for British India
1 Russell's India
1 Statutes relative to E. In. Company
2 Scott's Deckan
1 Persian Grammar
1 Account of 1st June
1 Memoir and Map of Indostan
2 McKenzie's War in Mysore

Vols.

1 Proceedings of Com^{ee} of Officers at home
1 Munro's Letters on ye last war
3 Dow's Indostan
3 Voltaire Fables
1 Hastings' memoirs
4 German dictionary
1 Jones' Persian Grammar
1 Arabick Grammar
1 Universal politician

57

Vols.

1 Hadley's Grammar
1 Papers on Maroon War
1 Hadley's Persian Grammar
2 Savary's letters
1 Savary Greece
1 Nadir Shah
1 Memoires Marshall Saxe
1 Abregé Chronologique Histoire de France

Vols.

1 Chapman Venereal disease
1 Transactions in India
1 McIntosh Vindiciæ Gallicæ
1 Cambridge's War in India
1 Cæsaris Commentaria
3 Vansittart's Narrative
1 Reynell's Marches of the B. Armies
1 Clarendon's Irish Affairs

No. 4

Vols.

1 Johnson's dictionary
1 Ainsworth's dictionary
2 Memoirs Baron de Tott
1 German Grammar
3 Gazetteer of France
3 Loyd's War in Germany
1 Dundas Quarto
  Proceedings of Officers
  Map of France
  Bengal Army List
  Roads of Bengal
1 Fullarton's India
1 Scrafton's reflections
1 Robertson's Historical Disquisition

Vols.

1 Dundas Cavalry Tackticks
1 Dumourier's campaign in Flanders
  Pamphlets
3 Dumourier's life
2 Histoire d'Hyder Ali
2 Bernier
1 Crebillon 2nd Vol.
1 Leonora
9 Royal register
  Pamphlets
  Allan's views of Hill Forts, &c.
7 Nouvelle Heloise
8 Robertson's works

This library was evidently formed before he left for India, though more than half of it consists of volumes that do not appear in Faulder's bill. The Colonel's list was made (for packing purposes, no doubt) on the occasion of his move from Calcutta to Madras in August, 1798. But one can hardly doubt that almost all the books had come with him from Europe. More than a hundred of the volumes had been bought in Bond Street just before he sailed; and the rest were palpable survivors from his Dublin library, since it was barely thinkable that Clarendon's *Sketch of the Revenue and Finances of Ireland* (sad relic of his vain designs upon the Irish Revenue Board) was bought for reading in Calcutta, and two items—*Papers on the Maroon War* and Edwards' *History, Civil and Ecclesiastical, of the British Colonies in the West Indies*—had manifestly been acquired when the Thirty-third were destined for that theatre of war. Besides, he had a habit of reading and was unlikely to discard his entire library in favour of the new books from Faulder's shop: a man, whose interests impel him (at a moment of financial stringency) to spend fifty pounds on books, inevitably has more books at home. So the list represents his choice of books at a decisive moment; and men reveal themselves in their selection of reading for a sea voyage of six months and a long residence abroad.

What does his library disclose? A military man of rather solemn tastes, whose books were almost all for use. There were no flourishes. His latest purchases reveal his concentration on India; for India filled his horizon. But there was more than India among his books. He was inclined to history and (the East apart) took out no less than thirty volumes, distributed between the venerated, if slightly alarming, names of Hume, Robertson, and Smollett. Nor were his thoughts confined to Britain, since French history was included. Even the Revolution engaged him, and from an unexpected angle. For he possessed a copy of Mackintosh's *Vindiciæ Gallicæ*, that judicious answer to Mr. Burke's fevered denunciations of French excesses. The Revolution was by far the most conspicuous fact in Europe; but one would expect a British Colonel to examine it (if he examined it at all) through the congenial medium of a hostile publication—unless, of course, he were genuinely concerned to ascertain what could be said in favour of it. But in that case he would be a most unusual Colonel. Perhaps he was. His literary tastes, indeed, might seem to show as much. For his light reading, apart from a new set of Swift, comprised two foreign authors who were, to say the least, unusual in military circles. King George's officers were seldom to be found with Rousseau in their hands. Yet seven volumes of his *Nouvelle Héloïse* accompanied the Colonel; and Arthur's sensibility could thrill with the melting *Julie* and enjoy the exquisite delineation of an English nobleman in *Mylord Édouard Bomston*. Voltaire, his second choice, displayed a more astringent quality that might well commend itself to a reader of Swift. But the combination of Voltaire with Rousseau on Arthur Wesley's shelves is undeniably intriguing. That he was not unacquainted with French literature in its naughtier moods is evident from his inclusion of an odd volume of *Crébillon*—with the appended note, touching to bibliophiles, "2nd vol." Apart from these, his literary tastes, though French, were almost commonplace. For he endured, it would appear, nine volumes of the *Woman of Pleasure*, to say nothing of ten more containing Louvet's

interminable *Aventures du Chevalier de Faublas,* and a translation of
the latest German romance, *Leonora.* An odd volume of the *Harleian
Miscellany* kept eccentric company with these sparks and nymphs, serving the Colonel, it would seem, for intellectual recreation between the
lilies and languors of Louvet and the roses and raptures of Rousseau.

His military reading was of a graver cast. Upon the present war in
Europe he was content with the writings of the refugee Dumouriez.
Dundas supplied a meagre textbook of drill and tactics. But Arthur's
choice of masters in the art of war was more significant. Frederick the
Great in fifteen small volumes, Marshal Saxe in quarto, and Lloyd's
*History of the late War in Germany between the King of Prussia and
the Empress of Germany and her Allies* formed his equipment. Frederick was plainly to be studied at full length in his own *Histoire de Mon
Temps* and *Histoire de la Guerre de Sept Ans.* (It may be justly doubted
how far the studious Colonel penetrated the last ten volumes of that
monarch's works, where the dust gathers on his odes, his rhymed
epistles, and his endless correspondence with the *coryphées* of French
philosophy.) But Frederick, however instructive in military practice,
rarely theorised upon the art of war. More theory, as well as sound cor-
rectives of undue subservience to Prussian views, was to be found in
Major-General Lloyd's volume of *Reflections on the General Principles
of War,* with which his narrative concluded. Slightly obsessed by the
eighteenth-century delusion that wars could be won without battles by
the simple (and magic) occupation of decisive points, and that "if you
possess these points, you may reduce military operations to geometrical
precision, and may for ever make war without ever being obliged to
fight," the General was fairly sound on strategy. His tactics, in spite
of an eccentric predilection for the pike, were more suggestive, since
he departed from the Frederician line, and proposed to meet cavalry
attacks with infantry formed into squares:

> "I will join the four companies, and form a complete square; can they
> break this? No; they will not say they can: for, exclusively of the musket,
> lances, and pikes, I will venture to say that no body of horse, with any
> degree of velocity, is able to break through a body of infantry of sixteen
> ranks, because the quantity of action produced by a horseman on full
> gallop (for one only shocks at a time) is not equal to the resistance of

21

sixteen men placed behind each other, so near as to support in a mass the shock of the horseman.

"I conclude that, armed as I propose, a battalion of infantry will beat in the open field twice the number or indeed any number of horsemen formed and armed as they are at present."

This was strange reading in 1796; but after Waterloo, perhaps it did not read so strangely.

The thoughtful Lloyd was equally inclined for change in his extended use of *tirailleurs*. Light infantry was to operate on a wide front before the troops in line.

"The fire of our two light companies will alone produce a greater effect than that of the enemy, for this obvious reason, that our light infantry acts where and how they please, aims at their leisure, crosses their fire along the enemy's whole front, goes upon their flanks, &c.; in short, it acts with all the advantage of real and expert chasseurs."

For these new purposes he recommends that their numbers should be expanded to one-fifth of each battalion:

"The number of the latter may appear too great; and in fact it is so, if they are confined to that kind of service only in which they are now employed. . . . But according to our plan, they will perform all the duties commonly done by light troops; and likewise in a day of action, they shall be employed in such a manner, as will enable them to render more real service than the heavy infantry."

Here, in his little library of 1796, was the germ that may have led an officer in 1809 to attach a rifle company to each brigade of his command in the Peninsula, to form Portuguese infantry brigades with one battalion to every five—Lloyd's exact proportion—trained and equipped as *Caçadores*, and to put out a line of skirmishers whose fire could invariably hold the French *voltigeurs*. So perhaps his country's debt was greater than it ever knew to Major-General Lloyd, late of the Austrian army, and variously denominated by a choleric historian of Frederick "Epimetheus Lloyd," "surly sagacious Lloyd," and "a man of great natural sagacity and insight; decidedly luminous and original, though of somewhat crabbed temper now and then; a man well worth hearing on this and on whatever else he handles."

Arthur's last military instructor was no less suggestive. For Marshal
Saxe survived in his *Reveries* as a singularly active mind, busy with
every topic from the desirability of body-armour to the endowment of
motherhood. Inclined by nature to an excessive ingenuity in details
of equipment that faintly recalls the preparations of the White Knight
for active service, that accomplished soldier was severely practical upon
the theory of war. The soldier's health engaged him; he was strong for
vinegar as the secret of Roman vigour, and insists in detail upon care
of the feet. He was admirable upon the leg—*"Le Principal de l'Exercice*   27
sont les jambes & non pas les bras: c'est dans les jambes qu'est tout le
secret des manœuvres, des combats, et c'est aux jambes qu'il faut
s'appliquer." (One almost catches, in this firm abstention from heroics,
the ring of a later voice.) Not that he failed to explore the higher regions
of the military art. He was sagacious on the merits of reserving fire till
the last moment—*Le quel emportera l'avantage, de celui qui s'est amusé*   28
à tirer ou celui qui n'aura pas tiré? Les gens habiles me diront que c'est
celui qui aura conservé son feu, et ils auront raison—a salutary lesson
which the French, omitting to absorb it from Saxe, had ample opportunities of learning on Peninsular battlefields. The villainy of army
contractors roused his invective; he was emphatic on the value of light
infantry; and his whole survey of warfare was conducted with the cold   29
gaze of a realist.

Such, if he read them, were Colonel Wesley's first masters in the
art of war. Saxe, Frederick, Dundas, Dumouriez, and Lloyd hung like
fairies, good or bad, above his professional cradle to bestow their gifts.
Not that war bulked largely in his library. For, India apart, it accounted
for barely twenty of his two hundred volumes. India was his main
interest; almost a quarter of his books related to the East. Yet he was
disinclined to think of India as a mere battlefield. For India had civil
problems, which were included in his studies. He could even refer them
to first principles, finding his politics in Bolingbroke, his law in Blackstone, and his economics in the *Wealth of Nations*. It was a statesman's
library in miniature—but all designed for use, and none to awe visitors.

His purchases revealed him, as another library, bought two years later
for another soldier, revealed its owner. For General Bonaparte, just leaving for the East and scrawling a list of purchases for Bourrienne in '98,

entered the same confessional. The list was more impressive. It was analytical and erudite. It had an air.

BIBLIOTHÈQUE DU CAMP

1° *Sciences et arts.*
2° *Géographie et voyages.*
3° *Histoire.*
4° *Poésie.*
5° *Romans.*
6° *Politique et morale.*

	Vol.
Justin	2
Arrien	3
Tacite	2
Tite-Live	
Thucydide	2
Vertot	4
Donina	8
Frédéric II	8

Sciences et Arts

	Vol.
Mondes de Fontenelle . . .	1
Lettres à une princesse d'Allemagne .	2
Le Cours de l'École-Normale . .	6
Aide nécessaire pour l'artillerie . .	1
Traité des Fortifications . .	3
Traité des Feux d'artifice . . .	1

Géographie et Voyages

Géographie de Barclay . . .	12
Voyages de Cook . . .	3
Voyages français de La Harpe . .	24

Histoire

Plutarque	12
Turenne	2
Condé	4
Villars	4
Luxembourg	2
Duguesclin	2
Saxe	3
Mémoires des Maréchaux de France .	20
Président Heinault . . .	4
Chronologie	2
Marlborough	4
Prince Eugène	6
Histoire philosophique de Indes .	12
D'Allemagne	2
Charles XII	1
Essai sur les mœurs des nations .	6
Pierre le Grand . . .	1
Polybe	6

Poésie

Ossian	1
Tasse	6
Arioste	6
Homère	6
Virgile	4
Henriade	1
Télémaque	2
Les Jardins	1
Les chefs-d'œuvre du Théâtre-Français	20
Poésies légères (choisies) . .	10
La Fontaine	

Romans

Voltaire	4
Héloïse	4
Werther	1
Marmontel	4
Romans anglais . . .	40
Le Sage	10
Prévost	10

Politique

Le Vieux Testament.	
Le Nouveau.	
Le Coran.	
Le Vedam.	
Mythologie.	
Montesquieu.	
L'Esprit des Lois.	

31   There were pretensions here. Besides, the General had ten thousand francs to spend, compared with Arthur's fifty pounds. So he bought three times as many volumes. Yet how few of all their purchases appeared in both selections. Both owned a set of Frederick the Great; each bought the *Reveries* of Saxe; they both agreed in reading Voltaire and the *Nouvelle Héloïse*; and both sailed with Plutarch in their baggage. That was the

mode, of course; and the coincidence of choice scarcely argues a taste in common. Born the same year and living in the last decade of the Eighteenth Century, they could scarcely hope to escape Plutarch. But it is pleasant to discover a classical allusion shared between these two admirable subjects for a Plutarchian diptych.

What else do the two trunks reveal? Arthur's was full of his resolve to master India, to learn Indian warfare and administration. But there was little about Egypt in Bonaparte's. He preferred to soar with *Orlando Furioso,* to explore the deeps of melancholy with *Werther,* or to draw a gentler sigh over the destinies of *Manon.* Even his military works ranged every age and nation; his classics were impressive; and his collection of travels qualified him rather for the conquest of the world than for an exact knowledge of the Syrian Desert. In fine, it was a gentleman's library in perfect miniature—perhaps a shade too perfect to be quite a gentleman's. "You find me," he could exclaim to callers, "among my books." Arthur's were far less universal. But then the Colonel of the Thirty-third would not have to sustain exhausting conversations with French *savants* on the voyage out. Neither was he inclined to class the Bible as *Politique et morale*; but then, perhaps, he did not need to buy one for the journey. Heroic poems had no charms for him; life would, it seemed, be tolerable for Arthur without the Iliad; he took no tragedies in verse. Indeed, had fate exchanged their trunks, one doubts how much of Bonaparte's he could have endured. Voltaire undoubtedly, and Rousseau, and the military history. But the sardonic amateur of Swift must have jettisoned almost all the other's lighter reading. For his choice was more austere. But then austerity is frequently the note of books selected by intending travellers. How many of them get a reading, how few survive the journey, are dark questions rarely answered. In Arthur's case, however, the later list remains to show how many of his purchases of '96 were still by him in '98. Swift survived; but Bolingbroke alas! had vanished. He had Locke and Paley with him still; his *Wealth of Nations* kept its charm, his Blackstone too. But though Cæsar was retained, the classics lost their hold on him. For the six volumes of Plutarch no longer darkened his bright Indian horizons. But as he waited for his passage out, his trunk was full of them, and he of a high resolve to read them.

He was at Portsmouth still in the last week of June, 1796, waiting for a wind for India to take himself, his sword, and the light baggage of his education ten thousand miles from England. For he was twenty-seven, his education ended now. It had been a singular affair from start to finish. His family, perhaps, had taught him least of all. They saw so little of him. Besides, their interest was always centred on Richard's bright ascent—Richard's success would surely atone for all his backward brothers. But if he learnt little from his family, had Eton taught him more? Angers, perhaps, imparted polish and a notable distinction of manners. And Dublin? Dublin and Trim had been his university, where he learned all the arts of management, the shifts of personal finance, Viceregal deportment, and the under-side of Parliamentary affairs. That had been his civilian education. As to his profession, had he not studied it in the sombre academy of his Dutch winter? Formed by a varied past, he waited for the wind at Portsmouth. A wind sprang up; the frigate sailed and Europe faded into the summer haze behind him.

Sepoy General

Contra la mar salada conpezo de guerrear
A oriente exe el sol e tornos a esa part.

Poema del Cid.

A TEDIUM inseparable from the professional recollections of retired administrators broods impenetrably above the brightest pages
of Anglo-Indian history. Besides, there are so many of them, and almost
uniformly bright. That glorious circumstance, perhaps, contains the
secret of their tedium; since bright surfaces repel protracted contemplation. Viewed by posterity, there is a lack of vicissitudes about them that
is almost distressing. That lofty destiny, those prescient forerunners, and
the long roll of their inevitable victories sweep past like a political
speech to its foregone conclusion. We see the goal; we note the all too
steady progress; and our starved dramatic sense cries out for a hitch
somewhere. But it cries in vain; and our ingratitude almost forgets
that no victory is inevitable until it has been won. Familiar in its
outline, the story seems to pall by reason of its very grandeur. For
a continent subdued is vastly less exciting than a city saved or an election
barely won. It has all the unimpressive vastness of astronomical dimensions, and fails as dismally of its effect upon our fainting comprehension.
Eastern history is often disappointing to the Western mind. Did not
Macaulay, in a famous Minute, expose to impolite derision "history
abounding with kings thirty feet high and reigns 30,000 years long,
and geography made up of seas of treacle and seas of butter"? Something, perhaps, of those staggering proportions survived to haunt the
latest phase of Indian history, to infect the conquerors themselves, and
touch the annals of the British conquest with Oriental tedium.

Yet India in the first stages of the British conquest was far from
tedious. Familiar objects of the Anglo-Indian horizon were not yet
conspicuous or existed only in the most rudimentary forms. Not yet
the grave Civilian; not yet his lady. The stupendous flood of Indian
reminiscence was a modest rill, still near its source. No voice rehearsed
the endless anecdote of how, "when we were at Dumdum in '36, we ate
some colt. Don't you remember Jubber's colt—Jubber of the Horse Artillery, General?" For India was still a land of promise, gleaming with faint
allurement over the edge of the world. But Eldorado draws livelier
company; and India, though less improving, was distinctly brighter. For

it was Hastings', Francis', Impey's, Hickey's India, where a cheerful world, pleasantly redolent of factors, writers, and supercargoes, defied the climate upon claret or withdrew sedately to more dignified repose beneath a Latin tag in a Calcutta graveyard. The scene was bright with powdered heads, with gentlemen in white, with smiling ladies who could smile the brightlier for a comforting knowledge that "the men are out of all proportion to the female world." They rode; they danced; sometimes they danced themselves into a decline. They strolled at sunset on the Fort or aired themselves in more adventurous mood upon the water. Oars dipped, as families reclined in pinnaces and bands of music floated by. For the Eighteenth Century, disinclined to pine in exile, viewed the waters of Babylon rather as an invitation to a water-concert than as a signal to hang up its harp. It was a masculine society, where life was planned delectably for male diversions; and the lively exiles ate the bread of affliction with a certain gusto. They ran wild for masquerades and supped heroically off oysters, while gentlemen amateurs unendingly rehearsed the parts that they could never get by heart. Life was inalterably eighteenth-century, as though Bengal had been a sultrier Bath and the Great Tank reflected the Piazza at Covent Garden. Did not the pen of *Asiaticus* deplore in a Calcutta journal the sad decease of a young lady "celebrated for her poetry and misfortunes," who—cruel to relate—had "died of pure sensibility"? How clear it rings, the authentic voice of the Eighteenth Century, speaking quite unmistakably with bland, familiar accents in its unusual surroundings. Europe might have its moments of uncertainty, as the harsh voices of the Revolution fell on its ear. Europe, perhaps, was changing now; something was stirring in the air of Europe that might mean a change of season, and the Eighteenth Century was putting on its wraps. But, whatever hour the clocks might chime in Paris, it was still the Eighteenth Century in India. A traveller would find it there and, once landed at Calcutta, need never leave his comfortable century. Indeed, the journey would prolong it, as summer is prolonged for travellers who follow summer round the world.

One traveller found it indubitably so, obtaining by his timely exile a prolongation of the Eighteenth Century, a reprieve for that delicious prisoner of Time, who lay in Europe under sentence. Born at its height behind a Dublin fanlight, he had passed his youth in it; for what was more *dix-huitième* than a Viceregal world and Dublin Castle? But as the glow began to fade from Europe, he passed on to India, where the world still walked by its unwavering light. Splintered at home, the mirror of the Eighteenth Century was still intact in India. The judicious traveller could point a toe in its smooth surface and survey himself still framed by its gracious gilding. For the century enclosed him still; there was no need for him to leave it yet. Had he not followed its summer round the world to India? He had always lived in its easy weather; and in India, it seemed, he would live in it still. Indeed, he would find it far from pleasant to encounter other seasons: they were unthinkable for him. Perhaps he would resist them, when they came.

I

The ship sailed on. Portsmouth was far behind them now, and the dim headlands of the Spanish coast. The road to India led southward down the broad sea-lanes of the Western Ocean, and Teneriffe stood up out of the summer sea to watch them pass. The summer turned to autumn, as they made the long haul past St. Helena to the Cape. Those were the days when travellers paused at the Cape to taste its wine and eat its grapes and stretch their legs with a ride to Constantia and a scramble up Table Mountain. But now the Cape was more congenial than ever, since British enterprise had lately rescued it from the unworthy Dutch. For though the French might overrun the Netherlands and indulge the antics of their preposterous Batavian Republic, they should never have the Cape: the sheltering arm of Britain would secure it from the dread contagion. Indeed, it had just done so, finding the rescue of Dutch colonies less arduous (and more rewarding) than that of Holland. So Colonel Wesley found himself ashore in the very latest British garrison. He found the Thirty-third as well, and resumed his regimental duties in the intervals of paying his respects in Cape Town to two young ladies, fresh from school in Bloomsbury and on their way to India. Miss Jemima Smith was gay, satirical, and enterprising; but Miss Henrietta, aged seventeen, conquered the Colonel with her more retiring manners, to say nothing of a "pretty little figure and lovely

neck." And a caller at the house found him "all life and spirits" and   5
the very image of John Philip Kemble. His blue eye was clear; his
nose was large; his speech was rapid, "with, I think, a very, very slight
lisp"; and a beard of obstinate growth placed him under the distressing
necessity of shaving twice a day. Before they sailed, he wrote in the
interests of his career to the Governor of Madras. Then they sailed on
to India, enduring "a most tedious passage" in the *Princess Charlotte*   6
East Indiaman. Even the composition of a second letter to Lord Hobart
failed to relieve the tedium. He had his regiment; he had his box of
books; he had his thoughts. But the bright spaces of the Indian Ocean
stretched endlessly away, and India still lurked somewhere behind the
haze. A line of coast appeared at last. The sea became the Roads; the
Roads dwindled to the Hooghly; the Hooghly turned to Garden Reach;
and halfway through February, 1797, the Colonel landed at Calcutta.

Once safe ashore, he had his duties. For there was the Governor-
General to be called upon. There was not a notion yet that Richard
might be summoned to fill that lofty throne. When Arthur sailed, Lord
Mornington was deep in politics at home with every expectation of
staying there; and Sir John Shore sat modestly in Warren Hastings'
seat. That potentate recalled (after a fitting interval) his first prophetic
estimate of Arthur. For the discerning Governor-General observed that
if Colonel Wesley should ever have the opportunity of distinguishing   7
himself, he would do it. He even found in the young man "a union of
strong sense and boyish playfulness." Both would find scope in India.
Indeed, his playfulness seemed likely to be called upon before his sense.
For one muggy night in March Mr. Hickey found him presiding at
the Calcutta dinner for St. Patrick's Day and doing the duties of the   8
Chair with peculiar credit to himself—and in matters of conviviality
Mr. Hickey's standards were exacting. Now he was in the cheerful
world that went for morning rides, paid calls, and made its bow at the
Governor-General's levée. It was Dublin Castle over again, but Dublin
Castle with a difference. For the Calcutta *ton* was often quite inseparable   9
from its hookah, drew fragrant puffs between the hands of cards, or
smoked discreetly in the back of theatre boxes. A mob of pipebearers
sometimes came in with the dessert, and furtive devotees had been
occasionally known to snatch a sly cheroot in guestrooms. Even the fair

could not escape the strange infection. (Here was a novelty for Arthur, a variation upon Dublin Castle.) For long years before the Nineteenth Century could draw its first emancipated whiff, pale ladies in Calcutta tasted smoke. But when they stooped to smoke, they smoked with grace; since eager beaux approaching with the pipe put a fresh mouthpiece on, uncoiled the snake, and offered it respectfully to the fair novice. Once that spring he went up the river to Chinsurah and stayed with Mr. Hickey and a men's party. The house was new, the company select; after mornings pleasantly divided between horse exercise and billiards they sat down twelve to table; and having dined, a cheerful company "pushed the claret about very freely," while somebody obliged with a song. He was there again in June. They rode races every morning, and the King's birthday was celebrated with loyal ceremony. For the convivial Hickey had procured a turtle and some venison, to say nothing of the very best champagne, hock, claret, Madeira, and "an eminent French cook" imported from Calcutta for the occasion. Small wonder that they fell to glees and catches, and a General rendered *The British Grenadiers* with the utmost spirit. But these diversions failed to distract the Colonel. His mind still ran on Indian campaigns; and when the General invited his opinion upon the introduction of light artillery, he could respond with a wealth of technicality, though not "regularly bred to artillery," in a paper citing the late wars in Mysore, the defects of recent operations, and the scarcity of horses in India. For he had read to some purpose his forbidding library of Indian history.

That summer a hope of active service dawned. For Spain, having rashly entered the war on the French side, the British formed a sage resolve to appropriate the Spanish colonies in the Pacific. The Philippines were most inviting; so were the Dutch establishments in Java; and a combined attack from India was freely talked of. While the expedition was deliberately fitting out, there was a chance that Arthur might be given command of the Bengal contingent. He was alert at once, drew plans for submission to the Governor-General, and displayed a terrifying intimacy with monsoons, the defences of Batavia ("surrounded by a slight brick wall, which has no defence. It has on the eastern side of it a citadel, which stands close to the bay, but which, however, is not within shot of the artillery-ground. . . . In the rear of the town, at some

73

distance, are two redoubts; in which, however, as I am informed, there
are no guns"), and the comparative merits of Malay harbours. The
Colonel was unusually thorough; and he wrote hopefully to Richard on
his prospects of the command.

> "I desired the person who communicated his wishes to me to decline   14
> it in my name, and to propose Doyle. If any thing should prevent Doyle
> . . . I intend to accept of it; taking the chance that the large force they
> intend to send, the known pusillanimity of the Enemy, and my exertions
> will compensate in some degree for my want of experience. I hope to be
> at least as successful as the people were to be to whom Hobart wishes to
> give the command. . . . Of course the Chief Command of this expedition
> would make my fortune; going upon it at all will enable me to free myself
> from debt."

The prospect was alluring; but the offer, alas! was not renewed. His
initial gesture of abnegation had been successful—more successful, possibly, than he intended—and he sailed with no higher rank than that of
Colonel commanding the Thirty-third. But before the expedition left,
he had a touch of fever. India, perhaps, seemed less attractive now—"I   15
have not yet met with a Hindoo who had one good quality, and the
Mussulmans are worse than they are. Their meekness and mildness do
not exist." Cruelty, deceit, and perjury formed a depressing background;
and he began to feel a little lonely, having "no news from England
since I left it, which is extraordinary, considering that that was in June
'96." Now it was July '97; and almost wistfully he asked his brother to
"let my mother, &c., know that I am well."

But within a fortnight a mail arrived with the sublime intelligence
that Richard was to come out to India as the next Governor-General.
So that bright promise was to be fulfilled at last, and Richard awaited
with serenity its rich fulfilment. Imperial attitudes had always suited
him, and his new appointment would enable him to strike the most
imperial of all. For what spoke plainlier of Rome, what more reminiscent
of the legions and the eagles, than a proconsul? Not that the prior associations of the office were conspicuously proconsular. His countrymen
had strikingly declined to award tht civic crown to Warren Hastings;
few warriors were less adapted to the pallium than Lord Cornwallis; and

the judicious qualities of Sir John Shore—"a good man, but cold as a greyhound's nose"—were scarcely of the order that cries out for bronze to be their record. But these predecessors could not conceal its rich
16 possibilities from the discerning Richard. It was, he could see that it was "the most distinguished situation in the British Empire after that of Prime Minister of England"; and he was modestly prepared to discharge its functions. Meanwhile (since Roman dignities were often followed by a Roman triumph) it would be just as well to think about
17 a marquessate, if one should come his way. For Mornington was quite resolved to be Marquess Wellesley; and Ulster King of Arms, in his secluded room at Dublin Castle, was kept busy with Richard's eager enquiries upon heraldic points—had he the right to quarter Cusack, Geneville, and De Lacey with Wellesley? who married Walter Cowley of Castle Carbury in the reign of Henry VIII? and what was known
18 about a shadowy ancestor traditionally thought to have been standard-bearer to Henry II and feudal holder of some lands near Wellington in Somerset? These lofty themes engaged him, as the new Governor-General prepared to enter on his splendid province. But he had living relatives as well, whose prospects might be gilded as Richard's luminary rose in the skies of patronage to become, in Burke's splendid image, "lord of the ascendant."

Richard, it seemed, had other views, though his brother Henry went with him as secretary. For his Roman qualities appeared to include the austerer forms of Roman virtue; and one hopeful applicant received the chilling answer that a young gentleman, for whom his favour was desired, would receive—

19 "every encouragement and assistance; and if he deserves it (not otherwise) I will take care that he shall rise as quickly as the Regulations of the Company's Service, and the attention due to the merits of others will permit; more I will not do for my own Brother; nor would I accept this high station, unless I were assured of my possessing firmness enough to govern the British Empire in India without favor or affection to a human being either in Europe or Asia. The integrity of my own character in such a government is the best provision which I can make for any branch of my family; and if this were not good policy, as well as morality, I have

vanity enough to be resolved to sacrifice every consideration (but the public interest) to the preservation of a just and well-founded fame."

This was austerity indeed; for it was the golden age of patronage, and India was almost sacred to nepotism. But Arthur was not unprepared for Richard's Roman virtues, since his reception of the news of the great appointment concluded with an almost formal offer of "service to you in your Government" and the rueful supplement that "such are the rules respecting the disposal of all patronage in this country, that   20
I can't expect to derive any advantage from it which I should not obtain if any other person were Governor-General." It gratified him, though. Had he not pressed his brother to entertain the appointment within a month of his own arrival in India? He even offered reasoned consolations for Richard's approaching separation from his domestic hearth, though "I acknowledge that I am a bad judge of the pain a man feels upon parting from his family." For the twelve months' absence of a line from home still seemed to rankle.

Meanwhile, with Richard brushing up his quarterings at home, Arthur went soberly about his duties, untroubled by heraldic problems or the lands once held by spectral ancestors near Wellington. What was Wellington to him? They would be sailing for Manilla soon; and the Colonel plagued Government for mess allowances and a prompt amend-   21
ment of the system by which ships' surgeons were to be made responsible for his soldiers' health at sea—"It takes out of my hands entirely the superintendence and control over the management of the sick. . . . I shall be deprived of that part of the superintendence over my corps which is most gratifying to me when they are embarked, and by exercising which I can render most service to the soldiers." For he was strong upon their health (had he not watched an army die in Holland?); and his regimental orders for the voyage were a judicious code of hygiene   22
that included frequent fumigation of the decks, daily exercise with dumb-bells, and the sterner prescription that "the men should be made to wash their feet and legs every morning and evening, and occasionally water should be thrown over every man; every day if possible." The new practitioner did not disdain such unheroic aids to war.

Not long before they sailed, he had a word with Mr. Hickey on a loftier theme. The Thirty-third, it seemed, were unprovided with a chaplain;   23

76

a friend of Mr. Hickey's had a nephew; and the Colonel "in the hand-
somest manner" promptly appointed him. The appointment, it must be
confessed, disclosed a somewhat languid interest in their spiritual health,
since the new chaplain was "a young clergyman of very eccentric and
peculiarly odd manners," whom he had met at Hickey's house. They
sailed in August; but the ships were barely three days out from land
before the new regimental chaplain disgraced himself completely. For
this unaccountable young man became intolerably drunk and gave
a public exhibition of extreme impropriety. Then, seized with con-
trition, he refused all nourishment and stayed secluded in his cabin.
The captain's consolation failing, Colonel Wesley came on board and
plied the penitent with kindly arguments—"that what had passed was
not of the least consequence, as no one would think the worse of him
for the little irregularities committed in a moment of forgetfulness:
that the most correct and cautious men were liable to be led astray
by convivial society, and no blame ought to attach to a cursory debauch."
But all in vain. The unhappy clergyman continued to repent, drooped
for a week or so, and died. Meanwhile, the little fleet pursued its way
through the still summer days, until they reached "the shallow sea
that foams and murmurs on the shores of the thousand islands, big and
little, which make up the Malay Archipelago." For the first stage was
ended in the long journey to Manilla; and Arthur Wesley walked ashore
among the palms that overlook Penang.

That regon of romance, of Malays and Chinamen, "of shallow waters
and forest-clad islands, that lies far east, and still mysterious between the
deep waters of two oceans," was more mysterious still in 1797. But the
Colonel seemed impervious to mystery and, Malays and palm-trees not-
withstanding, wrote sturdily to Dublin ordering some Irish linen for his
back. His tone was reassuring—"I don't think that people get quite so
rich in India as it is imagined in England that they do, but I must
say that I am richer now than I ever was & I hope in the course of
4 or 5 months to have it in my power to send you home at least a sufficiency to pay 2 years Interest on my debts." Here was good news for
an anxious agent, and the cheerful Colonel breathed the soft Malayan air
more lightly for its despatch. But before their first attack was launched
across the Straits upon the unsuspecting Dutch in Java, an impulsive

77

Government recalled the little force. The French, it seems, commanded by the atrocious Bonaparte, had lately made the most disquieting progress in Italy. Besides, the peace of India itself was vaguely threatened; and for these somewhat occult reasons it was thought well to concentrate the British forces in the East. So the expedition to Manilla sailed home again from Penang, and Arthur never walked the shadowy stage of romance, where silent rivers creep mysteriously past Malay Stockades and drums throb in vast, unlistening forests.

Indeed, he resolutely declined to see its mystery and instead composed a memorandum on the material advantages of holding Penang. Its defences, garrison, and revenue were minutely estimated; and the treatment of commercial problems seemed to shew that his Adam Smith was not unopened. This freight of views returned with him to India, where he was seen again at dinner with his mess or dining with a brother officer at Alipore. Hickey was with them more than once and found "eight as strongheaded fellows as could be found in Hindostan." After the cloth was off, they despatched twenty-two toasts "in glasses of considerable magnitude"; then discipline relaxed, the Chair considerably ruling that gentlemen might drink as little as they choose; but a cheerful company persisted bravely with the task until they staggered out to find their carriages and palanquins a little after two, leaving Mr. Hickey to enjoy an excruciating headache, which lasted forty-eight hours and extorted the impressive tribute that "a more severe debauch I never was engaged in in any part of the world." This was high praise indeed. Such relaxations aiding, Arthur resumed his regimental life. Not that his interests were exclusively military, since he still had his books and composed a lengthy memorandum in refutation of someone's heretical *Remarks upon the Present State of the Husbandry and Commerce of Bengal.* This malcontent had assailed the British connection through the East India Company, and the resourceful Colonel offered a detailed defence. His economics were self-taught; he ventured boldly on the sugar question and devised an ingenious naval argument in support of Great Britain's preferential tariffs in favour of West Indian produce by insisting upon the necessity of the Atlantic trade as a school of seamanship. The Colonel was growing positively encyclopædic; and he improved his Indian knowledge with a visit to Lord Hobart at Fort

28 St. George, where he found the little world of "hum-drum Madrassers"
and the more pressing problems of a Presidency which dwelt in uncomfortable proximity to the unrestful Tippoo. But he was back in
Calcutta on the May day in 1798 that Richard—dapper, aquiline, and
29 stately—made his auspicious landing. The frigate which had brought
him out was so "encumbered" (to the irreverent eye of the *Morning
Chronicle*) "with stores, carriages, and baggage, that should the rencontre of an enemy make it necessary to prepare for action, Lord Mornington will inevitably suffer from clearage in the course of six minutes
a loss of at least £2,000." Such were Richard's imperial paraphernalia.

Lord Mornington was still an Irish earl; but, halfway to his goal
already, he was Lord Wellesley in the English peerage now. They called
his brother Henry by the new name of Wellesley, too. Richard had
always seemed to prefer the fuller version, writing their surname, with a
30 faint contempt for its abbreviated form, "Wellesley, otherwise by corruption Wesley." It had an ampler air; and since the family must do their
loyal best to live up to Richard, Arthur felt bound to make the change
as well. For it would never do for Colonel Wesley to persist, when the
31 foremost name in India was Wellesley. So Arthur made the change;
and within two days of Richard's landing he signed his first letter in
the more impressive style of "Arthur Wellesley."

II

H<small>E WAS</small> a person of importance now, with Richard safely installed
in Warren Hastings' seat and Henry, his younger brother, at the
new Governor-General's elbow as private secretary. What could be of
better augury for Arthur than these highly-placed relations? Not that
their influence would waft him straight into preferment. For Calcutta
was not Dublin Castle; and the cruder forms of patronage were checked
effectively by the Company's regulations, to say nothing of Richard's
stern resolve to play the Roman parent. But Richard, however lofty, was
still Richard. Had he not always been the architect of Arthur's career,
brought him into Parliament for Trim, advanced the purchase price of
his promotion, even supported him in the vain pursuit of Irish places?
His principles might indispose him to endow his brother as an Indian
placeman; but Lord Mornington was not reluctant to use him for the
public service.

The new proconsul was inclined by nature to become a thunderbolt
of war. But the technique of war presents an obstacle that even the most
high-spirited of civilians find awkward; and Arthur was welcome to his
brother in the capacity of technical adviser. The post was strictly unofficial. But since the Company omitted to supply their Governor-General
with a military cabinet, that enterprising potentate proceeded to repair
the omission by employing Arthur Wellesley as an informal chief of
staff. Unofficial or not, the post was real enough; and Colonel Wellesley
was kept busy writing memoranda for the Governor-General upon a ¹
forward policy in Mysore, troop movements in the Carnatic, supply, fortifications, professional grievances in the Company's army, and the defences of the north-west frontier. His detail (he was always strong on
detail) was abundant; he projected forts without omitting to estimate
their armament, and "said nothing about Dindigul, as I have not seen ²
it, and don't understand anything relating to it." Supply engaged him
quite as deeply as strategy; and, always disinclined to soar, he kept his
feet firmly on the ground of practicable operations—"It is impossible to

3 carry on a war in India without bullocks. . . . Order that the collectors
of the different districts under the Company's Government should endeavour to ascertain the number of bullocks they have in their districts,
and what number they could collect without doing much injury to the
cultivation of the country." This was the prose of war; and few officers
were better fitted to dispense it than Lord Mornington's unofficial
chief of staff.

But Arthur Wellesley still remained a regimental officer. He was
a Colonel still. Not quite an ordinary Colonel, though. He had his
4 books; and in a list of them he made that summer there was abundant
evidence of reading that was far from habitual with Colonels in 1798.
He had discarded little of the library that had come out with him
two years before. His irony still fed on Swift; Paley and Locke still
guided him towards the eternal verities, Blackstone and Adam Smith
towards a just apprehension of earthly problems; and India still formed
the staple of his library. Cæsar, Saxe, Lloyd, and Frederick were still
his counsellors upon the art of war. Indeed, he found his Cæsar curiously
relevant to Indian military problems; for he confessed in later years
how much he learned from him, "fortifying my camp every night as
he did," and borrowing Cæsar's methods of crossing rivers by basket-
boats. But Bolingbroke had gone. Was it not Mr. Burke who had
uttered the scandalised enquiry, "Who now reads Bolingbroke?" Not
Arthur Wellesley, it would seem; and the attempt on Plutarch was
abandoned—or, his six volumes read, a triumphant reader had discarded them. He even weeded his light reading; and a judicious pen
was drawn through *Faublas* and the *Woman of Pleasure,* as he made his
5 list of books for packing. For he was ordered south that summer, and
Mr. Hickey was deprived of the society of the Thirty-third. They sailed
in August for Madras, and reached port after an arduous four weeks
6 of navigation, that comprised collision with a reef outside Calcutta, a
leak, a spell of pumping, and a supply of drinking water that spread
dysentery on board. Arthur was not immune himself, lost fifteen men,
and was left reviling the commissariat for its shortcomings—"I conceive
it to be very inconsistent with the principles of the Christian religion
to give people bad water when he had notice of the probability that it
would be so. . . . A Gentile could not have done worse than give us a

bottle of good rum by way of muster, and fill the casks with the worst
I ever saw." The convalescent was still fuming a month later—"It   7
is unpardonable, as I warned him of it, and I am afraid that I must
make a public complaint of him."

Now he was in Madras, where officers took evening rides on the
Mount Road acknowledging profound salaams from the old Nabob of
Arcot, as he rode, turbaned and long-bearded, in a venerable English   8
chaise behind his black postillions. But, his regiment apart, Colonel
Wellesley was in Madras on special duty. His enterprising brother at
Calcutta was inclined for war with Mysore. Somewhat unduly shocked by
an egregious gesture of the French, Lord Mornington fingered his   9
thunderbolts. For a flurried Frenchman at Mauritius had produced a
sonorous proclamation calling for volunteers and reciting that Tippoo   10
was only waiting for French aid to drive the British out of India.
Such ill-considered eloquence is habitual with revolutionaries. But
Mornington jumped almost fiercely to conclusions; and exasperating
visions of "Citizen Tippoo" planting trees of liberty, while grateful
Mysoreans performed the Carmagnole, danced angrily before his eyes.
The French were everywhere; they were in Egypt now; a draggled
shipload of them had even reached Mysore; and with India in danger
would not a prescient Governor-General be wise to strike before worse
happened? Besides, prompt action would enable him to settle the ancient
reckoning with Tippoo. Arthur, consulted on his policy, was less in-
flammable and wrote a chilling memorandum. The French alliance with
Mysore appeared to leave him singularly calm. While Richard's fancy
kindled with the dreadful prospect of Tippoo allied with the Republic,
One and Indivisible, Arthur was coldly counting heads—"the consequence of that alliance has been an addition to the forces of Tippoo   11
of 150 men at most." And even if the French should send a force from
Europe, he estimated that it could not exceed 3,000 men, who must
first elude the British squadrons at the Cape and in Indian waters
before they could appear in Mysore. Once there, a chain of causes
lovingly enumerated would reduce their efficacy by three-quarters. In fine,
the Colonel was not alarmed by the alliance and concluded that "if it
be possible to adopt a line of conduct which would not lead immediately
to war, provided it can be done with honour, which I think indispensable

in this Government, it ought to be adopted in preference to that proposed in the conversations. . . . Let the proclamation be sent to Tippoo
with a demand that he should explain it and the landing of the troops.
Don't give him reason to suppose that we imagine he has concluded an
alliance with the objects stated in the proclamation; and finding he has
derived so little benefit from the alliance, there is every probability that
he will deny the whole, and be glad of an opportunity of getting out
of the scrape. In the meantime we shall believe as much as we please,
and shall be prepared against all events." This was the wisdom of the
serpent. His chief of staff declined to soar with Richard; for soldiers are
sometimes less given to military moods than spirited civilians. The
Colonel's view received abundant confirmation and, to his brother's deep
regret, prevailed. The *rôle* of Mars postponed, Lord Mornington prepared his plans, organised allies, and waited for his moment.

Colonel Wellesley's mission in Madras was closely connected with
these preparations. He brought instructions to the Commander-in-Chief,
expounded Richard's strategy, wrote freely in cipher to Calcutta commenting on his seniors, and exercised unwearied pressure to secure a
degree of military readiness. His major task, more delicate, was to ensure
co-operation by the Governor of Madras. Lord Clive was difficult and dull,
cast in the mould that Nature favours to obstruct the bold designs of
clever men. His speech was slow, but easily kept pace with his thought;
and the resulting compound formed an unlikely partner for the leaping
Richard, who angrily enquired of a colleague, "How the Devil did he
get there?" Arthur, a shrewder judge, was doubtful "whether he is so
dull as he appears, or as people here imagine he is." So the judicious
Colonel took the slow-spoken peer in hand. Scarcely articulate themselves, such types are frequently impervious to the spoken word. But
Arthur's diplomacy prevailed; indeed, he was so far successful that there
was even a danger of his being almost permanently attached to this un-
inspiring duty, "merely because there is a chance that endeavours may be
made to set Lord Clive against the measures which the Supreme Government have thought necessary." Meanwhile, his backward pupil made
gratifying progress, and was presently discovered by Mornington to be
"a very sensible man . . . on the most intimate and cordial footing."
It was Arthur's first diplomatic triumph.

But his diplomacy found more strenuous exercise in importuning languid authorities to move the siege-train nearer to the frontier of Mysore, to have a plan of operations, to locate supplies "upon the line which it may be intended to follow," and to substitute effective commissaries for "the vague calculations of a parcel of blockheads, who know nothing, and have no data." His efforts, though extremely trying to the temper, were successful. But the success left him unsatisfied. He was still unconvinced that Richard's dashing policy was sound, and urged that Tippoo should not be pressed too far—"Nothing should be demanded which is not an object of immediate consequence. . . . I would confine the demand to his receiving an ambassador from us." Besides, his personal position as Richard's legate *in partibus infidelium* was particularly awkward; and his embarrassments were confided to his brother Henry with strict injunctions to say nothing of them to Mornington. They had a more material side as well. For his situation in Madras denied him all chances of obtaining a command elsewhere; and though his tone was highly disinterested—"whether I return £500 richer in consequence of having been in a command, or poorer in consequence of having been in Fort St. George, is a matter of indifference to me"—it was not surprising that his eye wandered in the direction of an impending vacancy in Ceylon, "if there be no war." But even if there were, his mood was curiously cool. It would, he felt, be long and doubtful; and he appeared to view with calm his own recall to Europe whenever seniority should make him a Major-General. Even when Mornington obligingly proposed him for the Staff in India, he acquiesced without marked enthusiasm, preferring European service, but conceding gloomily that "as I am obliged to serve in some part of the world, however disagreeable this country is, I don't know whether I may not as well remain here as go to any other place. I have been perfectly well in India, and I don't much care about being in a disagreeable place."

The drums of war, it seemed, scarcely made music in his ears. Meanwhile he struggled dutifully on, pestering supine officials and mitigating his exile with a shipment of delicacies from the Governor-General's *maître d'hôtel* and the more graceful *rôle* of witness at Belle Johnston's wedding. The tone of Richard's correspondence with Mysore began to deepen ominously. Tippoo was still profuse in his desire for "gladdening

23   letters notifying your welfare"; but Mornington, past compliments, responded grimly and with a creditable mastery of Oriental idiom) that "dangerous consequences result from the delay of arduous affairs." His correspondent countered with an exasperating rigmarole rich in allusions to Jamshyd, the major constellations, and his continuing anxiety for further intelligence of Richard's health, concluding with the unhelpful information that "being frequently disposed to make excursions and hunt, I am accordingly proceeding on a hunting expedition," adding however that a British envoy "slightly attended (or unattended)" would not be unwelcome. Lord Mornington, his moment come, permitted himself

24   the luxury of impatience; and Tippoo was informed that further negotiations would be conducted by the Commander-in-Chief of the British army in the field. Richard, it seemed, was going hunting too. Indeed,

25   he wrote almost savagely to England that "I have had the satisfaction to succeed completely in drawing the Beast of the jungle into the toils . . . our own army is the finest which ever took the field in India; and by dint of scolding and flattering I have equipped it within a period of time perfectly astonishing to the old school." Much of the scolding had been Arthur's.

26   The Colonel's preparations for the field included a soup-tureen and dishes for a mess of twelve. He was still deep in questions of supply and

27   earned the unusual tribute from the Commander-in-Chief that "the judicious and masterly arrangements in respect to supplies . . . were no less creditable to Colonel Wellesley than advantageous to the public service, and deservedly entitle him to my thanks and approbation." Small wonder that this adept viewed with profound disgust "two Company's officers; one of them . . . so stupid that I can make no use of him, and the other such a rascal that half of my occupation consists in watching him. . . . Besides this, they neither of them understand one syllable of the language; have never even been in a camp, much less on service." His own experience was scarcely extensive; but the young Colonel (he was close on thirty now) began to know his mind. Before they took the field, however, a trying incident engaged him. Consulted by an angry Colonel who was deep in an aimless wrangle with subordinates over a minor point of regimental accounting, Arthur advised him to abstain from issuing an irritating order. But since good advice is

rarely welcome, his incensed colleague insisted, and Arthur (always
eminently practical and excusably a trifle ruffled) enquired, "Then why,   29
if you had made up your mind to do so, consult me on the subject?"
The injudicious order issued, the inevitable duels followed between the
Colonel and his juniors; and the unhappy man, after a death-bed interview with his "dear Arthur," expired, another melancholy instance of
the degree to which a trying climate can exalt the sense of honour, as
well as of the prevailing taste—high-spirited, but how uncalled for—of
British officers for avoidable casualties.

The war was ready to begin. Arthur, who had been in temporary
charge of the whole army, commanded a division of native allies with
a slight stiffening of English troops, consisting (in his own enumeration)
of "the 33rd, six excellent battalions of the Company's sepoys, four   30
rapscallion battalions of the Nizam's, which, however, behaved well, and
really about 10,000 (which they called 25,000) cavalry of all nations,
some good and some bad, and twenty-six pieces of cannon"—a respectable
command, its nucleus being formed by the Nizam's contingent, whose
presence in the field was largely due to Mornington's acceptance of   31
Arthur's earlier advice to eliminate French influence at Hyderabad by a
prompt *coup de main*. The Colonel had been reading his Dumouriez—
"You have read Dumourier's account of his organizing the Poles; I am   32
employed in a business of much the same kind. My Poles fight too, and
that not badly, I assure you." The "ponderous machine" moved slowly
up towards the highlands of Mysore, and Arthur viewed without elation   33
the prospects of the war. His misgivings were sharply accentuated by an
enquiry from Madras whether Richard should take the field himself.
Arthur's negative was prompt and unqualified—"All I can say upon   34
the subject is, that if I were in General Harris's situation, and you joined
the army, I should quit it." Such frankness was, perhaps, a trifle more
than brotherly; but Richard, to his credit, took it extremely well, adding
his satisfaction at the general praise of Arthur's management—"I wish
to God the whole were under your direction; but even as it is, I think
our success is certain." Arthur did not. His mood was notably subdued. Henry was warned that "our war cannot be successful in one   35
campaign"; and he was at extreme pains to water Richard's wine more
liberally than any stranger would have dared—"I am glad that you are   36

86

prepared for a failure. . . . My despondency goes thus far, and no farther. . . . I think I have done better to make it known to you, than to tell you that it was impossible that we should not succeed. It is better to see and to communicate the difficulties and dangers of the enterprise, and to endeavour to overcome them, than to be blind to everything but success till the moment of difficulty comes, and then to despond."

His spirits rose a little as they penetrated deeper into Mysore—"There
37 is not *now* a doubt but that we shall bring that monstrous equipment to Seringapatam, and, in that case, we shall certainly take the place." They had a brush with the Mysoreans in the last week of March, and
38 the Thirty-third charged with the bayonet. His tone was higher now— "We are here with a strong, a healthy, and a brave army, with plenty of stores, guns, &c., &c., and we shall be masters of his place before much more time passes over our heads." But Arthur's health was slightly affected. His trying spell of duty in Madras left him a little low; and the heat of Mysore, in April combined with bad water
38 to bring on dysentery, "which did not confine me" (so Richard was informed), "but teased me much. I have nearly got the better of it, and I hope to be quite well in a few days." Before it left him, though, he was tried harder than is entirely good for any man with dysentery. For on the very night he wrote about his health to Richard, the Colonel was
39 in charge of a small column engaged in clearing the approaches to Seringapatam. The night was "dark as pitch *forward*, and in the *rear* towards our camp the fires and lights burnt brilliantly, which increased
40 the darkness in front." The column stumbled through the night into a little wood, which nobody had reconnoitred. Entangled in the darkness, they were heavily fired on and lost formation; the gloom filled suddenly with shots and shouting; a spent ball struck him on the knee; somewhere in front the leading files were captured in the night; and as confusion deepened, the Colonel—a trifle unaccountably—left them to report his failure. Shaken and unwell, he reeled back to camp. It was not far from midnight; and the exhausted man, his nerves all frayed, flung himself face down across the mess-table to sleep. Attacking in the morning, he retrieved himself and carried the position; but the night-
41 mare of the little wood had left him with the bitter flavour of defeat— "mad," as an officer recorded, "with this ill success"—explaining ruefully

to Richard his "determination, when in my power, never to suffer an 42
attack to be made by night upon an enemy who is prepared and strongly
posted, and whose posts have not been reconnoitred by daylight." And
forty years away he could still draw a sketch-map in explanation of the 40
affair at Sultanpettah Tope. For the unpleasing night lived in his
memory. Such lapses are occasionally final. Arthur's, happily, was not.
That icy rigour of control, it seems, which led his countrymen to an
unkind suspicion that nerves had been omitted from his composition,
came to him only by degrees. He was not born, but made himself, the
unmoving soldier of later years; and learning his lessons as they came,
he learned some of them (since night attacks are a rough school of
war) that night at Sultanpettah.

The siege was duly opened with the becoming ritual of parallels and
breaches; and Arthur found himself one evening in charge of a successful operation against an outlying work. But on the day of the assault 43
he was in reserve, commanding in the trenches, while General Baird enjoyed the unusual treat of storming a fortress in which he had once been
a prisoner. Baird's part was played to perfection; his sword was drawn;
his big voice roared, "Then forward, my lads"; a flag fluttered in the
breach; and panting Englishmen scrambled into Seringapatam. But when
they found Tippoo's body, Colonel Wellesley was at the eager General's 44
side, and Arthur's careful hand assured them that no life remained. The
captured fortress was a problem, since it contained vast quantities of
treasure and a scared native population. The situation plainly called for
skilful handling by the command; and the heroic Baird was scarcely
likely to display the requisite touch. Had not his mother, hearing years
before that he was chained to a fellow-captive at the tail of one of Tippoo's
guns, gaily exclaimed, "I pity the mon wha's tied to ma Davie." And 45
Arthur's portrait of him, drawn in later years, was no less distinct—"a
gallant hard-headed, lion-hearted officer; but he had no talent, no *tact*; had 46
strong prejudices against the natives; and he was peculiarly disqualified
from his manner, habits, &c., and it was supposed his temper, for the
management of them. He had been Tippoo's prisoner for years. He had
a strong feeling of the bad usage which he had received during his
captivity." This was unpromising for the prospects of good government
in Seringapatam; and Baird received a morning call from Colonel

Wellesley. He disliked the Colonel, since he had always resented Arthur's command of the Hyderabad contingent, overlooking the fact that Arthur was almost wholly responsible for its existence and that the Nizam's son had asked expressly for the Governor-General's brother to be appointed. Seated at breakfast with his staff in the palace, he heard the Colonel say, "General Baird, I am appointed to the command of Seringapatam, and here is the order of General Harris." The angry General rose, turned to his staff, and said, "Come, gentlemen, we have no longer any business here." But Arthur, upon whom rhetoric was invariably wasted, politely added, "Oh, pray finish your breakfast."

Such was Arthur Wellesley's entry on his first responsible command. His fiery senior departed in a blaze of protests, wrote angrily to the Commander-in-Chief, and received no vestige of satisfaction. For General Harris was not disposed to vary his selection, though he let Richard know that the appointment had occasioned comment. But Richard could reply with perfect justice that he had "never recommended my brother to you, and, of course, never suggested how or where he should be employed." He added, though, that Arthur was "the most proper for that service"; and Arthur's own reflections after thirty years confirmed his verdict—"I must say that I was the *fit person* to be selected. I had commanded the Nizam's army during the campaign, and had give universal satisfaction. I was liked by the natives." The choice, at any rate, was not his brother's. Arthur had earned the prize from the Commander-in-Chief; and if, as he declared in later years, "it is certainly true that this command afforded me the opportunities for distinction, and then opened the road to fame," he owed it to himself.

III

THE new Governor of Seringapatam succeeded at an awkward
moment, with half his subjects actuated by a strong desire to
plunder the other half. Indeed, for a brief interval the army enjoyed a
spell of looting, in which gold ingots changed hands for a bottle of
brandy and one judicious Scot acquired the Sultan's jewelled armlets at   1
a modest price from an impulsive private. Meanwhile the Colonel sent
grimly for the provost-marshal, and "by the greatest exertion, by hanging,
flogging, &c., &c., in the course of that day I restored order among the   2
troops." Four of the criminals were hanged and confidence returned to
the scared population, though the new commandant's embarrassments
were not diminished by the hungry presence of the late Sultan's collection of live tigers. Colonel Wellesley held himself responsible for Tippoo's
subjects, and urged with emphasis that "General Harris ought to go   3
away as soon as he can, as the plunderers of his army and that of the
Nizam still occasion great confusion and terror among the inhabitants,
and tend to obstruct our settlement of the country." He seemed to pride
himself that he had "gained the confidence of the people." For his mind
was busy with civilian problems; and Richard was advised at length
upon the future of Mysore. He still kept his independence though, insisting with his former clarity that Richard should not act the *rôle* of conqueror in person—"Many persons in camp . . . are exceedingly anxious   3
that you should come here to settle everything. I am (as I was upon a
former occasion) of a different opinion." The conquered state was duly
partitioned, surviving under British influence in a diminished form,
while the Company shared its remaining territories with Richard's native
allies. Freely consulted on the settlement, Arthur advised with all his
shrewdness—"I recommend it to you not to put the Company upon the   4
Mahratta frontier. It is impossible to expect to alter the nature of the Mahrattas; they will plunder their neighbours, be they ever so powerful. . . .
It will be better to put one of the powers in dependence upon the Com-

pany on the frontier, who, if plundered, are accustomed to it, know how to bear it and to retaliate, which we do not."

Richard, the war successfully concluded, prepared to bind his sheaves. The Cabinet was promptly informed that a marquessate, or else the Garter, would be acceptable. But the fountain of honour was distant, and mails were slow. Meanwhile the conquering army offered him the insignia of St. Patrick tastefully composed of Tippoo's jewels. Richard at first declined the gift; but the Company overbore his coy refusal, adding an offer of £100,000. Once more the Governor-General had scruples, whereupon his Board with sound commercial instincts substituted an annuity of about half the value. The news of victory reached England and elicited the thanks of Parliament; the fountain of honour began to play, and Richard's sovereign was pleased to advance him in the peerage as Marquess Wellesley. It was his marquessate at last; but the maquessate, alas! was Irish. His disgust was eloquent. A letter home was signed "Mornington (not having yet received my double-gilt potato)"; and the angry nobleman declared that "as I was confident there had been nothing Irish or pinchbeck in my conduct or in its results, I felt an equal confidence that I should find nothing Irish or pinchbeck in its reward." What now remained but for them to "dispatch the overland express; and for God's sake bring me home, home, home; home first, home last, home midst"?

Remote from these impassioned outcries, Arthur sedately governed Seringapatam. He had his troubles too, though the prize-money seemed to afford a brighter prospect. Richard was promptly advised that "my share . . . will enable me to pay the money which you advanced to purchase my lieutenant-colonelcy, and that which was borrowed from Captain Stapleton on our joint bond." But Mornington refused the offer with the utmost chivalry. Arthur was still embarrassed, though. Campaigning with a staff (and without increased allowances) had proved a heavy burden; his present post was quite as costly; and he concluded gloomily that "I am ruined." Yet he was disinclined to leave it. For when Richard proposed that he should go home with the trophies of Seringapatam, he made an unconvincing gesture of consent, "if it is thought that I can be of any use." But his pen was busy with reasons for remaining in Mysore. Had he not "the most respectable and the best

situation for me that I could have in India"? Besides, the thought of his
successors filled him with alarm—Baird was impossible, and Generals were
"generally so confoundedly inefficient." So, if the choice were left to
Arthur, he should prefer to stay; he might "render service to the public";
and as the year wore on, he was confirmed in command of the Company's forces in Mysore.

He was a satrap now, immersed in local administration and native
grievances. How seriously he took the last appears from his anxiety to
be dissociated from a somewhat ill-considered order of the Commander-
in-Chief, which outraged local feelings by a search of Tippoo's zenana
for hidden treasure—"I had nothing to do with it excepting that I obeyed   8
the General's order, and . . . I took every precaution to render the search
as decent and as little injurious to the feelings of the ladies as possible."
Indeed, before the year was out, he gave still stronger proof of his respect
for native customs. For when the redoubtable Abbé Dubois, labouring
in the Indian mission-field for a revival of native Christianity, demanded
the return of two hundred Christian women from the late Sultan's
zenana, Arthur reluctantly declined, "although the refusal is unjust,
because, the Company having taken this family under its protection, it   9
is not proper that anything should be done which can disgrace it in the
eyes of the Indian world, or which can in the most remote degree cast
a shade upon the dead, or violate the feelings of those who are alive."
The limit of his concessions was to demand a census of the Christian
women, which would enable the eager missionary to re-marry any members of his flock whose wives had died behind Tippoo's purdah; the
Sultan's heirs must be assured that "it is not intended to ask for a single
woman," though warned that refusal to comply would involve a reference to Government, which might be followed by unpleasant consequences, since "I am by no means certain that if the matter came before
Government they would not be obliged to give up every woman of
them. Justice and all our prejudices and passions are on the side of the
Christians. . . . If the Princes and the family here carry *their* prejudices
so far as to refuse compliance . . . the result will then be most probably,
that Government will give orders not only that every Christian woman,
but every woman detained in the Zenana against her consent, may be
allowed to depart." How many colonels in 1799 would have declined to

liberate the Christian captives of a defeated Moslem? This was moderation with a vengeance. Not that his temper was un-Christian, since he
submitted an official request for a chaplain, so that the garrison of Ser-
10 ingapatam might "have the advantage of regular divine service, and
other duties which a clergyman could perform." But he administered
an awkward province with a due sense of native rights; and when he
11 authorised a lengthy code of regulations for the re-establishment of native justice, he sanctioned separate tribunals for Hindu and Moslem law
(together with short forms of pleading and a compulsory reference to
arbitration before trial) in terms that reflected equal credit on his Blackstone and his Indian library.

The Colonel laboured to restore his province. The battered city was
12 rebuilt under a watchful eye—"This morning I was there at half-past
ten, and the people who mix up the chunam were then coming to work,
in number about 12, and there were no other persons near the work"—
and calm gradually returned to Seringapatam. But the country districts
were disturbed, and the remaining months of 1799 passed in the strenuous pursuit of an elusive enemy. The *terrain* was uninviting, since
guerilla warfare in the jungle is hardly favourable to the higher flights
of strategy; and Arthur found few openings for Frederician manœuvre,
though the ingenuities of Saxe were not without their lesson. Such operations (rendered acceptable to tender European consciences by the term
"pacification"), which are the aftermath of every conquest, normally
13 abound in opportunities for minor misadventure. But Arthur pacified
with skill, distributing his force in flying columns with defined objectives and orders that were invariably distinct and detailed. He took the
field himself and toured his frontier posts, enjoining a respect for native
feelings on troops engaged in punitive operations, and stigmatising ex-
14 actions from the villagers as a departure from "the first principle of a
soldier, which is fidelity to the trust reposed in him." He was still deep
in the absorbing task of pacification when Richard offered him a new
15 command. The unworthy Dutch were now to be relieved of Batavia;
the operations would be light, the credit ample, and the prize-money
more than rewarding. This lucrative excursion was proposed to Arthur,
"provided you can safely be spared from Mysore." But Mysore, alas!
16 had claims upon him. Madras was loud with outcries at the prospect

93

of his departure; Lord Clive grew almost eloquent upon the impossibility of replacing the energetic Colonel; and he regretfully put by the chance —"I do not deny that I should like much to go; but . . . my troops are   17 in the field"—assured consolingly by Richard that "you could not quit   18 Mysore at present. Your conduct there has secured your character and advancement for the remainder of your life, and you may trust me for making the best use of your merits in your future promotion."

Promotion tarried in the most provoking way; and Richard, who detected an affront to his own dignity in any check to Arthur, fumed over the fate of "Colonel Wellesley not only unnoticed but his promo-   19 tion protracted so studiously, that every Intriguer here believes it to be delayed for the express purpose of thwarting me." A Colonel still, he took the field again in 1800 to remove the last reproach of insurrection from his province. One *insoumis* still stained the bright horizon of Mysore, where Dhoondiah Waugh hung on the northern border, wear- ing the slightly excessive title of "King of the Two Worlds." Arthur, more modestly concerned with only one, resolved on "the destruction of   17 this man," and moved against him in force. His correspondence—a pro- tracted litany of bullocks and road-making—shewed how completely he   20 had mastered the lesson that transport is the key of war; and he was disinclined to linger on the awkward problem of Dhoondiah's precise status—"he either belongs to the Mahrattas, or he does not: if he belongs   21 to the Mahrattas, they ought to remove him to a greater distance, as no state has a right to assemble on the frontier of another such a force as he has on ours; if he does not belong to the Mahrattas, and he is there contrary to their inclination, they ought to allow us to drive him away, and to join with us in so doing." In May he started from Ser- ingapatam; in June he was one hundred and fifty miles to the north in   22 an exasperating region where rivers rose and fell at precisely the wrong moments; in July he was storming forts in the Mahratta country and, these obstacles removed, prepared for the agreeable *finale* of rounding up his adversary. But as the operation entered on its closing phase, the elusive Dhoondiah was far from passive in the hands of fate, and In- dian rivers almost uniformly failed to co-operate with Wellesley's time- table. In August the hunt turned eastward towards Hyderabad; the pursuing columns converged; and as the net was drawn round him,

Dhoondiah dashed at its meshes, encountering Colonel Wellesley and his cavalry. They met on a September day in 1800, and Arthur enjoyed the exhilarating luxury of leading a cavalry charge. Four regiments in line behind him drove at the enemy who broke, leaving the monarch of the Two Worlds (expelled with violence from one) to explore his other kingdom. The campaign had lasted fifteen weeks—the summer weeks of 1800, in which Bonaparte, First Consul now, dazzled the Austrians by the consummate swordsmanship of Marengo. Arthur was rounding up a robber-chief; and if his later exploits were a somewhat doubtful progeny of Eton playing-fields, the pursuit of Dhoondiah derived more obviously from hide-and-seek in Naylor's garden. For the Colonel had achieved a business-like triumph over a shadowy foe and the unmanageable facts of Indian climate and geography, leaving his brother to announce with sober exultation that "we have now proved (a perfect novelty in India) that we can hunt down the lightest footed and most rapid armies as well as we can destroy heavy troops and storm strong fortifications." The novelty and the proof were alike Arthur's.

The disturber of its peace removed, he was engaged once more in the settlement of Mysore. Land tenure, flying columns, and the incalculable proceedings of native potentates absorbed him. One night a dismissed favourite from Hyderabad poured endless grievances into his ear during the cheerful uproar of a nautch; and as duty kept him on the advancing frontier of Richard's empire, he surveyed the new problem of the Mahratta confederacy, where Scindia threatened to achieve "that which we learn that all our policy ought to be directed to prevent, viz. one man holding and exercising nearly all, if not all, the power of the Mahratta empire." Not that he favoured the heroic surgery of preventive war—"one country has no right to commence a war upon another because at some time or other that other may form an alliance with its enemy. . . . The question of peace or war is not, and cannot be, only the probability of success, but must depend upon other circumstances, and in this country must depend upon the prospect of being attacked by the power with which it is proposed to go to war." Late in the year these speculations were sharply interrupted by an order transferring him from Mysore, and a fresh prospect opened. For Richard's war-like eye, sweeping the western skies, observed the French to be more menacing than ever. Were they not still in Egypt? Besides, Marengo had been fought that summer. A British force was concentrating in Ceylon with the spirited design of making trouble for the French; and Colonel Welles-ley was to lead it, though Richard was perfectly aware that "great trouble will arise among the general officers in consequence of my em-   28 ploying you; but I employ you because I rely on your good sense, dis-cretion, activity, and spirit; and I cannot find all those qualities united in any other officer in India who could take such a command." So he departed from his province, leaving behind a military testament of im-   29 pressive detail, which enlightened his successor on the topography of Mysore, together with exhaustive notes upon supplies, civil government, and lines of operation; and for a time Seringapatam knew him no more.

IV

B EFORE the year was out, the Colonel was at Trincomalee (with
six cases of claret, six of Madeira, and six of port), deep in demands
for vinegar, tea, sugar, beef, Staff officers, and rum. Their destination
was a trifle vague. It seemed to oscillate between Mauritius and a voyage
through the Red Sea to take in rear the French whom Bonaparte had
left marooned in Egypt. Mauritius was their first objective; and Richard
offered the agreeable prospect that "if you should succeed in taking the
Isles of France and Bourbon, I mean to appoint you to the government
of them, with the chief military command annexed." Arthur was then to
choose between this novel eminence and a return to his command in
Mysore. Meanwhile he cross-examined likely informants on the approaches to Mauritius, the French defences, tides, landing-places, and
the unfamiliar problems of amphibious war. His little army waited in
Ceylon. But, the customary dislocation prevailing between the services,
the fleet was nowhere to be found; and its delays ended all hope of a
surprise attack upon the islands. Early in 1801 the Colonel warned his
brother of the altered prospect; the Admiral, a distant voice in the
Straits of Malacca, declined (from Penang) to attack Mauritius without
an order from the King; his muffled protest was decisive, and the expedition was diverted.

Richard's next notion, since Batavia was always tempting, was to send
them to attack the Dutch in Java. But before the plan matured, orders
from England changed their direction once again. Egypt was now their
goal; the waiting forces in Ceylon were destined for a protracted spring
across the Indian Ocean, past Aden and the bald Arabian littoral of the
Red Sea, and on to the Egyptian coast. Once there, they might reach
Suez, or a desert march from Kosseir would take them into Upper
Egypt. But Arthur's part in this amended programme was sadly diminished. For the angry Generals had prevailed, and Colonel Wellesley
was to sail (as Colonels should) as second in command—and second in
command, by an unhappy dispensation, to the most trying of his seniors,

Major-General Baird. Before this intimation reached him, he had gathered up his force, put it on board the transports, and shipped it to
Bombay *en route* for Egypt. The blow fell while he was still at sea.
Letters from the embarrassed Richard broke the news as best he might,   5
that potentate, in a rare mood that bordered on apology, explaining
almost timidly to Arthur that the postponed attack upon Mauritius
should be reserved as a tit-bit for him, that he could not have had the
command in Egypt without a breach of every service regulation, that
Baird should prove to be a charming colleague who was quite sure to
listen to his views, that Richard would not feel offended if Arthur chose
to return to Mysore, though he should much prefer him to remain with
Baird. But Richard's preferences were Arthur's last concern. He was
exceedingly annoyed. For this supersession seemed to his angry eye to
ruin his professional prospects; and the indignant Colonel rained re-   6
sentful letters on his brother Henry, who sent consoling answers but
discreetly kept the correspondence from the Marquess. Here he was—
"at the top of the tree in this country" and trusted equally by two Presi-   7
dencies—degraded suddenly, without stated cause, from an attractive
command. The General might be his senior; but Richard had no right
to raise his hopes, to make use of him for the preliminary drudgery,
and—least of all—to give no public explanation of the sudden change:
"I have not been guilty of robbery or murder, and he has certainly
changed his mind; but the world, which is always good-natured towards
those whose affairs do not exactly prosper, will not, or rather does not,
fail to suspect that both, or worse, have been the occasion of my being
banished, like General Kray, to my estate in Hungary." This was a
novel tone for Arthur, since he grew almost shrill at the thought of the
affront, of all his wasted efforts in Ceylon, of his subordinates misled
into an unpleasant trip with Baird, of his own career in danger.

That was a novel thought. Arthur—the patient, rather listless Arthur
—had a career. He had not seemed to think so in the bleak discomfort
of his Dutch campaign six years before, when his mind ran mainly upon
prospects of leave. Had he not done his best on his return to Dublin to
become something in the Irish Revenue? And even in India he seemed
almost indifferent as he balanced the prospects of a return to Europe
against an Indian career—"I don't know whether I may not as well re-

main here as go to any other place." His tone had mounted slightly, when he announced his preference for staying at Seringapatam; and now the angry Colonel, raging round Bombay in an unenviable mood, was anything but indifferent to his prospects.

His first impulse was to stay in India, to sulk anywhere in preference to serving under Baird. Before the month was out, however, his mood changed. News came in March that Abercromby was already striking at Egypt from the north; and if the Red Sea expedition was to serve any purpose, it must move at once. Baird had not yet arrived, and Arthur resolved to sail immediately and make a start in Upper Egypt—"my former letters will have shown you how much this will annoy me; but I have never had much value for the public spirit of any man who does not sacrifice his private views and convenience, when it is necessary." This was more soldierly. Not that Arthur was unconscious of his own virtue, since he wrote later of his "laudable and highly disagreeable intention." But the gesture was frustrated; for he was promptly taken ill. His illness was anything but diplomatic, since he was assailed after a touch of fever by an unpleasing malady termed the Malabar itch. The drastic therapeutics of Bombay plunged the sufferer into nitrous baths, which positively burned his towels; and as his cure progressed, the expedition sailed with Baird. The Colonel, partly reconciled by an unusual display of manners on the part of his chief, collaborated loyally with a voluminous memorandum on Egyptian warfare; he had been studying local politics, the desert, and the Nile and gave Baird the benefit of his researches. But Egypt in 1801 was not his destiny. Richard restored him to the command in Mysore, and he returned with evident relief to Seringapatam. The incident almost parted the brothers. For Arthur's "My dear Mornington" cooled instantly to "My Lord," reverted momentarily to "My dear Mornington," and was succeeded by an awful silence. The brothers ceased to correspond; and, this breach apart, the *imbroglio* of the Egyptian command revealed the interesting fact that Arthur had ambitions.

V

THAT summer he returned with sober elation to his province. The voyage south was uneventful; but once ashore the convalescent travelled at breakneck speed, lending interest to the long ride up-country by leaving his little escort far behind, and remarking cheerfully to a young captain, "If we are taken prisoners, I shall be hanged as being brother to the Governor-General, and you will be hanged for being found in bad company." A day was spent *en route* in courtesies to a native ruler, of which Arthur's Persian stood the strain admirably, even rising to corrections of the Company's interpreter. Then he resumed the dash to Seringapatam. On the road they heard of a promotion of Colonels to be Major-General; he brightened at the news and called for an Army List; but when he found that he was not included, he wistfully exclaimed, "My highest ambition is to be a Major-General in His Majesty's service."

A Colonel still, he entered on his little kingdom once again, assured by a consoling friend that honour and wealth awaited him at Seringapatam and by Henry that he was "still at the top of the tree as to character. . . . I have never heard any man so highly spoken of, nor do I know any person so generally looked up to. Your campaign against Dhoondiah. . . ." His lot was enviable enough, though his grievances still haunted him and he hinted darkly to Henry that "I have some thoughts of going home in the next winter if I don't see some prospect of being actively employed in India." But this was little more than a brotherly *boutade,* since he lived in a happy whirl of local administration and cheerful company. They sat down eight or ten to dinner in the old palace, the Colonel opposite his saddle of mutton. He ate well, though his recipe for health in India was "to live moderately, to drink little or no wine, to use exercise, to keep the mind employed, and, if possible, to keep in good humour with the world. The last is the most difficult, for, as you have often observed, there is scarcely a good-tempered man in India." Arthur was one of them, however; for roast mutton

8   was his chief indulgence. He rarely took more than four or five glasses
beyond his pint of claret; and such abstinence seemed almost total in
9   an age when military manners prescribed officially a monthly ration of
fifteen bottles of Madeira as the bare limit of necessity, with such extras
as beer and spirits and water by way of luxuries. Not that the abstemious
Colonel was a gloomy host. For he was always gay at his own table,
talking in his quick way of his past successes in the field (a meagre
theme for Wellesley in 1801), of intrusive seniors—"we want no Major-
Generals in Mysore"—and of commissariat iniquities, which moved him
to inform the mess one day that if he ever commanded an army of his
own, he should not hesitate to hang a commissary. So the lively Colonel
10 talked the afternoons away over his mutton and claret at Seringapatam.
He was just thirty-two, a little grey already about the temples; but that
was a mere legacy of fever, since his brown hair (he wore it cropped
and disapproved of powder on hygienic grounds) still crowned a young
man's face. Sometimes he got a game of billiards; and occasionally they
went after antelope with Tippoo's hunting leopards, the Colonel following the hunt in his own howdah. They had feminine society as well.
For wives were not excluded; and Arthur shewed a distinct partiality
11 for wives. A brother-officer recalled him as the wearer of "a very susceptible heart, particularly towards, I am sorry to say, married ladies." A
prudish aide-de-camp was shocked; an interfering lady interfered; but
if eyes were bright and husbands negligent, who could blame the Colonel? He might, perhaps, have thought of Kitty Pakenham. But Kitty
Pakenham was ten thousand miles away.

With these agreeable mitigations he laboured at his oar, writing in-
10 numerable letters about public works and army stores and the illimitable
theme of transport bullocks, or taking the garrison's salute after an early
morning parade in a cocked-hat, long coat, white pantaloons that ended
in Hessians and spurs, and an impressive sabre with a big silver hilt.
His official life from ten to four was mainly filled with a supremely
12 distasteful enquiry into the malversation of large quantities of stores. It
ended, after dragging him through "scenes of villainy which would disgrace the Newgate Calendar" in stern sentences upon the guilty officers.
But though the Colonel's duty was performed down to its most un-

pleasant particular, he was still capable of pity, writing to the Governor
of Madras:

> "I take the liberty of addressing your Lordship in favour of an old   13
> man, (the late) Lieutenant-Colonel ——, whom I have lately been the
> means of convicting of very serious crimes before a general court-martial;
> and I do so, not from any doubt that I entertain of the reality of his guilt,
> but from a conviction of his former good conduct as an officer, and of
> the extreme poverty and distress to which he has been reduced in con-
> sequence of the sentence of the general court-martial. I understand that
> when he will have paid the Company the sums which are due to them
> in consequence of that sentence, he will be left entirely destitute; and,
> without attempting to justify any part of his conduct, I may safely say
> that he becomes an object of charity.
>
> "Allow me, therefore, to entreat your Lordship to give him some small
> pension to enable him to support himself, or that you will recommend
> him for some provision to the Court of Directors on account of his long
> services and his present reduced situation."

Few causes have been better pleaded. For Arthur, incapable of false
sentiment, was genuinely moved to pity.

His other interests survived. He resumed the never-ending struggle
to secure respect for native rights and customs, though he had few illusions as to native virtues, writing acidly that "every native who gets a
paper signed by the name of a person having any power makes a bad   14
use of it and generally contrives by its means to extort something to
which he has no right." But he shielded villagers from requisitions;   15
insisted on behalf of Tippoo's zenana that "the greatest attention may
be paid to their prejudices and customs. . . . Keep everybody at a distance from them, and prevent all intrusion upon them, which can be
occasioned only by a desire to gratify a vain curiosity"; and even promul-
gated a sentence on an army surgeon for maltreating natives with the
stern comment that the prisoner "ought to have known that he is a
part of a body of troops placed in this country to protect the inhabitants, and not to oppress them." He had little taste for the strong hand—
"I long for the return of the civil government. Although a soldier myself,   16
I am not an advocate for placing extensive civil powers in the hands
of soldiers merely because they are of the military profession, and I have

always opposed the idea excepting in cases of necessity." His correspondence, though, was not uniformly official. A colleague was assured
that "I shall send to Mrs. Stevenson in two days some cabbage and
celery plants, and in about a week her rose-trees." He was a gardener
himself, sent cuttings to his friends, and quite early in his residence at
Seringapatam made judicious use of creepers on unsightly walls. Sometimes he enclosed drawings of native monuments with notes on Jain
theology; and once the Governor of Bombay received from Arthur a letter
that was positively arch. A young lady, it seems, had sent him a portrait
of himself; this tribute elicited the grim comment that "the two or three
glances which you mention made very little impression upon the fair
artist, as the picture is as like anybody else as it is to the person for
whom it is intended." This was ungrateful. But the Colonel's chivalry
was equal to the occasion, since he proposed to write to her himself,
"to tell her that I am glad to find that those few glances made an impression upon her memory so exceedingly favourable; and I have employed a gentleman here to draw the picture of a damsel in the character
of a shepherdess, which I shall also present as the effect of the impression
made upon my memory by the fair artist." Here was the Colonel in a
graceful mood.

He had other moods as well. An awful silence still prevailed between
him and Richard, and he seemed to view with equanimity his brother's
possible recall to England in 1802. His tone with Baird was friendly;
the rough General seemed to have won him in Bombay, and Arthur
wrote him all the news of India to brighten his campaign in Egypt. He
took the field himself quite soon in order to dispose of an insurgent
rajah in the west. This time, early in 1802, he undertook the complexities
of forest warfare; and the campaign in Bullum was a neat and punctual
operation by three converging columns. The leading rebel was run to
earth and hanged in pursuance of Arthur's grim determination on
"*the suspension* of the Rajah"; and the whole salutary process was concluded in three weeks. The expedition appeared to leave him with few
illusions on the subject of British authority in India, since he wrote that
year on the necessity of military power "for a government which exists
only by the sword." But he rarely generalised; the news from Europe
elicited little beyond gruff disapproval of Addington's limp pacificism—

"There is too much moderation and candour for these bad times. . . .   24
I see that they have submitted to abuse from the opposition, and instead
of retorting it according to the good old custom, they have deprecated
it"—and he was soon back at Seringapatam, lost in the familiar jungle
of timber contracts, errant subordinates on whom he sometimes turned
a slightly indulgent eye—"He has a wife and family (who in my eyes
cover a multitude of sins, &c.)"—and mess disputes that drew from him   25
the sage opinion that "a drunken quarrel is very bad, and is always   26
to be lamented, but probably the less it is inquired into the better." A
small godson engaged him, receiving kisses in the postscript of official
letters; and Arthur, with a sense of duty rare among god-parents, was   27
at pains to have his namesake submitted to the mysteries of vaccination
for the cowpox. He had lighter interests too. For that year the Colonel's
mess was swept, if one may judge from Arthur's bills, by a passion for
theatricals; and his purchases of plays appear among dozens of Madeira,
casks of ale, lamp-glasses, and potatoes. Some remain enigmatic; for
his acquisition of "1 Book plays" and "8 plays" reveal little of the sta-   28
tion's taste in drama. But Schiller's *Robbers* shewed them in a tragic
mood; though a sprightlier taste appeared in his purchase of Sheridan
(though no particular play was specified), no less than of Davies' *Plays
written for a Private Theatre*. The last, published in 1786, had just attained the degree of staleness appropriate to amateur performance, though
no record survives to shew whether Arthur played *General Blunder,
M.P.,* in *News the Malady*. The same account records his literary diversions, which consisted of a complete set of *The Novelist's Magazine*
and a French novel. Duty was tempered by these mild alleviations. Promotion came at last; gazetted in April, 1802, the news reached him in
December; and the world heard at length of Major-General Wellesley,
commanding the troops in Mysore, Malabar, and Canara.

Whilst Arthur loyally hewed regimental wood and drew provincial
water, Richard—a Marquess now—surveyed imperial horizons. The little
autocrat was more august than ever. Seated majestically in the stately
replica of Kedleston that rose at his command (to exasperate his parsi-
monious Directors with its "style of Asiatic pomp and display" and to
direct the juvenile attention of a successor to India, implanting "the   29
ambition, from an early age, to pass from a Kedleston in Derbyshire to a

Kedleston in Bengal"), Lord Wellesley held the gorgeous East in fee with peculiar enjoyment of the fact that it was gorgeous. "The drums and banners, the turbans and the flowing robes, the spears, the silver maces, the elephants with their canopies of State" entered his splendid repertory, as he "elevated" (in a successor's envious phrase) "the spectacular to the level of an exact science." His taste for grandeur found appropriate expression in an expanding Body Guard which, fifty strong at his accession, rose to two hundred in a year or so, mounted in two years more to three hundred men and two guns, and twelve months later reached the impressive total of four hundred men, two guns, and a band. Small wonder that Cornwallis was a little staggered on his arrival to succeed this Cæsar; the old soldier lost himself in endless corridors, was startled by Richard's innumerable sentries—"If I show my head outside a door, a fellow with a musket and fixed bayonet presents himself before me"—and the embarrassed veteran ended by ordering this galaxy of martial state back to the guard-room. Not that Richard's splendour was all for show. It was easy to ridicule "the sultanised Englishman"; but even Mr. Hickey, always a trifle fretful, could not withhold a tribute to "the pompous though undoubtedly able little Knight of St. Patrick." For he transformed "a little patchwork of crimson spots on the map of the Indian Continent" into an Indian empire. This process was observed with growing horror by an ungrateful Company. Leadenhall Street breathed its concern into the ear of Westminster; the Board of Control transmitted softened versions to the Governor-General; and that dignitary, resolved that India should be "ruled from a palace, not from a countinghouse; with the ideas of a Prince, not with those of a retail-dealer in muslins and indigo," and mounting

"the high horse he loved so well to ride,"

became increasingly impatient of restraints. His resignations grew in frequency, since he was by nature ill-adapted to a system of government based rather on the principles of ventriloquism than upon those of Montesquieu; and even Arthur, scarcely a sympathetic witness now, was moved to resentment of "the corrupt and vulgar interference of Leadenhall Street in the operations of his government." He felt for Arthur too, when an ill-timed economy curtailed his allowances for the Mysore com-

mand; for official disregard of Arthur's claims seemed to the angry
Richard to "have offered me the most direct, marked and disquieting   38
personal indignity." Their paths converged again, since he had work
for Arthur now.

The last stage in Lord Wellesley's strenuous conversion of "a British
Empire *in* India" into "the Empire *of* India" was the extension of British   39
influence to the vast territories of the Mahratta confederacy. As usual,
action was preceded by a preliminary phase of diplomacy. Arthur was
not consulted upon this stage, since the brothers' intimacy was still interrupted by their Egyptian misunderstanding. But Richard's finger,
vigorously thrust into the rich compound of Mahratta jealousies, drew
out the unquestionable plum of a treaty with the Peshwah, that dignitary   40
engaging to submit to British influence in exchange for restoration to
his throne. Arthur was promptly notified that his force in Mysore would   41
be required to take the necessary action. The order was not unexpected,
since he had composed a paper in the previous year on the subject of
operations against the Mahrattas; and he plunged with gusto into his
customary preparations. Bullocks and rice became the burden of his   42
official correspondence, because "if I had rice and bullocks I had men,
and if I had men I knew I could beat the enemy." His strategy was   43
simple:

> "It is obvious that the intentions of the British government regarding   44
> the affairs of the Mahratta empire cannot be carried into execution unless
> Holkar's army is either defeated or dissipated. The object of the campaign
> must therefore be to bring him to a general action at as early a period as
> possible. . . . If it be our intent to bring Holkar to a general action, it is
> his to avoid it; and it may be depended upon that he will avoid it as
> long as possible.
>
> "His army is light, and chiefly composed of cavalry. The whole composi-
> tion of our armies is heavy . . . Holkar, therefore, will have not only the
> inclination but the means of avoiding the result which, I take it for
> granted, can alone bring the war to a conclusion. . . . Therefore I con-
> clude that, after a certain period for which our stock of provisions will
> have been provided, we shall be obliged to return to our own country for
> a fresh supply.
>
> "There are but two modes of carrying on this war by which we may

avoid this disagreeable result: one is to place the seat of it in a country
. . . near our own resources . . . ; the other is to keep up our communication with our own country, whatever may be the distance from it
of the seat of war. In regard to the first, viz., to command the seat of war,
I have to observe that we shall no more be able to do that than we shall be
able to command its operations. . . .

"The second mode then is that alone by which we can succeed. By this
mode we shall always supply ourselves; the enemy may protract his defeat, but sooner or later it must happen."

This was clear-eyed. It was to be a commissariat war; and, omitting
all heroics, General Wellesley waded ankle-deep in questions of supply.
He called for beef; he called for sheep; he called for forage; he was
45   meticulous upon the packing of his provisions, specifying gunny bags
for his rice, kegs for his salt beef, and casks "with iron hoops of four
gallons each" for his arrack. Depots were stocked in northern Mysore
adjacent to the Mahratta border; and though operating from the south,
he conceived the unusual project of an advanced base somewhere along
46   the western coast, to which he could transfer his communications on
reaching the region of Poona—"by this arrangement we should carry on
the war at Poonah . . . with the resources of Bombay; and we should
shorten our line of communication many hundred miles." (The same
manœuvre was to shift a later army's base from Lisbon to the north coast
of Spain, as they worked northwards into the Pyrenees.) For months he
lived in an ecstasy of preparation; and though the breach with Richard
was not yet bridged by a single letter, Arthur's feelings were a shade
47   kinder now, since he urged him indirectly to come south to Madras
on the ground that "nothing but Lord Wellesley's presence can keep
the government of Madras in the direct line." The army moved in
February, 1803; in March they crossed the border; and at the moment
48   of invading Mahratta territory Arthur broke the long silence with a letter
to the Governor-General (though he was still "My Lord"), expressing
some uncertainty as to his own future in Mysore. Richard responded with
a whole-hearted testimonial to "his approved talents, firmness, temper, and
integrity," concluding with a vigorous insistence on his retention in the
49   Mysore command. These powers at peace once more, the war proceeded
smoothly. The long march was almost uneventful, and in April General

Wellesley rode into Poona after a final dash of sixty miles with four hundred cavalry. His dealings with the Mahrattas were almost uniformly satisfactory, and in the view of one highly competent observer this easy progress had been largely due "to the admiration which the Mahratta 50 chiefs entertain of that officer's military character, and the firm reliance which the inhabitants place on his justice and protection."

With the Peshwah safely restored to his throne at Poona, the first stage of the war was over. Richard was promptly notified of the success in terms which made it plain that Arthur approved his policy and would 51 deal faithfully with the "croaking" of his brother's critics; the family alliance was almost reconstituted now, the General resenting with exemplary warmth the latest slight upon the Governor-General—"the letter from the Court of Directors to the Governor of Fort St. George is shock- 52 ing. I hope that you do not propose to stay in India longer than the end of this year. Such masters do not deserve your services." At first it seemed unlikely that there would be any further need of military operations. Mahratta bands were still at large in the northern provinces, and for these his strategy was shrewd and practical:

"Press him with one or more corps capable of moving with tolerable 53 celerity. . . . The effect produced by this mode of operation is to oblige him to move constantly and with great celerity. . . . He cannot venture to stop to plunder the country, and he does comparatively but little mischief, at all events; the subsistence of his army becomes difficult and precarious; the horsemen become dissatisfied; they perceive that their situation is hopeless, and they desert in numbers daily; and the freebooter ends by having with him only a few adherents, and he is reduced to such a state as to be liable to be taken by any small body of country horse."

But he wrote cheerfully of his "great hopes . . . that the combination of 54 the northern Chiefs will end in nothing. . . . I think that, although there will be much bad temper and many threats, there will be no hostility." He made his preparations, though, his mind running on pontoons as a means of obtaining superior mobility by crossing rivers that remained impassable for native armies. His correspondence soon abounded in five- 55 inch cables, anchors, graplins, and measurements of boats; and as the work advanced, he discovered an increasing disrespect for native allies who "think that when once they have put the seal to a treaty with us, 56 they have nothing to do but to amuse themselves and sleep." (In a long experience of allies Arthur was generally disappointed.) The summer months of 1803 passed slowly by; and he was still detained in Poona by an endless web of Mahratta diplomacy. He was not altogether easy, since he seemed to have his doubts of Richard's eternal forward policy—"One bad consequence of these subsidiary treaties is, that they entirely annihilate the military power of the governments with which we contract them. . . . In my opinion we ought to withdraw from Poonah, and leave some chance that the principal chiefs may have the power of the state in their hands; . . . I would preserve the existence of the state; and guide its actions by the weight of British influence." The General was disinclined to war, if war could be avoided. He could still write in June, as interminable *pourparlers* proceeded with the Mahratta chiefs, that "my object is the preservation of peace"; in July he was a shade more sceptical—"If there be any truth in a Mahratta durbar, we shall have peace." Taking a hand himself in the negotiations (Richard presently conferred full powers on him in the most complimentary terms), he bluntly challenged Bhonsla and Scindia to withdraw their forces, still clinging gallantly to his conviction that peace was "very probable." But he wisely fixed no date for the expiry of his ultimatum from a practical desire "to keep in my own breast the period at which hostilities will be commenced; by which advantage it becomes more probable that I shall strike the first blow, if I should find hostile operations to be necessary." Then, as the last skein of procrastination wound slowly off the reel, he grimly informed his incorrigible correspondents in the first week of August that he had offered "peace on terms of equality, and honorable to all parties: you have chosen war, and are responsible for all consequences."

His first movement was a swift attack on Ahmednuggur. The place was stormed with a precision which elicited the rueful compliment that "these English are a strange people and their General a wonderful man. They came here in the morning, looked at the pettah-wall, walked over it, killed all the garrison, and returned to breakfast." This capture deftly covered Poona from the Mahrattas. Then he moved north to find them, crossing the Godavery in full flood by means of his precious basket boats. His plan was simple—"I do not expect that we shall be able to bring the enemy to an action, but we must try to keep him in movement,

and tire him out." He was at peace with Richard now, writing that
month to "My dear Mornington" once more; and his main preoccupa-   65
tions consisted of dealings with the natives, in which he lived up to an
exacting standard ("If we lose our character for truth and good faith,   66
we shall have but little to stand upon in this country"), and the eternal
problem of military hygiene—"I consider nothing in this country so
valuable as the life and health of the British soldier." After an interlude   67
of countermarching to the east and back again, he moved north and
stumbled on his enemy, a day earlier and in considerably greater force
than he anticipated, at Assaye.

The *rencontre* on September 23 was unexpected, since his intelligence
was far from perfect. Nearly half his force had been detached to follow   68
by another route, and the men with him had marched twenty miles that
morning. The odds were serious, since the enemy had 40,000 men in
line to his own 7,000; and the situation was uninviting, as they were
strongly posted in the angle formed by two rivers. Plainly he must attack at once, since his little force was manifestly unequal to sustaining
the weight of an attack by an enemy of six times their numbers. Success
depended on a double gamble. If the enemy would have the courtesy
to keep reasonably still, he might cross their front and reach their flank;
once there, if only they would oblige by still continuing to face in the
same direction, he might roll them up. His flank march across their front
was uninterrupted, and the first perilous throw succeeded. Guessing at a
ford, he got his force across one river, and drew it up with 40,000 men
in front and two rivers behind. This seemed a trifle reckless, although
the gamble might succeed, if an unwieldy enemy continued to expose an
unprotected flank to his impending blow. But the enemy, less unwieldy
than Wellesley had hoped, changed front with admirable precision and
faced his little force in its perilous peninsula. Then his attack was
launched, and the result was "one of the most furious battles that has   69
ever been fought in this country." With little scope for tactics, he handled
the attacking units well, led infantry charges against guns, and had two
horses killed under him. The Mahrattas were well drilled and amply
provided with artillery; they broke at last, however, leaving Wellesley
in possession of the ground and ninety-eight of their guns. But he was
almost spent; and that night Wellesley sat motionless among the casual-

70 ties, his head between his knees. His gay strategy—"Dash at the first fellows that make their appearance, and the campaign will be ours"— was justified, but at a singularly heavy price.

71 Richard received the news with stately raptures. He had observed their march "with much solicitude for the success of our operations on public grounds, and with every additional anxiety, which affection could inspire"; and now the watcher had been gratified in "all my affection and all the pride of my blood." He had foreseen it all—"It was not more than was expected from you"—and a majestic hand waved Arthur forward to his niche in a blaze of Ciceronian commendation. Arthur was melted visibly; and, until lately satisfied with a bare "Believe me, &c.,"

72 he now became ever Richard's most affectionately. Meanwhile, the army bound its wounds, assisted by a dozen of the General's own Madeira for

73 every tent of casualties, and moved off in pursuit. Two months of march-

74 ing, to an accompaniment of dilatory negotiations (and a touch of fever for the General), ended in a second encounter with the Mahrattas at Argaum on November 29. Unlike Assaye, this was premeditated; and

75 the affair proceeded with perfect regularity, though Arthur personally checked a panic of his native infantry. He wheeled his cavalry into position, riding sedately at their head, and presided calmly over an inexpensive victory. The last stage of the war was the storm of Bhonsla's fortress of Gawilghur. Arthur directed the attack against both faces of

76 the place, riding a daily circuit of fifty miles. It duly fell; and the year ended with a pair of peace-treaties which satisfied even Richard's exacting

77 notions of conquest, and left him in ecstasies over "a brilliant point in the history of this country, and a noble termination of your military glory."

By comparison, the next year was almost restful. Indeed, after three

78 years in tents the General began to need a rest; for early in 1804 he found himself "much annoyed by the lumbago." But his repose was interrupted by a minor operation, in which he moved five regiments sixty

79 miles in thirty hours and wrote exultantly that "we now begin to beat the Mahrattas by the celerity of our movements." Had he not once in-

80 sisted to a colleague that "time is everything in military operations"? Then he returned to Poona and received a presentation from his officers. The triumph continued at Bombay, where he rode through crowded

streets, received addresses, made sedate replies, dined at the theatre   81
(confronted by "an elegant transparency" of his own coat of arms), and
"had much conversation with mercantile gentlemen there." Even his
correspondence took a gentler turn; a Colonel's lady in Bombay was
asked to procure

> "some pickled oysters, and I wish you to prepare some and send them   82
> here. You must lose no time, as I understand that the oysters at Bombay
> become best when the rains commence.
>
> "Don't send them by Coleman, as he will eat more than his share before
> he reaches camp; nor by any of your great eaters, or I shall get none of
> them. . . .
>
> "Tell Colonel Gordon that I see that all the offices of subordinate Collec-
> tor in Malabar are filled up, and that his brother-in-law has no chance. But
> as a recommendation from a *great Man* is always a good thing I write this
> day to Lord Wm. Bentinck to recommend Captain Watson to him."

Arthur, it seems—unlike the stately Richard—could positively jest about
his greatness. His next letter was no less familiar, since it announced
with relish that

> "the oysters were excellent; everybody likes them. . . .   83
>
> "As for your susceptible youths, I consider three days full enough for
> them at Bombay, particularly when I want them elsewhere. But whenever
> you have a mind to detain one of my champions as you call them, you
> have my permission to do so, and I shall not be the 'Deaf Adder' of the
> reasons which you will give for detaining them, provided that you don't
> allow them to marry. After that they would not answer my purpose."

This was no grim disciplinarian. The sprightly General even pressed
his correspondent to visit them in camp:

> "We get on well, but we want you to enliven us. Allow me to prevail
> upon you. If you'll come I'll go and meet you with my Servts. at the top
> of the Ghaut, so that you will only have 24 miles to travel in palanqueen.
>
> "There is excellent galloping ground in the neighbourhood of camp,
> and the floor of my tent is in a fine state for dancing and the fiddlers of
> the Dragoons and the 78th and Bagpipes of the 74th play delightfully."

Here was a charming mood. His proximity to Bombay enabled him to
replenish his library as well; and purchases of books appear among   84

sword-belts, expensive saddlery, pale ale, York hams, and Gloucester cheeses. His taste for drama still prevailed; for Bell's Shakespeare (in nineteen volumes) and the *British Theatre* (in thirty-four) entered his library that year. Dow's *History of Hindostan* (to replace, perhaps, a missing copy, since he had brought out a set from England), together with a work on Egypt followed the line of his earlier reading, though the purchase of Gentz's survey of *The State of Europe before and after the French Revolution* showed plainly that his thoughts were turning homeward. A sheaf of pamphlets—*Brief Answer . . , Cursory Remarks . . , Substance of a Speech . . , Report of the Cause . .* —kept him abreast of current affairs. He bought some military books—two volumes of French tactics, Smirke's *Review of a Battalion of Infantry*, and Porter's *Military Instructions*, to say nothing of a *Summary Account and Military Character of the several European Armies that have been engaged during the late War*. For Arthur was beginning to envisage other theatres of war than Mysore and other enemies than contumacious rajahs. This work (which chilled its latest reader with the depressing observation that "an English general, who returns from India, is like an Admiral, who has been navigating the Lake of Geneva") surveyed the European armies. French methods were well summarised; the Austrians were sternly judged; and no reader could retain illusions as to the military efficiency of Spain after reading its choleric verdict—"a Spanish regiment . . . looks like an assemblage of beggars. . . . During a siege, they have been known to destroy the trenches . . . in order to steal the earth bags, and sell them for a few pence." A terrifying appendix warned readers of the *Parallel of the Policy, Power, and Means of the Ancient Romans and Modern French; shewing the real Designs of the latter against the Independence of Europe; particularly of Great Britain and Ireland.*

Not that Arthur's reading was exclusively professional. For at the same time he bought the *Sporting Magazine* for 1802–3, together with some odd numbers of the *Universal Magazine*. His latest acquisitions—dramatic, military, and miscellaneous—were added to the General's little library; and one work, a shade more unexpected than the rest, appeared in his bookseller's account. He positively bought a copy of Dr. Priestley's *Socrates and Jesus Compared,* and Arthur Wellesley faced that slightly condescending examination of the enlightened pagan. But his purchases were not invariably literary in design or male in destination. For "1 Brilliant hoop Ring and 2 pearl guards to ditto, 150 Rs." reveal a gentler mood. He was not easy, though, contemplating an early return to Europe and pressing Richard to resign before an ungrateful Company dismissed him. But Lord Wellesley, fairly launched on his career of conquest, was disinclined to stop. Fresh provinces beckoned him on to further wars; and Arthur wrote ruefully that "the system of moderation and conciliation by which, whether it be right or wrong, I made the treaties of peace . . . is now given up." His own principles were plain:

> "I would sacrifice Gwalior, or every frontier of India, ten times over, in order to preserve our credit for scrupulous good faith, and the advantages and honor we gained by the late war and the peace; and we must not fritter them away in arguments, drawn from over-strained principles of the laws of nations, which are not understood in this country. What brought me through many difficulties in the war, and the negociations for peace? The British good faith, and nothing else."

Small wonder that the questionable ingenuities of Richard's later diplomatic manner left him "dispirited and disgusted . . . beyond measure." War was resumed, with Arthur as a gloomy commentator. He watched the operations from a distance; but this time there were few victories, and the epitaph of the campaign was written in his grim comment that he did not "think that the Commander-in-Chief and I have carried on war so well by our deputies as we did ourselves." For Lake and Wellesley had made 1803 glorious by Laswaree and Assaye; but Monson's retreat and Lake's failure at Bhurtpore clouded 1804.

Arthur was growing restless now. Had he not "served as long in India as any man ought, who can serve any where else"? There was "a prospect of service in Europe, in which I should be more likely to get forward." (This seemed a trifle selfish; but his distaste for Richard's policy hardly increased the hold of India upon him.) Besides, his rheumatism would not be improved by another rainy season under canvas. The course of operations in 1804 rendered him almost superfluous; and after setting his administrative house in order, he withdrew to Calcutta, where he sat to Home for a head-and-shoulders at the modest price of

500 rupees, and assisted the Governor-General with a steady stream of memoranda, including a lengthy vindication of the earlier phases of his Mahratta policy. Calcutta had its softer side as well, attested by the purchase of a pearl necklace with some bracelets and a "silk worked shawl." But Monson's "retreat, defeats, disgraces, and disasters" (Arthur was not indulgent to these "woful examples of the risk to be incurred by advancing too far without competent supplies") recalled him to the south again, more convinced than ever that "against the Mahrattas in particular, but against all enemies, we should take care to be sure of plenty of provisions." Before the year was out, he was back at Seringapatam. The atmosphere was peaceful now; and the Colonel's lady from Bombay was informed of his "great dinners daily" and a sufficiency of dances, together with the General's gallant wishes for her return to Bombay "in high health and beauty to be again its ornament."

He was quite clear about his destination now—"I certainly do not propose to spend my life in the Deccan; and I should not think it necessary, in any event, to stay there one moment longer than the Governor-General should stay in India." The clouds were gathering round Richard —some foreshadowing resignation, others shaped perilously like dismissal; and Arthur foresaw "a variety of subjects in discussion, relating to this country, upon which some verbal explanation is absolutely necessary. I conceive, therefore, that in determining not to go into the Deccan, and to sail by the first opportunity for England, I consult the public interests not less than I do my own private convenience and wishes." India, he felt, had been a hard mistress, from whose penurious Directors he "had never received any thing but injury. . . . I am not very ambitious; and I acknowledge that I have never been very sanguine in my expectations that military services in India would be considered in the scale in which are considered similar services in other parts of the world. But I might have expected to be placed on the Staff in India. . . ." This was a standing grievance with him. Besides, British India was not in danger—had it been, he "should not hesitate a moment about staying, even for years" —and he concluded almost angrily that "these men or the public have no right to ask me to stay in India, merely because my presence in a particular quarter may be attended with convenience." His plans were

definite in the first days of 1805; he should resign, if quiet continued on
the northern borders of Mysore. Richard consented; and the General
promptly notified the authorities. A Madras official was advised of his
desire to secure a passage home—"I am not very particular about accom-
modation, and I would take any rather than lose the opportunity . . . and
I don't care a great deal about the price. I should prefer, however, either
half a round house or the starboard side of a quiet cabin; and I don't
much care who the captain is, or what the ship." This was almost precipitate. But his departure was delayed by endless complications—official
business to be wound up, his staff to be provided for, portraits distributed
to friends, and the safe bestowal of two elephants presented to the departing traveller by a devoted rajah at the last moment. Before he started,
he found time for an unusual act of kindness. Years before, when he
defeated Dhoondiah, the dead man's son was captured; Arthur had
taken the boy under his own protection; and on leaving India he settled
a sum of money on him, taking steps at the same time to assure his
future. Whilst he was waiting at Madras (and very far from well), he
received a pleasant piece of news which he passed on to Richard:

> "A fleet arrived from England this morning; it sailed on the 4th of
> Septr. I enclose a paper of the 3^d. containing an extract of the Gazette
> of the 1st Septr. by which it appears that General Lake is made Lord
> Lake of Delhi and Laswaree, and I a Knight of the Bath. I have
> heard no other news, excepting that Captain Fitzgerald of the 34th in-
> formed me that the fleet had spoken a Ship which left England the 27th
> Sept^r., the Captain of which ship informed them that there was every
> probability of war between France and the Northern Powers. He did not
> recollect the name of the ship, or of the Captain, or where he saw the ship."

So the world heard for the first time of Sir Arthur Wellesley, though
the recipient's sense of his new honour appeared to be almost effaced by
his contempt for Captain Fitzgerald's inexactitude of mind. A passenger
who went on board ten days later to find his own luggage informed
Sir Arthur that there was a box "kicking about the *Lord Keith*," which
contained his insignia. Then he prepared to start for home. His final
purchases comprised a selection of reading-matter for the voyage; and
it is pleasant to observe a marked deterioration in the severity of Sir

103 Arthur's tastes. Nine years before the Colonel had acquired a library which would not have disgraced a public institution. But Major-Generals need relaxation, and his choice of books in 1805 would have given entire satisfaction to a girls' school. *Love at First Sight* (in five volumes) was matched by *Lessons for Lovers* (in two); his fancy wandered from *Illicit Love* to *Filial Indiscretion or the Female Chevalier*. His bookseller supplied him with a dazzling array of the most brilliant popular successes in recent fiction, which appeared (if their titles could be trusted), to concentrate upon family complications. For the eager traveller was regaled with four volumes of *The Rival Mothers* and three of *The Supposed Daughter,* to say nothing of *The Disappointed Heir* and the wider horizons suggested by *Fashionable Involvements* and *The Fairy of Misfortunes*. In all, he bought twenty-six novels by authors ranging from Madame de Genlis to Mrs. Gunning. Almost the sole exception to his prevailing thirst for fiction was *Beauties of the Modern Dramatists,* a purchase which appeared to shew that his theatrical interests survived exile from the dramatic circle in Seringapatam. Nor was an earlier allegiance overlooked in his acquisition or Crébillon's *Letters of Madame de Pompadour*. The spirit of Crébillon almost seemed to haunt another entry in the same account, which debited Sir Arthur, homeward-bound, with ten pairs of ladies' shoes—small gifts of Oriental elegance for Western wearers.

104 The last farewells (including a convivial evening with the field officers and captains of the station, which "passed off with great harmony" and ended in a young gentleman's inexcusable refusal to sing and the arrest in error of a completely innocent captain by an inebriated Town Major) were safely said and due answers returned to the grateful addresses of Madras, Seringapatam, and his own Thirty-third. They sailed in March,

105 Sir Arthur with a comfortable conviction that "in India at present there is not, or will not in a short time, be anything for a military man to do."

106 But he had Richard's business to transact at home—"Send me all your commands to England; I shall have nothing to do excepting to attend to them, and I will exert myself to forward your views." Richard was

107 still his chief; though Arthur, who was nearly thirty-six, had learnt his trade and, in his own later judgment, "understood as much of military

matters as I have ever done since." Once more the breeze sprang up; a frigate sailed; and India faded behind him.

At midsummer an island stood up out of the sea; and Arthur Wellesley went ashore at St. Helena. His health, in spite of *mal de mer*, was better now; and he found "the interior of the island . . . beautiful, and 108 the climate apparently the most healthy that I have ever lived in." (Richard confirmed his view a few months later, deriving satisfaction from "its singular beauty and delightful climate," as well as from a congenial atmosphere of deference, and testifying to its beneficial effects upon a delicate young man, whose "health is restored by this climate.") Sir Arthur stayed there for three weeks, rode into Jamestown for a christening, and derived peculiar enjoyment from a Governor of antique cut—"a good 109 man, but a quiz, of a description that must have been extinct for nearly two centuries. I never saw anything like his wig or his coat." The General lodged at The Briars; the house (it had another lodger later) 110 lay pleasantly among the trees in a deep valley close by the road to Longwood. The names were unfamiliar to Sir Arthur—and still more so to an eager man, who waited in those summer weeks of 1805 for news of a fleet that he had flung halfway round the world to set a trap for Nelson, whilst his bugles rang upon the hills above Boulogne. But for three weeks in 1805 a malicious fate enjoyed the brief paradox of Napoleon at large and Wellington at St. Helena. Then, in July, Sir Arthur Wellesley sailed on to Europe: the island waited.

Dublin Castle

I

THE ship sailed home across the summer seas of 1805. Their course
was northward now; and as the bright Atlantic waves danced before *Trident*, Sir Arthur Wellesley sat writing in his cabin. His pen
was busy with a paper upon Indian famines, in which he wrote learnedly
of irrigation and native agriculture; and he replied at length to a proposal of Lord Castlereagh's for the employment of Indian troops in the
West Indies and the substitution in India of West Indian negroes.
Though strong upon the sepoy's virtues—"I have tried them on many
serious occasions, and they have never failed me"—he was sceptical of
the experiment, and suggested that Malays might answer better, whilst
he was more than doubtful about garrisoning India with negro slaves.

There was a pause in Europe; and as *Trident* brought Sir Arthur
home, the world was waiting. London, a little anxious, waited for news
of Nelson, last heard of halfway to America in pursuit of phantom
Frenchmen; the big hills above Boulogne waited to pour two hundred
thousand men across the Channel into Kent; Sir Robert Calder waited
doggedly off Finisterre to bar the road to England; and in a little room
behind Boulogne the Emperor was waiting for a fleet that never came.
Trident, in company "with about forty sail of Indiamen and Chinamen," sailed decorously homeward up the broad avenues of the Atlantic.
Far to the west Nelson, eager and miserable in his feverish pursuit of
Villeneuve, hunted the French towards their ports; and in those summer
weeks of 1805 Nelson and Wellesley both rocked to the Atlantic swell.
The General was nearing Europe now. Portugal heaved slowly out of
the sea as they sailed by, and the Spanish mountains stood ranged behind
the mists. But nothing stirred in the Peninsular sunshine. They passed
the coast of France; but all the hutted alleys of Boulogne were emptying. For the Emperor had changed front abruptly, turned a scornful back
on the derisive cliffs of Dover, and flung himself angrily against Vienna.
Eastwards across the world obedient Russians in the last of Mr. Pitt's
despairing Coalitions moved stiffly forward to the tap of their monotonous

drums, and Austrians fumbled with their arms, as the Emperor's *berline* rolled into Germany. Gold-braided Marshals in stupendous collars tilted hats of pantomime proportions; the French cavalry jogged eastwards through the blinding summer dust in the full coquetry of sabretache and dolman under a nodding avenue of busbies, shakoes, and immense brass helmets with plumes, with crests, with horse-hair tails, with strips of leopard-skin, with great imperial ciphers, as the long lines of bayonets wound across France behind their clanging bands to write Austerlitz upon their eagles.

Sir Arthur read his novels, walked the deck, and wrote notes to fellow-passengers. They reached England in September, and the General set off for London to lay siege to ministers in Richard's interests. One day he had a strange encounter in "the little waiting-room on the right hand" of   4
the old Colonial Office in Downing Street. Another visitor was waiting there already—a sad-eyed little man, "whom from his likeness to his pictures and the loss of an arm" Sir Arthur promptly recognized as Nelson, home from the sea and happy in a few weeks of Emma Hamilton and "dear, dear Merton." The Admiral began to talk and, as Wellesley recollected drily, "entered at once into conversation with me, if I can call it conversation, for it was almost all on his side and all about himself, and in, really, a style so vain and so silly as to surprise and almost disgust me." (Sir Arthur was unlikely to be captivated by the manner which, when expressed in an excess of stars and ribbons, had elicited from John Moore the pained comment that their wearer seemed "more like the Prince of an   5
Opera than the Conqueror of the Nile.") Then, suspecting something, the sailor left the room, learnt the identity of the spare military man, and came back transformed. All that the General "had thought a charlatan style had vanished, and he talked of the state of this country and of the aspect and probabilities of affairs on the Continent with a good sense, and a knowledge of subjects both at home and abroad, that surprised me equally and more agreeably than the first part of our interview had done; in fact, he talked like an officer and a statesman." So the French marched to Austerlitz, and the first broadsides of Trafalgar came faintly up the wind, as Nelson and Wellesley sat talking one September day in a room off Whitehall. Lord Castlereagh was busy; and they talked above half an hour. The talk stayed in Sir Arthur's memory; and after thirty years he

judged that "I don't know that I ever had a conversation that interested me more," adding the shrewd reflection that "if the Secretary of State had been punctual, and admitted Lord Nelson in the first quarter of an hour, I should have had the same impression of a light and trivial character that other people have had, but luckily I saw enough to be satisfied that he was really a very superior man; but certainly a more sudden and complete metamorphosis I never saw." They never met again.

6 All that autumn he besieged ministers with rare assiduity. His first assault was on Lord Castlereagh. Born the same year, they had seen something of each other in Dublin as young members of the Irish House of Commons. The other's legislative triumphs as Chief Secretary and pilot of the Act of Union through the muddy shallows had fallen in Sir Arthur's absence. But as Pitt's understudy Castlereagh now assisted another pilot to weather a severer storm, and the Secretary for War and President of the Board of Control took for his province the whole world (including India). Wellesley was soon correcting his Indian opinions, submitting memoranda, reading draft despatches, and setting Richard's proceedings in the most favourable light. He saw Lord Camden too, and told him bluntly that the Prime Minister's support of Richard left much to be desired. Pitt promptly sent for Sir Arthur; and, deep in Indian affairs, they rode slowly into town together—two noses of rare quality jogging comfortably side by side down the long road from Wimbledon. Then he was off to Cheltenham for a rest. Not that his visits were confined to ministers; for on the way he stopped at Stowe to prospect the Opposition. The Whigs were full of promises, pressed Richard to return to his old political friends, and to remember above all that the Prince of Wales was younger than the King. The shrewd General surveyed an unfamiliar problem, took counsel with his brothers, and reached the sage conclusion that Richard would be well advised "to remain neutral for some time and observe the course of events." This was judicious strategy.

His own prospects were slightly obscure. The Duke of York was gracious, and ministers shewed a mild tendency to make use of his advice on military questions. He met them all that autumn, when he was staying in Lord Camden's house at Chislehurst. They rode twenty miles a day;
7 and Mr. Pitt's invalid refreshment of steak and bottled porter was sent on ahead; then they rode home again to Camden Place, changed their

splashed clothes, and held a Cabinet on how to foil the French. (A strange irony sent the last Emperor of the French to die in the same house three-quarters of a century later.) Once or twice Sir Arthur was consulted upon proposals for Continental expeditions. At one moment it was hoped that Prussia could be induced to take the Emperor in rear; and the notion commended itself to Mr. Pitt, whose strategy consisted less in striking blows than in making agitated passes above the map of Europe. But this slightly feverish prestidigitation scarcely commended itself to Wellesley, who predicted grimly that the Prussians could not be "raised, equipped, and on the Danube in less than three months"; and the event proved him correct. These consultations left Sir Arthur with a less favourable impression of Mr. Pitt than Mr. Pitt's of him. For while the soldier gauged the civilian defects of the Prime Minister—"the fault of his character was being too sanguine . . . he conceived a project and then imagined it was done, and did not enter enough into the details"—the admiring statesman found that Sir Arthur "states every difficulty before he undertakes any service, but none after he has undertaken it." This was a blessing, after the querulous paladins with whom Pitt was normally condemned to work.

The autumn passed away. The sagacious Mack marched twenty thousand Austrians into the iron trap of Ulm; Nelson lay murmuring in the half-darkness of the cockpit; and one November night Sir Arthur at a table in Guildhall heard the Prime Minister returning thanks in two immortal sentences "for the honour you have done me; but Europe is not to be saved by any single man. England has saved herself by her exertions, and will, as I trust, save Europe by her example." One of the cheering voices was Sir Arthur Wellesley's. He soon had an opportunity to display the quality of uncomplaining service which had impressed Mr. Pitt. For in December, 1805, he was appointed to command a brigade in a Continental expedition affording the most ample grounds for complaint. A Hanoverian officer, who bore the slightly unpromising name of van der Decken, had proposed to plant a British army in Hanover with the laudable design of worrying the French; the Cabinet complied; and through the winter months of 1805 an aimless stream of reinforcements was maintained. An infantry brigade of three battalions was commanded by Sir Arthur Wellesley. He was a week at sea, passed an unpleasant Christmas Day in a gale among the sands of Heligoland, and landed below Bremen, seeing once more the unpleasing levels of the winter landscape which Colonel Wesley of the Thirty-third had left behind in '95. They saw the rain; they saw the unpleasing news of Austerlitz; they never saw the French. As the stricken Pitt dragged home from Bath to die, orders were sent to bring them home again; and Sir Arthur's second taste of European warfare—six uneventful weeks in the neighbourhood of Bremen—had been scarcely more inspiring than his first.

Returned to England in February, 1806, he subsided equably into the modest dignity of a brigade at Hastings, "in command of a few troops stationed in this part of the coast, the old landing place of William the Conqueror." The post, since all danger of invasion had perished with the French navy at Trafalgar, was not conspicuously exacting. But when someone asked how he endured it after his greater days in India, his answer was impressive—"I am *nimmukwallah*, as we say in the East; that is, I have ate of the King's salt, and, therefore, I conceive it to be my duty to serve with unhesitating zeal and cheerfulness, when and wherever the King or his government may think proper to employ me." Besides, the Whigs were in and Castlereagh was out; as Sir Arthur wrote to a friend in India, "*we* are not actually in opposition, but we have no power"; and it was hardly likely that professional plums would fall into his lap. Not that his situation was unfavourable; he was gazetted to the Staff as well as to the lucrative dignity of the colonelcy of his old regiment, and he wrote comfortably that these appointments "have made me rich."

Perhaps he needed to be rich in 1806. At any rate, he assumed at least one fresh liability that year. For in the spring he married. It was in some ways the most obscure of all his actions. There are no maps of such affairs; the heroine herself confessed that there were no love-letters; and the surviving facts barely suffice to indicate the meagre anatomy of his unpromising romance. He had loved at twenty-four, when the bright vision of Kitty Pakenham first danced before his eyes. Because he loved, his violin lay smouldering in a Dublin grate, and he resolved to be a soldier. That was in '93. A taste of soldiering in Holland almost cured him of military views. But love survived; and at twenty-six, a lover still, he set his modest hopes in '95 upon a civilian situation under the Irish Revenue and a home in Dublin. What felicity for Kitty Pakenham, designed by Providence to be his little Dublin wife. But Providence un-

kindly omitted to provide her with a Dublin husband. For in '96 the
quays, the Castle, and the Custom House receded; and for nine years he
walked an ampler stage under a deeper sky. At thirty-six the East restored
him. Was he her lover still? If so, he had been unusually passive. For
they never wrote. This singular departure from romantic ritual was confessed upon the highest authority. Kitty attested it herself in answer to
the Queen; for when she went to Court, the royal couple beamed ap-   16
proval. Her Majesty was pleased to be inquisitive—

"I am happy to see you at my court, so bright an example of constancy.
If anybody in this world deserves to be happy, you do. But did you really
never write *one* letter to Sir Arthur Wellesley during his long absence?"

"No, never, madam," answered Kitty.

"And did you never think of him?"

"Yes, madam, very often."

But fortunately his enquiring sovereign never asked Sir Arthur how
often he had thought of Kitty. Hardly, it would seem, with embarrassing
frequency. Never when writing letters; nor at the jeweller's. Yet during
their nine years of separation he both wrote to ladies and bought jewellery
—but not, it would appear, for Kitty, since she never wrote to thank him
for it.

Was he her lover, then? If he was, he scarcely seemed to know it. But
her world appeared to think so. Perhaps it was not, at first sight, the
sort of world that might be expected to carry weight with Sir Arthur.
For it was the slightly high-pitched world of Dublin beaux and Longford
belles, where young ladies romped and languished in provincial mansions
or flushed and paled in Merrion Square over matrimonial prospects.
Their skies were filled by her Excellency the Lord-Lieutenant's wife,
the Castle season, and the latest breath of London fashion; and when
little Miss Edgeworth of Edgeworthstown distilled her raptures over   17
"sweet Kitty Pakenham," she drew an air that was nothing if not provincial. But it was not unfamiliar to Sir Arthur. (How long was it since
Captain Wesley, a stiff Castle aide-de-camp, made his first awkward bows
in Dublin?) So he was not surprised to hear a Dublin voice one day at   18
Cheltenham, as General Sparrow's lady greeted him. She was a daughter
of Lord Gosford's; besides, he had seen something in the East of her

19 brother-in-law Lord William Bentinck, the Governor of Madras. But the Sparrow twittered; and Sir Arthur heard with more surprise her sudden assurance that Kitty Pakenham's sentiments towards him were still unchanged. What, the startled gentleman enquired, did she still remember him? And did the Sparrow think he should renew his offer? If so, he was prepared to. The chivalrous reply did credit to his self-command; and chivalry combined with Lady Olivia Sparrow to seal his fate. For Arthur Wellesley found himself Prince Charming unawares, hero (or victim) of a one-sided romance.

The next step was easy; for if Dublin drawing-rooms expected him to marry, what other course was open to a Castle aide-de-camp? His dignity (to say nothing of the lady's feelings) seemed to demand it. Besides, her attitude was distinctly flattering; and, his family apart, Sir Arthur was a little lonely. His friends were all in India, and the Longfords were a respectable connection. So he laid siege to Kitty in due form. Sieges were never his strong point; but it was the most successful of his sieges, though perhaps the fortress fell just a thought too easily. For Kitty Pakenham, at thirty-three, surrendered at discretion; Sir Arthur won his prize; and in the spring of 1806 he went to Ireland to bring home his bride. Pretty? Perhaps. Young? Well, not quite so young as she had been in Dublin. Devoted? Ah, devotion was her *forte.*

20 They married at St. George's, Hill Street; and every *amateur* of romance in Dublin thrilled with delight at the lovers parted for long years, the maiden's vigil, her knight in peril overseas, the hero's homecoming,
21 and then a leap into his arms, rapture, and wedding-bells. Miss Edgeworth plied a gleeful pen over "one of those tales of real life in which the romance is far superior to the generality of fictions," hoped ecstatically that "the imagination of this hero and heroine have not been too much exalted, and that they may not find the enjoyment of a happiness so long wished for inferior to what they expected," and asked with fervour what Sir Arthur looked like. An unreliable observer at the Castle informed her that he was "handsome, very brown, quite bald, and a hooked nose." But though he retained an admirable head of hair, he fell lamentably short of his romantic *rôle.* For his Irish wedding-trip was accomplished
22 inside a week; and when he sailed for England, he travelled by himself.

True, he had overstayed his leave to be with her. That was a saving touch
of romance. But was it kind to leave the bride to travel after him "under
the care of his brother, the clergyman"? It almost seemed to lend sub-   21
stance to the dreadful whisper that when the couple drove home from
the honeymoon, a startled world beheld the bride inside the carriage, the
bridegroom on the box. And yet, perhaps, she found it a relief: she was
always scared of him.

So Prince Charming, contrary to precedent, came home alone; and
the bride followed later in charge of a relation. This was a shade discouraging; but when his hands were full, Sir Arthur was not easily discouraged, and at the moment he had other things to think of. There was
his brigade at Hastings, which occupied him with agreeable problems
of coast-defence; he read stimulating papers on the Rye inundations and
the military virtues of Winchelsea Castle. Besides, that summer he went   23
into Parliament. His motive for the step was not ambition or any appetite for politics, but the defence of Richard. For, loyalty apart, the family
viewed Richard's fame as their main asset. Resigned at last, the splendid
Marquess was back in England, draped in the dignity peculiar to returned
proconsuls. But his attitude, though always regal, was not wholly free
from uneasiness. A pertinacious Anglo-Indian named Paull had dogged
him spitefully for years. This mischief-maker had succeeded in entering
the House of Commons, and was now engaged in a series of manœuvres
unpleasantly suggestive of impeachment. Impeachment was the mode
that year. Lord Melville was already well on the road to Westminster
Hall; and if Paull had his way, Lord Wellesley seemed likely to follow
him. (Such persecution seemed, if he might judge from the dismal precedent of Warren Hastings, the customary reward of Indian service.) If
Pitt had been alive, the Marquess might perhaps afford to disregard his
persecutor. But Pitt was gone; the obnoxious Paull had Whig connections; and it was doubtful how far Whig ministers would undertake
Richard's defence. Slightly alarmed, he mobilised his little cohort. Henry
was busy on official doorsteps; William was in the House already; and
in April Arthur was returned for Rye.

The campaign was not exacting, since the Rye electors listened more
closely to their proprietor than to any candidate. Their simple appetites   23
appear in his election accounts:

	£	s.	d.
Wine &c. &c. at the Meeting at the Court Hall	3	8	0
Supper for Corporation at Nomination	37	10	0
Cold Collation day of Election	15	8	0
Election Dinner Tea Supper &c.	123	0	6
do. do. for Freemen Wives & Families	88	12	6
Town Clerk's Fees &c. &c.	26	5	0
Serjeant's Fees	13	2	6
Ringers	5	5	0
Waiters at the Inn	5	5	0
Donation to the Poor in lieu of Garlands &c. &c.	50	0	0
	£367	17	0

The freemen dined; the corporation supped; the ringers rang; the waiters waited; the poor of Rye were richer by fifty pounds in lieu of wearing Wellesley's colours; and on these reasonable terms the obliging borough sent Sir Arthur to the House of Commons.

H<small>E TOOK</small> his seat in April, 1806, when politics were complicated by the strange ministerial interlude of "All the Talents," and the gunpowder muzzle of Charles Fox hung like a benevolent thundercloud over the Treasury Bench. Before the month was out, he was at grips with Paull, challenging his brother's assailant to state his charges; and Mr. Secretary Fox, who spoke in the debate, discovered a diminished taste for India impeachments in distressing contrast with his robust appetite when in Opposition. A few days later Mr. Paull launched his First Charge rather inaudibly, and only found a seconder after a most embarrassing pause. Sir Arthur followed with a fervent hope that the House would "consider the feelings of his noble relative, and come to such decision as would lead to a speedy and full discussion of the whole case"; and William testified with deep emotion to his respect for Richard. Unmoved by this affecting spectacle, the persevering Paull retorted in the subsequent debate that "the hon. but indiscreet Knight of the Bath was an accessory to many of the facts," eliciting from Sir Arthur the curt answer that "as to the observation that he himself was implicated in some of the proceedings, his short reply was, that what he did in India was in obedience to the orders he had received; and for the manner of that obedience, and its immediate result, he was ready to answer, either to that House, or to any other tribunal in the realm."

It was adroit of Arthur to appear as Richard's leading advocate. The laurels of Assaye formed a becoming ornament of the defence; and all through the summer, his days divided between rooms in Clifford Street, the House of Commons, and an uneasy feeling that he ought really to be back with his brigade at Hastings, he laboured at his forensic oar. He harried Mr. Paull with a zest once savoured in the pursuit of Mahratta chieftains, pressing him for specific charges, moving for papers, and scrambling over discovery of documents with a professional gusto worthy of the Temple. In July he made a Parliamentary appearance on a large scale, though India was still his theme; for he exercised himself at length

upon the Indian Budget, chosen hunting-ground of all sun-dried legislators, with a wealth of figures and a grasp of public finance highly creditable in a soldier. He spoke once on army matters in favour of increased
rates of pay for junior officers. Then the House rose, and he escaped from
Westminster.

Not that he found his *rôle* particularly congenial. The company was
stupid; and two sporting members, deep in discussion of their books,
were vastly entertained when the General, who sat between them, asked
gravely to what books they alluded. He informed a friend in India that
"I am in Parliament, and a most difficult and unpleasant game I have to
play in the present extraordinary state of parties." For it was not easy,
even for a skilled tactician, to align all parties in support of Richard,
though the egregious Paull ably seconded his efforts. Besides, there was
his own profession and the brigade at Hastings. After midsummer the
General resumed his military avocations in the plain little town, still
innocent of attractions and parades, where a green haze of tamarisks
hung about every street. But even there his pen was busy with a long
vindication of Richard's policy; and they still corresponded upon Parliamentary business. Sir Arthur was managing the St. Ives election for him,
securing the return of two members at the slightly exorbitant rate of
£3,500, payable within fourteen days after the meeting of Parliament.
But Westminster was plainly not his own destination. Sir Arthur was
growing restless, and his brother was informed that "it is such an object
to me to serve with some of the European Armies that I have written
to Lord Grenville upon the subject; & I hope that he will speak to the
Duke of York." His eyes had strayed from Mr. Paull to more interesting
horizons. For the war in 1806 was more widespread than ever, with the
French slowly bearing down on Prussia, a British army in the toe of
Italy, and unlikely Russians on the Adriatic. A military friend in Calabria
sent him a full account of the victory at Maida, which confirmed his own
impression that the French column could be beaten by British infantry
in line. There was even a vague notion of sending a small force to Portugal. Surely employment could be found somewhere in the world for
the Hastings brigadier.

Since his experience of active service was confined to Europe and Asia,
ministers consulted him exclusively upon operations in America. The war

with Spain had opened vast colonial perspectives; and delirious enter-
prises swam constantly before their eyes. Nine hundred bayonets, four
guns, and six dragoons were hopefully consigned into the vast spaces of   15
the Argentine to capture Buenos Ayres; five battalions were entrusted
with the flattering mission of rounding Cape Horn, occupying Chile, and
crossing the Andes; and the same lofty disregard of time and space dictated a third project, which verged on the sublime. Two forces starting
in two separate hemispheres were to converge on Mexico. One, based upon
Jamaica, had the relatively simple task of striking at the Atlantic sea-
board; but the other, destined for a simultaneous attack on the Pacific
coast, was to travel by a route devised in Bedlam. Embarking at Madras,
it was expected to proceed to Mexico by way of Singapore, the Philippines, and Botany Bay. The tedium of its voyage would be relieved by
capturing Manilla on the way; and having sailed halfway round the
world, it should arrive punctually in Mexico to co-operate with the contingent from Jamaica. This promising command was offered to Sir
Arthur, "if Lord Grenville can arrange it for me, & if upon the exam-   16
ination of the papers in the Secretary of State's office, & upon a conversation with the persons who have been in that Country I should think
the plan likely to succeed, & Gov^t. should still be of opinion that it is
desirable to obtain possession of Mexico." (The papers, it appeared, were
being studied at the moment by a Colonel Robert Craufurd, destined by
Government for another *rôle* in their South American extravaganza, with
whom Sir Arthur was to be better acquainted.) The General conferred
with the Prime Minister on the egregious project, and even wrote a
paper in which it was examined with perfect gravity, arguing with   17
painstaking lucidity that the time-table was wholly impracticable, that
a garrison of one thousand men could not maintain themselves with any
comfort on an island with a population of two millions, and that if
Mexico was to be attacked at all, the attack had better start from
Jamaica without Pacific complications.

Small wonder that he turned almost with relief to Richard's politics,
urging him to bow to the spirit of the age and seek journalistic allies—
"It appears that the Newspapers have at last made such progress in guid-   18
ing what is called publick opinion in this Country, that no Man who

looks to publick station can attain his objects, without a connection with & assistance from some of the Editors." Even editors and politicians might well seem preferable to Cabinet strategy; and in the autumn he expressed his own readiness to come into Parliament again and even to contribute to his brother's party fund. (That week the Emperor struck once again at Jena, and Prussia crumbled into dust.) The enterprising Richard hoped to mobilise a group of eight members with a total outlay of £7,000, which Sir Arthur judged to be "certainly cheap." He was prepared to sit with them himself, and to give £1,500; for his finances were distinctly brighter, and old Dublin debts began to melt before the rising sun of unaccustomed affluence. Not that he was reconciled in any way to a career as a back-bencher. His battalions were being steadily withdrawn for active service, and he was anxious to go with them—"and I don't care in what situation. I am only afraid that Lord Grenville does not understand that I don't want a Chief Command if it cannot be given to me; and that I should be very sorry to stay at home when others go abroad, only because I cannot command in Chief." This was a very different tone from the indignant outcries with which he had once refused to go to Egypt as second in command to Baird. But now all the world was in the field— John Moore and Lowry Cole in Sicily, Beresford on the River Plate, and even Craufurd off to some eccentric destination—and it would never do for Wellesley to remain in command of a few martello towers at Hastings.

The Cabinet detained him still with South American enquiries. He wrote copiously upon the coast of Mexico, and was condemned to the exasperating company of political exiles, spies, and noblemen with bright ideas. His views were shrewd, and on one vital point his grasp of Mexican realities was quite surprising:

"The French gentlemen who have turned their thoughts to this subject have recommended that one of the French princes should be established as king in New Spain, and the English and Spanish writers have recommended an independent government, without specifying of what nature it should be. None, however, have pointed out in what manner the government recommended to be established in that country should be kept in existence, carried on, and supported after the revolution should have been effected, particularly against the attempts which might be made upon it by the United States."

Such foresight, exercised two generations later, might have saved Maximilian and Bazaine; and uttered by Sir Arthur Wellesley in 1806, it came near to prophecy. But though vague on the political prospects, he was prepared to conquer Mexico with eleven thousand men and listed the requisite supplies with admirable precision. A sounder instinct than the French displayed in 1861 dictated that "the object . . . upon the arrival and disembarkation of the troops in Mexico must be to remove   22 them from the low countries on the coast to the higher and more healthy parts inland. I have asked for horses, mules, and pioneers, with a view to this object principally." But the mirage of Mexico dissolved; and he was left at Deal, writing stray paragraphs for Richard against the outrageous Paull.

That winter he returned to Parliament, elected in the first weeks of 1807 for a Cornish borough which lurked obscurely under the *aliases* of   23 St. Michael and Michael Midshall, otherwise Mitchell. He had a house in Harley Street; and in February, as the French felt their way across the snow to Eylau, a child was born there. He still favoured ministers with his opinions on Central America, commenting shrewdly that their   24 high-minded action in abolishing the slave trade would scarcely enlist the enthusiastic support of the slave-owners of Venezuela. The defence of Richard was resumed in Parliament; and once at least Sir Arthur left   25 his heir's cradle in Harley Street to get some hunting at Hatfield. But   26 before March was out, these agreeable exercises were sharply interrupted by a change of Government. A threat of toleration for his Catholic subjects aroused the sleeping dragons of King George's conscience, and Whig ministers were abruptly consigned to outer darkness. Pitt's heirs returned in force; Lord Castlereagh resumed the War Department, while Mr. Canning took the Foreign Office, and the Duke of Portland inspired general confidence as Prime Minister in time of war by the twin circumstances of being seventy years of age and in failing health. Sir Arthur Wellesley was invited to accept the post of Chief Secretary for Ireland. The offer marked him as a Tory. But the Tories had befriended Richard; and he accepted. His reasons, which were transmitted with unusual delicacy to the late Prime Minister, were almost wholly governed by the exigencies of his brother's position. As this manifestly demanded a **Tory** connection—

27   "the only doubt I had . . . was whether I should accept a civil office the duties of which might take me away from my profession. I have consulted the Duke of York upon this point, & he has told me, that he approves of my acceptance of the office, & that he does not conceive that it ought to operate to my prejudice; & the Ministers have told me that they consider me at liberty to give up the office in Ireland whenever an opportunity of employing me professionally will offer, & that my acceptance of this office, instead of being a prejudice to me in my profession, will be considered as giving me an additional claim to such employment."

A minister on this unusual tenure, he left his infantry brigade; and in March, 1807, his career as a back-bencher ended, Sir Arthur Wellesley was Chief Secretary for Ireland.

III

D ᴜʙʟɪɴ resumed him in the third week of April, 1807. It was ten years since he had lived there; and both of them were changed. His haunt was still the Castle. But the Castle aide-de-camp living a shade precariously on credit was now a Major-General, K.B., and Chief Secretary at the eccentric salary of £6,566. He was the great Sir Arthur now. And Dublin? Dublin had waned a little. For the slow poison of the Act of Union was working. There was no Parliament to meet on College Green; coaches were rarer now in Dame Street; and fewer gentlemen kept up their houses in Merrion Square. The city's pulse was slower. But Ireland was more feverish than ever. For deprived by Union of the traditional leadership of its resident gentry, an impatient country turned from its natural leaders to more exciting substitutes. The new Chief Secretary lost his illusions rapidly. Within a month he was assuring ministers that "no political measure which you could adopt would alter the temper of the people of this country. They are disaffected to the British Government; they don't feel the benefits of their situation; attempts to render it better either do not reach their minds, or they are represented to them as additional injuries; and in fact we have no strength here but our army." Relief for Catholics scarcely promised a solution, since he retained in later years a strong conviction that "Ireland has been kept connected with Great Britain by the distinction between Protestants and Catholics since the Act of Settlement. The Protestants were the English garrison. Abolish the distinction and all will be Irishmen alike, with similar Irish feelings. Shew me an Irishman and I'll shew you a man whose anxious wish it is to see his country independent of Great Britain. . . . I was astonished when I was in office to find the degree in which the opinion had grown that Ireland could stand alone as an independent country among gentlemen of property, persons in office, and connected with government. The connection with Great Britain has decreased in popularity since the Union, the abolition of jobs, the curtailment of the patronage of the Crown. . . ." Small wonder that as he paced a little

4   square in Portugal, he once proclaimed his belief that "independence is
what the Irish really aim at, and he is therefore for giving no more, but
proceeding upon King William's plan to keep them down by main force,
for he thinks that they have too much power already, and will only use
more to obtain more, and at length separation."

So Dublin Castle taught him to be a Tory. There are few better schools;
and Sir Arthur was a likely pupil. For the accident of his career had kept
him in the East for nine decisive years between 1796 and 1805. In those
years the movement of ideas at home sent many thoughtful men to study
unfamiliar topics, and the principles that underlay the Revolution were
viewed by calmer eyes than Burke's. Soldiers were not exempt from
such reflections; John Moore was something of a Whig; and Wellesley
himself had owned a copy of *Vindiciae Gallicae*. But whilst the leaven
of the Revolution was working in English minds, he was governing
Mysore. He stepped ashore again in 1805, quite untouched by any ques-
tionings. The accident of Richard's grievances aligned him with the
Tories; the Tories sent him to Dublin Castle; and the Castle made a
Tory of him.

5   Landed in Dublin after a most unpleasant crossing, he plunged into
his duties; and before the month was out, he was knee-deep in patronage,
dispensing promises with easy grace and draping refusals with profound
regrets. The dissolution of Parliament doubled his work, since the Chief
Secretary acted as head organiser for Government in all the Irish seats,
6   and he was soon desiring the Whips' office in London "to make me acquainted with the price of the day." Some borough-owners were reported
to sell to the highest bidder; others were more amenable, responding to
a timely hint of Church preferment for a brother. But in some lively instances his martial instinct was rewarded by the tumultuous delights of
a contested election; and he reported gleefully upon the prospects of
"beating out," and even "kicking out," an opposition candidate. An Irish
contest had a rare flavour, affording ample scope for military attainments
since, in *Charles O'Malley's* cheerful recollection—

7   "the adverse parties took the field, far less dependent for success upon
previous pledge or promise made them, than upon the actual strategem of
the day. Each went forth, like a general to battle, surrounded by a numerous and well-chosen staff; one party of friends, acting as commissariat, at-

137

tended to the victualling of the voters, that they obtained a due, or rather undue, allowance of liquor, and came properly drunk to the poll; others again broke into skirmishing parties, and, scattered over the country, cut off the enemy's supplies, breaking down their post-chaises, upsetting their jaunting cars, stealing their poll-books, and kidnapping their agents. Then there were secret service people, bribing the enemy and enticing them to desert; and lastly, there was a species of sapper-and-miner force, who invented false documents, denied the identity of the opposite party's people, and, when hard pushed, provided persons who took bribes from the enemy, and gave evidence afterwards on a petition."

Duels abounded; the military were present in force "which, when nothing pressing was doing, was regularly assailed by both parties"; and "the man who registered a vote without a cracked pate was regarded as a kind of natural phenomenon." Sir Arthur's bulletins recorded that Tipperary mobs, "parading through the country with green flags and feathers," had broken up conveyances taking electors to the poll; that the dragoons 8 were out; and that a Wexford candidate had killed his opponent in a duel, adding a little grimly that "as this is reckoned fair in Ireland, it created no sensation in the country." He pressed reluctant voters, reproached placemen whose support of Government left something to be 9 desired, suggested skilful arguments "on the ground of the Protestant interest and on Talbot's revolutionary speech on the first day of the election," and generally proved himself a worthy manipulator of the electoral machine. The experience was scarcely calculated to increase his respect for representative institutions. But the Irish elections of 1807 were, perhaps, the most remarkable (and not the least successful) of Wellington's campaigns.

His own electoral career was less adventurous. Relinquishing his Cornish seat on grounds which may be surmised from its earlier history (St. Michael had cost Clive so much that he was driven back to India and 10 glory on the field of Plassey), Sir Arthur stipulated that its successor must be inexpensive, rejected Ipswich, and with admirable simplicity "directed Justice Day to return me for Tralee." That luminary complied; though Sir Arthur was simultaneously returned for Newport, Isle of Wight, for which he subsequently elected to sit. His fellow-member was a fresh-faced young gentleman just down from Cambridge, who had succeeded

recently as Viscount Palmerston. Till the House met, work kept him at
his desk in Dublin. He was housed comfortably at the Chief Secretary's
Lodge in Phœnix Park, left his bow-fronted home each morning, and
rode across the Park with the Lord-Lieutenant's daughters. They parted
at the gate (as yet unshadowed by any Wellington Testimonial); and
he rode slowly down the quays towards the Castle. His work was waiting on the table in the Chief Secretary's room; and through the summer
days he sat writing courteous letters to his official correspondents. His
correspondents all had wishes; and with rare unanimity their wishes
seemed to run in one direction. For they invariably coincided in a disinterested anxiety to see deserving friends accommodated at the public
expense. A bland Chief Secretary was "concerned that he cannot adopt
this opportunity of gratifying your wishes," politely indicated obstacles
"which may, and indeed must, retard the accomplishment of your wishes,"
and confessed how happy he should have been "in being instrumental
in forwarding your wishes." The gentle sibilant ran, like a mild refrain,
through all his correspondence. But he could still be firm, refuse a pension to a peeress, and write firmly to his sister that there was no vacancy
in the Dublin packets, and that if there were "it may be expected that
the Duke of Richmond or I, who have been all over the world, have
naval friends of merit, but not rich, to whom we may be desirous of
giving such a provision." Matters of larger policy occasionally interrupted
the absorbing business of distributing loaves and fishes. He wrote wisely
on the defence of Ireland, dismissed martello towers in favour of mobile
naval defence, and assumed judiciously that "Ireland, in a view to military operations, must be considered as an enemy's country." But he was
capable of moderation, and could refuse leave for a Yeomanry celebration
of the events of '98 upon the admirable ground that "it appears impossible to celebrate the victory at Vinegar Hill without recalling . . . the
persons over whom that victory was gained, and all the unfortunate circumstances of the times which concurred to bring about that state of
affairs which rendered that battle and victory necessary. His Grace cannot believe that those who wish to commemorate their military achievement are desirous to hurt the feelings of others, however blameable and
guilty they may have been; and he does not suppose that they can wish
to perpetuate the memory of the unfortunate circumstances which led

to the contest in question." For long memories, the standing curse of Ireland, were best discouraged; and a wise Chief Secretary checked the throb of Orange drums.

Indeed, his ears were tuned that summer to the sound of other drums. For a rumour reached him of an expedition to the Baltic, and he was soon pressing Castlereagh to release him from his desk—"It will be understood and said that I had avoided or had not sought for an opportunity of serving abroad in order to hold a large civil office. As I am determined not to give up the military profession, and as I know that I can be of no service in it unless I have the confidence and esteem of the officers and soldiers of the army, I must shape my course in such a manner as to avoid this imputation. If, therefore, you send the expedition, I wish you would urge Lord Hawkesbury to fix upon a successor for me, as I positively cannot stay here whether I am to be employed with it or not." But, for the moment, duty called at Westminster, and Sir Arthur's eye surveyed civilian ranks. For the House met in June; an Irish relative was gaily informed that "we must get our troops over by the 22nd of this month . . . and I think your presence here in the next week to hurry the fellows away might have good consequences"; and before the month was out, he sailed for England. As they left Dublin, his observant eye was caught by a defective pier, and he learned something on the passage about the grievances of packet captains. Kitty was left behind in Phœnix Park. For she was his little Dublin wife; and, instinctively perhaps, she stayed behind in Dublin. But Sir Arthur was back at Harley Street, deep in correspondence upon Church patronage or speaking in the House of Commons on an Irish sinecure. He was still pressing the egregious Paull to state his charges against Richard; and the Chief Secretary found himself introducing a Coercion Bill inherited from his predecessor. In the best Castle style he proposed a duration of seven years, and experienced the unpleasant sensation of being thrown over in the debate by the Chancellor of the Exchequer. He was heard once again— this time on Indian finance—wrote countless letters about military loaves and ecclesiastical fishes, pressed a young sailor's claims upon the First Lord of the Admiralty with the dry commendation that they were "founded upon his being the favourite son of his mother, who was a favourite of yours about thirty years ago," and did his best to govern

Ireland from his room in Harley Street, opining tartly that "it would be best to take no further notice of the trees of liberty at Tipperary" because "Lord Landaff will be tired of furnishing trees as often as those planted will wither." One day in June, as the slow waters of a northern river mirrored a barge on which two Emperors shared out the world, Sir Arthur Wellesley was busy writing dutiful injunctions about a Castle informer.

Small wonder that he turned with evident relief to his own professional prospects. For the vague expedition to the Baltic had now a less uncertain outline. A descent on Denmark was suddenly projected; and in the last week of July ministers acceded to Sir Arthur's application to serve with the expedition—"I don't know, and I have not asked, whether I am to return to my office when this coup-de-main will have been struck or will have failed." Indeed, he scarcely seemed to mind. For war was his profession; and "no political office could compensate to me the loss of the situation which I hold in the army, and nothing shall induce me to give it up." They gave him a division; and, Chief Secretary still, the strange pluralist posted from Harley Street to Sheerness and sailed in the *Prometheus* fire-ship for Copenhagen.

IN THE Danish expedition of 1807 Great Britain's policy against
Napoleon became, for the first and last time, Napoleonic. A friendly
neutral was curtly summoned to give up its fleet. True, there was reason
to suppose that France was on the point of seizing it herself. Besides, 1
Great Britain undertook to hold the ceded warships as a "sacred pledge"
until the war was over. But Albion, rarely perfidious, seemed suddenly
resolved to earn her title. An unaccustomed ruthlessness transformed those
amiable features; scruples were hastily discarded by the vivacious Canning; King George appeared in the aggressor's *rôle*; and this departure
was rendered still more shocking by its complete success.

The expedition to the Baltic was hastily diverted from its random exploration of seaside resorts and strongly reinforced. Sir Arthur took command of the reserve, though he did not owe the appointment "to any
favour or confidence from the Horse Guards. . . . In the first place, they 2
thought very little of any one who had served in India. An Indian victory
was not only no ground of confidence, but it was actually a cause of
suspicion. Then because I was in Parliament, and connected with people
in office, I was a politician, and a politician never can be a soldier. Moreover, they looked upon me with a kind of jealousy, because I was a lord's
son, '*a sprig of nobility*,' who came into the army more for ornament than
use . . . they thought I could not be trusted alone with a division. . . .
When the Horse Guards are obliged to employ one of those fellows like
me in whom they have no confidence, they give him what is called a
second in command—one in whom they have confidence—a kind of *dry
nurse*." Sir Arthur's nurse, a thoughtful brigadier named Stewart, was
admirably chosen; and half his command came from the infantry train-
ing-camp at Shorncliffe, where John Moore forged the Light Brigade.
They sailed in summer weather, and he went ashore in the first week of 3
August beneath the battlements of Elsinore. His professional custodian
was discreetly helpful at every turn—"during the embarkation, the voy- 2
age out, and the disembarkation General Stewart did everything. I saw

no kind of objection to anything he suggested, and all went *à merveille.*" His command landed with "one simultaneous and tremendous cheer" in the summer dawn to the north of Copenhagen. The city was invested; and when a Danish force that had been left at large shewed a disturbing tendency to interrupt, Sir Arthur was detached to deal with it. His plan was simple: whilst he attacked the enemy in front, a second force was to sweep round and take them in rear. But chance, a broken bridge, and somebody's mishap denied him the complete success; and though he found the Danes at Kioge on August 29, attacked with spirit, and destroyed them, he was left lamenting that "not a man would have made his retreat if [General Linsingen] had carried into execution his part of the plan; but, as it is, they have been sufficiently beat to prevent their assembling again." It was a neat performance, and the credit was all his own. For when the helpful Stewart began to make suggestions, "I stopped him short with 'Come, come, 'tis my turn now.' I immediately made my own dispositions, assigned him the command of one of the wings, gave him his orders, attacked the enemy, and beat them. Stewart, like a man of sense, saw in a moment that I understood my business, and subsided with (as far as I saw) good humour into his proper place."

The British forces could dispose of Copenhagen at their leisure now. It was to be bombarded, though Sir Arthur felt a strong distaste for this form of coercion and would have preferred to starve the city. But the guns played on it, whilst he ranged the open country and exchanged chivalrous correspondence with defeated Danes. He met a gentleman named Rosencrantz, and resisted, as he afterwards confessed, a strong temptation to ask him after Guildenstern; a General conveyed his gratitude in imperfect English "for your human and generous conduct . . . it is a great pitty that political views should counteract the private feelings of the individuals"; one grateful Dane thanked him "sincerely and of my heart for the protection you have given me in these days your troops have laid in my neighbourhood"; and an indignant Princess, whose property had been tampered with, was so far mollified by his courtly apologies and its prompt restoration as to offer a shy gift of fruit—"*pleignant seulement qui'ils ne soyent pas meilleures*"—and to invite Sir Arthur, "*comme le Chevalier est amateur de chasse,*" to shoot her coverts. These amenities lasted into the autumn. The city fell; and in recognition of his services

at Kioge Sir Arthur was detailed to negotiate the terms of its capitulation.   10
Then he recalled that he was still Chief Secretary for Ireland, and that
the days were drawing in—"the *long nights* are approaching fast, and if
I am to have any concern in the government of that country, it is desir- 11
able that I should be there." So he was given leave at once and sailed
home, shortly followed by the surrendered Danish fleet. His sole memento
of the expedition was a likely colt named "Copenhagen."   12

V

THE world was more than usually out of joint that autumn; and England seemed to run before the gale under bare poles. How proudly she had sailed with Mr. Pitt for pilot and all the sails of Coalition set. But now the last shreds of her allies had vanished, as gust after gust swept across Europe from the west. Austerlitz had carried Austria away; Jena took off the Prussians; and the inconstant Czar, shaken at Eylau, went dancing down the wind of Friedland. There were no allies left for England excepting a mad King of Sweden, who was too mad even to change sides. Small wonder that the Emperor, parading Europe with a troupe of kings and dealing continents like cards, shared half the world with Alexander on the barge at Tilsit. For the world obeyed him now. His writ ran from Naples to the Baltic; and the Pope was a mere bishop—one of his bishops. He could make dukes like wild flowers (he made twenty-six that year), give laws to the whole Continent, leave England starving on its island, its goods shut out by his *douaniers* from every port. For every port seemed to be his. True, Portugal still kept a narrow doorway on the Atlantic. If so, then Portugal must take his orders; and when the Emperor commanded, who could deny him?

Sir Arthur Wellesley sailed sedately home from Copenhagen, landed
1 at Yarmouth, and was stopped at a country house in Suffolk to confer with Castlereagh. There was a notion of sending him back to Denmark
2 to continue the negotiations, but Lord Hawkesbury demurred. The traveller reached London "in high spirits." For the brush at Kioge stood to his credit, and ministers appeared to value him. Had not Lord Castle-
1 reagh written that "we shall want him for Flushing"? But fate spared him Walcheren; and he returned to Dublin, the Castle, and his Lodge in Phœnix Park. Not that he meant to stay there, since he assured a
3 friend in India that he was even ready to return to the East, though "I don't think it probable that I shall be called upon . . . men in power in England think very little of that country, and those who do think

of it feel very little inclination that I should go there. Besides that, I
have got pretty high upon the tree since I came home, and those in
power think I cannot well be spared from objects nearer home." So
Canning was informed that "I shall be happy to aid the government in   4
any manner they please, and am ready to set out for any part of the
world at a moment's notice." Meanwhile he governed Ireland.

His problems varied. There was still, there was always the multitude
waiting to be fed; and the Chief Secretary performed his daily miracle
from a diminishing supply of loaves and fishes. Tithes engaged him
deeply; and that adaptable intelligence produced a system of reform
which even included "a law to compel the residence of the clergy in   5
their benefices." (Junot's men were winding through the passes into
Spain.) His busy mind ran on Irish education; and though Sir Arthur
valued the curriculum less highly than public order—"I believe it will
turn out that there are more schools in Ireland, and more people taught   6
to read and write, than in England. We want discipline, not learning"
—he was still capable of writing with sudden enlightenment that "in
my opinion the great object of our policy in Ireland should be to en-   7
deavour to obliterate, as far as the law will allow us, the distinction
between Protestants and Catholics, and that we ought to avoid anything
which can induce either sect to recollect or believe that its interests are
separate and distinct from those of the other. I would apply this principle to the education which you intend to propose to the Board." (The
marching columns of the French had left Spain behind them now.)
Sir Arthur wrote respectfully to the Lord Primate of Ireland enclosing   8
a return of private schools to be filled up by his clergy; and that day
Junot's ragged infantry limped into Lisbon.

With the French in Portugal, official minds began to fear a raid on
Ireland, though Sir Arthur predicted wisely that the invader "must
make up his mind to the loss of his communication with France for   9
every purpose excepting that of intelligence." His plan for its defence
was drawn upon the sage assumption that "no position will be safe
excepting where the troops will be"; and quite unruffled, he returned to
tithes and education. One hopeful clergyman sent him a play to read,
which he undertook to "send and recommend to the manager of the
playhouse, but you must be aware that no recommendation of that sort   10

can ensure it success"; and as the year went out, he was opining that "Ireland is not a country on which the experiment of sudden and rapid reforms of abuses can be tried. However enormous the latter may be, they are too inveterate and of too long standing to bear the sudden application of the former; but I know that neither the abuses which exist, nor the reforms which can be applied to them, have been lost sight of since I have been in this country." How many tenants of the Chief Secretary's Lodge have stared across the Park and murmured the same good intentions towards the Wicklow mountains?

As 1808 came in, the Emperor pervaded Europe, and Sir Arthur Wellesley was signing departmental letters in a room at Dublin Castle. He would be forty soon; and Alexander had conquered the world at thirty-one. But as the *rôle* of Alexander seemed adequately filled at present, Sir Arthur was confined to writing lucidly upon the government of Ireland. His task was modest, since it scarcely amounted to more than the preservation of an English bridgehead on a hostile island. For Ireland, once a little parody of England, was barely more in war-time than a mere parody of Ireland. French agents flitted up and down; informers in back streets composed incredible reports or crept mysteriously to the Castle; the Tipperary mails were robbed; there was an argument about Maynooth; innumerable busybodies asked for official favours; and the Chief Secretary presided imperturbably over the simple operations of unrepresentative government upon a countryside whose leading crop was a luxuriant nobility. It was a singular employment for Sir Arthur, who gave no signs of impatience. His second son was born in January; and before the month was out, he left for England to attend the House of Commons. (He was unwell, and asked the Lord-Lieutenant to keep the news from Kitty "as it is only making a piece of work out nothing.") Business was unexciting. One afternoon he sat demurely in his place to listen to the Speaker's thanks for the Copenhagen expedition and managed a becoming answer. He was still capable of an injured speech upon the eternal charges against Richard; and when the virtuous Whitbread attacked the conduct of the troops in Denmark or grudged Lake a pension, he replied. Perhaps the predestined futility of all war-time Oppositions helped to make a thorough Tory of him. But he could navigate the vexed waters of a debate upon religious education with the rational

complaint that the Catholics instructed Irish children out of textbooks
calculated "to breed them up in a fixed and rooted hatred to Protestants,"   15
to say nothing of the dreaded writings of Tom Paine.

But he had other interests. For Castlereagh employed him to advise
once more on operations in America. The vague design of raising insurrection in the Spanish colonies persisted; and he conferred at length with
General Miranda, whose company was not congenial. The revolutionary
shocked him—"I always had a horror of revolutionising any country for   16
a political object. I always said, if they rise of themselves, well and good,
but do not stir them up; it is a fearful responsibility." Besides, he could
not bear Miranda's symmetrical constitutions "of a Republican form,   17
and too regularly constructed ever to answer any practical good effect.
. . . All the old institutions in the country ought in the first instance
to be maintained, and to be changed and amended only as time and
experience would point out what would suit both people and country
better." For Sir Arthur was still Chief Secretary; and it would never do to
concede in South America the very principles which he was combating
in Kerry. But he wrote careful memoranda on the prospects of a descent
on Venezuela and made detailed estimates of army stores.

As 1808 wore on, Sir Arthur seemed to be the military maid-of-all-work
of a bewildered Cabinet—"considered here very much in the light of   18
the *willing horse,* upon whose back every man thinks he has a right to
put the saddle." His views were asked for on a Swedish expedition en-   19
trusted to John Moore; and when France and Russia appeared to
contemplate a combined attack on India by way of Persia, he supplied
ministers with the lines of a defensive campaign. But his official skies   20
were filled with Ireland. There was still a full budget of outrages; he was
deep in a scheme for providing Dublin with a police force; and favours   21
were asked for daily, though he was learning to be stern with applicants,
regretting his inability to oblige even the Duke of Kent. One night he   22
confessed to the House of Commons in defence of an unduly sectarian
appointment that "his own opinion was, that without distinction of   23
religion, every man ought to be called upon to do service to the state,
where he was particularly qualified to do that service"; and he was
even capable of drafting regulations positively countenancing the attendance of Catholic soldiers at mass. But that week a longer shadow fell   24

across his office table. For "the Government have lately been talking to me about taking the command of the corps destined for Spain, which is to be assembled at Cork"; and 1808 moved to a livelier measure.

The air, as airs are apt to be in New Castile, was minor, the performers odd. King Charles of Spain—high-nosed for Bourbon and strongly, too strongly chinned for Hapsburg—performed an uncertain bass, Ferdinand his heir a piercing treble. Two voices rendered the melody—the Queen with amorous *roulades*, and Manuel Godoy, Prince of the Peace, with romantic *brio*. For Queen and Prince were lovers, son and father enemies. A deeper note intruded on this discord at Aranjuez as,

> Cannon his name,
> Cannon his voice,

Napoleon sounded the dominant fifth. The voices were unfairly matched; and the part-song became a solo. For it was barely human to put the ruthless purity of that Canova profile against the collective imbecility of a Bourbon family group by Goya. The sharp voice at Fontainebleau offered a principality in Portugal to Godoy, a French princess to Ferdinand, and in a swift aside called Joseph, King of Naples, to Bayonne. His troops were moving now. The marching columns wound through the pale winter sunshine of 1808 down the long road towards Madrid; Junot was safe in Lisbon; and Murat, furred and frogged, jingled through Burgos. The air quickened suddenly in March, as King Charles pronounced his abdication and, watched by incredulous French troopers, Ferdinand succeeded. The uneasy vocalists were summoned to Bayonne; and the sharp voice resolved their discords. One night in April King Ferdinand, who shambled in before the rest, received a message after dinner that the House of Bourbon had better cease to reign. (Sir Arthur Wellesley was busy with his papers, and wrote a few days later to the Lord-Lieutenant that "there is nothing new.") Before the month was out, the caste assembled at Bayonne for the strange harlequinade—the old King as Pantaloon, Godoy a sadly dishevelled Harlequin, and his devoted Queen an indomitable Columbine. The Emperor surveyed his troupe; and the charade began. (In the House of Commons Sir Arthur Wellesley was harmlessly augmenting the stipends of Irish curates.)

Charles abdicated first, then Ferdinand—and Spain was his to dispose
of. King Joseph waited for his cue. But Spain was not so passive. For
beyond the mountains Murat's cavalry was sabring the *Madrileños*, and
the dull volleys of his firing-parties rolled across Madrid: it was the first
gun-fire of the Peninsular War. (That day Sir Arthur wrote about a pier
in Meath.) Then, their *rôles* concluded, Clown, Harlequin, and Panta-   30
loon shuffled off the stage; the Emperor turned happily to other matters
—to Italy, to Poland, to the little son just born to Hortense (they had
better name him Charles-Louis-Napoléon), to the defences of Ancona,
to the fleet, to canals in Lombardy, to Marmont's defalcations in Dal-
matia and the prospects of a French mission to Morocco; while Sir Arthur
Wellesley thought of Church affairs and entertained the House of Commons with the innocent theme of first-fruits.   31

VI

THAT summer England heard the news from Spain. A little force was fitting out at Cork for a raid on Venezuela; and Sir Arthur Wellesley, just promoted Lieutenant-General and deep in preparations for his expedition, was quick to see the chance. Some months before he had sent out a spy to Spain "to pick up what he can find out." But when the news came in May, he wrote ministers a paper. For if Spain was really in revolt, "this would appear to be a crisis in which a great effort might be made with advantage; and it is certain that any measures which can distress the French in Spain must oblige them to delay for a season the execution of their plans upon Turkey, or to withdraw their armies from the north." He proposed to divert the Venezuela expedition to Gibraltar and to employ it in raising Spain against the French or organising a general exodus of Spaniards to South America upon the model of the loyal Portuguese, who had left Lisbon for Brazil. The notion was experimental—"one month would probably be sufficient to ascertain the chances of advantage to be derived from the temper of the people in Spain"—and if none appeared, the expedition could proceed to South America according to its former plan. But the chance of distracting the Emperor by a diversion in Spain appealed to him—"the manner in which his armies are now spread in all parts of Europe, each portion of them having great objects and ample employment, which cannot be given up without injury to his affairs, afford (*sic*) an opportunity which ought not to be passed by." This simple conception, born in May, 1808, somewhere between the Irish Office and his house in Harley Street, brought seven years of war to the Peninsula, and raised on the smooth surface of the Empire the "Spanish ulcer" (in Napoleon's unpleasing image) which ultimately drained its strength.

Ministers were more than usually receptive; and on June 1 Sir Arthur wrote in greater detail of "the plan of operations at present in contemplation," enumerating with precision the quantities of stores required for its two objectives. By June 4 ministers were talking of Wellesley for

151

the command; and two days later the plan had been officially espoused 6
by Castlereagh. Two lions waited in his path—Kitty's wifely tears and
the disappointed hopes of General Miranda. Both were alarming; and
Sir Arthur handled both with rare discretion, postponing Kitty with a
warning to the Lord-Lieutenant—"Don't mention this subject, as I don't 5
write it to Lady W. till it be positively determined"—and, by a wise precaution, breaking the unpleasant news to the Venezuelan patriot in a
London street "to prevent his bursting out. But even there he was so 7
loud and angry, that I told him I would walk on first a little that we
might not attract the notice of everybody passing. When I joined him
again he was cooler." But until he cooled, Sir Arthur was followed
down the street by Spanish curses. "You will be lost," the disappointed
patriot informed that trim, retreating back, "nothing can save you; that,
however, is your affair; but what grieves me is that there never was such
an opportunity thrown away." Yet Venezuela's loss was Spain's, Portugal's, and ultimately Europe's gain.

It was decided, then. They were to try their chance in Spain *en route*
for Venezuela; and if they made anything of Spain (the first month
or so would show), Sir Arthur Wellesley must win his laurels elsewhere than on the Orinoco. At any rate, there would be laurels to win,
since he had got a command. For on June 14 Majesty traced its large, 8
uncertain signature in the top, left-hand corner of a commission appointing him to command a force "employed on a particular service." That
evening Mr. Croker dined with them in Harley Street; Kitty, who had 9
come to town, was there as well. Their guest was to take charge of
Irish business in the House of Commons while the Chief Secretary was
abroad; and there was some conversation after dinner upon the rousing
theme of the Dublin Pipe Water Bill. Mr. Croker was inclined to argue,
and suggested that his host should write him on the subject. "No, no," Sir
Arthur said in his quick way, "I shall be no wiser to-morrow than I am
to-day. I have given you my reasons: you must decide for yourself."
Then his attention seemed to wander. He fell silent; and for a time
nothing was said in the dining-room at Harley Street, until his guest
enquired what he was thinking of. "Why, to say the truth," Sir Arthur
told him, "I am thinking of the French that I am going to fight. I have
not seen them since the campaign in Flanders, when they were capital

soldiers, and a dozen years of victory under Buonaparts must have made them better still. They have besides, it seems, a new system of strategy which has out-manœuvred and overwhelmed all the armies of Europe. 'Tis enough to make one thoughtful; but no matter: my die is cast, they may overwhelm me, but I don't think they will outmanœuvre me. First, because I am not afraid of them, as everybody else seems to be; and secondly, because if what I hear of their system of manœuvres be true, I think it a false one as against steady troops. I suspect all the continental armies were more than half beaten before the battle was begun. I, at least, will not be frightened beforehand." Thoughtful but unafraid, he soliloquised to Mr. Croker, and sat thinking in his chair in Harley Street of British infantry in line waiting for the French columns of attack.

10   At any rate, he would get back to his profession now. He had piloted the Dublin Police Bill through Committee, and politics were palling on
11 him. For the Opposition intoned an endless and repetitive litany of fault-finding, and even ministers seemed to fail lamentably in unanimity—the first duty of ministers, as viewed by Sir Arthur. Not that his tenure of the new command was quite secure. For the veiled deities of the Horse Guards were adverse. In those discriminating eyes he was still a novice and (what was worse) a politician. Venezuela, perhaps, might be entrusted to such hands with safety; but the command in Spain appeared
12 excessive for the youngest Lieutenant-General in the Army List. Ministers, of course, might feel a natural partiality for the Chief Secretary. But
13 while they did their best, the Duke of York had other views, and Majesty itself was understood to frown. The Horse Guards, by the customary
14 device, gave him a second in command; Sir Arthur dutifully visited Windsor; but the outraged gods were still unappeased.

15   In the third week of June he went off to Ireland to prepare the embarkation of his new command. He was seen driving down Whitehall
16 in a post-chaise and four, spent the evening at Coombe Wood with
17 Lord Liverpool, and slept at his married sister's. On the road to Holyhead he stopped to see some old friends of his mother's at Llangollen; and the inseparable Ladies made a peculiar addition to his equipment. For they supplied a Spanish prayer-book, from which Sir Arthur "learnt," as a grateful inscription testified, "what he knows of the Spanish lan-

guage." Armed with this unusual *vade mecum*, he prepared to start for
the Peninsula. His actual destination was uncertain, since Spain was
in an uproar. The cold voice of history, wiser than usual after the
event, may diagnose "the Spanish revolution, like a leafy shrub in a   18
violent gale of wind, greatly agitated but disclosing only slight un-
connected stems." But to contemporary eyes Spain in the early summer
of 1808 was a more heartening scene, where province after province
assembled an indignant *Junta*, declared its independence and rose. The
French, thrown suddenly on the defensive, fumbled a little; fortresses as
old as time, armed with museum pieces, failed to surrender at their
summons; and bewildered Generals faced the incalculable prospect of
an endless war against an unforgiving population. The infection of
revolt spread to the Portuguese, and Junot was forced back on Lisbon.
Great Britain, until recently so friendless, had her allies now. A pleading delegation from the north of Spain appeared in London; even the
Whigs, unmoved by monarchs in distress, were melted by the anguish
of a nation struggling to be free; and ministers enjoyed the rare and
pleasurable experience of hearing their noble sentiments echoed by
Opposition speakers, when they announced a crusade in the Peninsula. Its
precise destination, though, was still obscure. Sir Arthur was not unduly
sanguine—"I think the whole question depends upon whether the Junta   19
of Andalusia had been assembled. If they had, and had submitted to
the French Government, the game appears to be over." It had not ended
yet. Indeed, it had not quite begun, with the French staring helplessly
into Saragossa and Dupont groping among the hills of northern Andalusia. Sir Arthur's orders were to drive Junot out of Portugal. He was
to concentrate on that objective, though he might look in at Vigo or   20
Corunna on his passage out; and in a cheerful whirl he made his preparations for departure. Old habits revived; he gave directions for the troops   21
at Cork to be landed frequently from their transports, as "it will tend
much to the health of the men, and will make them feel less unpleasantly
the heat and confinement"; he wrote with eloquence on the superior   22
convenience of "small tin kettles"; and in utterances that recalled all
the bullocks of Mysore he made desperate endeavours to secure suf-   23
ficient transport. The troops were ready now; and he lay waiting for a
wind at Cork. Lord Castlereagh desired him to go straight to Portugal,   24

detaching someone to report on conditions in the north of Spain. But Sir Arthur thought better of it, and preferred to see the Spaniards for himself, since "it appeared to me that the intelligence which I should receive here might decide on the expedition, and that I could trust no person excepting myself with such a decision." He was not trustful. For it was his way to see for himself: his strength lay in the fact—and, perhaps, something of his weakness also. So he should sail ahead in a fast frigate, touch at Corunna, and rejoin the expedition before they came in sight of Portugal.

Through the first days of July, 1808, he lay waiting for the wind to set from Ireland towards Spain. He was to fight the Frenchmen whom he had not seen since Flanders; and what else had life formed him for, if not for fighting Frenchmen? For their unholy challenge threatened his whole tradition. His eyes had opened to the tap of heels on Dublin floors under the marble eyes of drawing-room divinities; his first games were played among the garden gods at Dangan; and he learned manners at the silken knees of the Eighteenth Century. Its sad, tinkling melody had filled his ears at home, at Dublin Castle, on College Green, at Westminster, in the Chief Secretary's lodge. The age enfolded him; and, inalterably eighteenth-century, he walked its minuet. But France turned violently from the Eighteenth Century and with an impious hand waved Europe on towards the witches' cauldron of the Nineteenth. The harsh challenge of the Revolution broke in upon the ordered dance. Hoarse voices called outside; there was a glare of torches, a sudden hammering on the doors. They splintered; and as the intruders flooded in with wild eyes and snatches of discordant song, the mounting numbers of the *Marseillaise* rose on the air. For the scared violins had fallen silent. The dance had stopped. They were not dancing now. But frightened ladies huddled into corners, and their angry partners confronted a new age with drawn swords. What other course but fighting Frenchmen was open to a gentleman?

Besides, it was his trade. He was by choice a soldier; and he found it more than usually congenial to fight in such a cause. For it engaged him as deeply as a duel engaged other men, since the issue of the war was, in its way, a duel. His home, his origins, his life, his century had all been challenged by the French; and now he was to meet them on the four-square ground of the Peninsula. The trim duellist of the *ancien régime* stepped smartly forward, measured the distance with a steady eye, tested his sword against the turf, and waited. A wind sprang up on July 12; he put to sea at last; and by the divine inconsequence of British institutions the Chief Secretary for Ireland sailed in a cruiser named *Crocodile* to deal a death-blow to the French Empire.

Peninsular

Devers Espaigne vei venir tel bruur,
Tanz blancs osbercs, tanz elmes
    flambïus!
Icist ferunt nos Franceis grant irur.
                    Chanson de Roland.

H E W A S at sea once more; and as the big Biscayan rollers staggered beneath a creaking ship, Sir Arthur crossed the Bay. It was past midsummer, 1808, and the Peninsula was waiting. That was where he was to fight the Frenchmen; and it was a noble theatre of war. For there would be room to fight in the Peninsula. Portugal, perhaps, was slightly cramped between the mountains and the sea. But Spain lay beyond; and he would find room enough in Spain. Those wide horizons would give him back the freedom of manœuvre that he had once known in India. For Spain, where interminable uplands stretched endlessly away to tall sierras, was the most spacious country in Europe—perhaps the only one (Russia alone excepted) where there was really room to fight. Vast, inhospitable distances lay between dead cities strung at intervals on crumbling roads; grey olives marched interminably across red, rounded, and unlikely hills; and discouraged rivers wandered aimlessly with shrunken waters past fantastic cliffs or died away in the wide spaces of immense, unwelcoming plains. It was all singularly baffling to Marshals trained on trim South German pastures or in the neatly chequered fields of Italy. For as they entered Spain, they passed beyond the certainties of Europe; Africa received them now; and they were left to stray disconsolately across an unfamiliar stage, where cues were missed, and the scenery was ill-adapted to the triumphant tableaux of Napoleonic warfare. But to eyes accustomed to the East, the Spanish scene was less bizarre; Indian experience might serve his turn in the Peninsula; and there would be room enough to fight.

There was one drawback, though. For it was an empty land; and to fight (he knew it well) one must indubitably feed. But armies left at large to wander down the broad corridors of Spain were lamentably apt to starve. They could not hope to live in the French style upon the country, since the country barely lived itself. Great armies could support themselves in Central Europe by wayside requisition; but in Spain they must transport their food. A war of transport and supply waged across starving provinces was novel to the French; but to a soldier of the East India Company it was the most familiar mode. He was accus-

tomed to intone an endless litany of commissariat bullocks, and had
mastered the eternal truth of Indian warfare that "if I had rice and bul-   1
locks I had men, and if I had men I knew I could beat the enemy."
So if it was to be the bullocks of Mysore over again, it was as well,
perhaps, to be a Sepoy General.

I

He was a week at sea. *Crocodile* was a fast sailer; Ireland faded into
the haze behind them; and in the third week of July, 1808, the sterner
outline of Corunna stood up out of the summer sea. The Spaniards in
the north, supported on a heady diet of non-existent victories, were most
encouraging; and Sir Arthur, whose credulity was still undimmed by intimacy (or any great command of Spanish), reported happily that "the
accounts of these successes, although credited, are only private; but I   2
credit them." Then he wrote a note to the Lord-Lieutenant about the   3
Clare election and sailed to meet his transports off Cape Finisterre. He
left the fleet again and landed at Oporto. The Portuguese were slightly
lacking in enthusiasm; but a startled bishop undertook to send five hundred mules to meet his force when it was landed. Sir Arthur sailed   4
again, rejoined his transports, and coasted southwards. They were to
land at the mouth of the Mondego and move on Lisbon. Meanwhile,
he found a moment for a line to the Home Secretary about some Customs patronage at Cork. Then he turned happily to more immediate   5
problems.

There was strange news from Spain. Far to the south Dupont and
eighteen thousand Frenchmen stumbling through the Andalusian glare,
where mud roads wander circuitously towards white villages, had walked
into a trap. Leaving Andujar in the plain, its brown towers aligned between the broad Guadalquivir and the green sierra, and groping uncertainly towards the hills, he found across his road to safety a Spanish army
under a Swiss commander with the unlikely name of Reding. The Swiss,
the Spaniards, and the French fought through a blazing summer day.
The Frenchman failed to clear Reding from his road; Castaños with
more Spaniards lay in his rear; and Dupont was trapped at Baylen. The
trap closed in due form with a capitulation; and when Dupont sur-

rendered, it dawned upon a pleased and startled world that the tricolour, in spite of eagles, Emperor, and *Marseillaise*, was not invincible—gratifying intelligence for a General hanging off the coast of Portugal with orders to drive it from the Peninsula.

His news from home was less exhilarating. For the veiled divinities of the Horse Guards had prevailed, and he was to be superseded in command of the expedition. Ministers had done their best for a colleague; but, as the austere Moore recorded, "he was so young a Lieutenant-General that the Duke had objected to it." Age would be served; the Cabinet succumbed; and as "the King and the Duke of York objected to him," something more venerable than Wellesley must be found to drive the French out of Portugal. For it would never do to win a battle with a junior Lieutenant-General. Greybeards abounded in the Army List; and a greybeard in command would at least save them from John Moore. For that Galahad was home from Sweden. His troops were added to the expedition; he had a perfect right to follow his command to the Peninsula; and if he went, he would command as Wellesley's senior. This prospect was distasteful to the Cabinet, exasperated by his Scottish rectitude, a slightly Whiggish flavour, and an unhappy aptitude for being very nearly always right. (Few qualities are less rewarding, since Cabinets, so apt to err themselves, prefer a saving touch of human frailty in their instruments.) It was resolved to irritate John Moore into resignation by a familiar artifice. For he was curtly informed that if he went to the Peninsula, he went as junior to Sir Hew Dalrymple and Sir Harry Burrard. These paladins, both Guardsmen, were of unquestionable seniority; one had served against Washington with Howe; and both now enjoyed the dignified repose reserved for governors of fortresses, Sir Hew residing in the flowered shades of the Convent at Gibraltar, and Sir Harry exercising a less arduous tutelage of Calshot Castle. The Cabinet, rendered aware of their existence by research (mitigated in the case of Sir Hew by some activity in his relations with the Spanish insurrection), decreed that they should take command in Portugal. This was a studied insult to John Moore, who was expected to throw up his *rôle* and go off to mutter in the wings. But though the fuse was lit, no explosion followed; for the tiresome man possessed, in addition to his other qualities, the virtue of long-suffering. Besides, he was determined not to miss a chance of active service. So he drove off to Portsmouth after a snappish interview with Castlereagh; and one more General was added to the lengthening list of Wellesley's seniors in the field.

The unpleasing news reached him as they lay off the Mondego. The blow was tempered by a note from Castlereagh assuring him that the Secretary of State had "made every effort to keep in your hands the greatest number of men, and for the longest time that circumstances would permit." For the Cabinet still favoured him; and Wellesley was commended to his new commander as "an officer of whom it is desirable for you, on all accounts, to make the most prominent use which the rules of the service will permit." This was promising. But with Sir Hew, Sir Harry, and Sir John each on his way to Portugal, Sir Arthur's days of command were numbered. He had a second in command as well; but "I came to an immediate explanation with him; I told him I did not know what the words '*Second in command*' meant, any more than third, fourth, or fifth in command; that I alone commanded the army, that the other general officers commanded their divisions; that if anything happened to me, the senior survivor would take the command; that in contemplation of such a possibility I would treat them, but him in particular, as next in succession, with the most entire confidence, and would leave none of my views or intentions unexplained; but that I would have no *second in command* in the sense of his having anything like a joint command or superintending control; and that, finally and above all, I would not only take but insist upon the whole and undivided responsibility of all that should happen while the army was under my command." This was plain: until Sir Harry or Sir Hew appeared, Sir Arthur would command.

As time was short, he prepared to land his force; and Portugal was told that her allies were fighting "for all that is dear to man—the protection of your wives and children; the restoration of your lawful Prince; the independence, nay, the very existence of your kingdom; and for the preservation of your holy religion." This was strange language from a Chief Secretary. But he was always tender of native customs (had he not kept a missionary out of Tippoo's zenana?); and in a General Order that would have scandalised Dublin Castle he prescribed a code of manners for the use of Protestant soldiery in a Catholic country:

13   "It is almost essential to the success of the army that the religious prejudices and opinions of the people of the country should be respected, and with this view the Lieutenant-General desires the following rules may be observed:

"1st. No officer or soldier belonging to the army is to go to any place of religious worship, during the performance of Divine service in such places, excepting with the permission of the officer commanding his regiment, and the General officer commanding the brigade to which he belongs.

"2nd. When an officer or soldier shall visit a church, or any other place of religious worship, from motives of curiosity, at periods when Divine service is not performed, he is to remain uncovered while in the church.

"3rd. When the Host passes in the streets, officers and soldiers, not on duty, are to halt and front it; the officers to pull off their hats, and the soldiers to put their hands to their caps. When it shall pass a guard, the guard will turn out and present arms; when a sentry, the sentry must present arms."

This was the statesmanship by which Mysore had once been governed. Indeed, it shewed a little more than judicious tenderness for local prejudices; for his little code concealed an ingenious measure of toleration for the Catholics in his command. As he wrote twelve months later,

14   "The soldiers of the army have permission to go to mass, so far as this: they are forbidden to go into the churches during the performance of divine service, unless they go to assist in the performance of the service. I could not do more, for in point of fact soldiers cannot by law attend the celebration of mass excepting in Ireland. The thing now stands exactly as it ought; any man may go to mass who chooses, and nobody makes any inquiry about it. The consequence is, that nobody goes to mass, and although we have whole regiments of Irishmen, and of course Roman Catholics, I have not seen one soldier perform any one act of religious worship in these Catholic countries, excepting making the sign of the cross to induce the people of the country to give them wine."

But his preparations were not entirely spiritual, since another order specified with his old precision the loads of pack-mules and bullock-waggons. For he was eternally the Sepoy General.

The surf that thunders along Portuguese beaches was roaring in their
15   ears, as they landed in the first week of August. That was the ground-

bass, audible ten miles out to sea and uncomfortably evident inshore in the form of drowned men and broken boats. They landed fifteen thousand strong; Sir Arthur came ashore; and presently the leading *motif* of his Peninsular symphony fell on their ears. For the dusty air filled with the shriek of solid wheels revolving slowly under bullock-carts. That shrill *falsetto* creaked its unchanging melody above all other noises; newcomers to the country always caught it first; the squealing axles were even audible to dashing Light Dragoons; and to the more delicate sensibilities of a German commissary "the scratching of a knife on a pewter plate is like the sweet sound of a flute beside them." With this music in their ears they toiled southward through the dust to find the French. They found them first across the road to Lisbon near Obidos on August 15. A scuffle ensued; and the French fell back upon an admirable position at Roliça, against which Sir Arthur two days later launched a serious attack. The ground was difficult, and he preferred to impose retreat upon his enemy by the persuasive method of outflanking rather than by the brutal (and costly) insistence of a frontal attack. But an impulsive Colonel compromised his plan, and it cost Sir Arthur close on five hundred casualties to dislodge the French from Roliça.

His southward thrust brought the French swarming out of Lisbon like angry wasps. Junot gathered thirteen thousand men and moved north to meet him. Sir Arthur's numbers were increasing now, as two more brigades from England had anchored off the coast; and he took post on the hills above Vimeiro to cover their landing. Unhappily they were accompanied by one of Wellesley's seniors. For Sir Harry Burrard was in the *Brazen* sloop; and his arrival automatically relieved Wellesley of the command. That afternoon (it was August 20), just as Sir Harry's boat was ordered to land him, Sir Arthur came on board. He was inclined to advance; but his senior, more cautious, favoured a waiting game; and Sir Arthur dutifully cancelled his orders for a fresh offensive, writing disconsolately to Castlereagh that "this determination is not in conformity with my opinion, and I only wish Sir Harry had landed and seen things with his own eyes before he had made it." Sir Harry did not land; like every traveller, he had letters to write; another night on board his sloop seemed preferable to the dubious hospitality of a Portuguese beach; and Wellesley remained in charge for a few hours longer. Perhaps it was as well. For the French moved that night; and two days later he could write gleefully to the Lord-Lieutenant that "as I am the most fortunate of men, Junot attacked us yesterday morning with his whole force, and we completely defeated him." Sir Harry landed in the morning, rode hurriedly inland to the sound of guns, and found the action in progress at Vimeiro. Sir Arthur "in few words explained to me the position occupied by the Army, and the steps taking to beat the enemy. . . . I had reason to be perfectly satisfied with his disposition, and the means he proposed to repulse them, and I directed him to go on with an operation he had so happily and so well begun." So, thanks to Sir Harry, Wellesley had his chance.

It was a simple affair. The French in their white summer uniforms came on in columns of attack, and the British waited on the ridge in scarlet lines. The columns panted uphill in the hot August sunshine, and the long lines received them with a volley and then the bayonet. As he recalled with a grim smile in later years, they came on "with more confidence, and seemed to *feel their way* less than I always found them to do *afterwards*. I received them in line, which they were not accustomed to." The columns broke; and this simple process having been repeated several times at various points, the shattered French drew off. Sir Arthur turned to his exiguous cavalry with a lift of his cocked hat and "Now, Twentieth, now is the time." He turned to Burrard too, who sat beside him on an indifferent mount, and watched proceedings through his glass, observing, "Sir Harry, now is your time to advance. The enemy are completely beaten, and we shall be in Lisbon in three days." But the rules of war lay heavy on Sir Harry. He was a pardonably cautious man; for his professional experience was almost limited to unsuccessful expeditions. So he resolved to wait once more; and once again delay was fatal to his own chances of distinction. For in the morning Sir Arthur, early on the beach, observed a fresh arrival and reported to Sir Harry, not without glee, that he was superseded in his turn by the appearance of Sir Hew Dalrymple. That thunderbolt of war was even less inclined to sudden action, since his last (and sole) experience of active service had been in Flanders fourteen years before with the Duke of York. He,

too, preferred to wait on events. What could Sir Arthur do? His seniors
chose to waste his victory, and he was irritably helpless.

Not that his victory was altogether wasted. For the French, with a
somewhat juster appreciation of the consequences of Vimeiro, surrendered. Their action caused a flutter, since an impulsive Portuguese
vedette had diagnosed the approach of a dismal little group, consisting
of two squadrons of dragoons with a white flag and a French General
with a slight grasp of English, as a French offensive. But when its nature
was disclosed, Sir Hew received the emissary. A long afternoon of
negotiation ensued—"from about halfpast two till near nine at night,
with the exception of the short time we sat at dinner"—in the hot little   25
room at Vimeiro. Sir Harry and Sir Arthur were both present, though
the latter was uneasy with his new commander and disliked the terms of   26
the armistice. As he wrote to Castlereagh on the next day, "I beg that you
will not believe that I negotiated it, that I approve of it, or that I had any
hand in wording it. It was negotiated by the General himself in my
presence and that of Sir Harry Burrard; and after it had been drawn out
by Kellermann himself, Sir Hew Dalrymple desired me to sign it." Wellesley dutifully complied, with the comment that it was an extraordinary
paper, promptly silenced by his superior's retort that it did not contain   26
anything that had not been settled.

He was extremely uncomfortable—"my situation in this army is a   27
very delicate one. I never saw Sir Hew Dalrymple till yesterday; and
it is not a very easy task to advise any man on the first day one meets
him. He must at least be prepared to receive advice." Sir Hew was not.
Advice from Wellesley was the last need he felt; and the veteran was not
rendered more receptive by Castlereagh's expressed desire that he should
make of Sir Arthur the most prominent use permitted by the rules of   10
the service. For, as he testified, "those rules, and my own feelings of   28
what was due to myself, and to the distinguished Officers senior to
Sir Arthur Wellesley . . . would not allow of my making any extensive
use of the talents of that General after my whole force was assembled."
Small wonder that Sir Arthur's letters grew almost plaintive—"I should
prefer going home to staying here. However, if you wish me to stay, I   27
will: I only beg that you will not blame me if things do not go on as
you and my friends in London wish they should." Things undeniably did

not. The imperfect armistice became a still more imperfect Convention; the French were to evacuate Portugal; but as the precious weeks before the autumn rains went by, the British hung uncertainly about the outskirts of Lisbon. Wellesley was more uncomfortable than ever. Slighted by Dalrymple, he found consolation in defiant presentations and addresses from his military colleagues and in angry letters home—"I am sick of all that is going here, and I heartily wish I had never come away from Ireland, and that I was back again with you." That might be compassed; but before he went, he made a singular approach to Moore. Drawn to him by a generous letter of congratulation after Vimeiro, Sir Arthur was still more attracted by Moore's chivalrous attitude: "I have told both Sir Hew and Sir Arthur that I wished not to interfere; that if the hostilities commenced, Sir Arthur had already done so much, that I thought it but fair he should have the command of whatever was brilliant in the finishing. I waived all pretensions as senior. I considered this as his expedition. . . . I should aid as far as I could for the good of the service, and, without interference with Sir Arthur, I should take any part that was allotted to me." These feelings were reciprocated on Sir Arthur's side by a positively mutinous determination to secure the substitution of Moore for Dalrymple in command of the expedition. He wrote to him at length, offering to press the Cabinet in this direction; they talked the matter over; but John Moore, always impeccable, replied a shade severely that he "could enter into no intrigue upon the subject." He was frankly disinclined to save ministerial faces by making "a submission, or anything that tended to it, which I thought unbecoming," though he admitted stiffly that he should be obliged to Wellesley or to any other friend who might remove the unfavourable impression that he had made upon the Cabinet.

There was no more for him to do in Portugal. He had declined a fatuous proposal of Sir Hew that he should go to Madrid upon a diplomatic mission; and he was equally unenthusiastic about a scheme of Castlereagh's for sending him to report upon the north of Spain—"I am not a draftsman, and but a bad hand at description. . . . I have told Sir Hew Dalrymple that I was not able to perform the duty in which you had desired I should be employed; that I was not a topographical engineer, and could not pretend to describe in writing such a country as the Asturias." He grasped the problem, though. Where soldiers like Moore irritably denounced Cabinet strategy as "a sort of gibberish which 35 men in office use and fancy themselves military men," Sir Arthur helped ministers towards a plan. Before he sailed from Portugal, he wrote a luminous survey of Spanish prospects. His estimate showed few illusions as to his country's allies:

"I doubt not that, if an accurate report could be made upon their state, 36 they want arms, ammunition, money, clothing, and military equipments of every description; and although such a body are very formidable and efficient in their own country, and probably equal to its defence, they must not be reckoned upon out of it; and in any case it is impossible to estimate the effect of their efforts. In some cases equal numbers will oppose with success the French troops; in others, 1,000 Frenchmen, with cavalry and artillery, will disperse thousands of them, and no reliance can be placed on them in their present state."

He was prepared to contemplate the conduct of combined operations with these allies by a British force of 15,000, which "should advance from Portugal, to which Kingdom it would be in the mean time a defence." But he drew a great distinction between the risks that could properly be taken with this relatively small British contingent and the bulk of the expeditionary force:

"The next consideration is the employment of the remainder of the army now in Portugal, amounting by estimate to about 10,000 men, with an additional corps of 10,000 men assembled and ready in England, and some cavalry. I acknowledge that I do not think the affairs in Spain are in so prosperous a state as that you can trust, in operations within that kingdom, the whole disposable force which England possesses, without adopting measures of precaution, which will render its retreat to the sea coast nearly certain. Besides this, I will not conceal from you that our people are so new in the field, that I do not know of persons capable of supplying, or, if supplied, of distributing the supplies, to an army of 40,000 men (British troops) acting together in a body. Even if plenty could be expected to exist, we should starve in the midst of it, for want of due arrangement. But the first objection is conclusive. We may depend upon it that whenever we shall assemble an army, the French will consider its defeat and destruction their first object, particularly if Buonaparte should be at the head of the French troops himself; and if the operations of our army should be near the French frontier, he will have the means of multiplying and will multiply the numbers upon our army in such a degree as must get the better of them. For the British army, therefore, we must have a retreat open, and that retreat must be the sea. . . .

"The only efficient plan of operations in which the British troops can be employed, consistently with this view, is upon the flank and rear of the enemy's advance towards Madrid, by an issue from the Asturias. If . it be true, as is stated by the Asturian deputies in London, that their country is remarkably strong, and that it is secure from French invasion —if it be true that the ports of Santander and Gijon, the former particularly, are secure harbours in the winter—and if the walls can give to both, or either, the means of making an embarkation, even if the enemy should be able to retreat through the mountains—the Asturias is the country we should secure immediately, in which we should assemble our disposable forces as soon as possible, and issue forth into the plains, either by Leon or the pass of Reynosa. The army could then have a short, although probably a difficult communication with the sea, which must be carried on by mules, of which there are plenty in the country. . . ."

Meanwhile the British striking force of 15,000 might join the Spaniards farther to the south. Their lot, he granted, would be more precarious; but he was prepared to face the risk.

"First, I conceive that there is a great deal of difference between the risk of the loss of such a corps as this, and that of the loss of the whole of the disposable force of Great Britain. Secondly, it does not follow that, because the whole British army could not make its retreat into Portugal, a corps of 15,000 could not. . . . I conclude, then, that although this corps might be risked, and its retreat to the sea should be considered in some degree *en l'air,* that of the whole disposable force of Great Britain ought to be, and must be, saved."

These bold designs differed completely from the prevailing character of British operations. For sea-power, which kept an easy line of retreat permanently open behind every British expedition, had largely atrophied strategical conceptions; and most contemporary soldiers were satisfied 37 with "our old style of expedition,—a landing, a short march, and a good fight, and then a lounge home again." Even John Moore had once made

use of the disastrous term, "a littoral warfare." But this innocuous form 38
of military "tip-and-run" was unlikely to modify the European situation.
For in 1808 the French Empire was broadbased upon its undefeated
armies. The last word of sea-power had been spoken at Trafalgar; and
if the world was ever to be freed, the victory must be won on land.
Baylen had shewn the way; Vimeiro followed; and Sir Arthur saw the
long road that lay before his country.

Meanwhile, there was no prospect of immediate operations. The French
were gone; the rains were imminent; a high official at Dublin Castle 39
had just died; and he applied for leave. He scarcely seemed to mind
what prospect offered, so long as Dalrymple did not darken it, since
he wrote to Castlereagh that "it is quite impossible for me to continue 40
any longer with this army; and I wish, therefore, that you would allow
me to return home and resume the duties of my office, if I should still
be in office, and it is convenient to the Government that I should still
retain it; or if not, that I should remain upon the Staff in England; or,
if that should not be practicable, that I should remain without employment." For Dublin Castle, the Horse Guards, or half-pay were preferable
to an endless farce with a cast consisting almost wholly of preposterous
veterans—of an old gentleman who habitually alluded to the Thames
when he meant the Tagus, and the less endearing figures of Sir Harry 41
and Sir Hew, who lived on in his exasperated memory as "the Gentlemen." So he turned an indignant back on Portugal, and went down to
the water-front at Lisbon. A ship received him; the brown forts of
Cascaes slid by; the tall hills above Cintra receded in the autumn mists;
and he was homeward bound once more.

II

H is homecoming was not triumphal—quite the reverse. For the
people of England, always a trifle irresponsible on military matters, had decided to resent the Convention under which the French
evacuated Portugal. Opinion settled down with gusto to a noisy hunt for
scapegoats, and from the accident that Dalrymple's despatch enclosing the
Convention was dated from Cintra,

1   "Britannia sickens, Cintra! at thy name."

This temper was excusable, since the treaty was a bitter disappointment.
A defeat would have been easier to bear; for defeats were usual. But to
be starved of victory for fifteen years, to thrill with the glad tidings of
Vimeiro, to wait on tip-toe for a crowning triumph, and then to learn
that the defeated enemy were to be shipped comfortably home was beyond
bearing. The mild eyes of Mr. Wordsworth flashed fury at the out-
2 rageous thought of "turning the British Lion into a beast of burthen, to
carry a vanquished enemy, with his load of iniquities, when and whither
it had pleased him." Small wonder that, in *Childe Harold's* memory,

3   "Pens, tongues, feet, hands combined in wild uproar;
             Mayors, Aldermen laid down the uplifted fork;
             The Bench of Bishops half forgot to snore;
             Stern Cobbett, who for one whole week forbore
             To question aught, once more with transport leapt,
             And bit his devilish quill agen, and swore
             With foes such treaty never should be kept,
         While roared the blatant Beast, and roared, and raged and—slept!"

The explosion was universal and ranged the whole gamut of abuse from
shrill invective in newspapers with funeral borders and angry caricatures
of the three Generals wearing white feathers or dangling from gallows
to Canning's bland announcement that he should in future spell "humiliation" with a "Hew."

These clouds were mounting in the sky, as Wellesley sailed for Eng-
4 land. He reached Plymouth on October 4 and gathered his forces to

resist the onslaught. His strategy was deft, since he promptly wrote a
friendly letter to a leading member of the Whig Opposition. As he had
written to John Moore, "I am no party man"; and at such moments there
was something to be said for a slight cultivation of the mammon of un-
righteousness. Not that he was afraid. For his sturdy temper appeared
in the note he sent to Richard upon reaching Harley Street once more:

> "I arrived here this day, and I don't know whether I am to be hanged
> drawn & quartered; or roasted alive. However I shall not allow the Mob
> of London to deprive me of my temper or my spirits; or of the satis-
> faction which I feel in the consciousness that I acted right."

The Wellesley clan was mobilised in his defence—William at the Admiralty, Henry at the Treasury, and Richard in the solemn shades where
returned proconsuls await the summons (often long delayed) to high
office—whilst angry Whigs confessed themselves "not sorry to see the
Wellesley pride a little lowered," and Cobbett railed against "the arro-
gance of that damned infernal family." The family, indeed, was veering
slightly. For their hopes, so long pinned upon Richard, were positively
turning to Arthur. Their mother, with a slight lapse of tact, congratulated
him on his younger brother's victory—"upon the glorious success of our
Beloved Hero! God bless him . . ."—and Richard was left brooding
darkly on the fate reserved for the brothers of great men. But he was still
head of the family; and Kitty, sometimes a little apt to gush, poured out
her troubles to him after Vimeiro.

> "Even the Hopes with which the Newspapers are filled are too agitating
> not to give great uneasiness. But I am a Soldier's Wife and the husband of
> whom it is the pride of my life to think shall find that he has no reason
> to be ashamed of me. All promises well, the Cause is a glorious one, and
> Please God we shall see our friends return safe and successful. My Boys
> are well and lovely."

Arthur's first errand was to Castlereagh, where he did his best for
Moore and reported to Sir John that "I am placed under your command,
than which nothing can be more satisfactory to me. I will go to Coruña
immediately, where I hope to find you." They never met, though; for a
postscript added that he must first appear in the enquiry to be held into
the Portuguese *imbroglio*. Tempers were rising; and when he asked

12 Castlereagh to drive him to the Levée, the cautious statesman "hemmed
and hawed, and said that there was so much ill-humour in the public
mind that it might produce inconvenience, and, in short, he advised me
not to go to the levée."

Sir Arthur had an answer ready. "When I first mentioned it," he said,
"I only thought it a matter of respect and duty to the King; I now look
upon it as a matter of self-respect and duty to my own character, and I
therefore insist on knowing whether this advice proceeds in any degree
from His Majesty, and I wish you distinctly to understand that I will go
to the levée to-morrow, or I never will go to a levée in my life."

Sir Arthur went.

His sovereign, who had faced mobs himself, was uncommonly civil;
13 and whilst he was at Court, the General enjoyed the spectacle of the
Corporation of London petitioning for an enquiry into the Convention
and being royally snubbed. But no Government could resist the public
14 pressure indefinitely, and a military tribunal was appointed to inquire
"into the late Armistice and Convention concluded in Portugal, and into
all the circumstances connected therewith." Meanwhile Sir Arthur went to
Ireland, saw Kitty once again, and steadily refused to take part in the
15 public controversy. Friends were informed that "I will publish nothing,
nor will authorise the publication of anything by others"; strangers who
volunteered assistance in the press were faced with a polite refusal to
furnish material or correct their text; and the obliging Croker, who had
laid his pen at the Chief Secretary's feet, learned that Sir Arthur had "not
read even one, much less all, the calumnies which have been circulated
against me during my absence in Portugal." Not that he was inactive.
For he corresponded with his Whig connections, read interminable arguments in his defence composed by William, and returned to London in
November, when the Board was ready to sit.

It was a strange tribunal. Solemnly convened at Chelsea Hospital by
royal warrant, the Board of General Officers met under the tall windows
16 of the Great Hall. There were seven of them—three peers, a baronet, two
commoners, and a knight. But the knight presided, since Sir David
Dundas was blest with seniority compared with which Sir Hew Dalrymple was a schoolboy. Had he not served on one of Chatham's expeditions in the Seven Years' War? The War of Independence found him

deep in military erudition; he wrote profusely upon tactics; at sixty he
commanded a brigade in Colonel Wesley's first campaign; and now at
seventy-three, known with affectionate derision as "Old Pivot," he presided in the court by which Sir Arthur and his seniors were to be tried.
The other members, a galaxy of minor talent with reminiscences of Bunker's Hill and Pitt's less successful expeditions, presented an array of
martial eminence less formidable in the field than in White's window.
Sir Hew, Sir Harry, and Sir Arthur were summoned to their bar in the
Great Hall at Chelsea, where they sat before mellow panelling not yet
ennobled by the names of Sir Arthur's victories. These instruments of
justice moved with becoming deliberation. They called for bales of correspondence; disdaining hasty study, they listened patiently whilst a clerk
recited it *vivâ voce*; they summoned witnesses and, with all eternity before them, invited written narratives. Sir Hew disclosed his spite against
Sir Arthur at the first opportunity, complaining of newspaper attacks "for
the purpose of rescuing a more favoured Officer from the unlooked for   17
unpopularity of a measure he most certainly approved." Wellesley retorted with a comprehensive denial of complicity in any press campaign
and blandly admitted his concurrence in "the principle of the measure,
viz. that the French should be allowed to evacuate Portugal," adding
that he "did not think it proper to refuse to sign the paper on account of
my disagreement on the details." (That day the Emperor beneath the
spires of Burgos watched his marching columns flooding southwards
across Old Castile; for the *Grande Armée* was bearing King Joseph back
to his capital.) Sir Arthur's narrative was put in evidence, and he met
a written cross-examination with bare, but convincing, references to the
correspondence. He was at pains to spare Sir Harry "not only out of
regard to him, but because I think it fatal to the public service to expose   18
officers to the treatment which I have received, and to punishment for
acting upon their own military opinions." His whole difference was with
Dalrymple, and his defence was plainly stated:

> "It is perfectly true that I advised the principle of the arrangement,   19
> that I assisted the Commander-in-Chief in discussing the different points
> with General Kellermann; and that I gave him my opinion when he asked
> it, and when I thought it desirable to give it him. But I was not the
> negociator, and could not be, and was not so considered, the Commander

of the Forces being present in the room, deciding upon all points, and taking part in all discussions. If indeed, the Commander of the forces had given me instructions to negociate this instrument, and I had then negociated it, I might have been responsible for its contents; or at all events, for the manner in which it was drawn up; but as it is, my signature is a mere form."

This was plain enough; and as the case went on, he called his witnesses. (The French were still in flood; Polish lancers cantered against entrenchments in the throat of a Spanish pass; and the Emperor breasted the mountains that look down on Madrid.) Sir Arthur was still answering questions beneath the picture of King Charles II, who caracoled across a wall in Chelsea resisting the discreet allurements of a whole bevy of feminine mythology. His closing speech was lucid and assured. The Board took three meetings to consider its Report, one more to draft it, and a final assembly for signature. It was December now. The French were marching north again. For John Moore, emerging warily from Portugal, had thrust into Leon "bridle in hand; for if the bubble bursts, we shall have a run for it." The run was just beginning; for the Emperor had divined the threat to the long road that wound behind him towards France and turned sharply north to meet the challenge. The hunt was up; John Moore edged northwards; and his pursuer crossed the Guadarrama in the teeth of a midwinter storm, tramping angrily among the freezing, cursing files with the snow driving in his face.

That day the Board at Chelsea Hospital signed their Report. It was a cautious document, less actuated by an overwhelming sense of justice than by a professional desire to spare everybody's feelings. It found the facts, praised Wellesley for Vimeiro, arrived at no decision on the sole point to be decided, and concluded in a mood of hazy benevolence that "no further military proceeding is necessary on the subject." The Duke of York perused it and unkindly pointed out the evasion, writing with unseasonable sharpness on Christmas Day that the Convention of Cintra "has been altogether omitted." Faced with the unpleasant necessity of making a decision, the Board (while Moore's rearguard were breaking bridges on the long road to the sea) had one meeting more and approved the armistice by six votes to one and the Convention by a narrower majority of four to three.

This terminated the proceedings, though the public mind continued to be exercised. Mr. Wordsworth, writing at some disadvantage from his retreat at Grasmere, explored the larger issues in the *Courier*. He quoted Milton and the Georgics and ransacked the outer regions of Petrarch and Dante for damaging quotations. But though he tramped up the bare shoulder of Dunmail Raise to meet the post, polemics at long range were 23 far from easy; and when his noble lucubrations were expanded into "the last great example of a Miltonic tract" and (De Quincey aiding with the proofs) put out in a pamphlet, few of the five hundred copies were sold, though Walter Scott agreed with his sentiments. But while disapproving 24 of the treaty, Scott was very far from disapproving of Sir Arthur—"I would to God Wellesley were now at the head of the English in Spain. 25 His late examination shows his acute and decisive talents for command; and although I believe in my conscience that when he found himself superseded, he suffered the pigs to run through the business, when he might in some measure have prevented them—

> 'Yet give the haughty devil his due,
> Though bold his quarterings, they are true.' "

But the haughty devil was relegated for the moment to the lowlier duties of Chief Secretary for Ireland and, as 1809 came in, sat modestly behind his writing-table at Dublin Castle. Moore's men, vowed unforgettably to "glory, disgrace, victory, and misfortune," were reeling through the snow 26 to Lugo, as Sir Arthur fingered official tape once more. Ireland was quite unchanged. The same gentlemen still asked for the same favours, and the same Yeomanry pursued the same offenders. But Wellesley was indisposed to govern it indefinitely. "I shall go to England for the meeting 27 of Parliament, and mean to join the army as soon afterwards as I shall be allowed to go." His martial inclinations were encouraged by loyal tributes from Londonderry and Limerick; and Castlereagh was duly advised of his intention to "join the army if it should remain on service 28 in Spain within a limited time." Meanwhile Sir Arthur wrote to the Lord Mayor of Dublin upon street improvements, and Moore turned to 29 bay on the jagged hills above Corunna.

The House met in January, 1809; and he was in his place to receive 30 the thanks of Parliament for Vimeiro. Kitty gave a parting ball in Dublin 31

and followed him to England. When his own pluralism was challenged
by the Opposition, he undertook to resign his civil office upon being appointed to another command; and to accelerate, perhaps, this welcome
event he spoke in defence of the Duke of York, now labouring in sad
disgrace by reason of unkind suggestions, the sprightly Mrs. Clarke, and
the list of promotions pinned to the royal bed-curtains. There was a
long debate on the Convention; and when Tarleton spoke against it, Sir
Arthur assured that dashing relic of the War of Independence that he
"would much rather follow his example in the field than his advice."
On the next day he testified before the Clarke committee to the excellence of the Duke of York's work for the army; and before March was
out, the House of Commons heard him on the blessings that canals
would confer on Irish agriculture. It was his swan-song. For on April 7
he resigned his seat.

There was more work for him abroad; and he escaped from Westminster with obvious relief. All Spain was now submerged by the
French tide; and as the rising waters flooded into Portugal, Cradock,
who had succeeded John Moore, waited uneasily near Lisbon. The Cabinet (as Cabinets will in times of military doubt) looked in two directions. For Canning fixed a fascinated stare upon Cadiz and thought hard
of campaigns in Andalusia, while Castlereagh's mind ran on Portugal.
The latter still relied on Wellesley for military advice. Sir Arthur had
not lost his confidence; his brother Charles still wrote to Castlereagh
from the Peninsula, "Would to God we had the hero of Vimeiro at our
head now"; and in March Wellesley wrote a paper for the Secretary of
State on the Defence of Portugal. His views were simple:

"I have always been of opinion that Portugal might be defended whatever might be the result of the contest in Spain; and that, in the mean
time, the measures adopted for the defence of Portugal would be highly
useful to the Spanish in their contest with the French. My notion was that
the Portuguese military establishments, upon the footing of 40,000 militia
and 30,000 regular troops, ought to be revived, and that, in addition to
these troops, his Majesty ought to employ an army in Portugal, amounting
to about 20,000 British troops, including about 4,000 cavalry. My opinion
was that, even if Spain should have been conquered, the French would
not have been able to overcome Portugal with a smaller force than 100,000

men; and that, so long as the contest should continue in Spain, this force, if it could be put in a state of activity, would be highly useful to the Spaniards, and might have eventually decided the contest. . . .

"The first measures to be adopted are to complete the army in Portugal with its cavalry and artillery, and to horse the ordnance as it ought to be. As soon as this shall be done, the General Staff officers should go out. . . ."

They took him at his word. For when Canning's Andalusian designs went thoroughly astray, Castlereagh prevailed and the Cabinet submitted Wellesley's name for the Portuguese command. Their tone, in writing to the King, was diffident. For "your Majesty's servants have not been   37
unmindful of the inconvenience that might arise, in case of any considerable increase of this force, from Sir Arthur Wellesley's being so young a Lieutenant-General. But, as any material increase of the army in Portugal cannot be at present looked to as probable . . . they humbly conceive that your Majesty's service (without prejudice to the claims of the distinguished officers in your Majesty's army who are his seniors) may have the benefit of Sir Arthur Wellesley's being employed where he has had the good fortune of being successful, and that it will remain open for your Majesty's future consideration to make a different arrangement of the command, if, under all the circumstances, it shall appear to your Majesty proper to confide it to a general officer of higher rank." This oddly apologetic tone served his turn; Majesty concurred; and Wellesley was appointed.

It was the end of March, 1809; and he was free to go. Ireland receded now (though there was still time for a note to the Irish Office upon Mr.   38
Croker's attitude towards the Dublin Paving Bill) and, his seat and office gleefully resigned, he made his preparations. As the Lodge in Phœnix Park was given up, Kitty would want a place in England. The Lord-Lieutenant offered obligingly to let them a small house near Goodwood;   39
but Sir Arthur thought she would be going to Malvern when the weather got warm enough. Then he went down to Portsmouth and waited for a   38
wind. Before sailing he called for a complete print of "the Spanish & Portuguese papers, including Mr. Frere's correspondence with Sir John Moore," together with a volume of evidence on Indian patronage for lighter reading in Portugal. He felt some scruples about superseding   40
Cradock and, with a lively recollection of his own embarrassments after

Vimeiro, declined to do so "if he had been in any manner successful"; for Sir Arthur was disinclined to play the *rôle* of Sir Hew. For days he stared across the Solent, waiting for a wind; and when it blew, it blew a gale. *Surveillante* sailed; and as they pitched down-Channel in the roaring darkness, the despairing captain thought of running them ashore on the Isle of Wight. It was just bedtime, when an excited aide-de-camp informed Sir Arthur that it would soon be all over with them. "In that case," his studiously undramatic chief replied, "I shall not take off my boots."

III

I T W A S the month of April, 1809, when he sailed once again for the Peninsula. Each time the curtain rose on a new scene to the same overture. For each chapter of his life appeared to open with the same interlude at sea. The boatswain piped, blocks creaked, the waves went dancing by, and the sea-wind sang in the halyards. Sometimes it was the Dublin packet taking a small boy to England, sometimes a transport ferrying an anxious Colonel to his first campaign; tall East Indiamen carried him round the Cape and up the Hooghly to Calcutta or, more respectful of their passenger, sailed up-Channel homeward bound with a tanned General. It was not long since *Crocodile* had stood across the Bay, taking an eager man to Portugal; and now he sailed in the same track for the last time. For five busy years he knew the sea no more, since the Peninsula was waiting, its mountains ranged behind the mists; and his road wound endlessly across the bare hillsides, past empty towns and dim cathedrals, until the folded mountains lay all behind him and he could look back to Spain. France lay before him then, mile after mile, spread out below the Pyrenees. When he next stepped on board ship (it was at Calais), a Duke came up the gangway and a discarded Emperor sat idly in the sunshine of 1814, watching the summer waves that broke on Elba. But now it was mid-April, 1809; and the long road still lay before him, winding all the way from Lisbon to the Pyrenees.

He would be forty in a week or so; and Alexander, he could still reflect, had conquered the world at thirty-one. But then, had Alexander governed Mysore or sat in the Chief Secretary's room at Dublin Castle? These odd preliminaries of conquest had filled Sir Arthur's life. (Perhaps they taught him lessons Alexander never knew.) Besides, Sir Arthur took his time. Rarely impulsive, he proceeded with a measured tread; and now his sober pace took him once more to Portugal. If fighting Frenchmen was his business in life, there were Frenchmen in abundance to be fought in the Peninsula. Life, indeed, seemed to hold little else for

180

him. For he was not leaving much behind. There was always Kitty,
to be sure. Poor, fluttered Kitty did her best to be "a Soldier's Wife." He
was her pride—the slightly alarming object of her veneration. But what
was she to him? When England dropped below the horizon, Kitty, one
feels, dropped with it. His fancy was unvisited by images of Kitty; or
if they came to him, they wore a slightly exasperating aspect—of Kitty
with her frightened manner running into debt, or sitting in the big
barouche with her face hidden in a book. He hated debts; he had seen
debts enough when he was young; but Kitty could never manage money
and was too shy to tell him until she had fallen into arrears. And then
she always read a book when she drove out, because she was dreadfully
short-sighted. For Kitty could never recognise the bowing figures in the
myopic haze along the pavement and sought refuge in her book—unworthy artifice for the wife of a coming man. Small wonder that, as he
rose steadily, she lagged a little. For she was born to be his Dublin
wife; and as Dublin receded, Kitty—short-sighted, muddled about accounts, and a little scared—receded with it. She was uneasy, too; for
at the news of his next victory, her brother expressed without undue
confidence a hope that "it may ultimately produce as much comfort to
his family as honour to his Country." It evidently had not brought
much comfort yet.

So Kitty waited for the news in Harley Street, and the ship sailed
on, taking Sir Arthur back to the Peninsula. He was not leaving much
behind. Perhaps the thought made him a little hard when other men
applied for leave. Perhaps the dusty distances of Spain dried up some
spring with him. At any rate, the void at home left him free to concentrate upon his problems. His plan was formulated on paper within
two days of his arrival at Lisbon:

"I intend to move towards Soult, and attack him, if I should be able
to make any arrangement in the neighborhood of Abrantes, which can give
me any security for the safety of this place during my absence to the
northward.

"I am not quite certain, however, that I should not do more good to the
general cause by combining with General Cuesta in an operation against
Victor; and I believe I should prefer this last, if Soult were not in possession of a part of this country which is very fertile in resources and of

the town of Oporto, and if to concert the operations with General Cuesta would not take time which might be profitably employed in operations against Soult.

"I think it probable, however, that Soult will not remain in Portugal when I shall pass the Mondego: if he does, I shall attack him. If he should retire, I am convinced that it would be most advantageous for the common cause, that we should remain on the defensive in the north of Portugal, and act vigorously in co-operation with Cuesta against Victor. . . .

"I am convinced that the French will be in serious danger in Spain only when a great force shall be assembled which will oblige them to collect their troops; and this combined operation of the force in this country, with that under General Cuesta, may be the groundwork of further measures of the same and a more extended description."

The design was simple—a thrust at Soult in northern Portugal, followed by a joint Anglo-Spanish attack upon the French in central Spain. He made his customary preparations, assembled bullock carts, called loudly for horse transport, and reviewed in detail the supply arrangements of his Portuguese allies. His flank was shielded from the French in Spain by the simple-minded expedient of collecting all the boats in which they might have crossed the flooded Tagus. Then he moved northwards against Soult. One novelty was introduced into his command. For he attached a company of riflemen to his infantry brigades —a memory, perhaps, of early reading in Lloyd's *History of the late War in Germany* (purchased by Colonel Wesley in 1796 before his voyage to India), assisted by his observation of the French columns of attack at Vimeiro. A strange interlude engaged him, when a French Captain of Dragoons appeared mysteriously in the British lines. His story was obscure. Soult, it appeared, assuming royal airs at Oporto, encouraged crowds of Portuguese to shout for "King Nicholas." After all, if Murat was King of Naples and Joseph Bonaparte of Spain, there could be no impropriety in Soult's becoming King of Northern Lusitania. Crowns were in fashion; but some of his brother-officers, either from envy or revolutionary austerity, resented the new mode and were prepared to kidnap the aspirant, if Wellesley would oblige with a timely offensive. Furtive interviews with mysterious strangers were not Sir Arthur's *forte*; nature had not designed him for a conspirator. But he saw Argenton and

picked up some useful information upon Soult's dispositions, though
8   he retained his determination that he "should not wait for a revolt,
but shall try my own means of subduing Soult." His visitor returned
9   one night. They met over a camp-fire beside the road; and Argenton repeated his incitements, obligingly presenting Wellesley with a paper upon
Soult's line of retreat. But Sir Arthur persisted in his endeavour to eject
Soult from Portugal by fair means, leaving Argenton to a feverish
career of hairbreadth escapes that was ended, before the year was out,
by a French firing-party at Grenelle.

His march towards the French continued through days bright with
10 flowers showering from grateful windows and nights thrilling with false
alarms and the never-ending song of frogs. Soult was still waiting for
him at Oporto, sweeping the seaward sky for a first glimpse of his sails.
But Sir Arthur was ashore and marching north. True, the broad Douro,
flowing beneath its cliffs, glinted between his marching columns and the
11 town; but had not fording Indian rivers formerly been one of his
accomplishments? Some barges were discovered; the bank was quite
unguarded; and one morning he launched a surprise attack with the
unobtrusive recklessness of his gruff "Well, let the men cross." The
astounding throw succeeded; and the French, surprised in broad daylight, were hustled out of Oporto on May 12 at a cost of one hundred and
twenty British casualties. Soult, headed off from every practicable road,
plunged miserably off in driving rain into the hills towards the north.
His guns, his bullion, and his stores were sacrificed; and after a week
of arduous retreat by winding tracks that hung precariously above terrifying gorges a starving, tattered mob, that had once been the Army of
Portugal, staggered to safety in the first Spanish town. Sir Arthur's
opening move was a complete success, though he wrote home resentfully
12 that "if the Portuguese troops had been worth their salt," his adversary "would have been hard pressed and probably could not have
escaped." A fortnight had sufficed him to manœuvre Soult out of Oporto,
and in less than four weeks from his landing he had cleared Portugal.
13   Then he turned south again to carry out the second part of his design
and deal with the French in central Spain, writing briskly to a colleague
that "as you have seen Soult out, you might as well see what we can
do with Victor." Much might be done with Victor. For the operations of

183

the French were unco-ordinated beyond Sir Arthur's wildest dreams. King Joseph hunted his rebellious subjects with a divergent pack of Marshals, who bayed in all directions—Junot and Mortier in Arragon, Ney in Galicia, St. Cyr in Catalonia, and Sebastiani among the dust and windmills of La Mancha. At intervals King Joseph sounded an ineffectual horn; and at longer intervals the post brought Imperial rescripts full of detailed instructions in the familiar *staccato* manner, months out of date and hopelessly inapplicable to Spanish conditions. The Emperor, deep in another war, was off again in Central Europe; and the sharp voice came faintlier now from bivouacs along the Danube—from Eck-mühl, from Ratisbon, and at length from the echoing corridors of Schönbrunn. Left almost to themselves, the Marshals plunged about Spain a little wildly, and Sir Arthur had an unequalled opportunity to inter-rupt their gambols. Far to the north Soult irritated Ney; Ney reviled Soult; their officers fought duels freely; and a Marshal's sword was positively drawn upon a brother-Marshal. Small wonder that their opera-tions lacked unity of purpose, and that the King of Spain was left to learn the news of Soult's eviction from Oporto by the circuitous route of a despatch from Paris. Victor, in this strategic whirlpool, had essayed an isolated thrust almost up to the Portuguese frontier; and if the riposte were swift, much might be done with Victor.

But Sir Arthur had allies, and the delights of combined operations with a Spanish army were new to him. He was already equal to the shaggy geniality of up-country *guerrilleros*, all side-arms and moustaches; but grave-eyed generals by Goya, whose elaborate courtesy almost invariably ran to full uniform and decorations but rarely kept appointments, were a more serious affair. His present collaborator was Don Gregorio de la Cuesta, Captain-General of Estremadura. This paladin, now rising seventy, was less menacing as an adversary than as an ally; for he looked back upon an uninterrupted record of sanguinary (and frequently avoid-able) defeat. Composed in equal parts of pride and failing health, he was the embodiment of Spain at its very worst—old, proud, incompetent, and ailing—and Sir Arthur could hardly hope to have a more instructive object-lesson in the joys of allied operations. With his illusions strong upon him he moved southward, while Cuesta proffered imbecile sug-gestions for a combined attack on Victor, which rested on the rosy hypothesis that Victor would oblige by keeping absolutely still while they annihilated him at leisure. But Victor, who had not been trained in Cuesta's school, fell back. Sir Arthur was not altogether easy, though for the moment the causes of his uneasiness were domestic. For his army gave him grave reason for dissatisfaction. Discipline left much to be desired. As he wrote, "we are not naturally a military people; the whole business of an army upon service is foreign to our habits . . . particularly in a poor country like this." He hated looting and wrote angrily that "I have long been of opinion that a British army could bear neither success nor failure, and I have had manifest proof of the truth of this opinion in the recent conduct of the soldiers of this army. They have plundered the country most terribly. . . ." The Government was pouring its best troops into the thirsty levels of Walcheren; and perhaps Sir Arthur got more than his share of Irish units. At any rate his complaints ended in a grim announcement: "the army behave terribly ill. They are a rabble who cannot bear success any more than Sir John Moore's army could bear failure. I am endeavouring to tame them. . . ." Besides, supplies were short (these were the days when he assured a ruffled commissary that if a General had really threatened to hang him, he would keep his word); and Mr. Huskisson at the Treasury was slow in meeting his demands for currency.

But he moved slowly forward, writing cheerfully that "the ball is now at my foot, and I hope I shall have strength enough to give it a good kick." In the last week of June they left Abrantes; on July 3 they passed the frontier into Spain; and for ten days they lay at Plasencia. Then he reviewed the Spanish army and knew the worst. He reviewed it, owing to a slight lapse of Spanish staff-work, at night; but even by torch-light the aspect of his allies was far from reassuring, and their commander's scarcely more so. For Cuesta, whose cavalry escaping hastily from his last defeat had ridden over him, was in the habit of commanding from a coach, though he had been hoisted for the occasion on to a horse, where he was precariously maintained by pride and two assistants. He had already impressed Sir Arthur in correspondence with being "as obstinate as any gentleman at the head of any army need be," and he was no easier in conference, where his refusals to comply with his ally's suggestions were filtered through an English-speaking Chief of Staff named

(with a friendly reminiscence of Dublin) O'Donoju. Victor was waiting
for them near Talavera by the slow waters of the Alberche. When they
came up with him, Cuesta was lifted from his coach, deposited upon its
cushions, and invited by Sir Arthur to co-operate in an attack; but the
chance was missed. The French fell back once more; and his enemy hav-   21
ing withdrawn, Cuesta became unnaturally enterprising. Faint but pursuing in his coach, he pressed after them across the endless plain that
rolled dustily towards Madrid, leaving Wellesley at Talavera darkly
resolved to go no farther. Cuesta grew "more and more impracticable   22
every day. It is impossible to do business with him, and very uncertain
that any operation will succeed in which he has any concern." Besides, he
could not move without supplies; the Spaniards fed themselves and left   23
their allies to starve. So he resolved to halt and, if necessary, withdraw
from Spain. Meanwhile, the impulsive Spaniards in full cry towards
Toledo and Madrid, stumbled into forty thousand Frenchmen with
Marshal Jourdan and King Joseph at their head and hastily fell back
towards Sir Arthur. He watched them streaming in and begged his colleague to retreat a little farther. The Spaniards, he conceived, would not
be at their best, if they engaged the French with a river immediately in
their own rear. So he sought Cuesta; but his ally was invisible. It was a
July afternoon, and the old General was (not unpardonably) sleeping off   24
his retreat. Sir Arthur interrupted his prolonged siesta and found him
more than usually obstinate. For if it was bitter to have lost the bright
vision of Madrid, whose gleaming towers had danced before his eager
eyes during the brief advance, would it not be galling beyond words to
watch his ragged, scared battalions trailing back under the cold eyes of a
contemptuous ally? Sir Arthur pleaded, argued, coaxed, and positively
knelt to the exacting mummy to whom fate had bound him as an ally.
Then the old *hidalgo's* pride was satisfied; and he consented to fall back
a little farther. The British were to stand on the green hills that shoulder
their way towards the plain of Talavera. The mules of Cuesta's coach
jingled incongruously by; and as the old gentleman sat in the shadow of a 25
cross on the roadside, his staff scandalised a German commissary by standing round with cigarettes. There was a scuffle, as the French passed the
Alberche; Sir Arthur galloped to the front and was almost caught among
their skirmishers. Then he rode off to rally the agitated Spaniards in the

dusty plain between Talavera and the green hills that climbed towards the tall sierra. Their officers appeared to have abdicated; and the Sepoy General, who was not unaccustomed to fluttered auxiliaries, took charge himself.

That night (it was July 27-28) his command was roughly aligned to the to north of Talavera facing eastwards, and the brook Portiña crawled along their front. The position—half hillside, half dusty levels—had nothing very much to commend it. But at least his troops were all assembled there, and the French, it seemed, would be good enough to attack. They were; indeed, they did so in the night. They attacked again at dawn; and through the heat of a long summer day they flung themselves against the scrubby sides of the Portiña gorge or streamed across the plain. Sometimes there was an interval, when panting men crept to the little stream between the armies and gulped its uninviting pools. But Wellesley cantered up the line or sat watching on the green hill that looks across Talavera and its brown towers to the carved cliffs beyond the Tagus. Once a spent bullet bruised his chest. But the day faded, and the French attacks died down. King Joseph saw his armies fail; and in the night they marched away. Judged by the strictest tests, it was a muddle. For Sir Arthur insisted upon doing everything himself; and as he could not be everywhere at once, there were imperfections. But a muddle ending in the retreat of forty thousand French before twenty thousand British was a victory.

He was more hopeful now, "after two days of the hardest fighting I have ever been a party to." For in the morning Robert Craufurd brought up the Light Brigade (which later years swelled to the Light Division), having marched to the sound of the guns and covered forty-three miles in twenty-two hours at Moore's celebrated quickstep of three paces at a walk alternating with three paces at a run. Small wonder that Sir Arthur wrote that day, "We shall certainly move towards Madrid, if not interrupted by some accident on our flank." But his instinct was sound enough. The accident occurred, since the next day brought news that the French had come down from the north behind him and were threatening his homeward road to Portugal. The pack of Marshals were all baying in the same direction now, Jourdan and Victor in front of him, and Ney and Soult behind. So there was nothing for it but retreat. That, indeed, would probably have been imperative even without the French. For if he stayed much longer in the parched valley of the Tagus, he was faced with a prospect of starvation. In the first week of August he wrote grimly that it was "almost impossible" for him to stay in Spain—"a starving army is   30 actually worse than none. The soldiers lose their discipline and their spirit. They plunder even in the presence of their officers . . . and with the army which a fortnight ago beat double their numbers, I should now hesitate to meet a French corps of half their strength." This was unpleasing; and their situation was not improved by their allies, who were apparently content to let them starve. Sir Arthur's pen poured acid in all directions. Lisbon was informed that "we are starving, and are ill-treated by the   31 Spaniards in every way. . . . There is not a man in the army who does not wish to return to Portugal"; Lord Castlereagh learnt that "we want   32 everything and can get nothing; and we are treated in no respect as we ought to be; and I might almost say not even as friends"; and Spanish statesmen were naturally aghast at his resolve to leave the country.

> "I am fully aware of the consequences which may follow my departure from Spain. . . . But I am not responsible for these consequences, what-   33 ever they may be. Those are responsible for them who, having been made acquainted with the wants of the British army more than a month ago, have taken no efficient measures to relieve them; who have allowed a brave army, that was rendering gratuitous services to Spain, that was able and willing to pay for every thing it received, to starve in the centre of their country, and to be reduced by want almost to a state of inefficiency; who refused or omitted to find carriages to remove the officers and soldiers who had been wounded in their service, and obliged me to give up the equipment of the army for the performance of this necessary duty of humanity."

Now he had no illusions left about his allies and wrote bitterly to Castlereagh that "the information which I have acquired in the last two   34 months has opened my eyes respecting the state of the war in the Peninsula." The sole accomplishment of Spanish troops appeared to be rapid dispersal followed by "reassembly in a state of nature"; and his angry litany was echoed in the shrinking ears of the Junta by a majestic voice. For Richard had consented to appear in Seville as Ambassador Extraordinary.

It was a strange reversal. For he was Arthur's armour-bearer now. There were odd visitors to the Peninsula that summer. Lord Byron walked the quays of Lisbon, admiring "Cintra's glorious Eden" and noting how

"Fandango twirls his jocund castanet,"

meditated freely upon history, legend, and current politics, and passed on to meditate at appropriate points along the Mediterranean and to carve his name upon selected fragments of the antique. But Lord Wellesley was a stranger visitor, running civilian errands in Seville, whilst Arthur won his battles. His family, which had no tact, was always congratulating him on Arthur's latest triumphs; and here he was, a mere second on the field of honour, writing dutiful reports to Canning in place of Mr. Frere. That adept at light verse had vanished; and, the sublime succeeding the ridiculous, Lord Wellesley occupied his post. But the requisite diplomacy was quite to Richard's taste, since his leading duty was to make the Spanish Government feel small. This feat was well within Lord Wellesley's range. Indeed, it was his *forte*. He echoed Arthur's strongest invectives to the embarrassed Spaniards and derived unlimited satisfaction from informing one of them with stately vehemence that he "would not trust the protection of a favourite dog to the whole Spanish Army."

But strong language could not mend Sir Arthur's case or feed his troops; and he retreated sulkily, slanting south-west towards the Portuguese frontier on the Guadiana. His mind was quite made up—"I have fished in many troubled waters, but Spanish troubled waters I will never fish in again." There were to be no more combined operations, and he lay irritably at Badajoz. But there were compensations. For Cuesta, worn out at last—or shocked by his unaccustomed participation in a victory—had a stroke. Besides, Talavera brought recognition to Sir Arthur. The Spaniards gave him presentation chargers and the rank of Captain-General (of which he declined the pay, refusing "to become a burden upon the finances of Spain during this contest for her independence"); the House of Commons voted him £2,000 a year for three years; and his sovereign was moved to elevate him to the peerage. He was to be a Viscount; and the problem of his title raised questions of rare delicacy which William handled for him, while Kitty and her boys were by the sea at Broadstairs. He could not well include Talavera in Arthur's style without Spanish

189

consent; and if he made any reference to Wellesley, what would Richard
say? Some feudal ancestor, it seemed, had held lands near Wellington. So   40
much was safe; and William risked the rest. The General should become
Baron Douro of Wellesley and Viscount Wellington of Talavera; and in
the autumn of 1809 Sir Arthur vanished in the new glory of Lord
Wellington.

IV

THE leaves of 1809 were falling, as the last addition to the Peerage
waited in Estremadura with his back to Portugal. He signed his
new name for the first time on September 16 to the usual letter about
biscuit and cash balances (for Lord Wellington was very like Sir Arthur),
adding a modest application to the Portuguese for leave to shoot a royal
covert across the frontier. (His prayer was granted, and subsequent
advices record his prowess with ball cartridge among the Braganza deer.)
But though Sir Arthur was unchanged, the scene was changing round
him. For the French wound homewards from Vienna with the name of
Wagram on their eagles. Now there was time for them to think of Spain
once more. Berthier was to be Chief of Staff there; a hundred thousand
men were on the march for the Pyrenees; and as his cavalry jogged southward once again and booted Marshals in their blue and gold tilted enormous hats and muttered about Spain, the Emperor spoke of going with
them. But he stayed behind that autumn, detained in Paris by an ageing,
pretty woman who trailed about the Tuileries holding her head low so
that they might not see how red her eyes were; and as Josephine dragged
miserably towards divorce, his armies surged into Spain once more.

The English, waiting for their impact, were a shade distracted by the
news from home. True, the new Viscount received the comforting intelligence that his brother Henry was to be Minister at Lisbon, prompting
Lord Byron to the ribald enquiry

> "How many Wellesleys did embark for Spain,"
> As if therein they meant to colonise.

But the family *bloc*—Arthur at Badajoz, Richard at Seville, and Henry at
Lisbon—was soon dislocated. For the Government collapsed with the
resonance peculiar to governments in war-time. The Duke of Portland,
who was still Prime Minister (if only people could remember it), was
taken ill. That did not matter much. But his surviving colleagues failed to
agree on a successor. The Foreign Secretary refused to serve under the

Chancellor of the Exchequer; the Chancellor returned the compliment; the Secretary of State for War resigned and (better still) fought a duel with the Foreign Secretary; the Prime Minister, who had been quite forgotten in the scuffle, resigned as well; and with these agreeable preliminaries his startled country passed to the rule of Mr. Spencer Perceval, K. C. This modest figure (one contemporary termed him with friendly disparagement an "honest little fellow") assumed the disconcerting task of forming a Cabinet in circumstances strongly reminiscent of Casabianca's. Canning and Castlereagh, the duellists of Putney Heath, had gone; but since the pressing needs of war and foreign policy had not gone with them, Perceval adopted the expedient of bringing Richard Wellesley home from Seville to the Foreign Office and giving the War Department to Lord Liverpool and the rosy-cheeked young Palmerston (who thought it "suited to a beginner"). This was grave for Wellington, since Castle- 6 reagh had always been his sponsor at the War Office, and he wrote to him in grateful terms:

> "It would appear that your friendship for me, of what I believe in the 7 instance referred to I ought more properly to call your sense of what was just to me and others, was the original cause of the dissatisfaction of your colleague. . . .
>
> "I have experienced many acts of friendship and kindness from you. If I had been your brother you could not have been more careful of my interests than you have been in late instances, and on every occasion it has always appeared to me that you sought for opportunities to oblige me and to mark your friendship for me; of all which I assure you that I am not forgetful."

The scene was changing fast. He had new masters now; that was a novel (and not particularly reassuring) circumstance in Wellington's rear. For who could tell how far Lord Liverpool would share Castlereagh's enlightened taste for Peninsular adventures? True, Richard could answer for his brother in Cabinet. But since Walcheren had failed, overseas expeditions were a trifle out of favour. In front of him the change was almost as disconcerting, since the French flood was gathering. The tramp of marching feet came nearer; the Young Guard were filing through the passes of the Pyrenees; and he could almost catch the sharp orders of the Emperor. There was one consolation, though: the Spaniards remained

almost wholly unaltered. For they passed the autumn in their customary
8   pastime of superfluous defeats, engaged, as he wrote bitterly, in "doing
Bonaparte's business for him as fast as possible"; and after Tamames and
Ocaña Wellington occupied the position of an allied General with the
unusual advantage that his allies had been annihilated.

But there was still Portugal; and while Portugal remained, he had his
plan. So early as the month of August, in the hot weeks that followed
Talavera, he faced the problem:

9   "The next point in this subject is, supposing the Portuguese army to be
rendered efficient, what can be done with it and Portugal, if the French
should obtain possession of the remainder of the Peninsula? My opinion
is, that we ought to be able to hold Portugal, if the Portuguese army and
militia are complete.

"The difficulty upon this sole question lies in the embarkation of the
British army. There are so many entrances into Portugal, the whole country
being frontier, that it would be very difficult to prevent the enemy from
penetrating; and it is probable that we should be obliged to confine ourselves to the preservation of that which is most important—the capital.

"It is difficult, if not impossible, to bring the contest for the capital to
extremities, and afterwards to embark the British army. . . . However, I
have not entirely made up my mind upon this interesting point. I have a
great deal of information upon it, but I should wish to have more before I
can decide upon it."

A sound instinct told him that when the French arrived in force, "their
first and great object will be to get the English out"; and as the autumn
passed, his mind was busy with his plan for a defensive. As usual he must
see the ground for himself; and in October he slipped away to Lisbon.
Twelve months before, in the exasperating days that followed Vimeiro, he
had tried to break into Lisbon, while Junot lay among the big hills in
front of Torres Vedras. He would see Torres Vedras once again; for Torres Vedras might serve his purpose now. So he spent half October riding
in and out among the great green hills that climb along the sky; the
square ruin of a Moorish keep above the little town watched him go by;
10 and before he left, he had composed a Memorandum of twenty-one precise instructions for his Engineers. He saw more besides; for that watchful
11 eye detected a mule-cart which a Major of Light Dragoons had appro-

priated for his own baggage, and a visit to a Lisbon theatre inspired the
acid comment that "officers who are absent from their duty on account of   12
sickness might as well not go to the playhouse, or at all events upon the
stage, and behind the scenes."

The plan was clearer now. He should not stand upon the frontier—
"the line of frontier of Portugal is so long in proportion to the extent and   13
means of the country, and the Tagus and the mountains separate the
parts of it so effectually from each other, and it is so open in many
parts, that it would be impossible for an army acting upon the defensive,
to carry on its operations upon the frontier without being cut off from the
capital." He should stand nearer to the sea, because (as he wrote later)
"when we do go, I feel a little anxiety to go, like gentlemen, out of the   14
hall door, particularly after the preparations which I have made to enable
us to do so, and not out of the back door, or by the area." So he prepared
the hall, devising for his adversary an impenetrable blend of field fortification and mountain warfare; and bewildered Portuguese were set
digging on the tumbled sky-line above Torres Vedras.

Then he was back at Badajoz, posted to Seville, saw Richard off to   15
England from Cadiz, and returned to his command once more. A busy
winter lay before him. For if he had resolved on making Portugal a
fortress, someone must organise the Portuguese. Their army and militia,
vigorously drilled by British officers and re-equipped in a fair semblance
of British uniform, were slowly coming into shape under Beresford. For
Wellington had little faith in patriotic emotion as an unaided instrument
of national defence and passed a shrewd judgment on the French:

> "As to the enthusiasm, about which so much noise has been made even   16
> in our own country, I am convinced the world has entirely mistaken its
> effects. I believe it only creates confusion where order ought to prevail . . .
> and I fancy that, upon reflection, it will be discovered that what was deemed
> enthusiasm among the French, which enabled them successfully to resist all
> Europe at the commencement of the revolution, was force acting through the
> medium of popular societies and assuming the name of enthusiasm, and
> that force, in a different shape, has completed the conquest of Europe and
> keeps the continent in subjection."

At any rate, the Portuguese (unlike the Spaniards) were to wear the
strait-jacket of British discipline; and, to do them justice, they wore it

with some credit. A sterner test awaited them, since his reading included
a "*Mémoire de la Campagne en Portugal, l'an 1762,*" and "Correspondence
relative to the War in 1762," and he had resolved to use their ancient
weapon of the *Ordenanza*. As an historian of the Spanish war of 1762 had
written, the King of Portugal commanded "his subjects to fall upon the
invaders, and the national hatred always excites them to execute the
'Ordinance.' As the Spanish army pushes on, the villages are depopulated,
and the inhabitants fall back on the capital." That was the plan—an
exodus before the French, leaving an empty countryside in front of them.
For starvation was to be the glacis of his fortress.

His mood was almost cheerful now, since the plan stood clearly in his
head. That autumn he got "pretty good sport" after the red deer near
Badajoz; and the new Cabinet agreed with his conviction "not only that
we cannot in good policy give up the Peninsula, but that we may be able
to continue the contest in Portugal with success, and that we shall finally
bring off our army." That was the comforting reflection which lay behind
his forecasts of the next campaign: their retreat was safe. For the new
Lines at Torres Vedras would, in the last resort, ensure a sheltered embarkation; and if they had to go, he meant to take the Portuguese, though
"I shall not have a single ton for a Spaniard." The campaign, of course,
would have to be defensive; there would be a dearth of brilliant deeds;
and he should "be most confoundedly abused, and in the end I may lose
the little character I have gained." But that would not greatly matter,
though he paid a shade more attention than usual to Opposition attacks
upon him, welcoming Mr. Croker's heroic poem upon Talavera and forwarding a narrative of the campaign of 1809 to a correspondent with an
unaccustomed warning: "If it is desired to publish anything upon the
subject founded upon the enclosed, pray let it be so disguised that it cannot be supposed to come from me. I think, however, that a publication
might be of some use." He was inclined to view the English critics with
philosophy—"You see the dash which the Common Council of the city
of London have made at me! I act with a sword hanging over me, which
will fall upon me whatever may be the result; but they may do what they
please. I shall not give up the game here as long as it can be played."

He saw clearly now, as the last weeks of 1809 went by, how he meant
to play it. The ground was chosen. For they turned their backs on Spain

before the year was out; and as 1810 came in, they were waiting for the
French among the piled and tumbled rocks of Beira. Best of all, he wrote   24
with gleeful underlinings that he had *"an unanimous army."* They were
not perfect (he complained to Liverpool that "if I succeed in executing   25
the arduous task which has devolved upon me, I may fairly say that I had
not the best instruments, in either officers or men, which the service
could have afforded"); but at least they did not argue with him. Indeed,
they trusted him—not yet, perhaps, with the blind confidence of later
years. But Lowry Cole, who had come out to take command of a Division,
bore striking testimony:

> "I never served under any Chief I like so much, Sir J. Moore always   26
> excepted, as Lord W. He has treated me with much more confidence than
> I had a right or could be expected from anyone. Few, I believe, possess a
> firmer mind or has, as far as I have heard, more the confidence of the Army."

Cole's good opinion was, it would appear, reciprocated; for his commander wrote to him that week, "I have got two dozen of excellent port   27
for you, which I do not know how to send you." (There were some compensations for making war in Portugal, though Lord Wellington's   28
anxieties sometimes included the delivery of his tea.)

The weeks went by; and he was waiting "in a situation in which no   29
mischief can be done to the army, or to any part of it; I am prepared for
all events; and if I am in a scrape, as appears to be the general belief in
England, although certainly not my own, I'll get out of it." He slipped
off to Lisbon in the winter for a final look at his new works; and from   30
the orders that he left behind, in case the French attacked in his absence,
it was plain that he had already chosen ground near Busaco for an action.   31
Then he returned to his position just inside the Portuguese frontier,
waiting, like any duellist, for some invisible second to give the signal. This
time his duel was to be fought with Masséna. He was ascending in the
scale of Marshals; and it was fitting that—with Junot, Soult, and Jourdan
already to his credit—he should be matched with Masséna. The Prince of
Essling was, at fifty-two, a shade past his prime, with a weakness for
feminine society in its more portable forms; but he was extremely able—   32
in his adversary's judgment, "the ablest after Napoleon." He was a little
tired, perhaps. But he brought nearly 80,000 Frenchmen into play against

Wellington's 25,000 British with the dubious addition of the Portuguese); and the long columns wound towards Portugal under the wide horizons of western Spain. Somewhere behind the blue distances Lord Wellington was waiting with his sober "doubt whether they can bring that force to bear upon Portugal without abandoning other objects, and exposing their whole fabric in Spain to great risk. If they should be able to invade it, and should not succeed in obliging us to evacuate the country, they will be in a very dangerous situation; and the longer we can oppose them, and delay their success, the more likely are they to suffer materially in Spain." That was his purpose now; that was the meaning of the Lines. There might be a battle, "if the enemy should invade this country with a force less than that which I should think so superior to ours as to create the necessity for embarking." But his taste for battles was very far from insatiable—"I am not so desirous as they imagine of fighting desperate battles; if I was, I might fight one any day I please. But I have kept the army for six months in two positions." Small wonder that impatient men grew more impatient, that the Staff gossiped and preferred "writing news and keeping coffee houses" to their own business, and positively croaked out their gloomy predictions, while their irritable chief expressed his displeasure with the doubters by continuing to entertain the meanest opinion of his instruments, professing to be "apprehensive of the consequence of trying them in any nice operation before the enemy, for they really forget every thing when plunder or wine is within their reach," and informing William (who was now Chief Secretary for Ireland) that "the army was, and indeed is still, the worst army that was ever sent from England." Nerves were a little strained by the long wait for Masséna. Sometimes, indeed, his outcries verged upon somewhat boisterous comedy:

> "I have received your letter announcing the appointment of Sir William Erskine, General Lumley, and General Hay to this army. The first I have generally understood to be a madman. . . . Really when I reflect upon the characters and attainments of some of the General officers of this army, and consider that these are the persons on whom I am to rely to lead columns against the French Generals, and who are to carry my instructions into execution, I tremble; and, as Lord Chesterfield said of the Generals of his day, 'I only hope that when the enemy reads the list of their names he trembles as I do.' Sir William Erskine and General Lumley will be a very

nice addition to this list! However, I pray God and the Horse Guards to
deliver me from General Lighthume and Colonel Sanders."

But he did not despair. For he retained a sound conviction that he knew
best—better than his subordinates, and far better than Masséna. Besides,
the new Government appeared to trust him; and Majesty itself positively
vouchsafed a favourable opinion of him before a final lapse into insan- 38
ity. Kitty was well; his little boys were over their whooping-cough; and
he waited briskly for the French.

They came slowly on, as summer mounted in the sky. He fell back
before them, curbing Robert Craufurd's inconvenient aptitude for expensive rearguard actions. For that eager warrior was ill-attuned to Fabian
exercises; and, as he disregarded orders, his blue chin projected farther
than ever above the high peak of his saddle. But he found Wellington
indulgent; for "if I am to be hanged for it, I cannot accuse a man who I 39
believe has meant well . . . although my errors, and those of others also,
are visited heavily upon me, that is not the way in which any, much less a
British army, can be commanded." Craufurd meant well enough; but his
alacrity marred the smooth perfection of their withdrawal from the Coa.
Then ill-luck took a hand; and a stray French shell sent up the powder-
magazine of Almeida in thunder—"a great and unexpected misfortune. 40
I had hoped that the place would have detained the Enemy for some time,
and that I might have relieved it if circumstances had favoured me."
But its guns were silent now, and they fell back upon the deep windings
of the upper Mondego. The French came slowly after them through a
jumble of fir-clad hills across the heather towards Busaco. The ground
was almost perfect for defence, and he stood to fight them on the tall
ridge. It was September 27; 60,000 Frenchmen faced 50,000 Allies, half of 41
whom were Portuguese; but through an autumn day Masséna launched
forty-five battalions against his twenty-four and failed to dislodge them.
The British fought according to their custom, and the Portuguese with a
new vigour. Their stout defence surprised Masséna; but that autumn
Masséna was not spared surprises. For a fortnight later, as he followed
Wellington's receding columns towards Lisbon and the sea, the big hills
of Torres Vedras climbed slowly up the sky, and he was faced by that
inspired introduction of the broad facts of geography into the art of war.

A nervous Staff excused itself for its omission to report upon the Lines by explaining apologetically that Lord Wellington had made them. *"Que diable,"* the Marshal snapped, *"Wellington n'a pas construit ces montagnes."*

They loomed stolidly in front of him, from the great bulk of Sao Vicente to the rectangular green slopes that curve away towards the gleaming reaches of the lower Tagus, where the Dutch sails of wherries seem to drift through the water-meadows. The whole foreground was full of mountains; and the mountains were all full of guns and Englishmen and Portuguese. It was most disconcerting. And that, though Masséna did not know it yet, was not the worst; for behind the Lines that filled his grey horizon a second line of field-works stood waiting for him on the big, bare hills beyond Mafra, and even a third traced in the dusty plain between the river and the Cintra hills. That was the triple keep of Wellington's enormous fortress, the citadel of Portugal.

It was October now; and the clouds hung low above the Lines. The autumn rain drove down, and the French were raking a dun wilderness of scrub for food. To Wellington's intense annoyance, they found a little. For the Portuguese, though improved out of all knowledge, had failed to rise completely to his Fabian conception of an evacuated desert (perhaps it is impracticable to play Roman *rôles* without a Roman Senate); and the Regency had left gaps in the projected glacis of starvation, which impelled their exasperated ally to fish at intervals in the muddy waters of Portuguese politics and even to the impassioned outcry that "if Principal Souza is to remain either a member of the Government, or to continue at Lisbon . . . he must quit the country or I shall." But the French lay hungrily before the Lines, hesitating to attack with a lively recollection of Busaco, and hoping with increasing fervour that Wellington would sally out. That wary fighter, finding himself "in sight of a very numerous but starving Army, which has been in our front now for ten days, and does not appear to like to attack us," looked down one day from a redoubt and thoughtfully remarked, "I could lick those fellows any day, but it would cost me 10,000 men, and, as this is the last army England has, we must take care of it." So he took care of it in the Lines. As he had written to Mr. Arbuthnot of the Treasury, "they won't draw me from my cautious system. I'll fight them only where I am pretty sure of success." Besides,

what need was there to fight a battle, when Masséna chose to starve himself? The "sure game" was best, and Wellington preferred to play it. He   47
watched them starving in the plain, as autumn turned to winter. But one
November night, as the fog lay in banks along the Lines, the French
slipped off. Their hungry columns groped northwards through the mist
towards Santarem, and he followed warily—"Feeling, as I do, all the   48
consequences which would ensue from the loss of a battle, and the risk
which I must incur, in the existing situation of affairs, if I should fight
one, I have determined to persevere in my cautious system, to operate
upon the flanks and rear of the enemy with my small and light detachments, and thus force them out of Portugal by the distresses they will
suffer, and do them all the mischief I can upon their retreat. Masséna is
an old fox and is as cautious as I am; he risks nothing." With an uneasy   49
feeling that he "could not attack them without incurring the risk of
placing the fate of the Peninsula on the result of a general action, in
which the advantage of ground would be much in favor of the enemy,"
Wellington remained almost stationary when Masséna halted for the
winter. The old fox had gone to ground, and a wary huntsman was
content to wait.

As 1810 went out, the French were still in Portugal. But so was Wellington. That was the miracle. The Emperor had put reinforcements into
the Peninsula to the surprising tune of 100,000 men; but by some strange
perversity the British still maintained their 25,000 there, and their commander wrote proudly home that "I am at the head of the only army re-   50
maining in the Peninsula—or, I believe, in Europe—that is capable and
willing to contend with the French." Small wonder the delighted Lowry
Cole wrote that "the ability displayed by Lord Wellington is universally   51
acknowledged and I hope the good folks in England will do him equal
justice. He certainly is in the literal sense of the word a fine fellow with
the best nerves of anyone I ever met with." Busaco and the Lines had
added Masséna to his bag of Marshals. Better still, a British army had
faced the Empire at its widest, when a man could walk from Genoa to the
Baltic on French soil, and had stared it out of countenance. The slow
tide was turning; and though the Peninsular War was not yet won, after
Torres Vedras it could not well be lost.

V

THE military problem of the Peninsula was almost maddeningly simple. The French objective, from which the Marshals were intermittently distracted by the allied lures of loot and sideshows, was to find and destroy the British expeditionary force. It was two years since the Emperor had announced, with a slightly hysterical blend of heraldry and natural history, that "the Leopard" would shortly be driven into the sea. That was the essence of French strategy. And the British problem was just as simple. For it presented two objectives—to avoid expulsion and then, resuming the offensive, to expel the French. The first goal was reached when Masséna, with the whole weight of the Empire behind him, turned back from Torres Vedras. It was plain from that moment that Wellington could not be driven out of the Peninsula. But could he drive out the French? That was his second problem, and in 1811 it was still unsolved. Its elements were simple, too. For the French occupation of Spain hung by one precarious chain—the great road from Bayonne to Madrid. If that were snapped, their armies must recoil from every province, since they could not maintain themselves with a British force across the road to France. If it were threatened, they must all come swarming north to safety. (Had not John Moore touched them on that nerve-centre in 1808 and seen the Emperor whip round towards him like an animal upon whose tail an unexpected foot had trodden?) If Wellington could get across their road to Paris, the game was won. That was the short way with the French. So he must thrust eastwards out of Portugal across Old Castile and break the road to France somewhere between Madrid and the Ebro. There was one point at which an angle of the road brought it nearer to him; the angle was at Burgos. That must be his goal, as it had once been John Moore's. But this time there would be no sudden dash for Burgos. For it was no part of his programme to make a gallant raid into Spain and scramble on board his transports at Corunna. The judicious Wellington was indisposed to risk himself beyond the shelter of his mountains, unless the gates of Portugal were safely held behind

him. He must be free to move decorously out of Portugal and to re-enter
it at will; and this privilege would not be his unless he held the gates. So
Badajoz and Ciudad Rodrigo must be his first objective; and, these once
secured, he might make his decisive thrust towards the road to Paris.

I

As 1811 opened, the deadlock on the Tagus held. Masséna's men
starved at Santarem with a will that impressed their adversary as "an
extraordinary instance of what a French army can do. It is positively   1
a fact that they brought no provisions with them, and they have not
even received a letter since they entered Portugal. With all our money,
and having in our favour the good inclinations of the country, I assure
you that I could not maintain one division in the district in which they
have maintained not less than 60,000 men and 20,000 animals for more
than two months." That was written in December; by the first week
of March their transport was a shadow, their shoes a memory, and
their supply the stray outcome of marauding forays across a chilly
waste of empty villages. Then, with Junot wounded and Ney frankly
mutinous, Masséna turned to go. Withdrawing deftly, he slipped off
towards the north with Wellington shepherding him on his way a
trifle gingerly. For he was disinclined to risk unnecessary battles, when
it was far simpler to preside over the inevitable disintegration of the
French from a safe distance. Had he not in his charge the last army of
England? Defeated, it would let the tide of war surge into Britain—"then
would His Majesty's subjects discover what are the miseries of war,   2
of which, by the blessing of God, they have hitherto had no knowledge;
and the cultivation, the beauty, and prosperity of the country, and the
virtue and happiness of its inhabitants would be destroyed, whatever
might be the result of the military operations. God forbid that I should
be a witness, much less an actor in the scene. . . ." But victorious, it
might be the instrument to end the interminable European war—"I am   3
equally certain that if Buonaparte cannot root us out of this country, he
must alter his system in Europe, and must give us such a peace as we
ought to accept." He saw the goal; and in his marching redcoats he saw
the means to reach it. For he had more work for them to do than win-

ning rearguard actions against Masséna. His mind was ranging eastward now towards the Spanish frontier; the gates of Portugal began to gleam on his horizon; and he preferred "to keep my own army entire, rather than to weaken myself by fighting them, and probably be so crippled as not to have the ascendant over the fresh troops on the frontiers. Almeida and Badajoz are to be retaken."

They were to be his next objective. Meanwhile, he followed warily as Masséna struggled back to Spain. They scuffled on the road at Pombal and again at Redinha, while Ney displayed the sombre aptitude for rearguard actions that was soon to light a larger army down a longer, darker road. (That month the guns in Paris flashed and boomed for an heir born to the Emperor: all that remained was to retain an Empire for him.) Masséna's ragged columns wound slowly through the mountains after a running fight at Foz d'Aronce; their road was littered with discarded transport, and they left a growing legacy of weary, barefoot men to be gathered in by their pursuers. The spring rains were falling now; Ney had gone raging off under virtual arrest, when the army of Portugal, enlivened by the *feux de joie* for the small King of Rome, fought a confused engagement in the fog at Sabugal, which only served to strengthen Wellington's conviction that "these combinations for engagements do not answer unless one is on the spot to direct every trifling movement." (Had he not been his own "general of cavalry and of the advanced guard, and leader of two or three columns, sometimes on the same day," throughout the long pursuit?) Then Masséna crept out of Portugal, leaving behind 8,000 prisoners and 17,000 dead, while Wellington proudly informed the Portuguese that the French invasion was at an end.

The first phase was over; and it remained to batter in the gates of Portugal. For the French still held Almeida (which guards the vestibule of Ciudad Rodrigo) and Badajoz; and Wellington directed simultaneous blows at both. Leaving Almeida in the grip of an investing force, he rode south to survey Badajoz, covering 135 miles in three April days, killing two horses, writing endless letters on the road, and losing two dragoons of his escort in a torrent. He reconnoitred Badajoz in person and drew up a detailed code of instructions for Beresford, who was to besiege the fortress; in case the French attempted to relieve it and Beresford resolved to fight, he was recommended to concentrate at Albuera. Then Wellington returned to the north. The French were on the move again; for Masséna, his gaps repaired with fresh troops, came marching to the rescue of Almeida. They faced him one May morning at Fuentes de Oñoro on the upland which parts the high prairies of western Spain from the tumbled rocks of Beira. All that day and the next the struggle swayed along the slopes. Then Masséna, groping round the British right, launched his attack on May 5. French cavalry charged British infantry in squares; the squares held (it was a lesson that Wellington observed); and whilst his infantry stood firm, his cavalry heavily outnumbered were ridden off the field, and two British guns by the supreme paradox of war charged and broke through a whirlpool of French horse. But, with his right in danger, Wellington swung it back with Frederician deliberation; and when the long day ended, his 37,000 men still lay between Almeida and its 47,000 rescuers. But he felt little pride in the achievement, writing to William that "Lord Liverpool was quite right not to move thanks for the battle at Fuentes, though it was the most difficult one I was ever concerned in. We had very nearly three to one against us engaged; above four to one of cavalry; and moreover our cavalry had not a gallop in them; while some of that of the enemy was fresh and in excellent order. If Boney had been there, we should have been beaten." But Boney was not there; and in his absence it might be permissible to take occasional liberties with the art of war.

Its fate duly sealed by the battle at its gates, Almeida fell. But to Wellington's acute annoyance the garrison escaped, and he was left reviling "the most disgraceful military event that has yet occurred," reaching the grim conclusion that "there is nothing on earth so stupid as a gallant officer." (Indeed, one unhappy object of his displeasure shot himself.) The spring campaign in the north had cleared the way to Ciudad Rodrigo and incidentally closed Masséna's career; for an ungrateful Emperor rewarded him with summary retirement, and Marmont commanded in his place.

But news from Badajoz drew Wellington's attentions south again. For Soult had pounded Beresford at Albuera—"a strange concern," as Wellington wrote. "They were never determined to fight it; they did not occupy the ground as they ought; they were ready to run away at

every moment from the time it commenced till the French retired."
Yet dogged gallantry prevailed; and Soult learned reluctantly, in Napier's
eloquent rhapsody, "with what a strength and majesty the British soldier
fights. . . . Nothing could stop that astonishing infantry . . . and fifteen
hundred unwounded men, the remnant of six thousand unconquerable
British soldiers, stood triumphant on the fatal hill!" But such heroic
exploits were not to Wellington's taste; and he was left writing grimly
that "another such battle would ruin us." Meanwhile, the summer was
before him; and he made a rush at Badajoz before the French could
return in force to relieve the fortress. But ample time is the essence of
successful sieges, and time was wanting. They were too quick for him;
and he drew off to safety, falling back once more to a strong position
just inside the Portuguese frontier. At midsummer the armies faced
one another in Estremadura. But the deadlock held; and the war drifted
north again along the frontier. For Wellington was still knocking at the
gates of Portugal; and having failed at Badajoz, he turned briskly to
Ciudad Rodrigo. That red-tiled fortress with its big brown church and
vaguely Mexican aspect was waiting in a broad green valley; and in
August he encircled it in preparation for a siege. But Marmont came up
in force to its relief; there was a scuffle on September 25 at El Bodon;
once more a British square held off the charging French; and Wellington again withdrew—without conspicuous assistance from the impulsive
Craufurd. He made a point of it on parade next morning.

"I am glad to see you safe, General Craufurd," he observed with
elaborate irony.

"I was never in danger," his rash subordinate replied.

"Oh! I was," said Wellington tartly.

"He's damned crusty this morning," muttered his unabashed lieutenant.

His designs on Ciudad Rodrigo postponed, Wellington fell back with
loving deliberation to a strong position on the Coa; but Marmont lay
watchfully in front of him and made no attack. The war was over
for the season now; and 1811 went out upon Wellington among the
rocky hills of Beira. It had been a fruitful year. He had cleared Portugal
and broken Masséna, and the gates of Portugal gleamed hopefully before
him. His business now lay with the frontier fortresses; and whilst they

lay waiting for his onslaught, the initiative had passed to him. Better still, he had transformed the war; as he wrote to Liverpool, "we have certainly altered the nature of the war in Spain; it has become, to a   15
certain degree, offensive on our part. The enemy are obliged to concentrate large corps to defend their own acquisitions; they are obliged to collect magazines to support their armies (Marmont says he can do nothing without magazines, which is quite a new era in the modern French military system); and I think it probable, from all that I hear, that they are either already reduced, or they must soon come, to the resources of France for the payment of those expenses which must be defrayed in money. As soon as this shall be the case, and as soon as the war will not produce resources to carry itself on, your Lordship may be certain that Buonaparte will be disposed to put an end to it, and will submit to anything rather than draw from France the resources which must be supplied in order to keep together his armies. I think it not unlikely, therefore, that peace is speculated upon in France."

Peace flushed the eastern sky, as he looked eastwards out of Portugal. Spain lay before him now, and beyond Spain the long line of the Pyrenees. That was the goal; his exclamation in a letter pointed it—

"You appear to think it probable that Buonaparte would be inclined or   16
obliged to withdraw from the Peninsula; and you ask, what would I do in that case? I answer, attack the most vulnerable frontier of France, that of the Pyrenees. Oblige the French to maintain in that quarter 200,000 men for their defence; touch them vitally there, when it will certainly be impossible to touch them elsewhere."

It was a lucid vision, and he followed it across his maps on a December day in 1811. He was still in Portugal, and between him and a sight of the Pyrenees lay Marmont, Soult, King Joseph, the French armies, and the long corridors of Spain; but the Pyrenees were waiting.

2

The war was forming him. Now he was nearly forty-three—high-nosed, clear-eyed, and confident. His nerves were always steady. That was his secret; Lowry Cole had pierced it, when he termed his com-

1   mander "a fine fellow with the best nerves of any one I ever met with."
For the sharp gaze never wavered, and the upper lip drew tightly down
over the slightly prominent teeth without a quiver. His nerves were
admirable; exercise, long days in the saddle, and plain fare helped to
keep them so. Did not Alava learn to dread his standing answer to the
question at what o'clock the Staff would move and what there was to be
for dinner? "At daylight," he invariably replied; and to the second in-
2   terrogation, "Cold meat." "*J'en ai pris en horreur*," the anguished Spaniard moaned, "*les deux mots* daylight *et* cold meat." But Wellington
3   throve on them. His night's rest varied between three hours and six; and
for his first four years in the Peninsula, although he was Commander-
in-Chief, he had reverted to the practice of his Indian campaigns and
4   slept in his clothes. His days were regular; rising at six, he wrote steadily
until breakfast at nine o'clock. Those quiet morning hours served to dispose of his enormous correspondence with incredible punctuality; for
5   "my rule always was to do the business of the day in the day." Then he
breakfasted and transacted military business with the Staff. This lasted all
the morning, except on hunting days when a gleeful Quartermaster-
6   General records that he "could get almost anything done, for Lord
Wellington stands whip in hand ready to start, and soon despatches all
business." Those were the days that startled Portuguese on lonely hillsides beheld an unprecedented cavalcade, heard view-halloos and the
sharp note of hounds, and marvelled at the strange proceedings of their
incomprehensible allies. "Here," as *Captain O'Malley* loved to recall,
7   "the shell-jacket of a heavy dragoon was seen storming the fence of a
vineyard. There the dark green of a rifleman was going the pace over
the plain. The unsportsmanlike figure of a staff officer might be observed
emerging from a drain, while some neck-or-nothing Irishman, with light
infantry wings, was flying at every fence before him"—and the Peer
8   himself followed his hounds in the sky-blue and black of the Salisbury
hunt. Such was the impressive apparatus with which Lord Wellington
toned his nerves in winter-quarters.

His nerves, indeed, were admirable; and a becoming sense of who
he was and what he had achieved contributed to steady them—"I am
9   the mainspring of all the other operations, but it is because I am Lord
Wellington; for I have neither influence nor support, nor the means

of acquiring influence, given to me by the government." Small wonder
that his correspondents never ventured upon a more familiar address
than "My dear Lord." Even behind his back he was "the Peer" to Gen-   10
erals and "our great Lord" to ardent subalterns; although an intoxicated   11
private once alluded (in the presence of a scandalised staff officer) to
"that long-nosed b——r that beats the French," and the army had been   12
known to call him "Atty." But such diminutives were rare; for he kept
his distance.

Not that he kept it by conventional distinctions of uniform and entourage. Headquarters, as one observer noted, were "strikingly quiet
and unostentatious. Had it not been known for a fact, no one would   13
have suspected that he was quartered in the town. There was no throng
of scented staff officers with plumed hats, orders and stars, no main
guard, no crowd of contractors, actors, cooks, valets, mistresses, equipages,
horses, dogs, forage and baggage wagons, as there is at French or
Russian headquarters! Just a few aides-de-camp, who went about the
streets alone and in their overcoats, a few guides, and a small staff guard;
that was all! About a dozen bullock carts were to be seen in the large
square of Fuente Guinaldo, which were used for bringing up straw
to headquarters; but apart from these no equipages or baggage trains
were visible." Perhaps he had seen quite enough of personal magnificence
in Richard's case to damp his taste for it. At any rate, his dress was unpretentious. A harassed army might echo *Micky Free's* lyrical complaint
to the Fourteenth Light Dragoons:

> Bad luck to this marching,   14
> Pipe-claying and starching;
> How neat one must be to be killed by the French!

But such niceties were scarcely to their commander's taste. One subaltern recorded that "provided we brought our men into the field well   15
appointed with their sixty rounds of ammunition each, he never looked
to see whether trousers were black, blue, or grey. . . . The consequence
was that scarcely any two officers were dressed alike! Some wore grey
braided coats, others brown: some again liked blue; many (from choice,
or perhaps necessity) stuck to the 'old red rag.'" His own opinions were
plainly stated to the Horse Guards:

16   "I hear that measures are in contemplation to alter the clothing, caps, &c. of the army.

"There is no subject of which I understand so little; and, abstractedly speaking, I think it indifferent how a soldier is clothed, provided it is in a uniform manner; and that he is forced to keep himself clean and smart, as a soldier ought to be. But there is one thing I deprecate, and that is any imitation of the French in any manner.

"It is impossible to form an idea of the inconveniences and injury which result from having anything like them. . . . I only beg that *we* may be as different as possible from the French in everything."

This was severely practical. So was his own costume, which generally ran to grey. His taste for personal reconnaissance inclined him to the
17   inconspicuous combination of a grey frock-coat worn with a low cocked-hat in an oil skin cover. It bore no plume; and before long Europe learned to know that austere silhouette. He was not altogether innocent of sartorial vanities, though, fancying the skirts of his coats a trifle
18   shorter than most men's in order (a Judge-Advocate conjectured) to set off a trim figure; nor was he without strong and individual opinions upon a novel cut of half-boots. But these effects were all contrived in the modest key of grey; and his entourage was equally inconspicuous. An unpretentious Staff, designed for use rather than ornament, was put to shame by the glory of gold lace and plumes that caracoled in the splendid wake of any Marshal of the Empire. But Wellington had little appetite for millinery. Besides, few Marshals shared his taste for solitary reconnaissance. He had unbounded faith in a strong glass and a fast horse, and often rode beyond his outposts, a lonely horseman in a cloak, with his perpetual desire to see things for himself—the French vedettes would never suspect a single figure in grey. So he dressed modestly below his military station, leaving the foppery of war to gaudier, if less successful, Marshals. Indeed, their master did the same. For Europe held another *redingote grise*: he might be matched against it one day.

Grey-coated, spare, and trim, the bleak figure, sharply outlined against the deep blue of Spanish skies, appears a shade incongruous. He never dressed the part; indeed, he had little taste for drama. When his advance-guard blundered into the whole French army, he greeted the alarming
19   intelligence with a casual, "Oh! they are all there, are they? Well, we

must mind a little what we are about then." And news that the French
were off, leaving Almeida in his grasp, reached him one morning early
whilst he was shaving. He lifted the razor from his cheek, remarking
"Ay, I thought they meant to be off; very well"; the shave resumed, and
nothing more was said. He specialised in a form of dry understatement
peculiarly unfriendly to heroics. Who else, addressing a charitable appeal
to the Prime Minister on behalf of a devastated ally, was capable of the
sublime exordium: "The village of Fuentes de Oñoro having been the   20
field of battle the other day, and not having been much improved by
this circumstance . . . ."? Few themes, indeed, moved him to eloquence
except the imperfections of his human instruments. But there his language often verged on the sublime. Unwearying himself, he was un-
merciful in his comments upon lack of energy in others; and exasperation frequently betrayed him into unpardonable generalisations. A fixed
belief that insufficient inducements were offered to recruits had led him
to the conclusion that "none but the worst description of men enter the   21
regular service"; and from this premise he proceeded to the gravest dis-
paragements of the men under his command. "The scum of the earth,"   22
he termed them, "the mere scum of the earth. . . . The English soldiers
are fellows who have all enlisted for drink—that is the plain fact—
they have all enlisted for drink." This tone became habitual with him in
later years, as a congenial antidote to the prevailing cant. For Wellington
could not bear his hearers to be romantic about soldiers—"people talk   23
of their enlisting from their fine military feeling—all stuff—no such
thing. Some of our men enlist from having got bastard children—some
for minor offences—many more for drink; but you can hardly conceive
such a set brought together, and it really is wonderful that we should
have made them the fine fellows they are." They were fine fellows, then.
He was prepared to admit as much; and for seven years in the Peninsula he toiled to make them so. Seven volumes of General Orders, drafted   24
in his own handwriting and traced endlessly across the paper with
"the short glazed pens" from Tabart's in New Bond Street, testify to his   25
parental care. "Crime" is duly present; the crackle of illicit pig-shooting
is heard; bee-hives are purloined; and the misdeeds peculiar to military
operations in wine-producing countries stalk through his pages. But
camp-kettles, shirts, and brushes haunted him; his dreams were full of

army biscuit; and his housekeeping anxieties are in strange contrast with the grave ablatives absolute of Cæsar or Napoleon's baroque eloquence. Supply was still the burden of his severely humdrum song. He

26 still insisted that "it is very necessary to attend to all this detail, and to trace a biscuit from Lisbon into the man's mouth on the frontier, and to provide for its removal from place to place, by land or by water, or no military operations can be carried on, and the troops must starve." Even his strategy was dominated by the practical consideration that

27 "a soldier with a musket could not fight without ammunition, and that in two hours he can expend all he can carry."

This was admirably unheroic. But in one particular he found his gallant subordinates more unheroic than himself. Uniformly indifferent to the risks of battle,

28

> "When, squadron square,
> We'll all be there,
> To meet the French in the morning,"

they failed to share his taste for uneventful winters in the discomfort of up-country billets in the hill villages of Beira. Moved with a simultaneous passion for the immediate transaction of urgent business at home, they applied for leave. Such unanimity was touching. But their commander was untouched; for leave was one of Wellington's blind spots. Lisbon leave was one thing. He could be positively debonair on

29 the subject of Lisbon leave, recording in a sardonic postscript that a subordinate "wants to go to Lisbon, and I have told him that he may stay there 48 hours which is as long as any reasonable man can wish to stay in bed with the same woman." But why gentlemen who had come all the way to the Peninsula in order, he presumed, to fight the French should wish to go home again entirely passed his comprehension. Ill-health might form a valid reason; but business grounds left him frankly incredulous. Even Craufurd was grudgingly informed that "Of-

30 ficers (General Officers in particular) are the best judges of their own private concerns; and, although my own opinion is that there is no private concern that cannot be settled by instruction and power of attorney, and that after all is not settled in this manner, I cannot refuse leave of absence to those who come to say that their business is of a

nature that requires their personal superintendence. But entertaining
these opinions, it is rather too much that I should not only give leave
of absence, but approve of the absence of any, particularly a General
Officer, from the army. . . . I may be obliged to consent to the absence
of an Officer, but I cannot approve of it. I repeat that you know the
situation of affairs as well as I do, and you have my leave to go to
England if you think proper." He could contrive a kindly refusal—"I   31
always feel much concern in being obliged to refuse officers who wish
to quit the army; indeed it is the most painful duty I have to perform.
But is must be performed; otherwise, between those absent on account
of wounds and sickness, and those absent on account of business or
pleasure, I should have no officers left." Indeed, he ultimately moved
the Horse Guards to confine Peninsular appointments to Generals pre-   32
pared to make a declaration in advance that they had no private business
likely to recall them to England. More romantic reasons moved him to
irony, although a hint from home that one young lady's continued separation from a love-lorn Major might be followed by fatal consequences
elicited a kindly, though terrifying, lecture on the course of love:

> "It appears to me that I should be guilty of a breach of discretion if I   33
> were to send for the fortunate object of this young lady's affections, and to
> apprise him of the pressing necessity for his early return to England: the
> application for permission ought to come from himself; and, at all events,
> the offer ought not to be made by me, and particularly not founded on the
> secret of this interesting young lady.
>
> "But this fortunate Major now commands his battalion, and I am very
> apprehensive that he could not with propriety quit it at present, even though
> the life of this female should depend upon it; and, therefore, I think that
> he will not ask for leave.
>
> "We read, occasionally, of desperate cases of this description, but I can-
> not say that I have ever yet known of a young lady dying of love. They
> contrive, in some manner to live, and look tolerably well, notwithstanding
> their despair and the continued absence of their lover; and some even have
> been known to recover so far as to be inclined to take another lover, if the
> absence of the first has lasted too long. I don't suppose that your *protégée*
> can ever recover so far, but I do hope that she will survive the continued
> necessary absence of the Major, and enjoy with him hereafter many happy
> days."

This was not unkindly. After all, Lord Wellington himself had the best reasons for believing in the capacity for survival of young ladies in love. Had not Kitty borne his own absence for nine years (and very nearly married Lowry Cole in the course of her vigil)? That, perhaps, was why he was a shade unsympathetic about leave. He had left so little behind him (his brother William was informed that "as for private concerns, I never trouble my head about them"), that home meant little to him; and why should it mean more to others?

Not that he was inhuman. He even had his moments of weakness. The day after Somers Cocks was killed at Burgos he came into someone's room, paced it for some time in silence, opened the door to go, and as he left exclaimed abruptly, "Cocks was killed last night." But his emotion was dry-eyed; how, with his work to do, could it be otherwise? High command is a supremely lonely business. Yet there were moments when he needed company. At four o'clock on winter afternoons he left his room "and then, for an hour or two, parades with any one whom he wants to talk to, up and down the little square of Frenada (amidst all the chattering Portuguese) in his grey great coat." The talk ran on anything—on India, on Ireland, on Mr. Canning's views about the Catholics—and the trim figure in grey paced up and down the little square among the staring drovers. He could be affable; and the Head-quarters mess grew familiar with his laugh—a terrifying cachinnation "very loud and long, like the whoop of the whooping cough often repeated."

The Peer kept his distance, though. For was it not almost his duty as Commander-in-Chief to be a shade aloof? Perhaps aloofness came natural to him. At any rate, it was his fate, his rather lonely fate, always to be a little different from his surroundings, his head held a trifle higher than his neighbours'. Had he not been an Englishman in Ireland, an Anglo-Indian in India, a soldier among politicians, and finally a politician among soldiers? He was invariably in contrast, never in perfect harmony with his assorted backgrounds; and the spare figure, tightly buttoned in its grey beneath a black cocked-hat, contrasted oddly with the glare of Spain. It was a lonely *rôle* to be Lord Wellington.

THE worst was over now. For it was 1812, and the slow tide of war began to ebb. They had withstood the full force of it since 1810, bearing up against the whole weight of the Empire. In those crucial years—the years of Busaco, of Torres Vedras, Masséna's retreat, and Fuentes de Oñoro—all Europe beyond the Pyrenees had been at peace, its Emperor at leisure to pour the flood-tide of his armies into Spain. But now the tide checked and, called by its unrestful luminary, began to ebb away towards the north, where the French faced about to meet another enemy. For Russian drums were tapping in the mist beyond the edge of Germany; the Czar's tall grenadiers were stiffly aligned; and the little Cossack ponies trotted smartly beneath the long lances of their bearded riders. Soon there would be more than Spain to think of. Spain must be held, of course; but now the Guard had gone, the Poles were going, and there would be no more reinforcements for King Joseph and the fretful Marshals. The tide was ebbing now. The French, evicted three times in four years from Portugal, were scarcely likely to return; although the Emperor seven hundred miles away in Paris still appeared to regard Lisbon as their objective, and pelted his Marshals with a succession of fantastic orders. These documents, in which Napoleon appears at his least impressive, were uniformly unhelpful, since the facts on which he founded his instructions originated almost exclusively in that powerful imagination, and the resulting orders (which bore no relation to Peninsular conditions) were invariably out of date when they arrived. Indeed, the least harmful to their recipients' chances of success were those which failed to arrive at all.

A fair proportion of these missives were diverted from their lawful destinations by the kindly forethought of *guerrilleros*; for the military genius of Spain, which had hitherto found infelicitous expression in a disastrous series of pitched battles, was admirably suited to the stealthier operations of the *petite guerre*—the *guerrilla*. Cloaked figures haunted Spanish defiles; French despatch-riders, ambling inattentively into the

throat of some dreadful gully, failed to emerge into the sunlight; and
as the empty road beyond wound dustily across the plain, eager knives
were slitting French saddlery in search of correspondence, to be for-
warded by faithful hands and lonely tracks and patiently deciphered at
Lord Wellington's headquarters. (If official Spain left much to be
desired as an ally, few armies have found more effective friends than
the Spanish *guerrillero*, who effaced the long French line of communications with grim persistence, rounding up the rumbling convoys,
rushing incautious posts, and imposing an escort of 1,800 men upon a
French General who wished to reach his destination.) From his perusal
of intercepted despatches Wellington might pardonably conclude that,
as an adversary at long range, the Emperor was fallible, and from the
tone which he habitually employed towards inferiors that Napoleon was
distinctly not a gentleman. This, indeed, became one of his fixed convictions. Did he not once inform a houseparty of Lord Hertford's that
"Buonaparte's mind was, in its details, low and ungentleman-like," a
defect which he charitably attributed to "the narrowness of his early
prospects and habits"? His fastidious taste was equally repelled by the
Emperor's frequent use of deception—"Buonaparte's whole life, civil,
political, and military was a fraud. There was not a transaction, great
or small, in which lying and fraud were not introduced. . . . Buonaparte's foreign policy was force and menace, aided by fraud and corruption. If the fraud was discovered, force and menace succeeded." Not that
he was convinced of their success—"I never was a believer in him,
and I always thought that in the long-run we should overturn him. He
never seemed himself at his ease, and even in the boldest things he did
there was always a mixture of apprehension and meanness. I used to
call him *Jonathan Wild the Great*, and at each new *coup* he made I
used to cry out 'Well done, Jonathan'." . . . As he read his papers
at Headquarters, this rich distaste, the full fruit of later years, was
slowly ripening.

But a more valuable discovery which emerged from the Emperor's
tangential dealings with King Joseph and the bewildered Marshals was
that Napoleon could err. Lord Wellington sat in his Portuguese headquarters above a village street and learned that serviceable lesson. Other
adversaries encountered the Emperor for the first time on battlefields,

and were appropriately awed into helpless immobility. But Wellington first came upon him in the more reassuring form of palpably absurd instructions to his deputies in Spain. "The habit of Napoleon," as Wellington wrote of him later, "had been to astonish and deceive mankind, and he had come at last to deceive himself." He did not fall into the vulgar error of underrating him, retaining a salutary belief that "his presence on the field made the difference of forty thousand men." But no student of his interventions in Peninsular affairs could retain in its full perfection the awe in which Europe held the white-breeched, green-coated figure. That, if Wellington was ever to meet him in the field, would be something gained.

Meanwhile, his problem waited. The French were still at large in Spain, and the strong places of the frontier barred his way. But if Ciudad Rodrigo and Badajoz awaited his attack, he enjoyed the rare advantage that he could choose his own moment for attacking them. For the initiative had passed to Wellington. He was at perfect liberty to move his pieces up and down the board, while the French could do little more than pant after him, parrying his blows. The cause was simple: Spain was a desert, and in desert warfare supply and transport are the only wings upon which armies can rise into motion. The Sepoy General had both; the French had neither.

Endowed with this superior mobility, he made a winter thrust at Ciudad Rodrigo. The January snow was deep in Leon as they moved against the fortress; and after twelve days in open trenches they stormed it on January 19—"in half the time" (as he wrote Liverpool with a rare note of triumph) "that I told you it would take, and in less than half that which the French spent in taking the same place from the Spaniards." His speed was costly, though; for the siege cost heavily in casualties, including Robert Craufurd, whose last words of reconciliation evoked the wondering comment that "Craufurd talked to me as they do in a novel." But speed was vital, if they were to snatch Ciudad Rodrigo before Marmont could return to its relief; and the sudden *coup* secured the northern gate of Portugal, eliciting for Wellington a Spanish dukedom from the grateful Cortes, a marquisate from Portugal, an earldom from the Prince Regent, and an annuity of £2,000 from Parliament.

The new Earl of Wellington and Duque de Ciudad Rodrigo surveyed the frontier with half the winter still before him. Badajoz remained, a rich prize to be seized before Soult from the south or Marmont from the north could intervene to rescue it. Time is the essence of siege-warfare—ample time for the slow ritual of investment, opening trenches, tracing parallels, saps, sorties, siting batteries, mining and countermining, and breaching scarps, the whole culminating in the triumphant *finale* of an assault and escalade. When conducted in due form, it had something of the grave decorum of a minuet (had not the Eighteenth Century once opened trenches to the sound of violins?); or it might be viewed under the guise of courtship—of a singularly formal courtship in which the gallant besieger drew a reluctant fortress with exquisite deliberation into the embraces of his parallels and saps. But time was the essence of this lingering procedure; and when time presses, besiegers are of necessity crude, hasty, and ungraceful. Wellington's approach to Badajoz was sadly lacking in the graces of unhurried siege-warfare, since his problem was to batter down the last remaining gate of Portugal before its guardians could return to save it. He moved south in February, with an agreeable pretence for the benefit of the French that he was "going to hunt . . . and you might even have a house arranged for the hounds at Aldea de Yeltes." Whilst his exceedingly impromptu siege-train jolted slowly forward towards Badajoz, he corresponded on the agreeable theme of his latest honours, even finding time for lengthy expositions of French finance and Indian army problems. News reached him that his brother Richard, whom the passing years rendered increasingly intractable, had resigned the Foreign Office and elicited the judicious comment that "in truth the republic of a cabinet is but little suited to any man of taste or of large views"—a sentiment of which he was himself to experience the justice later. Richard, indeed, was scarcely suited to republics; even a not too constitutional monarchy cramped him unduly. But his defection left Arthur as the leading Wellesley, though Henry still toiled patiently as British Ambassador at Cadiz—had laboured there, indeed, since Richard's translation to Downing Street—and now received the recognition of knighthood.

Meanwhile, the French still mounted guard in Badajoz. The siege began in March; the parallels crept closer; Easter went by; and on a

dark spring night (it was April 6) the attack was launched. For two
interminable hours it swayed round the fortress in a glare of port-fires,
as each storming column went roaring forward into failure. When the
news came to Wellington, the colour left his face and his jaw fell; but
he turned to give an order in that calm way of his, and even apologised
with formal courtesy for giving it to the wrong person. Then a report
arrived that Picton's men were in the fortress; the Staff hallooed; but
Wellington was still giving orders in his level voice. Badajoz was his.
Yet, for the moment, it was not Lord Wellington's, but his army's; and
for three nights and days of unprecedented riot they celebrated their
capture. Discipline dissolved in floods of wine; locks were shot open;
looting was universal; and scared nymphs (in comb and *mantilla*) fled
shrieking down the winding alleys before reeling fauns (in scarlet tunics).
Even the gaunt silhouette of gallows in the Plaza failed to check the
saturnalia, though their formidable master "fulminates orders and will
hardly thank the troops, so angry is he." But he was sad as well as
angry. For he had purchased Badajoz at a cruel price; and when he
saw the casualty returns, Wellington (for once not dry-eyed) wept
bitterly.

The first phase of 1812 was over. Badajoz and Ciudad Rodrigo secured, the gates of Portugal swung open; and in June they marched
eastwards into Spain, having the red earth underfoot and on their
right a line of snow mountains, until they saw the heaped brown cupolas
of Salamanca piled up against the eastern sky. That was the first stage
on the long road from Portugal to the Pyrenees. His blow was aimed at
Marmont in Leon rather than at Soult further to the south in Andalusia,
for the simple reason that French movements would be cramped by
starvation (had not hunger just recalled Marmont from a raid into
Portugal?) until the harvest ripened; and "the harvest in all the countries
north of the Tagus . . . is much later than it is to the southward. We
shall retain our advantages for a longer period of time in these countries than we should do to the southward." This was the application of
supply to strategy with a vengeance; and obedient to its dictates Wellington marched on Salamanca.

The French fell back, leaving a garrison to hold some forts; and early
one June morning Wellington rode in. The town was roaring; and he

rode slowly through the press, deafened with shrill *vivas*. Excited women crowded round him with tears, with kisses, with hoarse Spanish voices; and the still figure, writing orders on a sabretache, was almost pulled from his saddle. Three armies in four years had jingled spurs under the brown arcades of the Plaza Mayor—Moore's hurried redcoats racing against the Emperor in 1808, then an interminable succession of Frenchmen in blue, and now the redcoats once again. Some of them marched off to besiege the French remnant in the forts; the rest took post to the north of the city on the ridge of San Christoval, where Wellington hoped against hope that Marmont would attack him. That position, where he deliberately offered battle on two occasions in the course of 1812, was never fought over. But as the ideal is always more exquisitely rounded than the real, Wellington's conception of a defensive action is perfectly revealed in the unfought battle of San Christoval.

Exposing to the French a long and easy slope of innocent aspect and a blind skyline, the ridge dropped steeply on its inner face, affording perfect concealment to the defenders until the moment came to reveal them. For the Wellingtonian defensive had the splendid simplicity of a booby-trap. Its modest object was to spring unsuspected forces upon surprised attackers; and San Christoval (like Busaco before it and Waterloo a few years later) was admirably suited to this simple pleasantry. The attackers would pant uphill towards the blind skyline; somewhere behind the crest a line of British infantry would crouch, completely sheltered from artillery and waiting happily to fire its volley, utter its huzza, and leap forward with the bayonet. This game, if only Marmont would oblige with an attack, could be repeated three times on three successive ridges of identical conformation, before the French offensive could pierce through to Salamanca. One afternoon they came quite close to the position; and Wellington was heard muttering, "Damned tempting! I have a great mind to attack 'em." The French guns opened, and the round shot began to fall among his Staff quite close to where Wellington was standing with a map. He "moved a few paces, and continued his directions." But the moment passed; Marmont thought better of it, and drew off towards the north; and the battle of San Christoval—the perfect Wellingtonian battle—was never fought.

Twelve hundred miles away the Emperor, a squat figure in a great-

coat, whistled *Malbrouck s'en va't en guerre* and watched his long
columns wind slowly across a Polish river into Russia. Their bayonets
gleamed in the June sunshine, as the loaded caissons rumbled across
the bridges and the *Grande Armée* took the long road for Moscow. Then
the dust settled in the plain, and silence fell again behind them. In Spain
Marmont and Wellington were groping for one another outside Salamanca. At one moment the deadlock seemed complete, and the Peer
miraculously gave leave to a Staff officer, conjecturing that "you have
seen the end of it. . . . I shan't fight him without an advantage, nor he   14
me, I believe." There was an interlude of countermarching, in which
each followed suit with the precision of chess-players in the opening
moves. Marmont was edging round Salamanca towards the road to   15
Portugal. If that were threatened, Wellington must fall back; and the
two armies wheeled against the distant and unchanging background of
a tall sierra across a sort of dusty Wiltshire with long, marine horizons—
a reddish Wiltshire with tiled villages built of adobe—and this blend
of Mexico and Salisbury Plain appropriately evoked a series of precise
manœuvres. For they wheeled in full sight of one another, the two
armies racing southward side by side for the faint line of trees that
marked the Tormes. The air, oddly enough (since it was the third week
of July), was fresh, chilled by a biting wind off the sierra; and Wellington "never suffered more from cold." The focus shifted round   16
the city, as Marmont felt for the road behind his adversary; and as they
swung south of Salamanca, the French seemed to be leading in the
race. They could not be quite sure, though, how much of Wellington's
command was on the ground; for he had interposed a slope—one of
his favourite long slopes with a blind skyline—and three divisions were   17
concealed behind it. As the French headed for the west, they were strung
out a little in the race, gaily unaware that they were marching across
the front of Wellington's entire command. The morning of July 22
passed in this agreeable manner, Marmont "manœuvring" (as Wellington wrote) "in the usual French style, nobody knew with what object."   18
But about lunch-time the French lapse became manifest. Wellington was
"stumping about and munching" in a little farmyard among the brown
cottages of Los Arapiles, lunching apparently off alternate bites of chicken
and glances at the French through a telescope. (The occasion lingered

19 in Alava's memory because, for once, there was not cold meat.) The
Peer's lunch was interrupted by a final look towards the French. "By
God," he suddenly exclaimed, "that will do"—and scandalised Alava by
flinging far over his shoulder the leg of chicken which he had been
eating in his fingers. Then he cantered up the hill for a more comprehensive view, and the whole field was spread before him—the red
masses of his own command, the still country, and the marching French.
The game was in his hands: "*Mon cher Alava,*" he said cheerfully, "*Marmont est perdu,*" and rode off to launch the attack. For it was not his

20 way to entrust such vital missions to subordinates; and when he left
the stony hill, he galloped across level fields with one companion to give
his orders. Edward Pakenham, Kitty's brother, commanded the leading
column of attack.

"Ned," said his formidable brother-in-law, "move on with the Third
Division; take the heights on your front; and drive everything before
you."

"I will, my lord," he dutifully answered, "if you will give me your
hand."

There was a handshake; and the attack developed which "beat forty
thousand men in forty minutes." In the later phases he presided lov-

21 ingly over each turn of his battle; as Pakenham informed his mother,
"our Chief was every where and Sadly Exposed himself." For he was
seen riding forward with the advancing lines of his own infantry; and
when the heavy cavalry went thundering against the French (it was a
favourite hallucination of the Prince Regent in later years that he had
charged with them), Wellington was close enough to remark to their
commander, "By God, Cotton, I never saw anything so beautiful in
my life; the day is *yours.*" The day, at any rate, was England's. For
Wellington had launched twenty-eight battalions against seventy-eight
and sent them reeling eastwards into Castile; Marmont and Clausel, his
second in command and successor, were both wounded; and the Army
of Portugal hurried to shelter with a loss of fifteen thousand men and
twenty guns, a solid testimony to Wellington's ability to do something
more than defend strong positions of his own choice. Foy termed the
battle Frederician; and there were traces of the King of Prussia's "oblique
order" in the slanting thrust of Wellington's attack.

Indeed, the victory might have been still more crushing if a Spanish force, which he had posted at a ford behind the French, had been capable of simple obedience. But Carlos de España had decamped from Alba de Tormes, and the French slipped by. Spain was at Alba, though —the sinister, uncomprehended Spain of macabre *Caprichos* and sardonic portraits of egregious Bourbons and preposterous grandees— watching through the sharp eyes of Francisco Goya y Lucientes. For Goya watched him, as he rode in that night from Salamanca, if the note appended to his sketch can be believed; and the strange drawing, 22 with its unavoidable suggestion of an ascetic interrupted in his cell or a drowning man restored unexpectedly to the surface, records the exhausted victor—unshaven, hollow-eyed, the damp hair plastered to his forehead, a little shaken by the spent bullet which had bruised his thigh—a wild-eyed, unfamiliar Wellington, as Goya saw him on that summer night in a Spanish village.

The long corridors of Spain lay open to him now; and the French scurried wildly in all directions. Clausel drew off the wreckage of Salamanca towards the north; King Joseph hung disconsolately round Madrid; and Soult with infinite deliberation moved out of Andalusia to the rescue. Wellington, whose *forte* was not pursuit, shepherded Clausel warily towards Valladolid and the great road to France. A little artifice, framed to delude King Joseph's outposts, employed legitimate deception —"I shall stay here all day," he advised an officer in command of Portu- 23 guese cavalry, "and will act according to the Intelligence which I shall receive from you"; but an ingenious postscript enclosed "a letter which I beg you to send to the French advanced posts by an officer of the German Cavalry well-mounted with a well-mounted Escort. . . . Tell him to answer no questions and give no information excepting that Marmont's army is totally annihilated as a Military Body; and to get all the information he can. Desire him to say he does not know where I am, and that I move every day."

A choice, it would appear, was open to him between pressing still farther to the north, where Burgos beckoned at the angle of the road to France, and evicting Joseph from his capital. He chose the latter, very largely for the reason that "I could not go farther north without great 24 inconvenience, and I could at that moment do nothing else." Besides,

LORD WELLINGTON, 1812.
From a drawing by Goya, in the British Museum.

to send King Joseph scampering out of Madrid would deprive his government of all air of permanence; and the threat would almost certainly draw the French armies out of southern Spain. (Far beyond hearing now, behind the silence in the north, the long columns of the *Grande Armée* wound through the summer haze across the endless Russian plain. Napoleon was half inclined to reach Smolensk and halt, to check his senseless march deeper and deeper into Russia. But, as Wellington said of him later, "a conqueror, like a cannon-ball, must go on. If he rebounds, his career is over." So he went on into the silence.)

Bound for Madrid, Lord Wellington rode southward from Valladolid under the wide skies of Old Castile. Segovia watched him go by, the Roman arches of its aqueduct stepping serenely across the prostrate town; he passed the bald Guadarrama in the blazing August days; and within three weeks of Salamanca he was in the dusty plain below Madrid. King Joseph, a reluctant harbinger, scuttled before him into his capital and out again, bound for the distant security of Valencia with a retreating army and a vast convoy. For that unhappy monarch moved southward like a tribal migration in the choking dust of two thousand vehicles, whilst his capital made cheerful preparations to welcome the approaching British. They marched in on August 12, and found a city in the grip of the splendid dementia of which Southern capitals are occasionally capable. Bells pealed; the road ran wine and lemonade by turns, became a forest of waving palm-branches, and changed with dream-like ease into a *ballet* of young ladies pirouetting alongside the marching redcoats with offerings of grapes, of sticky sweets, of laurel leaves, and treating their impassive chief to worship that bordered perilously on the divine. For Wellington, high-nosed and silent, rode at the centre of the din with wild brunettes covering his hands, his sword, his boots, even his horse with Spanish kisses, and picked his cautious way across a bright sea of flowered shawls, until King Joseph's palace walls shut out the roaring city; and the new master of Madrid after this violent apotheosis resumed his problems.

Far behind him a grateful England, ringing with the news of Salamanca, poured out fresh honours. Official England was a little changed that summer, since a crazy pistol-shot had accounted for the inoffensive Perceval. But Liverpool assumed his place, Castlereagh returned to

office, and the Government was still in friendly hands. The Peer was to
be a Marquess now; and from his retirement Lord Wellesley, whose
sumptuous mind was always apt to run on heraldry, offered the generous suggestion that his victorious younger brother should be permitted   27
to augment his coat of arms with the French eagle. Ministers, consulted
on this vital problem, preferred the Union Jack; and Lord Wellington,
who felt that the French emblem "carries with it an appearance of
ostentation, of which I hope I am not guilty," concurred in their opinion. The Prime Minister was busy with the purchase of the manor of
Wellington on his behalf; and though cheerfully indifferent to his step   28
in the peerage (he asked someone, "What the devil is the use of making
me a Marquess?"), he took some interest in his new estates, and was not
above indicating that his allowances were quite inadequate to his expenses in the field. It was still raining Spanish honours, and his splendid
jewellery was augmented by the Golden Fleece.

Meanwhile, there were the French. He hoped to keep them busy in
the south with minor operations, whilst he secured the road to France
at Burgos. His tone was quite light-hearted—"Matters go on well, and   29
I hope before Christmas, if matters turn out as they ought, and Boney
requires all the reinforcements in the North, to have all the gentlemen
safe on the other side of the Ebro." (That day the swelling domes of
Moscow gleamed under a pale northern sky, and the French dead were
piled high round the Great Redoubt at Borodino.) Wellington turned
northwards now. Madrid was left behind; the blind windows of the
Escorial stared at the British columns, as they went by towards the
north; the French fell back before them; and one September day they
saw the spires of Burgos and the long saddle of the Castle. That obstacle
remained; and as Wellington saw it rising in tiers above the brown
roofs of the town to the crowning defiance of its embrasures, he was
inclined to "doubt . . . that I have means to take the castle, which is   30
very strong." (Doubt hung on the autumn air of 1812; for while the
Peer stared doubtfully at Burgos through his glass, a dreadful doubt
hung over Moscow. The bright domes were veiled in smoke; and as
the French marched away, they turned to stare over their shoulders at
the red glare on the sky behind them.) He was at Burgos for a month,
until the distant mountains were dusted with the October snows. Snow

fell in Russia, too—the first drifting flakes that fluttered harmlessly on the
still air, then powdered the interminable plain, until the winter skies
were dark above them, and they toiled endlessly through the white
silence. Wellington's three siege-guns—"Thunder," "Lightning," and
"Nelson" (who had lost a trunnion)—were banging bravely at the Castle.
He was still hopeful, though his hopes were chastened now—"Time is
wearing apace, and Soult is moving from the south; and I should not
be surprised if I were obliged to discontinue this operation in order to
collect the army." Headquarters were enlivened by an opinionated
Marine, whom the senior service had consigned to Burgos to enlighten
Wellington with demonstrations of "a new exercise of the bayonet, which
is to render a British soldier equal to 12 Frenchmen." This bright prospect opened one morning after breakfast; whereupon "after Lord W.
had looked and listened with some impatience, he gave his orders for
the day to the Adjutant-General, mounted his horse, and galloped to the
trenches." Marines, it would appear, were prodigal of bright ideas.
One had contrived an "artificial hill" for facilitating reconnaissance; but
his ingenuity faded before that of the learned Portuguese who "proposed
to burn the French army by means of convex glasses."

Burgos still barred the way; and impatient men stared from their
batteries at the brown roofs, the pointed spires, the trees along the
river, and the distant roads that wound across the plain like ribbons.
The autumn weeks were passing, and the French were gathering to
north and south of him. His parallels crept slowly forward; but the
rain drove down, flooding his trenches. He could not storm the place,
"having but little musket ammunition." Besides, he would not willingly
repeat the slaughter of Badajoz; when he stood at Cocks' graveside that
autumn, his face was wrung with pain. So he resolved to treat Burgos
a trifle summarily, as he had treated hill-forts in India, and resorted to
half-measures. But in war no half-measure succeeds. For mining, inadequate bombardment, and small storming-parties were no substitute for
the sustained exertions which had forced the gates of Portugal; and the
siege failed. As he wrote later in the year, "I played a game which might
succeed (the only one which could succeed), and pushed it to the last;
and the parts having failed, as I admit was to be expected," he faced the
consequences. He blamed no one else—"the Government had nothing to

say to the siege. It was entirely my own act. . . . That which was want-   36
ing . . . was means of transporting ordnance and military stores to the
place where it was desirable to use them." Transport, for once, had failed
him.

Regretfully he turned to go. Soult and the fluttered Joseph were work-   37
ing north towards Toledo; Madrid was threatened; and Wellington
could not maintain himself in his advanced position. They must turn
back from Burgos, as John Moore had once turned back from Sahagun
on the Burgos road; but (unlike Moore) they would not need to run
for their transports, since Portugal was safely held behind them. A grey
cathedral watched them file through the silent streets under the moon;
their wheels were muffled; but the Castle guns were silent. Within a week
they were behind the Douro at Valladolid, and November found them
on the familiar heights of San Christoval. The Peer breathed again,
having reassembled his forces without misadventure and "got clear in
a handsome manner from the worst scrape that he ever was in." Bare   38
countries are like ladders with few rungs; and having lost the rung of
Burgos, Wellington was forced to drop to the rung of Salamanca. He
hoped to hold it, though he had scarcely more than fifty thousand men
against ninety thousand. But once more the battle of San Christoval remained unfought. The French manoeuvred round his flank. Once again
the armies wheeled round Salamanca. But, unlike Marmont, Soult gave
no opening; the rain came driving down; and Wellington marched his
men off to Portugal.

The four final days of retreat were miserable. Supplies went astray;
starving men ate acorns and shot uncovenanted pigs; it rained incessantly;
and an exasperated chief presided over awkward moments in the rear,
confessing that, by God, it was too serious to say anything. Yet, serious
indeed, it was never dangerous; and he brought off his army "in face   39
of a superior enemy, with the deliberation of an ordinary march . . . and
the casualties from the sword under 850"—a lively contrast with the long
agony of the *Grande Armée.* For Wellington incurred no Beresina, and
did not require a Ney to fight heroic rearguard actions. He brought
his army off; and long before a pale, furred man in a sleigh drove
hurriedly from Smorgoni towards Paris, he had them safe in Portugal.

Not that he was content. An angry circular informed subordinates that

40 discipline was lax, that "the officers lost all command over their men" in the retreat, and that this lapse was solely attributable "to the habitual inattention of the Officers of the regiments to their duty." This ungentle document found its way into newspapers, and left a wholly false impression of a grim martinet. His irritation was excusable. For at some points on the long road from Burgos wine had been as plentiful—and almost as destructive—as snow in the retreat from Moscow. But it was all over now; and they were safe on the windy hills which look down into Portugal after a year in which British arms had secured two vital fortresses, taken twenty thousand prisoners, and cleared southern Spain of

35 the French. Small wonder that the Marquess wrote, "I believe that I
41 have done right"; while Pakenham reported him "in good health and temper, satisfied with himself." For 1812 was over. The South, the peerless South was free. The Frenchmen with their clanging bands were gone at last; and Seville throbbed with innumerable strings, while the soft wail of its own music stole through Granada. For the South was free, and Andalusia sang in the sunlight. Twelve hundred miles away the *Grande Armée* was dead.

VII

T HE pace was quickening, as 1812 passed into 1813. All Europe
was on the move that winter—France falling back across Germany,
Russia in ponderous pursuit, the Prussians drilling hopefully, and even
Italy stirring a little. The Emperor in Paris created, improvised, decreed,
and threatened. He must have fresh armies; and French drafts went
northwards now up the long road towards the Pyrenees. Valladolid and
Burgos, long accustomed to their south-bound convoys, watched the
changing tide and felt the wind of war set from a new quarter.

Not that Spain was to be left bare; for 200,000 men remained, of 1
whom nearly 100,000 faced Wellington. Once that winter he left his
village street in Beira to visit his allies. His first call was on the Spaniards, who had at last appointed him Commander-in-Chief. This honour
was delayed until the Spanish armies had exhausted the possibilities of
defeat under their own commanders; and the Peer accepted the command without enthusiasm. But it might be made to serve as a means
of co-ordination and control, and he defined his new authority in a
series of precise demands. Then he rode off through winter floods to
Cadiz and, enlivened by lumbago on the road, pressed his points in
person. This visit has inspired romantic guesses. But his main pursuits 2
during the sixteen days of its duration were far from Capuan; for he
negotiated with the Spanish Regency, addressed the Cortes in bad but
energetic Spanish, and wrote stately letters in rather stilted French to his
new subordinates. His task, as he defined it to a correspondent, was "to
try 'to organise the Poles,' which appears to be a work something of the 3
same kind with that which Dumouriez describes so well in his Life";
he had used the same comparison fourteen years earlier, when he was
organising the Nizam's army before Seringapatam—a testimonial to his
thorough reading of a book that had travelled from his Dublin lodgings
to Madras in Colonel Wesley's baggage. He judged that he had "made
some progress; but the libellers have set to work, and I am apprehensive
that the Cortes will take the alarm." For he found journalists and Parlia-

228

4 mentarians almost uniformly unhelpful. He was prepared, of course, to "fight for Spain as long as she is the enemy of France, whatever may be her system of government." But a constitution created "very much on the principle that a painter paints a picture, viz., to be looked at" failed to compel his admiration; and he was frankly derisive of "a sovereign popular assembly, calling itself 'Majesty' . . . and of an executive government called 'Highness' acting under the control of 'His Majesty' the assembly." He could see the menace.

> "The theory of all legislation is founded in justice; and, if we could be certain that all legislative assemblies would on all occasions act according to the principles of justice, there would be no occasion for those checks and guards which we have seen established under the best systems. Unfortunately, however, we have seen that legislative assemblies are swayed by the fears and passions of individuals; when unchecked, they are tyrannical and unjust; nay more: it unfortunately happens too frequently that the most tyrannical and unjust measures are the most popular. Those measures are particularly popular which deprive rich and powerful individuals of their properties under the pretence of the public advantage; and I tremble for a country in which, as in Spain, there is no barrier for the preservation of private property, excepting the justice of a legislative assembly possessing supreme powers."

So he proposed a House of Lords for Spain. Meanwhile, he "could wish that some of our reformers would go to Cadiz"; the lesson, he appeared to feel, might be salutary for Mr. Cobbett. For Cadiz marked a stage in Wellington's political education, serving to deepen his distaste for popular assemblies. Apart from Westminster, he had only known two legislative bodies intimately—the Irish House of Commons and the Cortes—and neither was calculated to make a democrat of him.

One ally grounded in the elements of military organisation, he passed on to his next pupil and rode off to Lisbon. Business was almost wholly precluded by four days of strenuous celebration. The anniversary of

5 Ciudad Rodrigo was honoured with a banquet; Captain Gurwood, who had commanded the "forlorn hope," arrived a trifle late and was exalted to the skies when his excuses were greeted with a genial "You were not too late this time last year." They all went to the Opera, where (for some reason buried deep in the Portuguese intelligence) doves fluttered in the

cheering auditorium, and one perched on the Peer's box. These arduous festivities concluded, he rode back to his village in the hills.

Life at Headquarters was not without its compensations. A buttoned figure still bent above its papers or tramped the little square on winter afternoons among the drovers. His hounds still hunted, and his talk was quite as varied as ever—how Ireland must be held by force, and   6
what a blunder his brother Richard and Mr. Canning made in taking up the Catholic question; how he meant to have twenty-five couples of hounds to hunt next winter; and how admirably the Peninsula was suited to warfare, because there was nothing in it for anyone to damage—"as, for instance, what is this village worth? burn it, and a few hundreds would make it as good as ever with a little labour"—but that he should be almost sorry to see such a war in Germany. Sometimes it was play-night in the Light Division, and he rode over to Gallegos for their theatricals. The programme (printed on War Department paper by the   7
army press at Freneda) announced *The Rivals* with a cast of Riflemen, a pink subaltern as *Lydia Languish,* and a small part for Havelock's elder brother—"after which a Variety of Comic Songs," the whole loyally con-cluding *Vivat Wellington.* For the Light Division Theatre was well aware of its position. But the great occasion was the ball at Rodrigo. That afternoon he had been working at Headquarters until half-past three; but he rode the seventeen miles in two hours, dined in his decora-   8
tions, danced, took supper, and set off at half-past three for a gallop home by moonlight. They sat down sixty-five to dinner, and two hun-dred guests came to the dance. The ball-room was a trifle draughty, as the siege had left a large gap in the roof. But they danced with spirit, though the floor left much to be desired, and a sentry had to be posted near a hole. Two Spanish couples obliged with the whirl and flutter of a *fandango* and a *bolero*; and a disapproving Judge-Advocate, who failed to relish

> "Fandango's wriggle, or Bolero's bound,"

observed that his allies twirled and handled their partners "a little more . . . than our fair ones would like at first," but was inclined to think that on the whole the English practice was for the best. They drank innumerable toasts—"The next campaign," "Death to all Frenchmen," and "King Ferdinand VII"—and when the ladies had retired, they taught the Spaniards how to say "Hip, hip, hip hurra" instead of "Viva," and chaired one another freely until someone dropped a General. Outside the moon was shining; it was freezing hard; a thoroughbred was clattering up mountain roads at a hand-gallop; and before dawn came to Ciudad Rodrigo, Lord Wellington was back at Headquarters.

He could be genial, though a snub could still be administered at need; and a bewhiskered aide-de-camp of the Prince Regent, appearing on parade in the full glory of a Hussar uniform, received no more from him than two fingers raised to a cocked hat at full gallop, followed by a resounding "Grant, if you will dine with me, I dine at six o'clock." But dinner at Headquarters had been known to end in a song; and he was apt to call without undue modesty for the song made in his honour by the Spaniards after Salamanca. The guitar spoke softly; long fingers plucked the strings; and, "*Ahe Marmont,*" the singer gloated, "*onde vai, Marmont?*" Wellington sat listening with composure to the lift and wail of the *copla.* Indeed, they noticed that he "hears his own praises in Spanish with considerable coolness"; and someone termed the song "Lord Wellington's favourite."

But life at Headquarters was not all dinners and fox-hunting. For there were still his endless papers—letters from ministers, from grandees of Spain, from half the Army List—all answered in his swift handwriting. His letters to the Spaniards were a complete correspondence-course in elementary administration, enlivened by sardonic comments to his brother Henry on the unsatisfactory progress of their backward pupils at Cadiz. Then there were endless courts-martial to be written upon or discussed with Mr. Larpent, departmental queries from young Lord Palmerston on the inspiring theme of regimental accounts, friendly notes from the Prime Minister about his new estate at Wellington, the eternal problem of cash payments, his regular report to the Secretary of State, and supplies to be collected for the spring campaign. A more agreeable category related to the fresh honours which came crowding on him. The Portuguese, not to be outdone by Spain, made him a Duke under the splendid style of Duque da Victoria; he became Colonel of the Blues and expressed his rapture in the shy confession that "there was never so fortunate or so favoured a man"; the Garter was conferred on him, and he wrote home

231

an anxious query over which shoulder he should wear the blue ribbon. An enticing offer of Russian troops for the Peninsula flits through his papers; but Spanish pride was, for some occult reason, offended by the thought; the offer turned out to be unauthorised; and, true to their invariable tradition, the phantom Russians never came.

There was no limit to the size, large or small, of the topics submitted to the Commander-in-Chief. He advised the Cabinet upon European strategy; and when Lieutenant Kelly of the Fortieth eloped with a young lady, the case received his best attention. He even interviewed the angry mother and undertook (in Portuguese) to restore the erring child on condition that she should not be ill-treated or consigned to a convent. Then he directed Lowry Cole to part the lovers. But Cole, impressed by the mother's menacing aspect, pointed out to the Commander-in-Chief the probable nature of the fair prodigal's welcome. Besides, the impulsive Kelly (as he reported) was quite prepared to make amends by marriage. Lord Wellington, more sceptical, could "not but observe that he has it in his power, whenever he pleases, to compensate in that manner the injury which he has done to the family"— and improved the occasion by an impressive homily upon the lamentable tendency of officers and men abroad to commit such outrages as they individually thought fit. But that very day the knot was tied by an army chaplain of Portuguese *Caçadores*. Propriety had received its due tribute and when the outraged parent called at Headquarters, she found a disobliging Wellington who declined to intervene and left his shrill visitor vociferating threats of sudden death for her offspring and transportation for the obliging chaplain. So romance was satisfied; and one more frontal attack upon a Wellington position had failed.

England was very far away; and the distance served to modify his attitude to politics. He had come out to Portugal as Chief Secretary in a Tory administration, returning from Vimeiro to dispense party arguments from the Treasury Bench without a conscious effort. But now his view of his position had changed; and when a Whig correspondent seemed to emphasise the party difference between them, he wrote that "as I have long ceased to think of home politics, it cannot be said that I am of a party different from that to which any other person belongs. I serve the country to the best of my ability abroad, leaving the Govern-

On the heights near Sobral,
June 19th 1813 ½ past 12 at
Noon. —

I have ordered the Light
Division to cross the River, &
to get possession of the Hill
on the enemy's left; and
fire in advance, & commence
them in front, & have your
Light Infantry across supporting
it by having by & heavy
Infantry —

There is a Bridge at the
village, & I understand a ford
just below —

I will make the light
division continue its
march till the head on
your right cols; and
you follow them up the
valley to the same point

Washington
½ before two P.M

21st M June 19

Since I wrote to you a [few?]
[days?] some ago I have
heard that the [_____] all
[_____] on the great
[_____] you had better
[_____] both when
you will have, as [_____]
the [_____] & [_____] up
such forts as you may
think [_____] — Wellington

ment at home to be contended for by the different parties as they may think proper." In fine, he was Lord Wellington and knew his duty.

Besides, the Peninsula still claimed his full attention. The French were now uneasily aligned on the great road to France; and the French monarchy in Spain was little more than a field-army. The South was up; the Catalans persisted bravely; *guerrilleros* went freely up and down the land; and the shaggy hills behind Bilbao were loud with drumming, as the North marched out to war behind its pipes. A French rearguard still occupied Madrid; but the King's headquarters were already far to the north in Valladolid; and his modest hope was to hold the line of the Douro against the British, who were bound to come marching up from Portugal by way of Salamanca. But were they? Lord Wellington had other views. For he was disinclined to force a passage of the Douro in face of a French army in strong prepared positions. He preferred to cross the river lower down its course, far behind the Portuguese frontier, and to appear in disagreeable force on the French bank. That, he surmised, would be an inexpensive method of dislodging them. So early as the third week of April his design was confided to Beresford:

14   "I propose to put the troops in motion in the first days of May. My intention is to make them cross the Douro in general within the Portuguese frontier, covering the movement of the left by the right of the army towards the Tormes. . . ."

This was simplicity itself. At the same time he chose a bold expedient to accelerate his spring towards the north. His base was now at Lisbon; and whilst it might be satisfactory to draw supplies thence so long as he was operating in Leon and Castile, his line of communications would be intolerably lengthened (and the resulting delays increased), if he succeeded in advancing further to the north. So he resolved upon the unusual measure of transferring his base to the north coast of Spain as soon as he

15   should reach the northern sphere of operations. (The same conception appears in the transfer of his base in 1803 from Mysore to the west coast of India.) Before his march began, the Admiral commanding on the sta-

16   tion was advised that Wellington thought it "not impossible that we may hereafter have to communicate with the shipping in one of the ports in the North of Spain"; and at a later stage his supply ships were definitely

ordered to the great bay of Santander, a striking instance of the superior   17
elasticity conferred by sea-power on land operations.

Now they were ready to advance; and symptoms of the move began to
appear at Headquarters, where the Peer's claret was reported to be pack-   18
ing. The date was fixed by the ripening of crops of forage for his horses.
But the spring rains were late that year, and slight delays in the arrival
of the bridging-train (he infuriated the artillery by taking their gun-teams
to draw pontoons) deferred his start—fortunately, perhaps, as Wellington
was visited by a devastating cold. They moved before the end of May;
and as they passed the frontier into Spain, he turned his horse and, with
a rare concession to drama, flourished his hat towards the rear with the   19
apostrophe, "Farewell, Portugal! I shall never see you again." He never
did.

For the hunt was up that sent the French behind the Pyrenees. Within
a fortnight he had manœuvred them off the Douro; and the bells were
clashing in Zamora, as a cloaked, grey figure rode in. He waved away the
dishes of an endless lunch; and disappointed Spaniards asked, "Is that   20
Lord Wellington? The man who is sitting there so meekly in a grey coat,
has only one officer at his side, and will not eat or drink anything? Good
God!" Delighted villages thumped tambourines; nuns showered rose-
leaves from the security of upper windows; but the advance went on, as
they moved steadily northwards up the broad corridors of Old Castile.
The Peer was on the move; and a hurried glimpse caught him pacing a
village street with Beresford, whilst his tent was being pitched and the   21
Military Secretary sat writing orders on his knee under a wall. The French
continually fell back, as rung after rung of the long Spanish ladder slipped
from their hands. They stood at Burgos; but its works were still unre-
paired. He was outflanking them again; and they fell back once more,
leaving a rearguard to destroy the Castle (and blow out the glass of the
cathedral). The roar of the explosion reached Wellington, who was on
their heels and promptly resolved to "*hustle* them out of Spain." His first
design had contemplated a formal siege of Burgos. But the French had   22
saved him the trouble; and his spirits mounted, as King Joseph's monarchy dwindled to an army in retreat. "Affairs are somewhat changed,"   23
he wrote, "since the period when the *frightened Leopard* was to have been
driven into the sea. I think that if the Powers of Europe chuse it we may

now carry on a successful War, or may force the Tyrant to make a peace
which shall give genuine tranquility to the World, & security to Independent States." (His spelling seemed to suffer slightly in the swift
advance.) The French were waiting for him now in the hills south of
Ebro. It was a strong position, approached precariously by a narrow road
that crawled beneath the wicked spires of Pancorbo. But Wellington had
little taste for frontal attacks on strong positions; and his columns slanted
northwards away from the main road to France by which he was expected. For he would get behind the French again. He was still groping
round their right; and their route lay by unlikely mountain paths, where
he walked his horse and the guns were man-handled as the teams stepped
gingerly over the boulders. The French were turned again and went disconsolately behind the Ebro, the Peer shepherding them; and his method
of command was neatly illustrated by three notes written in a single
afternoon to Lowry Cole:

24

"On the heights near Poder June 19th 1813 $\frac{1}{2}$ past 12 at Noon.
"I have ordered the Light Division to cross the River, & to get possession
of the Ridge on the Enemy's left; and you will advance, & cannonade them
in front, & push your Light Infantry across supporting it by Cavalry &
Heavy Infantry.
"There is a Bridge at the Village, & I understand several fords."

The affair developed, and a second note conveyed his further wishes:

"I will make the Light Division continue its march till the Ridge on
your right ends; & do you follow them up the valley to the same point.
"$\frac{1}{4}$ before two P.M.
"Let the Cavalry go with you."

A final scrap torn from his notebook warned the advancing Cole and left
him with a discretion that, from such a source, was both flattering and
rare:

2 P.M. June 19th.
"Since I wrote to you a quarter of an hour ago I have heard that the
Enemy are in strength on the great Road; you had better therefore halt
when you will have crossed the River; & taken up such Posts as you may
think proper."

235

His great sweep to the north had sent the French behind the Ebro and placed his own forces between Santander and the enemy. Now he could draw supplies by a short road from his new base; and if the French would fight, he was prepared to fight them.

He had come up with them at last; and their meeting-place was the great amphitheatre of Vitoria, where the last foothills of the Pyrenees look out across Castile. The hunted French—an army fifty thousand strong encumbered with a King, a Court, large portions of a Civil Service, and an extensive *smala* (someone irreverently remarked, *"Nous étions un bordel ambulant"*)—lay across the great road to France. Somewhere behind the hills Lord Wellington was waiting to attack. It was all a little like the last phase of a *corrida*, when the trim *matador* steps briskly sword in hand into the silent ring, watched by a weary bull. The French waited for the blow, watched by the distant circle of the hills. The blow prepared by Wellington was a miniature of the whole campaign, in which he had continually groped round the French right to place himself between them and their road to France. His groping left should swing behind them once again, cut the great road to Bayonne, and encircle them or (at the worst) deflect them from their natural line of retreat, leaving them to stumble towards Pamplona and the high passes of the Pyrenees. That was his plain design, and on June 21 he executed it. His sole uncertainty was the whereabouts of Clausel's command, which had been hunting *guerrilleros* in the north; but an obliging innkeeper rode twenty miles to tell him that Clausel was safely lodged in his *posada*. Lord Wellington had ridden over the ground; his troops were up; and as the guns began to speak in the mist of a June morning, Vitoria watched from all its belfries. The Peer, as usual, was everywhere, placing the troops and riding behind his infantry, as Picton led them into action in a cloud of blasphemy and a top-hat. Perhaps the full perfection of his scheme was slightly impaired by Wellington's practice of ubiquitous intervention, as an orchestral rendering would scarcely be improved by a conductor unable to restrain his virtuosity from playing half the parts himself. But his blow fell, though Graham on his left had failed to get behind them; and as the shadows lengthened, the French went reeling off towards the Pyrenees. They had lost all their guns but two, the loot of Spain, and (worse still) the great road by which they might have marched back to

27 Bayonne. Behind them in Vitoria excited redcoats were breaking open boxes full of Spanish dollars; while Portuguese capered in French Generals' uniforms, and by the light of flares a great fair was held where the whole *débris* of King Joseph's monarchy—pictures, books, currency, church-plate, and tapestry—was auctioned to perspiring men by bawling comrades. Wellington gave dinner to General Gazan's wife, who had been left behind. They asked her if another lady in the same plight was not a General's wife as well. *"Ah, pour cela—non,"* she answered brightly, *"elle est seulement sa femme de campagne."* The lure of loot was almost irresistible; and the pursuit left something to be desired, though a Light
28 Dragoon suggested that the cause was rather Wellington's reluctance "to entrust officers with detachments to act according to circumstances, and I am not quite clear if he approves of much success, excepting under his own immediate eye."

But the blow had fallen. In just a month from his adieu to Portugal the
29 French monarchy in Spain had ceased to exist; and the news rang through Europe. The *Gazette* with Wellington's despatch was printed in French, Dutch, and German and distributed broadcast; the unwelcome news was thrust upon French fishermen in the English Channel; a Russian *Te Deum*—the first ever sung for a foreign victory—greeted it; and the news sent Stadion running at midnight down the corridors of a Silesian
30 château, knocking at doors and greeting ruffled kings and ministers with the glad tidings that *"Le roi Joseph est —— en Espagne."* The tall Czar was radiant at the news; the dismal King of Prussia brightened; Bernadotte was a more loyal ally now; and even Austria veered towards action. For the guns of Vitoria echoed across the Continent, and Wellington had stepped from the Spanish to the European stage.

VIII

IT WAS midsummer, 1813; and as they went forward, a long line of
mountains climbed slowly up the sky, where all the folded Pyrenees
stood ranged in order. Beyond them lay the fields of France. For the long
road from Lisbon had brought the marching redcoats all the way from
Portugal, across the bare Castilian uplands, until they saw the last of
Spain and the curved skyline of the Pyrenees. Spain was behind them
now with its wide skies and crumbling cities; and their road wound
upwards, past the brown belfries of Pyrenean villages and the anfrac-
tuosities of Basque nomenclature, towards the gates of France. King
Joseph was a dejected phantom flitting through the passes to St. Jean de
Luz, his armies a receding line of bayonets winding beneath the dripping
trees through driving rain towards the frontier. Lord Wellington rode
irritably behind them, reviling the indiscipline of his own troops—"We
have in the service the scum of the earth as common soldiers; and of
late years we have been doing every thing in our power, both by law and   1
by publications, to relax the discipline by which alone such men can be
kept in order. . . . As to the non-commissioned officers, as I have re-
peatedly stated, they are as bad as the men. . . ." This angry mood
inspired the summary arrest of an unlucky gunner for disobedience. But   2
it soon subsided; and Pakenham reported him "vastly well and in high
spirits," whilst his indignation grumbled in the distance like a receding
storm as he reported to the Horse Guards that nobody in his army ever   3
thought of obeying an order, with the rare and generous admission that
it was "an unrivalled army for fighting, if the soldiers can only be kept in
their ranks during the battle."   4

The march went on towards the frontier. They heard the sea at last in
San Sebastian bay and saw the slow tide draw through the narrows of
Pasajes. France lay before them now. For there was nothing in their path
except the garrisons of San Sebastian and Pamplona; and they swept past
the fortresses, until they stared through the passes into France and
watched the smoke of French villages across the gleaming Bidassoa. (It

238

was six months before any other European army came in sight of France.) But the Peer was cautious, though civilian correspondents might expect an immediate invasion of France and began to count the days until he should ride into Paris; yet, as he drily pointed out, "none appear to have taken a correct view of our situation on the frontier, of which the enemy still possess all the strongholds within Spain itself; of which strongholds, or at least some of them, we must get possession before the season closes, or we shall have no communication whatever with the interior of Spain." Facile ministers might write smooth things about the prospects of his elevation to supreme command of the Allies in Germany (eliciting a dutiful statement that he was the Prince Regent's servant, would do what his masters pleased, but was far better where he was); and Prinny himself, to whom he had despatched Marshal Jourdan's *bâton* after Vitoria, responded in a slightly gushing letter that "you have sent me, among the trophies of your unrivalled fame, the staff of a French Marshal, and I send you in return that of England"—a gesture which caused some embarrassment to his advisers, since there was no such thing. But while the Horse Guards did their very best to design one for the occasion—with some misgivings lest the Prince, whom an official acidly denominated "the fountain of taste," might do it for himself—the new Field Marshal, raised at last to the very top of the military tree, obstinately declined to lose his head.

His sole objective, as he saw, was to prevent the French from reaching their isolated garrisons in San Sebastian and Pamplona. Soult was in front of him, selected by the Emperor (who was somewhere in Saxony at grips with half the Continent) as *"la seule tête militaire qu'il y eût en Espagne"*—a warier Soult than the light-hearted Marshal who had waited for Sir Arthur Wellesley at Oporto in 1809. A chastened order now directed all his smaller units to send their eagles back to the depots for safe custody; for now he had Lord Wellington to deal with. British guns were banging in the sunshine at the roofs of San Sebastian huddled beneath the slopes of Urgull; and Pamplona would be starving soon. It was time for the French to provide a distraction; and one morning in the third week of July (the Peer had a slight touch of rheumatism) sharp fighting on the bare hills behind Pamplona brought him to Sorauren. For Soult was thrusting southwards into Spain through Roncesvalles.

(Strange how that year's fighting hung about old scenes; for the Black Prince's men had drawn their bows at Vitoria, and now French bayonets wound through the pass where Charles the King had ridden and the last despairing echoes of Roland's horn once died away.) The French advance   8 was sharply pressed; and Wellington came up at a gallop, stopping to scrawl a hasty order on the stone parapet of a bridge with the Staff muttering all round him, "The French are coming." But he was off again before they came, the grey figure jolting in the saddle round corners and up mountain paths, until its trim silhouette was seen at the very summit —cocked-hat, frock-coat, and thoroughbred outlined against the summer sky. The Portuguese caught sight of him first; and their hoarse cries of "Douro" set the whole army roaring, until the cheers ran like a flame along the hillsides and far out of sight. Erect and silent, a trim figure sat its horse above the cheering, as the whole army roared its recognition of "our great Lord," in "that stern and appalling shout" (as Napier termed it in a famous rhapsody) "which the British soldier is wont to give upon the edge of battle." Since Vitoria they called him "the hero of Britain." They knew him now; and as he said that summer, "they will do for me what perhaps no one else can make them do." He could see the blue and gold of Soult and his staff across the narrow valley; and the wary Marshal deferred the French attack, spread out his maps, took lunch, and went to sleep, leaving a spirited junior to lean against a tree and positively beat his brow with blind exasperation at the thought of sleep at such a juncture. The attack followed on the morrow; but by now Wellington's command was comfortably aligned upon a ridge; and though he termed it "fair *bludgeon* work," the results were satisfactory. It had been a risky   9 business, though (he told someone afterwards that "at one time it was rather alarming certainly, and it was a close-run thing"); and he had little taste for mountain warfare, where the nature of the ground prevented him from being everywhere at once—"It is a great disadvantage   10 when the Officer Commanding in Chief must be absent, and probably at a distance. For this reason there is nothing I dislike so much as these extended operations, which I cannot direct myself."

There was an interval, while they were battering San Sebastian into readiness for an assault. The Peer was limping with lumbago (his health   11 gave him unusual trouble that year, with a spring catarrh, his rheumatism, and now his back; and a misadventure when a chimney at Head-quarters caught fire and sent him out to shout directions in the rain with a silk handkerchief over his head had scarcely helped). So when they dined in state for the Prince Regent's birthday, he rose with difficulty for the toasts, though a Spanish commissary rendered his favourite *Ahe Marmont*. His correspondence now was full of politics—of *haute politique* from Central Europe where a galaxy of Allied monarchs performed a highly complicated dance, and of the usual vexations from Cadiz where an accomplished troupe of Spanish politicians continued to exasperate his long-suffering brother Henry by striking progressive attitudes, when all that the situation called for was a single-minded prosecution of the war. The last evoked from Wellington a promise that he would not "miss a fair opportunity that may offer to give the democratical party a shake"; he was slightly favourable to an offer of royalist support in France by the plump Duc de Berry; but he was frankly disrespectful of the Allied sovereigns, whose endeavours to concert a plan of campaign were cheerfully dismissed as "loose conversations among Princes. For my part, I would not march even a corporal's guard upon such a system." His clear intelligence discerned that Allied war-aims must be harmonised before combined Allied strategy could be dreamt of, and he summed them up:

> "The object of each should be to diminish the power and influence of France, by which alone the peace of the world can be restored and maintained: and although the aggrandizement and security of the power of one's own country is the duty of every man, all nations may depend upon it that the best security for power, and for every advantage now possessed, or to be acquired, is to be found in the reduction of the power and influence of the grand disturber."

Meanwhile, he entrenched himself securely at the gates of France. The guns of San Sebastian still boomed; but on the very day that Soult made another thrust a little nearer to the sea, the place fell. Flames licked its crumbling houses, and the sea swung idly in the bay beneath the silent citadel. The road to France was clear—the long road that they had tramped, mile after mile, since they first heard the thunder of the surf along the beaches and the first creak of loaded ox-waggons in Portugal,

six years behind them now. They had seen Lisbon with its straight and
sheltered streets, the brown forts along the Tagus, cool hospitals in Belem,
and the big hills that guard Torres Vedras, as they tramped through
Portugal in the dusty sunshine and watched the cactus writhe silently
along the roads. The tall sierras of the frontier, where chilly rivers wind
through deep, slaty gorges, had seen them on the march; and they had
passed the empty distances of Spain, until they heard the torrents racing
through the shaggy Pyrenees. For those perspiring redcoats in their
black shakoes had tramped half the length and breadth of the Peninsula.
Choking inside their stocks and loaded with sixty pounds of kit and
rations and nine pounds of Brown Bess, they had marched all the way   14
from Portugal to France in scarlet faced with yellow, white, and blue,
and heavily cross-belted, through the blinding sunlight of six Peninsular
summers. Lord Wellington had formed them, corresponding endlessly
about their needs and husbanding them carefully; for when a French
adviser volunteered a wild strategical design, he opined that it "might
answer well enough if I could afford, or the British Government or na-   15
tion would allow of my being as prodigal of men as every French
General is. They forget, however, that we have but one army, and that
the same men who fought at Vimeiro and Talavera fought the other day
at Sorauren; and that, if I am to preserve that army, I must proceed
with caution." Now he was almost proud of them. Army orders might
abound with his customary fulminations against irregularity, and he
could still ingeminate that "there is no crime recorded in the Newgate
Calendar that is not committed by these soldiers, who quit their ranks   16
in search of plunder." But in the privacy of his despatches he informed
the Cabinet that "it is probably the most complete machine for its num-   17
bers now existing in Europe," adding in a letter to Dumouriez that his
command was *"plus en état de faire une campagne d'hiver qu'aucune
armée que j'aie jamais vu"*; and in later years he said proudly that "I   18
could have done *anything* with that army: it was in such splendid order."
For he was proud of them; and they responded with more warmth than
he was quite accustomed to, cheering his silent figure for miles along the
line at Sorauren and even in camp acclaiming him "not with three times
three, or nine times nine, but as long as they could see him."   19
   Now he had brought them to the edge of France; and in the autumn

weeks of 1813 the invasion was ready to begin. France had not been invaded since the wild days of the Republic, when the heads fell in Paris and Colonel Wesley of the Thirty-third beat his disconsolate retreat from the northern fortresses. But now his glass was busy among the red roofs and white walls of Basque villages; and in the first week of October they slipped across the river below the brown church-tower of Fuenterrabia. (Before the month was out, the Emperor faced a great ring of enemies in front of Leipzig, fought for three days, and trailed off in defeat towards the Rhine.) The strict exigencies of strategy, perhaps, demanded that Wellington, once comfortably established astride of the western Pyrenees, should turn eastwards and drive Suchet from Catalonia. He confessed as much to Dumouriez:

"La Catalogne m'a donné bien des mauvais momens pendant l'automne, et j'ai bien souvent pensé a y aller.

"Peut-être que, si je regardais seulement l'Espagne, ou même si je voyais les affaires sous un aspect militaire seulement, j' aurais du y aller, parcequ'il n'y a pas de doute que Buonaparte tient en Catalogne et tiendra les facilités pour rentrer en Espagne. Je dis peut-être, parceque, dans ce diable de pays, où j' ai fait la guerre pendant cinq ans, j'ai toujours trouvé, comme votre Henri Quatre, qu'avec des petits armées on ne faisait rien, et qu'avec des grandes armées on mourait de faim. . . . D'ailleurs il faut que la vue purement militaire cède à la politique. J'ai vu la marche des affaires en Allemagne, et, malgré les revers très graves qui sont arrivés; j'ai cru voir des germes des succès très considerables qui sont depuis arrivés.

"Si je ne me suis pas trompé, il est bien plus important aux alliés, et à l'Espagne même, que je me porte en avant en France, au lieu de faire une guerre de forteresse en Catalogne. . . ."

His steady reasoning gleams through the imperfect French; and he went forward into France. Pamplona fell behind them, and in November they drove the French from the Nivelle, where Soult had hoped to stand behind a miniature version of Torres Vedras. Now they were closing in on Bayonne, and Headquarters moved to St. Jean de Luz, between the blue Biscayan rollers and the carved hills behind. A conversation with a captured Colonel, to whom Wellington gave dinner, informed him of the Imperial *Götterdämmerung*. The Staff plied their unhappy guest with questions; but the discreet Peer "interfered quietly and whispered to them to let him alone, and that after a good dinner and a few glasses of Madeira our friend would mend." The treatment answered; and his host adroitly brought the conversation round to comforts at Headquarters— to the Emperor's recent experiences in that respect—and then, with the most casual air in the world, he launched a question.

"*Où était le quartier-général de l'Empereur,*" he innocently enquired, "*d'après les dernières nouvelles?*"

"*Nulle part,*" the Colonel answered gloomily, "*il n'y a plus de quartier-général.*"

"*Comment plus de quartier-général?*"

"*Monseigneur, il n'y a point de quartier-général, et point d'armée; l'affaire est finie.*"

But Soult was still in front of him, and the fortress of Bayonne was formidable. Besides, he had all the novel problems of an invasion—of French feelings to be handled with his invariable discretion, angry deputations to be soothed, and proclamations posted up in Basque. Perfect discipline became more necessary than ever, and the pardonable inclination of his Spanish troops to avenge the long French occupation by a carnival of theft and destruction caused him endless trouble. Indeed, his Peninsular allies were more than usually trying that season, and he wrote bitterly that "*le Démon de la discorde se plait à mêler des affaires de*   23 *la Péninsule.*" Wellington was rarely figurative; but the outbreak was not surprising, since he was afflicted with a Minister of War at Cadiz whom he stigmatised as "that greatest of all blackguards," and he was   24 unusually sensitive to the attacks of Spanish journalists upon alleged atrocities at San Sebastian.

A new complication threatened his peace, as he faced in his clear-headed way the problem of the future government of France. He had been thinking of it ever since he read a *Quarterly* review by Croker in 1811 of   25 a book by some exiled royalist; he read the book itself (it was Faber's *Notices sur l'Intérieur de la France*) and found it highly instructive; and when two rainy days confined him with the *curé* at St. Pé and his interlocutor confirmed his previous impressions of French opinion, he promptly advised the Government that France was weary, that the pre-   26 vailing hunger was for peace—peace, probably, without the Emperor. But he found no positive revival of royalist sentiment and advised peace

LORD WELLINGTON, 1813
From a sketch by T. Heaphy, in the National Portrait Gallery.

with Napoleon, if he was inclined to moderation. At the same time he hinted broadly that "if I were a Prince of the House of Bourbon, nothing should prevent me from now coming forward, not in a good house in London, but in the field in France; and if Great Britain would stand by him, I am certain he would succeed." He even sent a message to the same effect to Monsieur; and the majestic processes of the Bourbon mind, as-sisted by Wellington's report of his conversations with a village *curé*, evolved the project of despatching the Duc d'Angoulême to San Se-bastian. A grateful letter to Headquarters from Hartwell House even compared Wellington to Marlborough—strange praise from a great-great-grandson of Louis XIV—and advised him of the satisfaction with which Louis XVIII observed his entry into France.

There was a pause in drenching Pyrenean rain; and two brigades of Guards in scarlet tunics and white pantaloons attended divine worship on the sands at St. Jean de Luz, whilst Lord Wellington in full uniform stood near the drum-head. Then they attacked again, driving the French behind the Nive. But Soult struggled hard, and 1813 went out upon a week of stubborn fighting in the hills behind Biarritz. This year there could be no interlude of peaceful winter-quarters in his village street at Freneda. For the war scarcely halted except for a few weeks of leisure at St. Jean de Luz, when everybody strolled on the sea-wall from four o'clock till six "at a true twopenny postman's long trot," whilst languid Guardsmen (recently arrived and a shade exhausted by their unaccus-tomed activities) lounged on the parapet, and Lord Wellington himself was seen outraging military sensibilities with his frock-coat and top-hat or the sky-blue and black, no less civilian, of the Salisbury hunt. For he got in his hunting. The little streets were full of vociferating Spanish muleteers and the long strings of jingling mules; the little shop-windows offered the unaccustomed delights of butter and sardines; and obliging Frenchmen ran the blockade of their own sentries with poultry for their country's foes. For they preferred the invader's ready money (helped out with bags of sugar to which they had been strangers, thanks to the blockade, for seven years) to the less profitable traffic of Soult's requisi-tions. It had been the invariable practice of French armies to live upon the country; but when the country happened to be French as well, the practice failed to commend itself, and a shrewd countryside preferred to sell to Wellington's commissaries.

The French prince and his suite arrived, and nobody was much impressed—"Lord Wellington was in his manner droll towards them . . . they bowed and scraped right and left so oddly, and so actively, that he followed with a face much nearer a grin than a smile." There were balls at the *Mairie* (where an adventurous *gendarme* essayed a horn-pipe) and church parade on Sundays with the Guards in hollow square on the sands against a sunny background of blue sky and crowded shipping in the smooth blue bay—"quite," as a rapturous Judge-Advocate remarked, "a Vernet." But work crowded on the Peer. His next enterprise was to encircle Bayonne by bridging the wide Adour below the town while the February gales were still blowing; and someone saw him studying the sea from the sea-wall at halfpast seven one winter morning. The bold throw succeeded; and whilst they made it, Soult was distracted by an attack far inland, which drove him beyond Orthez on February 27. But for the first time Wellington was very nearly one of his own casualties. He was standing under fire with Alava, when a wounded Portuguese limped past, explaining that he was *"ofendido."* Something knocked over Alava; and Wellington was laughing at him, when he was hit himself. He fell and scrambled to his feet, remarking with cheerful blasphemy, "By God! I am *ofendido* this time." For a stray shot had driven his sword-hilt against his hip, bruising it and breaking the skin; but, though stiff, he was well enough to ride on the next day.

The French drew off along the Pyrenees; and the war rolled eastwards across France. The spring was bitter; and Lord Wellington rode after them with the snow driving in his face (that day his taste for inconspicuous costume selected a white cloak). In the north the Emperor was fencing desperately, as the net slowly tightened round him. The end was coming now; and hopeful kings revisited their kingdoms. King Ferdinand of Spain, more like a Goya than ever, lifted the questionable light of his unpleasing countenance upon Gerona; and Wellington remembered that he had got some pictures of King Joseph's after Vitoria, which might belong to Ferdinand. They had not impressed him at the time—not, that is to say, so much as the Raphaels which they had shewn him in Madrid —and he had "thought more of the prints and drawings, all of the

246

Italian school, which induced me to believe that the whole collection was robbed in Italy rather than in Spain." He sent them home for cleaning, but was now concerned to learn that they were finer than he had supposed. So Henry Wellesley was instructed to ascertain if they were Spanish royal property, as "I am desirous of restoring them to His Majesty." But he had Bourbons nearer home; and Wellington, now a convinced royalist on strictly military grounds, pressed the Prime Minister to take a stronger line in favour of the dynasty:

37   "Any declaration from us would, I am convinced, raise such a flame in the country as would soon spread from one end of it to the other, and would infallibly overturn him.

    "I cannot discover the policy of not hitting one's enemy as hard as one can, and in the most vulnerable place. I am certain that he would not so act by us, if he had the opportunity. He would certainly overturn the British authority in Ireland if it was in his power. . . ."

Then Angoulême, *incognito* discarded and a Royal Highness once again, rode into Bordeaux in the wake of Marshal Beresford; and the white cockades came out.

    The war rolled slowly east; and Wellington's paper-work was more
38 than usually exacting. Diplomacy absorbed him now; he was in the saddle all day long; and correspondence was reserved for after dinner. But the French were still in front of him. He had a brush with them at Tarbes, a slightly tangled affair with Soult in front and a town amicably bawling *"Vive le roi"* behind. Then he was facing Toulouse in the last week of March, with Soult comfortably ensconced behind the broad Garonne. There was endless trouble with the bridging-train; and he
39 went reconnoitring in his usual fashion, riding down to the river with an oilskin cover over his cocked-hat and positively chatting with a French vedette. Then he dismounted, strolled about, and having seen the ground rode off. (That week the heavy footsteps echoed in the deserted galleries of Fontainebleau, as Marshals came and went, until a lonely man sat huddled in an empty palace.) An excited note was on its way from
40 Paris, acquainting Wellington that "Glory to God and to yourself, the great man has fallen." But Soult was still in Toulouse; and on April 10

Wellington's attack was launched. It took liberties that in other circumstances would have been scarcely pardonable, and there were grave vicissitudes. But it succeeded; Wellington, for once, was playing high for victory; and Soult, driven from his stronghold, trailed off towards Carcassonne, while the Peer rode into Toulouse. They cheered him in the streets; and he had not been in the place an hour before a Colonel came 41
riding in with news from Bordeaux.

"I have extraordinary news for you."

"Ay," said the Peer, whom nothing could surprise, "I thought so. I knew we should have peace; I've long expected it."

"No," said the Colonel, "Napoleon has abdicated."

"How abdicated?" Wellington replied with cheerful incredulity. "Ay, 'tis time indeed. You don't say so, upon my honour! Hurrah!" And the Colonel enjoyed the unprecedented spectacle of Lord Wellington without his coat on spinning round and snapping his fingers.

He gave a ball at the *Préfecture* that night; and they sat down about forty to dinner. He gave them a new toast as well—"Louis XVIII"—and someone served out white cockades for them to wear. Then Alava stood 42
up and gave them *"El Liberador de España,"* whilst all the foreigners—French, Germans, Portuguese, and Spanish—toasted him in their own languages—*"Liberateur de la France," "Liberador da Portugal," "Liberateur de l'Europe."* They shouted for ten minutes; and then the embarrassed hero "bowed, confused, and immediately called for coffee." After that they all went to the play. Their white cockades were stared at; but when Wellington (who was in the stagebox with Picton and the Spaniards) laid his hat on the front of the box to shew the royal colours, the house roared. They played the royal anthem, too; and someone recited the new constitution from a box. The piece was admirably chosen. For it was Grétry's *Richard Cœur de Lion*; and when the band struck up the air, a vocalist sang the appeal of his devoted Queen disguised as Blondel—

"Ô Richard, ô mon roi, l'univers t'abandonne . . ."

and those excited soldiers heard the very air once sung to other soldiers, as a young Queen at Versailles walked graciously among them with a sleepy Dauphin in her arms. Dauphin and Queen were gone; but the wheel had come full circle. For King Louis reigned once more in France. Peace came within a week; Lord Wellington signed a Convention of Toulouse with less unhappy consequences than that of Cintra; and as the firing died away, the marching columns halted. There was a sudden silence, and the war was over.

IX

"—— and then all the people cheered again." For it was 1814—"the year of revelry," as someone called it, with Allied sovereigns bowing graciously in all directions, and Lord Byron writing *Lara* whilst undressing after balls and masquerades, and oxen roasting whole in country market-places, and mail-coaches bowling along every road in England trimmed with laurel leaves and rousing sentiments about "the Downfall of the Tyrant" and bright with transparencies of Lord Wellington. But Wellington was still at Toulouse. Army business kept him there a few 1 weeks longer, mitigated by more balls at the *Préfecture* and a little hunting, for within a week of the armistice he was riding to hounds at five o'clock one morning, and a distinguished soldier enquiring for his whereabouts was scandalised to learn the the Commander-in-Chief was believed to be somewhere in a forest about eighteen miles away. But his top-hat and blue frock-coat were seen about the streets, as he slipped unobtru- 2 sively out of Angoulême's *levée* on his way back to the *Hôtel de France*; arch whispers even hinted that his residence was rendered more attractive by the Spanish belle wedded to its proprietor—"I do not mean to be scandalous," as the Judge-Advocate primly observed, "but this, perhaps, may have decided the choice of the house." After all, the war was over. Now they were all discussing who goes to America; for "the government," as someone at the Horse Guards wrote, "have determined to give 3 Jonathan a good drubbing," and a large detachment of that incomparable army was to see the shining spaces of the Great Lakes, the flames of Washington, and the endless cane-brakes of Louisiana. But Wellington did not go with them. Another duty called. For Castlereagh invited him to take the British Embassy in Paris, and he accepted with a sober con- 4 viction that he "must serve the public in some manner or other; and as, under existing circumstances, I could not well do so at home, I must do so abroad." His acceptance alluded modestly to "a situation for which 5 I should never have thought myself qualified." But he was not too old to learn a new trade at forty-five; besides, six years of dealing with the

Spaniards and Portuguese were a respectable apprenticeship in diplomacy, and Henry wrote cheerfully from Madrid that he would find it "very pretty amusement."

6   Then he was off to Paris in the first week of May, arriving just in time to see the Russians march past the Allied sovereigns on the *Quai*. Those
7 exalted personages watched from a window in the Louvre; and King Louis XVIII sat composedly in an armchair, while the lean Emperor of Austria stood just behind him with the dismal King of Prussia, and the tight-waisted Czar did the honours. Lord Wellington saw the spectacle on horseback, riding between Castlereagh and his brother Charles. But he was quite a spectacle himself; for all the monarchs craned forward for a sight of him, where he sat his horse almost defiantly civilian in his blue frock-coat and top-hat. They introduced him to old Platow the Cossack; and when he saw the Russian cavalry, he said in his plain way, "Well, to be sure, we can't turn out anything like this." The Czar called on him that evening, and he looked in at a ball where the company was sublimely mixed—a *galimatias* of reigning princes, Blücher's moustaches, the red head of Ney, and the watchful eyes of Metternich. The Czar waltzed with Maréchale Ney, and Blücher kissed Lady Castlereagh's hand with gusto. Then he was introduced to Wellington and, in default of conversation, "they held each other's hands, and there was a great deal of hearty smiling"; someone interpreted; but the old Hussar looked merely puzzled. Wellington was a week in Paris. Whilst he was there, the news arrived that Liverpool and the Prince Regent had given one last turn to the fountain of honour, and so he was to be a Duke. Kitty had it
8 from the Prime Minister himself; and Richard, who was always strong upon such matters, was duly taken into counsel as to the proper title for him. So Arthur passed him in the race. For Richard was a Marquess still; but Arthur was to be a Duke—the Duke of Wellington. His hands were full; and it was three weeks before a brotherly postscript acquainted
9 Henry that "I believe I forgot to tell you I was made a Duke."

Before May was out, he was back at Toulouse on the road to Spain, where Ferdinand was rapidly reducing his long-lost subjects to distraction. But it would never do to inaugurate the new golden age with a civil war; and hopes were entertained that Wellington's familiar tones

might discipline the restive Spaniards and their unprepossessing king.
Castlereagh had thought him looking well in Paris; but an observer at   10
Toulouse found him a little thin and pulled down by a cold. Then he
posted off to Spain at eight o'clock one morning. The long road was
familiar; he saw Vitoria again, and the tall spires of Burgos; Valladolid
went by, and once more he came in sight of Madrid. He saw the King,
and thought him "by no means the idiot he is represented." But his min-   11
isters were quite deplorable; and Wellington discharged a heavy cargo   12
of good advice—that promiscuous arrests should be followed up by trial
or release, or, at the very least, by some kind of attempt to justify them;
that England would expect an effort to govern "on liberal principles";
and that, in certain circumstances, she might even undertake "to discourage and discountenance, by every means in our power, the rebellion
in the Spanish colonies." (For the time had not yet come for calling a
New World into being to redress the balance of the Old; besides, the
Duke of Wellington was not Mr. Canning.) This business was transacted
to an accompaniment of etiquette that varied between the impressive and   13
the imbecile. He stood with Ferdinand on a palace balcony and kept his
hat on, because he was a Grandee of Spain; and when he had his audience,
the simpering San Carlos asked him if he noticed how the guards had
stamped their feet. "That is only done," he added, "for a Grandee of the
first order—you must indeed be a happy man."

He was happy in his way; for he was fully occupied. His family displayed a tendency to share his happiness, since William had brought his
household to the Continent and joined him in Madrid. Soon he would
see them all; for he was on his way to England now. He stopped a few
days in Bordeaux writing farewell epistles, and a final Order was issued to
the army:

> "1. The Commander of the Forces, being upon the point of returning to   14
> England, again takes this opportunity of congratulating the army upon the
> recent events which have restored peace to their country and to the world.
> "2. The share which the British army has had in producing these events,
> and the high character with which the army will quit this country, must
> be especially satisfactory to every individual belonging to it, as they are to
> the Commander of the Forces; and he trusts that the troops will continue
> the same good conduct to the last.

"3. The Commander of the Forces once more requests the army to accept his thanks.

"4. Although circumstances may alter the relations in which he has stood towards them, so much to his satisfaction, he assures them that he shall never cease to feel the warmest interest in their welfare and honor; and that he will be at all times happy to be of any service to those to whose conduct, discipline, and gallantry their country is so much indebted."

The debt was honourably acknowledged; and he was granted nearly forty years for its discharge—forty years of begging-letters and hats touched by eager fingers as his horse went by. There was a loose sovereign ready in his waistcoat pocket for any old soldier who had served under him. His letter-bag was filled for nearly half a century with applications for every kind of favour; and can he be reproached if his replies more often than not were in the negative? Harrowing anecdotes are preserved of hungry veterans who, dining at his table, filled their pockets with the broken meats for starving families at home. An angry officer who had served with him in the East, endorsed his courteous confession of inability to find him employment with the angry query, "Can this Man have a Heart!!" Yet the indignant applicant had voluntarily retired from the service in 1812; and now he was inclined to blame the Duke for not employing him in 1828. (Indeed, his notion of the Duke's utility was even more extensive; since a note survives in which "the Duke of Wellington presents his Compliments to Mr. Elers, and is much obliged to him for his Letter of this day. The Duke has no occasion for a Newfoundland Dog, and will not deprive Mr. Elers of him.")

Had he a heart? The contrary is scarcely proved by the circumstance that he did not grant every favour that was asked of him. How could he? It was easy enough for Byron to reel off indignant stanzas inciting him to

> "go, and dine from off the plate
> Presented by the Prince of the Brazils;
> And send the sentinel before your gate
> A slice or two from your luxurious meals:
> He fought, but has not fed so well of late."

But to become the almoner of fifty thousand men drawn from the least provident classes of his fellow-subjects, to forward the professional ambitions of half the officers in the Army List, and to prolong these services into the second generation was utterly impossible. Besides, his hands were often tied by a strong sense of orderly administration. For how could responsible Departments ever do their work if the Duke of Wellington perpetually intervened in favour of innumerable *protégés*? That was the reason why his correspondents often received an irritating *non possumus*, and concluded angrily that they were forgotten. True, he had every excuse for not remembering them. For whilst they had ample leisure for their reminiscences, Wellington had something more to do than to perfect his recollections of the breach at Badajoz. His life was crowded almost to the end with diplomacy and politics and army administration. New faces and fresh problems perpetually engaged him; and Larpent once diagnosed his apparent neglect of old associations.

> "You ask me if Lord Wellington has recollected——with regard? He [17]
> seems to have had a great opinion of him, but scarcely ever mentioned him
> to me. In truth, I think Lord Wellington has an active, busy mind, always
> looking to the future, and is so used to lose a useful man, that as soon as
> gone he seldom thinks more of him. He would be always, no doubt, ready
> to serve any one who had been about him, or the friend of a deceased
> friend, but he seems not to think much about you when once out of the
> way. He has too much of everything and everybody always in his way to
> think much of the absent."

That was excusable; and if England omitted to make due provision for his soldiers, the fault was not Wellington's, but his country's.

France, from St. Jean de Luz to Calais, flowed past his carriage windows as he posted homewards through the summer days of 1814. He stopped long enough in Paris to transact some army business with the [18] Ministry of War, where Bourbon tact had installed the sleek Dupont; for that paladin reigned over the army of Austerlitz, wearing the withered laurels of Baylen—a defeat commanding twenty years of victory. Then Calais slipped behind him; and Wellington came in sight of England, last seen the gusty day he sailed for Portugal in 1809. The little streets of Dover rang with huzzas; and eager faces pressed against his carriage windows, as he drove through the cheering countryside. Kent and Surrey were one dusty, roaring lane of bawling Englishmen, and London was waiting to take out his horses. But he drove too fast for

19 them to Piccadilly, where he found Kitty and his boys in Hamilton Place —a smiling Kitty, more short-sighted than ever and a trifle breathless with her sudden rise from Countess to Marchioness, and now to the last dizzy empyrean of a Duchess. Besides, she had sustained exhausting conversations with foreign royalties. A crowd was cheering in the street; but he escaped by a back way into the Park, and slipped off to see his mother in Upper Brook Street, strolled down Oxford Street, met Richard in a cheering crowd, and went to see his married sister. Then he drove down to Portsmouth, where naval salutes were booming for the Allied sovereigns, and paid his respects to the Prince Regent. Next the protracted triumph—first popular, then royal—took a Parliamentary turn; and the new Peer put on his robes to take his seat in the House of Lords as Baron, Viscount, Earl, Marquess, and Duke. After the Lords it was the Commons' turn; and one afternoon he visited them. They had already voted money for the purchase of an estate; as Government

20 proposed £300,000, the Opposition outbidding them, as Oppositions will, carried £400,000 with Mr. Canning and Mr. Whitbread (who had once charged him with exaggerating Talavera) among the loudest voices. Now he was coming to the House in person. His voice had not been heard there since a few words on Irish agriculture and canals five years before. But now a chair was set for him at the Bar; the House rose at his entry, and he sat "for some time covered." The House was full of uniforms; the very mace assumed a military pose, since the Serjeant-at-arms had grounded it and stood beside him at attention. Then he made them a little speech of thanks—first to the Commons for their compliment, and then to the nation for its war-effort.

He was five weeks in England; and his days were loud with ceremonial eloquence and bright with presentations, whilst his evenings were an unending *levée* in the new Field Marshal's uniform. He went down to

21 Essex, and stayed with William's son at Wanstead. The Prince, the royal Dukes, and the whole Wellesley clan were there; and the adoring eyes of Lady Shelley were on him after dinner, when they drank to his father's memory and the Prince Regent proposed his health. The Duke rose, smiling broadly, and began:

"I want words to express . . ."

The Regent promptly interrupted him with royal geniality. "My dear

fellow," said Prinny, in his easy way, "we know your *actions*, and we
will excuse you your *words*, so sit down."

The Duke, always obedient to royalty, sat down "with all the delight
of a schoolboy who has been given an unexpected holiday." Then they
all drank to Richard, who replied (as might have been expected) at
considerable length. After dinner the Duke polonaised; Blücher performed a country dance; and old Platow gave a Cossack performance,
which convulsed the company and appeared to consist of nodding his
head and stamping like a horse.

He was all smiles that summer, savouring his triumph and saying
gaily to the lady on his arm, as the crowds outside the Opera parted
respectfully before them, "It's a fine thing to be a great man, is not it?"
He enjoyed the incense; and he could enjoy the general gaiety as well,
watching his aides-de-camp all dancing hard at Carlton House and asking cheerfully, "How would society get on without all my boys"? And   22
someone saw him "in great good humour apparently, and not squeezed
to death" at the great masquerade in Burlington House, where Hob-
house went as an Albanian; Byron was there dressed as a monk, and
Caroline Lamb was more outrageous than usual. A *Star* reporter grew
rapturously classical, recording that "the company did not separate from
the allurements of Terpsichore's court till Sol rose to light them to repose." But there was business to be done—prospective country houses to
be viewed with Mr. Wyatt, letters to Henry about Spanish policy, and
advice to ministers upon the American war. They consulted him about
an expedition to New Orleans, inspired by Cochrane's appetite for prize-
money; but the Duke was full of practical objections. He stated his opinion plainly; and when the failure had cost heavily in casualties (including Edward Pakenham), he wrote bluntly to his brother-in-law:

"We have one consolation, that he fell as he lived, in the honourable   23
discharge of his duty: and distinguished as a soldier & as a man.

"I cannot but regret however that he was ever employed on such a
service or with such a colleague.

"The expedition to New Orleans originated with that colleague, & plunder was its object. I knew & stated in July that the transports could not
approach within leagues of the landing place, & enquired what means were
provided to enable a sufficient body of troops with their artillery provisions

& stores to land, & afterwards to communicate with them. Then as plunder was the object, the Admiral took care to be attended by a sufficient number of *sharks*, to carry the plunder off from a place at which he knew well that he could not remain. The secret of the expedition was thus communicated & in this manner this evil design defeated its own end. The Americans were prepared with an army in a fortified position which still would have been carried, if the duties of others, that is of the Admiral, had been as well performed as that of him whom we lament.

"But Providence performed it otherwise & we must submit. . . ."

Then the cheers died away behind him; and he was off to the Continent once more. He did not go direct to Paris, but performed a minor military duty *en route* by reporting upon the defences of Belgium. This territory was now incorporated in a single kingdom with the Netherlands; and it was manifestly desirable to render its southern frontier impervious to French invasions. He reconnoitred for a fortnight, riding round the Belgian villages with three Colonels of Engineers; and his conclusions were embodied in a memorandum favouring a return to the Barrier line of fortresses. A brief examination of the country scarcely enabled him to be precise upon the probable course of military operations. But he indicated "good positions for an army" at various points, of which the last was "the entrance of the *forêt de Soignies* by the high road which leads to Brussels from Binch, Charleroi, and Namur": it was the ridge of Waterloo.

His reconnaissance concluded, Wellington resumed his new profession and became a diplomat. It was a pleasant change to bombard the French with arguments about the slave trade and mild remonstrances upon the misdeeds of American privateers. The French conception of neutrality was frankly scandalous; and the activities of the *True Blooded Yankee* kept his pen busy. One ardent privateer, whose appetites appeared to extend to monumental masonary, had even captured a recumbent statue of Queen Louise of Prussia; and tearful representations were made to Wellington to assist in its recovery for the mausoleum at Charlottenburg. But a large proportion of his work related to the slave trade. He had been startled whilst in England by "the degree of frenzy" felt in this admirable cause, the Lord Mayor positively hesitating to propose the health of King Ferdinand in the solemn shades of Guildhall in case the com-

pany refused the toast. But Paris brought Wellington a closer acquaintance
with the problem; for he was pelted with improving literature, inter-
viewed by Zachary Macaulay and the virtuous Clarkson, and positively   27
satisfied the latter that he had read through his *History of Abolition* and
Impolicy of the Slave Trade, to say nothing of a little thing by Mr.
Wilberforce and all the memoranda from the African Society—strange
reading for a conqueror. But his interest was genuine; and he gave
shrewd advice upon the management of French opinion, even volunteering to finance their publications out of public funds. Smaller matters   28
occasionally diversified his work; once he applied for special library
facilities on behalf of a Fellow of Trinity in uncertain health engaged
on an edition of Demosthenes; he argued with some reason in the interests of scholarship that the *Archives* might reasonably raise their ban
upon research into the reign of Louis XV; and that awful eye, before
which Generals had shrunk, was turned upon an irritable oculist who
had expected every facility for his scientific investigations in spite of a
total ignorance of French. Courtesy suggested that he should offer to
the King his pack of hounds—*"une meute des meilleures races d'Angle-*   29
terre"—a not unflattering description of the assorted hounds behind which
he had hunted all the way from Portugal to Toulouse.

Life was a pleasant relaxation—a shade too pleasant, if hostile whispers
were to be believed, since a Bonapartist lady circulated stories about a   30
prima donna. But Kitty was in Paris now; his boys were coming out
for Christmas; and if Grassini smiled, who could resist? Not that his
life in Paris was all triumphs and trivialities. Interminable papers brought
him accounts of the negotiations at Vienna, and his advice was sought
at every turn. He even advised upon the menace of the Regent's wife,
suggesting shrewdly that it might be "worth considering whether it is   31
not desirable that every facility should be given to the Princess of Wales
to amuse herself abroad, in order that she may not be induced to return
to England"—a rich example of the Wellingtonian horse-sense that was
requisitioned for the next half century upon every problem from the
future of Europe to the disposal of Mrs. Fitzherbert's papers. His own
affairs were relatively calm, though a libel in *The Times* moved him to
unaccustomed wrath. He could be philosophical enough in general, reminding sensitive acquaintances that "misrepresentation of facts is the   32

common practice of the writers of newspapers." But this time his patience failed; and William was instructed to set the Law Officers in motion. His indignation was sublime—

33   "If I possess any advantages in point of character, I consider myself bound to set the example to others of a determination to prevent the blackguard editors of papers from depriving us of our reputation by their vulgar insinuations.

"The truth is, I refused to employ a relation of the editor of the 'Times' in my family, and that is the reason he has accused me of corruption; but that is no reason why I should bear it."

That autumn ministers discovered a new cause for anxiety. The French were restless; a stout King in an arm-chair formed an imperfect substitute for an incomparable Emperor on horseback; veterans were muttering in corners; and there were grave fears for Wellington. His life was precious, and a military insurrection might endanger it—or at least detain him in
34   France and deprive the Allies of his services. The official mind was busy with pretexts for bringing him away. Could he not be sent for to advise the Congress? Once at Vienna, he need not return to Paris; and then he could be sent to take command in America. That was their real design.
35   The Regent felt that "nothing should be neglected to induce the Duke of Wellington to accept of the Chief Command in America as soon as possible, as his name alone will reconcile the whole view & opinion of the Country, & at the same time be the means of obviating as well as removing many difficulties which may afterwards arise." Lord Liverpool
36   concurred, and put it tentatively to the Duke, who felt "no disinclination to undertake the American concern," but demurred on purely European grounds to leaving Paris at the moment. It might, he thought, be possible in March, 1815; but at the moment he was strongly inclined to stay. There was no false modesty about his refusal—"I entertain a strong opinion that I *must* not be lost." But the very unrest, which was the reason for his recall, was in itself the strongest argument for retaining him in Europe—"In case of the occurrence of anything in Europe, there is nobody but myself in whom either yourselves or the country, or your Allies would feel any confidence." Besides, his presence in America would not make much difference, since "that which appears to me to be wanting

in America is not a General, or General officers and troops, but a naval
superiority on the Lakes"; without it he could do little more than "sign
a peace which might as well be signed now." Then he went on to
advise them bluntly to make peace without annexations. The dashing son   37
of solemn Mr. Gallatin, who was negotiating at Ghent, even believed
that Wellington in his eagerness for peace with the United States, corresponded directly with the American delegate, urging him to come to
terms and dwelling with some skill on Gallatin's Swiss origin. The effect,
if James Gallatin can be believed, was admirable—"Father, I think, was
pleased. He is a foreigner and is proud of it." For the Duke's diplomatic
accomplishments even included the art of charming that unpleasing
type of American whose chief pride is that he is not American. Once he
was almost persuaded to leave Paris, though he was still reluctant—"I   38
confess that I don't see the necessity for being in a hurry. . . . I really
don't like the way in which I am going away. . . . I don't like to be
frightened away." But he admitted the necessity for his recall, though
the American command had few attractions. A better plan was found
when Castlereagh, recalled to England by his Parliamentary duties,   39
invited Wellington to replace him at Vienna. This was respectable, and
he accepted.

The year went out upon a world at peace. For peace was positively
signed on Christmas Eve at Ghent between Great Britain and the United
States (personified by the pertinacious Adams, Bayard, Henry Clay, and
Mr. Gallatin, always comfortably aware of the nobility of his Swiss
blood). On the last day of the year Lord Liverpool wrote to the Duke   40
with evident relief about the mission to Vienna and a difficulty with
Murat at Naples and his own plans (the Prime Minister was hoping to
get down to Bath). Then Europe slept, and midnight sounded from the
steeples—from the tall spire above Vienna, from Ste. Gudule at Brussels
and Notre Dame (where Paris stirred a little in its sleep) and from the
little belfries, where a lonely man counted the hours on Elba—and as the
echoes died away, it was 1815.

1815

Waterloo! Waterloo! Waterloo! morne plaine!

LES CHÂTIMENTS.

WINTER

EUROPE was under snow. Lord Castlereagh, with something less than his customary tact, informed an after-dinner audience at Vienna that "*il commence l'âge d'or*" and was generally understood to have alluded to British subsidies; the Czar, acutely conscious of his virtue, was full of noble sentiments and frankly covetous of Poland; even the widowed King of Prussia forgot his mourning in a lively appetite for Saxon territory; and M. de Talleyrand limped deferentially among the gilded furniture with his thin smile. Two carriages rumbled along the miry roads, one taking Byron and his bride to their uncomfortable honeymoon; the Duke was in the other, rolling across the Continent towards Vienna. Behind him in Whitehall the Horse Guards struggled with the problem of Peninsular medals; the Prince Regent was at Brighton reading official papers and contemplating the Pavilion domes; and the Cabinet instructed Wellington upon the future of Corfu. He had a heavy cold when he arrived, and found the hot rooms of Vienna most exhausting. But it was winter still, and the hot rooms were full of bowing gentlemen in decorations. He saw Prince Metternich; he saw the Swedes; he saw the Poles. Life became an endless succession of interviews and drafts—drafts about Switzerland and Frankfort and the Valtelline. The Czar called one evening with a complicated grievance about the Danes and Bernadotte and the purchase price of Guadaloupe. He would be leaving soon for Russia; but Wellington seemed doomed to sit for ever manipulating drafts in stifling rooms. Would the spring never come?

It came that year a little early. For spring came with the violets in the first week of March. Prince Metternich had gone to bed at three one morning after a conference. He was not to be disturbed; but an officious servant brought in an envelope at six o'clock. The Prince looked at it and, observing without interest that it was merely from the Austrian Consul at Genoa, turned over again. But he failed to sleep; and about half past seven he opened it and read that Napoleon was missing from

263

Elba. Within an hour he saw three sleepy sovereigns; the Duke, who had a letter to the same effect, was told at ten; and when Talleyrand predicted that the Emperor would make for Switzerland, the Prince took another view—"*Il ira droit à Paris.*" Metternich was right: the spring had come.

SPRING

There was a sudden stir. The solemn exercises of Vienna were broken off, and diplomacy subsided like an interrupted minuet. Once again there was a sudden rapping on the doors; the music stopped, the dancers huddled into corners, and angry gentlemen drew swords. The Duke, three Princes, and fourteen assorted noblemen declared in the name of eight governments that Napoleon Buonaparte had forfeited all human rights. It was the dreadful cry once heard from revolutionary lips in Paris, when angry men with staring eyes bawled "*Hors la loi*" and dragged something shrinking to a scaffold. But it rang gravelier now; for it sounded from the solemn countenances of Wellington and Metternich and Nesselrode and Talleyrand, still wearing his thin smile. The Duke appeared to think at first that the King of France could do the business for himself; but he could see that Europe might have to inter- 4 vene, and he was hard at work among the excited Allies—"Here we are all zeal, and, I think, anxious to take the field. I moderate these sentiments as much as possible, and get them on paper. . . ." There was a notion of employing him as a courtly *attaché* to the Czar; but "as I should have neither character nor occupation in such a situation, I 5 should prefer to carry a musket." There would be ample opportunity, with all Europe marching upon France in a great crescent from the Alps to the North Sea. They gave him the command of an assorted force of Allies, which was to take the right of the line in the Low Countries. His tried battalions were largely in America or in mid-ocean; and his first instinct, in the absence of that incomparable army, was to call for a contingent of those Portuguese whom he had called 6 its "fighting cocks." A soldier once again, he turned briskly from di-plomacy and all its drafts—the protocol about the Swiss, the endless chicanery of the Dutch loan, and the Prince Regent's portrait on a

diamond-mounted snuff-box to be presented to the Bavarian—and posted
7 across Europe. He was at a party the night before he left Vienna; and
all the women kissed him, saying gaily that he would conquer Paris
and that in that event he might include them in his conquests. Once
more his carriage rumbled along miry roads; and at five o'clock one
morning in the first week of April he was in Brussels.

The city was not unfamiliar. He had passed through the country in
the previous summer; but it was twenty years since Lady Mornington
and her ungainly son had lodged in Brussels, where he learned French
and played his violin. His French was readier now, and he had manlier
8 accomplishments; but his mother was once more in Brussels. It was quite
fashionable that winter. The *ton*, denied all opportunities of Continental
travel by twenty years of war, was glad to make a jaunt to Brussels.
The Guards were there; Mr. Creevey took his wife and girls (was not
Becky Sharp seen chattering at the Opera?); and Lady Mornington,
released from Upper Brook Street was there as well, until her anxious
son arrived and packed her off to Antwerp. Then the town filled with
9 agitated Frenchmen; the royalties were all at Ghent; but Brussels had
its share of Marshals—Marmont at the *Hôtel d'Angleterre*, Victor (with
a pleasant echo of Talavera) at the *Hôtel Wellington*, and Berthier staying with friends. The Duke was seen at evening parties; and Mr.
Creevey, who had once crossed swords with him in Indian debates,
10 found him "very natural and good-humoured" and exceedingly communicative. For Wellington discussed the prospects freely, and Mr.
Creevey was not impressed. Opposition Whips are not easily impressed by military men; and when the Duke insisted that it would
never come to war, he left a poor impression of his perspicacity upon
the politician. But there was something to be said for using peaceful
language to members of an Opposition, which was busy denouncing
ministers for hurling Europe wantonly into another war. So Wellington
pained Mr. Creevey by his unintelligent insistence that the republicans
were bound to prevail in Paris and that in all probability some Brutus
would soon make an end of Buonaparte. Not that he thought so; for
on the very morning after his tone of stupid confidence shocked Mr.
11 Creevey he wrote to Blücher, "*Je ne serais pas étonné si la partie se
trouvait remise pour quelque temps. Mais nous l'aurons sûrement un jour*

ou l'autre . . ." But it would never do to use that language in Brussels *soirées,* where every sentence would be promptly echoed from the Opposition benches. So a military man, for once, was one too many for an Opposition Whip; and Mr. Creevey went to his grave convinced that Wellington had failed to grasp the gravity of the position in April, 1815.

He made a point of being cheerful, laughed when the *Champ de Mai* passed off successfully in Paris, and greeted any fresh desertion of the Emperor as evidence that his house was "tumbling about his ears." He gave innumerable balls and made everybody dance half the night. For the town was full of eyes; and it was just as well that Paris should believe that confidence prevailed in Brussels. But Brussels, if the truth were known, was anything but confident. The Duke, indeed, could scarcely be expected to be in high spirits with a discouraging command in which foreigners outnumbered British troops by more than two to one. His dealings with allies in Spain had made him an expert in the lukewarm; but this time their temperature was more discouraging than usual. His Dutch were poor, his Belgians unreliable; even his Hanoverians were hardly more than willing; and the King's German Legion alone came up to British standards. Not that his British troops were an inspiring spectacle. For out of twenty-five battalions only six had served in the Peninsula; the rest (except the Guards) were neither up to strength nor standard. His cavalry was tolerably abundant, since there had been no need for cavalry in America; but his demand for guns was answered by a grim intimation from the Ordnance that while guns abounded, "men and horses are the only difficulty I have." Even his Staff depressed him, since he inherited the Staff of a small army of occupation already in the Low Countries. But loud protests in his most emphatic manner gradually relieved him of them; the authorities were most obliging, though he complained bitterly of being "overloaded with people I have never seen before; and it appears to be purposely intended to keep those out of my way whom I wished to have"; and he ended with a Staff of thirty-three, of whom thirty-one had considerable Staff experience in the Peninsula. But at the outset it was not surprising that his correspondence rang with indignant outcries. April found him complaining that the British troops

12

13

14

15

16

266

were "not what they ought to be to enable us to maintain our military character in Europe. It appears to me that you have not taken in England a clear view of your situation, that you do not think war certain, and that a great effort must be made, if it is hoped that it shall be short." The month passed in a fever of preparations—of friendly correspondence with the Prussians on his left, of visits to the French royalties at Ghent, innumerable tangles of inter-Allied diplomacy, peculiar transactions with foreign potentates for the supply of infantry at a flat rate of £11 2s. a head, and ingenious rearrangements of the assorted nationalities in his command until the mosaic gave some promise of stability. But he could still write in May that he had "an infamous army, very weak and ill equipped, and a very inexperienced Staff." He was more hopeful now—"for an action in Belgium I can now put 70,000 men into the field, and Blücher 80,000; so that I hope we should give a good account even of Buonaparte." Besides, the need might not arise, since he was sometimes tempted to believe that internal politics might keep the Emperor in Paris. But he was haunted by his old desire for 40,000 British infantry; with them "I should be satisfied, and take my chance for the rest, and engage that we should play our part in the game."

That thought was in his mind one day, when he met Mr. Creevey in the Park at Brussels. The pert civilian asked a question.

"Will you let me ask you, Duke, what you think you will make of it?"

The blunt question stopped him in his walk. "By God," the Duke replied, "I think Blücher and myself can do the thing."

"Do you calculate upon any desertion in Buonaparte's army?"

"Not upon a man," said the Duke, "from the colonel to the private in a regiment—both inclusive. We may pick up a Marshal or two, perhaps; but not worth a damn."

Then Mr. Creevey asked him about the French royalists in Belgium.

"Oh!" said the Duke, "don't mention such fellows! No: I think Blücher and I can do the business."

At that moment his eye was caught by a British private in the green alleys of the Park; and as he watched the little scarlet figure staring at the foreign statues under the foreign trees, "There," said the Duke,

pointing a long forefinger, "it all depends upon that article whether we
do the business or not. Give me enough of it, and I am sure."

SUMMER

1. *Brussels*

Something was stirring behind the frontier. It was not altogether
easy to say precisely what it was, though spies reported copiously and
French deserters trickled in with unlikely stories. But secret agents
were lamentably apt to enrich the tedium of fact with those livelier
circumstances which they wished to happen—or which (better still) they
felt that their employers would wish to happen; and the Duke's writing-
table groaned under every form of voluminous misstatement. If his intelligence could be believed, the Empire was becoming momentarily
more precarious and the Emperor had developed an uncanny faculty
of being in several places at the same time—in Paris, in half the
fortresses along the northern frontier, even in Cherbourg on his way
to the United States—whilst his regiments appeared to be involved in an
endless saraband. They flitted up and down the frontier, were seen
drilling in unlikely places, and passed on every road by watchful
travellers. But they were plainly coming north. So much was evident.
But it was hardly possible to learn more about their strength and movements, since war had not been declared; and Wellington complained
bitterly that "in the situation in which we are placed at present, neither
at war nor at peace, unable on that account to patrole up to the enemy
and ascertain his position by view, or to act offensively upon any part
of his line, it is difficult, if not impossible, to combine an operation,
because there are no data on which to found any combination. All we
can do is to put our troops in such a situation as, in case of sudden
attack by the enemy, to render it easy to assemble, and to provide
against the chance of any being cut off from the rest." (This dismal
half-measure was the tribute paid to appearances, to the susceptibilities
of Opposition speakers who might otherwise have vituperated ministers
for being bellicose.) The army waited patiently in Belgian villages,
grooming their horses, cleaning side-arms, and counting champaigne at

4*s.* a bottle among their blessings. The Duke was busy with his papers, exchanging memoranda with the Allies upon the impending march of indignant Emperors on Paris timed for the end of June, studying bulky reports on the French army from the lucid pen of Marshal Clarke, Duc de Feltre (once the Emperor's, and now King Louis', Minister of War at Ghent), and reading fluttered notes from London about the misdeeds of the Opposition which had now been joined, for some inscrutable reason of enlightened views or disappointed pride, by the tangential Richard. Then there were quantities of good advice, and hopeful letters from the War Office promising to hire unemployed postboys to drive his guns, and indications that it might be possible to call out the Militia by the end of June, a line from Kitty with the news that Lowry Cole was getting married, and a helpful offer from a contractor who was prepared to manufacture howitzers of an entirely new pattern (grimly endorsed "Compliments; and I do not consider this to be a proper period to alter the equipments of the army or to try experiments"). Slightly inimical to innovations at the moment, he ordered the rocket troop to store its cherished weapons and use ordinary guns instead; and when someone urged that the change would break their Captain's heart, the implacable reply was, "Damn his heart, sir; let my order be obeyed."

Sometimes he was out reconnoitring in his usual fashion, riding alone with an orderly dragoon and studying the rolling ground between Brussels and the frontier. They would be moving soon, and he was thinking about the siege of Maubeuge. But he still regretted his lost Peninsular battalions, writing to Lowry Cole how much he wished that he "could bring every thing together as I had it when I took leave of the army in Bordeaux, and I would engage that we should not be the last in the race; but, as it is, I must manage matters as well as I can." He was still cheerful, though, with an agreeable tendency to crawl about the floor with children. The Duke of Richmond, under whom he had once served as Chief Secretary, had brought out his entire family; and in his circle Wellington revived old memories of the Viceregal Lodge and morning rides in Phœnix Park. One day he rode to Enghien with one of the girls to see a cricket match. But there is no need to diagnose a sudden taste for cricket, since the Guards were billeted at Enghien and the Duke could have a word with Maitland. For his pleasures were always apt to take a business turn, and the Peer's hounds in Portugal would often take him conveniently near a unit that stood in need of an inspection.

The June days went slowly by; and when he wrote to Graham ac- 28 cepting membership of a new military club, he added comfortably that the Emperor seemed unlikely to leave Paris at the moment—"I think we are now too strong for him here." But the reports came in —French *feux de joie* were heard at Maubeuge; Valenciennes was full of troops; the gates of Lille were closed; Soult was on the road; Grouchy had been seen reviewing cavalry; the Guard was on the march; the Emperor was everywhere at once. Something was stirring now behind the frontier.

2. *Waterloo*

The June days went by in Brussels. Late one Thursday carriages were clattering over the cobbles, and a sound of dance-music drifted into the summer night. The Duke was there. He had been working late 29 with Müffling and the Staff; for he had news that afternoon that the French had passed the frontier opposite the Prussians, and orders had been sent to move the army in the direction of Quatre Bras. But it was just as well to reassure the doubters by shewing up at the ball; and when he made his bow, Mr. Creevey's girls found him looking as composed as ever; though one young lady, who shared a sofa with him, thought him quite preoccupied and noticed how he kept turning round and giving orders. More news arrived while they were all at supper; and he desired the senior officers to leave unobtrusively. He said something civil to his host and slipped off with him to look at a map, remarking when the door closed behind them that Napoleon had *humbugged* him, by God! and gained twenty-four hours' march upon him. Asked his intentions, he replied that he proposed to concentrate at Quatre Bras— "but we shall not stop him there, and if so, I must fight him"—his thumb nail traced a line on the map behind Hougoumont and La Haye Sainte—"*here*." Then he went off to bed. It was a little after two; and

Mr. Creevey, who had stayed at home that evening and heard a deal of hammering on doors along his street, was writing in his Journal,

> "*June* 16. *Friday morning* ½ *past two.*—The girls just returned from a ball at the Duke of Richmond's. . . ."

The marching bayonets went down the empty streets, and in the summer dawn the pipes went by.

He followed them next morning (a gleeful English maid, who caught a glimpse of him as she was opening the shutters, cried, "O, my lady, get up quick; there he goes, God bless him, and he will not come back till he is King of France!"); and before noon he was staring at the woods beyond Quatre Bras. Then he rode over to the Prussians and had a word with Blücher. Their dispositions did not impress him, since they were rather recklessly aligned (in contrast with his own judicious practice) upon an exposed slope; and he said grimly that if they fought there, the would be damnably mauled. For his ally's benefit he translated this uncompromising view into the milder sentiment that every man, of course, knew his own troops, but that if his own were so disposed, he should expect them to be beaten. His expectation was not disappointed, since the Emperor shattered them that evening at Ligny. But Wellington employed the afternoon at Quatre Bras, where Ney flung four thousand men away in wild attacks. They heard the guns in Brussels; and the enquiring Creevey strolled on the ramparts, while sixteen miles away the Duke was steadying a line which was often far from steady. It was a wild affair of French lancers wheeling in the corn and redcoats hurrying up the long road from Brussels. Once Wellington was almost caught in a flurry of French cavalry far out beyond his firing-line. The ditch behind him was lined with Highlanders; and with a timely reminiscence of the hunting-field he shouted to them to lie still, put his horse at the unusual obstacle, and cleared it, resuming a less exciting position of command. And once his deep voice was heard calling, "Ninety-second, don't fire till I tell you." For he was everywhere as usual; while Ney, whose military talents were almost wholly pugilistic, raged up and down the line watching his cavalry surge vainly round the British squares. But the price paid was tolerably high, although a great lady in Brussels cooed consolingly

to a friend that poor Sir D. Pack is severely wounded, and the poor
Duke of Brunswick died of his wounds. . . . The Scotch were chiefly
engaged, so there are no officers wounded that one knows."

But the reverse at Ligny served to nullify any advantage gained by
the Duke at Quatre Bras; and he grimly observed that "old Blücher has
had a damned good hiding, and has gone eighteen miles to the rear.
We must do the same. I suppose they'll say in England that we have
been licked; well, I can't help that." He took this unpalatable decision
early the next morning; but (it was typical of him) the retreat was
deferred until his men had cooked a meal. With that inside them they
would, he felt, be more equal to the perils of a retirement with Napoleon
at their heels. The red columns filed off towards Brussels; and as they
went, the Duke remarked with obvious relief, "Well, there is the last
of the infantry gone, and I don't care now." The cavalry, he knew,
could look after themselves with a few guns to hold them. He watched
the perilous retreat, occasionally sitting in a field and laughing over
some old English newspapers or turning his glass on the immobile
French. The morning opened brightly; but as the day wore on, there
was a stillness, and a pile of leaden clouds climbed slowly up a sultry
sky. The storm broke in floods of rain, as his cavalry were drawing off;
and the thunder drowned the sharper note of guns, while the rockets
(in fulfilment of the Duke's most sceptical anticipations) sputtered and
fizzed and not infrequently exploded backwards. The rain drove down
and the long *pavé* gleamed before them, as they struggled back towards
the ridge in front of Waterloo, the French plodding after them across
the sodden fields.

There was a night of damp discomfort; but food was waiting in the
British bivouacs. They lit fires, and Peninsular veterans dispensed derisive
consolations, observing cheerfully to newcomers, "Oho, my boy! this
is but child's play to what *we* saw in Spain," and "Lord have mercy
upon your poor tender carcass. What would such as you have done in
the Pyrenees?" Uxbridge, his second-in-command, came to Wellington
and asked what he proposed to do. The Duke countered with a question.

"Who will attack the first to-morrow—I or Buonaparte?"

"Buonaparte."

"Well," said the Duke, "Buonaparte has not given me any idea of

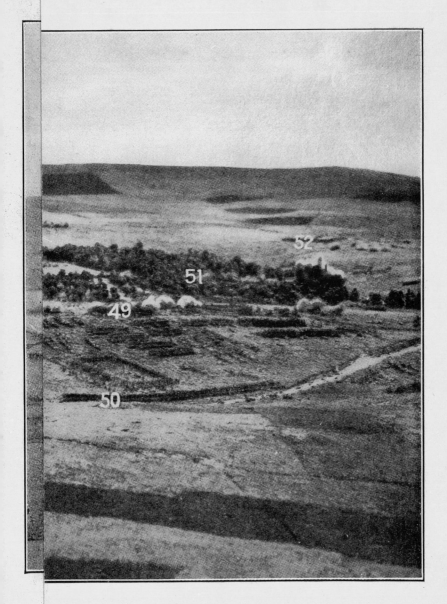

49 Byng
50 Vandeleur
51 HOUGOUMONT
52 Jérôme

his projects; and as my plans will depend upon his, how can you expect me to tell you what mine are?"

Then he rose and, laying a hand upon the other's shoulder, said kindly, "There is one thing certain, Uxbridge; that is, that whatever happens you and I will do our duty."

For his belief in plans was never strong. He once said pityingly of the Marshals that "they planned their campaigns just as you might make a splendid set of harness. It looks very well, and answers very well, until it gets broken; and then you are done for. Now, I made my campaigns of ropes. If anything went wrong, I tied a knot; and went on." Blücher had fallen back from Ligny; so Wellington had tied a knot, conforming with his ally's retreat by falling back to Waterloo. Now he was comfortably established on the ridge; but who could say what would happen next? If they attacked him in position, it might be Busaco over again. Or they might know their business better and edge round his right. In that event they might give an opening—and then it would be Salamanca—or they might manœuvre him from Waterloo without a battle. That would cost him Brussels and send the French royalties scampering from Ghent. It was too much to hope that Napoleon would choose a frontal attack, when the manœuvre round his flank promised so richly; and Wellington inclined to think that he would choose the latter course. So he sat writing in the night—to warn the royalties at Ghent, to suggest that Lady Frances Webster would be wise to leave at once for Antwerp, and to beg someone in authority in Brussels to "keep the English quiet if you can. Let them all prepare to move, but neither be in a hurry or a fright, as all will yet turn out well." And all night long the summer rain drove down on sodden fields; the trees dripped at Hougoumont; gleaming pools stood in the little farmyard at La Haye Sainte; somewhere across the darkness a square figure in a long grey coat was straining eager eyes into the night for a glimpse of Wellington's camp-fires; and two armies slept in the busy whisper of the rain.

A pale dawn broke over Belgium. The Emperor was breakfasting by eight o'clock. Soult was uneasy; Ney prophesied that Wellington would slip away again; but Napoleon swept away all objections.

"Il n'est plus temps. Wellington s'exposerait à une perte certaine.   40
Il a jeté les dés, et ils sont pour nous."

When Soult pressed him to call up reinforcements, he snapped contemptuously, *"Parce que vous avez été battu par Wellington, vous le regardez comme un grand général. Et, moi je vous dis que Wellington est un mauvais général, que les Anglais sont de mauvaises troupes, et que ce sera l'affaire d'un déjeuner."*

"Je le souhaite," replied the Marshal glumly.

The Emperor sailed before gusts of optimism that morning. Reille, who came in a little later, altogether failed to share his enthusiasm for a frontal attack on Wellington. But then Reille had served in Spain; even at Quatre Bras he shied nervously from an apparently unguarded position, because *"ce pourrait bien être une bataille d'Espagne—les troupes*   41
Anglaises se montreraient quand il en serait temps"; and now the sight of a British line behind an easy slope made him uncomfortable—he had seen something of the kind before. But the Emperor was rarely a good listener.

Besides, he meant to have his victory. A victory would mean so much —the road to Brussels open, France reassured by a familiar bulletin, King Louis made ridiculous again by further flight, the British driven into the sea at last, and (who knows?) a change of Government in London, the enlightened Whigs in office, and a world at peace with his tricolour floating peacefully above the Tuileries. The sky was clearing now; a breeze sprang up; the ground would soon be dry enough for guns to move. He would have his victory; and June 18 should take its place among his anniversaries.

"Nous coucherons ce soir," he said, *"à Bruxelles."*   40

Across the little valley Wellington was waiting on that Sunday morning in his blue frock-coat and the low cocked-hat that bore the black cockade of England with the colours of Spain, Portugal, and the Netherlands. His mixed command was, if anything more mixed than ever, since he had left some of his British troops to guard his right flank and the road to Ostend; and his foreigners outnumbered them by two to one. Still, he had got them in position on a ridge—one of his favourite ridges with an easy slope towards the enemy and shelter for his men behind its crest. The French outnumbered them; the Emperor had 70,000 men   42 to the Duke's 63,000; and he had only 156 guns against 266 in the hands of that incomparable artillerist. But if Blücher was to be believed, some Prussians would be coming later. The old *sabreur* had been unhorsed and ridden over at Ligny; but he dosed himself with a deadly brew of gin and rhubarb (and apologised to a British officer whom he embraced, observing cheerfully, "*Ich stinke etwas*"); and somewhere across the sodden fields his dark columns wound towards the Emperor's unguarded flank.

The Duke was waiting. As it was showery that morning, he kept putting on a cloak, "because I never get wet when I can help it." He waited for the French manœuvre to begin; had not Marmont manœuvred "in the usual French style" at Salamanca? But the Emperor made no attempt to manœuvre. Then it was not to be another Salamanca. For they came plunging straight at the British line in columns of attack, just as he had seen them when the French columns charged the heights above Vimeiro and Masséna's men struggled up the slope at Busaco. It was to be the old style of attack, to which he knew an answer that had never failed—the waiting line behind the crest, the volley long deferred, and then the bayonet. (As he wrote afterwards to Beresford, the Emperor "did not manœuvre at all. He just moved forward in the old style, in columns, and was driven off in the old style.") But there were variations; for the fighting surged round the outworks of his line at Hougoumont and La Haye Sainte. Then, the columns foiled, a stranger variation appeared, as the French cavalry came thundering uphill against his line. His infantry formed square to meet them, and the delighted gunners blazed into the advancing target, until they scampered off to safety in the nearest square bowling a wheel from each dismantled gun before them, as the bewildered horsemen rode helplessly among the bristling squares of inhospitable bayonets. It was a picturesque, but scarcely an alarming, experience. "I had the infantry," as he wrote afterwards, "for some time in squares, and we had the French cavalry walking about us as if they had been our own. I never saw the British infantry behave so well."

The Duke, as usual, was everywhere, fighting his line along the ridge as a commander fights his ship in action. He rode "Copenhagen"; and all day long the chestnut carried him along the lanes of weary men. Each shift of the interminable battle elicited a gruff comment or an order

scrawled on a scrap of parchment. He saw the Nassauers pressed out of
Hougoumont and acidly observed to an Austrian General, *"Mais enfin,
c'est avec ces Messieurs là qu'il faut que nous gagnions la bataille,"* put
in the Guards to retake the position with "There, my lads, in with you—
let me see no more of you," and watched Mercer's guns dash into place
between two squares with an appreciative "Ah! that's the way I like to
see horse-artillery move." When the Life Guards charged, a deep voice
was at hand to say, "Now, gentlemen, for the honour of the Household
Troops"; and when they rode back, a low cocked-hat was raised with
"Life Guards! I thank you." At one moment he formed a line of shaky
infantry himself, like any company-commander, within twenty yards of
the flash of an oncoming French column. And as the tide of cavalry was
ebbing down the trampled slope, he asked the Rifles in his quiet manner
to "drive those fellows away."

The light was failing now; and he rode down the line before the
Guard was launched in the last charge of the Empire. The shadows
lengthened from the west, as the tall bearskins came slowly on behind
six Generals and a Marshal walking (for it was Ney) with a drawn
sword. They were still coming on "in the old style"; and the waiting line
held back its fire in the Peninsular fashion until the Duke was heard
calling, "Now, Maitland! Now's your time." The volley crashed; and as
the smoke drifted into the sunset, the Guard broke—and with the Guard
the memory of Austerlitz, of Eylau, Friedland, Jena, Wagram, and Borodino melted upon the air. Then the Duke galloped off with a single
officer to order the advance. The smoke thinned for an instant; and a
trim, bare-headed figure was seen pointing a cocked-hat towards the
French. Someone enquired (a shade superfluously) which way to go; and
the Duke's voice answered him, "Right ahead, to be sure."

Late that night Blücher met him in the road on horseback and clasped
a weary Duke, exclaiming *"Mein lieber Kamerad"* and exhausting his
entire stock of French by adding a trifle inadequately, *"Quelle affaire."*
For the Emperor had shattered his last army in blind attacks upon the
ridge and then crushed it between Wellington and the Prussians. A
lonely, white-faced man, he stood in the moonlight waiting in a little
wood, waiting for troops that never came: his cheeks were wet with tears.

Far to the south the Prussian cavalry were sabring the last remnant of the *Grande Armée* under the moon. . . . "No more firing was heard at Brussels—the pursuit rolled miles away. Darkness came down on the field and city; and Amelia was praying for George, who was lying on his face, dead, with a bullet through his heart."

56   The Duke rode slowly back to Waterloo. There was no feeling of elation, and they were all exhausted. Besides, he had a solemn notion that, where so many had fallen close to him, he had somehow been preserved by Providence. "The finger of Providence was upon me," he wrote that night, "and I escaped unhurt"; and he repeated almost the same words in Paris later. Then they sat down to supper; the table had been laid for the usual number, but the Staff had suffered cruelly, and there were so many empty places. The Duke, who ate very little, kept looking at the door; and Alava knew that he was watching for the absent faces. When the meal was over, he left them. But as he rose, he lifted both hands saying, "The hand of God has been over me this day." Then he went out and began to write his despatch:

57   "My Lord,
              "Buonaparte having collected the 1st, 2nd, 3rd, 4th, and 6th corps of the French army, and the Imperial Guards . . ."

He asked them to bring in the casualty returns, and slept for a few hours. When he read them by the first morning light, he broke down. Picton, Ponsonby, De Lancey, Barnes, Gordon, Elley . . . it had been worse than Badajoz. Then he took his tea and toast, finished his despatch,
58   and rode sadly into Brussels. He saw Creevey from his hotel window and waved a signal to come in. He was quite solemn still and said that it had been a damned serious business—a damned nice thing—the nearest run thing you ever saw in your life. His mind ran on the losses, and he added grimly that Blücher got so damnably licked on Friday night that he could not find him on Saturday morning and was obliged to fall back to keep in touch with him. Then he walked up and down the room and praised his men. Creevey enquired if the French had fought better than usual.

     "No," said the Duke, "they have always fought the same since I first saw them at Vimeiro. By God! I don't think it would have been done if I had not been there."

3. *Paris*

In twelve days they were in front of Paris. There was a spectral interlude, in which ghosts walked the Paris streets. For the long figure of La Fayette, last seen when Marie Antoinette was Queen of France, leaned from the tribune; and men heard a voice of 1790 unmake the Empire. It was as though Mirabeau had spoken. The Emperor, almost a ghost already, haunted the green alleys of Malmaison like an uneasy spirit. The little house among the trees filled with Imperial *revenants*. His brother Joseph came, the shadow of a King of Spain, and Jerome, faint simulacrum of a King of Westphalia; less shadowy, the indomitable Madame Mère took leave of him; Walewska came to sob out the last echoes of their love in Warsaw; and Hortense made a last home for him among her mother's flowers. His tired eyes watched round every corner for the lost figure of an Empress bending over her roses; for the roses were in bloom at Malmaison.

Uneasy gentlemen flitted in all directions—to safety in the south, to make their peace with the returning King, to Wellington's headquarters with bewildering proposals for an armistice. He had one answer for them all, since in his clear way he discerned the objects of the war. Long before Waterloo he had stated them to Marmont:

> "*La France n'a pas d'ennemis que je connaisse. . . . Nous sommes les* 59
> *ennemis d'un seul homme, et de ses adhérens. . . . La situation où nous*
> *allons nous trouver ne peut pas donc s'appeler un état de guerre contre la*
> *France, mais bien une guerre de la part de toute l'Europe, y inclus la France,*
> *contre Buonaparte, et contre son armée, de laquelle la mauvaise conduite a*
> *donné occasion aux malheurs qui vont arriver, et que nous déplorons tous.*"

With these opinions it was not surprising that he reminded the invading army that "their respective Sovereigns are the Allies of His Majesty the 60 King of France, and that France ought, therefore, to be treated as a friendly country." But these refinements were far beyond the simple-minded Prussians, who clung to the consoling thought that France,

278

which had so recently dominated Germany, was now defenceless, and behaved accordingly. The Duke, on the other hand, burned with the chivalry peculiar to citizens of uninvaded countries. Even his troops were slightly irked by his tendency to side with the civil population; and

61 ministers grew almost plaintive over his leniency. "It is quite right," wrote Liverpool, "to prevent plunder of every description, but France must bear a part of the expenses of the war. . . . We do not exactly know what course in this respect the Duke of Wellington has been following. . . . I trust, however, that you will be able to satisfy him that the French nation ought to bear a part of the expense."

Not that his chivalry was mere knight-errantry. For it had a distinct and practical purpose, since he was determined to restore King Louis. His devotion to the Bourbons was anything but sentimental. Long before

62 Waterloo he had described their restoration as "the measure most likely to insure the tranquillity of Europe for a short time." He recognised that their cause did not command unanimous enthusiasm, but wrote cheer-

63 fully to Henry Wellesley that "if we are stout we shall save the King, whose government affords the only chance of peace." After the victory

64 he moved King Louis into the neighbourhood of Paris on his own authority, because he "wished His Majesty should be on the spot, or as near it

65 as circumstances would permit." He told the delegates from Paris that he "conceived the best security for Europe was the restoration of the King, and that the establishment of any other government than the King's in France must inevitably lead to new and endless wars." With that in view it was vital to avoid anything that might render him distasteful to his subjects. It was unhappily inevitable that King Louis should return *dans les fourgons de l'ennemi*; but if that enemy were only reasonably well-behaved, his subjects might forgive his choice of a conveyance. So the Duke's army orders became a protracted correspondence-course in good manners, and his command found that its business with the French had been changed from winning battles to the more exacting task of winning golden opinions.

Prince Blücher, a devoted partner in the field, was disinclined to enter this tournament of chivalry. Prussia had bitter memories (as well as natural bad manners), which it was comforting to gratify by scaring French villagers and devastating French country houses. So Müffling,

279

duly installed as Governor of Paris, proposed to apply himself with gusto
to the collection of a fine of 100,000,000 francs. And was it reasonable of
Wellington to discover scruples about blowing up a Paris bridge, whose
mere existence was an affront to his allies, since it was named *Pont
d'Iéna?* Blücher was strong for it, although the French offered helplessly
to rename the offensive structure *Pont Louis XVIII*; and when Wellington still pleaded for the bridge, the old man tartly enquired what would   66
have been the fate of any bridge in Washington named after Saratoga.
But the Duke summarily closed the discussion by the heroic measure of
posting a British sentry on the bridge; the Prussians, it was thought,
would hesitate to blow up an Allied soldier. But this view was based
upon an under-estimate of their distaste for ill-timed historical allusions.
For, less sentimental, Blücher's engineers promptly set to work upon the
simple problem of destruction; but though thoroughly determined, they
did not know their business; and the bridge, which ultimately survived
under the abject name of *Pont des Invalides,* was saved by their complete
incompetence rather than by British chivalry.

It was a reasoned chivalry; for the Duke insisted that "if one shot is   67
fired in Paris, the whole country will rise against us." That would mean a
war of conquest for the Allies and a civil war for Louis XVIII. If such
disasters were to be avoided, France must be reconciled to the new terms
of peace. It was hardly customary to consider the feelings of defeated
states; but the Duke's reasoning rendered this novel course inevitable. It
followed that the terms must be of a character that would command
French consent; and this effectually precluded further annexations. As
the Duke wrote, *"nous avons raison de croire que la France cédera sans*   68
grande difficulté sur le système qu'on veut adopter, et que la nation
entière s'opposerait à son démembrement." The problem was not simple,
since *ex hypothesi* France was still a European menace standing in grave
need of restraint; but the restraining measures must be such as would be
acceptable to France. Lord Castlereagh devised an ingenious expedient;
but since its character was wholly military, it depended upon Wellington's
support. His views were as clear as ever:

> "In my opinion . . . the Allies have no just right to make any material   69
> inroad on the treaty of Paris, although that treaty leaves France too strong
> in relation to other powers; but I think I can show that the real interests of

the Allies should lead them to adopt the measures which justice in this instance requires from them. . . .

"My objection to the demand of a great cession from France upon this occasion is, that it will defeat the object which the Allies have held out to themselves in the present and the preceding wars.

"That which has been their object has been to put an end to the French Revolution, to obtain peace for themselves and their people, to have the power of reducing their overgrown military establishments, and the leisure to attend to the internal concerns of their several nations, and to improve the situation of their people. The Allies took up arms against Buonaparte because it was certain that the world could not be at peace as long as he should possess, or should be in a situation to attain, supreme power in France; and care must be taken, in making the arrangements consequent upon our success, that we do not leave the world in the same unfortunate situation respecting France that it would have been in if Buonaparte had continued in possession of his power. . . .

"If the King were to refuse to agree to the cession, and were to throw himself upon his people, there can be no doubt that those divisions would cease which have hitherto occasioned the weakness of France. The Allies might take the fortresses and provinces which might suit them, but there would be no genuine peace for the world, no nation could disarm, no Sovereign could turn his attention from the affairs of this country. . . . We must, on the contrary, if we take this large cession, consider the operations of the war as deferred till France shall find a suitable opportunity of endeavouring to regain what she has lost; and, after having wasted our resources in the maintenance of overgrown military establishments in time of peace, we shall find how little useful the cessions we shall have acquired will be against a national effort to regain them.

"In my opinion, then, we ought to continue to keep our great object, the genuine peace and tranquillity of the world, in our view, and shape our arrangement so as to provide for it.

"Revolutionary France is more likely to distress the world than France, however strong in her frontier, under a regular Government; and that is the situation in which we ought to endeavour to place her.

"With this view I prefer the temporary occupation of some of the strong places, and to maintain for a time a strong force in France, both at the expense of the French Government, and under strict regulation, to the permanent cession of even all the places which in my opinion ought to be occupied for a time. These measures will not only give us, during the period of occupation, all the military security which could be expected from the permanent cession, but, if carried into execution in the spirit in which they are conceived, they are in themselves the bond of peace."

He added shrewdly that "the troops of those Sovereigns should be selected   70
for this service who would have the least inclination to remain in possession of the fortresses at the termination of the period."

A later paper neatly summarised the choice before the Allies:

"If the policy of the united powers of Europe is to weaken France, let   71
them do so in reality. Let them take from that country its population and
resources as well as a few fortresses. If they are not prepared for that
decisive measure, if peace and tranquillity for a few years is their object,
they must make an arrangement which will suit the interests of all the
parties to it, and of which the justice and expediency will be so evident that
they will tend to carry it into execution."

Other Allies at the end of other wars have faced the choice between a
negotiated and a dictated peace; but the alternatives were not so clearly
stated, and the statement did not emanate from their leading soldier.

The Allied policy of moderation in 1815 owed its main driving-force to
Wellington. His lucid reasoning served largely to impose it on a reluctant
Cabinet and unenthusiastic Allies; but his reasoning prevailed less because it was lucid than because it was his. For the Prime Minister referred
to it respectfully as "the Duke of Wellington's projet," and its reasonable-   72
ness was gilded by the prestige of Waterloo. Other problems faced him,
as the Allies mounted guard in Paris and irreverent Parisians enjoyed the
unwanted spectacle of redcoats in the Bois and bewildered Cossacks staring at the Palais Royal, of "Prussian and Russian officers in blue or green   73
uniforms, waists drawn in like a wasp's, breasts sticking out like a
pigeon's; long sashes, with huge tassels of gold or silver, hanging halfway down their legs—pretty red and white boyish faces, with an enormous
bush of hair over each ear; lancers in square-topped caps and waving
plumes; hussars in various rich uniforms . . . Austrian officers in plain
white uniforms, turned up with red." Whilst Europe strolled on the boule-
vards in every colour of the rainbow, the Emperor, in Europe still, admired the coast of Devonshire from *Bellerophon*; and the Prime Minister
discussed his destination with the First Lord of the Admiralty. His pres-

74 ence was embarrassing; but Lord Liverpool, stifling a hearty wish that "the King of France would hang or shoot Buonaparte as the best termination of the business," was prepared, if necessary, to take him into custody. The Duke, for once, was not consulted; he had already expressed a strong distaste for Blücher's bloodthirsty opinions on the subject, stating firmly

75 that "if the Sovereigns wished to put him to death they should appoint an executioner which should not be me." And when Napoleon's surrender was announced in Paris, they heard the Duke say that he must have an

76 interview with him, and that he ought to be imprisoned at Madras. But Mr. Barrow, of the Admiralty, recommended St. Helena; Sir Hudson Lowe accepted the appointment; and Lord Bathurst anticipated com-

77 fortably that "Bonaparte's existence will soon be forgotten." Charged with this hopeful mission, *Northumberland* sailed through the summer days into the south, until the roar of Europe sank to a distant murmur and the Western Ocean fell silent round them.

In France the Duke of Wellington attended conferences, inspected troops, and drafted inexhaustibly. It was still raining decorations; his uniform became a gallery of European orders of chivalry, as the long procession of saints and heraldic monsters resumed with St. Andrew of

78 Russia, the Black Eagle of Prussia, and the Elephant of Denmark. The stout King of France detached the ribbon of the Saint-Esprit from his own sacred person, hung it on the Duke, and offered him a park; though Wellington's good sense preserved him from the *gaucherie* of celebrating a French defeat with an estate in France. The grateful Netherlands, going one better than the rest of Europe, made him a Prince—the Prince of Waterloo. But his own country was a shade embarrassed by the problem of its gratitude, since he had everything already. He was a Duke; he had the Garter; so they were reduced to voting him a further £200,000 towards the purchase of an estate. But though the fountain of honour had run dry, the Regent could still gush; and that royal hand

79 acquainted his dear Wellington that even the consummate skill of the Corsican could not withstand the superior genius of our own hero, and that England once more fulfilled a glorious destiny under the auspices of her transcendent General, adding with condescension that his most sincere friend was George, P.R.

The Duke went cheerfully about his business. The worst was over now.

The King of France was on his throne again; and Wellington, more than any other man, had seated him there. For the second Restoration was the outcome of his prompt initiative after Waterloo and those endless conferences in the Paris suburbs, when Wellington, watched by the narrow eyes of Fouché, imposed the King and (stranger still) imposed a minister upon him who had sent his brother to the guillotine in '93. He had kept uncongenial company, with Talleyrand limping beside him and Fouché's whisper in his ear; and clever Count Molé thought him so innocent. But Wellington was a deft match-maker; the King's reluctant hand lodged safely in the old regicide's, the peculiar *mariage de convenance* was successfully contrived; and King Louis, to the Duke's infinite relief, reigned in France once more. Not that his troubles ended there. For the peace-treaty was still on the anvil. He knew his own mind, which was in complete agreement with Castlereagh; but there was still the Cabinet to be persuaded, and the Allies had strong opinions of their own. For Allies, once wooed (like Danaë) in a shower of gold, grew sadly independent with no further British subsidies in prospect. The Prussians were stiff-necked by nature; Metternich was sly; and the Czar was torn as usual between Russian interests and the Sermon on the Mount. But Russia being largely satisfied, his better self prevailed. Besides, the Duke required a counterpoise to the dead weight of Central European reaction; and there was less than usual to fear from what he used to term Alexander's "Jacobinical flights."

There were distractions, though; for the Paris season of 1815 was an endless whirl of balls and reviews. Half London was in Paris to renew the glorious emotions of that unforgettable June evening when a chaise drove up Whitehall with the Waterloo despatch and a French eagle sticking out of each window. Croker was there, rejoiced by the spectacle of "the old Life Guards patrolling the Boulevard last night, as they used to do Charing Cross during the Corn riots"; Walter Scott came, thrilling with patriotic fire; and Palmerston prepared to leave the War Department (and Lady Cowper's smiles) for a lounge round Paris. They strolled about the conquered streets, linked arms with friends in uniform, and filled the theatres every night. Not that Paris minded; for that mercurial city was in raptures over a ballet in which Waterloo was positively mimed and a grateful *ballerina* received her wounded lover from the hands of a

284

noble-hearted Briton. Britons were quite the mode, and kilted Highlanders the rage. But though gentlemen abounded, the town seemed to be fuller still of ladies. All the world was there; white shoulders gleamed in all directions and curls shook at every turn, though Kitty lingered in England, mildly astonished by the accuracy of her own presentiment

83   (confided to Scott long before the battle) that when her hero met Buonaparte, he would destroy him at *one* blow. But the bright eyes of half the Continent followed the Duke, as he went briskly about Paris in his blue frock-coat. None followed him more closely than the adoring gaze of Lady Shelley. That devotee was among the earliest arrivals; and as Lady

84   Granville acidly observed, she and her husband "ran after the great Duke in a very disgusting way, but as they were together, *'sans peur et sans reproche.'* " Expanding slightly in the sunshine of her simple-minded

85   worship, he talked to her about the battle, said solemnly, "The finger of God was upon me," and let her cut off a lock of his hair in the reassuring presence of her husband. Her sensibility was quite prodigious; for a *tête-à-tête* with the Duke was almost too much for her; and (as she told someone) it was positively sacrilegious to degrade her adoration with the coarse name of love. But she drew him out. One day he shewed her all his gold boxes with the portraits of European monarchs, and let her watch him answering his letters. He liked to talk to her about the battle, and tell her what he said to Uxbridge and how experience gave him a pull over other soldiers. Not that he struck martial attitudes before her. "I hope to God," he said, "that I have fought my last battle. It is a bad thing to be always fighting. While in the thick of it, I am too much occupied to feel anything; but it is wretched just after." He told her that next to a battle lost the greatest misery was a battle gained, and that he

86   was only just recovering his spirits. (He could write more cheerfully about the losses now—"Never did I see such a pounding match. Both were what the boxers call gluttons. . . .") Now he looked forward to a cheerful life—"I must always have my house full. For sixteen years I have always been at the head of our army, and I must have these gay fellows round me." Flushed with these confidences, she glowed with pride in being born an Englishwoman and living in the same age with this

87   great being, though the sharp eye of Lady Granville observed the Duke to be a trifle inattentive to her strenuous pursuit.

The bright round continued, with reviews by day and parties almost every night. Lady Castlereagh's were dull (though she did her best to enliven them by wearing her husband's Garter as a hair-ornament); and Wellington preferred more cheerful company. So he was sometimes to be found in a livelier *milieu* than the grave-eyed world of monarchs and diplomatists. Caroline Lamb (who startled Paris with a purple riding-habit) amused him with her outbursts; and French ladies were a little apt to express their royalist opinions by embracing him in public. Had not a roomful of beauty in Vienna offered him a vista of conquests beyond the dreams of Alexander? The world whispered (and even wrote) unseemly things about his friendship with Lady Frances Webster, though the world knew nothing of the hurried note which he had scrawled to her in the rainy darkness of the night before Waterloo advising her to remove from Brussels. But Lady Shelley, whose devoted gaze rarely left him, remained quite convinced of their perfect innocence. He seemed so simple and so fatherly. But then Lady Shelley was a goose.

He was the saviour of Europe, just forty-six, with a trim figure and a handsome face. He dressed the part at last; and an admiring world crowded to watch him bow by candlelight or sit his horse in Field Marshal's uniform with his sword drawn as the long lines of infantry went stiffly by. In the Peninsula they had sometimes called him "the Dandy"; now he was "the Beau"; and what is a Beau without his due accompaniment of belles? Sometimes he rode with Lady Shelley; and how it thrilled her to hear him say, "Stick close to me." Once she was actually close enough to hear him order an aide-de-camp to "tell that damned adjutant he can't ride: tell him to get off his horse." It positively made her feel as though she could have charged up to the cannon's mouth under her hero's orders. He shewed her how the infantry formed square at Waterloo, and once he told her how much he disliked cheering in the ranks—"I hate that cheering. If once you allow soldiers to express an opinion, they may on some other occasion hiss instead of cheer." They dined at Malmaison one night; and after dinner she walked in the dark garden with him and explored Josephine's conservatory by the uncertain light of a few candles. Not that their evenings were invariably so restful, since he once polonaised with her all through the house. He let her ride on "Copenhagen"; and one hot afternoon, as they were sitting in a

THE DUKE OF WELLINGTON, 1815
From a painting by Sir T. Lawrence, R.A., at Apsley House.
By permission of the Duke of Wellington, K.G.

garden, she watched him playing with a grubby little child—he positively took a bite out of its apple and sat the urchin on his knee. Then they all went off to a fair and rode on the merry-go-round, the ladies circulating gaily upon swans and the Duke more suitably accommodated with a wooden horse.

90   But there were statelier occasions, when he received his guests. All Europe came; and the Duke bowed them in—sovereigns, Field Marshals, Allies, Frenchmen, diplomats, and Cossacks. M. de Talleyrand limped up the stairs; Fouché was there; and the big double doors flew open, as the footmen bawled, *"Sa Majesté le Roi de Prusse."* Walter Scott was there as well; and his eyes filled with tears as he saw Wellington shake hands with Blücher. Paris was full of thrills for Scott; did not old Platow dismount and kiss him in the Rue de la Paix? Besides, he had been presented to the Czar, wearing his blue and scarlet Selkirkshire uniform; and royalty, eyeing his lame leg, floored him at once by asking in what affair he had been wounded. The Duke awed him; he told someone that he had never felt abashed except before the Duke, because Wellington—the greatest living soldier and statesman—possessed every mighty quality of the mind in a higher degree than any other man did or had ever done. But that evening Walter Scott sat down to supper with him and two ladies. The royalties were supping somewhere; but the Duke apparently preferred the company of Scott and Lady Caroline Lamb, who punctuated their repast "by an occasional scream." There was a bust above his head, which displayed (the house had once belonged to Junot) the marble features of the Emperor; and two thousand miles away *Northumberland* sailed on into the South Atlantic.

AUTUMN

The ship sailed on below the horizon; and the leaves fell in Europe. Waterloo was fading into retrospect, and the Duke wrote polite discouragements to eager historians. For he was quite convinced that no true account of it could be written, and that it was just as well.

91   "The object which you propose to yourself is very difficult of attainment, and, if really attained, is not a little invidious. The history of a battle is not unlike the history of a ball. Some individuals may recollect all the little

events of which the great result is the battle won or lost; but no individual can recollect the order in which, or the exact moment at which, they occurred, which makes all the difference as to their value or importance.

"Then the faults or the misbehaviour of some gave occasion for the distinction of others, and perhaps were the cause of material losses; and you cannot write a true history of a battle without including the faults and misbehaviour of part at least of those engaged.

"Believe me that every man you see in a military uniform is not a hero; and that, although in the account given of a general action, such as that of Waterloo, many instances of individual heroism must be passed over unrelated, it is better for the general interests to leave those parts of the story untold, than to tell the whole truth."

He was prepared to help, but added ominously "Remember, I recommend you to leave the battle of Waterloo as it is." For he was grimly positive that "if it is to be a history, it must be the truth. . . . But if a true history is written, what will become of the reputation of half of those who have acquired reputation, and who deserve it for their gallantry, but who, if their mistakes and casual misconduct were made public, would not be so well thought of?" With these opinions it was not surprising that in later years "the Duke entertains no hopes of ever seeing an account of all its details which shall be true." Truth, he believed, might well be damaging; and he was disinclined to expose brave men to undiluted truth. Besides, he was more indulgent now and even pleaded with the Horse Guards for a delinquent, whom a later age would have diagnosed unhesitatingly as a case of shell-shock:

92
93
94

"Many a brave man, and I believe even some very great men, have been found a little terrified by such a battle as that, and have behaved afterwards remarkably well."

95

(Had he, one wonders, any recollection of the distant night when a scared young Colonel staggered into camp from Sultanpettah Tope?) His diagnosis was sympathetic:

"From what I have heard of the case since I received your letter, it appears that, —— —— having left the field as wounded, the surgeon of the regiment could not return him in the list of wounded. It will turn, first, upon whether the surgeon was right or wrong; and, secondly, whether he was not so stunned as to be obliged to quit the field, although not in such a state afterwards as that the surgeon ought to have returned him as wounded."

But now the Duke was busy with a fresh problem. For the Allies, denied any further opportunities of territorial gain, developed a wholly unexpected passion for the fine arts. There were excuses, since France under the Empire had been a connoisseur of comprehensive tastes, appropriating every major work of art from The Hague to Rome, until the Paris galleries came to resemble less a national collection than a complete history of European painting and sculpture. Laocoon writhed in the Louvre; the horses of St. Mark's stepped decorously on the arch outside the Tuileries; Apollo Belvedere posed in his niche; and, far from her native Florence, Venus dei Medici simpered in exile. Art had indubitably followed the eagles, though in the opposite direction; and the liquidation of this sumptuous collection promised the Allies all the delights of a gigantic jumble-sale where there was nothing to pay. Vast inventories were prepared; military working-parties took pictures down from walls and handled unaccustomed packages; Canova came from Rome with an interminable list of Papal property; there were the Hessian pictures at Malmaison, the Dutch pictures in the Louvre, and the Pope's statuary everywhere; and Prussia developed a wholly unsuspected wealth of art-treasures. The Venetian horses gave endless trouble, since they were now Austrian property; but the Austrians, who had no tools, were quite incapable of moving them. They requisitioned British Engineers, lined the Place du Carrousel with a guard of white-coats, and slung the horses down under the watchful eye of Lord Palmerston, who clambered up the arch himself. These exercises somewhat dimmed the lustre of the Duke's popularity in Paris, since the recovery of stolen property is rarely popular among receivers.

Major and minor diplomacy absorbed him; and he corresponded vigorously upon the composition of the Allied army of occupation for north-eastern France. The Duke was to command it in the name of the Allied monarchs; and he was full of cares about the British contingent. Ministers, in a sudden access of post-war economy, were demolishing the army, and he advised them gravely that "my opinion is that the best troops we have, probably the best in the world, are the British infantry, particularly the old infantry that has served in Spain. This is what we ought to keep up; and what I wish above all others to retain." He had his fill of troops that summer; for it was the season of the great reviews in Paris, when the streets were lined with every colour of the Allied rainbow, and Wellington took the salute in the Place Louis XV beside a King and two Emperors. He watched the Prussians at Grenelle, the Russian Guard at Neuilly,   98 and expounded the superiority of line over column to Palmerston, a fresh-faced young gentleman who had figured in his correspondence as the source of irritating departmental queries. He told the attentive Secretary at War that he had started in the last campaign with the very worst army that was ever got together, fortunately leavened by four or five of his Peninsular regiments. Nothing, he thought, could equal British soldiers in the field. They might not look quite so well as others at reviews, because appearance was, he felt, a trifle underrated. But in the field he was always confident that a detachment would maintain its post against any force until they dropped. So he was proud of them, as he shewed off their paces in the fields beyond Montmartre. It was a replica of Salamanca, faultlessly performed without rehearsals. The Prussians were apt to require two days of preparation for such performances and to peg the ground with finger-posts. But Wellington, who saw the *terrain* for the first time that morning, took it impromptu; and the watching foreigners were vastly impressed as the long scarlet lines wheeled and deployed with the added (and, in Paris, wholly irresistible) fascination of swinging kilts.

Diplomacy recurred in an unusual form that autumn. For while negotiations for the peace-treaty followed a comparatively normal course, the Czar soared beyond protocols into a region inhabited by the sublime platitudes of revealed religion. This revelation was principally vouchsafed through the ecstatic agency of Baroness von Krüdener, whom Castlereagh described irreverently as "an old fanatic, who has a considerable reputa-   99 tion amongst the few highflyers in religion that are to be found at Paris." Her vein was highly mystical; she had a Swiss disciple, a private entrance to the Elysée, and a flow of words by which the Czar was frequently reduced to tears. But tears were not enough; for action was required of a repentant Czar. His noble attitudes had already inspired disrespectful

British to term him "the Magnanimous Dandy"; but refreshed by nightly draughts from her apocalyptic well, his magnanimity dilated to more than Wilsonian proportions. Not that she led him towards a novel idea; since he had been vaguely haunted for more than ten years by the nebulous conception of a European union of Christian states, which now emerged, wreathed in sanctimonious garlands of Scriptural allusion. Diplomacy raised polite eyebrows. Prince Metternich concluded that the Romanoff "mind was affected"; Lord Castlereagh agreed that it was "not completely sound"; the Duke was present when the plan was mooted by its Imperial patentee, and experienced some difficulty in keeping a straight face. The Foreign Secretary thought it a "piece of sublime mysticism," and its proposal "what may be called a scrape." But if the Czar derived satisfaction from addressing autograph letters to the Prince Regent inviting him to conduct his policy upon the principles of Holy Writ, it was not easy to refuse him; and as the October days drew in, they signed the blameless articles of the Holy Alliance in Paris, Alexander glowing with a slightly evangelical pride at the circumstance of their signature in that godless capital.

Far to the south the ship sailed on into silence. South of the Line an island waited. It was the island where Sir Arthur Wellesley had stayed ten years before on his way home from India. Fate had transposed them now; for he commanded on the soil of France, while the Emperor descended at the very house where he had stopped on St. Helena in 1805. In those October days a lonely figure paced the garden of The Briars, while kings and emperors in Paris subscribed their august signatures to the Holy Alliance. Europe was growing chilly now; the year was almost over; winter had come again.

Occupied Territory

Nations are never so grateful as their benefactors expect.—WELLINGTON TO CANNING, DEC. 15, 1814.

Was this the summit? Field Marshal, Duke—three times a Duke and once a Prince—he had dethroned an emperor and restored a king. His victories had saved Europe, as he had heard Pitt prophesy ten years before, when he sat unrecognised at a long table in Guildhall; and the greatest soldier in the world had fled before him. Monarchs accepted his rebuke, and respectful nations did as he told them. Cheers were the least part of his incense, although he savoured them. For one summer evening he had stood beside King Louis at a palace window; candles were set to light their faces; and when the sea of waiting Frenchmen outside the Tuileries saw their sovereign smiling beside the foreign Duke, they cheered and cheered. The cheers found softer echoes, where adoring ladies flocked after him at evening parties. Aloof from cheering crowds, he was rarely indifferent to ladies' homage; and it was generously offered. He liked to talk to them about himself; they listened prettily; though if they were inclined (like de Staël) to unwomanly accomplishments, he took a manly pleasure in alarming them. For while the wide-eyed Lady Shelly might ask favours freely, he wrote with wicked glee that "I am on proper terms with the Staël—that is, she is confoundedly afraid of me." So the indulgent hero mounted them on "Copenhagen," rode with them in the Bois, took them to boxes at the Opera; and a skirt generally fluttered among his staff at a review. It was a cheerful picture, although Kitty was not in it. His Duchess was detained in England, since a brief experience of her in the year before had left him disinclined to expose her to the risks of Paris. For her accounts were always in inextricable confusion, and a big establishment was sure to be too much for her. Besides, there were his boys to be looked after. And she was so short-sighted, too; his vast international parties called for arts of management that lay far beyond her Dublin range. Did not Miss Edgeworth, of Edgeworthstown, write appreciatively, when she called on St. Patrick's Day and found a plate of shamrocks on her table, that "nothing could be more like Kitty Pakenham" than the Duchess of Wellington? So she was left in England; and he kept house for himself. Almost a widower already, he tasted bachelor delights, was free to choose his own com-

295

panions, and walked briskly down the long avenue of smiling faces. He
was the Duke. Indeed, he was something more, since an impressive
protocol signed by four Powers appointed him Commander-in-Chief of
an international army of occupation. Russians, Austrians, Germans, and
British presented arms at his approach; he reigned in seven Departments
from Calais down to Bâle with 150,000 men; and an Ambassadors' Conference sat in Paris to be the vehicle of his communications. Small wonder
that Miss Berry found that when "talking of the allied sovereigns . . .   4
he says *we* found so-and-so—*we* intend such-and-such thing—quite treating *de Couronne à Couronne*." For the Duke of Wellington had positively
become a European Power with his own army, territory, and diplomatic
relations. Was this the summit?

I

Unpleasant problems faced him before 1815 was out, since Ney, always
injudicious, contrived to get arrested. A frantic wife besieged the Duke   5
with prayers to intercede with the King, and Ney added something
soldierly relying on the general amnesty embodied in the capitulation of
Paris after Waterloo. The Duke was disinclined to help, since Ney's
treachery to King Louis in the spring had been exceptionally gross, and
settled government would become wholly impossible in France if such
treason went unpunished. Besides, the Cabinet were pressing with civilian
sternness for an example to be made in the interests of public order, and
Wellington concurred; for he was unlikely to lag behind Liverpool and
Castlereagh upon a question of elementary discipline. The King apparently expected him to intervene on behalf of the Marshal, and avoided
giving him an audience. Wellington, who had no such intention, resented
the discourtesy with a tremendous intimation that, as commanding the   6
troops, he should remain and do whatever was officially required of him,
but that he was likewise an English gentleman, that the King of France
had insulted him, and that until the insult was atoned for he should
never go near him except on public business. Meanwhile he made no
move in favour of the Marshal, who fell to a French firing-party; and
angry Bonapartists were convinced that he was a victim to Wellington's
jealousy of his military achievement, while lively Radicals in England

embraced the martyr's cause and lampooned the Duke for a cold-hearted refusal to interfere with the course of French justice, *Don Juan* ingeminating

7
> "Glory like yours should any dare gainsay,
> Humanity would rise and thunder, 'Nay!'"

and adding in a footnote with a grin, "Query, *Ney?—Printer's Devil.*"

Now it was 1816, and the world began to settle down. The Duke left Paris in the spring and installed his headquarters at Cambrai. There were as many papers as ever on his table—papers about mad Englishmen in Paris who got themselves into scrapes by plotting against the King, complaints from Zieten about the treatment of the Prussians, a polite request that Fouché would discourage the French authorities from their enterprising plan of opening gaming-houses in occupied territory for the benefit of the Allied troops, and a note from Hill who had gone home and found his family in some embarrassment (eliciting the kindly an-

8 swer that the Duke possessed "a large sum of money which is entirely at my command, and . . . I could not apply it in a manner more satisfactory to me than in accommodating you, my dear Hill, to whom I am under so many obligations"). He wrote judicious letters on French politics to

9 Louis and his ministers, pleaded for General Mouton (whose conduct in the Hundred Days, though he commanded a corps at Ligny, had not been actively treasonable), and positively prolonged his residence in Paris at the King's request. How many conquerors have been invited to extend their stay in a conquered capital? Small wonder that he wrote that "there is not much confidence in anybody either here or in England, excepting myself." Then he was off to The Hague; the Netherlands were full of problems—French refugees in Brussels, the new fortresses along the frontier, and a growing tendency in Belgian quarters to resent Dutch predominance. In June he was brought back to Paris for a French royal

10 wedding. The Shelleys were there; and he told her that he was not well and had been recommended to try Cheltenham. He took them to the play and carried her off to drink tea in his favourite social haunts. One evening he gave dinner to the Spaniards, and she saw him in his Spanish uniform. She had been going on to a reception at the Duchesse de Berry's; but he pressed her to stay; and as the royal invitation was for ladies only,

she "felt that it would be monstrous dull" and stayed. After the guests
had gone, she heard him talking about Spain and about the blunder they
had made in abolishing the Inquisition; someone, it seemed, had proposed it in his time, but he had told them shrewdly, *"Quoi, vous voulez
me donner un autre ennemi à combattre! J'aurai tous les curés de la
Castille contre moi. L'Inquisition se meurt d'elle même. Voyez le Portugal; nous ne l'avons pas aboli là, et cependant elle n'existe plus. Ce sera de
même ici. Si vous l'abolissez, elle existera toujours."* Reformers of abuses
have received worse advice.

He gave a ball of his own; and Lady Shelley, who came a little early,
found him by himself moving the chairs about; for he was always strong
on detail. That evening he took in Marmont's wife to supper; but afterwards he sat with Lady Shelley until he went off to bed at four o'clock in
the morning. He told her that he should be going home in a few days—
"You must dine with me every day until I go." They rode together, and
she talked about her husband's political affairs. "What," said the Duke,
"are quarrels to be eternal? I hate these party squabbles." For he was an
indifferent partisan; and when an injudicious letter from Lord Grey to
an arrested Englishman fell into his hands, he returned it unopened to
the Whig leader. They had their last ride, and Lady Shelley felt quite
sad; indeed, she was completely overcome that evening by the delicacy
of Biggotini's dancing in the affecting ballet of *Nina*. Then he was off at
three o'clock one morning, jolting along the road to Calais. The roads of
1816 were full of travellers. That summer Lord Byron swept the Continent again with his sombre regard. It was just seven years since he had
meditated on the quays of Lisbon, while Sir Arthur waited for the
French at Talavera. Still faithful to Sir Arthur's footsteps, he meditated
now in Brussels. He was a trifle patronising with Waterloo (though he
compared it favourably with Troy, Mantinea, Leuctra, Marathon, and
several other sites of his acquaintance) and, having noted the rare lyric
possibilities of a sound of revelry by night, passed on to meditate
elsewhere.

II

I T W A S past midsummer, 1816, when he saw England once again.
The cliffs of Dover gleamed, onlookers cheered, and he drove off to
1 Richard's house not far from Ramsgate. Richard, an enigmatic figure
in these days with the air of an imperfectly extinct volcano that is inseparable from a career of Empire-building, was getting on for sixty now.
Once a master of the art of resignation, he had nothing left to resign; but
he was still prepared to favour correspondents and the House of Lords
with his unnaturally progressive opinions upon the Catholics and fiscal
2 policy. Besides, there was his toilet; for Richard was arranged with care.
When Lawrence painted him a few years earlier, he noticed that his
sitter's lips already owed something to art; and some years later a malicious eye observed his blackened eyebrows, rouged cheeks, and awful
brow whose lofty pallor, alas! was not innocent of artificial aid. The
Duke called on this ageing Cæsar and posted on to London. But London
3 in July was hardly restful. The Regent claimed him for dinner; he dined
out assiduously and took a hand in a feminine cabal at Almack's against
the autocracy of Lady Jersey. The London round seemed to revive him.
4 Then he was off to Cheltenham for his cure. The spa received him with
triumphal arches and illuminations; he sipped his water in Well Walk,
gossiped with a few Peninsular acquaintances, and strolled with Kitty
and his boys. She wrote off delighted bulletins, informing the anxious
Ladies at Llangollen that

5 "he for whom all the world is so justly anxious is considerably better both
in looks and spirits since his arrival in England.
"I think I perceive an amendment every day. This happens to be the
time of the holidays of our Boys, and I say with delight they are as fond
of and as familiar with their noble and beloved Father as if they had never
been separated from him. They accompany him in his walks, *chat* with him,
play with him. In short they are the chosen companions of each other. . . ."

He had always got on well with children, and could get on with these,

299

even if they were his own. Kitty might have her faults; her trick of ad- 6
miring him in public was particularly trying. But that summer he was
at his gentlest. When someone hinted that he sometimes failed his friends,
he defended himself with warmth—"The truth is that for fifteen or sixteen years I have been at the head of armies with but little intermission; 3
and I have long found it necessary to lay aside all private motives in considering publick affairs. I hope that this practice does not make me cold-
hearted, or feel a diminished interest for those I am inclined to love. If
I may judge by what I feel, I should say it does not. . . ." And judged by
what he did, it did not either. For ne was busying himself to obtain 7
public aid for Sheridan's impoverished family. His benefactions were
often gruff; and a formal manner sometimes left a suitor under the
impression that his petition had been dismissed, when it was generously
granted. Thus, he reported to a friend of Indian days in search of an
appointment that he had spoken for him without success and "I now
recommend you to let the matter drop. . . . You may be quite certain 8
that great situations are not obtained in this country by personal exertion
and interest. Let a man show that he has talents, integrity, and enlarged
views, and he may depend upon it that if employment abroad is his
object, he is more likely to obtain it without solicitation than by making
the most active exertions." The recipient of this homily might be excused
for concluding that the Duke had done with his affairs. But without his
knowledge Wellington wrote the same day to urge his claims upon the
Company, dilating on his zeal, integrity, and talents, and concluding that
they could not do better than employ him in a great situation, such as the
governorship of Bombay. He always hated to raise hopes or to parade his
services; and they were often rendered under cover of a curt reply.

Another suitor haunted him that season; for the French were pressing
for a reduction of the army of occupation, and its commander was felt to
be the likeliest person to view their request with favour. M. de Richelieu
had seen him on the subject before he came home on leave; he advised 9
Castlereagh that there was no danger in the proposed reduction, and gave
the French the benefit of his guidance as to the best moment to put forward their demand. His leave was ending now; the walks with his two
boys at Cheltenham were over; and he was back in London. One afternoon he rode as far as Kensington. For Graham took him out to Wilkie's 10

studio in Lower Phillimore Place, and he called on the respectful painter with Lady Argyll and the Duke and Duchess of Bedford. The painter had been warned, his mother and sister posted to watch the great arrival from behind the parlour curtains, and his works judiciously disposed about the studio. The Duke surveyed them and approved, remarking in his decided tone "Very good" and "Capital." Then he sat down to study one of them; and Lady Argyll began to tell the artist that Wellington wished him to paint a picture. The Duke tilted his chair back and proposed a group of old soldiers outside a public-house chewing tobacco and telling stories; he should not be particular about their uniforms and suggested that the public-house might be located in the King's Road, Chelsea. Wilkie concurred with rapture, adding that the picture only wanted a story. Wellington said that perhaps it would do if they were playing skittles. Wilkie proposed a reading from a newspaper, to which the Duke was perfectly agreeable and added that the sketch might be sent to him abroad. Then he stood up, took out his watch, and informed the company that he was dining with the Duke of Cambridge. He turned to Wilkie with a bow and asked when he should hear from him. The artist answered that he could not get the picture done for two years. "Very well," replied the art patron, "that will be soon enough for me." He went downstairs, bowed once more to his host, saw old Mrs. Wilkie at the parlour window and bowed to her, mounted his horse, and then rode off. The little windows were all full of faces; two Guardsmen watched him from the corner; and as the sound of hoofs died away down Lower Phillimore Place, they were tying ribbons on the historic chair which he had honoured. His leave was over now; and before August was out, he was in France again.

III

B^{A C K} once more in his little kingdom, Wellington resumed the endless correspondence about his troops, about the new Barrier fortresses
on the Belgian frontier, about Bonapartist exiles who misbehaved themselves in Brussels, and British officers who misbehaved nearer home in the
theatre at Boulogne. Canning passed through on his way back to Lisbon;   1
and the Duke, whose enthusiasm for abolition had manifestly waned
since the days when he discussed slavery with Clarkson in the Paris embassy, disliked his notion of awarding British support to Portugal or
Spain according to their respective display of abolitionist virtue—"nonsense and folly" was his brief description of the philanthropic policy.
Then he had his autumn reviews, graced by the royal Dukes of Kent and   2
Cambridge and a due accompaniment of evening parties. The Dukes were
hardly to his taste; as he told Creevey afterwards, "they are the damnedest
millstone about the necks of any Government that can be imagined. They
have insulted—*personally* insulted—two-thirds of the gentlemen of Eng-   3
land." But he had more congenial guests; for the Duchess of Richmond
brought out her girls to stay with him at Cambrai. He had written
charmingly to Lady Shelley, telling her how much he missed his "absent
A.D.C." at the reviews. But she was far away in Vienna, and now other
belles rode "Copenhagen." Georgy Lenox found him a rather trying
mount from an unpleasing mannerism of neighing violently at the sight   4
of troops (an authentic instance of a war-horse laughing "ha-ha" to the
trumpeters); and one day when she found herself inside a square with
him, she overheard the ranks remarking, "Take care of that 'ere horse;
he kicks out; we knew him well in Spain." The house at Mont St.
Martin was crowded and cheerful with incessant amateur theatricals and
a more violent diversion known as "riding in the coach," which appeared
to consist of dragging ladies down interminable corridors on rugs. The
gentlemen were harnessed; even the Duke did not disdain this humble
office, though he occasionally mounted the rug himself, and Wellington

302

drove through Headquarters behind a team of ladies. A bulletin from his own hand describes the romping:

> "We are going on here as usual—'Riding in the coach,' dancing the Mazurka, &c., &c. The house is as full as it can hold. Yesterday was a very bad day, and I went to Cambray, and I understand that they hunted Lord C—— through all the corridors, even that in the roof. At night we had an improvement on the coach. Two goats were brought in and harnessed, but instead of being horses and assisting to draw, they chose to lie down and be drawn. The night before, the ladies drew me the *petty* tour, and afterwards Lord Hill the *grand* tour, but the 'fat, fair and forty,' and M—— were so knocked up that some of us were obliged to go into the harness, although we had already run many stages."

This cheerful horseplay filled his evenings. For he could romp with his own circle, though the outer world found him less oncoming, the indomitable de Staël concluding bitterly that as she had done everything to fascinate him without success, the glacial Duke must be devoid of all *"cœur pour l'amour."* But he had little taste for clever women. His days were rendered quite sufficiently exhausting by clever men; and in the evenings he might be excused for preferring something a trifle less exacting.

His days, indeed, were full of problems. He did not spare much attention for the gathering storm at home (which he was inclined to attribute to the sudden "reduction of our war establishments . . . the rage for travelling of all our gentry, which have deprived some of our people of employment, and lastly and principally . . . the idleness, dissipation and improvidence of all the middling and lower classes in England, produced by a long course of prosperity and of flattery of their vices by the higher orders and the government"). His interests were, of necessity, almost entirely Continental; but in that sphere no problem, however civilian, was beyond his range. He was the guardian of the peace-treaties; and finance, the inseparable (though often insubordinate) hand-maid of peace-treaties, came within his survey. The French were bound by treaty to pay an indemnity of 700 million francs in five annuities, in addition to the costs of the Allied occupation; and the Duke picked his way through a morass of foreign loans, of rates of interest, of scrip, of currency, of interviews with Mr. Baring. He favoured the financing of France by an issue of *Rentes* to leading houses in London and Amsterdam, and expressed his view that "unless some arrangement of the description proposed is adopted, France will be aground this year, and our settlement of last year will be entirely destroyed." That degree of common sense in post-war settlements was not reached by later generations without years of blundering and controversy. But Wellington could grasp the point. Embodying the wisdom vainly sought by his successors in endless Conferences at unnumbered health-resorts, he saw the bankers for himself and faced the still more tangled problem of French Reparations. He had some experience of finance, since remittances to his army in the Peninsula had always involved complicated banking transactions. But the Reparations question in 1817 was worse than financial, since it included the awkward problem of distribution between hungry Allies as well as that of French ability to pay; and Wellington was finally enthroned, on the proposal of the Czar, as supreme arbiter of all Allied claims. How many men would rather deal with Napoleon than with Reparations? But Wellington faced both; and what is more, he faced Reparations single-handed.

Not that the French were grateful. For nations rarely are; and Paris theatres rang with denunciations of *"le tyran de Cambrai"* and little jokes on *"Vilainton,"* whilst he took care never to "go into any blackguard mob or place in which a fellow might insult me with impunity." He went about his business, as the months slipped by, reviewing troops inspecting Belgian counterscarps, discussing Mr. Rothschild's dealing in exchange, and maintaining order in occupied territory. His own affairs scarcely engaged him, though he was still at the Spaniards for a decision about the royal pictures which he had captured at Vitoria; and when it was suggested that his boys should be educated at the Military College, he was strong for "the education usually given to English gentlemen" in preference to anything more technical. He ran across to England more than once in the course of 1817. On one visit he attended the Prince Regent's inauguration of Mr. Rennie's new Strand bridge; and once he was besieged by James Ward, the Academician, who had just won a prize with his design for an "Allegory of Waterloo." This masterpiece, a terrifying composition in which mythology predominated, involved a sitting from the Duke, whose lifelong servitude to painters was just beginning. He saw Mr. Ward and, stifling his objection to being painted by an artist whose leading triumphs had hitherto been achieved in the depiction of bulls, made the valid excuse that he was just off to the Continent.

"My lord," said the determined painter, "I will follow you there."

"Ah, Mr. Ward," the deep voice replied, " a man that has five thousand troops under his command knows not where he may be one day after another. But I will sit to you on my return."

13 He was back again before the year was out to view another country house. This time it was Lord Rivers' place near Reading; the splendid avenue of trees found favour in his eyes; and the purchase of Stratfield Saye for £263,000 was approved. But his concerns were still wholly Continental; and as 1817 wore on, he was kept busy with a tour of inspection in Alsace, his autumn reviews, and the absorbing business of checking

14 the sporting and pugilistic proclivities of his command in France. Kitty came out to him that autumn; and he wrote sternly to complain that someone had been using in her carriage horses belonging to the pon-

15 toon train. He had other pets as well; since a Foreign Office messenger was once charged with a "black and tan dog of the Duke of Norfolk's breed" for the Commander-in-Chief, and Lady Castlereagh recruited his kennels with two boar-hound puppies. But life at Cambrai was not all hunting and house-parties. For French politics were far from reassuring

16 in the first weeks of 1818, and the Duke feared gravely for the dynasty— "I entertain no doubt how this contest will end. The descendants of Louis XV will not reign in France; and I must say, that it is the fault of Monsieur and his adherents. . . . I wish Monsieur would read the histories of our Restoration and subsequent Revolution, or that he would recollect what passed under his own view, probably at his own instigation, in the Revolution." Besides, there was the endless wrangle over Reparations;

17 and Wellington reported that "since Baring left me, as I generally spend the greatest part of every morning now with money-changers, Rothschild has been with me." It was not simple to assess the damages resulting from twenty years of European war; and the Duke struggled bravely

18 with the appetites of half the Continent. As he wrote, "my plan is first to ascertain what will really and ought to satisfy each nation. . . . I will then, secondly, negotiate with the French government to obtain that sum in the mode which will be most advantageous to the Allies, and least injurious to the other operations of the French government." The goal

was plain enough, though it was less readily accessible; for the intervening region was inextricably tangled with tales of ancient outrages committed by the armies of the First Republic and every exaction of the Empire in its career of conquest. But he laboured on untiringly, and the Allied claims were ultimately reduced by his industry to 240 million francs.

One February night these labours were almost interrupted, as he was driving home in Paris after a party. A shot rang out; he saw the flash himself and suspected nothing, though he was perfectly aware that his life was threatened; a sound of running footsteps died away down the dark street, as he got out at his own door and asked the coachman with some heat what he had meant by driving in at such a pace. The coachman answered that he had seen a man fire at his Grace. The news affected Europe variously. Prinny was shocked beyond belief, writing in almost tearful terms to his "dear Friend" and eliciting the courtly answer that if anything could reconcile a man to such attempts upon his life, it was the reception of such letters from one to whom he owed all his success; old soldiers in French *cafés* muttered in deep moustaches that Waterloo had been avenged; King Louis fluttered, and his ministers entered with gusto on a series of promiscuous arrests in the best manner of Continental justice; while poor Kitty sobbed out her relief at his escape in a note to Richard—

"I cannot bear that you should run the hazard of hearing reports so alarming whilst I have the blessing of knowing that he is safe. Thank God, thank God, my dear Lord Wellesley, my Husband is perfectly safe but his life has been attempted as he returned home on Wednesday night at his own door a pistol was fired at him, but he ever was he still continued the special charge of Heaven tho' so close he was not touched neither is there the smallest mark on the carriage why did not the footman seize the varlet for it appears that he stood near the sentry box and that they must have seen him, but he has none but French footmen. . . . My next wish to thanking God for the preservation of the most precious life, is to save you from anxiety."

She was still fluttering, when she wrote to him again:

"Tho' still far from well I am so anxious to see you for many reasons. . . . I wish to rejoice with you on the success of my dear and excellent

husband, his very narrow escape which I am not yet warrior enough (tho'
I have thought myself very valiant) to think of it without agitation. . . ."

While the French police stirred muddy waters by haphazard arrests
of Bonapartist malcontents, his own Government ordered the Duke to
leave Paris forthwith and withdraw to Cambrai. He did not relish the
retreat and fenced with their command, complaining that he had not
been consulted in a matter in which he was "principally and personally
concerned," and politely deploring the necessity for disobeying orders.
But he disobeyed them; and Wellington's one act of mutiny was concealed in a blandly phrased expectation that "the Prince Regent and his
government will agree with me in thinking that I ought to delay to
obey His Royal Highness's commands." He even took the unusual
liberty of examining the desirability of such commands being given at
all. For why should he be any safer at Cambrai? And if not at Cambrai,
why anywhere on the Continent? In that event he would become "the
ridicule of the world, and I should by this very act deprive myself of
the means of serving you in future in any capacity." This was unanswer-
able; and the Duke stayed in Paris.

There was so much for him to do—French Reparations to be settled,
French politics to be supervised, and the Allied occupation to be brought
somehow to an end. His own affair was soon disposed of, when they
arrested a Bonapartist *bravo* of the name of Cantillon, who was manifestly
guilty (though a French jury subsequently acquitted him). The news
reached St. Helena, where an ageing, lonely man noted Cantillon's
name. Paris echoed this unpleasing temper, though King Louis was
almost tender now, sending the Duke a little present of old Sèvres with
a shy intimation that he felt himself *encouragé dans cette démarche par
un vieux proverbe que je vais tâcher de rendre dans votre langue:* Do
little gifts—keep friendship alive." Friendship, alas! was sadly strained
by Reparations in 1818. But the Duke persisted, revising Allied claims,
conferring endlessly with bankers, and running backwards and forwards
between Paris, Cambrai, and London. He had a new address in town;
for that spring he dated his first letter from Apsley House, which he had
bought from Richard. He had a fresh problem, too. For Spain and
Portugal were drifting into war over the rebellious Spanish colonies in

307

South America. The Duke, it was believed, might intervene in the commanding character of uncle to the Peninsula; but this view reckoned without the towering altitude of Spanish pride; and his intervention, when it came, rather resembled the tentative intrusion of a nephew between two punctilious uncles. His views were plain enough. No notion of calling a New World into being to redress the balance of the Old had crossed his mind; he was not Canning, and he disapproved of revolutions. Besides, his main anxiety was lest the United States might   26 seize the opportunity of recognising infant nations struggling to be free in South America; and he pressed the Spaniards to prompt action in the River Plate before this calamity could supervene.

His hands were full that summer, though life at Cambrai was still cheerful. Creevey came over and found him riding out to see a cricket   27 match with two belles from Baltimore. Wellington talked freely after dinner about the royal Dukes and their bad manners, and how the House of Commons could not be blamed for making difficulties about their allowances, as it was their only opportunity of revenge, and he thought, by God! they were quite right to use it. This was strange language from a pillar of the throne to a former Opposition Whip. But the Duke did not see himself as a strict Tory, and he enquired with friendly interest about the problem of Whig leadership; Tierney might do, he thought, though Romilly was strange to him—but then, the House of Commons never cared for lawyers. He was less Tory than ever when he discussed the Regent—"By God! you never saw such a figure in your life as he is. Then he speaks and swears so like old Falstaff, that damn me if I was not ashamed to walk into a room with him." They dined together again in a French provincial inn; and Creevey was quite shocked when two grubby maids brought in two partridges, a fowl, and a fricasse to set before six hungry gentlemen. The Duke, who had driven from Paris on the meagre support of a cold chicken eaten in his carriage, seemed to enjoy it all. The champagne was poor; the tea at breakfast the next morning came out of an enormous coffee-pot; there were no saucers; but when Creevey opined that this formidable brew was a creditable product for Vitry, Wellington remarked "with that curious simplicity of his" that he had brought it all the way from Paris. Then Creevey saw his coach driving away at breakneck speed; for Wellington had got wind of the approaching Duke of Kent, and incontinently bolted. But the royal Duke caught him up at Valenciennes. His troubles multiplied, since the new Duchess of Kent accompanied him, to say nothing of a German lady-in-waiting of the most austere appearance. There was a dinner-party, and Wellington went grumbling round the Staff, enquiring who the devil was to take out the maid of honour. An anxious silence ended in a flash of inspiration—"Damme, Fremantle, find out the Mayor and let him do it." After all, the French had lost the war; they were in occupied territory; and the invitation was a mild, but pardonable, *væ victis*. They dined; they danced; the Duke of Kent amused them all by his new-found solicitude about his lady's health (he positively stroked her cheek after a waltz in order to ascertain if she was overheated); and Creevey regaled his host with a sanctimonious saying of the Duke of Kent's about his aged mother's illness. The delighted Wellington took Creevey by the button and, remarking "God damme! d'ye know what his sisters call him? By God! they call him Joseph Surface," exploded into one of his tremendous laughs which startled the entire ball-room. But the Duke of Kent always amused him. Wellington called him "the Corporal," from an untidy habit of appearing in undress uniform; and he could never forget the broad comedy of his confessions to Creevey about his royal sacrifices of domestic happiness on the altar of dynastic duty. He relished simple fun; and the Duke of Kent afforded ample opportunities, especially when he got them all up at dawn for an inspection, and kept poor Creevey waiting for his breakfast until the shower of royal interrogations had rained itself out. Wellington advised the starving gossip that it was always wise on such occasions to take his breakfast first and went chuckling round the Staff, pointing at Creevey and repeating with wicked glee, *"Voilà, le monsieur qui n'a pas déjeuné."* He liked the little man, savoured his anecdotes, and spoke civilly to him about the Whigs, praising Grey and Lansdowne, and deploring the fact that they were buried in the House of Lords—"Nobody cares a damn for the House of Lords; the House of Commons is everything in England, and the House of Lords nothing." And Creevey liked him in return: the Duke's simplicity impressed him—"that curious simplicity of his . . . his comical simplicity . . . the uniform frankness and simplicity of Wellington in all the conversations I have heard him

engaged in, coupled with the unparalleled situation he holds in the world
for an English subject, make him to me the most interesting object I
have ever seen in my life."

His reign at Cambrai was ending now. For the world met once more
in conference that autumn to resettle the peace of Europe and to end
the Allied occupation. Lord Castlereagh passed through *en route* for Aix-
la-Chapelle; the Czar descended from his distant Sinai; and the statesmen furbished up their decorations, polished their protocols, and prepared
themselves for the invigorating processes of another Congress. He was
in Brussels just before it opened, and once more Creevey met him strolling
in the Park.

"Well now, Duke, let me ask you, don't you think Lowe a very un-   28
necessarily harsh gaoler of Buonaparte at St. Helena?"

"By God! I don't know. Buonaparte is so damned intractable a fellow
there is no knowing how to deal with him. To be sure, as to the means
employed to keep him there, there never was anything so damned absurd.
I know the island of St. Helena well. . . ."

His view of Lowe was simple—"as for Lowe, he is a damned fool."
But one evening when Creevey was at him again at Lady Charlotte
Greville's about a newspaper report that he was to join the Cabinet, he
answered with a grunt.

Then he was off to Aix-la-Chapelle for the Congress. He and Castlereagh formed the British delegation and he played his part in the
agreeable charade of Continental unity. The Foreign Secretary was
"quite convinced that past habits, common glory, and these occasional   29
meetings, displays, and repledges, are among the best securities Europe
has now for a durable peace"; and if the common past of the Allies
was to be recalled, the Duke was a notable exhibit. He gave the Czar
a great review, composing for the occasion the libretto of a sham fight
which made him feel as if he had been "writing a Harlequin Farce."
The ceremonial round began once more—review, ball, dinner, play—and   30
Palmerston was vastly impressed by the perfection of his manners, "the
extreme respect and deference paid by all to the Duke, and, on the other
hand, the manly but respectful manner with which he treats the
sovereigns." The Prussians, by an odd twist of fate, gave their display at
Donchery, outside Sedan, where Prussia was to wait in spiked helmets

for the sword of another Emperor. The Duke talked a good deal to Palmerston, telling him all about line and column and how it was his practice to meet French attacks behind the shelter of a little ridge. He pointed at a Prussian column.

"Look how formidable that looks; and yet I defy the French" (the Duke clapped his hands) "to mention any one instance in the whole war in which these masses had made the least impression on our lines."

Then he described the process in detail—the British volley and the scattered reply of the advancing French, the wavering of the attackers, and the odd way in which their columns always frayed out from the rear—"As the French column ran from the rear, one used to see the men huddling together and running to the right and left, just as they saw the means of sheltering themselves behind a body of fellow-fugitives, so that at a little distance they went waddling like ducks." That was his simple picture of the tactics by which the Empire had been broken.

The business of Europe was transacted at Aix-la-Chappelle: the Allied occupation was to end, and Wellington was liberated from his duties in a fresh shower of military honours. For he became a Marshal of the Russian, Austrian, and Prussian armies. At one moment his functions were almost extended beyond Europe, since it was proposed that Wellington should mediate in the name of the Great Powers between Spain and her colonies. But he replied judiciously from the depth of *"mon expérience et ma connaissance intime du caractère Espagnol"* that *"il n'y a pas sur la terre une nation si jalouse que l'Espagne de l'intervention dans ses affaires des Puissances Etrangères."* Had he not fought a war in the Peninsula to convince the French of that simple truth? The notion dropped; and he was left with the less exacting duty of evacuating France. The last time-tables were prepared; the Allies who had brought down Napoleon parted for the last time; the bayonets wound homewards across France in opposite directions; the British sailed; the Russians and the Germans marched; and before 1818 was out, Wellington was left alone in Paris. He went home by way of Brussels, and by Christmas he was safe at Apsley House.

The long task was over; but it was unthinkable that Wellington should fade discreetly into private life. He was far too useful; and ministers, who had found him, a judicious colleague since 1814, still desired his

company. Now there was nothing for it but the Cabinet. They had a
notion that he might join without portfolio; but it was felt to be more   33
appropriate to bring him in as Master-General of the Ordnance. Lord
Liverpool made him the offer, and he accepted on slightly peculiar terms.
Accustomed to the public service, he was prepared to serve. But he was
at pains to divest his acceptance of all party connotations:

> "I don't doubt that the party of which the present government are the   34
> head will give me credit for being sincerely attached to them and to their
> interests; but I hope that, in case any circumstances should occur to remove
> them from power, they will allow me to consider myself at liberty to take
> any line I may at the time think proper. The experience which I have ac-
> quired during my long service abroad has convinced me that a factious op-
> position to the government is highly injurious to the interests of the country;
> and thinking as I do now I could not become a party to such an opposition,
> and I wish that this may be clearly understood by those persons with whom
> I am now about to engage as a colleague in government."

In other words, he was prepared to sit with them in Cabinet, but by no
means to go out of office with them, as a good Tory should. For it was
possible that some other Prime Minister might require his services; and
Wellington plainly viewed himself as a public servant, not as a Tory politician. It was his sense of public duty, not party affiliations, that brought
the Duke home from France in 1818 to be a Cabinet minister. For he
was still "*nimmukwallah*"; he had eaten the King's salt and would serve
him still, even among the politicians.

The Cabinet

And what is a great man? Is it a Minister of State? Is it a victorious General? A gentleman in the Windsor uniform? A Field-Marshal covered with stars?—CONINGSBY.

I

I T W A S 1819, and this handsome, greying man of fifty was home again. Home would be quite a novelty, since he had been a wanderer for twenty years. Indeed, it was not easy to recall a time when he had lived at home. School, Brussels, Angers, Dublin lodgings, freezing camps in Holland, Dublin once more, eight years of Indian cantonments, his Irish interlude divided between the Lodge in Phœnix Park and Harley Street, an endless succession of Peninsular billets, the Paris embassy, a hotel at Brussels, Paris again, and then headquarters at Cambrai—it was a gipsy record; and home would be a new experience for Wellington. Not that he was unfitted for home life. Quite the reverse; since all his inclinations appeared to lie in that direction. For he liked nothing better than a house full of guests and cheerful evenings in society where all the men were well-connected and nearly all the women pretty. How he had enjoyed watching his "boys" dancing, and confessed to Lady Shelley that he must always have his house full—"for sixteen years I have always been at the head of our army, and I must have these gay fellows round me." The mood recurred with him; and his house-parties at Cambrai were an attempt to satisfy it. Perhaps it had been easier for him to play the smiling host abroad than it would be in his new mansion at Hyde Park Corner and the big house in Hampshire. For Kitty would be there as well; and Kitty seemed to fail him somehow. Sadly deficient in the arts of household management (her finances on his return from the Peninsula had been as involved as a French loan), she was afraid of him; and her fears were often hidden in an irritating trick of gushing over him in public. Besides, her eyes were always weak; and she was quite unequal to the exacting duty of recognising all London and half Europe. The Duke could always manage a nod at the right moment; but his short-sighted Duchess hid her embarrassment behind an open book when she drove out. And was she quite so beautiful as all the smiling faces that had shone like stars on him in Paris? Or so intelligent? He had no taste for bluestockings; but when he talked, he liked to be understood. He once

315

defined feminine ability as "anticipating one's meaning; that is what a
clever woman does—she sees what you mean." Poor Kitty was not clever,
though; she never knew what Arthur meant; and it was more than
doubtful how far home would disappoint him.

But his own part, if he had leisure, could be played to perfection. Trim,
handsome, and mature, he was "the Beau" indeed, a figure made for
admiration. Not that his countrymen outside Society were particularly
ready to admire. For the first rapture of public worship that succeeded
Waterloo had evaporated; he had not banked its fires by public appearances in England; and England, in its odd way, had grown slightly indifferent to the man who won the war. But the wanderer returned to a
cheerful scene; for London in the last year of the Regency was nothing
if not cheerful. It was the gay arena of *Tom and Jerry*, where Vestris
danced, Grimaldi clowned, the Regent's tilbury spun through the Park,
and Almack's was a nightly galaxy where the Lieven looked sharply
about her and Lord Palmerston quadrilled with Lady Cowper. The town
quoted *Don Juan*; Corinthians in vast top-hats boxed uncomplaining
watchmen or strolled through Piccadilly in the tightest garments; there
was a pleasant buzz about the turf, the masquerade, the ring, and
Tattersall's; and the *ton* gathered nightly in opera boxes to talk its
Frenchified slang and to exchange the latest wisdom of George Brummell for the last impudence of Harriette Wilson. Somewhere beyond
the town angry provincials tramped to mass-meetings and stood in rows
to stare at banners with exciting mottoes and listen to the most disturbing speeches. There was a new stir in the air that alarmed the Cabinet
and left county magistrates bewildered. For misguided men appeared
unable to appreciate that change was anathema, that Waterloo had been
a final victory over change, that change had been exiled to St. Helena.
Why had King George fought the Revolution to a finish, if his victorious
subjects were to be gnawed by revolutionary cravings? Small wonder that
his ministers looked anxious. For their endless talk about the Sinking
Fund and currency reform concealed deeper misgivings. The Whigs
might be too strong for them. But was that the worst? Something of
graver menace stirred in the shadows behind the Whigs. No Whig
avowed it; it was remote from Ricardo's blameless calculations; and in
their wildest moments Hunt and Cobbett refrained from naming it.

But it hung on the dusty air above the lines of sullen Yorkshiremen tramping to meetings. Half seen in the grey skies over Manchester, it struck a distant spark where Shelley, writing by an Italian bay, mouthed his unforgettable

3
> "I met Murder on the way—
> He had a mask like Castlereagh—
> Very smooth he looked, yet grim;
> Seven blood-hounds followed him,"

and as his voice rose in the direct appeal of

> "Men of England, wherefore plough
> For the lords who lay ye low?
> Wherefore weave with toil and care
> The rich robes your tyrants wear?"

he broke into the marching-song of the English revolution.

Such prospects rendered Wellington a welcome recruit to the harassed Cabinet which, having won the war, found peace a trifle baffling. The
4 glowing memory of *Coningsby* recalled the event—"a Mediocrity, not without repugnance, was induced to withdraw, and the great name of Wellington supplied his place in council. The talents of the Duke, as they were then understood, were not exactly of the kind most required by the cabinet, and his colleagues were careful that he should not occupy too prominent a post; but still it was an impressive acquisition, and imparted to the ministry a semblance of renown." There was no trace as
5 yet of that pre-eminence which inspired Disraeli's later comment on "the aquiline supremacy of the Cæsars." But the Duke was a valued colleague with interests extending far beyond the somewhat limited concerns of the Ordnance Office; and it was unlikely that he would be left in peace to rearrange his Paris furniture at Apsley House, stare at King Joseph's pictures on the walls, and hang his latest purchases of the Dutch school. His Parliamentary appearances were, with one exception, slight. But foreign diplomats corresponded freely with him on the prospects of
6 European stability (eliciting the shrewd advice, *"Soyez sûr qu'en politique il n'y a rien de stable que ce qui convient aux intérêts de tout le monde; et qu'il faut regarder un peu plus loin que soi-même"*); and upon foreign policy he was treated by Liverpool and Castlereagh as a member of the inner Cabinet.

His grasp of home affairs was more intermittent, since they came before him mainly in the form of applications by local commanders for Ordnance stores with a view to maintaining public order. He had no doubts upon the subject, since nothing in his previous experience had led him to believe in the divine nature of *vox populi*. Had he not governed Ireland from a room in Dublin Castle? Few Chief Secretaries are democrats. His long professional career had been an uninterrupted war against French democracy. He was the natural enemy of Jacobins; and nothing that he had seen of the Spanish Cortes modified his distaste for democrats. His contempt for governments founded upon *"la popularité vulgaire"* was unconcealed. He watched this lamentable tendency abroad— 7
"Le grand mal en France est, qu'on croit pouvoir gouverner par la popularité, et gagner la popularité en flattant les viles passions de la classe la plus avilie et la plus corrompue de la nation." Ignoble abroad, was there the slightest reason to believe that popular appetites in England were any more exalted? He could see none; and the Duke diagnosed the objective of the democratic movement as "neither more nor less than 8 the Radical plunder of the rich towns and houses which will fall in their way." This simplified the question. If robbery and arson were in prospect, the Duke knew where he stood. It was just possible, of course, that he misjudged the movement, that it derived its impetus from something nobler than an ill-regulated impulse for destruction. England was deeply moved that autumn; for 1819 saw the first stirrings of democracy. But democracy was hardly likely to be more congenial to Wellington than arson. For the sanctity of numbers made no particular appeal to him. Less interested in the numerical support for any policy than in its merits, he was no democrat. How could he be? He had passed a lifetime in the constant endeavour to act wisely; and in almost every case wise action had been diametrically opposed to a crowd's desires. Indian administration in 1802 was a poor school for democrats; Dublin Castle was an embodied denial of democracy; and he was unlikely to absorb its tenets in the Peninsula, since generals in the field are not dependent on securing a majority of votes in favour of next season's plan of operations. Besides, the crowds of his experience had been almost invariably wrong. A London mob had hooted him for the Convention of Cintra; and as he bled the French Empire to death in the Peninsula, he

had been pursued by Opposition invectives. It was French mobs that had infected Paris with the Terror and inflicted upon Europe the long nightmare of the Empire; even now their sudden fevers were a constant menace to European peace. Spanish mobs had inspired the ignoble babble of the Cortes and deepened their country's peril in its darkest hour. And was there any ground for hope that English mobs would be wiser?

With these convictions he was single-minded in his resolve to check the English revolution. Not that he had the slightest taste for military rule. That might do well enough for France—he told Decazes as much, but added that *"il faut envisager l'armée en France sous un point de vue tout à fait différent de celui où nous envisageons l'armée dans ce pays-ci."* England, so far as he could see, was well served by its civilian institutions; and he was stout in their defence. His advice was practical. Local commanders should keep their forces concentrated and quarter them outside the towns; their health should be considered, and it would be as well to attach a field-gun to each column. The law must be administered—"Don't let us be reproached again with having omitted to carry into execution the laws. . . . Rely upon it that, in the circumstances in which we are placed, impression on either side is everything." The ship rocked a little after Peterloo; but the country came safely through the autumn of 1819, and the Duke was writing cheerfully to friends abroad that the crisis had passed. The return to firm government in the Six Acts raised his spirits. For he had been thoroughly uneasy in the intervening months before the strong hand was brought into play, writing almost feverishly to Lady Shelley that "if our wise laws allow 60,000 people to assemble to deliberate, what Government can prevent it? If they allow secret societies, having for their professed object the overthrow of the Establishments, the forging of pikes, and the training of the people to the use of them, I am sure there is no Opposition member's wife . . . who would wish the Government to overstep the law in order to prevent the people from the exercise of these valuable and useful privileges. Then every man who attends one of these meetings—whether for the purpose of deliberation or crime, or for that of secret conspiracy —thinks, and boasts, that he is performing a public duty; and it would be a sin to deprive the people of this gratification." His irony had the

319

metallic ring of an impatient man who found himself a little out of sympathy with his surroundings. But he was heartened in the autumn by a general rally of the propertied classes to the existing order. For he was convinced that the palladium of English liberty reposed mysteriously in the alliance of property with ordered freedom—a blend too subtle for its Continental imitators. As he wrote to Alava,

> "On veut notre constitution en Europe; mais ce qu'on ne veut pas c'est la   13
> sûreté, la conservation des propriétés, que chez nous en fait la base et la
> force. Observez aussi que c'est cette conservation que nous faisons marcher
> de front avec nos libertés, et qui en est le garant qui nous rend ennemie
> toute la classe soi-disant Libérale en France, dans les Pays-Bas, et en Al-
> lemagne. Pourquoi? Parce qu'ils ne veulent que voler, ils ne parlent de
> liberté qu'avec l'objet d'empocher le bien d'autrui; et ils ne peuvent pas
> souffrir un pays où la liberté est établie et fondée sur l'ordre, et sur la
> sécurité des propriétés."

His estimate of democratic motives might be unduly low; but there could be no doubt of his belief in the British compound of private property and freedom. Indeed, his faith in it was almost mystic—and there are few states of mind more perilous than a mystical attachment to any set of institutions. For his fervour inspired him ten years later to an untimely intimation that the human mind could scarcely attain such excellence as the unreformed constitution—a saying which served to precipitate Reform. His faith was stated in the first week of 1820, when he informed a foreign correspondent that "*grâces à Dieu et à nos Insti-*   14 *tutions miraculeuses*" the danger was, for the moment over, adding shrewdly that "*se qu'on appelle içi les anciens abus, ce dont les Reforma-teurs modernes voudraient se defaire et ce que nos voisins et imitateurs liberaux ne veulent pas imiter, sont les circonstances qui nous donnent un appui notable dans toutes nos difficultés.*"

That month

An old, mad, blind, despised, and dying king

faded out of his long dream at Windsor into eternity; and his kingdom passed to George IV. The change was far from sedative, since his domestic infelicity supplied a grateful country with a new form of sport. There was a carnival of indecorum; and the Queen's virtue became a party question, the Crown challenging and Whigs defending that somewhat battered fortress. Prinny appeared in the unusual *rôle* of an injured husband; and Opposition speakers, long accustomed to baiting the Prince Regent, found themselves denouncing the sovereign. Attacks upon the monarch were barely distinguishable from attacks upon the monarchy; and as the coarse fun of the Queen's divorce proceeded, Whiggery itself drifted perilously near to republicanism. The Duke's alignment was inevitable. He was a minister; he viewed his sovereign (since he was a gentleman) without enthusiasm; but he kept official company. He had spent Christmas at Stratfield Saye with the Castlereaghs, two foreign diplomats, Mr. Arbuthnot of the Treasury (and his handsome wife), and Mr. Planta of the Foreign Office. Kitty was there, of course; but an observant Austrian found the house "not very comfortable, the park ugly, the living mediocre, the whole indeed indicating the lack of sympathy existing between the Duke and his Duchess." Poor Kitty's tragedy was known already; and the Duke went his social rounds without her. Wellington went on to Woburn, where he found the Lievens and the Duke of York. Such company was scarcely likely to make him a *frondeur*.

Besides, the dark forces of disorder were more menacing than ever. There was a plot to murder the Cabinet one night at the Spanish embassy; but Life Guards cleared the street, and a constable secured a halter thoughtfully provided for hanging Castlereagh on a lamp-post. One evening someone hung about outside the Ordnance Office to stab the Duke, as he walked home across the Park to Apsley House. But that night Fitzroy Somerset happened to meet him in the street; the two men strolled along arm in arm; and the pair of friendly backs alarmed an unheroic murderer. Then there were whispers of a dark design to invade the Cabinet at dinner in Grosvenor Square, murder them all, parade Castlereagh's head on a pike down Oxford Street, attack the Bank, break open Newgate, and finish up a crowded evening after the best French precedents by proclaiming the Republic at the Mansion House. Few things are more depressing than the exaggerated deference of English revolutionaries to foreign models; but their sense of detail was creditable, since a thoughtful butcher had provided two bags for the heads (though the defence contended later that they were destined for

the gentler office of carrying off Lord Harrowby's plate). The Cabinet
was warned in time; and the Duke, true to his usual tactics, proposed
to await the attack in a favourable defensive position. Ministers, he
thought, should take pistols in to dinner with them and await develop-
ments. But his civilian colleagues found the proposal unattractive. Indeed, from the civilian point of view it had its flaws; and they preferred to dine elsewhere, while the Bow Street magistrate rounded up
Thistlewood and his associates in a back-street off Edgeware Road.

It was a dark, tumultuous time, when Castlereagh carried pocket pistols
at the dinner-table; and the Duke's distaste for democrats deepened
excusably. So, it must be confessed, did theirs for him. For the first
ecstasy of public admiration had faded before he joined the Cabinet; he
had been cheered at the opening of Parliament the year before; but in   18
the restive mood of 1820 opinion involved all persons in authority in a
common unpopularity. Its manifestations were occasionally harmless, as
when the roadmenders in Grosvenor Place shouldered their pickaxes   19
and stopped his horse on the way home to Apsley House, insisting that
he should say "God save the Queen." The Duke complied.

"Well, gentlemen," he said obligingly "since you will have it so,
God save the Queen—and may all your wives be like her."

In a year of breaking glass his windows were respected. But he was
hooted by an English crowd for the first time since 1808. For that
autumn Creevey heard them booing him in the Park, though they   20
scattered hurriedly as the Duke reined in. Not that it embittered him
against the Opposition, since he could manage a good-humoured nod
to the little Whig above the hooting mob and strolled up to him in
the Argyle Rooms with a genial "Well, Creevey; so you gave us a blast
last night. . . ." But his contempt for crowds was scored a little deeper— 21
"The mob are too contemptible to be thought about for a moment!   22
About thirty of them ran away from me in the Park this morning, because I pulled up my horse when they were *hooting*! They thought I
was going to fall upon them and give them what they deserved!" As the
unpleasing scuffle of the Queen's divorce proceeded with its long procession of preposterous and perjured foreigners, his sense of public
dignity was gravely offended. His shrewd advice at the beginning of
the affair had been to avert the danger by selecting a handsome young   23

diplomat (Fred Lamb, a favourite of Miss Harriette Wilson, struck him as being suitable) and sending him to the Queen's hangers-on abroad with the judicious warning, "You are going to lose your golden eggs— you are going to kill your goose! Once in England, and you will not be able to live with her on your present footing and retain your present allowances." But the moment passed; the monumental farce of the royal trial was mounted in the House of Lords; and when somebody objected to its effects upon the Crown's prestige, Wellington replied bitterly that the King was degraded as low as he could be already.

The constant threat to public order filled his mind. He settled routes for cavalry patrols through West End streets with the detail appropriate to the march of armies, sending six men to Portman Square, twelve more to Cavendish Square by way of Wigmore Street, and posting a vedette in Brooks Street as though Soult and all his men had been expected from the direction of Park Lane; and when the Guards alarmed them all that summer with dangerous symptoms of mutiny, his common-sense evolved the first proposal of a separate police-force. Not that he had become a frozen pillar of reaction. For he was quite prepared to recognise inevitable changes, insisting that the Spaniards could not hope to recover their rebellious colonies—"One would suppose that the reconquest of their colonies by force of arms would be out of the question even to them . . . Considering that their colonies must now be considered as lost. . . ." He was no less positive upon a policy of non-interference in Spain itself, adducing the whole course of the Penin-sular War as evidence that Spain would never tolerate foreign inter-vention, and adding generously that "this result of the war may in part be attributed to the operations of the Allied Armies in the Peninsula; but those would form a very erroneous notion of the fact who should not attribute a fair proportion of it to the effects of the enmity of the people of Spain." Even the settlement of 1815 seemed to lose something of its sanctity for him at times, since he confessed one night at Almack's that he was beginning to doubt how long the restored dynasties would last; though when Naples rose, he urged the Austrians to act promptly, as they could do with 80,000 men now what they might fail to do with 200,000 later. For he had a constitutional distaste for revolutions.

He saw a good deal of the Lievans. It was a time when London society seemed to be full of foreigners; Allies abounded in all directions; Esterhazy and Palmella were seen everywhere; Alava told his stories; and tame cossacks chattered in opera boxes. The Duke met the Lievens everywhere, and seemed to find the unwearied Dorothea agreeable. There was no accounting for her triumphs, since a meagre throat surmounted by an indifferent profile formed an inadequate equipment, and malicious rhymesters were inclined to dwell upon her accessories:

> *"Des broderies, des bouderies,*
> *Des garnitures—comme quatre—*
> *Voilà l'Ambassadrice à la façon de Barbarie."*

30

But there was no denying her success; for those curls were shaken at every magnifico in Europe; Metternich himself succumbed at Aix-la-Chapelle; and lively malice termed her latest child "*l'enfant du Congrès.*" This *vivandière* of diplomacy set her snares for Wellington; and he yielded so far as to act in country-house charades with her. Indeed, his lifelong renunciation of musical performances were momentarily relaxed, when she played the latest waltzes on the pianoforte; for the Duke accompanied her on the blameless triangle. He talked freely to her and (greatest test of all) answered politely when she asked him which of his battles he liked best.

31
32

33

Not that he lived entirely in a world of foreigners. For he had his English friends. Lady Shelley, home from her travels, conversed with him at evening parties and found him a little scared by thoughts of the old age of Marlborough. They rode together in the Green Park, where he passed an hour most afternoons between office and the House of Lords; she dined at Apsley House, where she found Caroline Lamb and Mrs. Arbuthnot, and they saw all his treasures. She loved to hear him talk; his friendship was discreet; and they never knew what dreadful things "my husband's young kinsman, Percy Shelley, who seems disposed to become a poet" was writing about the Government. The great day arrived when he came to stay with them in the country. Her devotion had roused the countryside, and forty mounted farmers rode beside his carriage; they took out the horses and dragged it up the hill; and as his hostess heard the cheers, she very nearly fainted. But the Duke's smile revived her; even her nervous headache vanished; and she dis-

34

35

36

charged her social duties. He was quite wonderful at dinner, scrawling a plan of Toulouse upon a scrap of paper (carefully preserved) and sketching Orthez on the knee of his evening breeches (which were not available as a souvenir) "with an eagerness and intentness which were quite delightful." She showed him a French account, which he dismissed as "all a lie. The French were much superior to us in force." (His enemies, it may be observed, began about this time to shew a striking tendency to grow in numbers when he discussed his battles.) They talked till midnight, and he entertained them with a full description of the new breakwater at Plymouth and its dimensions. At breakfast the next morning he was quite delightful with her children; and everything was going *à merveille*. Then they went off to shoot, and Lady Shelley breathed again. Not that she breathed for long; for as a marksman the Duke was anything but commonplace. The terror of his country's foes, he terrified her little girl by letting off his gun in all directions. "What's this, Fanny?" cried Lady Shelley. "Fear in the presence of the Lord of Waterloo! Fie! Stand close behind the Duke of Wellington: he will protect you." Indeed, it was the safest place.

He shot a dog, then a keeper, and finally an aged cottager who had been rash enough to do her washing near an open window.

"I'm wounded, Milady," cried his victim.

"My good woman," she replied, "this ought to be the proudest moment of your life. You have had the distinction of being shot by the great Duke of Wellington!"

An embarrassed Duke assisted her sense of history with a guinea. But she was not his only bag, since he positively shot a pheasant which his pious hostess had stuffed and added to the museum of Wellingtoniana in her dressing-room, where it stared glassily down upon the coffee-cup which he had used before Waterloo and the chair on which he dined with her in 1814.

37   They shared a rather schoolgirl joke about Mrs. Arbuthnot and her dominion over him, giggling together over "*La Tyranna*" and her uncertain temper, and keeping up the agreeable legend that he lived in abject terror of her and was under the necessity of seizing favourable opportunities to get her leave to visit Lady Shelley. The Duke vastly enjoyed his mythical subordination and was almost kittenish—"I have

taken advantage of a favourable moment and have obtained *permission.
. . . When the cat's away the mice go and play*, and as she is at her
brother's in Lincolnshire, and at her mother's, I have taken leave to ask
you to Stratfield Saye. . . ." So Mrs. Arbuthnot's leave, not Kitty's, was
the requisite. Kitty wrote dutifully, sending Lady Shelley news about
her boys and farmyard fatalities, and was "quite sorry we are deprived
of your company." But Mrs. Arbuthnot played her part according to
their standing joke, writing to Frances Shelley in her most commanding
tones that "the slave (poor creature!) has asked my leave to invite you
to dinner next Saturday, and, in order to bribe me into compliance, has
invited me to meet you and keep watch, in order to prevent any attacks
being made upon my legitimate authority. I have been very magnanimous
about it, and I beg you will return me your best thanks. I have given
permission. . . ." It was a mild diversion; and the Duke supported his
rôle admirably with nervous bulletins about his tyrant's moods. Other
news sometimes crept in; his shooting was improving; Charterhouse was
a better school than Eton (strenuously denied by Kitty); he had known
so many instances of boys going through Eton without learning anything;
Free Trade in 1821 would mean free, irretrievable ruin; Buonaparte was
printing lies about Waterloo; but "supposing I *was* surprised: I won the
battle; and what could you have had more even if I had not been
surprised?"

They prattled pleasantly enough, as he went his rounds among the
country houses. Once he was near his mother's old friends at Llangollen,
but not near enough to call, though he sent a charming note. House-
parties and official papers filled his life; and he still had leisure sometimes to give sittings to an artist. Lawrence painted him that year for
Robert Peel's collection of notabilities, and he sat without undue protest.
For he was not overwhelmed with business, though he took his position
in public life seriously enough. He was, he knew he was more than
Master-General of the Ordnance with a seat in the Cabinet. For he was
the Duke of Wellington; and when the King displayed an awkward
tendency to dismiss the Government, the Duke favoured him with a
long memorandum of personal advice. He had been accustomed to deal
with Continental kings and emperors, as someone said of him in Paris,

"*de Couronne à Couronne*"; and having managed Louis and Alexander as equals, why should he shrink from George IV?

Politics were still lively in 1821, though the ferment was dying down. The ground-swell of revolution, which had menaced 1819, was subsiding now. But there were still breakers on the surface. For one evening early in the year, when the King risked himself at Drury Lane, a disrespectful playgoer in the gallery addressed the royal box with the stentorian enquiry, "Where's your wife, Georgy?" But a loyal audience sang *Rule Britannia* and positively rendered *God Save the King* three times. The crowds outside the theatre were immense. A slightly officious loyalist insisted upon making a lane for Wellington, returned into the crowd, performed the same kind of office for Lord Palmerton, felt in his fob, and then made the disastrous discovery that his seals were missing. As he had made four journeys through a crowd within five minutes' walk of Seven Dials, this was not surprising. But he appeared to think that his loss established some claim upon the Duke. The Duke, with slightly chilling courtesy, disabused him of the notion. Admitting that he perfectly recollected the incident, he pointed out that "this service, if it can be so called, was purely voluntary on the part of this gentleman. The Duke is as well able as any other man to make his way through a crowd even if there existed any disposition to impede his progress, which did not appear, and therefore the assistance of this gentleman was not necessary; and, moreover, the Duke's footman attended him." This was unkind; although the next paragraph expressed his grateful thanks for the stranger's courtesy. His sole objection was to the resulting claim for compensation, which he met with a denial of liability that would have done credit to a solicitor, pointing out that the loss was not discovered until after the journey with Lord Palmerston and, alternatively, that even if it had been suffered on his journey with the Duke, the journey was itself wholly superfluous—*volenti*, in fact, *non fit injuria*. But the Duke did not rest wholly upon his Common Law rights; for as the claimant "may be a gentleman in circumstances not able to bear the expense of such a loss, and as the Duke certainly considered his conduct towards him as very polite, the Duke feels no objection to assist him to replace the loss he has sustained," adding the excellent advice "in future to omit to render these acts of unsolicited and unnecessary politeness unless he should be in a situation to bear the probable or possible consequences." The whole effect, it must be confessed, was chilling; and the result upon his unknown benefactor's politics remains unknown. How long did he remain a Tory? Or did he go straight home, stopping on the way to buy a pike, and join a secret society? Yet Wellington had granted his request for compensation. Only the kindness had been done, as usual, a trifle gruffly. For the Duke had been at pains not to create a precedent. It was a wise precaution, since, after all, he passed his life in crowds; he had numerous admirers; and if it were known that he was willing to replace all missing jewellery, where would it end?

The year wore on with preparations for the Coronation, and the King plunged with gusto into the details of that sartorial apotheosis. His ministers struggled with the unholy forces of economics and the more sanctified obstacle provided by the claims of Roman Catholics to citizenship. The Duke appeared to hold a somewhat Dublin Castle view. In former days he used to tell the Duke of Richmond that "it was nonsense to talk of the Church and State being in danger; English influence and connection were in danger if the Catholic Emancipation were ever carried." But he had spoken on the question in the House of Lords in 1819, 43 arguing with simple-minded emphasis that the whole question turned upon how far the Protestant Church could be safeguarded in Ireland, and that in view of the fact that it had been established "at the point of the sword and by means of confiscations," the Roman Catholics were quite certain to be inspired "by the remembrance of the events to which I have alluded and the idea of unmerited and mutual suffering." These were generous admissions. But the Duke's conclusion, though he appeared to realise the whole tragedy of Ireland, was that it was wholly unsafe to leave the future of Protestantism in the hands of men who had passed through such fires. For Protestantism must, in his view, come first. Not that he was a bigot, since he declined to become an Orangeman 44 upon the ground that Roman Catholics were excluded and that, their faith apart, he had always found them loyal subjects. Besides, that year he began to press Lord Liverpool to take Canning back into the Cabinet; 45 and Canning's views on that and other questions were more advanced. The Duke discerned a useful colleague, though his own convictions did not incline him further towards respect for democracy, since he shocked politicians in 1821 by his blunt statement that, after getting 9,000 signatures to a petition, it was superfluous "to go through the farce of a county meeting." The Whigs were deeply pained; but as he regarded it as a national calamity to "give up the Government to the Whigs and Radicals, or, in other words, the country in all its relations to irretrievable ruin," he did not greatly care. This was a very different tone from his non-partisan acceptance of office three years before. But the disorders of 1819, followed by the addiction of democrats in 1820 to the meaner forms of murder, had changed his views; and he was a Tory now.

One day that spring a lonely, dying man was making his will seven thousand miles away. He left 10,000 francs to the *sous-officier* Cantillon, acquitted by a French jury on a charge of attempting to murder Wellington three years before: the Duke had always been convinced that Napoleon was not a gentleman. But Providence designed one of its neatest repartees. For at his funeral (he died within the month) the battle-honours on the colours dipped at the Emperor's grave-side were "Talavera" and "Pyrenees": the last word, one feels, was Wellington's. The news came to London in the summer days when the town was buzzing with the Coronation. The great day arrived at last; and Wellington fitted on his coronet, while Benjamin Robert Haydon hurried round London in an ecstasy of patriotism borrowing the items of his Court suit. The Abbey was a sea of ermine, swayed by the stately tides of the Coronation Service; although the streets outside witnessed a slight, but farcical, recrudescence of the Queen. Westminster Hall moved Haydon to a page of perfect prose. The royal epiphany was comparable to the sun's—"There are indications which announce the luminary's approach; a streak of light—the tipping of a cloud—the singing of the lark—the brilliance of the sky, till the cloud edges get brighter and brighter, and he rises majestically into the heavens." Cast for this splendid *rôle*, George IV enraptured his beholder—"A whisper of mystery turns all eyes to the throne. . . . Then three or four of high rank appear from behind the throne; an interval is left; the crowds scarce breathe. Something rustles, and a being buried in satin, feathers, and diamonds rolls gracefully into his seat. The room rises with a sort of feathered, silken thunder. . . . As he looked towards the peeresses and foreign ambassadors he shewed like some gorgeous bird of the East." Wellington, in his brightest plumage, figured in this ornamental aviary. As the banquet opened, he walked down the Hall in his coronet, cheered by the Guards, and returned on horseback. He rode up to the throne and (oh, miracle) backed his horse to the door and out of it. Next he was seen beside the armoured figure of the King's Champion. He saw a good deal of the King that summer, since he was commanded to go with him   48 as far as Brussels, when he went abroad. Privileged to escort his sovereign to Waterloo, the Duke explained the action; and the lucidity of his explanations doubtless contributed to the King's lifelong belief that he had fought himself, though Wellington recalled that "His Majesty took it very coolly; indeed, never asked me a single question, nor said one word, till I showed him where Lord Anglesey's leg was buried, and then he burst into tears."

The year went out upon an increase of Irish anxieties; and early in 1822 they had a notion of sending him to Dublin as Lord-Lieutenant. But his reply was shrewd—"I am ready to go anywhere you please, but   49 remember my going will attract notice not only in England but in Europe. Take care that you don't let off your great gun against a sparrow! What is it you want me to do for you? If you want me to put down *the row*, I will do that easily enough; but if afterwards I am merely to continue the divided system—a Lord-Lieutenant one way and a Secretary the other—I tell you fairly I don't expect any good from it." So Richard went instead. He had subsided now into the shadow of his junior, murmuring to Wyatt, the architect, "Aye! Arthur is a much cleverer fellow than I am, you may depend upon it." Was there a touch of irony? If so, it might be forgiven; for Arthur had passed him in the race. He was the greatest Wellesley of them all, with Richard's place as head of the family, the dukedom Richard might have had, and even Richard's house at Hyde Park Corner; and now Richard went to the Viceregal Lodge because Arthur would not go. It is a slightly melancholy part to play Quintus Cicero.

Not that Arthur was devoid of opinions upon Irish matters. He ex-   pressed a healthy appetite for Coercion in the House of Lords, though   50 he was equally emphatic on the dereliction of absentee landlords, who ought to have "gone over to look at their properties instead of *brawling*   51

330

GEORGE IV WITH THE DUKE OF WELLINGTON ON THE FIELD OF WATERLOO, 1821

From a drawing by Sir Robert Ker Porter, in the author's possession.

and *balling* in London. . . . A population of seven millions, increasing in an immense proportion, without employment, . . . getting in fact nothing for the produce of their country . . . appears to be a dangerous phenomenon in political economy. I believe we have not yet seen the last call of the Irish population on the charity of their English countrymen; and we shall yet have something more to do for them than give charity balls and brawl upon distress. We want in Ireland the influence of manners as well as laws. How we are to get the former in the absence of nearly all the landed proprietors is more than I can tell." This was sensible; and it shewed a laudable desire to do something more with Ireland than repress it. Other problems faced them, as the summer months of 1822 stole by—resurgent Greece, insurgent Mexico, a restless mood in Italy, Spain ringing with Riego's hymn, and the ferment of revolution working wherever Metternich turned his uneasy eye. There was another Conference in prospect. For the perambulating Areopagus was to meet at Vienna in the autumn and disolve these menaces by the magic of collective wisdom. Castlereagh (he was Lord Londonderry now) was busy on his own Instructions; and no clouds as yet obscured that "splendid summit of bright and polished frost which, like the travellers
52   in Switzerland, we all admire; but no one can hope, and few would wish to reach." The Duke took delivery of Wilkie's pictures, ordered six years before and now astonishing the Academy with the diversity and
53   liveliness of its Chelsea pensioners. The painter asked £1,260; and as the Duke counted out the notes himself, Wilkie suggested that a cheque might be more convenient.

"Do you think," replied his patron, "I like Coutts' clerks always to know how foolishly I spend my money?"

That summer the Park wall was breached not far from Apsley House;
54   a shrouded figure trundled through; workmen were busy on the mound across the road; and on the anniversary of Waterloo "Achilles" was unveiled just outside his library windows. Midsummer passed; and the candles on Castlereagh's table burned low, as the bowed figure wrote and wrote his inexhaustible despatches, conjuring an ordered world out of the tumult of 1822. The burden weighed him down; and the dying light flickered suddenly. For at his farewell audience before leaving
55   for the Continent he scared the King by talking wildly; his mind was

an unhappy whirl of plots; he started at chance words; and when the Duke observed it, he warned him with terrible lucidity. The two men were alone. Wellington looked into the white face of Castlereagh and spoke.

"From what you have said, I am bound to warn you that you cannot   56 be in your right mind."

This must be the truth. The Duke would not deceive him. The unhappy man covered his tortured face and answered from the sofa.

"Since you say so, I fear it must be so."

Castlereagh was sobbing bitterly. Wellington offered kindly to stay with him; but he declined, since the world must not suspect. The Duke warned the doctors—those sagacious doctors whose sole specific was to bleed and bleed. But Castlereagh escaped them all one summer morning, clutching a little knife. A gloating mob outside the abbey cheered his coffin (the mourners took it to be a cheer for Wellington, since crowds cheered   57 him still); and Lord Byron exclaimed with his customary felicity,

> "So *He* has cut his throat at last!—He! Who?
> The man who cut his country's long ago."

But Wellington was deeply grieved; for he had lost his oldest friend in politics.

II

THE age of Castlereagh was over. Who was to succeed him at the Foreign Office? But there was a more immediate question. Who was to take his place at the impending Conference? They settled that within a week. For Wellington received the King's command to attend it, and he was writing to assure Metternich *"de ma bonne volonté, et de mon zèle pour consolider l'alliance générale, et le système de l'Europe."* The choice was natural, since the Duke was now the sole survivor of the diplomatic campaigns of Vienna, Paris, and Aix-la-Chapelle. Besides, he knew everyone in Europe, and everyone knew him; and Europe, it was to be hoped, had retained its habit of attending to the Duke.

But the main problem still confronted them. Who was to take the Foreign Office? The choice was difficult, since it was complicated by Parliamentary considerations. For the Government was lamentably weak in the House of Commons, and it was vital to reinforce the Treasury Bench, where Mr. Peel, Home Secretary at thirty-four, withstood the nightly onslaught of the Whigs almost unaided. If they promoted Peel to lead the House, were his lieutenants adequate? The best was Palmerston; and Palmerston, in the thirteenth year of his uneventful tenure of the War Department, was scarcely an exciting figure. He had been introducing Army estimates since 1809; he wrote a sound official letter; his defence of flogging was an annual event; and he had earned from Mr. Croker the doubtful compliment of being judged "as powerful in intellect as Robinson, and much more to be relied on in readiness and nerve." But he was no Rupert of debate; and, Palmerston apart, the rest was silence. For ability in its more glaring forms was hardly countenanced in Lord Liverpool's administration. There was one possibility, since the first orator in England was Canning; and Canning was at Liverpool, waiting for his passage to India as Governor-General. It had been a strange career. The favourite disciple, as he liked to think, of Pitt, he had proved a sad embarrassment to Pitt's successors. For he was highly unaccountable. A splendid flourish had proclaimed that his

political allegiance lay buried in Pitt's grave; and it was undeniable that   3
his loyalty resided in no very accessible spot. His course had always been
uncertain. Resigning on a deadly feud (and an exchange of pistol-shots)
with Castlereagh in 1810, he had hung insecurely in the Parliamentary
firmament, until he dropped suddenly like an erratic meteor towards
the west. For in 1814 he demobilised his few supporters and departed to
the British embassy at Lisbon, content apparently to serve Castlereagh
as an official subordinate at an augmented salary of £14,400. Then he
returned, rejoined the Cabinet, and administered Indian affairs until
his second resignation—this time upon the treatment of Queen Caroline.
After an interlude he had accepted the Governor-Generalship of India,
consenting, it would seem, to abandon his political ambitions for that
opulence which is the last refuge of disappointed politicians. His disappointment was not surprising, since every avenue was closed to
Canning in 1822. The King could not forgive his attitude of chivalry
towards the Queen, even professing to regard him as her accepted lover;
the Whigs bore too many scars of his corrosive wit; and Tories sar-
donically wished him "very well whatever part of the world he might   4
go to." This was a melancholy harvest to reap at fifty-two; and that
summer Canning waited disconsolately for his passage to the East.

   The scene was changed suddenly by the tragedy at Cray; and he
was waiting now for Castlereagh's succession. He would take nothing
less; his mind was quite made up; it must be "the whole heritage"—   5
the Foreign Office with the leadership of the House of Commons—
or nothing. Embarrassed Tories hoped to see Peel lead the Commons
and the Duke at the Foreign Office. But the Duke had other views.   6
For he had favoured Canning's readmission to the Cabinet since 1821,
although it was not easy for him to control the situation now, since   7
he was seriously indisposed. A light-hearted aurist, in a bold attempt
to cure his ear-ache, had inserted caustic in the ear, destroyed its hear-   8
ing, and very nearly destroyed his patient at the same time—a notable
achievement for British medicine, which already numbered Castlereagh
among its victims for the year. But the King waited on the Duke's
opinion. Each found the other slightly trying; for the King's exuberance
jarred on the Duke, and the Duke was apt to differ from George IV on
military topics, forcing his sovereign to the painful avowal that "it is not   9

for me to dispute on such a subject with your Grace." But the King knew a loyal adviser, and the Duke knew his duty. Wellington was still in
10 bed; but a royal emissary was assiduous at his bedside, and the King even deferred his interview with the Prime Minister until he knew the Duke's opinion. Wellington expressed it plainly; Canning, he felt, was a necessary reinforcement and would prove a loyal minister in spite of his eccentric views upon the Roman Catholic question. As to the King's personal objections, did not the sovereign's honour consist in doing acts of mercy? This was the height of tact; and the King's self-esteem expanded in the sunshine of conscious virtue. He positively revelled in his own magnanimity. Indeed, the Duke had almost over-done it; since the King, borrowing his line from Wellington, sum-
11 moned Canning to office with an unduly gracious intimation that "the King is aware that the brightest ornament of his crown is the power of extending grace and favour to a subject who may have incurred his displeasure." This was too much for Canning, who was narrowly re-strained by Wellington from making a reply. But the Duke, always practical, advised him that "as he intended to accept, he had better take no further notice of the paper." The King and Canning were not his only charges, since his Tory colleagues were a trifle fretful, and he was even compelled to pacify Castlereagh's reproachful widow with a lengthy argument, in which he urged shrewdly that "nothing can be so erroneous as to place any individual of great activity and talents in a situation in which there is no scope for his activity, and in which he must feel that his talents are thrown away. His views must always be directed to dis-turb rather than to preserve the existing order of things, in order that out of a new arrangement he may find himself in a position better suited to him." This danger was averted now; Canning was safely in-stalled as Castlereagh's successor; and the Prime Minister wrote grate-fully that without Wellington's assistance "it never might have been brought to such a result."

2

Within a fortnight he was on the Continent, bound for Vienna. He stopped in Paris to confer with French ministers, resumed his

journey, and plunged into the latest Congress. For a melancholy irony
compelled Mr. Canning, who had once gleefully announced that "we
shall have no more congresses, thank God!" to direct British policy in   12
a Congress. But events had an unpleasant trick of following a course
precisely opposite to that laid down for them by Mr. Canning. The
business before the Congress was highly variegated—the Greek insurrection, Spanish colonies, the Austrians in Italy, and an awkward
tendency on the part of Russia to claim the coast of British Columbia.
They were to meet at Vienna; but the Congress was transferred to Verona,
and Byron welcomed them to Italy with elaborate raillery at

> "Proud Wellington, with eagle beak so curl'd,   13
> That nose, the hook where he suspends the world!
> And Waterloo—and trade—and—(hush! not yet
> A syllable of imports or of debt)—
> And ne'er (enough) lamented Castlereagh,
> Whose penknife slit a goose-quill t'other day—
> And 'pilots who have weathered every storm,'—
> (But, no, not even for rhyme's sake name Reform).

.   .   .   .   .

> "Strange sight this Congress! destined to unite
> All that's incongruous, all that's opposite.
> I speak not of the sovereigns—they're alike,
> As common coin as ever mint could strike;
> But those who sway the puppets, pull the strings,
> Have more of motley than their kings.
> Jews, authors, generals, charlatans, combine,
> While Europe wonders at the vast design:
> There Metternich, power's foremost parasite,
> Cajoles; there Wellington forgets to fight;
> There Chateaubriand forms new books of martyrs;
> And subtle Gauls intrigue for stupid Tartars;
> There Montmorenci. . . ."

The French delegate played a leading part. For the chief item on
the agenda was Spain, where the French were shewing awkward signs
of intervening in a civil war. There was no doubt of British views upon
foreign intervention; the Duke had made them clear to Castlereagh six
months before; Castlereagh concurred in his disapproval; and Canning   14
followed suit after knocking impressively at the open door and instruct-
ing Wellington "frankly and peremptorily to declare, that to any such   15

interference, come what may, his Majesty will not be a party." There
was no difference between them, and the Duke did not feel the slightest
difficulty in conveying that "we had insuperable objections to interfere
in the internal concerns of any country" and, more formally, that "to
animadvert upon the internal transactions of an independent State, unless
such transactions affect the essential interests of his Majesty's subjects,
is inconsistent with those principles on which his Majesty has invariably
acted in all questions relating to the internal concerns of other countries;
that such animadversions, if made, must involve his Majesty in serious
responsibility if they should produce any effect, and must irritate if
they should not." The doctrine of non-intervention in Spain was quite
congenial to Wellington, since he had argued it at length before Canning
came to the Foreign Office; and now he argued it once more before
a highly unsympathetic audience of foreign diplomats. The French were
spoiling for a fight against a paralytic enemy; and the Czar was haunted
by a disturbing dream of marching Russian armies across Europe in the
sacred name of counter-revolution. The Duke, who diagnosed him
shrewdly—"The Emperor would have no objection to a war, but it
must be on a stage on which he would have the eyes of all Europe upon
him and the applause of the world"—laboured steadily to damp the universal ardour in a modest hope "that we shall get through these difficulties
in a creditable manner, and that we may be able to maintain the
peace of the world." He had no difficulty in enlisting Austrian apprehensions of the Russian design; and the danger of a general conflagra-
tion was averted by his downright dissociation of Great Britain from
common action at Madrid, which immobilised the Alliance. This disposed of Alexander's vision of 150,000 Russians tramping through Austria
to Milan *en route* for the Pyrenees. But the uneasy possibility remained
that France might intervene alone. Wellington had preached reason on
his way through Paris; but when Villèle disclosed the military details of
the French plan for invading Spain, he had not refrained from practical
comments. It was his vanity, as a sharp woman guessed, to know "how
to do everything, and to do it better than anyone else." The problem
of invading Spain interested him professionally. After all, he was the
greatest living expert on Peninsular wars; and he could scarcely be
expected to pass by in silence such alluring topics as the line of the

Ebro and the military effects of occupying Madrid. Always a strong
believer in the virtues of prompt action for the suppression of revolutions
(had he not prescribed it unofficially in the case of Naples two years
before?), he was perfectly convinced that "the French will meet with
no more resistance in marching to Madrid than he does in going to the
Ordnance Office." But it scarcely follows that he told them so. There is
no evidence that Wellington encouraged them to try the experiment and
that, as a learned fantasy suggests, he was deliberately false to Canning's
policy by privately inciting France to intervene in Spain. Such treachery
was not in his manner. Besides, he had just been at considerable pains
to instal Canning at the Foreign Office; and, in any case, the policy of
opposing intervention in Spain was Wellington's as well as Canning's.
In reality he laboured to avert the war; and if he failed, at least he had
succeeded in preventing a general explosion.

On minor matters he was still more successful. Russia was checked
in North America; Austria was pressed discreetly to repay war-time
loans; and he made some progress with the abolition of the slave trade.
Upon the question of the Spanish colonies he served Canning as a
loyal mouthpiece—"I shall of course follow what is laid down in your
despatch." But he followed it with evident distaste, finding the rebels
uncongenial company and deploring undue haste—"I know that we must
at last recognise all these governments, but I would recognise them when
necessary, and only when really constituted and become powers, instead
of seeking for reasons for recognizing them, and by recognizing them
constitute them." This was rational; and he restated his position—"I
consider it a point of honour that we should not be in a hurry to recognise that independence, and that the measure should be forced upon us
by circumstances rather than we should seek for occasions to adopt it. . . .
I therefore have always been for going as far as was necessary, and
never further." Canning recognised his fairness in a final tribute to his
work at Verona—"You have done, in respect to that question (of
Spanish America), all that could be desired; and upon the slave trade,
more than could have been expected."

It had been a strange affair. The Congress of Verona with its *parterre
de rois*—two emperors, three kings, a cardinal, three grand-dukes, twenty
ambassadors, twelve ministers, and three foreign secretaries—had been

the last parade of a vanishing Europe, where Metternich whispered his sharp asides and the Duke moved in splendid profile through a lane of bowing gentlemen in stars. They had their relaxations too. There was the great Roman amphitheatre for their plays, and for lighter entertainment Dorothea Lieven and the Récamier with her echoes of Directoire *salons* and the distant days when Josephine was gay and General Bona-
27 parte an awkward lover. A stranger echo hung about a stout and smiling archduchess, where Marie Louise, Duchess of Parma, played écarté with Wellington. As the cards fell between them, they settled their accounts in *napoléons*; and when he dined with her, she told the Duke how sorry she was that she had failed to get his favourite roast mutton for him. For Napoleon's widow studied Wellington's tastes. He saw something of her son as well, finding him "a fine lad, educated just like the archdukes"; and the Duke told someone later that "he was very civil to me." Then he was off to Paris by way of Milan and Lyon,
28 having loyally applied the policy which enabled Canning to write triumphantly "For 'Alliance' read 'England.'"
29 He had business in Paris, where he still hoped to check the French. Canning instructed him to offer British mediation; the Duke, fearing a rebuff in Paris, delayed the offer; Canning insisted; and the Duke predicted gloomily that "the government have mistaken this case, and that the mediation will be rejected on the ground on which it was rejected at Verona." The Duke was right; and Canning's insistence got nothing more for his country than "a parting blow." But Wellington had done his duty in Paris. Indeed, he had done more, since Lady Shelley had entrusted him with an important mission concerning a blouse. Less arduous than Mr. Canning's, he discharged it to a nicety and could
30 report in triumph that "your blouse goes to you by the stage tomorrow. But mind! You are to wear it the first time you dine with me, with the Tiranna!" He took the road again and was at Apsley House for Christmas, 1822.

3

The new year opened pleasantly enough with house-parties at Stratfield Saye. The Duke of York came to shoot with the lugubrious Leopold;

he asked the Shelleys; but their meeting was delayed, since a week later
he was still pressing her to come with the Liverpools and Madame Lieven   31
—and "mind you bring the blouse!"—and when Neumann came, he
found the Arbuthnots there with the Lievens and Prince Esterhazy. But
Spain still filled his horizon, and he loyally seconded Canning's efforts to
deter the French from intervention, even adding the unique resources
of his personal position to the exiguous armoury of the Foreign Office.
For in his character as a Grandee of Spain he sent Fitzroy Somerset to
Madrid with sedative advice. Canning struck martial attitudes (he had
already written gaily that the French tone "really stirs one's blood . . .   32
in the good old constitutional way in which France and England used
to hate and provoke each other") and flung his thunderbolts about with
a fine carelessness. He talked of his own "itch for war," made dashing
speeches in the House of Commons, increased the Navy, and laid papers
—the normal prelude of a declaration of war. In Canning's case, however, the free publication of diplomatic correspondence formed part of a
design for invoking public opinion on matters of high policy and, perhaps,
owed a little to the pardonable pride which literary men feel in their
own compositions. These proceedings were unspeakably distasteful to
the Duke, though they were still on friendly terms, Canning begging
him expansively never to stand on ceremony in volunteering comments   33
upon policy. But though Wellington defended his own action in the   34
longest speech that he had yet delivered in the House of Lords, it was
unpleasing to be dragged in Mr. Canning's foaming wake. He had misgivings now, warning Lord Liverpool that a draft of Canning's "would
go to a break up of the Alliance; and I don't believe that any of us, not   35
even Mr. Canning himself, thinks that the affairs of Europe are in such
a state that the Alliance provided in the Second Article of the Treaty of
1815 may not be necessary." Canning's pyrotechnics failed to exhilarate
him:

"We have given the Spaniards reason to believe that we should assist   36
them, and we have shaken the confidence of France in our desire of maintaining peace for her sake as well as our own. Then at home, nobody knows
what the policy of the Government is, and it will turn out at last that the
country and Parliament will declare for neutrality before the government will
have an opportunity of doing so; and it will be believed that the govern-

ment have been forced by the country to be neutral, their intentions having been to interfere in favour of Spain."

37 A series of false positions, however brilliant, was distasteful to the Duke. He disliked the promiscuous publication of official documents; and it was disconcerting to encounter the pitying regard of his Continental associates. For the French ambassador wrote patronisingly that he

38 was *"guerrier peu redoutable sur les champs de l'intrigue"*; and Metter-

39 nich, deep in Vienna, recorded with regret, *"Quel dommage que Wellington soit si craintif, lui qui a un cœur si droit et une si honnête figure!"*

So he went the round of country houses in 1823, while Canning issued his challenges. The Duke moved from Stratfield Saye to Wherstead, from Wherstead to Maresfield, on to the Pavilion, and from Beaudesert to Hatfield. It was a stately progress; and the red boxes followed him with their depressing tale of Canning's extravagances. There was no war with France; no one had ever meant to have one; and if they had, there was no time, since Spain collapsed before the French invasion with the most disconcerting suddenness and left Mr. Canning thundering in spite of

40 everything to delighted crowds about the might of England. It was far pleasanter to sit to Hayter in his cloak; for Mrs. Arbuthnot had consented to Lady Shelley having a portrait of him, "provided the picture is not painted by Sir Thomas Lawrence, and is not so good as hers." So the

41 Duke went his social rounds and made a charming offer to Alava, exiled by the turmoil of Spanish politics, of a home with him in England.

But 1824 renewed his cares. He still maintained a correspondence upon foreign affairs with Metternich and with those embassies abroad where he

42 had a brother or a friend; and early in the year he confessed to Henry Wellesley that "we are radically defective in our diplomatic head-quarters here." He disliked the hail of Blue-books, with which Canning sought

43 to captivate his countrymen; for such publications seemed to lead inevitably to the renunciation of Cabinet control of foreign policy. Mr. Canning might prefer to have his policy debated in a wider circle than the *champ clos* of Downing Street, where ageing Tories sat round the table with

20 disapproving faces; but the Duke did not. Trained in an older school, he valued secrecy—hardly for its own sake (though Madame Lieven hinted that he loved a secret), but for the greater freedom of manœuvre

which secrecy confers. He was not greatly interested in evoking cheers. Besides, he disapproved the drift of Canning's policy, writing to Metternich that "I feel as you do the *isolement* of the British government; and I am equally aware with you of the mischief which it does to us as well as to the world; probably more to the world than to us." Canning might proclaim the dissolution of the Alliance in the gloating formula, "Every nation for itself, and God for us all." But was it reasonable to expect the Duke to part from it without a pang? The Allied ministers were men with whom he had worked in close confidence since the great days of 1815. They had shared common dangers, won wars together, and settled Europe in agreement. The endless conferences that followed Waterloo had left a certain *camaraderie* among them, which Wellington could not easily forget; and, slow to make new friends, he was as slow at losing old ones. But his Continental ties were something more than personal. He had his principles, though they were less articulate than Mr. Canning's; and it was wholly inevitable that his point of view should be more European. It was scarcely possible to be a Duke in four countries and a Marshal of every Continental army, to have served two emperors and half a dozen kings in command of an international army of occupation, to make an annual tour of inspection of the new Belgian fortresses—and to retain in its perfection that insularity which was now Mr. Canning's pride. Besides, the settlement of 1815 owed so much to his work. He had won Waterloo; his diplomacy restored Louis XVIII; the peace-treaty bore his signature; the Reparations settlement was his personal achievement; and if Canning could intimate in a celebrated flourish that he had called a New World into existence, it was almost as true that Wellington had called the Old.

The two were bound to clash. Canning owed his promotion almost wholly to the Duke's intervention; but even gratitude will not enable oil to mix with water. Their views were poles apart; their methods were discordant; and what soldier relishes the sight of a civilian flourishing a sword? Viewed by the Duke, the Foreign Secretary was hasty, ill-advised, and quite unbearably dramatic; his popular appeals were most distasteful; and—the uneasy question rose in Wellington—was he quite a gentleman? These discontents found a sympathetic audience at Windsor, where his sovereign fished disconsolately in Virginia Water. He did not fish alone; for Lady Conyngham was there, and they had week-end parties at the Cottage. The life was not conspicuously gay. The King

46   breakfasted alone, the Duke with Lady Conyngham; they met at three; phaetons were at the door; the guests paired off and drove—a gentleman and lady between each spinning pair of wheels—till five; sometimes the royal drive was diversified by brandy and water at a park lodge; then dinner in the pagoda, conversation until ten, and cards till midnight.

47   But the "Cottage Coterie"—a pair of Austrians, two Lievens, and the French ambassador—was anything but favourable to Mr. Canning; and the Duke was admitted to their circle. He talked freely to them, though he was hardly a party to their drawing-room conspiracy "*de faire sauter*

48   *M. Canning*." But that autumn he involved himself in a dispute with Canning on the latter's plan of visiting Paris; Canning suspected royal intrigues and retorted sharply that "it is high time to look about me, and to beware of what Burke calls 'traps and mines.' " The Duke was not a plotter; but it was comforting to pour his views into receptive ears. He was distressed by Canning's eagerness to sanctify South

49   American revolutionaries with British recognition, pleading in vain that "considering what is passing in Ireland, and what all expect will occur in that country before long, the bad with hope, the good with apprehension and dread, we must take care not to give additional examples in these times of the encouragement of insurrection, and we must not be induced by clamour, by self-interested views, by stock-jobbing, or by faction, to give the sanction of our approbation to what are called the governments of these insurgent provinces." The analogy of Ireland haunted him: how could Dublin Castle extend a hand to Buenos

50   Ayres? He reasoned lucidly that "if you hold that the people of Colombia have been guilty of no crime, and that Bolivar is a hero and no rebel, then you ought not to prosecute O'Connell." This was logical; and in the last weeks of 1824 he carried his objections to the length of offering

51   to resign. There were struggles in the Cabinet; the King almost mutinied; but Canning got his way. Lord Liverpool was on his side, and the

52   Duke ultimately acquiesced, admitting to a foreign diplomat that he regretted having introduced Canning to the Cabinet, but that it was impossible to dismiss him. So the New World was duly conjured into being. Not that Canning's policy was a romantic gesture towards the

great open spaces, since in its later phases it was partly inspired by a legitimate anxiety to forestall the United States; "Spanish America," as he wrote gaily, "is free, and if we do not mismanage our affairs sadly she is English. The Yankees will shout in triumph, but it is they who lose most by our decision."

The Duke's skies were darkening. Madame Lieven wrote that "Mr. Canning poses as a Radical to please the populace—the other Ministers smile approvingly to keep their places. The Duke of Wellington alone is prepared to break a lance for the good cause." Ireland was full of menace, and the Roman Catholic question began to loom with unpleasant urgency. His shooting was improving, though; and he could report a bag of fourteen rabbits, a dozen hares, a brace of pheasants, and a partridge. One theme alone seemed to inspire him with no misgivings; for national defence found him as calm as ever—"I confess that I am one of those who do not much apprehend invasion. I think steam navigation has in some degree altered that question to our disadvantage. . . . But I confess that I think a solid invasion of the country . . . is out of the question." His nerves were always steady, and the soldier in him was still reassured; but as he went to Windsor for Christmas, 1824, the statesman was distinctly uneasy. For the world was full of awkward problems. Portugal was in an uproar; Byron had died at Missolonghi; and British sympathy seemed to be solicited on behalf of revolutionaries in every hemisphere. Nearer home the Irish situation increased in gravity; and the Duke corresponded copiously with Peel, who was now the guardian of public order at the Home Office. The two men drew together. Their convergence, as *Coningsby* diagnosed it, "was the sympathetic result of superior minds placed among inferior intelligences, and was, doubtless, assisted by a then mutual conviction, that the difference of age, the circumstance of sitting in different houses, and the general contrast of their previous pursuits and accomplishments, rendered personal rivalry out of the question." Besides, they both distrusted Canning. As 1825 wore on, the King surrendered to his Foreign Secretary; but his colleagues surrendered none of their misgivings.

The Duke passed the year among his customary employments. The Ordnance Office kept him busy with revetments, counterscarps, and barracks at Bermuda; he was consulted upon Indian affairs; and his

views about the Greeks were plainly expressed. "The establishment of
a new Power in Europe, which must be founded on the principles of
modern democracy, and therefore inimical to this country," filled him
with no enthusiasm. Not that he loved the Turk, admitting frankly that
"the Turkish government is so oppressive and odious to all mankind,
that we could scarcely expect to carry the country with us in a course
of policy . . . the result of which is to be to maintain by the exercise
of our power that government at Constantinople." But he viewed the
expansion of Russian influence with genuine concern. His minor interests were less absorbing. He defended spring guns in the House of
Lords for the simple reason that they checked poachers, and he favoured
Lady Shelley with a discourse on education:

> "As for John, you must impress upon his mind, first, that he is coming
> into the world at an age at which he who knows nothing will be noth-
> ing. . . .
>
> "If he means to rise in the military profession—I don't mean as high as
> I am, as that is very rare—he must be master of languages, of the mathe-
> matics, of military tactics of course, and of all the duties of an officer in all
> situations.
>
> "He will not be able to converse or write like a gentleman . . . unless
> he understands the classics; and by neglecting them, moreover, he will lose
> much gratification which the perusal of them will always afford him; and
> a great deal of professional information and instruction.
>
> "He must be master of history and geography, and the laws of his country
> and of nations. . . .
>
> "Impress all this upon his mind; and moreover tell him that there is
> nothing like never having an idle moment. . . ."

For he was still the young Colonel with a habit of private reading, who
thirty years before had filled his trunk for India with improving books,
who took his Blackstone with him and learned from Cæsar how to cross
a river.

As he sat to Hayter, the tide of his patience mounted. For portrait-painters were rapidly becoming one of the burdens of his life.
They talked; they borrowed all his clothes; and, what was worse, they
could not paint. Even Lawrence kept him standing for three hours with
folded arms, and then produced a complete travesty of his sword. This

must plainly be put right at once. The painter made excuses; but the Duke insisted.

"Do it now."

"I must go to the Princess Augusta's."

"Oh no; you must put my sword right. It is really bad."

After all, he had more experience of swords—and of portraits—than most men.

In the last days of 1825 a diversion offered itself. For Alexander died at Taganrog, and the King and Canning tentatively suggested (with profuse expressions of anxiety for the Duke's health) that he should go   61 to Russia on a special mission to the new Emperor. The prospect was uninviting, since he was far from well and the road from London to St. Petersburg in mid-winter was long. Besides, it was proposed that he should do his best to stop the Russians from going to war with Turkey in the cause of reek independence. Preventing wars was his *métier*; but this war could only be prevented if the Porte could be prevailed on to make concessions to the Greeks; and it was doubtful how far the Duke would relish being made an instrument of Greek emancipation. Madame Lieven gleefully proclaimed that his mission was "*une idée bouffonne et grande* . . . side by side with the salaam the Duke is to make should   62 he come to an understanding on the question of Greece." The ingenious Canning, she thought, would thus contrive to "compromise him and mock him at the same time—a double pleasure." But how could he refuse? "I don't see how I, who have always been preaching the doctrine of going wherever we are desired to go, who had consented   63 to go and command in Canada, could decline to accept the offer of this mission." So he announced himself "at all times ready and willing to serve your Majesty in any station" and accepted. Indeed, if Canning told the truth, he "not only accepted but *jumped* at the proposal." But   62 his alacrity is doubtful, since the world whispered that Canning would not be inconsolable if this Arctic journey proved too much for him; and the Duke seemed to share the world's misgivings. Rarely emotional, he took leave of his friends with unusual tenderness; Alava had never seen   64 him so profoundly moved; he parted from his mother with emotion; and the tears streamed down his cheeks, as he left Lady Burghersh.

4

Wellington entered upon his Russian campaign in February, 1826. The journey was to take three weeks; and to elude the minor irritants of Polish inns he adopted the ingenious expedient of a silk mattress; silk, it was hoped, would be impenetrable to invaders; and he had chosen a light material, upon which they would be more conspicuous. Such ingenuity was not unworthy of a great tactician. Besides, there was a strong element of the White Knight in the Duke's composition. A lifetime in the field will often implant a taste for minor ingenuities; for the exigencies of campaigning tend to stimulate such proclivities; and the returning veteran will sometimes carry them into the less exacting conditions of civilian life. Was he not the inventor of a patent finger-bandage, which he demonstrated incessantly? Were not his later years delighted by the dual precaution of a sword-umbrella? So the ingenuity of his travelling bed (explained with pride to Lady Shelley after his return) was quite in character.

He went by way of Berlin, where he called upon the King of Prussia and wrote to Canning five times in one day. He was frankly sceptical of his prospects of success in Russia; if the Russians chose to go to war with Turkey, he should not be able to stop them. But his major object was to localise the conflict to prevent a scuffle in the Balkans from developing into a European war. "The question of Greek and Turk is trifling in comparison"; and he was infinitely less concerned with the brutalities of Pashas and the indomitable Ypsilanti than with the major problem of European peace. As to the Greeks, he was prepared for "an arrangement short of independence." But peace must be preserved in Europe; and he agreed with Canning in believing that another Congress was the last way to preserve it. His carriage rumbled across Poland and the sad Livonian levels, and he reached St. Petersburg in the first week of March. That evening he saw Nesselrode and called upon the Emperor Nicholas on the next day. The Czar seemed eminently reasonable about the Greeks; and Wellington plunged into a vortex of diplomacy, mitigated by that Russian official hospitality which consisted of "pallid asparagus and fœtid oysters." His nights, as someone wrote, were "nothing but blow-outs for the Duke," his days all "politics and pipe-clay." Stiff Russian guardsmen in tall shakoes and tight tunics presented arms; stiffer generals raised fingers to preposterous cocked-hats; the Czar gave him a regiment of infantry on the anniversary of the Allies' entry to Paris; and he visited a stupendous girls' school, where he watched young ladies curtsey by platoons and heard twenty-five pianos in simultaneous action. He managed to survive it somehow, without even getting one of his customary colds. Indeed, the chief thing that impressed the Duke in Russia was that no one seemed to have a cold. He drafted endless protocols and spoke his mind to Nicholas, warning him "that he can fix the moment when, and the point at which the first shot will be fired; but that he may as well talk of stopping the course of the Neva as of fixing the limits of his operations if once he goes to war." The Russians listened blandly; but it is doubtful how far his presence in St. Petersburg modified their course. Indeed, he was a shade perplexed by the Byzantine complications of palace politics, confessing to his brother that "it is difficult to judge of matters here, and whether there is any Minister or not, and who is the adviser. We have some great diplomatic characters here, but I believe they are all as much in the dark as I am." He worked assiduously to avert a Russo-Turkish war or, at the worst, to localise it. That was his main objective, and he succeeded in attaining it; for there was no European war. As to the Greeks, he was already reconciled to seeing them with something short of independence; and when the persuasive Lievens represented that Russian policy was not aimed at abetting revolutionaries, but at the re-establishment of order in Greece—"a regular state of things, a hierarchical discipline"—the Duke was charmed. His pen grew busy with more drafts; and a Protocol emerged which guaranteed to Greece a qualified degree of independence under Anglo-Russian auspices. Canning was slightly rueful, since the Protocol committed England to Greek independence far beyond his original instructions to the Duke. But Wellington was three weeks distant from the Foreign Office and acted on his own discretion. Canning could have no grievance, since the Duke followed lines that were perfectly consistent with a disinterested support of Greek emancipation. Peace was preserved; the world was spared the horrors of another Congress; and a ray of hope fell across Greece. The

69

70

71

Duke was moving with the times (though his critics have preferred to think that he was unaware of what he was doing); and if the Russians rejoiced, it does not follow that British interests had been betrayed. Imperial gratitude expressed itself, as always, in terms of sables and malachite vases; and at four o'clock one April morning Wellington started for home again. He might have stayed in Russia for the coronation; but he preferred to leave. The work was over; and Peel, who had acted as his Cabinet correspondent, was pressing him not to delay his return "a single day beyond absolute necessity." Once again duty called; this time it was his duty to the Tories. For his Tory colleagues were uncomfortable without him. He travelled by Warsaw and Berlin, where he stopped long enough to receive the honour of a Prussian infantry regiment; and before the month was out, he was in Apsley House once more.

5

Wellington's Russian campaign was over. It had been a picturesque interlude, and the walls of Stratfield Saye bore traces of it in the form of innumerable engravings of high-collared autocrats, of sleighs, of snowy scenes, of angry bears, of the tall buildings of St. Petersburg. But no musical composer was ever moved to celebrate his *1812*, no painter to depict him in the snow. Yet, like Napoleon, he had returned without his army; but, unlike the Emperor, he had left home without it too.

Home was a trifle unattractive in April, 1826. Canning was high in the ascendant, and the skies were darkened by "the three C's," as Croker called them, "Corn, Currency, and Catholics." The eager Huskisson must really be restrained from committing ministers to repeal the Corn Laws. The Duke would go no further than an undertaking that they should be "fairly considered" in the next session; while the Government's nice equipoise upon the Catholic question must be maintained. That summer he found greater comfort in the past—in dining at the Admiralty with Croker and the Duke of York and recalling how the French cavalry at Waterloo in their cuirasses and jack-boots "lay sprawling and kicking like so many turned turtles," and regaling a house-party of Lord Hertford's with reminiscences of Spain and Paris and the distant days of his campaign in Denmark. But the unpleasing present still persisted; red boxes

349

followed him with their distasteful reminders of the world of 1826; and
at sight of them he grew almost peevish. Canning was worse than ever—
"a most extraordinary man. Either his mind does not seize a case ac-
curately; or he forgets the impressions which ought to be received from
what he reads, or is stated to him; or knowing and remembering the
accurate state of the case, he distorts and misrepresents facts in his instructions to his ministers with a view to entrap the consent of the Cabinet to
some principle on which he would found a new-fangled system." The
Foreign Office papers failed to circulate for Cabinet approval; and when
the British minister was suddenly withdrawn from Spain without notice
to the Cabinet, Wellington complained bitterly to the Prime Minister:

> "Here we are with a step taken which will be considered as a signal of
> war throughout Europe . . . without any one of the ministers being aware
> of the existence even of discussion.
>
> "I am certain that Mr. Canning would not consent to such a proceeding
> by any other man. There is no person who (with propriety, in my opinion)
> reserves to himself more frequently the right of judging for himself of the
> cases for which he is to be held responsible. I am certain, likewise, that you
> will admit that this is not the mode in which the business of this country
> ever has been, or can be carried on."

But Canning was incorrigible. His latest escapade was the defence of
Portugal—of Portugal lately turned constitutional and acidly described
by the Duke as "Constitutional Portugal, I mean in the modern sense
with licentious Chambers sitting in Lisbon and publishing their debates
and a licentious press." This victim of repression failed to stir his sympathies. It had been one thing to rescue decorous Braganza Portugal and
Bourbon Spain from the revolutionary legions of the French; but this
was quite another matter. However, Mr. Canning and the Cabinet
thought otherwise. A splendid declamation was pronounced in the House
of Commons—"We go to plant the Standard of England on the well-
known heights of Lisbon. Where that Standard is planted, foreign dominion shall not come . . ."—and while Mr. Canning stirred members'
pulses, the Duke conveyed the same intelligence to the Lords in nine
sentences. Even the prospect of a new war in the Peninsula failed to move
him to eloquence. For Great Britain intervened at last—in the sacred

name of non-intervention—and when a brigade sailed for the Tagus,
80 Wellington dutifully acquiesced with notes for the commanding officer
on the familiar topic of bullock-carts.

The year ended with a menace of still further change. For the Duke
of York was dying, mourned by the tearful King in the congruous la-
81 ment, "Alas! my poor brother!" He had commanded the army (with a
brief interruption due to the vivacious Mrs. Clarke) since the distant
days when Arthur Wesley was a Colonel; and his broad figure formed
an unchanging part of the architecture of the Horse Guards. He died in
the first week of 1827, and the world waited for a new Commander-in-
Chief. There was one soldier with transcendent claims. But Peel warned
the Duke that his sovereign contemplated taking the command in person. Was it not a royal hallucination that he had charged with the heavy
cavalry at Salamanca? Besides, the post-war exercises of the British army
had been mainly sartorial; and the King played a splendid part in military tailoring. Wellington received the warning with a bitter intimation
that he had been promised the succession, but that he always viewed the
82 royal promise, "like many others, as so many empty and unmeaning
words and phrases." The fancy passed, however; and Wellington was
83 duly installed as Commander-in-Chief, taking command in a General
Order consisting of a single sentence.

Now there could be no more promotion. For he had reached the very
summit of his profession. How could he rise further? There were still
politics, of course; in civil life he was no more than a mere minister;
84 but if a vacancy occurred, could a Commander-in-Chief hope to become
Prime Minister? Croker, at any rate, thought not; the way, he felt, was
clear for Canning now. The vacancy occurred within a month. For the
Prime Minister collapsed in February; and the age, the interminable age
of Liverpool was over.

6

Who was to be Prime Minister? There was an eager scurry; and the
Duke spoke his mind at the breakfast-table at Apsley House. The pres-
84 ent Government, he said, must be kept together for everybody's sakes—
"After them comes chaos." Croker agreed, adding that it would all have

been so simple if he had not become Commander-in-Chief, but that put him out of the question as Prime Minister.

"Yes, yes, I am in my proper place, in the place to which I was destined by my trade. I am a soldier, and I am in my place at the head of the army, as the Chancellor, who is a lawyer, is in his place on the woolsack. We have each of us a trade, and are in our proper position when we are exercising it."

This was admirable; but who was to be Prime Minister? Canning felt no uncertainties: his moment had arrived. But even Canning required colleagues; and his Tory colleagues were frankly hostile to the notion of a Canning administration. For, all else apart, his Catholic opinions scared them. They scared the Duke as well, who could not bear his methods at the Foreign Office and confessed to Arbuthnot (who passed it on to Peel) that he detected "much of trickery; he sees that the sons and relations of our most vehement opponents are taken into employ; and he cannot divest himself of the idea that, directly or indirectly, there has been an understanding with some of the leaders of the Opposition." If Canning was in league with the Whigs, it was quite impossible for the Duke to serve under him. At any rate, he did not mean to. Four years of Canning had made him a Tory of the strictest sect. But he played scrupulously fair; and when the King summoned him to Brighton, Wellington sent word that "he had nothing to say to him, and that it would not be fair to his colleagues that he should see the King at such a moment." But his own opinions were developing. For the ardent Protestants besieged him with suggestions that he should manœuvre Canning out of the new Cabinet; the Duke, however, favouring a continuance of the *status quo*, repelled them. They even proposed that he should take the Premiership himself; but Wellington put by the crown, though he confessed that "circumstances might be conceived under which it would be his duty to accept the situation if he was called upon by the King to do so." His views inclined, however, to the substitution of Mr. Robinson as Prime Minister; Canning, he thought, would be content to serve under Mr. Robinson. Canning, however, was indisposed to become the major ornament of a Robinson administration, suspecting that "the Protestant part of the Government wished to have me as *cheap* as possible, to task me to the utmost for their support in the House of Commons and in the

Foreign Office . . . but to repress all higher aspirations as strictly as if I were of another species than their Lordships." Perhaps he was.

The tension lasted from mid-February to the second week of April. London buzzed with rumours; Taper and Tadpole were on tip-toe; and Mr. Croker lived in an ecstasy of exclusive information. But perhaps George IV enjoyed this interlude more than any of his subjects, except when agitated Tory magnates addressed him in the most unbecoming terms. For the King presided over the *imbroglio* in a mood that was positively Puckish. He had suffered much from his ministers, and it was a treat for him to keep them dangling. Once, indeed, he asked the leading characters in the official comedy to Windsor. It was an uncomfortable house-party; and when Wellington passed the whole morning with the King, Canning aged visibly. Besides, the royal mood at lunch was plainly favourable to the Duke. After lunch the customary phaetons came. The royal Puck, with perfect malice, sent the Duke for a drive with Princess Lieven, a fervent Canningite, and kept Canning at home for a talk. The drive was trying; and it was painfully significant to find on their return that the impartial King had passed the entire afternoon with Canning. But nothing came of it. For when the rival statesmen met, each asked the other if he knew anything; but their elusive sovereign, deep in his delicious game of hide-and-seek, had said precisely nothing.

Yet even royal games must end at last; and Canning's firm refusal of any compromise won the trick. No Government could live without him; and if he could not have Tory colleagues, he should bring in the Whigs. A cold exchange of letters with the Duke ensued. His Grace's sincere and faithful servant, George Canning, advised him that he had his Majesty's commands to reconstruct the administration, that it was his wish to adhere to the principles on which Lord Liverpool's had so long acted together, and that his Grace's continuance as a colleague was essential. The Duke replied with a polite enquiry of his dear Mr. Canning who was to be Prime Minister. Canning responded in a didactic vein that he had believed it to be generally understood that the person charged with the formation of a Government was apt to be Prime Minister, that this course would be followed in the present instance, and that the King approved. The letters rang like pistol-shots on a frosty morning. The Duke was winged. One shot remained, however, and he fired it. Writing

in a cold fury, he expressed his inability to believe that any Government
of Canning's could follow the ancient ways of Lord Liverpool's, or that
anyone would ever think so, or that its policy could serve either King or
country. So he resigned. His resignation of the Ordnance, which was a
Cabinet office, was natural. But he declined to serve Canning as Commander-in-Chief and resigned the Horse Guards too; and for the first
time in forty years the Duke was out of place.

III

The Duke was out; and gleeful caricatures depicted *Achilles in the Sulks, or the Great Captain on the Stool of Repentance,* with a figure, angry and aquiline, sitting in Apsley House and exclaiming bitterly,

> "Here for brutal courage far renowned,
> I live an idle burden to the ground.
> (*Others* in *counsel* fam'd for nobler skill
> More useful to *preserve* than *I* to *kill*.)"

Lately Commander-in-Chief and Master-General of the Ordnance, he was now a comparatively private individual, a mere Field Marshal with marked Tory leanings. Opinion was a trifle shocked, although strict Protestants nodded approval when he resigned. A file of Tory colleagues followed. For the Duke's resignation was a signal to Peel and the older Tories. He was a party-leader now; Peel was his aide-de-camp; and the ranged nobility awaited his commands. For he had travelled far in the eight years since he accepted office from Lord Liverpool on an express understanding that he should not be bound to go into Opposition with his colleagues. That reservation had once served to mark him as a public servant still, to distinguish him from the humbler breed of politicians. But he was a politician now; and, like any politician, he resigned.

The Duke was out; and the King was left almost alone with Mr. Canning and the Whigs. This was a shade alarming, since the royal conscience was firmly opposed to Catholic Emancipation, and the sovereign was left feeling "very sore at his notion of desertion by those who forced Mr. Canning on him originally." The royal irritation was expressed in a curt acceptance of the Duke's double resignation. But how could he complain? Wellington could scarcely be expected to serve in Mr. Canning's Cabinet. That disposed of the Ordnance. Could he retain the Horse Guards? The office of Commander-in-Chief was not political. But Wellington chose to view Canning's second letter as "a rebuke for which I had given no provocation, and in which the authority of the King's

355

name was very unnecessarily introduced." His honour, the last refuge of
an angry statesman, was involved. Besides, there would have to be frequent consultation between Prime Minister and Commander-in-Chief;   3
questions were bound to arise on pay, on garrisons, on the troops in
Portugal; and manifestly he did not possess the Prime Minister's confidence. The fact was that his dislike of Canning was too strong for any
form of official co-operation. For he was writing vehemently of "this   4
charlatan" and the "foolish, insulting and indecent manner of his behaviour to me." Yet Wellington was not the man to act impulsively
from motives of merely personal distaste. He saw a larger issue, to which
his quarrel with Canning was only incidental. Was not the world of 1827
full of threats to the existing order?

> "Rely upon it, my dear Charles, the object of the great aristocracy, and   5
> of the *parti conservateur* of this country, is to secure the Crown from the
> mischief with which it is threatened, by moderation, by consistency, by firm-
> ness and good temper. Matters have been brought to the state in which they
> are by a man (for after all there is but one man) who does not possess a
> particle of any one of those qualities. The aristocracy must not aid his
> views. They must not render perpetual the unfortunate separation between
> the Crown and the party to which I have above referred. I earnestly recom-
> mend, then, moderation and temper, and above all, respect for the Crown
> and for the person of the King."

This had the firm tone of a party-leader—of the new leader of the *parti
conservateur* and its natural allies, the aristocracy. For though Mrs.   6
Arbuthnot could still describe him as "of *no party*," Wellington was now
the rising hope of the stern, unbending Tories.

The spring passed in irritable explanations, while the army lived under
a confused interregnum with Lord Palmerston, that hermit of the War
Department, for its temporary and civilian Commander-in-Chief. The   7
Duke made a reasoned statement on his resignation in the House of
Lords, which compelled the praises of Lord Ashley for its manly virtue.
How could their Lordships have supposed him capable of a desire to be
Prime Minister—"a station, to the duties of which I was unaccustomed,
in which I was not wished, and for which I was not qualified; as it must
be obvious to your Lordships, that not being in the habit of addressing
your Lordships, I should have been found, besides other qualifications,

incapable of displaying, as they ought to be displayed, or of defending the measures of government as they ought to be defended in this House, by the person thus honoured by his Majesty's confidence? My Lords, I should have been worse than mad if I had thought of such a thing." This was putting it a trifle high. Besides, his disclaimer gave awkward hostages to the enemy if an opportunity of office should recur. (*"En politique,"* as a judicious Emperor remarked to an impulsive politician, *"il ne faut point dire 'Jamais.'"*) But statesmen are frequently carried away by their own abnegation, when they disclaim their own ambitions.

8   There was an awkward interchange of correspondence with Canning, discontinued by the latter from an anxiety (which seemed a shade belated) that it might not "degenerate into controversy." The King, a little nervous now, intimated that the command of the new army was still open; but the Duke's frowns persisted. His brother William was the

9   bearer of a furtive invitation (promptly disavowed to Canning by the courageous monarch) to call at Windsor. The Duke went at duty's summons; and London buzzed again. The irrepressible Creevey met him

10   one afternoon coming out of Arbuthnot's front-door in Parliament Street and promptly buttonholed him with "Curious times these, Duke." The Duke agreed, put his arm through the inquisitive Whig's, swung him right round, and marched him off towards the House of Lords. He sent a civil message through Creevey to Lord Grey and spoke with heat of Canning, stopping at intervals to emphasise his points and very nearly pulling the button off Creevey's coat in the process. No one, he said, could act with Canning; and his temper was quite sure to blow him up. Others noticed it as well that summer, a sharp American observer re-

11   cording that "Mr. Canning's temper has become most uncertain." Canning, it seemed, was growing odd; office had broken stronger men; and the Duke watched him with genuine concern. One evening the Prime Minister bore down upon the American ambassador with an unprovoked tirade against the aristocracy; and Wellington drew up a chair between Gallatin and Humboldt, looked anxious, and asked suddenly if they found anything odd in Mr. Canning's manner. He had seen such things before; could it be possible that Canning might be going the same way as Castlereagh? While the Duke looked on, he did not play an active

12   part in Parliament, though he spoke once or twice on the Corn Bill with

a clear repudiation of "any feeling of party or of faction, or of the least desire to embarrass His Majesty's Government." For he had not learnt—perhaps he never mastered—the ways of Opposition. He had served the State far too long to distinguish readily between Opposition and sedition. He might resign: that was permissible. But the Duke could rarely bring himself to oppose a Government, even if it was Mr. Canning's.

The House rose in July; and the Prime Minister was far from well. He had never managed to throw off a cold contracted at the Duke of York's funeral in the previous winter, when they were all kept standing on cold pavements; he had persuaded Eldon to stand on the Lord Chancellor's cocked hat and written gaily to the Duke that "Mr. Mash, or   13 whoever filched the cloth or the matting from under our feet in the aisle, had bets or insurances against the lives of the Cabinet." He had been ailing all the summer; and now the bet was almost won. For "it was a rich, warm night at the beginning of August, when a gentleman enveloped in a cloak, for he was in evening dress, emerged from a club-house at the top of St. James' Street, and descended that celebrated eminence." He paused, as readers of *Endymion* know, to impart the news that Mr. Canning was *in extremis*. That brief reign was over now; it had lasted for three months. Strange how the Duke's customary allowance of power to his opponents was a Hundred Days.

His epitaph on Canning was laconic—"I hear that Dr. Farr says that   14 it was Canning's temper that killed him." This was unkind; but he spoke   15 kindly of him in company, admiring his rare gifts of speech and writing and the patience with which Canning had permitted him to "cut and hack" his drafts. But he deplored the ungovernable rages with which he often greeted differences in council; and Canning impressed him as "one of the idlest of men." For industry of the Duke's order often suspects more rapid methods. Idle or not, Canning was gone; and the King was left to find a new Prime Minister. There was a flutter among the expectant Tories. Would the Duke be sent for? He was not; for by a pleasing irony the King, averse to further changes and dreading the humiliation of a summons to the evicted Tories, summoned the shadowy presence of Mr. Robinson, now ennobled as Lord Goderich, to keep Canning's Government together. That "transient and embarrassed phantom" reigned without distinction and with a growing personal discom-   16 fort, until he vanished like an uneasy spirit at cockcrow. To steer a course with a mixed crew of Whigs and Tory Canningites might have tasked stronger nerves than his; and his nerves were anything but strong. A later age views nervous ailments with an indulgent eye. But to the full-blooded world of 1827 an intermittently lachrymose Prime Minister was merely comic. Lord Goderich whimpered through five months of office; and when he made his final exit behind a borrowed royal handkerchief, a heartless world guffawed. Not much had been accomplished, though Wellington had been induced to resume his post as Commander-in-Chief. He took command "as of an Army in the Field" without political considerations, although his action was submitted for approval to his Tory friends; for the Duke felt his new position as a party-leader with responsibilities towards his political associates.

17
18

The reign of Goderich was a conscious interlude; and Wellington watched from his Tory fastness. One day before the summer ended he strolled in to the "Social Day" of a new sculptor's exhibition. A respectful circle in the gallery marked the majestic presence of Mrs. Siddons in tow of an Academician. The Duke's air was less sublime; Haydon, indeed, was positively disappointed and "never saw one whose air and presence were so unlike genius or heroism." But, thanks to the Elgin Marbles, Haydon's standards of the heroic were unduly elevated. He thought that Wellington "seemed embarrassed, and as if he felt he was unpopular." That was quite possible in a year in which he had endured distinct rebuffs. But he was not too embarrassed to admire the sculpture, stepping to the order-book and inscribing himself for a *Milo* and a *Samson*. One of the artist's friends came up to thank him. "He should go abroad," said the clear military voice. This sentence of exile sounding a little unpropitious, he added hastily, "Not to stay, but to see—eh—the—eh—great works as others have done." Then he wheeled briskly round, lifted a martial finger to his hat, and left the gallery, his duty to the arts accomplished. In the autumn he paid a round of visits in the north, and was triumphantly received, even Grey recording that his "course has been one continued scene of rejoicing." The cheers melted his diffidence. He was a coming man once more, though he shot worse than ever. They were all at Stratfield Saye; the Duchess was unwell and kept her room, where Mrs. Arbuthnot bore with fortitude the tedium of her conversa-

19

20

21

tion. Downstairs Alava told his stories and Lady Jersey aired her charms, while the gentlemen expressed their sympathies with Turkey at the outrageous violence of Navarino. The Duke was in the grip of one of his tremendous colds; the subject of catarrh appeared to fascinate him, and 22 he was apt to send detailed directions for its treatment to his relations, confiding sovereign remedies to diplomatic bags. They had lent Apsley House to the Shelleys; and poor Kitty wrote from Stratfield Saye begging 23 Lady Shelley to stay on in London, adding, "I hope you like my Douro upon further acquaintance! Is he not the living image of his father?" For she was still devoted to her alarming Duke.

Then he was back in London, while Lord Goderich, a tearful Sisyphus, administered his country. Wellington's infrequent sense of family loyalty 24 impelled him to press his brother Henry's claims to a peerage; Henry's ambition was to figure as Lord Cowley, if that spelling of their former name was correct, although he had "a decided aversion to the name of Colley." His wish was gratified, and Lord Cowley joined the Duke, Lord Wellesley, and Lord Maryborough in the family peerage; for with the sole exception of Gerald, who was in the Church, they were all peers now. The weeks went by; Lord Goderich's outcries became more audible; and as his tears flowed faster, he resigned.

The question, the eternal question which had haunted 1827, was raised again in the first week of 1828. Who was to be Prime Minister? There 25 had been a notion of Lord Harrowby; but he refused. Richard was even spoken of. But the King knew his own mind at last; for nine months of keeping company with Whigs had roused his sleeping fervour for the Reformation, and he was now an ardent Protestant. That meant a Tory Government; a Tory Government meant Wellington; and the Duke was sent for. His audience was highly unusual; for the King was ill. A cheer- 26 ful voice, owned by an unbecoming figure in a dirty silk jacket, exclaimed from the recesses of a royal bed, "Arthur, the Cabinet is defunct." The royal head was crowned by a singularly greasy turban; and royal art proceeded to enliven the occasion with a perfect rendering of the deportment of his late ministers. His visitor was then requested to form a Gov- 27 ernment upon the understanding that Catholic Emancipation should form no part of Cabinet policy. The Duke was guarded. In view of his position as Commander-in-Chief, he must consult his friends. He asked for time, but went so far as to elicit royal wishes for and against individuals. The King had no objections except to Lord Grey; the Government, he thought, should be composed of persons of both opinions upon the Catholic question; and he repeated frequently that he desired nothing more than a strong Government. The Duke returned to town and sent for Peel—Peel was his second-in-command—and he would speak to nobody till Peel had been consulted. Peel's advice was plain. Their course, he felt, would be anything but simple, since the Tories had been split by Canning and the tide of Catholic Emancipation was rising. But he was content to serve under Wellington in a reunited Tory administration, and was decidedly of opinion that the Duke should be Prime Minister. Canning had once objected to "the union of the whole power of the State, civil and military, in the same hands" as being "a station too great for *any subject*, however eminent, or however meritorious, and one incompatible with the practice of a free constitution." The Duke himself had termed it madness. But his view was changed. He could do better than Goderich. Besides, the Tories looked to him; the King was quite subdued; and was it not his duty to accept public situations? So the Duke, at fifty-eight, became Prime Minister.

Prime Minister

The man of the age is clearly the Duke, the saviour of Europe, in the perfection of manhood, and with an iron constitution.—ENDYMION.

H E W A S to govern England now; and an expectant world took his success for granted. Wellington had never failed; his long career had been a mere procession of success; and what civilian task could find him wanting? After all, he was no stranger to administration. Eight years in the Cabinet were a respectable apprenticeship; he had once governed Ireland, to say nothing of his administrative experience in Portugal, Mysore, and France. Diplomacy could hold no mysteries for him, since he had attended Congresses with Castlereagh, conferred with kings and emperors on equal terms, and corresponded with half the Continent. It was an adequate equipment; and the world was not in the least surprised that, in *Endymion's* phrase, "England should be ruled by the most eminent man of the age, and the most illustrious of her citizens."

The task was formidable, though. The auguries were good—"the conviction that the Duke's government would only cease with the termination of his public career was so general, that, the moment he was installed in office, the Whigs smiled on him; political conciliation became the slang of the day, and the fusion of parties the babble of clubs and the tattle of boudoirs." But the task was formidable. Could he perform the duties of Prime Minister? Pure administration had no terrors, since he knew his mind, could make decisions, and always answered letters. A slightly excessive sense of detail might, perhaps, encumber him. Soldiers are bred to detail, since there is nothing in the world (as Napoleon III once wrote to a War Minister) with so much detail about it as an army; and the Duke's passion for exactitude was sometimes lost among *minutiæ*, as when he accompanied an offer to keep an appointment in Westminster Hall with the somewhat exaggerated caution that "it will take me a quarter of an hour to go from the Ordnance to Westminster Hall; and as much for the Man who is to go for me." He could face all the paperwork, since Wellington had been writing State papers for as long as his countrymen could remember. There would be public speaking to be done, of course, and he was not a speaker. But the House of Lords must put up with his plain manner of debating, once described by Walter Scott as "slicing the argument into two or three parts and helping himself to the best." That would suffice; for the world did not expect him to give performances like Mr. Canning's. His colleagues could do all the talking. But could he manage them? That was, perhaps, more doubtful, since he was accustomed to the simple compliance of a staff; and a staff is not a Cabinet. Staff officers can be trusted not to resign at awkward moments. But Cabinets require arts of management that are wholly unfamiliar to commanders in the field. Generals of division act upon instructions; the Quartermaster-General is rarely troubled by his conscience in performing simple departmental duties; but would Secretaries of State be equally reliable? As he complained later, "One man wants one thing and one another; they agree to what I say in the morning, and then in the evening up they start with some crotchet which deranges the whole plan. I have not been used to that in all the early part of my life. I have been accustomed to carry on things in quite a different manner: I assembled my officers and laid down my plan, and it was carried into effect without any more words."

But Cabinets work upon different lines. For Cabinets consist of colleagues; and the Duke was more accustomed to subordinates. Would he be happy as the head of such a republic? There was his party, too. A lifetime in the field had trained him to expect obedience in the ranks; they were not called on to concur, but merely to obey; and he applied the same simple canons of duty to his political followers. "The party!" he exclaimed with irritable emphasis. "What is the meaning of a party if they don't follow their leaders? Damn 'em! let 'em go!" And it is hardly to be wondered at that they occasionally went. For even party men have been known to require something more than to be led.

These were the limitations of his splendid equipment for civilian office. Mechanically perfect, he was defective in the minor art of persuasion. The defect was inherent in his nature and aggravated by his training. For he was anything but pliant; and there had been no need for him to persuade anyone at Headquarters. If *Endymion's* glowing forecast of "a dictatorship of patriotism" was correct, all would be well. Few men were better qualified to be dictator. But if dictation failed, if a need arose to persuade colleagues or fellow-citizens that he was in the right, his prospects of success were questionable. He might, perhaps, succeed so long as operations were confined to the familiar political *terrain* over which he had manœuvred with Lord Liverpool and Mr. Canning. So long as politics remained a highly complicated game played by well-connected persons within the limits of the Parliamentary board, he played with tolerable skill. But when the board was suddenly enlarged and new pieces with strange moves appeared upon it, he was baffled. This was not politics as he had learnt them. For politics according to the rules were a genteel affair in which residents in Mayfair governed England by the simple process of making speeches to one another in Westminster. That was the old *terrain*, on which he could manœuvre with fair proficiency. But now the ground was unfamiliar; Westminster had ceased to be the sole battlefield of politics, and operations were in progress all over England; strange, unauthorised belligerents had elbowed the recognised players into corners; and where once the game of politics had turned upon the evolutions of competing groups, it now depended on the incalculable appetites of crowds. The Duke was never at his best with crowds; he had no taste for them, whether they cheered or hooted him; besides, the best years of his life had been devoted to obstructing their desires. For a Chief Secretary learns to be indifferent to Irish crowds; and the long war against the French was little more than an attempt to discipline the Paris mob. He had learnt a deep distaste for democracy in the dark, tumultuous years when murder was its leading argument and Thistlewood its chief apostle; and if crowds were to be the arbiters of politics, the Duke would stand his ground. He was a shade bewildered, as he faced the new attack. There was no precedent (outside the unpleasing precedents of France) for politics on such a scale. For this was something wholly different from the orderly manœuvres of political parties. The rules of war were openly defied, and the *terrain* had been transformed out of all recognition. It seemed to have no limits now; and where were the familiar mountain-ranges, which had once prescribed the course of operations? He could not have been more at sea, if fate had suddenly transferred Headquarters from the Lines of Torres Vedras, where he could foresee with precision the direction of the next French offensive, to Nelson's quarter-deck surrounded by a shifting element and exposed to attack from every point of the compass.

But the Duke stood his ground. Indeed, resistance was his main conception of a statesman's duty. Not that his mind was purely negative.
But he had not been the chosen swordsman of the *ancien régime* for
nothing. What had he fought the French for, if not to check the tide
of change? He had resisted change at Busaco and Salamanca and
Waterloo; and it was too much to hope that he would welcome it
in England. He had lived half a lifetime with the sound of the French
guns in his ears; he was the saviour of Europe; and was it reasonable
to expect him to applaud the principles from which he had saved it?
His country must be saved again. The need to save it from the French
had passed; but there were still the Whigs. For those misguided men
were on the path which led direct to the French Revolution; and it
was vital at all costs to bar them out of office. So early as 1821 he had
urged Liverpool to pocket his official pride for the compelling reason
that the dread alternative was to "give up the government to the Whigs   7
and Radicals, or, in other words, the country in all its relations to irretrievable ruin"; in 1827, when Liverpool collapsed and the Tory dams
began to break, he had told Croker that "after them comes chaos"; and
now the Whigs were at the gates.   8

How to exclude them? He was too intelligent to oppose a front of
mere negation. That was the Tory system; but the Duke was more than
a mere "pig-tail" Tory. A master of defensive strategy, he was well aware
that at a certain stage resistance becomes dangerous to the defenders. It
had never been his habit to defend positions after they had become indefensible. That was the moment for a neat withdrawal to his next position.
When he commanded the last army of England in the Peninsula, he
stood to fight at Busaco, fell back to Torres Vedras, and stood to fight
again; and he proposed to execute the same manœuvre in defence of
social order. He always said that the best test of a great general was "to   9
know when to retreat, and to dare to do it"; and statesmen might do
worse than learn the lesson. It would be madness to risk the safety of the
constitution in an affair of outposts; that had always been poor Craufurd's
weakness, and the Duke found Tory braves almost as uncontrollable. But
they must choose their ground with care, defend a strong position as long
as it could be defended, and then, if circumstances unfortunately turned

it, fall back to the next. For a judicious strategy of retreat might, if persisted in, keep the Whigs perpetually in Opposition and save the State.

That was his design. It would require a mobile force for its successful
execution; and his Cabinet, the Tory party, and the King were anything
but mobile. Politicians had an awkward weakness for consistency, which
inclined them to defend positions long after a retreat had become imperative; and the King was now afflicted with an exceptionally trying conscience upon religious questions. But the Duke took command. He had
led highly miscellaneous armies in his time; and in 1828 he led another.

II

His methods of recruitment were simple but effective. All the week he sat in Apsley House with Arbuthnot at his elbow interviewing candidates for office and writing briefly to likely recruits. Croker found him one day in the later stages, when his patience was wearing a little thin. The Duke compared himself to a dog with a can tied to its tail and pointed irritably to a formidable mountain of red boxes and green bags. "There," he explained, "is the business of the country, which I have not time to look at—all my time being employed in assuaging what gentlemen call their feelings." This was a novelty; staff officers had had no feelings. But politicians were less reasonable; and he assumed with evident distaste the unfamiliar task of persuading these unmanageable creatures. His object was to repair the damage done by Mr. Canning, to reunite the Tory party by retaining Canning's misguided followers in a Tory administration. They gave him endless trouble, since Mr. Huskisson, who led the little group, was full of stipulations. First there were his leanings towards fiscal freedom. Then, if he was to stay at the Colonial Office, Lamb must remain Chief Secretary; that would be a guarantee that strict neutrality would be observed upon the Catholic question. The cheerful Palmerston must be promoted to the Cabinet. And was the Duke prepared to apply the principles of Mr. Canning in foreign affairs? His recent treaty about Greece went further than the Duke's Protocol of 1826. But Wellington satisfied their scruples by declaring that "the King's treaties must be observed" and appointing one of the group to the Foreign Office. The Canningites were duly enlisted; but their inclusion involved sacrifices. For Tories of the older school were dropped in order to make room for them; but as he banished them, Wellington wrote ruefully that "the King's service must be carried on." He was less tender with the normal appetites which beset Prime Ministers, informing one persistent applicant for a peerage that as there had been twenty-six creations in the last two years, it was his duty "to discourage and protest against any more being created unless some public service of magnitude

370

or public emergency should require it. If this duty is not performed, either the House of Lords will become a democratic body and a nuisance, or contemptible and useless. In either case the constitution of the country will be overturned." Few party-leaders can afford to tell their followers that the House of Lords will be unduly adulterated by their ennoblement; but the Duke was never a master of the soft answer. He was prepared to govern England and, for that purpose, to enlist a Government; but minor arts of management were far beyond him, and he totally disdained the latest mode of popular conciliation. Canning had always shown a weakness for the Press; but the Duke was frankly hostile. Journalists, in his experience, existed for the propagation of falsehoods; and he asked helplessly, "What can we do with these sort of fellows? We have no power over them, and, for my part, I will have no communication with any of them."

The voyage opened with a further sacrifice. Pressure was put on the Prime Minister to resign the office of Commander-in-Chief, and he reluctantly acceded. Work crowded on him; as he wrote grimly to an apologetic correspondent, "If you were to see the number of plans which I receive every day upon every description of subject, all of which I am obliged to peruse, you would admit there was no necessity for having any scruple about sending me your plan for diminishing the pay of the army." Stray callers were occasionally informed a shade ungraciously by letter that the Prime Minister, having learnt the object of their unsuccessful visit, did not regret not having seen them and must be acquitted, never having heard of them, of any disrespect. But Creevey found him "rising most rapidly in the market as a practical man of business. All the deputations come away charmed with him. But woe to them that are too late! He is punctual to a second himself, and waits for no man." He found little pleasure in his situation, writing to the Prince of Orange that he was involved in duties for which he was "not qualified, and they are very disagreeable to me"; but he added in a more cheerful tone that the Government was an unqualified success.

"There is in fact but little, if any, opposition to it. This state of things cannot last, I know. But as the whole of the landed and great commercial and monied interests of the country are decidedly with us, I hope that, if

371

the existing state of tranquillity in this country should terminate, we shall remain still with a strong government.

"Your Royal Highness would scarcely recognise England again if you were now to come here. There is no party remaining. The ladies and the youth of the country in particular are with us, and I could almost count upon my fingers those who are hostile to the government."

This was a glowing picture. But though beauty smiled upon the Government, his colleagues did not always smile on one another. The Canningites were fretful from the first; groups of bereaved politicians attached to statesmen recently deceased are rarely enlivening companions. He was prepared to make concessions about Corn; but they found him unhelpful towards Greece. This was embarrassing, since Greek independence was prominent in the political testament of Mr. Canning; Wellington had assured the House of Lords that he must claim "the right of not being included in the number of Mr. Canning's enemies," and introduced a Bill pensioning his family. But it was more questionable how far the Duke could be regarded as Mr. Canning's intellectual heir, since he displayed a strong distaste for the Greek legacy. For Mr. Canning, they felt sure, would never have termed Navarino an "untoward event" in the King's Speech. The watchful Palmerston diagnosed strong anti-Russian leanings, which he was inclined to attribute to the Duke's past encounters with the Lievens and some imagined slight at St. Petersburg; besides, the energetic Dorothea was unpopular with Lady Jersey and Mrs. Arbuthnot, the twin stars of the Duke's firmament. There were endless Cabinets on Greece with "much discussion and entire difference of opinion." Spring turned to summer, and they continued uncomfortably "differing upon almost every question . . . meeting to debate and dispute, and separating without deciding." For the leaven of Mr. Canning's principles was having difficulty with the Tory lump. His followers grew still more restive. The Duke found them uneasy bedfellows, confessing to Arbuthnot that he regretted their inclusion, and complaining of "the manner in which the *four* hang together" to Ellenborough, who confirmed his view with an unpleasing panorama of the Canningite revolt—Palmerston "always *pecking*," Grant "obstinate and useless," and the innocuous Dudley incited to rebellion by the more active Huskisson. Huskisson was always trying; Lord Palmerston was bad enough—the exasperated Prime Minister had once termed him a mutineer; but Huskisson was quite unbearable. Persons who believe themselves possessed of an economic gospel are frequently distinguished by an offensive air of conscious superiority. Besides, he was the leader of the little group; and as the vicar of Mr. Canning upon earth he could scarcely hope to engage the Duke's affections.

Relief came from an unexpected quarter, as the long shadow of Reform fell across the scene. That rock was, to all appearances, one of the few on which the Cabinet was unlikely to split. For Mr. Canning had opposed Reform; the Duke was no Reformer; and, however they might disagree upon Corn, Portugal, and Greece, they might reasonably be expected to maintain a united front upon Reform. Indeed, the problem of Reform itself appeared to be in a fair way towards solution by simpler methods in the best English manner, since they were extremely practical and quite devoid of logic. Thorough-paced Reformers argued that the whole system of representation stood in need of drastic overhaul; but reasonable men, unwilling to admit the need, met it unobtrusively. For as the more outrageous boroughs disqualified themselves by electoral misdeeds, their members were inconspicuously transferred to the new industrial towns, a practical device which robbed Reformers of their grievance whilst enabling Tories to admire the incomparable outline of the existing constitution. In the spring of 1828 East Retford was available for redistribution, and the inheritance was disputed between industry and agriculture; for the Whigs wished to transfer its member to Birmingham, while Tory ministers preferred to add him to the county members. The matter was discussed in Cabinet, where Huskisson regarded himself as committed by a previous utterance to the Opposition view, and it appeared to be agreed to leave it as an open question. Accordingly (not without pressure from the enterprising Palmerston) he voted with the Opposition. That night, seized with a pardonable scruple after voting against his colleagues, Huskisson wrote to the Duke offering his resignation and expecting that the offer would be gracefully refused. But the Duke thought otherwise. Fine shades were never to his taste; and it was quite beyond him that there were degrees of resignation. If a gentleman resigned, Wellington assumed that he meant it. Besides, a resignation from Huskisson was too good to be overlooked. Marmont had once exposed a flank to him at Salamanca; and now Huskisson had done the same, and with similar results. For the Duke positively swooped.

After a decent interval he hurried to the King; and the startled Huskisson, expecting to be pressed to stay, received instead a curt intimation that the sovereign had been made aware of his intentions. There was a flutter among the Canningites. Lord Dudley saw the Duke, who was blandly unaware that there could be any mistake. Palmerston pursued him to the House of Lords and had half an hour's conversation. They paced up and down the Long Gallery, as Palmerston unfolded Huskisson's slightly involved apologia and Wellington stared at the ground. But the Duke insisted that the letter meant what it said; that Peel had thought the same; that this had been coming for some time; and that such behaviour would soon bring him into as much discredit as Lord Goderich. Besides, he could not go upon all fours to Mr. Huskisson and ask him to remain. (That was his ruling thought: if Canningites chose to resign, why should the Duke prevent them?) Lord Palmerston was still plying him with arguments; and when he intimated that he should feel bound to go out with Huskisson, the Duke raised his eyes, looked sharply at him, and resumed their walk. But they reached no conclusion.

Then Palmerston returned to his colleague; and they concocted a second letter to the Duke, endeavouring to make him responsible if Huskisson left office. A brief reply from Apsley House informed them that it was better to lose Huskisson than to submit to the humiliation of begging him to stay. For the Duke's *amour propre* was stirred. As he said afterwards, "I told Dudley and Palmerston that I had no objection, nay, I wished, that they and Huskisson could get out of the scrape, but that I begged on my own part to decline taking a roll in the mud with them. This was not a very elegant expression, but it was a sincere one." The *imbroglio* dragged on to an accompaniment of protracted explanations. But Wellington could not escape from his initial belief that a man must be taken to mean what he said. There was no difference of principle—"There is not the idea of a principle in all these papers. . . . We hear a great deal of Whig principles, and Tory principles, and Liberal principles, and Mr. Canning's principles; but I confess that I have never seen a definition of any of them, and cannot make to myself a clear idea of what any of them mean." Political ideas were wholly irrelevant; the

19

20

21

22

374

simple point was that Huskisson had providentially resigned, and the Duke meant to hold him to it.

He was victorious, although the victory gave him a little trouble; and in the middle of it all he had to dine at the Mansion House. A colleague found him looking "ill, and as if he had been annoyed; but he was quite in good spirits with his reception, *elated*." He rather enjoyed the duel and was quite determined not to submit to Huskisson; as for Palmerston, he "did not choose to fire great guns at sparrows"; and, to Ellenborough's eye, he was "completely roused, and seems to feel as he did at Waterloo." In the last days of May silence descended on the field; the Canningites resigned; and *Endymion's* lovely mother heard a Tory hostess exclaim in triumph, "They are all four out. . . . The only mistake was ever to have admitted them. I think now we have got rid of Liberalism for ever." It was a sweeping forecast.

III

HIS forces had begun to shrink. For the little group had been his Light Division, whose agility would have been of value if he desired to manœuvre towards the Left. Henceforward he was left with a residue of solid Tories, whose inclinations lay all towards the Right. The Canningites were gone, each to his destiny—for Palmerston a drift towards the Whigs, the Foreign Office, and a reign (nearly thirty years away) over Victorian England; for Lamb his father's coronet and the unaccustomed exercise of Melbourne's endless conversations with a schoolgirl Queen; and for Huskisson the fatal locomotive. Their simultaneous departure left the Duke undismayed. He was not sorry to be rid of them. Their presence had endangered Cabinet discipline; and in replacing them he took steps to remedy the defect. For two of the vacancies were filled by military men. Sir George Murray, a Peninsular veteran, went to the Colonial Office in succession to the fretful Huskisson; and Sir Henry Hardinge, who had been his *liaison* officer with Blücher, replaced Lord Palmerston. The Prime Minister found the change congenial, as his late Quartermaster-General was unlikely to waste valuable time in unnecessary disputation, though the Opposition found derisive things to say about a "military and aide-de-campish" Government; and [1] when a minister said that their minds were a blank sheet upon some question, a House of Commons wit remarked that it must be cartridge-paper.

But their prestige was unimpaired. For there was no effective Opposition; and the Duke exasperated Princess Lieven by saying, "I am the most popular Minister that England has ever seen; take my word for it, [2] I am very strong." It was not like him to be boastful; but when he saw Dorothea, he seemed to harp upon his popularity. She was a sounding-board; and it was just as well for St. Petersburg to understand that Wellington was firmly seated in office. For his policy had a distinctly anti-Russian flavour; and the Russians would be more respectful if they realised that his reign was more than a passing episode of politics. He

376

3   reigned securely now. His brother Henry, to whom he was unlikely to
exaggerate, was informed that "we are going on well here. The government is very popular; and indeed there is but little opposition." His
4   Chancellor found him an admirable man of business, and Aberdeen, the
new Foreign Secretary, worked under his direction; "for almost every
5   despatch of the following years there is a draft memorandum, preserved
in Wellington's correspondence, and often embodied with just the necessary diplomatic wrappings from which his own peculiar telegraphic style
was so refreshingly free." Foreign affairs were a shade trying, as he found
the legacies of Canning's policy distinctly embarrassing. Russia was at
war with Turkey in spite of all his efforts; the French were straining
at the leash; and the territorial claims of Greece were growing every day.
The Eastern Question had passed momentarily beyond control; and the
Duke was limited by circumstances to a glum acquiescence in the inevitable. In Portugal he was compelled to witness the exact reverse of what
Mr. Canning had intended. The Portuguese declined to rally to the
constitution in defence of which Canning had struck his splendid attitude. For the British standard had been duly planted on the heights of
Lisbon; but no one seemed to mind. This was a shade humiliating. Indeed, a flavour of humiliation seemed to infect foreign affairs, as the
rather ruffled birds of Mr. Canning's policy came home to roost. But Mr.
Canning, *felix opportunitate mortis,* was not there to smooth them; and
it was left to Wellington to put the best face upon a series of unpleasing
situations.

His hands were full that summer, and his friends found him looking
6   white and overworked. His days were arduous—the Treasury at noon,
business till five, and then the House of Lords, followed by a dull dinner
7   and more papers until bed. Even when he dined with Mrs. Arbuthnot,
"poor fellow! the moment he had some coffee he sat down and read,
and wrote papers till past twelve o'clock at night! I told him he would
soon have no eyes left." But he got away to Cheltenham, when the
House rose, and recuperated in those decorous alleys. He sipped his water
every morning early and strolled in the Montpellier Gardens. Each after-
8   noon he took his bath; this relaxation lasted an hour, and he mitigated
the tedium with an armful of newspapers. (Always the White Knight,
he had a frame put across the bath to support his paper, thus solving a

377

problem that has often baffled meaner intellects.) The summer passed;
and the autumn Cabinets came round with his autumn colds, though
Mrs. Arbuthnot found that he was "wonderfully improved by Cheltenham, has got a *brown*, healthy colour, and seems to have got his head and   9
stomach quite right"; and he was well enough to wing a keeper of
Lord Hertford's. They were still busy with the Eastern Question; and
William, Duke of Clarence, afforded occasional diversion by his vagaries
as Lord High Admiral. For this elderly eccentric, flown (as royal personages sometimes are) by a titular dignity, endangered naval discipline
by irregular exercises of authority. He was a royal duke and, what was
more, the next King of England; but Wellington had faced more formidable foes and checked him with such firmness that his future sovereign resigned. Indeed, he simultaneously refused a favour asked by the
Duchess of Kent, now Queen-mother presumptive, who was anxious to   10
instal Sir John Conroy in an Ordnance job. For Wellington was rarely
prone to seek royal smiles.

The Prime Minister drafted indefatigably on every subject; as Dorothea
Lieven bitterly observed, he was "the universal man." His pen was busy
with the problems of both hemispheres—with the next war in North   11
America, with the Persian Gulf (where Bagdad and Persia should, he
felt, be strengthened as outworks of India against Russian aggression),   12
with an offensive classical quotation by which a legal luminary had once
annoyed the King, with a fantastic allegation in *The Times* that he was
selling gunpowder to Russia, and the vast burden of a correspondence
affording him "the advantage which I possess in the proffered assistance
of nearly every gentleman in England, who has nothing to do but to
amuse himself, and is tired of his usual amusements, and of reading the
newspapers." The indomitable Haydon, in the thick of "Eucles arriving
with the news of Marathon," wrote asking leave to dedicate a pamphlet
upon State encouragement of the nobler forms of art, and received a
prompt refusal "in his own immortal hand." A more detailed proposal
for the embellishment of the House of Lords with scenes illustrative of
constitutional principles alternating with portraits of King Alfred, Bacon,
Nelson, and the Duke failed to excite him, since he responded with a
bare acknowledgment and left Haydon with a suspicion that he was
"innately modest." Haydon, quite undeterred, sent him a copy of his

pamphlet (duly acknowledged), and proposed a public grant of £4,000 for historical paintings. The Duke's attitude was highly unpromising; for he first asked for details and, when he got them, objected that the scheme was not officially before him and that, in any case, he was opposed "to the grant of any public money for the object." He read everything and wrote voluminously; even Marie Louise received a civil message from the Duke condoling with her on the illness of Count Neipperg (her first husband's death at St. Helena had caused him less concern); and, to make all things worse, his London house was full of workmen. For they were reconstructing Apsley House upon a more majestic scale; and in the midst of the confusion the Duke's mind was busy with the Catholics.

The problem had been looming for a generation, ever since Mr. Pitt fell back defeated by the conscience of George III. That was a formidable fortress; and until it fell, the road to Catholic Emancipation was effectually blocked. Time had removed it now. But, strange to record, the royal conscience was inherited by George IV; and those rococo battlements still barred the way. Would the Duke succeed where Pitt had failed? It was not certain that he would make the attempt, since he had little taste for superfluous reforms; though Creevey wrote at the very outset of his term of office that "my sincere opinion is—and I beg to record it thus early— that the Beau *will* do something for the Catholics of Ireland." He knew his Beau; the Beau knew his Ireland; and if Catholic Emancipation became a practical necessity, he was quite capable of acting. The obstacles were grave, since the royal conscience and the Tory faith were equally opposed to it. But could Wellington be seriously asked to respect the scruples of a king who fished all day at Virginia Water and came to Council meetings in a blue surtout covered with gold frogs in order to exchange racing tips with Greville behind a royal hand? If he did not respect the royal person, he was unlikely to respect the royal scruples. The Tories were a graver obstacle, since the Government had been formed upon an express understanding that "the Roman Catholic question should be considered as one not to be brought forward by the Cabinet." But troops embarked for one objective had very frequently been transferred to another; after all, he had begun the war in the Peninsula (and won Vimeiro) with a force designed to operate in Venezuela. The only doubt was how far his present command would be capable of this manœuvre. The Tory mind was not adaptable; besides, there was the Tory past upon the Catholic question. But the last thing that the Duke thought of was his army's mind; they were not asked to have one; he did not invite the rank and file to make his plans; that was his duty. It might be awkward for them to have to contradict their former speeches; civilian politicians were apt to over-value consistency. But a retreat was sometimes the soundest strategy; he knew the value of a well-timed retreat; and if the situation called for one, they must abandon the position.

His mind was quickened by the events of 1828. The air was full of toleration. For the Whigs secured relief for Dissenters by the repeal of the Test and Corporation Acts. The Duke had little taste for Nonconformists; Methodist conventicles in the Peninsula had evoked the slightly grudging comment that "the meeting of soldiers in their cantonments to [18] sing psalms, or to hear a sermon read by one of their comrades is, in the abstract, perfectly innocent." But when the House of Commons chose to emancipate them, he urged the Lords to concur, though his mind was still adverse to the Catholic claims. That was in April. Events moved [19] swiftly in the summer, since the House of Commons positively carried a motion in favour of Catholic Emancipation by six votes, and an Irish by-election resulted in the impressive march of regimented voters headed by their parish priests to return a Catholic for County Clare. O'Connell, though ineligible, was elected; and the Catholic claims became an urgent problem, if Ireland was to be governed. Wellington spoke on the question [20] in June. His tone was guarded, and his sympathies were carefully extended to both sides. Disclaiming all doctrinal objections, he proclaimed the issue "to be a question entirely of expediency," an intimation with which politicians frequently preface a change of front. He concentrated on the practical difficulties of devising a *Concordat*, and hinted that something might be managed, if only an arrangement could be found whereby "the King shall have the power to control the appointment of the hierarchy, and their intercourse with the See of Rome, and which shall connect the Roman Catholic Church in Ireland with the Government." His peroration was a *staccato* plea for calm reflection:

"If the public mind was suffered to rest; if the agitators of Ireland would only be quiet; if the difficulties of this question were not aggravated by these perpetual discussions; and if men could have time to reflect upon the state of this question, they might become more satisfied, and it might then become more possible to discover the means of doing something."

So Mr. Creevey had been right. The Beau was perfectly prepared to do something for the Catholics, if only they would let him alone. It was a conversion as momentous (and far swifter in its consequences) than Mr. Gladstone's to Home Rule.

21   In August he approached the King for leave "to take into consideration the whole case of Ireland, with a view to the adoption of some measure to be proposed to Parliament for the pacification of that country." He faced the facts in his plain fashion:

> "The influence and the powers of Government in that country are no longer in the hands of the officers of the government, but have been usurped by the demagogues of the Roman Catholic Association; who, acting through the influence of the Roman Catholic clergy, direct the country as they think proper. . . .
>
> "We have a rebellion impending over us in Ireland . . . and we have in England a Parliament which we cannot dissolve, the majority of which is of opinion, with many wise and able men, that the remedy is to be found in Roman Catholic emancipation, and they would unwillingly enter into the contest without making such an endeavour to pacify the country."

That was his notion. If the citadel of public order was to be defended, the advanced position from which Eldonian Tories still defied the Catholics must be abandoned. Peel had reached the same conclusion, although he felt compelled by his own record as an uncompromising Protestant to
22   warn the Duke "that it would not conduce to the satisfactory adjustment of the question, that the charge of it in the House of Commons should be committed to my hands." A reluctant convert, he proposed to an-
23   nounce his own conversion and resign. The Duke wrestled stoutly with his scruples. He had lost his Light Division, when the Canningites resigned; in all probability his next step would cost him a brigade of Tories; Peel was his chief ally; and his ally must be retained at all costs. But his next objective was the royal conscience; and all through the
24   autumn his guns played upon that flimsy fortress. His policy was formulated in detail, though he still maintained silence in public; for secrecy

must be maintained on the eve of a retreat. He proposed to enfranchise the Catholics and admit them to public life in exchange for a few formal safeguards and the dissolution of their Association. A hint of his intentions crept into a letter, which startled a Catholic correspondent with an intimation that if the question could be sunk "in oblivion for a short time . . . I should not despair of seeing a satisfactory remedy," though he still professed to "see no prospect of such a settlement." Such Delphic utterances brought indignant charges of duplicity from angry Protestants when the mine was fired in the next year; and Wellington was afterwards reduced to a blunt admission in debate that his letter "had been better let alone. Indeed, I shall take care not to write such a letter again to such an individual." But could he help himself? He was not yet authorised to formulate—much less to announce—a policy; and until the King released him, he was bound to work on in silence.

A new year opened; and in the first days of 1829 the Duke was busy sounding Bishops, coaxing Peel, and managing the King. He was successful in persuading Peel not to abandon the ship in heavy weather. But if persuasion was a new art to him, George IV gave him ample opportunities for learning it. The Duke's system was simplicity itself—"I make it a rule never to interrupt him, and when in this way he tries to get rid of a subject in the way of business which he does not like, I let him talk himself out, and then quietly put before him the matter in question, so that he cannot escape from it." For George IV, no more amenable than Burgos to surprise attacks, required a siege *en règle*; and the Duke laid siege to him with infinite patience. His parallels crept slowly towards the doomed fortress; and one by one the royal outworks fell, until the last remnant of the King's conscience sought refuge in the citadel itself. It was Ciudad Rodrigo over again; for the unhappy King, whose favourite delusion was that he had fought in Spain, at least enjoyed the rare distinction of a siege by Wellington. His pressure was relentless. In January he broke down the embargo on Cabinet consideration of the problem. That month the King assented gloomily—"Damn it, you mean to let them into Parliament?"—to a plain announcement of Catholic Emancipation in the Speech from the Throne; and in February the murder was out. The Whigs, robbed of their leading grievance, were sulky; for the Duke had outmanœuvred them by falling back from an untenable position. But his Tory forces had little relish for the manœuvre. He spoke almost nightly in the House of Lords; and though a derisive

30 Whig conjectured that his utterances could be summarised as "My Lords! Attention! Right about face! Quick march!" he grew positively persuasive. It was a new experience for him; there had been no need to persuade his army to fall back to Torres Vedras; but the Tories were more trouble-

31 some, and even Mrs. Arbuthnot shewed signs of mutiny. The storm broke in March. Peel, who had honourably resigned his seat at Oxford, was defeated by wild clergymen; the King was breathing treason to his circle; but Wellington persisted grimly. As he told Arbuthnot, "I have under-

32 taken this business, and I am determined to go through with it. . . . I will succeed, but I am as in a field of battle, and I must fight it out in

33 my own way." His royal master whimpered about abdication, though the audience was ended by a royal kiss (not, one feels, the least distasteful

34 of the Duke's official duties). But a final plunge of his galled charger almost unseated him. For the King, positively frantic with Protestant apprehension, refused the final jump. He had been drinking brandy and water, when the Duke arrived with Peel and Lyndhurst. Their audience was painful, as the King talked for six hours. At intervals he took more brandy; at intervals they made an interjection. But the racing stream of royal indignation poured over their attentive heads. He should postpone the Bill—the Bishops must advise him—besides, there was his oath. He was not sure precisely what it was; but he had taken one; and so the Bill must go. They intimated that the Government went with it. But the interminable harangue proceeded with an uncomfortable echo of the dreadful garrulity which had marked the onset of his father's madness.

35 The Duke was quite convinced that he was mad; he hated to be cruel to a monarch in distress; but resignation was the only course that might restore the royal senses. So they resigned. Three rigid backs were turned on Windsor, and three gentlemen returned to London. The cure was efficacious, as a prompt recantation followed them, with the affecting post-

36 script, "God knows what pain it costs me to write these words. G.R." The careful Premier extracted a more specific statement of the royal approval, and the King complied. The long siege was over; and the Duke's flag fluttered on the captured citadel.

It remained to pass the Bill. The King would march with him; but

could he discipline the Tory peers into a wise retreat? His own authority
was sadly shaken by the violence of Protestant attacks—"If my physician
called upon me, it was for treasonable purposes. If I said a word whether   37
in Parliament or elsewhere, it was misrepresented for the purpose of fixing upon me some gross delusion or falsehood." In fine, there was a
distinct danger that the Duke himself would be discredited; and if his
name lost its magic, who would remain to give orders to a distracted
nation? Something must be done in order to restore his credit; and in
his sober way he made up his mind to do it. Among the most vociferous
of his opponents was Lord Winchilsea, an unimportant peer distinguished   38
by a loud voice, a mannerism of flourishing a large white handkerchief
when making speeches, and the *abandon* of his Protestant invective. This
zealot in an ecstasy of indignation composed a letter to the Press, in
which he charged the Duke with a mean subterfuge contrived in order   39
that he "might the more effectually, under the cloak of some outward
show of zeal for the Protestant religion, carry on his insidious designs,
for the infringement of our liberties, and the introduction of Popery into
every department of the State." This was too much. He had resolved to
make an example, and Lord Winchilsea would serve. The imputation of
dishonest motives must be stopped—if necessary, by a challenge. Duelling
was never to his taste; he had discountenanced it strongly in the Peninsula, since he disapproved of officers on active service running unnecessary
risks in private quarrels. He was on active service now; but he reflected
with complete detachment that a quarrel with Lord Winchilsea would
serve a public end, since it might dispel the prevailing "atmosphere of
calumny" and restore his personal authority. Then the Prime Minister   37
proceeded to pick his quarrel. Lord Winchilsea was asked in a curt note
if he was the author of the offending letter. When he admitted it, the   39
Duke demanded an apology. The Secretary at War acted for him, thus
demonstrating the utility of staff officers in a Government, when the
Prime Minister proposes to indulge in affairs of honour. The correspondence followed its appointed course: stiff gentlemen waited on one another; solemn memoranda were drawn up; the Duke demanded "that
satisfaction . . . which a gentleman has a right to require, and which
a gentleman never refuses to give"; and in the mist of a March morning
he rode out to Battersea. The Duke was punctual, and his opponent kept

384

40   him waiting. A round-eyed doctor, fetched early out of bed, recognised his formidable patient, who cheerfully remarked, "Well, I dare say you little expected it was I who wanted you to be here." Then they rode up and down till Winchilsea arrived; and the little party—four gentlemen, a doctor, and a case of pistols—proceeded on foot to a quiet corner. The Duke turned to his second.

"Now then, Hardinge, look sharp and step out the ground. I have no time to waste. Damn it! don't stick him up so near the ditch. If I hit him, he will tumble in."

There was a pause. The seconds had a final conference; and the Duke waited with a smile. Then Hardinge handed him a pistol. He had been wondering all the morning whether to shoot his man. It would be awkward if he killed him; he supposed he would have to go to prison until he could be tried; so he resolved to shoot him in the leg. A steady voice said "Fire"; and the Duke raised his pistol. But Winchilsea's was still pointing at the ground. The Duke paused for an instant, fired, and hit his coat. Then Winchilsea fired in the air. His second flourished a paper, which contained a withdrawal of the offensive charge. The Duke listened carefully. "This won't do," he said, "it is no apology." Then someone pencilled in the mystic word; the Duke distributed a chilly bow to each of his adversaries, lifted two fingers to his hat, and rode away. He went straight to Mrs. Arbuthnot's; walked in upon her at breakfast, and startled her by asking what she thought of a gentleman who had been fighting a duel; and later in the day he told the King at Windsor. "I

41   have another subject," he remarked, "to mention to your Majesty, personal to myself. I have been fighting a duel this morning." His sovereign graciously replied that he was glad of it. That mirror of deportment told someone that he was delighted with the Duke's conduct, that gentlemen must not stand upon their privileges, and that he should have done the same himself (and malice added that he would soon believe he had). But it elicited a wail of horror from Jeremy

42   Bentham, who favoured Wellington with a strange effusion beginning "Ill-advised Man!" dwelling in gratifying terms on the disastrous consequences of his removal from public life, and bleakly endorsed by the recipient, "Compliments. The Duke has received his letter." This prompt reply stirred Bentham's gratitude, and evoked further warnings against

385

the perils of assassination, with slightly rambling reminiscences of Aaron Burr, John Wilkes, and Nelson's signal at Trafalgar.

The duel served its purpose. His motives were unquestioned now: "the system of calumny was discontinued. Men were ashamed of repeating what had been told to them. . . . I am afraid that the event itself shocked many good men. But I am certain that the public interests at the moment required I should do what I did." The House of Lords resumed the Bill; and he argued manfully. They listened, and a respectful House heard Wellington warn the extremists:

37

> "I am one of those who have probably passed a longer period of my life engaged in war than most men, and principally in civil war; and I must say this, that if I could avoid, by any sacrifice whatever, even one month of civil war in the country to which I was attached, I would sacrifice my life in order to do it. . . ."

43

This was far more impressive than all his laboured disquisitions on the Bill of Rights, the House of Stuart, and the *Concordat* of Rhenish Prussia. But he debated endlessly against the sullen legions of outraged Protestantism, until the Bill passed its final stage. Then he allowed himself a modest *Te Deum* in the House of Lords.

44

It was thirty-six years since Captain Wesley in a maiden speech counselled the Irish House of Commons to use the Catholics with moderation. The encyclopædic Croker disinterred the speech; but the Duke had quite forgotten it. For he was always more anxious to be right than to be consistent; though in the present case he happened to be both.

45

T̶HE campaign of Catholic Emancipation was over. Its strategy—
the swift recognition that Ireland had become ungovernable, the
abandonment of an untenable position, and the bold retreat—was eminently characteristic; and it had ended, as the Duke's campaigns were
apt to end, in victory. Wellington had never failed. Indeed,. he was almost
coming to believe in his own luck; for one day when Croker called, the
Duke cheerfully remarked, "Yes, 'tis all my good luck, my Fortunatus's
cap," lifting a finger to the small red Cossack cap that he wore indoors
in cold weather. Where Pitt had failed, where Canning had not even
summoned up courage for an attempt, Wellington had achieved success.
The Whigs were dished; the House of Lords was silenced; and the King
had been outflanked. The siege of Windsor was, perhaps, the most
brilliant of Wellington's campaigns; for the victory was single-handed.
His personal authority had been his only weapon; and when the fortress
of the King's elusive conscience fell, it capitulated to one besieger. Small
wonder that his sovereign remarked sulkily that "Arthur is King of
England, O'Connell King of Ireland, and myself Canon of Windsor."
A teasing Guelph had done his best to irritate King George against the
Duke by terming him "King Arthur"; and there was something in the
accusation. For in his lonely mastery of King and Lords the Duke of
Wellington came near to being a fourth estate of the realm in his own
person.

Successful in its outcome, his Catholic campaign had been less satisfactory in its effect upon his followers. For discipline is always strained
by a retreat; and the Tory squadrons had found the retreat anything but
enjoyable. Mobility was not their *forte*; designed by nature for the fixed
defence of suitable positions, they were as unhandy as fortress artillery
in a sudden evacuation; and it was not surprising that some of the
heavier pieces had been left behind in the Duke's swift retreat. This was
distinctly awkward. Guns can be spiked; but it is not so easy to silence
politicians; and there was an uncomfortable possibility that some of

his Tory artillery, fallen into the enemy's hands, would be turned against
his lines. For High Tories were now leagued with Whigs in Opposition.
The Duke's apostasy had roused them to excesses of bitterness; during
the debates some humorist imported a rat into the House of Lords; and
the Duchess of Richmond adorned her drawing-room with an array
of stuffed rats under glass labelled with the names of leading Protestant
apostates. In such a mood there was not much prospect of Tory unity,
and the Duke's Parliamentary forces were sadly diminished. He had
already lost the Canningites; the solid Tories were departing now;
there was still Peel, of course. Peel was an invaluable ally. But with his
Light Division gone and his main body wavering, could the Duke hope
to win the war with the Portuguese?

Precarious in Parliament, the Duke's position was not greatly strengthened in the country. Peel's adherence was an indication that Wellington was allied with the new forces of industrial progress. But the alliance had not yet borne fruit in progressive legislation. Besides, his
main achievement was scarcely of a nature to evoke English gratitude.
He had emancipated the Catholics, and grateful Irishmen passed glowing
resolutions; O'Connell himself sat with a Catholic committee to raise
funds and decorate the Phœnix Park with a towering Wellington Testimonial. But Irish gratitude is an uncertain passport to British affections.
Few statesmen have survived after rendering a service to Ireland. The
bare attempt cost Mr. Gladstone his career, and subsequently an all-
powerful dictator fell from the summit of his Coalition within a year
of making peace in Ireland. It would almost seem that acts of justice
towards Ireland must be their own reward; for English politics hold
no other.

2

He was just sixty now, a trim frock-coated figure with a head
growing frosty and the profile that political cartoonists loved to draw.
Coloured or plain, his eye was always sharp; the splendid hatchet of
his nose was etched upon the background; and his tight-lipped smile
was visible in whatever disguise the caricaturist's fancy had suggested—
a mute's, a rat-catcher's, an Egyptian mummy's, or the sporting hat and

THE DUKE OF WELLINGTON, *circa* 1835
From a painting attributed to John Simpson, at Apsley House
By permission of the Duke of Wellington, K.G.

multitudinous capes of *The Man wot drives the Sovereign.* The gentler pencil of H. B. began its work with him that year; and the Duke, always recognisable, took the centre of the political stage. Even the grateful *Edinburgh* exclaimed "A greater than Cæsar is here, one who has not destroyed in peace the country he had saved by his sword."

The effort had been great. He had endured torrents of abuse, and done more public speaking on the Relief Bill than in the previous twenty years of his life. Abuse was a small matter; but he found oratory an uncongenial exercise and derived little pleasure from addressing the House of Lords with a bad cold, to sink back into his seat and wrap his cloak tightly round him. It was some satisfaction to compose a lengthy memorandum on army discipline and to confront reformers with the grim apophthegm, "I know the British army, and I dare not." The old martinet had "always considered this desire to alter the system of discipline of the army as one of the morbid symptoms of the times. It is like the notion that thieves ought not to be punished . . ."; and his conviction, that "the man who enlists into the British army is, in general, the most drunken and probably the worst man of the trade or profession to which he belongs, or of the village or town in which he lives," still burned as brightly as though Badajoz had been sacked a week before. But his real pride in the army appeared when he informed a correspondent that "its conduct in the field is unrivalled. Its officers are gentlemen, and moreover the gentlemen of England. . . ." His military duties cost him a fall that summer, when his horse threw him at a review in the Park. He was unhurt; and as he rode off the ground, they cheered him to the echo, crowding round to shake his hand. The ubiquitous Creevey met him the same afternoon riding down a side street in the West End, and congratulated him upon his Irish achievement.

"You must have had tough work," said the pert little Whig, "to get thro'."

"Oh, terrible, I assure you," replied the unruffled Duke, and rode off down the street.

He could return to business now; and, in all conscience, there was quite enough of it, with Ireland and the Russo-Turkish war and currency and Portugal and the London traffic problem. It was a relief for

him to manage a Civil List pension for Miss Ponsonby, the Lady of
Llangollen and his mother's friend; for he was capable of a friendly job   11
at need. Indeed, he took endless trouble to do something for George
Brummell. That exquisite, a stranger to the Duke, was languishing at
Calais; and Wellington had done his best to provide him with a post
in the consular service. But his Foreign Secretaries were uniformly
unhelpful; Dudley objected that the King would not like it; the Duke   12
appealed to Cæsar, who remarked without sympathy that Brummell
was a damned fellow and had behaved very ill to him; but Wellington
persisted, and his sovereign acquiesced. Then Dudley was obstructive; and
after him Aberdeen was nervous, until the Duke assured him that he
would take full responsibility. So, thanks to Wellington, George Brummell got his post, though with a final gesture of dandyism he subsequently recommended that it should be suppressed as a sinecure.

He went his autumn rounds among the country houses, and someone
engineered a meeting with Huskisson at Lord Hertford's. Would he take   13
back the Canningites? That was an intriguing question. There was some
evidence besides that the Whigs themselves might join his forces; and
Arbuthnot, his intelligence officer, was out taking soundings. But, for   14
the moment, he continued with his force of Tories, though the appointment of a Whig as Privy Seal indicated that he was prepared for a
manœuvre towards the Left. No party man, the Duke had strong
prejudices in favour of a national administration. Indeed, his Catholic
policy had been undertaken with the sole object of uniting all parties
in support of firm government in Ireland. But politicians were unreason-   15
able, and he found the King more trying than ever. The royal intellect
was busy with alterations in the Guards' uniform; deep in the mysteries
of tailoring, George held a daily review of pattern coats. His mind was   16
full of collars; but it was not too full to make difficulties for the Prime
Minister. The Duke retained his confidence that "nobody can manage   17
him but me," though once a bitter cry escaped him:

> "If I had known in January 1828 one tithe of what I do now, and of   18
> what I discovered in one month after I was in office, I should have never
> been the King's minister, and should have avoided loads of misery! How-
> ever, I trust that God Almighty will soon determine that I have been suf-
> ficiently punished for my sins, and will relieve me from the unhappy lot

which has befallen me! I believe there never was a man suffered so much; and for so little purpose!"

The mood, which was unlike him, passed; but whilst it lasted, he found less pleasure in his public duties than in going to the play to see Fanny Kemble as *Juliet*. Foreign affairs were uninviting, since Canning's gay commitments had destroyed in advance the positions from which he might have made some resistance to the advancing tide of Russia; as he wrote ruefully, "Mr. Canning and Madame de Lieven have much to answer for!" His mood was irritable, and his Greek policy was little more than a bad-tempered rearguard action; though a sudden gleam from Mr. Canning illumined him when a hint of a French monarchy in Colombia elicited from Wellington an unexpected echo of the Monroe Doctrine, with a sardonic reservation in favour of the exportation of the Duke of Cumberland. His diplomacy was firmly based upon the principle of non-intervention, by which (unlike its other exponents) he meant what he said, and not—in Talleyrand's malicious phrase— "*un mot metaphysique et politique qui signifie à peu près la même chose qu'intervention.*" So the Duke kept the peace of Europe; and as the year went out, the world passed into 1830.

3

The year 1830 opened uneventfully. The calendars announced a new decade; but calendars were often wrong. The world, to all appearances, was very much what it had been since Waterloo. Canning and Castlereagh were gone; but the Duke and Metternich remained. Europe was still a symphony in white—in France a white ground sprinkled with the lilies of the Most Christian King; in Russia the white silence, mile after mile, where the Czar reigned behind the winter mists; in Italy the white gleam of Austrian uniforms, as Uhlans jingled by and *Kaiserlicks* hummed airs from Schubert. England was chilled that winter; and as it starved, the Duke sat answering his letters. Because he answered them in country houses, there was unkind comment about "gadding about, visiting, and shooting while the country is in difficulty, and it is argued that he must be very unfeeling and indifferent to it all to amuse himself in this manner." But Greville, who noted it, termed the impression "most

false and unjust," allowing that Wellington needed a little relaxation, and that, "all things considered, it is not extraordinary he should prefer other people's houses to his own." Besides, he never missed his work, opening every letter and answering them all himself. The miscellany was amazing—currency, a king for Greece, screw steamers, agricultural distress, West Indians complaining that they could no longer supply rum to the United States, French designs on Algiers, low wages at Birmingham (with a sample bag of assorted hardware), and a proposal that Buckinghamshire lace should be made compulsory at Court, eliciting the grim reply that "if the use of lace is the fashion it will be worn whether   26
the King orders the use of it or not. If it is not the fashion it will not be worn, though the King might order the use of it." He seemed to have an eye for everything—even for the exasperating swarm of inventors, "who speculate upon inventing plans and projects for government when   27
they have nothing else to do. There are thousands of them at present in England; as well as I believe elsewhere; the offspring of the march of intellect. Their object is money; which, please God, they shall not get from the Public Treasury."

The King's health was failing now; and party politics were in inextricable confusion. For the Duke had split the Tories; the Whigs were split already; and the Canningites hung impartially on the flank of either army. Bewildered groups steered intersecting courses in an endless saraband, and the Duke might have his choice of partners for the Parliamentary dance. He could recall the Canningites; but Huskisson was a distasteful colleague. Or he might beckon to Lord Grey and strengthen his depleted ranks with a Whig reinforcement. But he guessed   28
that "all these parties prefer the Government to any other," and made no sign. For, if the truth were known, he was not greatly interested in colleagues. His Catholic campaign had shewn him that he could manage the House of Lords; and he was quite content to leave the Commons to Peel. The Government's position there was frankly precarious, since Peel's majority depended upon casual support; and a derisive   29
Opposition said scornful things about "a good weak Government." But what risk was there in an unguarded flank in the absence of any enemy strong enough to take advantage of it? That spring they were defeated twice on unimportant questions, of which a Jews' Relief Bill pro-

30 voked Wellington to write that "this Christian community will not much like to have Jewish magistrates and rulers. . . . It besides gives a false colouring, and throws ridicule upon the great measures of 1828 and 1829, which it resembles only in name." For he was no friend of emancipation for its own sake. He had been perfectly prepared to emancipate the Catholics in order to ensure strong government in Ireland; but Jews were quite another matter.

Spring turned to summer; and the King, "very nervous but very brave," was dying by inches. Once he called for the *Racing Calendar*, and almost to the last he talked of horses. The Duke was often at his bedside; and
31 the prospect of a new sovereign filled him with misgivings, since King William would probably suggest that they should take in Lord Grey. But Wellington was not inclined to admit him as a colleague—"I would infinitely prefer that he should be at the head of the Government to belonging to a Government of which he was a member." For he had little taste for Coalitions. He would not find it more congenial to sit in Cabinet with the Canningites. So it was probable that Whigs, Radicals, and Canningites would unite in Opposition under Grey. What would happen then? The House of Commons would plainly be the main theatre of war; and the Duke and Peel "must look not to what is personal to ourselves, but what is necessary for the King's service, and we must make sacrifices to provide for its security. I have long been of opinion that it is desirable that the power of the government should be concentrated in one hand, and that hand that of the leader of the House of Commons." So he pressed Peel to take his place, and offered to serve
32 under him. Such abnegation was uncommon; but nothing came of it. The King died in June—"poor Prinney," as Creevey wrote, "is really dead"—and the Duke saw a faded ribbon round his neck tied to a miniature. The portrait was a woman's, and he recognised Mrs. Fitzherbert.

The world was changing now; and he watched King William with
33 some apprehension, as he launched into a little speech at his accession Council. But it turned out to be nothing worse than a becoming epitaph upon his brother. The Duke breathed again. Perhaps his new master would prove more reasonable than his antecedents gave any grounds to
34 hope. The streets, at any rate, were still for Wellington, since he was

"much cheered by the people"; and King William seemed to share their
views. For the Duke told Greville that he found him both reasonable
and tractable, and that he could do more business with him in ten   35
minutes than with George IV in ten days. He had his weaknesses, of
course. For it was highly disturbing to receive twelve hours' notice that
the King proposed to bring the King and Queen of Wurtemberg to   36
dine at Apsley House. And the festivity itself was more disturbing still.
The royal guests were late, to start with; but, once at Apsley House,
King William threw himself into the entertainment with terrifying zest.
For an unsuspected appetite for after-dinner speaking developed under
the Duke's hospitality. The least felicitous of his allusions was a warm
panegyric on the married virtues, highly flattering to the Queen of
Wurtemberg but inappropriate to Wellington. Then he desired the band
to play, *See the conquering hero comes*, and addressed himself to his
embarrassed host. The theme inspired him. He spoke of Marlborough,
Queen Anne, Vimeiro, and the defeated French; then, with a sudden
memory that the French ambassador was present he argued with
creditable ingenuity that the Duke's victories were not over the armies
of his ally and friend, the King of France, but over those of a usurper.
Refreshed by this excess of royal tact (quite wasted on the French ambassador, who did not know a word of English and was restrained
with difficulty from bowing his acknowledgments), he returned to the
main theme, spoke once more of Marlborough, and closed with an
expansive vote of royal confidence in the present administration, which
had been, he thought, and would be highly beneficial to the country, and
should retain his confidence as long as he was on the throne. Such
tributes were unusual from such a quarter; and the Duke's reply was
brief. A startled company dispersed to set the clubs buzzing with the
story. Happy the nation with an impromptu speaker for its king; but
less happy its Prime Minister.

Things might have been far worse, though. For the eccentric monarch
gave no sign of Whig opinions, and the Duke was left undisturbed
in office. But his Parliamentary weakness persisted; and before the
summer ended, he signalled to the Canningites for reinforcements.
Lord Melbourne was approached, and intimated that he could not   37
join without Grey and Huckisson. This was too much for Wellington;

Huskisson might be endured, but he declined to swallow Grey. So there were no Canningite recruits. A demise of the Crown involved a General Election, and he faced the contest with undiminished confidence. His team was weak enough (even Greville wrote contemptuously of "the Duke's awkard squad"); but the issues were unexciting. For it was improbable that feelings would run high upon economy and slavery. The contest opened quietly; but as it proceeded, a long shadow fell across the hustings. For strange news began to come from France. The Paris streets had risen in the last days of July; the troops were helpless; Marmont tasted the flavour of defeat once more; and Charles X was off to England. This was revolution. All its familiar badges reappeared —the National Guard, M. de La Fayette, and the tricolour. Was 1830 to revisit the familiar scenes of 1789? One thing was certain: the world was changing fast.

4

The Duke still went about his business in a changing world. He recognised the change, writing quietly to the Prince of Orange that "it will be scarcely possible that we can all feel the same confidence in the duration of peace hereafter, as we have done heretofore from the year 1815 up to the 25th of last month." The age of Waterloo was ending; but he kept his head. The last revolution in Paris had cost Europe twenty years of war. But Wellington had no wish to see another. A word from him might have set armies on the move from Poland to the Rhine. Louis Philippe had made his revolution; and Europe, if its leaders chose, might oblige him with his Valmy, his campaign of France, his Waterloo. The Duke need only raise a finger. Metternich would not be unwilling; for Metternich lived in the age of Waterloo. But Wellington, oddly enough, had quite outlived it.

For his main desire was to preserve the peace of Europe, and he was prepared to do so at any reasonable cost. The chastisement of France, which had once been his leading accomplishment, had no attractions for him now. In consequence the Duke was rigidly opposed to intervention, informing Greville that "we should not take any part, and that no other Government ought or could." There must be no war;

he wrote to Aberdeen that "there are some bitter pills to swallow. . . .   41
However, the best chance of peace is to swallow them all." For he was
disinclined to treat the settlement of 1815 as sacrosanct, concluding that
"good policy requires that we should recognize the Duc d'Orléans as   42
King at an early period." Few men are reconciled so easily to the destruction of their own handiwork; and his self-control endured a further
strain in August, when a Brussels mob streamed out of a theatre and
rioted against the Dutch connection. For the waves of revolution,
spreading beyond France, threatened the counter-revolutionary dykes
erected in 1815. If anything was the Duke's own creation, it was the
Kingdom of the Netherlands, the child of Waterloo. Its armies had
served under him; its Barrier fortresses along the French frontier had
been his own peculiar charge; and now its southern province was in
insurrection. There was every temptation to rush to the rescue. But
the Duke resisted it. For his belief in peace was still stronger than his
belief in the peace-treaties of Vienna.

Europe was changing round him, and he kept his head. But the
change in Europe found an uncomfortable echo nearer home. England
was polling in those summer weeks; and as the news came in from
France, the tone of the elections changed. There was a sudden sense
that the old order was passing away; Reform, of which little had been   43
heard in the opening phases, became a leading issue; and Palmerston
wrote gleefully that "this event is decisive of the ascendancy of Liberal
Principles throughout Europe. . . . The reign of Metternich over and
the days of the Duke's policy might be measured by algebra, if not by
arithmetic." Besides, there was an odd belief that Wellington was somehow identified with the fallen Polignac, whose crude efforts at reaction
had provoked the July Revolution. Progressive persons whispered that
the Duke had caused Charles X to appoint him, and had even written
to prescribe the due reactionary lines which he should follow. But Grey
doubted the story; Wellington told Lady Jersey that he had not written   44
to King Charles since his accession; and his denial in a letter to Alava
was explicit.

"Por lo que toca á mi nombramiento del ministerio de Polignac, creo que   45
no está en Europa hombre político que tiene ménos que yo á decir á ese
asunto. Jamas me habló Polignac sobre sus intenciones. Jamas le he escrito,

ni al Rey, despues del nascimiento del Duque de Bordeaux, ni al Duque d'Angoulême; ni he comunicado can ninguno en Francia sobre las cosas internas."

This was plain enough; but an untrue belief is frequently as influential as the truth itself. Besides, the fact remained that a Paris mob had challenged law and order with undeniable success and reversed the immutable decrees of 1815. The Duke was the embodiment of law and order; he was 1815 incarnate; and if these things could be done in France, why not in England?

The fall of Polignac was promptly echoed beyond the Channel in an unpleasing change of temper. The impassive Place recorded that "the impression the events in Paris made on even the least intelligent of the people was such as will never either be effaced or to any extent forgotten by them"; an *Edinburgh* reviewer cried that "the battle of English liberty has really been fought and won at Paris"; Cobbett was in *staccato* raptures; and Brougham thundered before Yorkshire crowds. If 1830 was to be a year of revolutions, English Radicals would not be left behind; and the Whigs followed at a more becoming pace. For the near prospect of office had its customary effect on a divided Opposition, and the Whig party was reforming its disunited ranks. The skies began to darken, and the gloomy Eldon predicted "a storm for changes here, especially for Reform in Parliament." If there was to be an English Revolution, that was its most likely theme.

Reform was looming nearer now. Detained for years upon the fringe of politics, it had been a topic for occasional declamations by Parliamentary faddists and a dangerous toy for Radicals to play with. But in 1830 it took the centre of the stage, and every candidate who had a real constituency was forced to talk Reform. How would the Duke regard it? Canning had opposed Reform: that was one thing in its favour. But Wellington was hardly likely to tamper with the constitution. Democracy, even in the comparatively blameless form of a proposal to enfranchise the middle class, was not to his taste. He had small respect for elected persons, and was not greatly interested in the constituencies by which they might be elected. He had seen Parliamentary democracy at close range in Cadiz; and the example of Spain was not

encouraging. For her colonies had gone, and he was inclined to think that
"no country in what is now called a modern constitutional state can keep   48
a dependency." This was unpromising for England. Besides, the times
were scarcely propitious for constitutional experiments, with open revolution in the streets of Paris and Brussels in a heady uproar. Indeed, the
troubles on the Continent hardened his inclination to resist Reform and
induced a fatal mood of complacency. For in a document suspiciously
resembling a draft for a newspaper article he painted an unpleasing pic-   49
ture of events abroad, concluding that these facts, "if viewed in their
true light, will give the people of this country fresh reason every day to
be satisfied with their own institutions." This comfortable temper was
unfriendly to Reform; and an ugly stir among the agricultural labourers
sent him still further to the Right. For there was rioting that autumn in
sixteen counties; the invisible "Captain Swing" summoned his rustic
followers; the Oldham colliers were out; and the new cotton towns were
seething. Was it a moment for concessions? The Duke thought not.
Misled by Catholic Emancipation, his critics have enquired why he
did not concede Reform. But he never made concessions for their own
sake. Catholic Relief had been undertaken in order to unite responsible
opinion in support of strong government in Ireland. His whole administration was a campaign in defence of social order; and the concession
to the Catholics had been no more than a deft withdrawal to a stronger
position in rear. But if his troops fell back before Reform and admitted
democracy to Parliament, what would remain? There was no further
retreat possible, and he resolved to hold his ground. For 1829 had been
his Busaco. Now he had reached Torres Vedras. The sea was at his
back; and he must stand to fight.

He took his own decision in his own solitary fashion. There were no
Cabinets upon Reform, and Peel was not consulted. Peel, indeed, was
understood to complain that the Prime Minister was never influenced
by men—only by women, and those invariably silly. The Duke's little   50
camarilla, whom Greville impolitely termed "the women and the toad-
eaters," were not Reformers; and no influences checked his drift towards
the Right. His mind was thoroughly made up, and a later letter to a
colleague shews how impossible it was for him to repeat the brilliant
manœuvre of Catholic Emancipation:

51   "I have not leisure to discuss Parliamentary Reform either in writing or in conversation. I confess that I doubt whether it will be carried in Parliament.

"If it should be carried it must occasion a total change in the whole system of that society called the British Empire; and I don't see how I could be a party to such changes, entertaining the opinions that I do.

"To tell you the truth I must add that I feel no strength excepting in my character for plain manly dealing. I could not pretend that I wished sincerely well to the measures, which I should become not merely a party but the principal in recommending.

"I shall sincerely lament if I should be mistaken, and that Parliament should adopt the new course proposed. I foresee nothing but a series of misfortunes for the country in all its interests, and even affecting its safety. I cannot be a party in inflicting those misfortunes."

It is impossible to say that he misjudged the moment for retreat, since he would have regarded the retreat itself as an inadmissible surrender. For Reform in 1830 was a subject on which he was incapable of compromise. The brilliant opportunism of Catholic Emancipation could not be repeated; and there was no alternative to resistance.

What other course was open? Crowds were on the move, and he instinctively resisted crowds. Gentlemen could be bargained with; but crowds must be resisted. He had resisted them before. The age of Castlereagh had been a generous education in resistance, and the Duke had served his apprenticeship as a Cabinet minister under the beneficent
52   rule of the Six Acts. If it was to be 1819 over again, he knew the method; and he was soon provisioning his garrisons and warning officers against the narrow streets of Manchester as though he were still Lord Liverpool's Master-General of the Ordnance. The age of Cato Street seemed to
53   return, as warnings reached him of plots against his life. He informed a young colleague that "I never neglect and never believe these things," and had bolts put inside his carriage doors. Quite undeterred, he went to the unruly North. It might have a good effect if the Duke shewed himself in Lancashire. There was a railway to be opened between Liverpool and Manchester; and Huskisson, who was the local member, was
54   a share resentful that "the Great Captain is to be there with all his tail. Of course, one object is to throw me into the background." But Huskisson, alas! retained the centre of the stage. The Duke's train

399

was a sumptuous affair, crowned with a canopy that could be lowered
for tunnels. Wellington arrived wearing his Spanish cloak, entrained at   55
Liverpool, and laughed heartily at his unusual situation. A vast company rose to receive him; the band played *See the conquering hero
comes*; a gun boomed; and his strange conveyance rumbled majestically
into the tunnel. After a dreadful interval the train emerged, and anxious
multitudes observed its progress through the cuttings until "the flying
machines sped through the awful chasm at the speed of 24 miles an
hour." (Even the Duke with his sharp eyes could not read the mile-
stones.) This breathless flight could scarcely be maintained; and they
halted at Parkside for water. The halt was pleasingly diversified by
a march-past of trains, which were reviewed by Wellington from his
state carriage. Gentlemen got down to stretch their legs, and the Prime
Minister shook hands with Huskisson from his door. They were both
talking to Mrs. Arbuthnot, when there was a sudden cry. The "Rocket"
was approaching. Men ran to safety from the monster; but the unhappy
Huskisson, who lost his head, limped helplessly all ways at once and
clung to a carriage door in panic. The engine swept him off; and a dispirited procession reached Manchester, where they feasted in a dismal
hush. But the Duke was cheered to the echo, and both his hands were
nearly shaken off.

So Huskisson was gone; and within a fortnight Wellington renewed
his signals to the Canningites. For the elections had increased his weakness in the House of Commons. The Whigs appeared to be united now;
and it was no longer safe to leave his Parliamentary flank uncovered.
Peel was clamouring for reinforcements. Besides, the Canningites would
be more palatable without poor Huskisson. So he sent somebody to
Palmerston with a direct offer; but Palmerston refused to join without
his Canningite associates and the Whig leaders. This was too much for   56
Wellington, and Palmerston went off to Paris. For the Duke, quite
prepared to re-enlist his Light Division, could scarcely be expected to
take in the enemy as well. A final effort was no more successful, when
Lord Palmerston spent six minutes at Apsley House, insisted on a
thorough reconstruction of the Government, and was bowed out.

The Duke was still busy with the peace of Europe, insisting that a
Conference about the Netherlands should meet in London; and his   57

letter-bag still yielded a fair number of communications from Mr. Haydon, who was pressing indomitably for a State subsidy for art. Wellington responded bleakly that "no minister could go to Parliament with a proposition for a vote for a picture to be painted," and left poor Haydon (who was quite overwhelmed by tradesmen, babies, and a colossal canvas of Xenophon arriving in sight of the sea) convinced that "impossibility, from Wellington's mouth, must be impossibility indeed." As for Reform, he spoke his mind upon it in the House of Lords:

58

"I never read or heard of any measure up to the present moment which in any degree satisfies my mind that the state of the representation can be improved. . . . I am fully convinced that the country possesses at the present moment a Legislature which answers all the good purposes of legislation, and this to a greater degree than any Legislature ever has answered in any country whatever. I will go further, and say, that the Legislature and the system of representation possess the full and entire confidence of the country. . . . I will go still further, and say, that if at the present moment I had imposed upon me the duty of forming a Legislature for any country, and particularly for a country like this, in possession of great property of various descriptions,—I do not mean to assert that I could form such a Legislature as we possess now, for the nature of man is incapable of reaching such excellence at once,—but my great endeavor would be, to form some description of Legislature which would produce the same results. The representation of the people at present contains a large body of the property of the country, and in which the landed interest has a preponderating influence. Under these circumstances, I am not prepared to bring forward any measure of the description alluded to by the noble Lord. And I am not only not prepared to bring forward any measure of this nature, but I will at once declare that, as far as I am concerned, as long as I hold any station in the government of the country, I shall always feel it my duty to resist such measures when proposed by others."

This was plain speaking. As he sat down, the Duke turned to Aber-
59 deen.

"I have not said too much, have I?"

His colleague guardedly replied that he would hear of it. But the cautious Foreign Secretary gave a more significant summary of the Duke's speech to an enquirer—"*He said that we are going out.*"

Their weakness in the House of Commons was a real menace now. For he had openly defied Reform, and Reformers were in a majority there. He still professed to think that things might do, and said to Lady Jersey, "Lord, I shall not go out—you will see we shall go on very well," while Mrs. Arbuthnot echoed him faithfully. He trusted that his enemies —Whigs, Radicals, High Tories, and Canningites—were too divided to combine against him. Besides, the country gave him something more serious to think about than Parliamentary manœuvres. Tempers were rising now, and London did its best to behave like Paris. Excited meetings roared every evening in the Rotunda, Blackfriars; informers scrawled their apprehensions to the Home Office; and the new Police, with every hair on end, found *caches* of tricolour cockades. The Duke was in his element, took pistols with him in his carriage, and drafted operation orders for the defence of Apsley House with armed men at every window and one in poor Kitty's bath-room. But, all things considered, it would be just as well to postpone the royal visit to the City. The King was to have gone in state to the Lord Mayor's Dinner; but there was evidence that Wellington was to be attacked. He was quite equal to attempts upon his life. But a disorderly attack on the procession in the King's presence was quite another matter; and the Duke, by what Lord Wellesley termed a little bitterly "the boldest act of cowardice he had ever known," decided to postpone it. The postponement was a grave humiliation; stocks fell; and an Opposition bard chanted derisively,

> "Charles the Tenth is at Holie-Rode,
>   Louis Philippe will sone be going;
> Ferdinand wyse and Miguel good
>   Mourne o'er the dedes their people are doing;
> . And ye Kynge of Great Britain, whom Godde defende,
> Dare not go out to dine with a frende."

Outnumbered in the House of Commons, the Government had now confessed its inability to preserve the normal life of London. Hats were still raised to Wellington as he rode down to Whitehall, though a few boys hooted him. But his Government was a doomed fortress; its guns were silent now; and the garrison waited behind battered walls for the last assault. Reform was looming in the Commons; but before they reached it, ministers were defeated on the Civil List. The Duke was frankly startled. He had a dinner at Apsley House that evening (it was November 15); an excited gentleman came in with the news; and the Prime Minister, who was no feminist, said, "Do not tell the women."

He took a night to think it over and resigned. If they stayed in, Brougham's motion on Reform would be carried against them; but a timely resignation served to postpone it—"indeed it was with that view that I thought it best to lose no time in sending it." Forced to abandon his position, he could still fire a shot against Reform from his retreating rearguard. But the Duke was out.

Rearguard Action

"What is the best test of a great general?"
"To know when to retreat, and to dare to do it."—WELLINGTON.

I

T H E Duke, a private gentleman once more, surveyed the unpleasing scene, while Grey assembled the incongruous elements of the first Whig administration since the distant days of Fox. As he sat musing by the fire at Mrs. Arbuthnot's, they overheard him thinking aloud.

"They want me to place myself at the head of a faction; but I say to them, I have now served my country for forty years—for twenty I have commanded her armies, and for ten I have sat in the Cabinet—and I will not now place myself at the head of a faction."

For he was disinclined to lead the Opposition; the old gamekeeper could not turn poacher. A life of public service is an indifferent training for the Opposition, since he had served the King too long to acquire the habit of obstructing the King's ministers; and Rogers, who was listening, would take his message to Lord Grey. A private gentleman once more, he was still the leading gentleman in England; and gentlemen in 1830 had work to do. County magistrates and Yeomanry must maintain order in the countryside, where something unusual was brewing. Wellington was Lord-Lieutenant of Hampshire; he had already sent all the Hampshire gentlemen out of town; and the deep voice still rumbled on.

"When I lay down my office to-morrow, I will go down into my county and do what I can to restore order and peace. And in my place in Parliament, when I can, I will approve; when I cannot, I will dissent; but I will never agree to be the leader of a faction."

A rare mood of despair was on him. "Bad business," was his verdict in Peel's drawing-room, "devilish bad business"; and he looked so grave as he walked out of Downing Street and stepped into his cabriolet that Greville (though he got his customary nod) did not like to speak to him. The times were out of joint. For he was quite convinced that the French meant to go to war, and there was every sign of an impending revolution. The French, of course, were at the bottom of it—"I entertain no doubt that there exists a formidable conspiracy. . . . I am in-

407

clined to think that the operations of the conspirators in his country are conducted by Englishmen. But that the original focus is at Paris." French gold enabled agitators to flit about in gigs; and the Duke waited grimly for the explosion. He was inclined to blame himself for allowing "a licentious press to repeat *usque ad nauseam* the misrepresentations of all parties." But what hope was there that a misguided public could be preserved by Grey and his Whig colleagues? "The gentlemen now in power are committed to Revolution by the applause with which, as private persons, they greeted those in Paris and Brussels." Besides, their policies were a delirious and conflicting blend of Opposition pledges. And there was little salvation to be hoped for from the Crown. He had once said that where kings can ride on horseback and inflict punishment, revolution is impossible. Russia, perhaps, enjoyed that happy state; but it was evident that such feats of equitation were far beyond William IV.

What was to be done? The Duke performed his county duties and returned to town. His first reluctance to lead his friends in Opposition was passing now; and he gave fifty of his late colleagues a dinner at Apsley House. They dined in the great gallery among his Spanish pictures; and when the Duke of Richmond proposed his health with the sentiment that he hoped their host would soon give them the word of command "As you were," Wellington replied almost cheerfully, "No, not as you were, but much better." This was a trifle more encouraging, though he still counselled his retreating followers "to remain quiet till they see real cause to take an active part." For in rearguard actions unnecessary conflicts were to be discouraged. So they fell slowly back, as 1830 went out.

2

The world in 1831 was not more cheerful; and Mr. Croker found the Duke "in very low spirits about politics," though he still could not see his way to open fire as leader of an organised Opposition. But when the Reform Bill was produced, he knew his mind clearly enough, opining that the measure would, "by due course of law, destroy the country," while the disfranchisement of existing boroughs would give "a shake . . . to the property of every individual in the country." For he was more interested in the sanctity of vested interests than in the forms of Parliamentary representation. But party discipline presented irritating problems. It had already been revealed to him that a Prime Minister's authority over his followers is considerably less than that of a commander in the field; and he now discovered that an Opposition leader's is more slender still, complaining bitterly that "nobody does anything but what he likes, excepting myself. We are all commanders, and there are no troops. Nobody obeys or ever listens to advice but myself. Then I am abused because things do not go right." Even the faithful Peel—"that fellow in the House of Commons"—was trying. "One can't go on without him; but he is so vacillating and crotchety that there's no getting on with him. I did pretty well with him when we were in office, but I can't manage him now at all. . . ." Wellington was determined to defeat the Bill and had little patience with half-measures. His views were plainly stated; but his popularity seemed almost unimpaired. For one day in February he was thrown from his horse at Oxford Circus; they took him to a shop, where he announced that he was not seriously injured and requested that the mud might be removed from his clothes; a cab was called; and as he entered it, the Duke was loudly cheered. But he still argued stoutly in the House of Lords that Reform involved "the downfall of the constitution," contending shrewdly that Whig declamations on the toiling masses should be discounted because nobody proposed to enfranchise them, and that it was wise "to consider what a House of Commons ought to be, and not what the constituents ought to be" (a devastating test by which to judge some later extensions of the franchise). His strategy was simple—"to reject the Reform Bill, if only to gain time"—and in order to render their defensive tactics effective he was urging the divided Tories to close their ranks. In April a Government defeat in the House of Commons was followed by a dissolution. There was an afternoon of wild confusion in the Lords; peers shook their fists and bawled abuse at one another; the Lord Chancellor bounded about the Chamber; and guns boomed the tidings that King William had left his palace for the House.

But the Duke was absent. He was at Apsley House by Kitty's bedside. For poor, faded Kitty was sadly ailing. An Irish friend, who saw
her early in the year, was shocked to find her on a sofa, "paler than   17
marble . . . a miniature figure of herself in wax-work." A tiny head
on a big pillow, she stirred a little as her visitor arrived; and a familiar
voice said faintly, "O! Miss Edgeworth, you are the truest of the true
—the kindest of the kind." A thin white hand stole out to greet her,
and a faint touch of colour returned with the shadow of a smile. She lay
on the ground-floor of his great London house among the trophies—
glass cases full of china given by respectful monarchs, stupendous can-
delabra from the Portuguese, and the Homeric shield, gift of a grateful
City. Her visitor stared at them; and a faint voice behind her murmured,
"All tributes to merit! there's the value, all pure, no corruption ever
suspected even. Even of the Duke of Marlborough that could not be said
so truly." For her Duke was perfect, though he could never bear it when
she told him so. He alarmed her sometimes. But then great men were
bound to be alarming; and her brother's boys used to run up the
back-stairs, when they came to see her, for fear of an encounter with   18
their terrifying uncle. He was gentle with her now and positively wrote
to Alava about her health. She seemed to rally in the spring; but he still   19
sat with her. Her thin fingers strayed inside his sleeve and found a
circlet fastened on his arm years before by Kitty Pakenham. The guns   20
were booming for King William now across the Park. That afternoon
the House of Lords was full of agitated peers; but her Duke was there
beside her, as his poor, faded Kitty died.

Parliament had been dissolved, and London illuminated for Reform.
A cheerful mob paraded Piccadilly on the look-out for recalcitrant house-
holders. Dark windows meant a Tory occupant; and the great house at
Hyde Park Corner with its tall portico stood out against the summer
night in sombre outline. Mourning apart, the Duke was the last man
in London who was likely to put candles in his windows for Reform in
order to oblige a mob; and presently the stones began to crash into
the silent rooms (one did some damage to a picture), until a servant   21
on the roof let off a blunderbuss, and the crowd moved off to draw Park
Lane for Tories.

TAKING AN AIRING IN HYDE PARK
A PORTRAIT
Framed but not yet Glazed

THE DUKE OF WELLINGTON, 1833
From a lithograph by James Doyle, in the author's possession.

3

The twin scourges of Reform and cholera strode on through 1831. Reform was grave enough; but the Duke was not afraid of cholera— "the only thing I am afraid of is fear. . . . If three or four hundred *Notables* were to leave London for fear of it, they would be followed by three or four hundred thousand, and then this country would be plunged into greater confusion than had been known for hundreds of years." But Reform was a more formidable menace. His fears of violent revolution had vanished now; but he was frankly alarmed by the prospect of a measure which "totally alters all the existing political interests of the country, creates one-fourth entirely new interests . . . and this at the most critical period in the history of the world." He was inclined to blame himself for the destructive power of the press—"I allowed my contempt for the newspapers—a contempt founded upon the experience of a long life, of their utter inefficiency to do an individual any mischief . . . —to influence my conduct in respect to the press, when I was in office. The press is an engine of a very different description, when it attacks individuals, and when it attacks the institutions of the country. It is powerful in respect to the latter, and no man can blame my own neglect more than I do." Meanwhile, deluded citizens were voting steadily for Reform; there would be a majority of Reformers in the new House of Commons; and what was to be done? It might be comforting to sit at Walmer talking of old times to Alava and Croker. But what was he to do? Reform was a chimera menacing the "last asylum of peace and happiness," where great towns with no members of Parliament enjoyed "the benefit of being governed by the system of the British constitution without the evil of elections" and an eccentric franchise secured the Parliamentary services of steady persons whose presence "constitutes the great difference between the House of Commons and those assemblies abroad called Chambers of Deputies." His contempt for the new members was profound—"they dare not vote according to the suggestions of their own judgment after discussion; they are sent as delegates for a particular purpose under particular instructions, and not members of Parliament sent to deliver it *de arduis*

411

regni." He was acting on the defensive now; and the first necessity was to
unite his forces. This was achieved by midsummer. Peel was still enig-   26
matic; but the Tories were aligned behind the Duke. Even Lord Winchilsea was reconciled, and Wellington went over to inspect his Yeomanry.

Their course in Parliament was plain. The Bill must be defeated,
though the Duke retained his old reluctance to declare a general war
upon the Whigs—"I could not be a party to any violent or factious   27
opposition against any government named by the King." For he was
a public servant; and his services were at Lord Grey's disposal upon
matters of foreign policy. He even waited on the Prime Minister in
Downing Street, and wrote long memoranda for his guidance. But he
was quite unbending on Reform. If the Commons passed the Bill, the
Lords must throw it out. For time, he felt convinced, was on their side;
rejection meant delay; and under cover of delay sanity might yet pre-   28
vail. He was in town that autumn; Greville attended a great dinner at
Apsley House, where the Duke told him stories about George IV and   29
all the trinkets they had found in his belongings—gloves, *gages d'amour*,
and women's hair of every colour with the powder and pomatum still
upon it—and what a trial the Duchess of Kent had been with her commanding ways. But with Reform impending it was impossible for him
to find a refuge in talk about old times. The Tory peers must be convened, and he wrote argumentative letters in all directions. That autumn
his old mother died at eighty-nine, having seen her incomparable pair
of Gracchi on every eminence in two continents. The Opposition leaders
met at Apsley House, and Eldon came in after dinner, post-prandial in   30
the extreme. If the Bill passed the Commons, the Lords must do their
duty. Wellington informed his peers that Reform was synonymous with
democracy—"this fierce democracy"—and that democracy involved an
immediate onslaught upon property:

> "A democracy has never been established in any part of the world, that   31
> it has not immediately declared war against property—against the payment
> of the public debt—and against all the principles of conservation, which are
> secured by, and are in fact the principal objects of the British Constitution,
> as it now exists. Property and its possessors will become the common
> enemy. . . ."

The Spanish precedent still haunted him; for he insisted that Reform would paralyse "the strength which is necessary to enable his Majesty to protect and keep in order his foreign dominions, and to ensure the obedience of their inhabitants. We shall lose these colonies and foreign possessions, and with them our authority and influence abroad." Four days later angry Reformers read in black-edged newspapers that the Bill was dead, rejected by the House of Lords. An undergraduate was driving back to Christ Church in the Oxford coach, and confided to his diary Gladstone's impressions of his first debate.

The Bill was dead; but, with the country in an ugly ferment, it might rise again. The Duke's windows suffered once more; and when he went to Walmer, six gentlemen, headed by a fighting Army chaplain, rode as his escort. It was November now, and Wellington drove in his britzka—that open carriage in which everyone caught colds—with an armed servant on the box and a brace of double-barrelled pistols by his side. The Arbuthnots were at the Castle; and his tone was frankly pessimistic. Then Croker and a house-party arrived; Lord Stanhope began asking him questions about the Peninsula, retiring to his room to write down all his answers; and they found the Duke looking grave. He faced the facts about Reform, announcing that "the disfranchisement of any place is a painful thing to swallow. I don't mean that we shan't be obliged to swallow it—but it is a monstrous gulp." The closing sentence of his speech had urged the Lords to leave the door open:

> "In recommending to your Lordships to vote against this Bill, I earnestly entreat you to avoid pledging yourselves, whether in public or private, against any other measure that may be brought forward. I recommend to you to keep yourselves free to adopt any measure upon this subject which shall secure to this country the blessings of a government."

This was the strategy of retreat once more: the enemy were pressing hard, and it might be necessary to fall back to the next ridge. But warfare extended now far beyond the walls of Parliament; for crowds were on the move in every quarter of the kingdom, and Wellington's first instinct was to repress them. Crowds almost invariably warped his judgment. He sent his sovereign a warning letter on the subject of the Political Unions; they were reported to be arming now, and he advised their prompt suppression, pointing his advice with the alarming prec-

413

edents of the National Guard and the Irish Volunteers. The letter con- 36
veyed a hint that Wellington was prepared to take the helm again,
rescue the King from his Whig captors, fight a General Election upon
the issue of public order, and restore England to her senses. But his
bewildered sovereign was unresponsive.

To restore public order was the main problem now. As the Duke
wrote, "that once done, the reform of the Parliament might be consid- 37
ered with honour and safety, if not with advantage. Till these unions
are put down, it does not much signify, in reality, what course is taken."
In this mood he was frankly indifferent to the negotiations in progress
between ministers and the more cautious of his Tory followers in the
House of Lords. What did the details of Reform matter, if revolution
went unchallenged on its way? But the Duke could see that events had
made Reform quite inevitable—"the King has . . . pronounced himself
for Reform, and it would not be easy to govern in his name without 38
Reform. But the more gentle and more gradual the reform, the better
for the country. . . ." His mind was moving towards a fresh stage in
the long retreat; but he must not be hurried.

4

The next attack would come in 1832. For the Bill was passing through
the Commons for the third time. How was it to be received when it
reached the House of Lords? That fortress was not quite impregnable,
since it was generally known that Grey proposed to spike its slightly
antiquated guns by a creation of sufficient peers to pass the Bill; and
in January one enthusiast was pressing Wellington to see the King,
advise him to refuse this exercise of the prerogative, form a Tory
Government, and go to the country. But the Duke refused. He always 36
thought of details; and one detail of Parliamentary routine stood in the
way. For this exhilarating programme would leave no time for Parliament to renew the Mutiny Act before a dissolution. Besides, he doubted
how far the King would play his part. He had every reason to, since
when he had been prepared to act on similar lines in the autumn, the
King hung back and the moment for the *sortie* passed. Now there was

nothing to be done except to stand on the defensive; and he waited for the Bill behind the ramparts of the House of Lords.

39   An unwise "endeavour to bully slight colds" had ended in a temperature, and shooting gave him bad headaches before Christmas; but he was soon restored, out in the saddle through six hours of February rain, and riding sixty miles a day to hounds. As for the situation, he was

40   past tactics now. A gloomy certainty possessed him that "we are governed by the mob and its organ—a licentious press . . . the mob and Mr.

41   Place the tailor!" Convinced that "the monarchy . . . approaches its termination," he was averse from ingenious manœuvres designed to avert the creation of Whig peers. Indeed, he rather welcomed this ex-

42   pedient, since its very ruthlessness would expose Grey's *coup d'état* in all its nudity and spare noblemen the degradation of changing their minds.

43   The King might still prevent it—"The King of this country is a tower of strength"—but Wellington would put no pressure on him.

     The Bill reached the House of Lords in March, and Wellington fired a warning shot from the battlements. Even Greville, who had been busy

44   in the negotiations for a compromise, found his tone "fair and gentlemanlike . . . a speech creditable to himself, useful and becoming . . .

45   a very handsome speech." He opposed the second reading at length, though in a tone of marked restraint. But months of negotiation between Whig ministers and "Waverers" had weakened his defences; and the Bill passed its second reading. The enemy had penetrated his position now; for the Lords' vote admitted that there was to be a Reform Bill

46   of some sort, and the Duke faced the uncomfortable fact—"my own opinion is, that we shall not escape a Reform Bill on the principle of that now in the House of Lords, and that the efforts of all ought to be directed to render that bill as little noxious as possible." The threatened fortress was quite indefensible, and the heroic gesture of a last stand among the ruins made no appeal to Wellington. Always practical, he was prepared to abandon the position and fall back fighting. But he had few illusions as to the final outcome since he was frankly sceptical of the value of any possible amendments of the Bill. What else was there to do, though, unless the King came to his senses? The world was more than usually out of joint; for Wellington could scarcely take

47   a ride in London without hearing angry cries though Croker was con-

soled to notice "with what respectful, I should say *increased* attention
he is received by every well-dressed person, and even by a vast majority
of the lower orders." But his health was glaringly omitted from a long   48
toast-list at the King's dinner to the East India directors. The skies were
dark indeed; and the Duke ruefully confessed that "I am out of the   49
whole affair."

Grey's temper changed the situation. The Bill was in committee now;
and when the House of Lords shewed signs of independence in the first
week of May, the Prime Minister posted off to Windsor with a peremp-
tory demand for the creation of fifty peers. This was too much for his
much-enduring sovereign, who refused to give the required assurances.
The Government resigned; King William sent for Lyndhurst; and, in
Endymion's gleeful narrative, "the bold chief baron advised His Majesty   50
to consult the Duke of Wellington."

5

Was he to be Prime Minister again? He had his chance; and this
was the precise situation for which he had played in November, 1831—
the King at bay, the Whigs dismissed, and loyal subjects to the rescue.
But the *sortie*, which might have saved the fortress six months before,
was now little more than a forlorn hope. For it was 1832. However, it
might still serve a useful purpose; for Wellington was thoroughly alive
to "the advantage of taking the King out of the hands of the Radicals—   51
that is, in reality—of giving the country the benefit of some government"—and taking the sting out of the Reform Bill.

It was a Thursday when Lord Lyndhurst saw him, and they went off   52
in search of Peel. The three men met at Apsley House; Croker was there
as well, and asked who was to be Prime Minister. Lyndhurst nodded
towards Peel, and said that he must tell them. Peel spoke with unaccustomed emphasis: if the new Government proposed to carry a Reform Bill, he could not and would not have anything to do with it. He
had already made a *volte face* on Catholic Relief, and was quite determined not to repeat the experience. Croker suggested that Lord
Harrowby, who had been prominent among the "Waverers," might fill
the part; but the Duke disliked the idea, doubting if Harrowby would

be acceptable to the Tory peers. That night he wrote a note to Lynd-hurst:

53

> "I shall be very much concerned indeed if we cannot at least make an effort to enable the King to shake off the trammels of his tyrannical Minis-ter. I am perfectly ready to do whatever his Majesty may command me. I am as much averse to the Reform as ever I was. No embarrassment of that kind, no private consideration, shall prevent me from making every effort to serve the King."

So he was prepared to abandon his defensive strategy and lead the for-lorn hope; and on Friday Lyndhurst went down to Windsor and in-formed the King.

Croker saw the Duke again on Saturday, and found him grim, but not uncommunicative. "Well," he remarked, "we are in a fine scrape, and I really do not see how we are to get out of it." Harrowby, he said, had declined; so had the Speaker; and if no one else would act, he must form a Government himself. As the Duke remarked to Croker, he had passed his whole life in troubles and was now in troubles again, but it was his duty to stand by the King. That was his leading thought; the royal summons was a command to Wellington; and he pressed Croker to let Peel know that he would serve with him or under him or in any way that Peel might think best for the common cause. But Peel had little taste for a second recantation followed by a second martyrdom, and
54 kept carefully aloof. That day the printers were at work on Place's wily placard, "To stop the Duke, go for Gold"; a general run on the banks might paralyse the new Tory Government; and windows in Birming-ham already displayed the threat, "No taxes paid here until the Reform Bill is passed." But though the King was hissed as he drove up from Windsor, a crowd cheered Wellington outside the palace. He told the King that, "happen what would, he would stand by him and endeavour to extricate him from the difficulty in which he was placed." But he must have colleagues; and the King, who took a hand in the Duke's game, had no success with Peel or the Speaker. That afternoon Wellington inter-viewed a long procession of reluctant Tories; but none of them would serve except his military stalwarts, Murray and Hardinge. For the Tory intellect was not equal to the Duke's conception of a rearguard action in

politics, his incessant series of retreats to the next ridge in rear; and their civilian weakness for consistency was strangely troubled by the prospect of helping to pass Reform after resisting it so long. But they all dined together at the Carlton Club that night. The Duke was in the chair and listened to innumerable speeches, followed by a long session with the reluctant Speaker.

More interviews filled Sunday. His patience was beginning to wear a little thin, since he observed to Croker (who was hanging back) that in such a crisis, if a man put himself on the shelf, it might not be so easy to take him off the shelf when he perhaps might desire it. That night he saw the Speaker once again without success; for that dignitary's eloquence, repressed by his official situation, found release in a disquisition that lasted for three hours, led nowhere, and provoked from Lyndhurst the disrespectful comment that his prospective colleague was "a damned tiresome old bitch." The Speaker asked for time; but on Monday night the House of Commons intervened with a debate, which proved conclusively that the Duke's forces were inadequate. He faced the facts at once, and informed the King on Tuesday morning that he could not form a Government.

The *sortie*, which lasted for five breathless days, had failed; and the long siege was nearly over. For Wellington had failed to break the Whig blockade of the House of Lords. The Whigs were back again in office; and the peers, surrounded by a hostile Government and an angry House of Commons, were bound to capitulate. But it had been a gallant effort, though *Coningsby* conjectures that "the future historian of the country will be perplexed to ascertain what was the distinct object which the Duke of Wellington proposed to himself in the political manœuvres of May 1832," and concludes disapprovingly that "this premature effort of the Anti-Reform leader to thrust himself again into the conduct of public affairs . . . savoured rather of restlessness than of energy." But did it? His objectives were plain enough—to form a Tory Government which would preserve public order and pass a moderate Reform Bill. If he failed, it was because his followers permitted him to fail. Opponents of Reform, they were unable to share his willingness to pass the Bill. For they viewed it as good partisans were bound to view it: Reform was not a Tory measure, and what Tory could square his princples with voting for it? The Duke took another view. Never a good party man, he was prepared to sacrifice Tory orthodoxy in a crisis. Indeed, he did not regard himself as a mere party leader—"I was not acting for any body of men, but for the King." That was the key to all his actions. The King was in difficulties, and must be rescued; the King had summoned Wellington, and Wellington had eaten the King's salt. However desperate the adventure, he could not refuse. He did not spare himself, offering to serve under Peel and enduring endless interviews with his reluctant followers. But persuasion was not his *forte*; and if his followers thought more of Tory principles than of the King's dilemma, the Duke was not to blame.

Reform rolled on implacably; and Wellington, determined to avert the final ignominy of a wholesale creation of Whig peers by an unwilling King, withdrew his opposition to the Bill; his followers "skulked in clubs and country houses," whilst it passed through its remaining stages; and on a summer afternoon Whigs crowded to the House of Lords to hear the royal assent recited to the empty benches opposite.

6

One June morning he rode out of Apsley House to give a sitting to Pistrucci at the Mint. An ugly crowd collected in the City to wait for him on his return, and a magistrate offered his assistance. The Duke's reply was practical.

"You can do nothing. The only thing you can help me in is to tell me exactly the road I am to take to get to Lincoln's Inn; for the great danger would be in my missing my way and having to turn back on the mob."

He started with his groom, and the mob followed them. They tried to drag him from his horse in Fenchurch Street; but two Chelsea pensioners appeared, whom he stationed at each stirrup with orders to face about whenever he was forced to halt. There was some stone-throwing in Holborn; and when he saw a coal-cart in the distance, "Hillo!" said the Duke in a grim aside, "here's the Artillery coming up; we must look out." But an obliging gentleman, who drove a tilbury behind him for some time, gave valuable cover, and earned the Duke's esteem by "never looking towards me for any notice." Two policemen joined the little party; and the Duke disposed them at his horse's head as an advance guard. When they reached Lincoln's Inn, the mob was still at his heels. He surveyed the situation and enquired if there was another exit. It seemed there was. "Then be so good," said the Duke, "as to shut the gate." The enemy detained by this simple strategem, he rode out into Lincoln's Inn Fields; but the mob was after him again. His horse was walking, and an excited gentleman named Martin Tupper leapt on the steps of Surgeons' Hall, exclaiming loudly, "Waterloo, Waterloo!" The mob was slightly awed; the Duke raised two fingers to his hat; and the strange ride went on, "the cast-metal man" (as Carlyle wrote to his mother) "riding slowly five long miles all the way like a pillar of *glar!*" He had a little escort now, as they went up the Strand and along Pall Mall; gentlemen in club windows saw him staring straight between his horse's ears. They rode up Constitution Hill; but the mob headed him by a dash across the Park; and they were waiting outside Apsley House to hoot, as he reached home at last. It was June 18. "An odd day to choose," the Duke said to somebody. "Good morning."

II

THE new world, where Reform was law and Mr. Creevey boarded
his first omnibus, filled Wellington with grave misgivings. He was
quite convinced that the revolution had begun, and waited for the end
with dignity. The least of troubles was his personal unpopularity. An
emblem of opposition to Reform, he was continually hooted; but he
had grown accustomed to the mob outside his house, and even to the
groans of village Radicals as he rode home from hunting. He faced it
in his quiet way, reporting calmly that "I think that I have got the better
of the mobs in London by walking about the town very quietly, not-
withstanding their insults and outrages. It is certain that the better class
are ashamed of them, and take pains upon all occasions to testify every
mark of respect for me." But the prospect was dark—"the government of
England is destroyed"—and his mind ran on revolutionary precedents.
The monarchy might still survive, if only the army remained sound; but
the Jacobins were in the saddle, and he might live to see a National
Guard. He even detected symptoms of the Great Rebellion—"the times
are much more similar to those of Charles I than people are aware of.
The same parties, almost under the same denominations, are *en presence*.
. . ." But the French precedents unnerved him; for it was 1789 over again.
The road had forked once more towards safety or revolution; and
when his countrymen made the wrong choice, how could the old duellist of the *ancien régime* feel anything but dark forebodings? "Our wise
rulers prefer the course which faction suggested forty years ago to
that of wisdom, of experience, and reflection. God knows what will
happen to the world."

His course was clear, though. A Tory clergyman, who was inclined
to emigrate from his ungrateful country, had asked for the Duke's
advice.

"You have, I understand, a cure of souls. Can you abandon your post
in a moment of crisis and dangers for worldly objects? Your flock ought to

provide for your decent and comfortable subsistence; and they not only do not perfom that duty, but they persecute you! Still, ought you to abandon them? Is it not your duty to remain at your post? Expect better times. Make every exertion, every sacrifice to enable you to do justice by everybody, including your family; but I confess, if I was in your situation, I would not quit my post."

The parable applied as plainly to himself: he could not quit his post. For though the Duke was out of office, he was keenly aware that, politics apart, he was a public institution. As the late King's executor, he had assumed peculiar and delicate duties towards the Crown. Besides, the world conspired to regard him as a universal dispensary of good advice. "Every man," as he once wrote, "has one resource only; that is, to apply to the Duke of Wellington." A mannerism grew upon him of alluding to himself in the third person. Cæsar had done the same; but in Cæsar's case the habit was a mere convenience for narrative. In Wellington's it served to indicate an odd dualism. For he seemed to recognise two persons in himself—an ageing gentleman of modest tastes who could be happy in congenial society, and a public figure whose requirements were often more majestic. In this mood of queer detachment he wrote to Croker of his own state appearance as Chancellor of Oxford, "I am the Duke of Wellington, and, *bon gré mal gré*, must do as the Duke of Wellington doth." That was his duty for the future. It was far pleasanter, no doubt, to sit gossiping about the past in the low rooms at Stratfield Saye, or to pace the sunny flagstones of his battlements at Walmer eluding Stanhope's endless questions. But there was his duty to be done. He could not quit his post; the splendid *rôle* must be played out to the end.

The new Parliament met early in 1833; and Wellington returned from a stroll into the House of Commons to view the children of Reform with the chilly verdict, "I never saw so many shocking bad hats in my life." He feared the worst, informing Greville that his first consideration was to keep a roof over his head, the next to support Grey as the sole alternative to anarchy; for "I consider Lord Grey's Government as the last prop of the Monarchy." Besides, Opposition had never been his *forte*—"I have been in office, and have served the King throughout my life; and I know all the difficulties in which the Government are placed."

But since the revolution was over and the House of Lords had ceased to count, he saw no reason for regular attendance. Now he was almost irresponsible, and wrote cheerfully that "I have been here generally amusing myself with the Foxhounds," gaily attired in a scarlet coat, strapped trousers, and a lilac waistcoat. But he was in the Lords sometimes; and the devoted Haydon watched him speaking with such a manly air or deliberately fetching out his glasses to read a quotation. He was in calmer water now; and someone who rode with him in St. James's Park noticed how everyone got up and all hats came off at his approach. He was still convinced that "we are going, but I think it will be gradually. There will be no catastrophe; we are not equal to one. We shall be destroyed by the due course of law, unless the Virgin of the Pillar or some miracle saves us." But the process was comfortingly gradual; and when the King came to his Waterloo banquet that year, he had his windows mended for the occasion.

Not that he mitigated his despair, writing to Stanhope that he would "do anything to be able to quit this unfortunate and unhappy country." But how could he? There was nothing for it but to visit country houses, attend the House of Lords, and install a novel system of warming Stratfield Saye by hot-water pipes. (He was a domestic pioneer, even achieving triumphs in the uncharted field of household sanitation.) This mild routine carried him through 1833, until the University of Oxford brought him upon the stage again as Chancellor. The honour pleased him, though he protested that he "knew no more of Greek and Latin than an Eton boy in the remove." H. B. poked pleasant fun at *A Great Doctor of Cannon Law*, and the Duke conjectured gaily that "I shall get to the Woolsack at last." In June, 1834, he went to Oxford for his installation. It was a great occasion, with the Sheldonian packed to receive him and Mrs. Arbuthnot there to share his triumph. The Oxford Tories took him to their bosoms; Eldon was there as well, and the Duke gave a degree to his old adversary, Winchilsea. He had learnt with some apprehension that a speech in Latin was expected—"Now, any speech is difficult, but a Latin one was impossible; so in this dilemma I applied to my physician, as most likely, from his prescriptions, to know Latin, and he made me a speech, which answered very well. I believe it was a very good speech, but I did not know much of the matter." His Latin quantities were uncertain, and a shocked university heard its heroic Chancellor affront the rules by mispronouncing *Jacobus* as three short syllables. This was encouraging for the prospects of *Carolus*; but the incalculable Latinist defied convention once again with a protracted "o." False quantities were all forgiven, when a tactful prizewinner declaimed the Newdigate and reached the apostrophe,

> "And the stern soul the world could scarce subdue
> Bowed to thy Genius, Chief of Waterloo."

The packed Sheldonian rose at the Chancellor, roaring its homage; caps waved, feet stamped, and an impassive figure was seen rigid in its seat through a haze of dust. He noticed them at last, lifted his tasselled cap, and signalled to the poet to proceed; and then the cheerful uproar broke out again.

The Arbuthnots went off to Woodford. They were to meet again as usual in the autumn; but she died with dreadful suddenness in August. "Only think," wrote Mr. Creevey in his unpleasant idiom, "of the Beau's flirt, Mrs. Arbuthnot, being dead!" He was at Hatfield, when the news arrived. The letter fell from his hand, and he flung himself down on a sofa; then he rose on the verge of sobs and paced the room. That night he thought of poor Arbuthnot. They had both loved her; and the Duke felt that he must go to him. Early the next morning he posted off to console the widower. But the loss was Wellington's. For he had lost the only home that he had ever had. An exile until middle life, he had returned at fifty to his two big houses where poor, fluttered Kitty muddled accounts and failed to recognise his guests. That had been nothing like a home. But he was always at his ease in his chair at Mrs. Arbuthnot's. They had met first in Paris, when it was no novelty for Wellington to meet handsome women. Harriett Arbuthnot was quite as handsome as the rest, and far more sensible. She listened well, entered into politics, and could be trusted not to talk. She did not gush over him in public; and her slight tendency to order him about was an agreeable change for an authoritative man. Besides, her husband was an invaluable subordinate with vast official knowledge; and Wellington could always find sanctuary at her house in Parliament Street. All this was ended now; there would be no more talks beside her fire, no more little jokes

20

424

about the implacable *Tiranna* and her Slave. There was still Arbuthnot; and the two lonely men drew silently together. He had once shared Arbuthnot's home with him, and now the Duke gave Arbuthnot a shelter. They would be widowers together. But when the world watched him speaking calmly in the House of Lords that week, it thought him hard. For the world knew nothing of his stricken letters to Frances Shelley, who had once shared their jokes—all ended now.

2

An ageing, lonely man, he had his work, his friends, and his interminable correspondence. His friends receded now behind the distances which separate deaf men from the world; their voices came to him across the silence, and he answered loudly from the farther shore. But his contact with the world was principally maintained on paper; and he had little reason to complain of any lack of it. For everybody wrote to him; and from a constitutional inability to ignore a letter he wrote back to everyone. Stray correspondents invariably received the Duke's compliments and a full, if occasionally acid, statement of his point of view. Remedies for ailments from which he did not suffer were civilly returned; and unsolicited precautions for his spiritual welfare received due acknowledgment. For he was never frivolous about religion. A faithful Churchman, he was no church-goer in London because "in point of fact, I never hear more than what I know by heart of the Church service, and never one word of the sermon"; besides, the precious remnants of his hearing would be imperilled by sitting "for two hours every week uncovered in a cold church." He had tried St. James's, Piccadilly, and found it too chilly for him. But he invariably attended divine worship at Stratfield Saye and Walmer, where "my presence at church can operate as an example." He explained, for his correspondent's benefit, that he was not "a person without any sense of religion. If I am so, I am unpardonable; as I have had opportunities to acquire, and have acquired a good deal of knowledge upon the subject. . . . I am not ostentatious about anything. I am not a 'Bible Society man' upon principle, and I make no ostentatious display either of charity or of other Christian virtues."

His correspondent in this instance was a zealous bishop. But he had other correspondents upon spiritual themes. Early in 1834 he received an exhortation from a young lady much addicted to good works and   22 playing on the harp, who had been encouraged by her success with a convicted murderer to try her hand upon the Duke. Exhorted to spiritual rebirth by a total stranger, he answered promptly. Two blots, an error, and the circumstance that he misdated his reply convinced her that the Duke was overwhelmed by his emotions, although the month was January when the most hardened sinners frequently mistake the year without spiritual commotion, and he had made precisely the same error when writing to the King about his Cabinet in January, 1828. Heartened by   23 this conviction, Miss Jenkins called at Apsley House and left a Bible. The Duke resisted the temptation to present his compliments and acquaint Miss Jenkins that there were several in the house already. Indeed, he made no reply, although the gift was accompanied by a "suitable   24 note." This was in April; and Miss Jenkins' note remained unanswered for four months. But Mrs. Arbuthnot died in the first week of August; and before the month was out, the Duke's mind had turned to his religious correspondent, who received an answer (addressed to "Mrs. Jenkins") acknowledging her gift and asking whether he might have the pleasure of meeting her. It was most unlike him to wait four months before answering a letter or, having waited so long, to answer it at all. But in the interval something had gone out of his life with Mrs. Arbuthnot; was it possible that Mrs. Jenkins might replace her? Her reply enlightened him, revealing that, though willing to receive him, she was *Miss* Jenkins after all. The young evangelist had reached this great decision in consultation with her friend, Mrs. L., "a perfect woman of the world." The Duke, a little startled, rejoined that he was not "in the habit of visiting young unmarried ladies with whom he is not ac-   25 quainted"; but he proposed to call, when he was next in town.

He called upon her in November. Miss J. was fortified by prayer for the ordeal, "praying to God to be with me every moment of the time, directing even my dress." Divine guidance had indicated her old dark green merino as most suitable for the occasion; and as she went downstairs to receive her formidable guest, dear Mrs. L. cried after her, "Now if the Lord should send His arrow into his soul!" The Duke was standing by the fire; and she was quite surprised to notice that he had "such a beautiful silver head, such as I always from my childhood admired." Her mission would, it seemed, be less distasteful than she had feared. "This," she remarked, "is very kind of your Grace." He took her hand without a word; and the odd pair sat in two chairs on each side of the little fire. Miss Jenkins rose, exclaiming, "I will show you *my Treasure*"; the Duke got up politely; and his hostess returned to her seat clasping an enormous Bible. Then she began to read, announcing that her reading was from the third chapter of the Gospel according to St. John:

"There was a man of the Pharisees, named Nicodemus, a ruler of the Jews: The same came to Jesus by night, and said unto him, Rabbi, we know that thou art a teacher come from God: for no man can do these miracles that thou doest, except God be with him. Jesus answered and said unto him, Verily, verily, I say unto thee, Except a man be born again, he cannot see the kingdom of God. Nicodemus saith unto him, How can a man be born when he is old? can he enter the second time into his mother's womb, and be born? Jesus answered, Verily, verily, I say unto thee, Except a man be born of water and of the Spirit, he cannot enter into the kingdom of God. That which is born of the flesh is flesh; and that which is born of the Spirit is spirit. Marvel not that I said unto thee, Ye must be born again. . . ."

As she reached these words, Miss Jenkins emphasised her Scripture lesson by pointing at the Duke. His reply was slightly unexpected, since he promptly clasped her outstretched hand and said with emphasis, "Oh, how I love you! how I love you!" Some arrow, as Mrs. L. had hoped upstairs, had pierced him; but was it quite the arrow for which Mrs. L. had hoped? His hearing was imperfect, and it may be doubted whether he had caught the sacred words. But his sight was unimpaired; and he could see a pretty girl in a green dress.

He left, saying that he should call again, and made Miss Jenkins promise to write to him. She made several attempts, but finally desisted from this arduous composition, "considering such was not the will of God." The weeks went by, and his time was fully occupied. For the Whigs were out; Sir Robert Peel was on his way from Rome; and the Duke held the fort, acting temporarily as Prime Minister and all three

Secretaries of State. These administrative exercises would have kept most men busy at sixty-five. But though the Duke was the entire Cabinet in his own person, he found time in those crowded weeks for a note to Miss   26 Jenkins asking the reason of her silence and proposing to visit her again. Her silence was unbroken; but the Duke persisted. He called one Sunday afternoon and seemed a little flurried. It appeared that he was going on a visit to the King, on hearing which his pious hostess expressed a wish that it had been to the King of Kings. His conversation was exciting, since he alluded once more to his feelings for her and exclaimed: "This must be for life!" Indeed, he said it twice, and positively asked her if she felt sufficient for him to be with him a whole life. Miss Jenkins, who was quite prepared to be a Duchess, modestly replied: "If it be the will of God." He left her hurriedly and was a shade annoyed to find on his return that she had locked the door. Her explanation, which he received in silence, was that she had shut herself in to pray. He asked her why she had not written; and when she pleaded divine guidance, he was silent again. A doubt was growing on him. Locked doors, excessive piety, devotions at unseasonable moments, and a tendency to confuse the King of Kings with William IV—these were disturbing symptoms. Was Miss Jenkins all that the Duke had hoped?

He kept his distance for a fortnight; and as the days went by, a dreadful doubt grew on Miss J. as well. Was she to be a Duchess after all? A newspaper (for she did not disdain earthly means of intelligence) informed her that he was in town; and she put the matter to the test by a note entreating him to cease his visits. Her love for him was can-   27 didly avowed; she was fully aware that his intentions could not be otherwise than strictly honourable; but for religious reasons (which were set out at length) it was advisable that their meetings should remain purely spiritual. The Duke's reply conveyed (in three sentences) his entire con-   28 currence. Miss J. was horrified. His answer had confirmed her worst suspicions, and her racing pen bombarded him with texts. Page after page informed him of his degradation and excused her own prompt acceptance of his proposal by her firm conviction—how could he have ever doubted it?—that Miss Jenkins would "confer as high an honour on a Prince in bestowing my hand on him as he would on me in receiving it." He answered almost humbly:

29   "I beg your pardon if I have written a line or used an expression which
could annoy you. Believe me; it is the thing of all others that I would wish
to avoid! And that there is nobody more strongly impressed than I am
with veneration for your Virtues, attainments, and Sentiments!"

But though his tone was highly apologetic, there was nothing here
about marriage. Quite undeterred, Miss Jenkins received his letter with
the raptures appropriate to a repentant sinner. For a Duke penitent
might be a Duke redeemed, a Duke set on the right path and looking
for a Duchess. That was her dream; she never wavered in her faith that

30   Providence had "influenced the Duke of Wellington to love me above
every other lady upon earth from the first moment he beheld me." Her
devoted Mrs. L. was of the same opinion; and how could Mrs. L.—"a
perfect woman of the world in her early life"—be wrong?

There was an interval from January to June, 1835; and then the
extraordinary couple resumed their comedy—she still convinced of her
power to elevate him (as well as his to do the same for her), and he anything but reluctant to continue his association with a pretty girl. For
the attentions of twenty-one are flattering to sixty-six. Besides, if she
was so uncompromisingly good, she would at least be safe. Letters written to Miss J. would hardly find their way into the newspapers; she was

31   unlikely to divert the town (like Miss Harriette Wilson) by publishing
her reminiscences; and he could meet her without fear of awkward
consequences. So by midsummer their meetings were resumed. She
had been writing letters to him without posting them; he asked to
see them and was favoured with the loan of much improving literature. He seemed to enjoy her narratives of conversation with irreligious
strangers in stage coaches, discussed the merits of a preacher whose
ministrations she enjoyed at Ramsgate, and was almost meek in his
request that her more voluminous epistles should (in view of excess postage) be confided to several envelopes. He asked to see her; but the
adroit Miss Jenkins practised with skill the tactics of the flying nymph.
He took pleasure in their correspondence. For it was always to his taste
to be treated without undue deference; Mrs. Arbuthnot had continually
ordered him about; and Miss Jenkins, with all Scripture at her back, was
nothing if not authoritative. Indeed, her habits of command impelled
her to rebuke him for ceasing to seal his notes with a coronet and signing

them with a bare initial. This was gross disrespect—she should return
his letters and receive none from him in future unless they bore his full
insignia. It was years since anyone had dared to question the Duke's
conduct; and he replied with the familiar irony that he had "always
understood that the important parts of a Letter were its Contents. I never
much considered the Signature; provided I knew the handwriting; or
the Seal provided it effectually closed the Letter." But he accepted the
rebuke and undertook that future letters should be "properly signed and
sealed to your Satisfaction," noting with some relief that she proposed
to send him back his letters and adding helpfully that he would save
her the trouble of burning them. Before this olive-branch appeased her,
a second furious epistle sped from Miss J. to Apsley House. This was
too much for Wellington, who took refuge in his chilliest third person,
presented compliments, repeated his apology, and gave detailed instructions for the return of his letters. Miss Jenkins was distracted. Should
she abandon her letters and her Duke? The tactics of the flying nymph
had yielded excellent results; she had sixty letters from him; and
she spread them out before the Lord, asking His guidance as to their disposal. Her prayer was answered when Mrs. L., always the woman of
the world, advised her not to part with them. It was His will; for had not
Miss J. "asked the Lord to put it into her heart to advise me agreeably
to His will"? So Mrs. L. prevailed; Miss Jenkins kept her letters; and
an irritated Duke informed her coldly that "it is a matter of Indifference
whether Miss J. has burnt the Letters; or kept them; or sent them back."

They corresponded still; for Wellington lived in the grip of a nervous
inability to refrain from answering letters. Composing suitable replies
was, with him, an automatic reaction. But he was chilly now, regretting
bleakly that "Miss J. is not satisfied with the formal style of his Notes.   32
She was not satisfied when he wrote to her in a form more consistent
with familiarity. . . . The Duke assures Miss J. that he can reply to any
letter which she may think proper to address the Duke as fully in one
form as the other." When she asked him to return one of her letters, he
replied coldly that as "they are in general long and they succeed each
other rapidly," it was his practice to destroy them. She pelted him with
tracts and hymns in manuscript adorned with four distinct grades of
underlining; on one sublime occasion she ran to "nineteen sides of

paper under three covers"; each family bereavement brought him her consolations; and she formed an irritating habit of entrusting him with bulky letters for transmission to royal personages on the subject of Sunday observance, the rates of Marlborough House (upon which she had some texts unfamiliar to rating lawyers), and more eternal themes.

33 They met once in 1836, with Mrs. L. safely ensconced behind the folding doors. But this time there were no scenes; and the female Polonius heard little more than her fearless friend admonishing the Duke; though when Miss Jenkins asked about the trouble in his knee, he seemed quite gratified, drawing his chair a little nearer, "which of course met with the withdrawal on my part due to Christianity."

They did not meet again for years, although the nymph was now

34 pursuing. She sent him wipers for his spectacles and for his pens; she offered him a Bible in large print, which elicited the cautious answer that "that which I now have answers perfectly, and I will not deprive you of another." For he was wary now and less inclined to notify her of his movements. By 1840, faint but pursuing, she was offering to come and nurse him; but he assured her of his perfect health, adding defensively that "he has no reason to believe that he will have occasion to trouble her upon any subject whatever." For she was quite unbearable, writing with alarming frequency and getting little in return beyond bare acknowledgments, until "the Duke would recommend [her] to save herself from such anxiety in future by omitting to write to him." His last shot was still more final—"to avoid disappointment he now tells her that he will write no more."

Was this the end? Plainly, if Wellington had anything to do with it. But four years of silence were too much for Miss J.; and in 1844 she opened fire again. His replies at first were passive—he was obliged for

35 her kind enquiries, reluctant to embark upon religious topics, and re-
36 lieved to learn that her misunderstanding with Mrs. L. was at an end. But that year he called on her again and, on leaving, found quite a crowd round his horses. Indeed, he sent her his sole recorded present— a wax impression of his features on half a ducal visiting-card. This treasure left her in grave doubt as to its ultimate disposal—whether it should repose for ever in the British Museum or be realised in order that its proceeds might be sent upon the thankless task of propagating the Gos-

pel among the Jews. More visits followed; and his notes grew friendlier again, though they were mainly filled with brave assertions of his rude health and the intolerable burden of affairs. (Her new *rôle* as the Lady with the Lamp must be repelled at all costs.) But she soon grew exacting, expecting him to answer every letter. This was bad enough; but when she wrote a rambling story about money troubles, his patience finally ran out:

> "I will give her any reasonable assistance she may require from me; 37
> when she will let me know in clear distinct Terms what is the Sum she
> requires.
> "But I announce again; that I will never write upon any other Subject."

Such brutality sent her into apocalyptic transports; she even contemplated returning the precious seal and a lock of his hair. But Mrs. L., still worldly, pressed her to keep them both; and the Duke, sternly apprised that he had totally misunderstood, was unexpectedly apologetic—'P.S.," wrote Wellington, "I never will offend again in any manner." His 38 humility was quite astonishing. He had been humouring his fractious correspondent for twelve years, and her most extravagant *boutades* seemed powerless to exasperate him into a final breach. He made one attempt in 1847, in which "Field Marshal the Duke of Wellington presents his 39 Compliments. . . . He declines to [write] anything further to Miss J., being convinced that as usual any correspondence will end in his giving her Offence, however much he may desire and endeavour to please her." But this attempted *Nunc dimittis* elicited no more than a stern intimation that his correspondent "cared no more for his Field Marshalship than his Generalship"; and within three months they were both corresponding hard, the Duke complaining helplessly that "you write at great length; 40 with much celerity, in light coloured Ink." He seemed to find distraction in the taming of this spiritual shrew. It was such a change to encounter someone who stood up to him; he always liked commanding women. Besides, he was not far off eighty; and the solicitude of thirty-three for his welfare was distinctly gratifying. But when she favoured him with letters for transmission to Miss Coutts and Sir Robert Peel, he sent them back with a sharp intimation that "I am not the Post Man! nor the Secre- 41 tary of Sir Robert Peel nor your Secretary!" His patience was evaporating once again, and in a *cri de cœur* he wrote that "to read one letter from you is as much as I can do."

A gleam of hope appeared in 1850, when she announced her impending departure to the United States, and the Duke eagerly enquired her new address. But she stayed on relentlessly; and with exaggerated caution for her health he begged her to avoid fatiguing herself by excessive letter-writing. His request was vain; for shortly afterwards he received a wild farrago, in which her pen wandered distractedly among her symptoms, linseed poultices, the cost of jellies, and the inadequacy of her income, the whole richly decorated with appropriate texts. He asked how much she needed and what was her banker's name—"all this *legibly written*!" But she answered him with more texts. The Duke was helpless; and when Miss Jenkins grew reproachful, he bowed himself out with awful courtesy in a note concluding, "He thus finally takes his Leave!" But he did nothing of the kind. Involved in her epistolatory toils, he was as helpless as Laocoon. When she informed him of her health, the force of habit was too strong for him, and he replied. The stern pietist was soon rebuking him for regular attendance at earthly ceremonies; but he answered (with fervent requests that she should write no more) that he "considers it his Duty to serve the Public to the best of his Ability." That was in March, 1851. She never heard from him again, though he heard frequently from her. Indeed, a letter to the Duke was waiting on her table to be posted when the doctor called eighteen months later. He was always so kind about posting her letters. "That," she remarked, "is for the Duke." But he informed her gently that there was no Duke to read it. He had eluded her at last; and she departed for New York, to qualify still further for her heavenly crown by writing up her Journal, re-reading his three hundred and ninety letters, and reposing in the happy consciousness of a Duke very nearly saved from the burning.

42

43

44

433

III

IT WAS still 1834, and the Duke stared about him in the uncomfortable world created by Reform. But there were compensations; for the Whigs were breaking fast. First, Lord Grey resigned; Melbourne succeeded him; but when Lord Spencer died, removing Althorp to the Lords, there was a sudden buzz.

"It is an immense event," said Tadpole.

"I don't see my way," said Taper.

"When did he die?" said Lord Fitz-Booby.

"I don't believe it," said Mr. Rigby.

"They have got their man ready," said Tadpole.

"It is impossible to say what will happen," said Taper.

"Now is the time for an amendment on the address," said Fitz-Booby.

"There are two reasons which convince me that Lord Spencer is not dead," said Mr. Rigby.

But Mr. Rigby was wrong as usual. Spencer was dead beyond a doubt; Althorp succeeded to the title; and Lord Melbourne must find someone else to lead the House of Commons. His sovereign made difficulties and, with a sudden access of resolution, dismissed his ministers. For there were still the Tories; and the King sent for Wellington. The Duke was at Stratfield Saye. He was up early that November morning; for he was going hunting. But the King's letter came at six o'clock. His hunters countermanded, he ordered post-horses, was off by eight, and by dinnertime had seen the King at Brighton. His sovereign asked him to form a Government; but he "told his Majesty that the difficulty of the task consisted in the state of the House of Commons, and that all our efforts must be turned to get the better of these difficulties, that I earnestly recommended to his Majesty to choose a Minister in the House of Commons," and that Peel should be his choice. This was rare unselfishness, since their relations had been a little strained by Peel's refusal to join him in the forlorn hope of 1832. But the Duke's mind was quite made up that Peel must be Prime Minister; Arbuthnot had conveyed as much to

434

Sir Robert in the summer; and now Wellington informed the King. But where was Peel? With rare improvidence he was abroad. For Sir Robert had gone off to Italy. He must be sent for. Meanwhile, the Duke and Lyndhurst could govern England until he returned. Lyndhurst was to be Lord Chancellor, and the Duke calmly assumed all the remaining offices of state, writing gleefully that "I am in harness again; and I have sent to bring home Sir Robert Peel."

He was indeed in harness; for that week, "after much fumbling for his spectacles," he was sworn in as First Lord of the Treasury, Home Secretary, Foreign Secretary, and Secretary of State for War and the Colonies. He was the government of England. H. B. portrayed a solitary figure at the head of the Cabinet table asking two lines of empty chairs, "How is the King's Government to be carried on?—that is the question"; whilst a rival caricaturist depicted *The United Administration*, all clean-shaven, trim, and aquiline—Wellingtons to a man—in red, in blue, in black, in wig and gown, in capes, frock-coats, and robes, voting with splendid unanimity and encouraged by their sovereign's exclamation, "Now, my chosen friends and Ministers, I sincerely hope there will be none of those dissensions and disputes between you there were with the last." Their offices and titles filled the margin of this pleasing scene:

First Lord of the Treasury . . .	DUKE OF WELLINGTON
Home Secretary	DUKE OF VITTORIA
Foreign Secretary	PRINCE OF WATERLOO
War and Colonies	DUKE OF CIUDAD RODRIGO
Lord Privy Seal	COUNT VIMIERA
First Lord of the Admiralty . . .	BARON DOURO
Chancellor of the Exchequer . .	ARTHUR WELLESLEY
Lord High Chancellor	VISCOUNT WELLINGTON

And for three flurried weeks the charge was very nearly true. Taking possession as Home Secretary before his predecessor's papers had been cleared away, he was reported by scared officials to have "fixed his headquarters at the Home Office, and occasionally roves over the rest." His policy was simple: "all that he knew, which he told in his curt, husky manner, was, that he had to carry on the King's government." This was an infinite relief after the crotchets of the Whigs; and the world shared Lady Salisbury's consciousness that "it was really a moment worth living for to see that great man once more where he ought to be, appreciated as he deserves by his King, and at the head of this great country." For there could be few finer sights than the industrious old hero in temporary charge of England.

But Mr. Hudson reached Rome at last; Sir Robert raced across the Alps, "the great man in a great position, summoned from Rome to govern England"; and the Duke subsided into the Foreign Office, where he soon impressed ambassadors that "thirty minutes with him suffice to transact what can never be accomplished in as many hours with our wavering ministers of France." For Wellington was still as punctual and decisive as ever. But administrative virtues could not win General Elections, and the future of Peel's Government depended on the polls. Electioneering was hardly the Duke's province, though echoes of the distant warfare sometimes came his way. A young gentleman with slightly fluctuating principles, who had once asked him (without success) to accept the dedication of an epic poem, wrote imploring his support at High Wycombe. But nothing came of it; his correspondent was at the bottom of the poll once more, exclaiming darkly that he was now a cipher and chivalrously assuring the Duke that he might always count on the support of Benjamin Disraeli.

The elections went against them; and Wellington was soon assuring country neighbours that, "whatever way the Cats jump in this Quarter," he would not miss his hunting in the autumn of 1835. They had been five months in office; they would be out again at any moment; and when Peel was threatened with a final defeat in the House of Commons, an obliging colleague offered to send news of the division to Apsley House. But the Duke was perfectly prepared to wait until the morning.

"I am quite satisfied to have it when the newspapers come in at ten o'clock. If I could do any good by having it earlier, I would; but as I can't, I'd just as soon wait."

A friend interposed, remarking that he took it coolly and enquiring if anxiety ever kept him awake.

"No," said the Duke, "I don't like lying awake; it does no good. I make a point never to lie awake."

IV

THE brief interlude of Tory government worked wonders with the Duke's popularity. Oxford in 1834 had marked his readmission to the canon of Tory saints; but the next year restored him to a wider circle of good graces. Not that the world of 1835 had any wish to be governed by the Tories. But it was profoundly touched by the spectacle of Wellington in harness once again. His obvious good faith, his chivalry towards Peel, his willingness to serve under a younger man were in vivid contrast with the normal appetites of party politics; and the old man resumed his place in popular regard as a national institution. He went to Cambridge in the summer and was triumphantly received by town, gown, and Yeomanry; Vauxhall shouted itself hoarse when he appeared; and roaring crowds greeted him at a Hyde Park review. His pessimism had begun to melt.

"It is very bad," he observed to somebody at dinner, "but I consider the country on its legs again."

"Do you?" said Greville. "I am glad you think so."

"Oh yes," the Duke replied, "I think that, however this may end; I think the country is on its legs again."

Even his Parliamentary authority was recovering. The House of Lords had never lost its habit of attending to his simple arguments; as young Disraeli allowed, "there is a gruff, husky sort of a downright Montaignish naïveté about him, which is quaint, unusual, and tells." But when he silenced Brougham, the Boanerges of the new era, in mid-flight by lifting a warning forefinger and murmuring across the House, "Now, take care what you say next," it was a veritable triumph. For he had come into his own again. Young men of promise in 1836 noted signs of his approval with avidity, Disraeli writing gleefully that the Duke had told somebody at dinner that his Aylesbury speech was "the most manly thing done yet" and positively asked, "When will he come into Parliament?" And the less ardent Gladstone, who met him at Sir Robert Peel's and noted that "he receives remarks made to him very frequently with no more than 'Ha!' a convenient suspensive expression, which acknowledges the arrival of the observation and no more," commented favourably on his mental powers.

His life was easier again; and he could return to his normal occupations. The past absorbed him now; for Gurwood was editing his *Dispatches*, and the Duke turned over old papers to elucidate doubtful points. Then there were endless sittings to be given to portrait-painters. Indeed, the reckless Haydon had laid siege to him whilst he was still in office; but Wellington refused to sit. Quite undeterred, the painter called at Apsley House, borrowed his clothes, and asked the Duke to look at the completed picture. This was too much. The indignant hero had "no objection to any gentleman painting any picture of me that he may think proper; but if I am to have anything to say to the picture, either in the way of sitting or sending a dress, I consider myself, and shall be considered by others, as responsible for it. . . . Paint it, if you please, but I will have nothing to say to it. To paint the Emperor Napoleon on the rock of St. Helena is quite a different thing from painting me on the field of battle of Waterloo. The Emperor Napoleon did not consent to be painted. But I am to be supposed to consent; and moreover, I on the field of battle of Waterloo am not exactly in the situation in which Napoleon stood on the rock of St. Helena." This was discouraging; but Haydon urged that with six children to support he could scarely ignore a good commission. The Duke, who felt that Haydon had made free with his wardrobe, was obdurate, though he consented rather sulkily to the persisent artist "painting and engraving a picture of me in any way you please, and in any costume."

But his defence was not always so successful; and in his later years artists became a plague. Indeed, the pestilence was almost endemic. As he wrote helplessly from Walmer, "I did not . . . ask you to come here . . . as I expected a descent of artists. I have had one; some still remain, and more are coming—two from Scotland. I literally lead the life of the subaltern officer of a regiment. I parade, dressed for duty, at nine in the morning, and again once or twice a day. There is not a moment of the day or night that I can call my own. These gentlemen are at breakfast, dinner, and supper, and all the evening my existence is at their pleasure; I cannot move along the passage, or on the staircase, or the ramparts, without meeting them. . . ."

He had his public duties, too—meetings of Tory peers at Apsley House, dinners at Kensington with Princess Victoria and her overpowering mamma, his correspondence with Sir Robert on Opposition tactics, and regular attendance in the House of Lords where he spoke twenty-one times in 1836 upon every topic from insolvent debtors to railways. His course in politics was slightly complicated by his leader; for he had a leader now. Peel was sometimes a little trying, though the Duke was on better terms with him and took his hunting-coat to Drayton with a gay intimation that he was "prepared to do whatever you please." But Sir Robert's aptitude for chilling followers was impressive; even Wellington complained that "our leader does not excite enthusiasm"; and their relations sometimes resembled an exchange of signals between passing icebergs. But it was no time for dashing tactics, as the Tory rearguard receded slowly before Melbourne's languid advance. It was the dawn of a new age, although the dawn crept imperceptibly up the sky, until the apprehensive gaze of Wellington grew almost accustomed to the change of colouring.

A new age was dawning, although Greville wrote comfortably that "*nothing* will happen, because, in this country, *nothing* ever does." Familiar outlines of the night began to vanish. Beaux of the Regency crept silently away; royal uncles receded; and Mrs. Fitzherbert died among her memories. The Duke appeared in Tilney Street. He was the late King's executor, and Mrs. Fitzherbert's papers had presented problems of unusual delicacy which he had dealt with while she was still alive. Some had been sealed up and sent to Coutts' Bank; but the grate received a generous supply; and as the fire roared up, Wellington said grimly to his companion, "I think, my lord, we had better hold our hand for a while, or we shall set the old woman's chimney on fire." A new day was climbing up the sky; and as Kensington flushed in the summer dawn of 1837, two kneeling men informed a sleepy girl that she was Queen of England.

439

Apotheosis

O good gray head which all men knew.

ODE ON THE DEATH OF THE
DUKE OF WELLINGTON.

THE past receded now—the legendary past, where Nelson walked his quarter-deck and Mr. Pitt, sharp-nosed among the candles of Guildhall, urged England to save Europe, and a trim frock-coated figure cantered along the lines to lift a low cocked hat and point through the thinning smoke towards the French. The past receded into a middle distance hazy with patriotic folklore, a region of soldiers' tales and steel engravings. But one figure held the foreground still, where Wellington lingered indomitably on the bright Victorian scene. A hero of the last reign but two, he was the past incarnate. Men saw his profile and heard the guns of Badajoz; a spare, familiar figure brought back forgotten echoes; and the deep voice took them into their fathers' memories of days before Reform, before Waterloo, before Vimeiro, before . . . His
1 walks abroad became a progress, upon which the London streets turned respectfully to watch the past go by. Every hat came off; genteel persons made excuses to stop and stare; across the way young surgeons crowded on the steps of St. George's Hospital to watch him pass; and as he turned slowly in at Apsley House, the butcher's boy pulled up his cart
2 to see. Not that he was a passive spectacle. A cheering crowd once followed him up Constitution Hill until he reached his gate; he turned in the saddle, pointed to the iron shutters on the windows that they had broken once, swept them a bow, and then rode in without a word.
3 The roads near Walmer knew him well, driving a pair-horse phaeton from the left-hand seat in order that his companion might have his good ear. His driving was a little wild, but his talk was always on the target
4 —economy, dockyard employment as a method of reducing the poorrate, the futility of supposing that England would be the workshop of the world for ever, foreign markets, means of securing them by lower costs of manufacture (they were just driving into Ramsgate and stopped at the first draper's shop where he bought a white cotton handkerchief with red spots, emerging with the sage reflection that it had only cost a shilling and was an article which, one would think, might find a mar-

443

ket anywhere), and so back to Walmer, dinner at seven o'clock, a little talk, and candles at eleven. For the Duke lived on, half national monument, half Delphic oracle.

I

His talk was never better than in those later years. It had lost nothing of its astringent quality; yet somehow it was mellower. For he could be almost genial with the omniscient Croker, stepping in from the battlements at Walmer with a sardonic intimation that "I've just been receiving a lecture from Croker on fortification," and protesting amiably at the   4 dinner-table, "My dear Croker, I can yield to your superior information on most points, and you may perhaps know a great deal more of what passed at Waterloo than myself; but, as a sportsman, I will maintain my point about the percussion caps."

This was the speech of his briefest sayings. Uttered in his distinct voice, these oracles were patiently collected, not infrequently improved upon, and assembled like Sibylline leaves to form a canon of *staccato* wisdom. Debt, discretion, habits of industry, and early rising were among his austere themes; his views were obstinately normal, and his conclusions wholly to the taste of the age of Samuel Smiles. If he spoke at any length, it was generally about the past. Respectful interlocutors headed him firmly in the direction of the Peninsula and pelted him with questions. Stanhope was quite incorrigible in this vein, making a torment of his evenings, when the old man would have so much preferred a quiet hour between his candles with a paper. But the implacable inquisitor nightly perched beside him on his reading-table, until a thought-   5 ful lady piled it high with books. Quite undeterred, the relentless Stanhope took them off and installed himself as usual.

"I don't think much of your fortifications," said a deep voice from the Duke's armchair.

Not that his topics were exclusively martial. For one day he read them   6 the report of *Bardell* v. *Pickwick*; and he was occasionally engaged by deeper themes provided by his religious correspondents. Someone found him deep in a forbidding work by Habershon upon the Prophecies, and he was known to recommend a learned publication which proved (by the aid of Scripture) that the aboriginal population of America had originally come from Tyre. He found it quite convincing and regarded their successful navigation of the Atlantic without compasses as conclusive evidence of the activities of a higher Power. Then he talked of old times in India, told stories about Talleyrand, and went off on the campaign of Vimeiro. For it was more comforting to recall the past than to contemplate a present where O'Connell was haranguing crowds. Crowds always irritated him; as he thought of them, a little rhyme came back to him—

> *"Pour la canaille*
> *Faut la mitraille"*

and he murmured it quite lovingly as they went in to dinner. But his old despairs had very nearly vanished, since his countrymen showed sense enough to discard the Whigs; and though there were difficulties in sight, "I do not conceive them to be insurmountable, and I have good hopes for the future." For though the world was changing fast, perhaps it would not change too much.

2

The customary scene was Walmer, though the big house at Hyde Park Corner and the long rooms at Stratfield Saye still knew their master. But his most frequent setting in those later years was the low, castellated house beside the Kentish sea. Its aspect, like the Lord Warden's, was strictly military. But time had made them both civilians; its portholes were bedroom windows now, its platform a verandah, and the moat performed the peaceful office of a kitchen-garden. No less civilian, the Duke, white-trousered and blue-coated, emerged at six o'clock, tramped up and down his battlements, enjoyed the morning sun, and reappeared at breakfast. A morning with his papers, a ride to Dover in the afternoon, another turn upon the flagstones, dinner, a quiet evening unless Stanhope was in the house), and a bowed figure with a silver head lit the flat candlesticks and wished them all good-night.

His life was easy there, though he had his Cinque Ports business, giving the countersign to the Dover garrison each day and walking through Walmer in procession with the pilots when his Court was held. He

445

was a friendly neighbour, strolling unasked into Deal lodging-houses
in order to invite a wholly unimportant stranger to shoot his woodcock,
or sending somebody at Dover his garden key. Stray visitors with children found themselves miraculously asked to dinner; and when someone   11
in the neighbourhood complained of the devastations of the Castle
rooks, he replied meekly that they should be destroyed. He had his
sterner moments, though, when a female was summarily deported from
the neighbourhood; and a letter asking him to make some charitable   12
award to a young lady, who pleaded that she was eligible for an annuity
bequeathed to Kentish girls and that her father (whom she supported by
dressmaking) was seventy-eight, provoked the Duke's compliments and
his desire "that she will specify in clear and distinct terms what is the
benefit in the way of annuity which is in the gift of the Duke; which he
has the power of conferring on young ladies *seventy-eight years old* of the
County of Kent."

He had his garden; though he was no gardener, admitting to an ap-   13
plicant for employment who had confessed that he knew nothing of
gardening, "No more do I, but you can learn." His grounds were full
of robins, because the wintry old man had quite a feeling for them.   14
But a slow walk up and down the ramparts was his invariable resource.
He tramped them with Arbuthnot; and an indulgent housekeeper enjoyed the sight of "our two dear old gentlemen so happy together."   15
The Duke, however, was the younger, and on occasion youth would assert
itself. For sometimes as they paced the path along the beach at dusk,
the younger man halted.

"Now, Arbuthnot," said a deep voice, "you've been out long enough.   16
The dew is falling and you'll catch cold; you must go in."

So Arbuthnot, slightly protesting, went back to the Castle; and the
Duke tramped on alone.

A cloud of witnesses observed him, but none more eagerly than Haydon. The preliminaries of his visit were much as usual. A Liverpool
committee had commissioned a large picture of the Duke musing on   17
the field of Waterloo. True, he had never mused there; but the sublime
in art is not easily discouraged, and Haydon leapt at the canvas with
a muttered prayer that he might be no less victorious than his heroic
subject. In the intervals of lecturing all over the country and designing a

Nelson monument, he painted hard. Would the Duke sit to him? There was a chance. Meanwhile, the busy painter improved the occasion by writing to him on the subject of the Nelson project (eliciting the slightly ominous reply that Wellington was "not the committee, nor the *secretary to the committee*; and, above all, not the *corresponding secretary*"). He painted hard, borrowed a sketch of "Copenhagen," and traced his saddler; and when that deserving tradesman revealed that he had made all the Duke's saddles from Salamanca to Waterloo, this information "so increased my reverence I offered him my arm." Small wonder that he glowed over the discovery of a small niece of Wellington's who called her uncle, "Dukey." "The terror of Napoleon—Dukey to his niece!" But there were still the elusive clothes. The Duke remained inexorable and "hopes that he will have some cessation of note-writing about pictures. The Duke knows nothing about the picture Mr. Haydon proposes to paint. At all events, he must decline to lend to anybody his clothes, arms and equipments." Was this the end? In spite of everything his picture grew; D'Orsay called at the studio one day, sublime in scented gloves, white greatcoat, blue cravat, and "hat of the primest curve and purest water," picked up a brush and gave a touch. This would never do— "a Frenchman touch Copenhagen!"—and the indignant patriot rubbed out the sacrilegious brushwork. The Duke's clothes still defeated him. But not for long, since the indomitable Haydon had traced his tailor and ordered himself a pair of trousers of the Duke's own pattern, "so that I shall kill two birds with one stone,—wear 'em and paint 'em. So, my Duke, I *do* you in spite of you."

Not quite in spite of him; for one October day the postman brought an invitation to go down to Walmer. The eager guest set off by way of Ramsgate; the Castle bell was sounded when he arrived; and he met the party at dinner. He found them gossiping about a circus lady, coast erosion, and Napoleonic personages. The Duke averred that the French system was "bullying and driving—they robbed each other, and then poured out on Europe to fill their stomachs and pockets by robbing others." So much for the French. As for Don Carlos, he was "a poor creature." Mankind in general, it seemed, was not much better, since that evening Wellington was of the opinion that the natural state of man was plunder; society was founded upon property, and that was going fast. The talk strayed, as usual, to Spain—how they had burnt houses for fuel and how the British soldier must always have a home to go to at night.

"Your Grace," Haydon courageously remarked, "the French always bivouac."

"Yes," said the Duke, "because French, Spanish and all other nations lie anywhere. It is their habit. They have no homes."

Arbuthnot nodded in his chair; Haydon was studying the Duke's head, until the hero gave a tremendous yawn and rang for candles. He lighted two and gave one to his latest guest. "God bless your Grace," said Haydon, and retired to struggle with the inspiring consciousness of the greatest man on earth asleep just through the wall.

They breakfasted at ten. "Which will ye have," asked Wellington, "black tea or green?" Six children clamoured at the windows. "Let them in," said Wellington. The invading hordes arrived, charging the Duke with cries of "How d'ye do, Duke? how d'ye do, Duke?" One urchin clamoured thirstily, "I want some tea, Duke."

"You shall have it, if you promise not to slop it over me, as you did yesterday."

The speaker hugged them, three a side; and then they all romped wildly up and down the ramparts, with the Duke in full cry after a small girl. "I'll catch ye," said the Duke, "ha, ha, I've got ye."

He went out hunting in the morning; and after hunting he sat to Haydon, "like an eagle of the gods who had put on human shape, and had got silvery with age and service." His ride had made him "rosy and dozy"; and after dinner he read the *Standard* until bedtime. The next day was Sunday; and Haydon very nearly sat in the Duke's pew, profoundly affected by the spectacle of the conqueror in church. That night he read his paper again. He seemed a little aged when he sat again on Monday, "like an aged eagle beginning to totter from his perch." But a Russian diplomat appeared at lunch; and the Duke "put on a fine dashing waistcoat" for the occasion. More sketching in the afternoon with Lady Burghersh to keep his subject talking. But he was done at last.

"It's very fine," said Lady Burghersh.

"Is it though?" said the Duke. "I'm very glad." He never looked at it. But Arbuthnot and Lady Burghersh both begged Haydon not to alter

448

THE DUKE OF WELLINGTON, 1839
From a painting by Benjamin Robert Haydon, at Apsley House.
By permission of the Duke of Wellington, K.G.

it, as he had caught the likeness. One more evening at the Castle; then candles and a loud good-night, and Haydon ended his last day at Walmer.

But sometimes they had statelier visitors. The Duke always prided himself that he possessed "the most charming marine residence he had ever seen—that the Queen herself had nothing to be compared with it." And one day in 1842 he received an intimation of the royal pleasure to visit him in force. The preparations were extensive; Pitt's room was hastily partitioned off and gaily papered to form a royal dining-room; the village carpenter put up a little shelf to hold a timepiece in view of the royal bed (understood to be required for Albert's full happiness); and their careful host gave detailed directions for the guard of honour to parade "at a distance from the road and the Castle; so as not to frighten the Queen's horses." The Duke himself removed to the Ship Hotel at Dover. Even his laundry, evacuated by the Duke's mangle, became a royal guard-room; and H. B. depicted him surrendering his fortress and retreating with Lady Douro and his humble belongings. It was all a great success. The Duke rode over every day; the royal couple read Hallam's *Constitutional History* (varied with doses of St. Simon by way of light refreshment) or went out for excursions. But they found the house a little draughty; the Queen caught a cold; and it was three weeks before the Duke got back his Castle. Someone remarked that they had knocked about his rooms a little.

"Yes," he replied with a little smile, "yes, oh yes, they have rather. Cut up Mr. Pitt's room and turned it into a dining-room, but it don't signify, I'll soon knock all that down again."

For it was not so easy to displace the past at Walmer.

3

His thoughts were much in the past. With Arbuthnot dozing in his chair and Alava's endless Spanish chatter, how could he escape the past? Not that his life was a mere retrospect, since it was full of children. They came to stay with him, made havoc of his breakfast, played hide-and-seek with him along the ramparts, and bombarded him with cushions in the drawing-room. The *rôle* was most unlikely; but, as he wrote, "it is my fate to be all things to all men, women, and children." Indeed, a small boy, interrupted in a raid upon the Walmer fruit-trees, paid him an unusual compliment—"Never mind, let's go to the Duke; he always allows everything and gives you what you like directly."

He had been fond of children in the East; the war deprived him of the nursery days of his own sons; and when he was restored to them, they were too old for him to do much more than give directions to their tutors, pay their bills, and send their Latin verses to Richard for that connoisseur's approval. But his later years were bright with children. Dickens once saw him at Vauxhall "in a bright white overcoat" with two little girls and Lady Douro; grave visitors to Stratfield Saye were slightly embarrassed at being received by an old gentleman on all fours among the crumbs under the dining-table; and a staid individual who warned a fellow-traveller on the Deal steam-boat that he should really tell his little girl not to romance, as she had just told him that she had a pillow-fight with the Duke of Wellington, was pained to learn that it was the strictest truth. When children stayed with him, he sometimes wrote them letters to arrive by post; his bulletins to anxious parents were rich in detail—"Bo was indisposed while I was away. He says himself that his Indisposition was occasioned by his eating too much dinner; which is not unlikely." He shipped them off to France with the precautions appropriate to a well-timed invasion; and when he wrote to them, he was particularly careful not to write to their parents by the same post, "as I recollected that it was necessary that a letter should be brought for herself by the Postman in order to produce all the Satisfaction that it was capable of producing." His evening pillow-fight (known as the "battle of Waterloo," conducted in the drawing-room and usually opened by a judicious cushion hurled through his newspaper) was almost a ritual; and he had a pleasing habit of carrying a store of shillings hung on red and blue ribbons for distribution to stray children. "Are you for Navy," asked the Duke, "or Army?" Intending sailors got a blue ribbon and soldiers scarlet, though in one disastrous instance a small child, to whom he had promised a commission in the Guards, objected loudly: "But I am a dirl, Mr. Dook." It was all, as Dickens wrote, "good, and aged, and odd."

There was a saving streak of oddity about him. With strongly individual tastes and personal requirements he ran largely to unusual contraptions;

and his mind, as fertile as the White Knight's in strange devices of his own invention, soared far beyond the commonplace in household and personal appointments. The lives of visitors were darkened by a teapot perched in some complicated way on a hot-water jug, which appeared to possess no merit except that of capsizing more easily than usual; he loved to demonstrate his patent finger-bandage; a supply of sword-umbrellas afforded him protection against assassins in wet weather; and he gratified his fancy by appearing on the road in queer, boat-like conveyances of personal design. Strange clothing fascinated him in later years. Always susceptible to colds, he had a weakness for unusual cloaks and mufflers; overalls of strange construction seemed to appeal to him; and he had been known to appear on horseback with a fur collar and an umbrella. His passion for such ingenuities had made him a domestic pioneer. Guests at Stratfield Saye were nearly suffocated by his novel heating system; and, born a century before his time, he was a sanitary enthusiast.

His tastes were simple. A modest standard of barrack-room discomfort satisfied him, though he was conscious of the arts. The windfall of King Joseph's coach at Vitoria gave him the nucleus of a picture gallery, supplemented by judicious purchases in Paris. He was still buying Dutch and Italian pictures; and occasionally he took a fancy to commission a particular scene. Wilkie's *Chelsea Pensioners* originated in one of his ideas, and he had the notion of setting Landseer to paint a dramatic moment in a lion-tamer's exhibition. But he was more at home in music. His guests were firmly led off to the Ancient Concerts, where he was sometimes gratified by hearing his father's compositions; Grisi was brought down to sing at Walmer; and he arranged his programmes with precision—a selected vocalist and instrumentalists to taste ("If they want the horn I'll have Puzzi. I used to like the violincello").

So he lived on amongst his friends. Douro was married to a charming young lady, of whom he saw a great deal; and sometimes there were additions to his circle, when Alava made him receive "Mons. Merimée . . . a sort of lion." But strange faces were infrequent among his grown-up visitors; for his taste in acquaintances was formed. He had a home at last, a refuge from the innumerable contacts of his official life. The world complained that he did not surround himself with Peninsular veterans. But why should he? He had lived half his life among them; and it was far pleasanter to gossip to his little court. Gossip, alas! was not so easy across the silence of his deafness; and he turned increasingly to paper, writing innumerable little notes to privileged young ladies about his garden and the weather and the vexations of his public life. Almost indecipherable now, those scribbled pages, where a rose-leaf or a lock of his white hair is often pressed, hold in their trivialities the brave secret of his long struggle against loneliness and silence.

But he could still be formidable. The uneasy figure of John Gurwood   37 moved in the outer circle of his intimates. Brought into early prominence by reckless galantry at Ciudad Rodrigo, his subsequent career failed to live up to his own expectations. A slight display of temperament before Waterloo was scarcely helpful; and he spent the next few years in almost constant disappointments and the gloomy survey of *Gazettes* in which his name did not appear. An obscure love-affair assisted his decline, and so early as 1823 his nerves were gravely shaken by a hold-up in Spain. But the Duke, on taking over at the Horse Guards, promptly promoted him; and Gurwood responded by publishing his master's *General Orders*. This led him to a larger project, and he prepared to edit the entire *corpus* of Wellington's *Dispatches*. Close association with the Duke made him a devotee; and when the work concluded, the Duke reciprocated by obtaining him a pension and the post (after a struggle with Macaulay) of Deputy-Lieutenant of the Tower. Gurwood expanded in the sunshine of success. It was extremely pleasant to frequent the little circle at Stratfield Saye—so pleasant that he consented to be seen there without his wife. For Mrs. Gurwood's antecedents would hardly bear the strict examination to which pedigrees were subjected in the Duke's social neighbourhood. A bright Parisian *brunette*, she was unlikely to associate on easy terms with Lady Douro. First heard of as the widow of an invisible M. Mayer, deceased (it was charitably supposed) in Africa, Fanny Gurwood, *née* Kreilssamner, of Mulhouse, had two sisters of whom one worked at a Paris dressmaker's, while the other enjoyed the less arduous protection of the Director of the *Comédie Française*; and it was Gurwood's practice to accept the Duke's invitations as a bachelor. But in spite of everything his nerves continued to grow worse; and they were not improved by a sharp controversy with Napier, in which his

Peninsular laurels were impugned. As years went by, he had recourse to mediums; animal magnetism fascinated him; and he dabbled in the new wonders of mesmerism. His work grew heavier than ever, as he was now deep in an enlarged edition of the *Dispatches*. Mountains of documents confronted him, all clamouring to be copied out, arranged in order, printed, and indexed. At last he finished them; but the index was too much for him. Sleep left him; he was dreadfully depressed, spending a good deal of his time burning his precious papers; and the Duke gave him leave to go to Brighton, where he sat brooding in his lodgings until one afternoon he cut his throat. The Duke's consolations to his widow included a request for papers; for Wellington, it seemed, had heard from somebody that Gurwood had kept notes of his conversation. But Fanny answered that the unhappy man had destroyed all his documents "from an overstrained sense of delicacy towards Your Grace." The Duke replied with a detailed reiteration of the story:

> "A few days after the funeral of the lamented Colonel Gurwood, the Duke was informed by different persons, by some verbally, by others in writing, that the Colonel had been in the habit, when associating with him, of retiring to his room early at night, or as soon as possible, in order to write down a memorandum of what the Duke had said. . . .
>
> "The Duke does not believe that there is an instance in history of a similar act. It is anti-social; it puts an end to all the charms of society, to all familiar and private communication of thought between man and man; and, in fact, it places every individual in familiar society in the situation in which he puts himself in a publick assembly, with a gentleman of the press to report what he says. . . ."

Sublimely unaware that Stanhope had been doing the same thing for years, the Duke continued in a tone of stern reproof. He was at pains to demonstrate the depravity of such a practice in order to establish that the notes had better be destroyed for Gurwood's sake. This was too much for Fanny Gurwood, who answered hotly. Wellington, quite unabashed, restated his position at length, reminding Mrs. Gurwood a shade unkindly that "he was in the habit of daily intercourse with the Colonel, that he has had the pleasure of receiving him at his house in Hampshire, and at Walmer Castle, to both of which he was constantly invited, and always welcome whenever he chose to come, and that he did come frequently; but the Duke had never had the honour of receiving Mrs. Gurwood, excepting at balls, concerts, or publick breakfasts"; and that, in consequence, she was without sufficient knowledge of her late husband's practice when in contact with the Duke. He was still painfully explicit upon the story which had reached him and the iniquity, if credible, of such proceedings. It was all a trifle heavy-handed, although Fanny had given quite as good as she got. But the calm waters of his later years were rarely ruffled; and his letters dealt more frequently with less exciting themes, as the sea-wind rattled his windows and the sun crept along his battlements.

THE long procession of public life went slowly by, and the Duke rode with it. Indeed, he rode in the procession now rather than at its head. His juniors tasted the doubtful joys of leadership, whilst he played to perfection the *rôle* of Elder Statesman. It was a rewarding part, invariably greeted by rounds of affectionate applause. For they cheered him now. Cæsar's Commentaries were unfavourably compared with his *Dispatches*, and "Atticus" wrote respectful things about "the aquiline supremacy of the Cæsars" in a prose style that bore a strong resemblance to Disraeli's. Dispraise of him was out of fashion; only perverse persons like Mr. Borrow, who had once used his fists upon a Radical in the Duke's defence, were goaded into finding fault with him for being overrated and with "the loathsome sycophantic nonsense which it has been the fashion to use with respect to Wellington these last twenty years." Even the sharp eye of Jane Carlyle was melted by his "dear kind face"; and her formidable mate, who once heard him for a quarter of an hour in the House of Lords, confessed that "Wellington hawking, haing, humming—the worst speaker I had ever heard—etched and scratched me out gradually a recognisable *portrait of the fact*, and was the only noble lord who had *spoken* at all." Indeed, a glimpse of Wellington, seen at a ball of Lady Ashburton's in 1850, moved Carlyle to rhapsodies—"Truly a beautiful old man; I had never seen till now how beautiful, and what an expression of graceful simplicity, veracity, and nobleness there is about the old hero when you see him close at hand. His very size had hitherto deceived me. He is a shortish slightish figure, about five feet eight, of good breadth however, and all muscle or bone. His legs, I think, must be the short part of him, for certainly on horseback I have always taken him to be tall. Eyes beautiful light blue, full of mild valour, with infinitely more faculty and geniality than I had fancied before; the face wholly gentle, wise, valiant, and venerable. The voice too, as I again heard, is "aquiline," clear, perfectly equable—uncracked, that is—and perhaps almost musical, but essentially tenor or almost treble voice—eighty-two, I understand. He glided slowly along, slightly saluting this and that other, clear, clean, fresh as this June evening itself, till the silver buckle of his stock vanished into the door of the next room and I saw him no more."

He was sometimes a spectator now, watching the young Queen at her first Council and telling somebody that if she had been his own daughter he could not have desired to see her perform her part better, watching her Coronation, and watching her reviews a shade derisively— "Much better come in her carriage." What was a young lady doing on horseback "surrounded only by such youths as Lord Hill and me, Lord Albemarle and the Duke of Argyll—and if it rains and she gets wet, or if any other *contretemps* happens, what is to be done? All these things sound very little, but they must be considered in a display of that sort. As to the soldiers, I know *them*; they won't care about it one sixpence. It is a childish fancy, because she has read of Queen Elizabeth at Tilbury Fort; but *then* there was threat of foreign invasion, which was an occasion calling for display; what occasion is there now?" Such was the chilly welcome offered by one legendary figure to its successor.

He watched her hanging on Lord Melbourne's words and drew the sage conclusion that "she does nothing without consulting him, even up to the time of quitting the table after dinner and retiring to bed at night." But he was disinclined to active Opposition, though he assured Arbuthnot that "I have always been and shall always be in front of the Battle. I cannot hold back." He could not, if by holding back he meant retirement into private life. For the Duke of Wellington, that public character which he sustained with an increasing effort, still made demands upon him which were not to be denied. He must continue to speak his mind in public and, in that sense, to stand in the forefront of the battle. The only doubt that Tories sometimes felt was upon which side he was fighting. The Duke had never been a good Tory. Indeed, his hostility to all the arts of party was frankly expressed—"There is nobody who dislikes so much as I do, and who knows so little of Party Management. I hate it. . . ." Such prejudices were a rare handicap to leadership in Opposition. Besides, he often had his doubts; and Opposi-

tion leaders who give way to doubts are lost. There was so much to be
said for a Government supported by all moderate men. Not that he
had the slightest taste for Coalitions; Canning had formed a Coalition
once; and "the truth is that *Coalitions* have a bad name!" But, from his
point of view, there were worse fates than being governed by Lord Melbourne; and it would be extremely awkward to impose the Tories on
the House of Commons, the country, and the Queen. His sense of
public duty always kept him in close relations with the Government,
writing memoranda for their guidance on Canada and Indian defence.
Indeed, he often felt himself obliged to intervene in their support. This
was exasperating to eager Tories, who muttered angrily about his failing
powers; for what could be more distressing to the Greeks than to observe
their great Achilles in a constant posture of defence over the body of a
Whig Patroclus? But the Whigs acclaimed his statesmanship; and
even from a Tory standpoint there was something to be said for his
magnanimity, if England was to be preserved by perpetuating Melbourne and averting a dark future ruled by O'Connell and the Radicals.

The past engaged him too, when Soult came to London for the
Coronation and the Duke tactfully postponed publication of the Toulouse
volume of his *Dispatches*. The long pursuit across the Pyrenees was
ended in a drawing-room at Buckingham Palace, when Wellington came
up with Soult at last; and Soult even went to Apsley House. The Duke
was civil; but when somebody proposed that he should give the health
of the French army, "Damn 'em," he said, "I'll have nothing to do with
'em but beat 'em."

2

He was just seventy, when his course was sharply interrupted. The failing Whigs resigned in 1839, and Melbourne advised his sovereign to
send for the Duke. They spoke about his deafness, and Lord M. impressed her to be sure that the old man understood what she said to him.
She talked to Wellington for twenty minutes and found him kind. He
received her news with concern; but when she asked him to form a
Government, the Duke replied that he had no power over the House of

Commons, that they were sure to contradict him, and that she had better send for Peel. Then she expressed a hope that Wellington would take a place in the Cabinet. He made objections, saying that he was old and deaf and unfit for discussion, but that if he could serve her comfort, he should accept. She mentioned something about the Household; but he advised her not to make stipulations before anything was proposed. Then she saw Peel; and "the Queen don't like his manner after—oh! how different, how dreadfully so, to that frank, open, natural and most kind, warm manner of Lord Melbourne." Their interview was highly unpromising, with Sir Robert stiff and shy and the Queen shy and petulant. When she announced that she should not part with her Ladies, he started visibly and said that he must consult the Duke. They both returned on the next afternoon, and Wellington tried his hand with her alone. She had been pressing Peel to make him drop his notion of joining the Cabinet as leader in the House of Lords without office and become Foreign Secretary instead. She asked the old man thoughtfully whether it would not be too much for him.

"I'm able to do anything," he said in his decided way.

Then they discussed her Ladies; and the Duke repeated all his arguments—how their opinions were of no significance, but the principle involved had some importance. The Queen was obdurate; the Duke, not unaccustomed to young ladies, was less persuasive than usual; they failed to solve the problem; and Conservatism subsided once more into Opposition, "brained" (in Disraeli's figure) "by a fan," whilst H. B. [13] was moved to unusual bitterness and Alava remarked derisively, "*Je croyais que c'était seulement en Espagne que ces sortes de choses arrivaient.*"

They were all at a Palace ball on the next evening, and their triumphant sovereign wrote that "Peel and the Duke of Wellington came by looking very much put out." But were they? Not Wellington, at any rate; for [12] that day he had been writing gleefully to countless applicants for office that he "found himself under the necessity of declining to undertake the [14] Commission with which the Queen was pleased to offer to entrust me and recommended that it should be entrusted to Sir Robert Peel. Thank God! He has resigned the same. . . ."

3

The old man resumed his sentry-go over the Queen, her ministers, and his innumerable charges. It was a weary round. "Rest!" he cried bitterly that autumn. "Every other animal—even a donkey, a coster-monger's donkey—is allowed some rest, but the Duke of Wellington never! There is no help for it. As long as I am able to go on, they will put the saddle upon my back and make me go." The load grew heavier—or did it only seem heavier now? "It is like everything else," he wrote. "Nobody else will do it. The Duke of Wellington *must*." That *rôle* absorbed him, when he would gladly have subsided into leisure. "I am the Duke of Wellington," as he confessed, "and an officer of the army. But there is not an affair of any kind in which I am not required to be a party. And each of these cases is attended by consequences. I am now re-quired to be a party to the establishment of a college in Kent to teach agriculture. . . ." This was too much; his ordinary business included giving brides away, the House of Lords, Sinque Ports matters, and writing sympathetic letters to maiden ladies who enquired about the weight of baggage carried by soldiers on the march. But agriculture was really quite outside his province; and with his customary ardour of exposition he took several pages to say so. That was his Achilles' heel: he could not resist answering his letters. Such fatal regularity breeds correspondence; and as his wrist grew more rheumatic, the notion spread that there was no topic in the world upon which a letter to the Duke would be out of place, until he was left protesting angrily that "they forget that the Duke of Wellington has only one pair of eyes, and only a certain number of hours in the day like other people," or (more touchingly) "that which people will not understand is that the whole labour and business and ceremony and everything else of the world cannot be thrown upon one man, and that an old one!!"

He was unequal to it now. At seventy his health began to fail under his incorrigible abstemiousness. Indeed, a breakfast of dry bread was a poor preparation for a morning ride on a November day, enlivened by showers of icy rain and conversation on bimetallism. Chilled to the bone, he sat down to his papers, munched half an Abernethy biscuit, and

collapsed. But his collapse was brief. In a few hours the still figure on the little bed was up and giving orders once again; in a few days he answered letters as usual, paid the household bills, attended to his charities, tramped up and down the drawing-room urging a visitor to "tell them at Dover that you have seen me walking—and well—instead of lying speechless at your feet," and posted off in his open britzka for an eight hours' drive to London, where he sat in Council to hear his sovereign announce that she proposed to marry Prince Albert of Saxe-Coburg-Gotha. But the attacks recurred in 1840 and 1841; for he was ageing now, and his austerity impaired his powers of resistance. Did not   22
Mr. Greville notice how loosely the clothes hung on him and think him "only a ruin"? His face grew thinner, and he stooped noticeably; he was   23
a little apt to drop asleep over the fire; his step was firm enough, but he swayed in the saddle (*Punch* turned a kindly eye upon "the neat white-haired old gentleman, whom we have all seen rolling upon his horse in the Park and Pall Mall—a wonder to all bystanders that he did   24
not topple over," and one eye-witness recalls him in the saddle at a perilous tilt, the crop in his right hand rising and falling in a continuous salute all down the Row). There was no more hunting now; and as it tried his eyes to read without his spectacles, he could not hope to shoot. His recreations were all gone. Even music failed to entertain him, as the silence of his deafness deepened; and, once a connoisseur of Grisi and Tamburini, he seemed listless now and rarely called for his favorite airs. "One by one," as an observant neighbour wrote, "all his pleasures   23
have dropped from him like leaves from a tree in winter." For it was winter now, and the bare boughs of Wellington stood in bleak outline.

He still cast a shadow on the House of Lords, speaking assiduously on topics of all dimensions from foreign policy to penny postage and the comparative futility of Indian missions. His vast knowledge was fortified by an extensive correspondence with contemporary observers. Mr. Raikes had constituted himself the Duke's Paris correspondent (rewarded by an unsuccessful effort to get him Consular employment) and elicited   25
his comments on the shifting phases of Palmerstonian diplomacy. The Duke was frankly sceptical of the advantages of international controversy conducted "for the same cause as those who quarrel in Billingsgate;   26
that is for language rather than substance." His aims were simpler—"to

bring the French government back into its real and beneficial position in the councils of Europe." For splendid isolation was little to his taste —"I have no confidence in the system of *isolement*. It does not answer in social life for individuals, nor in politics for nations. Man is a social animal. I have still less confidence in *paix armée*. I will do everything that a private individual can do to conciliate and procure peace." (Had

27 he not informed the House of Lords that he was "one of those who consider that the greatest political interest of this country is to remain at

28 peace and amity with all the nations of the world"?) His comments ranged over the distant past, as he recalled "our absurd declaration of the independence of the colonies of Spain" or thought of Portugal, which once "was not only sound, but, with our assistance, formidable: it was the basis on which the machinery was founded which finally overturned the world."

But the past was very distant now; and the Duke almost felt that he belonged to it. For when news arrived of armed insurrection in the Welsh mining valleys and shooting in the streets of Newport, he raised

29 two hands in helpless protest and exclaimed, "Oh! if I were only twenty years younger!" That would have made him only fifty; at fifty he had helped Liverpool and Castlereagh to tame democracy; but he was

30 seventy—and times had changed. "In these times," as he noted later, "and since the Reform Act, a Tory Government is not to be expected." Schedule A and the extended franchise had done their work, and politics appeared to be reduced to a mere scramble between democracy and property, in which no single individual counted for anything and ministers were under the degrading necessity "of taking their course, not according to their notions of what may be wise for the country; but of what they may be able to carry through both Houses of Parliament." In such a world what place was there for Wellington? He could still do his military duty and assist in the smooth operation of the House of Lords; but he found the part increasingly distasteful.

It was some consolation, when Peel brought the Conservatives to power in 1841. Lord M. departed, and Sir Robert took his place. This time

31 there was no suggestion that the Duke should form a Government, although he was still bravely willing "to do anything, go anywhere, and hold any office, or no office, as may be thought most desirable or ex-

pedient for the Queen's service." Indeed, the King of Prussia had en-   32
quired during the alarums of Palmerston's Egyptian crisis in 1840 if
Wellington would command the German armies against France; and
the old man replied that, subject to the Queen's consent, he felt as
equal to the task as ever. But when Peel formed his Government, the
Queen recognised that Wellington's health was "too uncertain, and   33
himself too prone to sleep coming over him—as Peel expressed it—to
admit of his taking an office in which he would have much to do." So
he joined the Cabinet with the less arduous responsibility of leading
the House of Lords. His health had rallied, and Greville found him in   34
better trim. But the fresh burden of official business told upon his
temper. His duties were discharged; but their discharge was painful
now, and his tired fancy magnified them, until he thought himself too
busy to see anyone and refused interviews with terrifying rudeness.

He laboured through the years of Peel's administration. Indeed, when
Hill died in 1842, he resumed the post of Commander-in-Chief, adding
the Horse Guards to his cares at seventy-three. State ceremonies still
engaged him—he received the King of Prussia in his Prussian uniform
and the Czar in his Russian kit; the Queen came to Stratfield Saye; and   35
when the Prince of Wales was christened, he bore the Sword of State.
The return to duty seemed to revive him; for in 1843 he "spoke with   36
extraordinary vigour, and surprised everybody. He is certainly a much
better man in all respects this year than he was two years ago, mind and
body more firm." His private comments were as tart as ever; and he
received the news of Ellenborough's Indian enthronement among scenes
of Curzonian magnificence with the grim observation that "he ought to
sit upon it in a strait waistcoat." The Cabinet was almost tender with   37
him, each minister rising from his place when he had anything to say
and going to the chair beside the Duke in order that his views might   38
be audible to their old colleague. He had strong opinions of his own
on national defence, which were accentuated by the rising temper of the
French; and among graver problems the proposal for a Peninsular medal
recurred. He had never reconciled himself to the notion of a general
award of medals. But when his sovereign deftly combined it with a sug-   39
gestion that his veterans would value a memento of the Duke, he was
outmanœuvred; and forty years after Vimeiro a medal was issued to

all survivors of the war, bearing on its reverse a figure of Wellington kneeling to Queen Victoria.

But home affairs absorbed them, when the rains of 1845 destroyed the
40 Irish crop. Peel's mind moved rapidly towards Free Trade. The Duke was sceptical. "Rotten potatoes," he remarked without enthusiasm, "have done it all; they have put Peel in his d——d fright." He was an old Protectionist; but caring less for Protection than for national stability,
41 he argued stoutly that "a good government for the country is more important than the Corn Laws or any other consideration." Unlike the
42 Prime Minister, he was no convert to Free Trade— "My position is not the Corn Law; but it is to maintain a Government in the country." This
43 faith made him a loyal Peelite; long afterwards he wrote that "having in 1834 brought Sir Robert Peel from Rome and handed over to him the government of the country, and having once found that he possessed the confidence of the sovereign, of Parliament, and of the country, and thinking that a *government* is of more importance than any measure or particular law, since the passing of the Reform Act—I have been most anxious that Sir Robert Peel shall retain power in his hands; and I did everything in my power on the one hand to induce him to modify his proposed measures, and to take time for carrying them into execution, in order that they might satisfy those who supported his Government, and on the other to persuade his colleagues in office to go on."

That was his simple reasoning, when he informed the Cabinet in 1846
44 that "the Corn Law was a subordinate consideration." The major problem was the government of England; and when Croker bombarded
45 him with Protectionist orthodoxy, he replied majestically, "I am the *retained* servant of the Sovereign of this empire," and refused to be distracted from the larger issue. Who was to govern England? His angry correspondent would prefer the Corn Laws to be repealed, if they must, by Mr. Cobden. That was politician's logic. But the Duke would have none of it. He had seen the fatal consequences of permitting Whigs and Radicals to carry Reform in 1832 instead of letting Tories do it with a slight sacrifice of consistency; and he was not prepared for a repetition of the same mistake in 1846—"I will not be instrumental in placing the Government in the hands of the League and the Radicals." That was his guiding principle. It was his old strategy of retreat—the

deft withdrawal to the next position in rear, which would keep safe
men in office and leave dangerous characters in Opposition. He had employed it with success on Catholic Emancipation; his own supporters
failed him, when he applied it to Reform; and it was his guide along
the twisting path that led towards Free Trade. He faced with equanimity
the prospect of separation from a large section of the Tory Party—"I have
. . . put an end to the connection between the Party and me." Party   46
loyalties were a secondary matter, if the country was to be saved from
the dubious embraces of Mr. Cobden. Better Free Trade, he reasoned,
with Sir Robert Peel than Free Trade and the mob. Free Trade was
quite inevitable either way; and, as in 1829, he gave his orders to the
House of Lords—"My lords! Attention! Right about face! March!" They
wheeled obediently and repealed the Corn Laws at the Duke's command. It was the last and most beneficent of his retreats. The Bill was
passed; and as the old man left the House in the summer dawn, a little
crowd began to cheer. "God bless you, Duke," a workman shouted. "For   47
Heaven's sake, people," the gruff answer came, "let me get on my
horse."

4

Peel fell within the month, and the Duke was out again. But Opposition was no place for him; he had never shewn the slightest aptitude
for it; and his position was now more anomalous than ever. His views
were still Conservative; but it was quite impossible for him to "act with
a party in Parliament," since he was Commander-in-Chief to a Whig   48
Prime Minister. Lord John was tactful; and the watchful Greville noted
that "it is curious to see what good terms he is on with the Duke of   49
Wellington, who is much more cordial and communicative with him
than he was with his former colleagues." They corresponded freely on
India and army matters; and the Duke's letters almost relaxed the cus-   50
tomary stiffness of his official tone. Not that his approval was extended to
all John Russell's colleagues. Lord Palmerston was at the Foreign Office;
and the livelier excursions of Palmerstonian diplomacy failed to commend themselves to Wellington, who was profoundly shocked by spirited
interventions on behalf of British tourists:

51   "Only conceive calling upon an independent Sovereign to punish one of
his subjects *severely* for anything! . . . What we require is to be able to
flatter up the vanity of the sovereign people! to be cried up by their vile
Press as a Government bullying the world in protection of the sole amusement and habits of each thirty-millionth part of the sovereign people wan-
dering about in search of amusement."

The Duke, it is evident, would not have indulged in heroics over Don
52   Pacifico. His patriotism, though, burned brightly still. For he was quite
obsessed by national defence; Arbuthnot reported that "it haunted the
Duke of Wellington, and deprived him of rest, and night and day he
was occupied with the unhappy state of our foreign relations, the
danger of war, and the defenceless state of our coasts." His views were
53   vigorously expressed to the Prime Minister; and a letter to the Inspector-
General of Fortifications, dwelling in harrowing detail upon the dangers
of invasion and closing with a prayer "that the Almighty may protect
me from being the witness of the tragedy, which I cannot persuade my
contemporaries to take measures to avert," occasioned general alarm.
This document was confidential; but the recipient showed it to Lady
Shelley, who lent copies to half the House of Lords. It reached a newspaper; and the Duke's annoyance was extreme. His indignation smoul-
dered for two years, until he met her husband out one evening.

"Good evening, Duke," said Shelley. "Do you know, it has been said
by someone, who must have been present, that the cackling of geese
once saved Rome. I have been thinking that perhaps the cackling of
my old goose may yet save England."

The Duke stared at him and laughed. "By God, Shelley," he said,
"you are right. Give me your honest hand." And an old friendship
had been saved.

He still had his friends, his walks upon the Walmer battlements, and
his correspondence. Mr. Haydon still left little notes at Apsley House
54   asking for an authentic hat to paint from. An application to the Duke
elicited the stern reply that "those to whom he gives his hats and clothes
know best what to do with them"; but a sympathetic valet heard the
painter's prayer and succumbed to a sovereign (of which poor Haydon
had few to spare); and the triumphant hero-worshipper "carried off a

genuine hat—the glorious hat which had encircled the laurelled head
of Wellington! I trusted it to nobody; I took it in the hat-box, called a
cab, and gloried in it." The Duke's life was a protracted triumph now.
Warned by the dismal fate of Marlborough, he watched his dignity with   55
care—"The Duke of Marlborough, because he was an old man, was
treated like an old woman. I won't be." No problem caused him more
anxiety than his own statue. In the beginning he had viewed it with a
fine indifference, asking "to be considered as *dead* upon all matters   56
relating to the statue," and writing that "the Duke is the man of all
men in England who has the least to do with the affair." When it was
erected on the arch opposite his house, Arbuthnot wrote almost shyly
to him that "it seems as if it would be a Gala day in London." But   57
when it was proposed (on purely æsthetic grounds) to move it, he took
legitimate offence. Even the Queen, it seemed, took sides against him.
More sensitive than anybody seemed to realise, he felt as though the
world was all united in execration of him, "as . . . in 1808, when I was   58
persecuted by all factions, out of doors as well as in Parliament; and the
Lord Mayor and the City of London, wishing to treat a general officer
according to the precedent of Admiral Byng, petitioned the King
George III, in my own presence, to bring me by name to trial before a
general court-martial. I faced them all. . . ." The topic became dangerous;
even the Prime Minister asked Greville nervously if he should mention   59
it at Apsley House; and it provoked the Duke to a rare degree of
self-consciousness. Reminding Croker that "more than forty years ago   60
Mr. Pitt observed that I talked as little of myself or my acts as if
I had been an assistant-surgeon of the army," he launched into a vigorous
protest against the fancied slight. The Prime Minister received a fuller
version of the same theme, in which indignation moved him to unusual   61
eloquence—"Without conviction or trial for offence, or complaint al-
ledged, or even whispered or suspected; displeasure is marked with my
conduct, as according to the Hypothesis stated in this letter will be the
opinion founded on the removal of the Statue from its pedestal"—and
he came near threatening to resign the command of the army. His
thunderbolts prevailed; the Queen surrendered; and the Duke con-   62
tinued to ride sedately on his arch.

5

He was not far off eighty when the warning bells of 1848 began to clang. Half Europe was in flames; and a dull glare on the sky warned London, where half a million Chartists were on the march. The Duke was studiously calm and did his best to steady nervous ministers, beckon-
63 ing one across the House of Lords to inform him that "we shall be as quiet on Monday as we are at this hour, and it will end to the credit of the Government and the country." It did; but not without his help. For when the Cabinet decided to stop the Chartist march on Westminster, the Duke was sent for. This was a military matter; and military matters were plainly for the Duke. The old man came promptly; returns were called for; maps were unfolded on the Cabinet table; and as he gripped the problem, his swift decisions put courage into them all. Macaulay was profoundly impressed and thought it the most interesting spectacle that he had ever witnessed. (He told somebody that he should remember it to his dying day; but then Macaulay remembered everything.) The Duke made his plan on Sunday. If London was to be defended, he was a master of the defensive. He had the Guards, some guns, and three regiments of foot. But it had never been his way to show the enemy his strength. Besides, the military were a last resource; for the police might be sufficient. On Monday there was nothing to be seen about the streets except police and special constables (a nephew of the Emperor was on a beat in Piccadilly). Somewhere behind them the troops were wait-ing, as they had waited behind the slope at Salamanca and the long ridge of Waterloo. But they were never needed; for the great demonstration melted before a few police inspectors, and revolution drove respectfully to Westminster with its petition in a four-wheeled cab.

But the storms of 1848 brought shipwrecked mariners for consola-
64 tion to the Duke. The Prince of Prussia came to stay at Stratfield Saye; and when Wellington got back to London, he called every day on Metternich at the Brunswick Hotel in Hanover Square. The exiles from Vienna came to Apsley House to see the table laid for his Waterloo banquet; and when Radetzky thrashed the Italians, the Duke wrote to congratulate him. The world was sadly changed, and universal revolu-

tion had made havoc of the settlement of 1815; but it was some
consolation to visit the Metternichs on Richmond Green (and give the
Prince a little overcoat of his peculiar design). It was a most disturbing
time, when France resumed the tricolour and Lamartine sent pacific
messages to Wellington and Lord Palmerston had questionable dealings
with the most revolutionary governments; but though the world was
changed, the Duke lived bravely on.

III

A NEW decade—his ninth—was opening. His ninth? In one sense it was the tenth decade that Wellington had seen. For his eyes had opened in 1769; and here was 1850. He was past eighty now; and time had left the old man almost alone upon an emptying stage. They were all gone; his colleagues waited for him in stiff, marble attitudes upon their monuments; the Emperor was at the Invalides, watched by a silent circle of tall Caryatids; Lord Liverpool was gone, with Castlereagh and Canning; and now his juniors were going. Melbourne flickered out; a sudden accident took Peel; and when the old man spoke a few sentences about him in the House of Lords, his voice was broken. He was a lonely figure; and as he stood beside his brother Richard's open grave in Eton Chapel, his mouth quivered. Even the faithful Arbuthnot deserted him at last. The Duke saw the doctor in his little room at Apsley House and drew a chair close to catch his words.

"No, no," he said, taking the doctor's hand between his own and rubbing it, "he's not very ill, not very bad—he'll get better."

The old man stared hopefully into the doctor's eyes. "It's only his stomach which is out of order," he suggested. "He'll not die."

But there was no hope. Arbuthnot died with his hand in Wellington's, "quite tranquil" (the Duke wrote), "as a flame extinguishes when the substance which keeps it alive is consumed"; and the last echo of Harriett Arbuthnot died with him.

His life was full of dying echoes now—of lost ladies and forgotten ministers and his poor fluttered Kitty in her white muslin without jewellery sitting apart and talking to her boys' tutor instead of to the guest of honour, pausing at intervals to gaze with embarrassing devotion in his own direction. One echo pleased him; for though he had worn mourning for his friend at Hatfield, he took pleasure now in writing little notes to a new Lady Salisbury. Sometimes she shared his daily tramp along the Piccadilly side of the Green Park; and she was always glad to have his letters. She told him so, and he was no less glad to write

them. "They amuse me," he wrote, "as they do you, and I laugh
while writing them, thinking of the amusement they will afford you." So
she heard all about his minor worries and affairs of state and local politics
at Walmer and cures for colds and Palmerston's iniquities and the deplorable irregularity of brides' mothers who expected him to give away
their daughters without informing him whether to meet them at the
hotel or at St. George's, Hanover Square, and if at the church, whether
at the door or in the vestry. His daily gossip with her was a real pleasure
to him. For the deaf talk freely on paper; and as the silence deepened
round him, the little scribbled notes became his only form of conversation.

His correspondence was still a burden, though. "It is quite curious,"   8
he noted, "with what a number of Insane persons I am in relation. Mad
retired Officers, Mad Women. . . ." But he was gradually learning to
elude his persecutors, announcing with an air of discovery that "some
write in order to get an answer which they shew." Indeed, he speculated   9
innocently whether Cæsar and Hannibal had been exposed to the same
form of persecution. He was to blame, he felt, for letting it be thought
that he was "a good-natured Man, with whom Persons may venture
to take liberties, and what the French call serviceable." (Serviceable
indeed to the widowed lady at Boulogne who asked him for five pounds
to get her back to England and, when he sent it, asked five more because
his unexpected bounty had moved her to break a looking-glass with
a large piece of statuary.) Small wonder the Mendicity Society was invoked for his protection and made matters worse by advertising the
extent to which he had been imposed upon; for a migratory troop of
beggars followed him about and encamped before his doors. The White
Knight was still strong in him; and he was fascinated by the new electric
cable at Dover, though slightly troubled by the problem of avoiding   10
injury from passing ships by fastening it securely to the bottom of the
sea. A terrifying machine, known as the "Jump Baby" or "Baby Jumper"
engaged him deeply; and Lady Salisbury received a gift of one with
profuse instructions how to screw it to the nursery ceiling and no less
than three reminders that Lord Salisbury or the house carpenter should
test it before a small Cecil was entrusted to this "delightful instrument."
He had less taste for large-scale inventions, since the railway failed to

commend itself to Wellington, who felt that it was fraught with peculiar
perils for ladies. "I cannot bear," he wrote, "seeing or hearing of ladies
going alone by the Trains on the Rail Roads. It is true that you have
with you your children. But still the protection of a Gentleman is necessary." The gentry, he conceived, had allowed themselves "to be cheated
and bustled . . . out of the best system and establishment for travelling
that existed in any part of the World. England did not require Rail
Roads." But, however uncalled for, they had come; and though he used
them on occasion, he remained gravely impressed with their mysterious
menace to England's womanhood—"If I could attain the object, no lady
should ever go by a Train, at all events without protection. It is horrible
altogether." His greatest heights of ingenuity were reserved, as usual,
for sartorial invention. Lady Salisbury, whose taste in costume was unusual,
received consignments of his waistcoats with detailed instructions for
their adaptation; and when the polite world giggled discreetly over Mrs.
Bloomer's epoch-making innovation, the Duke was highly interested. "I
am vastly amused," he wrote, "by the Bloomer discussions! I understand
them, being somewhat of a Taylor." But the contemplated revolution in
female apparel was too much for him; and he concluded that "it is
impossible that the Costume should be adopted!"

The roar of public life receded. But when patriotic draymen mobbed
the unpleasant Haynau, he commented grimly that "the travellers of
the Bull family will suffer for it." He made a strenuous attempt to induce
Prince Albert to be his successor at the Horse Guards. Not that he had
the least intention of resigning; for he told the Prince that he was,
thank God, very well and strong and ready to do anything. But he was
nearly eighty-one; and it was most desirable, he felt, that the Crown
should control the army in these democratic times—"the democrats
would blow me up if they could, but they find me too heavy for them."
He said the same thing to the Queen, who countered that Albert already
acted as her private secretary and worked far harder than she liked, and
that these extra duties might be too much for him. There were more
conferences; memoranda were exchanged; but the proposal dropped. A
livelier business occupied him, when a prince was born on May 1, 1850.
The lyre was struck by Thackeray:

"To Hapsley Ouse next day
    Drives up a Broosh, and for,
A gracious prince sits in that Shay
    (I mention him with Hor!)

"They ring upon the bell,
    The Porter shows his Ed
(He fought at Vaterloo as vell,
    And vears a Veskit red).

"To see that carriage come
    The people round it press:
'And is the galliant Duke at ome?'
    'Your Royal Ighness, yes.'

"He stepps from out the Broosh,
    And in the gate is gone;
And X, although the people push,
    Says wery kind, 'Move hon.'

"The Royal Prince unto
    The galliant Duke did say,
'Dear Duke, my little son and you
    Was born the self-same day.

" 'The Lady of the land,
    My wife and Sovring dear,
It is by her horgust command
    I wait upon you here.

" 'That lady is as well
    As can expected be;
And to your Grace she bids me tell
    This gracious message free.

" 'That offspring of our race
    Whom yesterday you see,
To show our honour for your Grace,
    Prince Arthur he shall be.

            .   .   .   .   .

" 'You fought with Bonypart,
    And likewise Tippoo Saib;
I name you then with all my heart
    The Godsire of this babe.' "

472

Albert recorded their selection with a less sprightly pen, reporting for
16 the eye of Stockmar that "his first name is in compliment to the good
old Duke, on whose eighty-first birthday he first saw the light. Patrick is
in remembrance of our recent visit to Ireland; William, of the Prince
of Prussia, whom we shall ask to be godfather, and also in remembrance of poor Queen Adelaide, on whose account we have also selected
the Duchess Ida of Saxe-Weimar as godmother. My name the Queen
insists on retaining by way of *coda*. I hope you will approve the arrangement. The Exhibition is making good progress. . . ."

The Duke had his cares as Ranger of Hyde Park. For his territory had
17 been invaded by a determined female, who was unlawfully established in
a hut by the Serpentine and was suspected of intent to sell cakes and
oranges. "We must proceed," he wrote, "with caution and Regularity";
and he rode out to reconnoitre her position as thoroughly as though
she had been Masséna. He viewed the ground with care; but before his
offensive could develop, the enemy decamped, leaving the Duke victorious again. He had one more victory in 1851, when the Great Exhibition glittered in the Park. The watchful Commons had insisted that
no trees should be cut down. A dreadful consequence ensued. For when
the marvels of art and industry were exposed to view, the lively sparrows began to spoil them. The dilemma was agonising, since it was
impossible to shoot the sparrows without breaking half the glass in
the great building. What was to be done? His country turned, as usual,
to Wellington. The Duke was sent for; and the Queen herself explained
the difficulty. "Try sparrow-hawks, Ma'am," he replied. It was Wellington's last victory.

He found the Exhibition a great resource, rode up to see it every
18 day, talked to the stall-keepers, made appointments to meet ladies in
"the Glass Palace," and bought Miss Coutts a bracelet there. That sum-
19 mer he met Thiers and "had to make him some phrases about the Em-
20 peror Napoleon." There was a fancy ball in Queen Anne costume, to
which he dutifully went in powder and three-cornered hat, remembering to show the children how to walk a minuet before he went. Politics
were a receding murmur now, though early in the year he had been
called on to advise the Queen, when John Russell resigned and nobody
21 would form a Government. The Duke was sent for and advised his

sovereign to try Lord John again. Not that he had turned Whig, since
he called on Derby afterwards to express his satisfaction and said,
"Well, they are in the mud, and now you can look about you." He was
quite right; for the Conservatives came in the next year. He sat beside
the new Prime Minister in the House of Lords; and as he strained to
catch the unfamiliar names of the new Cabinet (a Mr. Disraeli was
to be Chancellor of the Exchequer), the old man kept asking Derby,
"Who? Who?" So somebody nicknamed the Government of 1852 "the   22
Who? Who? Ministry."

The slow weeks of 1852 went by; and Wellington still went his rounds.
That summer he made quite a long speech in the House of Lords on   23
the Militia Bill; and when the stooping figure rose at the Academy   24
banquet, they heard him speak of the admirable discipline which had
prevailed on board the sinking *Birkenhead*. He spoke a final sentence   25
on the same subject in the House of Lords. Then the House rose for
the recess, and England went on holiday. The Duke, as usual, was at
Walmer, pacing slowly up and down his battlements or writing letters   26
in his little room. (His standing-desk stood in the recess that looked
towards the sea and caught the morning sun; and his camp-bed, with
the silk mattress which he had devised for Russia in 1825, was in the
corner of the room.) A Grand-Duchess and her husband came to stay,
and there were moments when their host could "wish my Imperial   27
Royalties were in Russia." But he saw them off from Dover and returned to his little fortress with relief. That was the worst of being deaf
—"one gets bored in boring others, and one becomes too happy to get   28
home." Deafness apart, he had little fault to find with life at eighty-
three—"I really believe that there is not a youth in London who could
enjoy the world more than myself . . . but being deaf, the spirit, not the
body, tires!" The body, indeed, was strictly mortified by his remarkable régime, which comprised systematic starving and massage with
vinegar and water.

September came; and he rode into Dover and caught the train to
Folkestone for a call on Mr. Croker. They told him at the station that   29
the house was only half a mile away. So the Duke started out to walk
there and discovered that it was a three-mile walk ending with a climb
up a steep hill; and at the end of it he found that Croker had gone into

Dover. He started home again, ordered a fly to take him to the station, but positively walked part of the way until his conveyance overtook him. A meeting was arranged with more success a few days later; and the two old men sat gossiping about the past. They talked of old Irish Office Bills which he had left in Croker's charge when he went out to take command in the Peninsula, of the forgotten Parliament on College Green, of his horse "Copenhagen," and the endless complexities of Reparations in 1818. The Duke began to tell a story about a Spanish lady at Salamanca who had hidden some papers about herself, and broke off to spare Mrs. Croker's blushes. Then he explained to her that "all the business of war, and indeed all the business of life, is to endeavour to find out what you don't know by what you do; that's what I call 'guessing what was at the other side of the hill.' " The talk ran on French generals, and he said reminiscently that the Emperor was the best of them all. His own success in Spain had come, he thought, because he was "a *conquérant sans ambition*. I had for a time a sovereign power there, but no one suspected me of any design to become King of Spain or Portugal, like Joseph or Soult or Junot. I *was* almost King of Spain. . . ." The time slipped by; and when his carriage came, the Duke walked slowly down the steps counting them aloud for Croker's guidance. A slightly intoxicated Irishman with a Peninsular medal besieged him at the station and received the invariable sovereign. Then the Duke went back to Walmer.

He was not lonely, though; for his son Charles was at the Castle with his children. Besides, there was his correspondence—eight pages of Spanish in pale ink from Ciudad Rodrigo about a local grievance, his daily gossip with Lady Salisbury, and all his begging letters. His mind was running on the past; and he wrote off a long account of the mob that followed him through London in 1832, and how pleased the King had been when Oxford made him Chancellor. He had a letter from a madman, who proposed to call with a message from the Lord. But he was expecting more normal visitors; for Lady Burghersh was due to arrive on Tuesday and Lady Salisbury on Wednesday. He seemed quite well on Monday; and when his servant went to him on Tuesday morning (it was September 14), he ordered his carriage for a drive to Dover. But a little later he felt unwell and, methodical as ever, said: "I feel very ill; send for the apothecary." It was his last order; for the Duke never spoke again. He had been born beside the sea, where the long tide crept slowly round the bay from Dalkey to the hill of Howth; and the sea whispered still beyond the window of his silent room, as the tide ebbed slowly and the Duke sat on, a huddled figure in a high-back chair.

IV

ALL through the long November night it rained. The rain fell relentlessly, and London waited for the dawn with gleaming pavements. The Park trees stood dripping in the downpour outside a shuttered house at Hyde Park Corner. It drummed on the Great Hall at Chelsea, where two hundred thousand people had trooped by candlelight for five days past a still pageant of black velvet and silver stars, watched by immobile sentries resting stiffly on their arms reversed. Eastwards across the darkness a gilded cross dripped in the winter night on the Cathedral dome that waited for the day with all its windows darkened; and midway the hours chimed slowly from the Horse Guards. Outside on the parade the water stood in pools, and the rain whispered round the tent where men were working all night long on the great car. The night was paling now; and as it turned to grey, a darker mass was etched upon it, where the long lines of troops moved into place. There was a steady tramp of marching feet; cavalry went jingling by; words of command hung on the chilly morning air; and as the pale winter day came up, the rain checked. For the Duke was riding out again; and it was his way to ride out after rain. (Had it not rained that night before he rode to Waterloo?) It was broad daylight now. A gun thudded in the Park. The ranks stiffened; and as the bands wailed out the slow refrain, his last ride began.

> Duke of Wellington, Marquis of Wellington, Marquis of Douro, Earl of Wellington in Somerset, Viscount Wellington of Talavera, Baron Douro of Wellesley, Prince of Waterloo in the Netherlands, Duke of Ciudad Rodrigo in Spain, Duke of Brunoy in France, Duke of Vittoria, Marquis of Torres Vedras, Count of Vimiero in Portugal, a Grandee of the First Class in Spain, a Privy Councillor, Commander-in-Chief of the British Army, Colonel of the Grenadier Guards, Colonel of . . .

The minute-guns spoke slowly from the Park; and the car—twenty-

477

seven feet of assorted allegory—"rolled," in its proud creator's words, "majestically forth." It was a triumph in its way—a triumph over Banting, the undertaker, who had submitted drawings made (*proh pudor!*) by a Frenchman; a triumph for the new superintendent of the Department of Practical Art, whose modest sketch had drawn from Prince Albert the rapturous exclamation, "This is the thing." Small wonder that this sublime vehicle, all black and gold, was generously adorned with lions' heads, with sabres, with laurel wreaths; and in case its delicate symbolism should be missed, a thoughtful hand had added an immense trophy of real swords and muskets. One witness might observe a trifle bleakly that something in its outline recalled a railway truck. But *The Times'* enraptured eye was fastened on "the magnificent dolphins, symbolical of maritime supremacy, playfully wrought out along the spokes . . . the sumptuous pall, powdered with silver embroiderings—and the not less superb canopy of silver tissue, after an Indian pattern, manufactured with unexampled rapidity and skill by Keith & Co., of Wood-street." Nor was the *Illustrated London News* blind to the marvels of the canopy's supports, since they were halberts—no ordinary halberts, though, but halberts rising from ornamental tripods and "lowered by machinery in passing through Temple Bar," itself surmounted by vases burning incense and transformed into the semblance of a procenium arch for some sepulchral pantomime. This portent had a stormy birth. Competing Government Departments hung like rival fairies above its cradle. The Lord Chamberlain was gravely exercised; the Board of Works had a word to say; the War Department intervened; and for some occult departmental reason the Board of Trade conceived the matter to be its own sole concern. Six foundries struggled with the castings; the ladies of the School of Art stitched with demented fingers; and in three weeks this monument of art and industry rumbled across the Horse Guards. It rumbled, to be more precise, into the Mall; and there, just opposite the Duke of York's column, it gave a dreadful lurch and stayed. For the sodden roadway had collapsed under its weight, and the great wheels were buried up to the lions on their axles. Twelve dray-horses, sublime with funeral feathers, strained vainly at the traces. But five dozen constables leaned on a cable; and the stupendous hearse staggered once more into motion. The slow march resumed; and from the Park the minute-guns still thudded on the damp morning air—

> . . . *Field-Marshal of Great Britain, a Marshal of Russia, a Marshal of Austria, a Marshal of France, a Marshal of Prussia, a Marshal of Spain, a Marshal of Portugal, a Marshal of the Netherlands, a Knight of the Garter, a Knight of the Holy Ghost, a Knight of the Golden Fleece, a Knight Grand Cross of the Bath, a Knight Grand Cross of Hanover, a Knight of the Black Eagle, a Knight . . .*

The Queen was waiting at the Palace with a melancholy conviction that "we shall soon stand sadly alone; Aberdeen is almost the only personal friend of that kind we have left. Melbourne, Peel, Liverpool—and now the Duke—*all* gone!" The news had reached them in the Highlands on an excursion from Allt-na-Giuthasach, whilst they were sitting by the side of the Dhu Loch, one of the severest, wildest spots imaginable"; and her pen promptly underlined his epitaph—"the pride and the *bon génie*, as it were, of this country. He was the GREATEST man this country ever produced, and the most *devoted* and *loyal* subject, and the staunchest supporter the Crown ever had. He was to us a true kind friend and most valuable adviser. . . . Albert is much grieved. The dear Duke showed him great confidence and kindness." Even his small godson, Arthur of Connaught, kept murmuring, "The Duke of Wellikon, little Arta's God-papa"; for the pair of them had rambled through the big rooms at Apsley House together, when the Queen sent the baby round for the last anniversary of Waterloo. Small wonder that the long procession and the silent crowds made "a deep and *wehmütige* impression," as the old man passed her Palace windows for the last time. Albert rode with mournful thoughts in the *cortège*. He felt the loss as well, "as if in a tissue a particular thread which is worked into every pattern was suddenly withdrawn." Stockmar responded with a thoughtful analysis of human greatness, concluding with a slightly condescending estimate—"His intellect was not many-sided and mobile, but with all its one-sidedness it was always clear and sound, so that although the principles which lay at the foundation of his character were not of the noblest kind, still they contained a good sprinkling of practical truth, justice, and honesty." His object, it would seem, was to incite his princely pupil "to

replace the Duke for the country and the world." The country was less
ardent to accept the substitute; and a notion that the Prince might be
Wellington's successor as Commander-in-Chief occasioned general alarm.
But he retained his sober predilection for "*silent* influence," and drove
sedately in a mourning carriage. Half England rode in the procession,
watched by the silent pavements. There was no sound along the route
except a sudden, scattered cry of "Hats off" above the rolling of the
wheels, the wail of military bands, the thud of muffled drums, the slow
beat of hoofs, and the dull pulse of tramping men.

> *. . . Knight of the Sword of Sweden, a Knight of St. Andrew of
> Russia, a Knight of the Annunciado of Sardinia, a Knight of the Ele-
> phant of Denmark, a Knight of Maria Theresa, a Knight of St. George
> of Russia, a Knight of the Crown of Rue of Saxony, a Knight of
> Fidelity of Baden, a Knight of Maximilian Joseph of Bavaria, a Knight
> of St. Alexander Newsky of Russia, a Knight of St. Hermenegilda of
> Spain, a Knight of the Red Eagle of Brandenburgh, a Knight of St.
> Januarius, a Knight of the Golden Lion of Hesse-Cassel, a Knight of
> the Lion of . . .*

Still they went by. Three thousand foot brought on the slow *cortège*;
eight squadrons followed, and three batteries of guns clanked past. It was
the strangest medley of his long career slowly passing by. East Indian
Directors; one rigid private of every British regiment with arms reversed;
Chelsea Pensioners marching a little stiffly; then the civilians—the Bench,
the Cabinet, and Mr. Disraeli in a mourning coach wishing that his
memory of Thiers' obituary of a French Marshal had not been quite so
perfect as to obtrude itself almost *verbatim* into his funeral oration.
The new Laureate, whose *Ode* was out that morning, watched from a
window and was "struck with the look of sober manhood in the British
soldier," as he marched to bury the great Duke; and by the strangest
irony of all a son of the Emperor was waiting gravely at St. Paul's
in diplomatic uniform. For when Walewski hesitated, the Prince-Presi-
dent had sent him orders to attend; and Napoleon's son mourned Wellington by order of Napoleon's nephew, his bland Russian colleague encouraging him with "*Mon cher, si nous allions ressusciter ce pauvre
duc, je comprends que vous pourriez vous dispenser d'assister à cette*

cérémonie; mais puisque nous sommes invités pour l'enterrer. . . ." Mr. Carlyle, much tried by "all the empty fools of creation" crowding to Chelsea, mourned "the one true man of official men in England, or that I know of in Europe," from a second-floor in Bath House. Generous to "the *last* perfectly honest and perfectly brave public man," he was highly disrespectful to the car—"of all the objects I ever saw the abominably ugliest, or nearly so. An incoherent huddle of expensive palls, flags, sheets, and gilt emblems and cross poles, more like one of the street carts that hawk door-mats than a bier for a hero . . . this vile *ne plus ultra* of Cockneyism; but poor Wellington lay dead beneath it faring dumb to his long home." That thought almost stifled Lord Shaftesbury's austere disapproval of so much secular magnificence—"fine, very fine, but hardly impressive; signs of mortality but none of resurrection; much of a great man in his generation, but nothing of a great spirit in another; not a trace of religion, not a shadow of eternity. . . . Stupendously grand in troops and music. It was solemn, and even touching; but it was a show, an eye-tickler to 999 out of every thousand—a mere amusement." Perhaps. Yet the crowds watched bareheaded all through the winter morning (outside St. Paul's they were so closely packed that the lamplighters never reached the street-lamps, and the lights burned all day above the silent throng); and as the long procession passed, band after band caught up the slow refrain—

> *. . . The Lord High Constable of England, the Constable of the Tower, the Constable of Dover Castle, Warden of the Cinque Ports, Chancellor of the Cinque Ports, Admiral of the Cinque Ports, Lord-Lieutenant of Hampshire, Lord-Lieutenant of the Tower Hamlets, Ranger of St. James's Park, Ranger of Hyde Park, Chancellor of the University of Oxford . . .*

The long lines went by, wound slowly through the Park and past the blind windows of his empty house, down the long hill towards the City, until the trumpets died away.

Authorities

THE EDUCATION OF ARTHUR WESLEY

I

1. Lecky, W. E. H.: *History of Ireland in the Eighteenth Century*, 1892, I, 289–90.

2. Georgian Society: *Records of Eighteenth-Century Domestic Architecture and Decoration in Ireland*, 1909–13, V, 65.

3. Walpole, Horace: *Letters* (ed. Paget Toynbee), 1903–25, VIII, 256.

4. Georgian Society: *op. cit.*, V, *passim.*

5. Lecky, W. E. H.: *op. cit.*, I, 285–6.   6. *Ibid.*, III, 413.

7. *Ibid.*, I, 293.   8. *Ibid.*, I, 282.   9. *Ibid.*, II, 188.

10. Georgian Society: *op. cit.*, I–IV, *passim.*

11. Walpole, Horace: *op. cit.*, III, 209.   12. *Ibid.*, V, 129.

13. Lecky, W. E. H.: *op. cit.*, II, 22.

14. Dublin Mercury: April 29–May 2, 1769.

15. Assignment of 6 Merrion Street by Earl of Antrim to Earl of Mornington for £2,697. August 16, 1769, Registry of Deeds, Dublin.

16. Georgian Society: *op. cit.*, I, 13–14, 37, Plates XXXIX–XL.

17. Murray, J.: *Lost Escutcheon*, 1850; *Birthplace of Wellington*, 1852; *Wellington: the Place and Day of his Birth*, 1852. Burke, Sir B.: *Rise of Great Families*, 1873, 94–107. Notes and Queries, 4th Series, X, 443; 7th Series, XI, 35. The Times, June 3, 4, 7, 8, 10, 19, 1926.

A. Birthplace.—The following have been suggested:

> (*i*) Mornington House, 6 Merrion Street (now 24 Upper Merrion Street), Dublin.
> (*ii*) Grafton Street, Dublin.
> (*iii*) Dangan, co. Meath.
> (*iv*) Trim, co. Meath.
> (*v*) Mornington, co. Meath.
> (*vi*) Athy, co. Kildare.
> (*vii*) Between Dangan and Dublin.
> (*viii*) At sea off Dublin.

All except (*i*) are disposed of by the fact that the four contemporary Irish newspapers which record the event place it "in Merrion Street" (*Dublin Gazette*, May 2–4; *Dublin Mercury*, May 4; *Pue's Occurrences*, May 6; *Public Register or Freeman's Journal*, May 6, 1769). Merrion Street being established as the locality, there is little uncertainty as to the actual house. A shadowy tradition founded on oral evidence and recorded in *Complete Peer-*

age, places the event in an unidentified house belonging to Provost Andrews, of Trinity College, which is stated to have been lent to the Morningtons whilst their new residence was getting ready. But it seems hardly likely that an unmarried Provost was still in possession of a house in Merrion Street in addition to his official residence at a date ten years after his own appointment. No lease of it in his name is to be found in the Registry of Deeds, and contemporary Directories are unanimous in giving Trinity College as his sole address. There is, however, a bare possibility that the event occurred during a brief tenancy of these premises, of which no tangible evidence exists. But, on the whole, it is reasonable to assume that Lord Mornington's occupation of No. 6 preceded his formal acquisition of the house on Aug. 16, 1769; and (*i*) may therefore be adopted with confidence.

B. DATE OF BIRTH.—Two dates have been suggested:

    (*i*) April 29.

    (*ii*) May 1.

(*i*) is supported by (*a*) notice of birth on April 29 in *Exshaw's Gentleman's Magazine,* May, 1769; (*b*) entry of baptism on April 30 in Register of St. Peter's, Dublin; and (*c*) copy of prescription by Sir Fielding Ould, M.D., dispensed by Messrs. Evans, 9 Dawson Street, Dublin, on April 30 for Lady Mornington and "the young child."

(*ii*) is supported by (*a*) Lord Mornington's attestation of April 1, 1779 (Lord's Entries, Office of Arms, Dublin Castle); (*b*) Lady Mornington's statement of April 6, 1815 (MURRAY, W.: *The Place and Day of his Birth,* 20); and (*c*) W.'s lifelong belief.

The evidence in support of (*i*) is scarcely satisfactory, since the prescription for "the young child" proves on examination to have been wholly unsuited to a new-born infant, and was therefore written for his sister Ann, then twelve months old. As to the notices in *Exshaw* and St. Peter's Register, the former was a monthly magazine of frequent inaccuracy, and Irish parish registers of this period are unreliable as to dates. If, moreover, both are accepted as correct, it would follow that W. was baptised on the day following his birth, a circumstance which presupposes that the infant was thought to be in danger of immediate death. But there is no trace whatever of this remarkable fact either in tradition (though it is not easy to believe that so precarious an opening of so long and eminent a career could have passed wholly unnoticed) or in the chemist's books, since Arthur's first medicine (and that a mere lotion) was not made up until July 1, 1769.

In the absence, therefore, of reliable evidence in support of (*i*), I incline to (*ii*), which rests upon the belief of W. and of both his parents, and is supported by the father's sworn evidence in a public document of great formality.

II

1. DELANY, MRS.: *Autobiography and Correspondence,* 1861, I, 348–9.
2. *Ibid.,* I, 406. 3. *Ibid.,* I, 361. 4. *Ibid.,* I, 345.
5. BARRINGTON, D.: *Miscellanies,* 1781, 317.
6. DELANY, MRS.: *op. cit.,* I, 409. 7. *Ibid.,* II, 501.
8. BARRINGTON, D.: *op. cit.,* 318–19.
9. DELANY, MRS.: *op. cit.,* III, 546. 10. *Ibid.,* III, 535.
11. GEORGIAN SOCIETY: *op. cit.,* III, 75.
12. DELANY, MRS.: *op. cit.,* III, 514–15. 13. *Ibid.,* III, 539.
14. *Ibid.,* III, 540, 546.
15. PUBLIC GAZETTEER: June 21, 1760.
16. DELANY, MRS.: *op. cit.,* 531–2.
17. LECKY, W. E. H.: *op. cit.,* I, 342.
18. BARRINGTON, D.: *op. cit.,* 320.

III

1. WALPOLE, HORACE: *op. cit.,* VII, 197. 2. *Ibid.,* VII, 293.
3. *Ibid.,* VIII, 317–18.
4. GEORGIAN SOCIETY: *op. cit.,* II, 205.
5. DELANY, MRS.: *op. cit.,* V, 408.
6. Information supplied by Mr. Reginald Blunt. The school was at 185 King's Road, Chelsea, on the south side, a little west of the present Town Hall.
7. MORNINGTON, EARL OF: *Letter to Dublin agent,* Oct. 7, 1780. In the possession of Lord Gerald Wellesley.
8. LYNDON, W.: *Letter to Lord Wellesley,* undated. In the possession of Lord Gerald Wellesley. Cf. Mortgage £1,000 of March 4, 1774, by Earl of Mornington to C. P. Leslie and S. Gardiner. Registry of Deeds, Dublin.
9. Account for funeral expenses of Lord Mornington. In the possession of Lord Gerald Wellesley.
10. THACKERAY, W. M.: *Lines on a Late Hospicious Ewent,* 1850.

IV

1. Mortgage of Laracor, Great Ginnetts, Little Ginnetts, Clonemeath, and Doolestown, co. Meath, by Earl of Mornington to Rt. Hon. D. La Touche, of Dublin, for £8,000, July 4, 1781. Registry of Deeds, Dublin.
2. MAXWELL LYTE, H. C.: *History of Eton College,* 1889, 334.
3. ETON COLLEGE REGISTER, 1921.
4. MAXWELL LYTE, H. C.: *op. cit.,* 323.
5. ETON COLLEGE LISTS, 1678–1790. Ed. R. A. Austen-Leigh, 1907.
6. MAXWELL LYTE, H. C.: *op. cit.,* 300–1.

7. FRASER, SIR W.: *Words on Wellington*, 1900, 122, 161.

8. MAXWELL LYTE, H. C.: *op. cit.*, 305.

9. MAXWELL, SIR H.: *Life of Wellington*, 1899, I, 4.

10. VILLEBIOT, G. DE LA: *L'Académie d'Équitation et les Origines de l'enseignement équestre à Angers,* (Angers) 1909.

11. STANHOPE, EARL: *Conversations with the Duke of Wellington*, 1888, 164–7.

12. BRIALMONT AND GLEIG: *Life of Wellington*, 1858, I, 6.

13. MAXWELL, SIR H.: *op. cit.*, I, 5–6.

14. Mortgage of Dangan, Ballymaglasson, Mornington, Laracor, Oldrath, Great Ginnetts, Little Ginnetts, Clonemeath, Doolestown, and Moygare to Hon. R. Annesley and H. Gorges, of Dublin, for £10,000. May 24, 1785. Registry of Deeds, Dublin.

15. DICTIONARY OF NATIONAL BIOGRAPHY: *s. v.* Wellington.

V

1. CROKER, J. W.: *Correspondence and Diaries,* 1885, I, 337.

2. MORNINGTON, COUNTESS OF: *Letter to Miss Butler and Miss Ponsonby, Llangollen,* Nov. 26, 1787. In the possession of C. Hamilton, Esq., Hamwood, Dunboyne, co. Meath.

3. MORNINGTON, COUNTESS OF: *Letter to Miss Butler and Miss Ponsonby, Llangollen,* Dec. 17, 1787. *Ibid.*

4. *The Hamwood Papers of the Ladies of Llangollen* (ed. Bell), 1930, 72.

5. FRASER, SIR W.: *op. cit.*, 206.

6. GRIFFITHS, A.: *Wellington, his Comrades and Contemporaries,* 1897, 3.

7. *Ibid.*, 4–5.

8. MAXWELL, W. H.: *Life of Wellington*, 1839, I, 12.

9. WELLINGTON: *Bond for* £100, Dec. 1789, *Apsley House Papers.*

10. WESLEY, ANNE: *Letter to Miss Butler, Llangollen,* Sept. 15, 1789. In the possession of C. Hamilton, Esq. *Ibid.*

11. LECKY, W. E. H.: *op. cit.*, II, 209.   12. *Ibid.*, II, 252.

13. WELLINGTON: *Letter to Earl of Mornington,* March 20, 1790, *Apsley House Papers.*

14. WELLINGTON: *Letter to Earl of Mornington,* June 14, 1790, *Apsley House Papers.*

15. WELLINGTON: *Letter to Earl of Mornington,* June 18, 1790, *Apsley House Papers.*

16. PARLIAMENTARY REGISTER, XI, Dublin, 1791.

17. LECKY, W. E. H.: *op. cit.*, II, 408–9, 430; III, 3, 79.

18. WELLINGTON: *Letter to Page,* Ap., 1792, *Apsley House Papers.*

19. MAXWELL, W. H.: *op. cit.*, I, 10–11.

20. LECKY, W. E. H.: *op. cit.*, III, 194.

21. 82 Grafton Street: *Apsley House Papers*.

22. WELLESLEY PAPERS, 1914, I, 121.

23. PEARCE, R. R.: *Memoirs and Correspondence of Richard, Marquess Wellesley*, 1846, I, 44.

24. WELLINGTON: *Letter to Page*, Oct. 1792, *Apsley House Papers*.

25. LECKY, W. E. H.: *op. cit.*, III, 7.

26. WELLINGTON: *Letter to Page*, Sept. 1792, *Apsley House Papers*.

27. MORNINGTON, EARL OF: *Letter to Sir Chichester Fortescue*, June 20, 1796. In the possession of Lord Gerald Wellesley (partly printed in *Supplementary Despatches*, XIII, 3).

28. PARLIAMENTARY REGISTER (IRELAND), 1793, XIII, 5.

29. LECKY, W. E. H.: *op. cit.*, III, 140.

30. PARLIAMENTARY REGISTER (IRELAND), XIII, 313.

31. FORTESCUE, HON. J.: *Wellington*, 1925, 12.

32. CROKER, J. W.: *op. cit.*, I, 337.

33. ELLESMERE, EARL OF: *Personal Reminiscences of the Duke of Wellington*, 1904, 79–80; CROKER, J. W.: *loc. cit.*

34. FRASER, SIR W.: *op. cit.*, 32–3; GLEIG, G. R.: *Personal Reminiscences of the Duke of Wellington*, 1904, 283.

35. FRASER, SIR W.: *op. cit.*, 10.

VI

1. ROSE, J. HOLLAND: *William Pitt and the Great War*, 1911, 32.

2. *Ibid.*, 118.

3. GIBBON, E.: *Autobiography* (ed. Everyman's Library), 178.

4. WRIGHT, T.: *Caricature History of the Georges*, 1867, 479.

5. MAXWELL, SIR H.: *op. cit.*, I, 8.

6. FORTESCUE, HON. J.: *History of the British Army*, IV, 354.

7. WILSON, HARRIETTE: *Memoirs* (ed. Davies), 1929, 1.

8. HUGO, V.: *Quatrevingt-Treize* (ed. Nelson), 159.

9. WRIGHT, T.: *op. cit.*, 380.

10. Conveyance of Dangan by Earl of Mornington to T. Burrowes for £25,000, Sept. 18, 1793. Registry of Deeds, Dublin.

11. CARLYLE, T.: *French Revolution* (ed. J. Holland Rose), 1902, III, 254.

12. GRIFFITHS, A.: *op. cit.*, 7.

13. Regimental accounts, Dublin, Nov. 1793, *Apsley House Papers*.

14. BRIALMONT AND GLEIG: *op. cit.*, I, 12.

15. MAXWELL, W. H.: *op. cit.*, I, 13–14.

16. FORTESCUE, HON. J.: *British Army*, IV, 141, 145, 154–5, 157.

17. W.O.: 12, 4804, *Public Record Office*.

18. Regimental accounts, Cork, April 1794, *Apsley House Papers*.

19. Regimental accounts, Cork, May 1794. *Ibid.*

20. FORTESCUE, HON. J.: *Wellington*, 13; *British Army*, IV, 282.

21. STANHOPE, EARL: *op. cit.*, 111.

22. MAXWELL, SIR H.: *op. cit.*, I, 11.

23. BUNBURY, SIR H.: *Narratives of Some Passages in the Great War with France* (ed. Fortescue), 1927, 29.

24. WELLINGTON: *Letter to Mornington*, Sept. 19, 1794, B.M. Add. MSS. 37308, 15.

25. STANHOPE, EARL: *op. cit.*, 182.

26. WELLINGTON: *Letter to General Cunninghame*, Yzendoom, Nov. 19, 1794, *Apsley House Papers*.

27. *Supplementary Despatches*, 1871, XIII, 2.

28. Regimental accounts, Dec. 1794. In W.'s writing, *Apsley House Papers*.

29. FORTESCUE, HON. J.: *British Army*, IV, 320–2.

30. *MS. General and Brigade Orderly Book*, Feb. 16–April 11, 1795. In the author's possession.

31. WELLINGTON: *Letter to Earl Camden*, June 26, 1795: ". . . as I told you in London" (BRIALMONT AND GLEIG, *op. cit.*, I, 22). Camden entered Dublin March 31, 1795 (LECKY, W. E. H.: *op. cit.*, III, 325). It follows that W.'s London interview with him took place between his appointment as Lord-Lieutenant and his departure for Ireland—both in March, 1795.

VII

1. BRIALMONT AND GLEIG: *op. cit.*, I, 22–3.

2. Bill £14 12s. 1d. for cloth supplied by Lucas, Dublin, 1795. Paid May 30, 1807, *Apsley House Papers*.

3. WELLINGTON: *Letter to Earl Camden*, April 29, 1795, *Camden Papers*.

4. MORNINGTON, EARL OF: *Letter to Earl Camden*, April 24, 1795. *Ibid.*

5. PARLIAMENTARY REGISTER (IRELAND): 1795, XV, 376–81.

6. *Ibid.*, 381.

7. WELLINGTON: Fragment of letter to Earl Camden. Undated (for date cf. "the expedition to the Coast of France will not last for ever" and FORTESCUE: *British Army*, IV, 416–18), *Camden Papers*.

8. IRISH ALMANACK, 1795.

9. CAMDEN, EARL: *Letter to Lt.-Col. Wesley*, Sept. 15, 1793, *Apsley House Papers* (Copy in *Camden Papers*).

10. Prescription, *Apsley House Papers*.

11. FORTESCUE, J.: *British Army*, IV, 477–81.

12. MAXWELL, SIR H.: *op. cit.*, I, 18.

13. MORNINGTON, EARL OF: *Letter to Sir Chichester Fortescue*, June 20, 1796. (Partly printed in *Supplementary Despatches*, XIII, 3.) In the possession of Lord Gerald Wellesley.

14. CAMDEN, EARL: *Letter to W.*, June 5th, 1796, *Apsley House Papers*.

15. CAMDEN, EARL: *Letter to Earl Mornington*, undated (misplaced in 1795), *Apsley House Papers*.

16. LECKY, W. E. H.: *op. cit.*, III, 322.

17. PAGE: *Letter to W.*, June, 1796, *Apsley House Papers*.

18. Account of R. Faulder, June 6, 1796, *Apsley House Papers*.

19. MORNINGTON, EARL OF: *Letter to Sir Chichester Fortescue*, Aug. 5, 1797. In the possession of Lord Gerald Wellesley.

List of books in W.'s writing, endorsed in another hand "August 1798," and (more faintly) ". . . from Calcutta to Madras," *Apsley House Papers*.

21. LLOYD, W.: *History of the Late War in Germany between the King of Prussia and the Empress of Germany and her Allies*, 2 vols. (Vol. I bound in 2 parts), 1781–90. Vol. I, part II, 46.   22. *Ibid.*, 44.

23. *Ibid.*, 51–2.

24. OMAN, C. W. C.: *Wellington's Army*, 1912, 82–6; *Column and Line in the Peninsular War*, 17.

25. CARLYLE, T.: *Frederick the Great* (Centenary Edition), VI, 72–3; 273.

26. HART, B. H. LIDDELL: *Great Captains Unveiled*, 1927, 37–74.

27. SAXE, MAURICE COMTE DE: *Les Reveries ou Memoires sur l'Art de la Guerre*, 1758, 22.   28. *Ibid.*, 28.   29. *Ibid.*, 49.

30. BOURRIENNE, L. A. F. DE: *Memoires sur Napoléon*, 1831, II, 231–3.

31. NAPOLÉON: *Correspondance*, No. 2458.

SEPOY GENERAL

I

1. MUIR, RAMSAY: *Making of British India*, 1915, 301.

2. THACKERAY, W. M.: *Adventures of Philip*, 1862, cap. xvi.

3. BUSTEED, H. E.: *Echoes from Old Calcutta*, 1897, 110–51.

4. ELERS, G.: *Memoirs* (ed. Monson and Leveson Gower), 1903, 46–7.

5. *Ibid.*, 55–6.

6. WELLINGTON: *Letter to General Cunninghame*, March 9, 1797, *Apsley House Papers*.

7. PEARCE, R. R.: *op. cit.*, I, 308.

8. HICKEY, W.: *Memoirs*, 1913–23, IV, 154.

9. BUSTEED, H. E.: *op. cit.*, 127.

10. HICKEY, W.: *op. cit.*, IV, 155–8.   11. *Ibid.*, IV, 160–1.

12. *Supplementary Despatches*, I, 1–3.   13. *Ibid.*, I, 4–5.

14. WELLINGTON: *Letter to Earl of Mornington*, April 17, 1797, *Apsley House Papers* (printed incomplete, without indication of omissions, in *Supplementary Despatches*, I, 4–6).

15. *Supplementary Despatches,* I, 12–17.

16. MORNINGTON, EARL OF: *Letter to Sir Chichester Fortescue,* July 5, 1797. In the possession of Lord Gerald Wellesley.

17. MORNINGTON, EARL OF: *Letter to Sir Chichester Fortescue,* Aug. 5, 1797. *Ibid.*

18. MORNINGTON, EARL OF: *Letter to Sir Chichester Fortescue,* Oct. 14, 1797. *Ibid.*

19. *Supplementary Despatches,* XIII, 3 (misdated May 1, 1797; original in the possession of Lord Gerald Wellesley, dated May 2, 1797).

20. *Ibid.,* I, 18.   21. *Ibid.,* I, 9–12.   22. *Ibid.,* I, 19–24.

23. HICKEY, W.: *op. cit.,* 171–2.

24. WELLINGTON: *Letter to Page,* Prince of Wales's Island, Sept. 10, 1797, *Apsley House Papers.*

25. *Supplementary Despatches,* I, 24–34.

26. HICKEY, W.: *op. cit.,* IV., 190–1.

27. *Supplementary Despatches,* I, 34–49.

28. BRIALMONT AND GLEIG: *op. cit.,* I, 29.

29. CURZON, MARQUESS: *British Government in India,* 1925, I, 208.

30. MORNINGTON, EARL OF: *Letter to Sir Chichester Fortescue,* Nov. 30, 1796. In the possession of Lord Gerald Wellesley.

31. *Supplementary Despatches,* I, 51–2.

II

1. *Supplementary Despatches,* I, 52–83.

2. *Ibid.,* I, 67.   3. *Ibid.,* I, 57.

4. List of books in W.'s writing, endorsed Aug. 1798 (cf. *Education of Arthur Wesley,* VII, *n.* 20), *Apsley House Papers.* For W.'s later reference to his study of Cæsar, see ROGERS, SAMUEL: *Recollections,* 1859, 227–8 ELLESMERE, EARL OF: *op. cit.,* 97.

5. HICKEY, W.: *op. cit.,* IV, 201.

6. *Supplementary Despatches,* I, 84–5.   7. *Ibid.,* I, 96, 112–13.

8. ELERS, G.: *op. cit.,* 63–4.

9. ROBERTS, P. E.: *India under Wellesley,* 1929, 41–6.

10. PEARCE, R. R.: *op. cit.,* I, 178–80.

11. *Supplementary Despatches,* I, 52–5.   12. *Ibid.,* I, 86, 118.

13. ROBERTS, P. E.: *op. cit.,* 48.

14. *Supplementary Despatches,* I, 87.   15. *Ibid.,* I, 95.

16. *Ibid.,* I, 97.   17. *Ibid.,* I, 126.   18. *Ibid.,* I, 111-12.

19. *Ibid.,* I, 110.   20. *Ibid.,* I, 118–19.   21. *Ibid.,* I, 140.

22. *Genealogist: New Series,* XXI, 101; HICKEY, W.: *op. cit.,* III, 99.

23. PEARCE, R. R.: *op. cit.,* I, 217, 245, 248.

24. WELLESLEY, MARQUESS: *Dispatches,* 1840, I, 454.

25. ROBERTS, P. E.: *op. cit.*, 50.

26. *Supplementary Despatches,* I, 107.

27. *Ibid.,* XIII, 4.   28. *Ibid.,* I, 167.

29. ELERS, G.: *op. cit.*, 83–5; *Supplementary Despatches,* I, 160–5.

30. *Supplementary Despatches,* I, 203.   31. *Ibid.,* I, 73, 215.

32. *Ibid.,* I, 200.   33. *Ibid.,* I, 192.   34. *Ibid.,* I, 187–8.

35. *Ibid.,* I, 153.   36. *Ibid.,* I, 195–6.   37. *Ibid.,* I, 206.

38. *Ibid.,* I, 208.

39. ELERS, G.: *op. cit.*, 101–3.

40. MAXWELL, SIR H.: *op. cit.*, I, 32–3; 404. MS. Diary of Capt. J. Malcolm, B.M. Add. MSS. 13664, 45.

41. FORTESCUE, J.: *British Army,* IV, 736.

42. *Supplementary Despatches,* I, 209.

43. FORTESCUE, J.: *British Army,* IV, 738.

44. MAXWELL, W. H., *op. cit.*, I, 62–3.

45. HUTTON, W. H.: *Marquess Wellesley,* 1893, 33.

46. CROKER, J. W.: *op. cit.*, II, 102–3.

47. ELERS, G.: *op. cit.*, 103.

48. PEARCE, R. R.: *op. cit.*, I, 307–14, 425–31.

49. MAXWELL, SIR H.: *op. cit.*, I, 36.

III

1. ELERS, G.: *op. cit.*, 99–100.

2. *Dispatches,* I, 36–8; *Supplementary Despatches,* I, 213.

3. *Supplementary Despatches,* I, 215.   4. *Ibid.,* I, 250–1.

5. ROBERTS, P. E.: *op. cit.*, 70–1.

6. PEARCE, R. R.: *op. cit.*, I, 335–8.

7. *Supplementary Despatches,* I, 245–6.   8. *Ibid.,* I, 278.

9. *Ibid.,* I, 419–21, 440.   10. *Ibid.,* I, 403.

11. *Ibid.,* I, 258–72.   12. *Ibid.,* I, 226.

13. FORTESCUE, J.: *British Army,* IV, 750–2.

14. *Supplementary Despatches,* I, 376–7.

15. *Dispatches,* I, 125–7.   16. *Ibid.,* I, 129–30.

17. *Ibid.,* I, 133–4.   18. *Ibid.,* I, 135.

19. ROBERTS, P. E.: *op. cit.*, 75.

20. *Supplementary Despatches,* I, 433–4, 480.   21. *Ibid.,* I, 529.

22. FORTESCUE, J.: *British Army,* IV, 753–9.

23. ROBERTS, P. E.: *op. cit.*, 68.

24. *Supplementary Despatches,* II, 174–81.   25. *Ibid.,* II, 109.

26. *Ibid.,* II, 255–6.   27. *Ibid.,* II, 263.

28. *Ibid.,* II, 315.   29. *Ibid.,* II, 284–9.

IV

1. *Dispatches*, I, 275: *Supplementary Despatches*, II, 331.
2. *Supplementary Despatches*, II, 315.
3. *Ibid.*, II, 318–22.
4. *Dispatches*, I, 281–3.
5. *Supplementary Despatches*, II, 333, 356–7.　　　　6. *Ibid.*, II, 364.
7. *Dispatches*, I, 305–6.
8. *Ibid.*, I, 307.　　　　9. *Ibid.*, I, 321.
10. STANHOPE, EARL: *op. cit.*, 103.
11. *Dispatches*, I, 313–19.

V

1. *Supplementary Despatches*, II, 368.
2. ELERS, G.: *op. cit.*, 116–17.
3. *Ibid.*, 119.　　　　4. *Ibid.*, 122.
5. *Supplementary Despatches*, II, 364.
6. *Ibid.*, 409.　　　　7. *Ibid.*, 501.
8. ELERS, G.: *op. cit.*, 120–1.
9. ERCK, J. C. W.: *History of the 83rd Wallajahbad Light Infantry* (Cannanore), 1910, 65–6.
10. ELERS, G.: *op. cit.*, 116, 124.　　　　11. *Ibid.*, 126.
12. *Supplementary Despatches*, II, 489.　　　　13. *Ibid.*, II, 592.
14. *Ibid.*, III, 239.　　　　15. *Ibid.*, II, 405, 439–41, 456, 520.
16. *Ibid.*, II, 594.　　　　17. *Ibid.*, II, 631.
18. *Dispatches*, I, 52–3.
19. *Supplementary Despatches*, II, 451.
20. *Ibid.*, II, 614.　　　　21. *Ibid.*, II, 625.
22. *Ibid.*, III, *passim*; FORTESCUE, J.: *Wellington*, 40–1.
23. *Ibid.*, III, 109.　　　　24. *Ibid.*, III, 15–16.
25. *Ibid.*, III, 65.　　　26. *Ibid.*, III, 185.　　　27. *Ibid.*, III, 501.
28. Account of Hope, Reynolds, & Griffith, Madras, Ap. 1802, *Apsley House Papers*.
29. CURZON, MARQUESS: *op. cit.*, I, 43, 64.
30. MACAULAY, LORD: *Essay on Warren Hastings*, 1841.
31. CURZON, MARQUESS: *op. cit.*, I, 208.　　　　32. *Ibid.*, I, 241.
33. HICKEY, W.: *op. cit.*, IV, 329–30.　　　　34. *Ibid.*, IV, 287.
35. CURZON, MARQUESS: *op. cit.*, I, xvi.　　　　36. *Ibid.*, I, 71.
37. *Supplementary Despatches*, III, 150.
38. ROBERTS, P. E.: *op. cit.*, 178.
39. OWEN, S. J.: *Selection from the Despatches, Memoranda, and other Papers relating to India of Field-Marshal the Duke of Wellington*, 1880, xlvi.

40. ROBERTS, P. E.: *op. cit.*, 182–208; MUIR, RAMSAY: *op. cit.*, 201–5, 239–40.
41. *Supplementary Despatches*, III, 386–7.
42. *Dispatches*, I, 357–65.
43. GRIFFITHS, A.: *op. cit.*, 16.
44. *Supplementary Despatches*, III, 432–3.
45. *Dispatches*, I, 367–83.　　　　　46. *Ibid.*, I, 393–5.
47. *Supplementary Despatches*, III, 461.
48. *Dispatches*, I, 432–3, 467–9.
49. FORTESCUE, J.: *British Army*, V, 7–9.
50. *Dispatches*, I, 464.
51. *Ibid.*, I, 506–9.　　　　　52. *Ibid.*, I, 595–6.
53. *Supplementary Despatches*, IV, 97.
54. *Dispatches*, I, 520–1.　　　　　55. *Ibid.*, I, 484–7.
56. *Supplementary Despatches*, IV, 117.
57. *Dispatches*, II, 21–2.
58. *Supplementary Despatches*, IV, 126–7.　　　　　59. *Ibid.*, IV, 143.
60. *Dispatches*, II, 91.
61. *Ibid.*, II, 98.　　　　　62. *Ibid.*, II, 179.
63. FORTESCUE, J.: *British Army*, V, 13–19.
64. *Dispatches*, II, 257.
65. *Supplementary Despatches*, IV, 153.
66. *Dispatches*, II, 309.　　　　　67. *Ibid.*, II, 222.
68. FORTESCUE, J.: *British Army*, V, 22–34; MAXWELL, SIR H.: *op. cit.*, I, 55–60.
69. *Dispatches*, II, 356.　　　　　70. *Ibid.*, II, 219.
71. *Supplementary Despatches*, IV, 187–8.　　　　　72. *Ibid.*, IV, 289.
73. *Dispatches*, II, 457.
74. *Supplementary Despatches*, IV, 205.
75. FORTESCUE, J.: *British Army*, V, 39–41.
76. STANHOPE, EARL: *op. cit.*, 57.
77. *Dispatches*, II, 647.　　　　　78. *Ibid.*, II, 700.
79. FORTESCUE, J.: *British Army*, V, 73; CROKER, J. W.: *op. cit.*, II, 232–3; BRIALMONT AND GLEIG: *op. cit.*, I, 123–4.
80. *Dispatches*, II, 514.
81. *Ibid.*, III, 144–8; DOUGLAS, J.: *Bombay and Western India*, 1893, II, 26.
82. WELLINGTON: *Letter to Mrs. Gordon, Bombay*, May 18, 1804. In the possession of C. A. Oliver, Esq.
83. WELLINGTON: *Letter to Mrs. Gordon, Bombay*, dated May 18, 1804, but written at Chinchore, which W. did not reach until June 4, 1804. *Ibid.*
84. Accounts of Bombay tradesmen, May–Sept. 1804, *Apsley House Papers*.
85. *Supplementary Despatches*, IV, 334–7.　　　　　86. *Ibid.*, IV, 385.
87. *Dispatches*, III, 168.　　　　　88. *Ibid.*, III, 193.

89. *Ibid.*, III, 444.   90. *Ibid.*, III, 339.

91. Receipt of R. Home, *Apsley House Papers.*

92. Accounts of Calcutta tradesmen, Sept. 1804, *Ibid.*

93. *Supplementary Despatches*, IV, 466.

94. *Dispatches*, III, 462.

95. WELLINGTON: *Letters to Mrs. Gordon*, Dec. 7 and 20, 1804. In the possession of C. A. Oliver, Esq.

96. *Dispatches*, III, 593–4.

97. *Supplementary Despatches*, IV, 479; *Dispatches*, III, 631, 648–50.

98. *Supplementary Despatches*, IV, 487.

99. *Ibid.*, IV, 489, 493; *Dispatches*, III, 673.

100. *Ibid.*, IV, 500; *Dispatches*, III, 663.

101. WELLINGTON: *Letter to Lord Wellesley*, Feb. 17, 1805. In the author's possession (cf. *Dispatches*, III, 683).

102. *Supplementary Despatches*, IV, 496.

103. Account of Miss Hope, Madras, March 1, 1805, *Apsley House Papers.*

104. ELERS, G.: *op. cit.*, 173–5.

105. *Supplementary Despatches*, IV, 503.   106. *Ibid.*, IV, 497.

107. STANHOPE, EARL: *op. cit.*, 130.

108. *Dispatches*, III, 686; *Supplementary Despatches*, IV, 507–11.

109. STANHOPE, EARL: *op. cit.*, 259.

110. YOUNG, N.: *Napoleon in Exile: St. Helena*, 1915, I, 95.

DUBLIN CASTLE

I

1. *Supplementary Despatches*, IV, 514–20.

2. *Ibid.*, IV, 520–32.   3. *Ibid.*, IV, 512.

4. CROKER, J. W.: *op. cit.*, II, 233–4.

5. MOORE, SIR J.: *Diary* (ed. Maurice), 1904, I, 367.

6. *Supplementary Despatches*, IV, 533–41.

7. STANHOPE, EARL: *op. cit.*, 117–18.

8. MAXWELL, SIR H.: *op. cit.*, I, 75.

9. SWINTON, J. R.: *Sketch of the Life of Georgiana, Lady de Ros*, 1893, 173.

10. ROSE, J. H.: *op. cit.*, 556.

11. FORTESCUE, J.: *British Army*, V, 285–99.

12. CASTLEREAGH, VISCOUNT: *Correspondence*, VI, 93–4, 97.

13. *Supplementary Despatches*, IV, 587.

14. *Dispatches*, IV, 2.

15. *Supplementary Despatches*, XIII, 279.

16. EDGEWORTH, MARIA: *Life and Letters* (ed. Hare), 1894, I, 151.

17. *Ibid.*, I, 145.

18. BURKE, SIR B.: *Peerage*, 1929, *s.v.* Gosford; *Landed Gentry*, 1921, *s.v.* Bence.

19. MAXWELL, SIR H.: *op. cit.*, I, 78.

20. GEORGIAN SOCIETY: *op. cit.*, III, 106.

21. EDGEWORTH, MARIA: *op. cit.*, I, 150.

22. WELLINGTON: *Letter to Page*, April 8, 1806, *Apsley House Papers*.

23. *Apsley House Papers*, 1806.

24. *Return of Members of Parliament*, 1213-1874, 1878, II. (W. returned for Rye, April 1, 1806.)

II

1. COBBETT, W.: *Parliamentary Debates*, April 18, 1806.

2. *Ibid.*, April 22, 1806.   3. *Ibid.*, April 28, 1906.

4. WELLINGTON: *Letter to Page*, 14 Clifford Street, May 3, 1806, *Apsley House Papers*.

5. COBBETT, W.: *op. cit.*, May 8, 12; June 5, 20, 1806.

6. *Ibid.*, July 10, 1806.   7. *Ibid.*, July 14, 1806.

8. SWINTON, J. R.: *op. cit.*, 179.

9. *Supplementary Despatches*, IV, 587.   10. *Ibid.*, IV, 546-86.

11. WELLINGTON: *Letter to Marquess Wellesley*, Hastings, Sept. 14, 1806, B.M. Add. MSS. 37415, f. 15.

12. MACLEOD, COL.: *Letter to W.*, July 7, 1806, *Apsley House Papers*.

13. OMAN, C. W. C.: *Wellington's Army*, 78.

14. FORTESCUE, J.: *British Army*, V, 366.

15. *Ibid.*, V, 313, 375-7.

16. WELLINGTON: *Letter to Marquess Wellesley*, Oct. 3, 1806, B.M. Add. MSS. 37415, f. 17.

17. *Supplementary Despatches*, VI, 35-8.

18. WELLINGTON: *Letter to Marquess Wellesley*, Oct. 3, 1806, B.M. Add. MSS. 37415, f. 19.

19. WELLINGTON: *Letter to Marquess Wellesley*, Oct. 22, 1806, B.M. Add. MSS. 37415, f. 21.

20. WELLINGTON: *Letter to Marquess Wellesley*, Oct. 26, 1806, B.M. Add. MSS. 37415, f. 23.

21. *Supplementary Despatches*, VI, 50.   22. *Ibid.*, VI, 51.

23. *Return of Members of Parliament*, 1213-1874, II. (W. returned for Michael Midshall, Jan. 15, 1807.)

24. WELLINGTON: *Letters to Windham*, 11 Harley Street (renumbered 24 Harley St. in 1866), Jan. 25, Feb. 16, 1807, B.M. Add. MSS. 37852, ff. 15, 24. *Supplementary Despatches*, VI, 55-61.

25. COBBETT, W.: *Parliamentary Debates*, Feb. 26, 1807.

26. *Supplementary Despatches*, IV, 590.

27. WELLINGTON: *Letter to Marquess Wellesley*, March 27, 1807, B.M. Add. MSS. 37415, f. 39. Cf. *Supplementary Despatches*, XIII, 285–6.

III

1. *Third Report of the Committee on Finance*, 1808.

2. *Supplementary Despatches*, V, 33.   3. *Ibid.*, VII, 353.

4. LARPENT, F. S.: *Private Journal*, 1854, 75.

5. *Supplementary Despatches*, V, 5.   6. *Ibid.*, V, 18–19, 22.

7. LEVER, C.: *Charles O'Malley, the Irish Dragoon* (ed. 1905), 61.

8. *Supplementary Despatches*, V, 67, 69.   9. *Ibid.*, V, 52, 61.

10. *Ibid.*, V, 21, 48; *Return of Members of Parliament*, 1213–1874, II (W. returned for Newport, Isle of Wight, May 8; returned for Tralee, May 21; elects to sit for Newport, July 27, 1807); NAMIER, L. B.: *Structure of Politics at the Accession of George III*, 1929, 386 n.

11. SWINTON, J. R.: *op. cit.*, 118.

12. *Supplementary Despatches*, V, 69–71, 75, 82.

13. *Ibid.*, V, 28–36.   14. *Ibid.*, V, 71.   15. *Ibid.*, V, 66–7.

16. *Ibid.*, V, 79.   17. *Ibid.*, V, 86.   18. *Ibid.*, V, 126.

19. COBBETT, W.: *Parliamentary Debates*, June 29, July 1, 9, 16, 1807.

20. *Supplementary Despatches*, V, 108, 124.   21. *Ibid.*, V, 92.

22. *Ibid.*, V, 125.   23. *Ibid.*, V, 129.   24. *Ibid.*, V, 132, 135.

IV

1. ROSE, J. H.: *Life of Napoleon I*, 1903, II, 140–3; *Napoleonic Studies*, 1904, 133–65.

2. CROKER, J. W.: *op. cit.*, I, 342–3.

3. *Supplementary Despatches*, VI, 1.

4. *Ibid.*, VI, 3; HARRIS, RIFLEMAN: *Recollections* (ed. Davies), 1928, 11.

5. FORTESCUE, J.: *British Army*, VI, 70–2.

6. *Supplementary Despatches*, VI, 15.   7. *Ibid.*, VI, 9.

8. CROKER, J. W.: *op. cit.*, II, 120.

9. *Supplementary Despatches*, VI, 12–13, 18–19, 25.

10. *Dispatches*, IV, 5.

11. *Supplementary Despatches*, VI, 24.

12. MAXWELL, W. H.: *op. cit.*, I, 230.

V

1. CASTLEREAGH, VISCOUNT: *Correspondence*, VI, 186–8.

2. WYATT, B.: *Letter to Sir. E. Littlehales*, Oct. 1, 1807, *State Paper Office, Dublin Castle*.

3. *Supplementary Despatches*, XIII, 288.   4. *Ibid.*, V, 139.

5. *Ibid.*, V, 150, 167.   6. *Ibid.*, V, 151.   7. *Ibid.*, V, 185.

8. *Ibid.*, V, 200–1.   9. *Ibid.*, V., 192, 202–3.

10. *Ibid.*, V, 214.   11. *Ibid.*, V, 247.

12. *Hibernian Magazine*, Jan. 1808.

13. *Supplementary Despatches*, V, 317.

14. COBBETT, W.: *Parliamentary Debates*, Feb. 1, 9, 23, 25, 29, 1808.

15. *Ibid.*, April 14, 1808.

16. STANHOPE, EARL: *op. cit.*, 68–9.

17. *Supplementary Despatches*, VI, 65–6.   18. *Ibid.*, V, 341.

19. CASTLEREAGH, VISCOUNT: *Correspondence*, VI, 230–1.

20. *Supplementary Despatches*, IV, 592–601.

21. *Supplementary Despatches*, V, 330.   22. *Ibid.*, V, 405.

23. COBBETT, W.: *Parliamentary Debates*, May 11, 1808.

24. *Supplementary Despatches*, V, 442–3.   25. *Ibid.*, V, 444.

26. OMAN, C. W. C.: *History of the Peninsular War*, 1902–22, I, 1–56; ROSE, J. H.: *Napoleon I*, II, 159–68.

27. FORTESCUE, J.: *British Army*, VI, 148–50.

28. *Supplementary Despatches*, V, 405.

29. COBBETT, W.: *Parliamentary Debates*, April 26, 1808.

30. *Supplementary Despatches*, V, 406.

31. COBBETT, W.: *Parliamentary Despatches*, May 16, 1808.

VI

1. *Dispatches*, IV, 31.

2. *Supplementary Despatches*, V, 462.   3. *Ibid.*, VI, 80–2.

4. *Ibid.*, VI, 68.   5. *Ibid.*, V, 444.   6. *Ibid.*, VI, 73.

7. STANHOPE, EARL: *op. cit.*, 69.

8. Commission to Sir A. Wellesley, June 14, 1808, *Apsley House Papers*.

9. CROKER, J. W.: *op. cit.*, I, 12–13.

10. *Supplementary Despatches*, V, 453.   11. *Ibid.*, V, 365, 447.

12. MOORE, SIR J.: *op. cit.*, II, 239, 250.

13. CROKER, J. W.: *op. cit.*, I, 343.

14. WELLINGTON: *Letter to Marquess Wellesley*, Windsor, June 17, 1808, B.M. Add. MSS. 37415, f. 42.

15. *Supplementary Despatches*, V, 454.

16. STANHOPE, EARL: *op. cit.*, 227.

17. *Ibid.*, 291; SWINTON, J. R.: *op. cit.*, 149–50.

18. NAPIER, W. F. P.: *History of the War in the Peninsula*, 1828, I, 42.

19. *Supplementary Despatches*, V, 457.

20. *Dispatches*, IV, 16–19.   21. *Ibid.*, IV, 16.

22. *Ibid.*, IV, 25.

23. FORTESCUE, J.: *British Army*, VI, 188–9.
24. *Dispatches*, IV, 20, 24.
25. *Supplementary Despatches*, VI, 89.

PENINSULAR

I

1. GRIFFITHS, A.: *op. cit.*, 16.
2. *Supplementary Despatches*, VI, 89.   3. *Ibid.*, V, 473.
4. *Dispatches*, IV, 47.
5. *Supplementary Despatches*, V, 473–4.
6. *Dispatches*, IV, 50.
7. MOORE, SIR J.: *op. cit.*, II, 239, 250.
8. FORTESCUE, J.: *British Army*, VI, 192–9.
9. CASTLEREAGH, VISCOUNT, *op. cit.*, VI, 385.
10. *Dispatches*, IV, 31 *n.*
11. CROKER, J. W.: *op. cit.*, I, 343–4.
12. *Dispatches*, IV, 59.
13. *Supplementary Despatches*, VI, 91–2.
14. Dispatches, V, 134–5.
15. LARPENT, F. S.: *op. cit.*, 4.
16. TOMKINSON, W.: *Diary of a Cavalry Officer*, 1894, 12; SCHAUMANN, A. L. F.: *On the Road with Wellington*, 1924, 9, 11.
17. FORTESCUE, J.: *British Army*, VI, 206; OMAN, C. W. C.: *Peninsular War*, I, 236.
18. *Ibid.*, VI, 207–14; I, 237–40.
19. *Ibid.*, VI, 214–34; I, 242–62.
20. *Dispatches*, IV, 107.
21. *Supplementary Despatches*, VI, 122.
22. *Proceedings upon the Inquiry relative to the Armistice and Convention, &c. made and concluded in Portugal, in August, 1808, between the Commanders of the British and French Armies*, 1809, 87.
23. CROKER, J. W.: *op. cit.*, II, 122.   24. *Ibid.*, 89.
25. *Ibid.*, 16.   26. *Ibid.*, 56–9.
27. *Supplementary Despatches*, VI, 122–4.
28. *Inquiry*, 39.
29. *Supplementary Despatches*, VI, 132–3.
30. MOORE, SIR J.: *op. cit.*, II, 256–9.
31. *Dispatches*, IV, 156–7.
32. MOORE, SIR J.: *op. cit.*, II, 264–6.

33. *Supplementary Despatches*, VI, 134.
34. *Ibid.*, VI, 143; *Dispatches*, IV, 146.
35. MOORE, SIR J.: *op. cit.*, II, 261.
36. *Despatches*, IV, 142–4.
37. LARPENT, F. S.: *op. cit.*, 318.
38. MOORE, SIR J.: *op. cit.*, II, 205.
39. *Dispatches*, IV, 158–9.   40. *Ibid.*, IV, 147.
41. CROKER, J. W.: *op. cit.*, II, 123.

II

1. BYRON, LORD: *Childe Harold's Pilgrimage*, 1812, I, xxvi.
2. WORDSWORTH: *Concerning the Relations of Great Britain, Spain, and Portugal, to each other, and to the Common Enemy, at this Crisis; and specifically as affected by the Convention of Cintra: The whole brought to the Test of those Principles, by which alone the Independence and Freedom of Nations can be Preserved or Recovered*, 1809 (ed. Dicey, 1915), 50–1.
3. BYRON, LORD: *op. cit.*, I, xxv. Suppressed stanzas.
4. *Supplementary Despatches*, VI, 149.   5. *Ibid.*, VI, 148.
6. *Dispatches*, IV, 157.
7. WELLINGTON: *Letter to Marquess Wellesley*, London, Oct. 5, 1808, B.M. Add. MSS. 37415, f. 47.
8. CREEVEY, T.: *Papers* (ed. in 1 vol.), 1912, 89–90.
9. MORNINGTON, LADY: *Letter to Marquess Wellesley*, Sept. 3, 1808, B.M. Add. MSS. 37315, f. 56.
10. WELLESLEY, LADY: *Letter to Marquess Wellesley*, Phœnix Park, Aug. 13, 1808, B.M. Add. MSS. 37315, f. 54.
11. *Supplementary Despatches*, VI, 150–1.
12. CROKER, J. W.: *op. cit.*, I, 344.
13. STANHOPE, EARL: *op. cit.*, 243; OMAN, C. W. C.: *Peninsular War*, I, 292–4.
14. *Inquiry*, 5.
15. *Supplementary Despatches*, VI, 153, 169, 184; XIII, 310.
16. *Inquiry*, 12.   17. *Ibid.*, 15–17.
18. *Supplementary Despatches*, VI, 153.
19. *Inquiry*, 59.
20. MOORE, SIR J.: *op. cit.*, II, 303.
21. *Inquiry*, 120–1.   22. *Ibid.*, 122.
23. HARPER, G. M.: *William Wordsworth*, 1916, 174, 176–8.
24. WORDSWORTH, W.: *op. cit.*, xxxii.
25. LOCKHART, J.: *Life of Scott*, II, 226 (quoted in MAXWELL, SIR H.: *op. cit.*, I, 127).

26. SMITH, SIR HARRY: *Autobiography* (quoted in ROBINSON, MAJOR-GEN. C. W.: *Wellington's Campaigns*, 1914, I, 66).

27. *Supplementary Despatches*, V, 525.

28. *Ibid.*, VI, 196–200; V, 526.   29. *Ibid.*, V, 536.

30. COBBETT, W.: *Parliamentary Debates*, Jan. 27, 1809.

31. EDGEWORTH, M.: *op. cit.*, I, 160.

32. COBBETT, W.: *op. cit.*, Feb. 6, 1809.

33. *Ibid.*, Feb. 21, 22, 1809.   34. *Ibid.*, March 28, 1809.

35. FORTESCUE, J.: *British Army*, VI, 319.

36. CASTLEREAGH, VISCOUNT: *op. cit.*, VII, 39–41; FORTESCUE, J.: *British Army*, VII, 125–8; *Dispatches*, IV, 261–3.

37. CASTLEREAGH, VISCOUNT: *op. cit.*, VII, 43–4.

38. WELLINGTON: *Letter to C. Flint*, April 14, 1809. In the possession of F. M. Guedalla, Esq.

39. *Supplementary Despatches*, V, 643; VI, 209.

40. *Ibid.*, VI, 222–4.

41. BRETT, O.: *Wellington*, 1928, 60–1.

III

1. Information supplied by Georgiana, Viscountess Gough.

2. *Pakenham Letters, 1800–1815* (privately printed), 1914, 45.

3. *Dispatches*, IV, 267–8.

4. FORTESCUE, J.: *British Army*, VII, 146.   5. *Ibid.*, VII, 149.

6. OMAN, C. W. C.: *Wellington's Army*, 82–6.

7. GUILLON, E.: *Les Complots Militaires sous le Consulat et l'Empire,* 1894, 48–144; OMAN, C. W. C.: *Peninsular War*, II, 315, 321, 632–9; CASTLEREAGH, VISCOUNT: *op. cit.*, VII, 64–8.

8. *Dispatches*, IV, 276.   9. *Ibid.*, IV, 308.

10. TOMKINSON, W.: *op. cit.*, 3.

11. FORTESCUE, J.: *British Army*, VII, 158–63.

12. WELLINGTON: *Letter to C. Flint,* May 7, 1809. In the possession of F. M. Guedalla, Esq.

13. *Supplementary Despatches*, VI, 270.

14. *Dispatches*, IV, 371.

15. *Ibid.*, IV, 374.   16. *Ibid.*, IV, 380.

17. *Ibid.*, IV, 373–4; FORTESCUE, J.: *British Army*, VII, 202.

18. *Ibid.*, IV, 412.

19. FORTESCUE, J.: *British Army*, VII, 207; OMAN, C. W. C.: *Peninsular War*, II, 471.

20. *Dispatches*, IV, 430.

21. FORTESCUE, J.: *British Army*, VII, 215–16.

22. *Dispatches*, IV, 526.   23. *Ibid.*, IV, 524–5, 528.

24. FORTESCUE, J.: *British Army*, VII, 222.
25. SCHAUMANN, A. L. F.: *op. cit.*, 182.
26. FORTESCUE, J.: *British Army*, VII, 226–7.
27. *Ibid.*, VII, 232–61.
28. *Dispatches*, IV, 543.　　　　　　29. *Ibid.*, IV, 544–6.
30. *Ibid.*, V, 15.　　　31. *Ibid.*, V, 31.　　　32. *Ibid.*, V, 73.
33. *Ibid.*, V, 59.　　　34. *Ibid.*, V. 82–5.
35. BYRON, LORD: *Childe Harold's Pilgrimage*, I, xvi, xlvii.
36. *Supplementary Despatches*, VI, 373.
37. FORTESCUE, J.: *Wellington*, 112.
38. *Dispatches*, V, 3.
39. *Supplementary Despatches*, VI, 332.　　　40. *Ibid.*, VI, 360–1.

IV

1. *Dispatches*, V, 158.
2. *Supplementary Despatches*, XIII, 377.
3. FORTESCUE, J.: *British Army*, VII, 372–5.
4. *Supplementary Despatches*, VI, 383.
5. BYRON, LORD: *Childe Harold's Pilgrimage*, I, lxxxvii (suppressed stanza).
6. GUEDALLA, P.: *Palmerston*, 1926, 60.
7. *Supplementary Despatches*, VI, 401–2.
8. WELLINGTON: *Letter to C. Flint*, Dec. 7, 1809. In the possession of F. M. Guedalla, Esq.
9. *Dispatches*, V, 89.　　　　10. *Ibid.*, V, 234–9.
11. *Ibid.*, V, 215–16.　　　12. *Ibid.*, V, 247.
13. *Ibid.*, V, 245.　　　　14. *Ibid.*, VI, 9.
15. OMAN, C. W. C.: *Peninsular War*, III, 107.
16. *Supplementary Despatches*, VI, 388.　　　17. *Ibid.*, XIII, 396–7.
18. OMAN, C. W. C.: *Peninsular War*, III, 185 (citing *Continuation of Vertot*, II, 51).
19. *Dispatches*, V, 37.　　　　20. *Ibid.*, V, 563.
21. CROKER, J. W.: *op. cit.*, I, 24.
22. *Supplementary Despatches*, VI, 434.
23. *Dispatches*, V, 403.
24. *Dispatches*, V, 331–2.　　　25. *Ibid.*, V, 384.
26. COLE, LOWRY: *Letter to Hon. Henrietta Cole*, Guarda, Feb. 28, 1810, *Lowry Cole Papers*.
27. *Dispatches*, V, 515.　　　28. *Ibid.*, V, 500.
29. *Ibid.*, V, 611.　　　　30. *Ibid.*, V, 466, 473.
31. *Ibid.*, V, 475.

32. STANHOPE, EARL: *op. cit.*, 20.

33. *Dispatches*, VI, 6–9.

34. *Ibid.*, VI, 200, 287, 417, 429. 35. *Ibid.*, VI, 33.

36. *Supplementary Despatches*, VI, 588. 37. *Ibid.*, VI, 582.

38. *Ibid.*, VI, 515. (Names inserted from original in *Apsley House Papers*.)

39. *Ibid.*, VI, 564.

40. WELLINGTON: *Letter to C. Flint*, Aug. 29, 1810. In the possession of F. M. Guedalla, Esq.

41. FORTESCUE, J.: *British Army*, VII, 506–32; OMAN, C. W. C.: *Peninsular War*, III, 359–86.

42. MAXWELL, SIR H.: *op. cit.*, I, 202.

43. *Dispatches*, VI, 494.

44. WELLINGTON: *Letter to C. Flint*, Oct. 20, 1810. In the possession of F. M. Guedalla, Esq.

45. FORTESCUE, J.: *British Army*, VII, 547.

46. *Supplementary Despatches*, VI, 612.

47. *Dispatches*, VI, 555.

48. *Supplementary Despatches*, VII, 1–2.

49. *Dispatches*, VII, 7.

50. *Supplementary Despatches*, XIII, 526.

51. COLE, LOWRY: *Letter to Hon. Henrietta Cole*, Nov. 3, 1810, *Lowry Cole Papers*.

V

I

1. *Dispatches*, VII, 59–60. 2. *Ibid.*, VII, 392.

3. *Supplementary Despatches*, VII, 43.

4. *Dispatches* (cited in ROBINSON, C. W.: *Wellington's Campaigns*, I, 177).

5. *Dispatches*, VII, 428.

6. FORTESCUE, J.: *British Army*, VIII, 110, 116.

7. SCHAUMANN, A. L. F.: *op. cit.*, 306.

8. FORTESCUE, J.: *British Army*, VIII, 142; *Dispatches*, VII, 490–6.

9. FORTESCUE, J.: *British Army*, VIII, 153–75.

10. *Supplementary Despatches*, VII, 176–7.

11. *Ibid.*, VII, 123; *Dispatches*, VII, 547.

12. NAPIER, W. F. P.: *op. cit.*, III, 540–1.

13. *Dispatches*, VII, 583.

14. FRASER, SIR W.: *op. cit.*, 164.

15. *Dispatches*, VIII, 232–3.

16. *Supplementary Despatches*, VII, 245.

AUTHORITIES

2

1. *Peninsular*, IV, *n.* 51.
2. STANHOPE, EARL: *op. cit.*, 29.
3. ROGERS, S.: *Recollections*, 204.
4. TOMLINSON, W.: *op. cit.*, 108.
5. STANHOPE, EARL: *op. cit.*, 71.
6. LARPENT, F. S.: *op. cit.*, 96.
7. LEVER, C.: *Charles O'Malley* (ed. 1905), 571.
8. LARPENT, F. S.: *op. cit.*, 357.
9. *Supplementary Despatches*, VII, 43.
10. FORTESCUE, J.: *British Army*, VII, 420.
11. SIMMONS, G.: *A British Rifle Man*, 1899, 305.
12. TOMKINSON, W.: *op. cit.*, 117.
13. SCHAUMANN, A. L. F.: *op. cit.*, 317.
14. LEVER, C.: *op. cit.*, 554.
15. OMAN, C. W. C.: *Wellington's Army*, 295.
16. *Dispatches*, VIII, 378–9.
17. GLEIG, G. R.: *Personal Reminiscences of the Duke of Wellington*, 1904, 19.
18. LARPENT, F. S.: *op. cit.*, 403.   19. *Ibid.*, 68.
20. *Dispatches*, VII, 587.   21. *Ibid.*, VII, 202.
22. STANHOPE, EARL: *op. cit.*, 14.   23. *Ibid.*, 18.
24. *General Orders* (ed. Gurwood), 1837, xxv.
25. WELLINGTON: *Letter to C. Flint*, May 7, 1809. In the possession of F. M. Guedalla, Esq.
26. *Dispatches*, VII, 406.   27. *Ibid.*, VII, 641.
28. LEVER, C.: *op. cit.*, 277.
29. WELLINGTON: *Letter to Major-General Stopford*, Freneda, Nov. 9, 1811. In the possession of Lord Gerald Wellesley.
30. *Dispatches*, VII, 198.   31. *Ibid.*, IX, 75.
32. *Ibid.*, VII, 393.
33. *Supplementary Despatches*, VII, 171–2.   34. *Ibid.*, VII, 5.
35. ROGERS, S.: *op. cit.*, 207.
36. LARPENT, F. S.: *op. cit.*, 52–3, 75.
37. ROGERS, S.: *op. cit.*, 217.

VI

1. CROKER, J. W.: *op. cit.*, I, 339–40; II, 285–6; FRASER, SIR W.: *op. cit.*, 183.
2. GLEIG, G. R.: *Personal Reminiscences of Wellington*, 388.
3. STANHOPE, EARL: *op. cit.*, 9.
4. *Dispatches*, VIII, 557.

505

5. FORTESCUE, J.: *British Army*, VII, 349–68; FRASER, SIR W., *op. cit.*, 165.

6. *Dispatches*, VIII, 650.   7. *Ibid.*, VIII, 581–6, 656–8, 661–3.

8. *Supplementary Despatches*, VII, 307.

9. FORTESCUE, J.: *British Army*, VIII, 393–410.

10. *Dispatches*, IX, 173.

11. TOMKINSON, W.: *op. cit.*, 162.

12. FORTESCUE, J.: *British Army*, VIII, 462.

13. TOMKINSON, W.: *op. cit.*, 165.

14. FORTESCUE, J.: *British Army*, VIII, 471.

15. *Ibid.*, VIII, 473–80.

16. STANHOPE, EARL: *op. cit.*, 51–2.

17. FORTESCUE, J.: *British Army*, VIII, 480–513; OMAN, C. W. C.: *Peninsular War*, V, 418–74.

18. *Dispatches*, IX, 310.

19. CROKER, J. W.: *op. cit.*, II, 120.

20. D'URBAN, B.: *Peninsular Journal* (ed. I. J. Rousseau), 1930, 274.

21. *Pakenham Letters*, 170.

22. GOYA, F. LUCIENTES Y: *Drawing of Wellington*, British Museum, Department of Prints and Drawings; BERUETE, A. DE: *Goya as Portrait Painter* (tr. S. Brinton), 1922, 147; *Dispatches*, IX, 299 (for W.'s presence "On the heights near Alba de Tormes," July 23, 1812); ROGERS, S.: *Recollections*, 204 (for W.'s habit of shaving overnight); FORTESCUE, J.: *British Army*, VIII, 506 (for W.'s wound).

The following is the text of the note appended by a member of Goya's family to the British Museum drawing:

Un dibujo hecho en Alba de Tormes despues de la batalla de Arapiles de Duque de Wellington por el que se hizo el retrato.

It appears to follow that Goya's three oil paintings of W. (equestrian portrait painted for W., now at Stratfield Saye; portrait with hat, formerly in the possession of Alava, now in U.S.A.; portrait without hat in the possession of Duke of Leeds, now in National Portrait Gallery) were founded on the British Museum drawing. If this view is accepted, the agreeable anecdotes of Goya's violent onslaughts on W. during a sitting at Madrid must be dismissed.

23. ROUSSEAU, I. J.: *Unpublished Letters of Wellington, July–August, 1812,* Cambridge Historical Journal, III, i, 99.

24. *Dispatches*, IX, 351.

25. ROGERS, S.: *op. cit.*, 195.

26. OMAN, C. W. C.: *Peninsular War*, V, 514–15.

27. *Supplementary Despatches*, VII, 406, 414.

28. *Ibid.*, VII, 432; *Dispatches*, IX, 378, 432.

29. *Dispatches*, IX, 398.   30. *Ibid.*, IX, 434.

31. ROBINSON, C. W.: *op. cit.*, II, 281.

32. *Dispatches*, IX, 465.

33. *Supplementary Despatches*, VII, 443.

34. *Dispatches*, IX, 479.

35. *Supplementary Despatches*, VII, 478.

36. *Dispatches*, IX, 574.

37. FORTESCUE, J.: *British Army*, VIII, 572–91.

38. *Ibid.*, VIII, 608.

39. D'URBAN, B.: *op. cit.*, 301.

40. *Dispatches*, IX, 582–5.

41. *Pakenham Letters*, 185.

VII

1. OMAN, C. W. C.: *Peninsular War*, VI, 244–6.

2. FORTESCUE, J.: *British Army*, IX, 75; *Dispatches*, X, 26–7.

3. *Dispatches*, X, 19; cf. *Sepoy General*, II, *n.* 32.

4. *Ibid.*, X, 53–4, 63–5.

5. WARD, C. H. DUDLEY: *A Romance of the Nineteenth Century*, 1923, 82.

6. LARPENT, F. S.: *op. cit.*, 75, 82, 98.   7. *Ibid.*, 56.

8. *Ibid.*, 71–4.

9. SCHAUMANN, A. L. F.: *op. cit.*, 365–6.

10. LARPENT, F. S.: *op. cit.*, 60, 229.

11. *Dispatches*, X, 73, 371.

12. *Ibid.*, X, 209, 231; LARPENT, F. S.: *op. cit.*, 80; COLE, SIR G. LOWRY: *Letters to Wellington*, March 22, 26, 1813, *Lowry Cole Papers*.

13. *Dispatches*, X, 117.   14. *Ibid.*, X, 322.

15. Cf. *Sepoy General*, V, *n.* 46.

16. *Dispatches*, X, 334.

17. *Ibid.*, X, 429; Playbill, Light Division Theatre, Gallegos, Feb. 4, 1813, *Lowry Cole Papers*.

18. LARPENT, F. S., *op. cit.*, 112.

19. MAXWELL, SIR H.: *op. cit.*, I, 310.

20. SCHAUMANN, A. L. F.: *op. cit.*, 369–70.

21. LARPENT, F. S.: *op. cit.*, 148.

22. CROKER, J. W.: *op. cit.*, I, 336; II, 307.

23. WELLINGTON: *Letter to C. Flint*, June 10, 1813. In the possession of F. M. Guedalla, Esq.

24. WELLINGTON: *Orders to Sir G. Lowry Cole*, June 19, 1813, *Lowry Cole Papers*.

25. FORTESCUE, J.: *British Army*, IX, 162–94; OMAN, C. W. C.: *Peninsular War*, VI, 384–450.

26. CROKER, J. W.: *op. cit.*, II, 232.

27. TOMKINSON, W.: *op. cit.,* 254; MAXWELL, SIR H.: *op. cit.,* I, 322.
28. *Ibid.,* 253.
29. BEATSON, F. C.: *With Wellington in the Pyrenees,* 1914, 2; ROSE, J. H.: *Life of Napoleon I,* II, 321.
30. CROKER, J. W.: *op. cit.,* I, 337; II, 307.

VIII

1. *Dispatches,* X, 496.
2. FORTESCUE, J.: *British Army,* IX, 199.
3. *Pakenham Letters,* 217.
4. *Dispatches,* X, 539.   5. *Ibid.,* X, 613–14.
6. *Ibid.,* X, 524; *Supplementary Despatches,* VIII, 17.
7. *Ibid.,* X, 532; *Supplementary Despatches,* VIII, 95.
8. LARPENT, F. S.: *op. cit.,* 227, 242; BEATSON, F. C.: *op. cit.,* 158; FORTESCUE, J.: *British Army,* IX, 272; OMAN, C. W. C.: *Peninsular War,* VI, 662.
9. *Dispatches,* X, 602.   10. *Ibid.,* X, 596.
11. *Ibid.,* X, 593; LARPENT, F. S.: *op. cit.,* 183, 229.
12. *Ibid.,* X, 612–15.   13. *Ibid.,* X, 639–40.
14. OMAN, C. W. C.: *Wellington's Army,* 295, 301.
15. *Dispatches,* XI, 35.
16. *Supplementary Despatches,* VIII, 626–7.
17. *Dispatches,* XI, 306, 309.
18. MAXWELL, SIR H.: *op. cit.,* I, 373.
19. ROBINSON, C. W.: *op. cit.,* II, 372.
20. FORTESCUE, J.: *British Army,* IX, 396–407.
21. *Ibid.,* IX, 422–42.
22. *Dispatches,* XI, 275; MAXWELL, SIR H.: *op. cit.,* I, 357; CROKER, J. W.: *op. cit.,* I, 340.
23. *Ibid.,* XI, 230.   24. *Ibid.,* XI, 301.
25. CROKER, J. W.: *op. cit.,* I, 341.
26. *Dispatches,* XI, 304–6.
27. *Supplementary Despatches,* VIII, 411.
28. LARPENT, F. S.: *op. cit.,* 307; GLEIG, G. R.: *op. cit.,* 21.
29. FORTESCUE, J.: *British Army,* IX, 449–72.
30. LARPENT, F. S.: *op. cit.,* 357–60.   31. *Ibid.,* 385.
32. *Ibid.,* 382.   33. *Ibid.,* 398.
34. *Ibid.,* 422, 425; MAXWELL, SIR H., *op. cit.,* I, 366; STANHOPE, EARL: *op. cit.,* 184.   35. *Ibid.,* 428.
36. *Dispatches,* XI, 586; *Supplementary Despatches,* VIII, 707.
37. *Dispatches,* XI, 547.   38. *Ibid.,* XI, 607.
39. LARPENT, F. S.: *op. cit.,* 476.
40. *Supplementary Despatches,* VIII, 725.

41. BROUGHTON, LORD: *Recollections of a Long Life*, 1909, I, 190.
42. LARPENT, F. S.: *op. cit.*, 485–8.

IX

1. LARPENT, F. S.: *op. cit.*, 496–7, 500.   2. *Ibid.*, 508–9.
3. *Supplementary Despatches*, IX, 58.
4. *Dispatches*, XI, 681.   5. *Ibid.*, XI, 668.
6. *Supplementary Despatches*, IX, 74.
7. BROUGHTON, LORD: *op. cit.*, I, 111–14; *Supplementary Despatches*, IX, 64.
8. *Supplementary Despatches*, IX, 29.   9. *Ibid.*, IX, 100.
10. LARPENT, F. S.: *op. cit.*, 529.
11. CROKER, J. W.: *op. cit.*, I, 334.
12. *Dispatches*, XII, 28, 38, 44.
13. CROKER, J. W.: *op. cit.*, I, 333; MAXWELL, SIR H.: *op. cit.*, I, 379.
14. *Dispatches*, XII, 62.
15. ELERS, G.: *op. cit.*, 272–4; CROKER, J. W.: *op. cit.*, III, 280.
16. BYRON, LORD: *Don Juan*, IX, vi.
17. LARPENT, F. S.: *op. cit.*, 227.
18. *Dispatches*, XII, 51.
19. BRIALMONT AND GLEIG: *op. cit.*, II, 355; SHELLEY, FRANCES LADY: *Diary* (ed. Edgcumbe), 1912–13, I, 61, 66; *The Courier*, June 24, 1814.
20. *Dispatches*, XII, 66–9; CREEVEY, T.: *op. cit.*, 102–5.
21. SHELLEY, FRANCES LADY: *op. cit.*, 67-71.
22. BROUGHTON, LORD: *op. cit.*, I, 156–7; *The Star*, July 2, 1814.
23. WELLINGTON: *Letter to Earl of Longford*, Brussels, May 22, 1815. In the possession of Lord Longford.
24. *Dispatches*, XII, 123–9.
25. *Supplementary Despatches*, XIV, 537.
26. *Dispatches*, XII, 77.
27. *Ibid.*, XII, 95, 107–8, 114; *Supplementary Despatches*, IX, 228.
28. *Dispatches*, XII, 138, 181, 208.   29. *Ibid.*, XII, 199.
30. BROUGHTON, LORD: *op. cit.*, I, 258; *Dispatches*, XII, 218.
31. *Supplementary Despatches*, IX, 241.
32. *Dispatches*, XII, 9.
33. *Supplementary Despatches*, IX, 467.   34. *Ibid.*, IX, 405–6.
35. GEORGE, PRINCE REGENT: *Letter to Earl Bathurst*, Brighton, Nov. 19, 1814. Catalogue No. 90 (1926), H. Sotheran & Co., London.
36. *Supplementary Despatches*, IX, 422–3, 425–6.
37. GALLATIN, T.: *A Great Peace Maker* (ed. Gallatin), 1914, 34–5.
38. *Supplementary Despatches*, IX, 434–7, 439.
39. *Ibid.*, IX, 459.   40. *Ibid.*, IX, 517–19.

1815

1. *Supplementary Despatches*, IX, 552, 582, 588.
2. *Ibid.*, IX, 586–7.
3. METTERNICH, PRINCE DE: *Mémoires, Documents et Ecrits Divers,* 1880, I, 205–6; STANHOPE, EARL: *op. cit.,* 25–6; *Supplementary Despatches,* IX, 583–4.
4. *Supplementary Despatches,* XIV, 539; HOUSSAYE, H., *1815,* 1911, I, 202, *n.* 2.
5. *Dispatches,* XII, 268.
6. *Supplementary Despatches,* XIV, 539–40.
7. SHELLEY, FRANCES LADY: *op. cit.,* 112.
8. ROGERS, S.: *op. cit.,* 214.
9. CREEVEY, T.: *op. cit.,* 225.   10. *Ibid.,* 215, 226–7.
11. *Dispatches,* XII, 324.
12. FORTESCUE, J.: *British Army,* X, 238, 243–8, 430.
13. *Ibid.,* X, 233, 237.
14. *Supplementary Despatches,* X, 18.
15. FORTESCUE, J.: *British Army,* X, 239–42; *Supplementary Despatches,* X, 219; EDMUND, BRIG.-GEN. SIR J.: *Wellington's Staff at Waterloo* (unpublished note).
16. *Dispatches,* XII, 291–2.   17. *Ibid.,* XII, 358.
18. *Dispatches,* XII, 346.   19. *Ibid.,* XII, 378.
20. CREEVEY, T.: *op. cit.,* 228.
21. *Dispatches,* XII, 375–6.
22. *Supplementary Despatches,* X, 183, 244.
23. MERCER, C.: *Journal of the Waterloo Campaign* (ed. Fortescue), 1927, 91–2.   24. *Ibid.,* 107.
25. *Dispatches,* XII, 433, 438, 472.   26. *Ibid.,* XII, 435.
27. MAXWELL, SIR H.: *op. cit.,* II, 10.
28. *Dispatches,* XII, 462.
29. FORTESCUE, J.: *British Army,* X, 278–83; *Supplementary Despatches,* X, 509–10; MAXWELL, SIR H.: *op. cit.,* II, 13–14; CREEVEY, T.: *op. cit.,* 223, 229; FRASER, SIR W.: *op. cit.,* 257–310; SWINTON, J. R.: *op. cit.,* 133.
30. FORTESCUE, J.: *British Army,* X, 289–325; STANHOPE, EARL: *op. cit.,* 109; CREEVEY, T.: *op. cit.,* 230; OMAN, C. W. C.: *Wellington's Army,* 81; HOUSSAYE, H.: *op. cit.,* II, 211; ELLESMERE, EARL OF: *op. cit.,* 170.
31. MAXWELL, SIR H.: *op. cit.,* II, 27.   32. *Ibid.,* II, 37–8.
33. *Supplementary Despatches,* XII, 512.
34. FORTESCUE, J.: *British Army,* X, 332–3.
35. MERCER, C.: *op. cit.,* 147–53.   36. *Ibid.,* 157.
37. FRASER, SIR W.: *op. cit.,* 2–4.   38. *Ibid.,* 35.
39. *Dispatches,* XII, 476–7; *Supplementary Despatches,* X, 501.

40. Houssaye, H.: *op. cit.*, II, 318–20.

41. Oman, C. W. C.: *Wellington's Army*, 81.

42. Fortescue, J.: *British Army*, X, 352–4.

43. Stanhope, Earl: *op. cit.*, 110.

44. Maxwell, Sir H.: *op. cit.*, II, 57.

45. *Dispatches*, XII, 529.

46. Maxwell, Sir H.: *op. cit.*, II, 67, 75.

47. Stanhope, Earl: *op. cit.*, 221.

48. Shelley, Frances Lady: *op. cit.*, I, 169.

49. Mercer, C.: *op. cit.*, 171.

50. Fraser, Sir W.: *op. cit.*, 80–1.

51. Palmerston, Viscount: *Selections from Private Journals of Tours in France in 1815 and 1818*, 1871, 54.

52. Fortescue, J.: *British Army*, X, 380.

53. *Ibid.*, X, 389.   54. *Ibid.*, X, 392.

55. Stanhope, Earl: *op. cit.*, 245.

56. Fortescue, J.: *British Army*, X, 394; Maxwell, Sir H.: *op. cit.*, II, 92; *Supplementary Despatches*, X, 531; Ellesmere, Earl of: *op. cit.*, 172; Shelley, Frances Lady: *op. cit.*, I, 103.

57. *Dispatches*, XII, 478.

58. Creevey, T.: *op. cit.*, 236–7.

59. *Dispatches*, XII, 441.   60. *Ibid.*, XII, 493.

61. *Supplementary Despatches*, XI, 24–5.

62. *Ibid.*, X, 147.   63. *Ibid.*, X, 169, 231.

64. *Dispatches*, XII, 502.   65. *Ibid.*, XII, 534.

66. *Supplementary Despatches*, XI, 21.

67. *Dispatches*, XII, 558.   68. *Ibid.*, XII, 581.

69. *Ibid.*, XII, 597–9.   70. *Ibid.*, XII, 601.

71. *Ibid.*, XII, 623.

72. *Supplementary Despatches*, XI, 130.

73. Mercer, C.: *op. cit.*, 284.

74. *Supplementary Despatches*, XI, 47.

75. *Dispatches*, XII, 516.

76. Shelley, Frances Lady: *op. cit.*, I, 105.

77. *Supplementary Despatches*, XI, 55.

78. Croker, J. W.: *op. cit.*, I, 332.

79. *Supplementary Despatches*, X, 553–4.

80. Molé, Comte: *Mémoires*, 1922, I, 266–7.

81. *Supplementary Despatches*, X, 275.

82. Croker, J. W.: *op. cit.*, I, 61.

83. Simpson, J.: *Paris after Waterloo*, 1853, 129.

84. Granville, Harriet Countess: *Letters* (ed. Leveson Gower) 1894, I, 62.

85. Shelley, Frances Lady: *op. cit.*, I, 96, 102–3, 106, 125, 127, 129.

86. *Dispatches,* XII, 529.

87. Granville, Harriet Countess: *op. cit.*, I, 68.

88. *Ibid.*, I, 74, 109.

89. Shelley, Frances Lady: *op. cit.*, I, 112–13, 116, 128, 133–5, 137, 145–6; II, 9.

90. Simpson, J.: *op. cit.*, 192–7; Lockhart, J. G.: *Life of Sir Walter Scott,* V, 82–4, 91; Scott, Sir W.: *Paul's Letters to his Kinsfolk.*

91. *Dispatches,* XII, 590.   92. *Ibid.*, XII, 610.

93. *Supplementary Despatches,* XIV, 619.   94. *Ibid.*, X, 507.

95. *Dispatches,* XII, 691.

96. Palmerston, Viscount: *op. cit.*, 33–5.

97. *Dispatches,* XII, 668.

98. Palmerston, Viscount: *op. cit.*, 12–16.

99. *Supplementary Despatches,* XI, 175–80; Phillips, W. Alison, *Confederation of Europe,* 1914, 123–56; Webster, C. K.; *Pacification of Europe, 1813–1815,* in *Cambridge History of British Foreign Policy,* 1922, I, 514–17.

OCCUPIED TERRITORY

1. Phillips, W. Alison: *op. cit.*, 126.

2. Burghersh, Lady: *Correspondence with the Duke of Wellington* (ed. Weigall), 1903, 16.

3. Edgeworth, Maria: *op. cit.*, I, 265.

4. Berry, M.: *op. cit.*, III, 78.

I

5. *Dispatches,* XII, 694–6; *Supplementary Despatches,* XI, 231–8; Webster, C. K.: *op. cit.*, in *Cambridge History of British Foreign Policy,* I, 506–7.

6. Gleig, G. R.: *op. cit.*, 309.

7. Byron, Lord, *Don Juan,* IX, i.

8. *Supplementary Despatches,* XI, 305.

9. *Ibid.*, XI, 273, 301, 309–10, 313–16.

10. Shelley, Frances Lady: *op. cit.*, I, 196–205.

II

1. Shelley, Frances Lady: *op. cit.*, 205.

2. Curzon, Marquis: *British Government in India,* 1925, II, 180–1.

3. SHELLEY, FRANCES LADY: *op. cit.*, I, 229–30.

4. WELLESLEY, LORD GERALD: *Cheltenham Spa* in *Country Life*, Jan. 16, 1926.

5. WELLINGTON, DUCHESS OF: *Letter to Lady Eleanor Butler and Miss Ponsonby, Cheltenham,* July 18 (year omitted, but evidently 1816 from references to W.'s health and temporary absence from Cheltenham. Cf. SHELLEY, FRANCES LADY: *op. cit.*, I, 229). In the possession of C. Hamilton, Esq., Hamwood, Dunboyne, co. Meath.

6. GLEIG, G. R.: *op. cit.*, 275.

7. *Supplementary Despatches*, XI, 434, 449.

8. *Ibid.*, XI, 458–9.   9. *Ibid.*, XI, 427, 441–2.

10. HAYDON, B. R.: *Autobiography* (ed. Davies), 1926, I, 245–7.

III

1. *Supplementary Despatches*, XI, 513, 533.

2. SHELLEY, FRANCES LADY: *op. cit.*, I, 308–9.

3. CREEVEY, T.: *op. cit.*, 277.

4. SWINTON, S. R.: *op. cit.*, 142–6.

5. BURGHERSH, LADY: *op. cit.*, 16.

6. *Supplementary Despatches*, XI, 561.   7. *Ibid.*, XI, 564.

8. WEBSTER, C. K.: *Foreign Policy of Castlereagh, 1815–1822,* 1925, 82–6; *Supplementary Despatches*, XI, 751–2; XII, 13–17, 119, 156–74, 190–1, 193.

9. *Supplementary Despatches*, XI, 745.

10. *Ibid.*, XI, 500; XIV, 655.   11. *Ibid.*, XI, 687.

12. *Dictionary of National Biography, s.v.* WARD, JAMES: *Art Journal*, 1849; WARD, J.: *The Battle of Waterloo in an Allegory painted for exhibiting at the Egyptian Hall, Piccadilly,* 1821.

The oil sketch for the large picture (afterwards hung in Chelsea Hospital), now in the writer's possession, is reproduced as Frontispiece.

13. BURGHERSH, LADY: *op. cit.*, 21; *Supplementary Despatches*, XII, 118.

14. *Supplementary Despatches*, XII, 92.   15. *Ibid.*, XII, 183.

16. *Ibid.*, XII, 213.   17. *Ibid.*, XII, 261.

18. *Ibid.*, XII, 289–90.

19. *Ibid.*, XII, 271; MAXWELL, SIR H.: *op. cit.*, II, 115.

20. *Ibid.*, XII, 285, 302.

21. WELLINGTON, DUCHESS OF: *Letter to Lord Wellesley* (undated), B.M. Add. MSS. 37315, f. 256.

22. WELLINGTON, DUCHESS OF: *Letter to Lord Wellesley* (undated), B.M. Add. MSS. 37316.

23. *Supplementary Despatches*, XII, 325–6, 333–4.

24. *Ibid.*, XII, 430.   25. *Ibid.*, XII, 513.

26. *Ibid.*, XII, 547–8.

27. CREEVEY, T.: *op. cit.*, 276–88.

28. *Ibid.*, 288–9; *Supplementary Despatches*, XII, 678.

29. *Supplementary Despatches*, XII, 722.

30. PALMERSTON, VISCOUNT: *op. cit.*, 46, 49, 53; *Supplementary Despatches*, XII, 735.

31. *Supplementary Despatches*, XII, 848.

32. *Ibid.*, XII, 874, 879. 33. *Ibid.*, XII, 776.

34. *Ibid.*, XII, 813.

THE CABINET

I

1. SHELLEY, FRANCES LADY: *op. cit.*, I, 71, 106.

2. MAXWELL, SIR H.: *op. cit.*, II, 260.

3. SHELLEY, P. B.: *Mask of Anarchy*, ii; *Song to the Men of England*, i.

4. DISRAELI, B.: *Coningsby*, 1844, II, i.

5. DISRAELI, B.: *Whigs and Whiggism* (ed. Hutcheon), 1913, 379.

6. *Dispatches, New Series*, I, 96. 7. *Ibid.*, I, 7, 13, 66, 69.

8. *Ibid.*, I, 80–1.

9. *Ibid.*, I, 56; cf. HALÉVY, É.: *History of the English People* (tr. Watkin), 1926, II, 72, for a romantic inference that W. favoured military dictatorship. This picturesque suggestion is neatly contradicted by W. himself in the continuation of the passage quoted by Prof. Halévy.

10. *Ibid.*, I, 89. 11. *Ibid.*, I, 87.

12. SHELLEY, FRANCES LADY: *op. cit.*, II, 65–6.

13. *Dispatches, New Series*, I, 101.

14. WELLINGTON: *Letter to Baron Vincent*, Jan. 5, 1820, *Apsley House Papers*.

15. NEUMANN, P. VON: *Diary* (ed. Beresford Chancellor), 1928, I, 13.

16. GREVILLE, C. C. F.: *Journal of the Reigns of King George IV and King William IV*, 1875, I, 23.

17. NEUMANN, P. V.: *op. cit.*, I, 18; GREVILLE, C. C. F.: *op. cit.*, I, 26–7; MAXWELL, SIR H.: *op. cit.*, II, 150–1; OMAN, C. W. C.: *The Unfortunate Colonel Despard and other Studies*, 1922, 22–48.

18. SHELLEY, FRANCES LADY: *op. cit.*, II, 86.

19. RUSSELL, G. W. E.: *Collections and Recollections*, 1898, 22.

20. CREEVEY, T.: *op. cit.*, 337. 21. *Ibid.*, 312.

22. SHELLEY, FRANCES LADY: *op. cit.*, II, 104.

23. STANHOPE, EARL: *op. cit.*, 92.

24. GREVILLE, C. C. F.: *op. cit.*, I, 37.

25. *Dispatches, New Series,* I, 131–2.   26. *Ibid.,* I, 128.

27. *Ibid.,* I, 97–8, 101.   28. *Ibid.,* I, 116–21.

29. NEUMANN, P. v.: *op. cit.,* I, 30.

30. SHELLEY, FRANCES LADY: *op. cit.,* II, 139.

31. LIEVEN, PRINCESS: *Diary* (ed. Temperley), 1925, 43.

32. ELLESMERE, EARL OF: *op. cit.,* 80–1.

33. NEUMANN, P. v.: *op. cit.,* I, 48.

34. SHELLEY, FRANCES LADY: *op. cit.,* II, 34, 37.

35. *Ibid.,* II, 49.   36. *Ibid.,* II, 66–8, 73–6, 81.

37. *Ibid.,* II, 93–113.

38. *Hamwood Papers,* 352.

39. WELLINGTON: *Letter to Sir T. Lawrence,* Oct. 20, 1820, B.M. Add. MSS. 12102; *Dictionary of National Biography, s.v.* SIR T. LAWRENCE.

40. *Dispatches, New Series,* I, 150–3.

41. GREVILLE, C. C. F.: *op. cit.,* I, 43; NEUMANN, P. v., *op. cit.,* I, 50–1.

42. *Dispatches, New Series,* I, 154–5.

43. PARKER, C. S.: *Sir Robert Peel from his Private Papers,* 1891, I, 83; *Parliamentary Debates,* Dec. 10, 1819.

44. *Dispatches, New Series,* I, 155–6.   45. *Ibid.,* I, 192–6.

46. *Parliamentary Debates,* Jan. 25, 1821.

47. HAYDON, B. R.: *Autobiography* (ed. Davies), I, 313–14.

48. SHELLEY, FRANCES LADY: *op. cit.,* II, 110; BRIALMONT AND GLEIG, *op. cit.,* III, 115.

49. STANHOPE, EARL: *op. cit.,* 44, 289.

50. *Parliamentary Debates,* Feb. 9, 1822.

51. *Dispatches, New Series,* I, 241.

52. CROKER, J. W.: *op. cit.,* I, 225.

53. CUNNINGHAM, A.: *Life of Sir David Wilkie,* 1843, II, 73; WELLINGTON, EVELYN DUCHESS OF: *op. cit.,* I, 83.

54. ASHTON, J.: *Hyde Park,* 1896, 268.

55. GREVILLE, C. C. F.: *op. cit.,* I, 54–5; CROKER, J. W.: *op. cit.,* I, 224.

56. STANHOPE, EARL: *op. cit.,* 126; *Dispatches, New Series,* I, 255–8.

57. CROKER, J. W.: *op. cit.,* I, 226; BYRON, LORD: *Occasional Pieces;* NEUMANN, P. v.: *op. cit.,* I, 102; *Dispatches, New Series,* I, 263.

II

1. *Dispatches, New Series,* I, 264.

2. CROKER, J. W.: *op. cit.,* I, 230.

3. PHILLIPS, W. ALISON: *George Canning,* 1903, 60.

4. HALÉVY, É.: *op. cit.,* II, 156.

5. TEMPERLEY, H. W. V.: *Foreign Policy of Canning,* 1925, 28.

6. HALÉVY, É.: *op. cit.,* II, 157; CREEVEY, I.: *op. cit.,* 386.

7. *Dispatches, New Series,* I, 192.

8. NEUMANN, P. v.: *op. cit.,* I, 102–3.

9. GREVILLE, C. C. F.: *op. cit.,* I, 51.

10. *Dispatches, New Series,* I, 273–9.

11. PARKER, C. S.: *op. cit.,* I, 336; NEUMANN, P. v.: *op. cit.,* I, 103.

12. TEMPERLEY, H. W. V.: *op. cit.,* 45.

13. BYRON, LORD: *The Age of Bronze,* xiii, xvi.

14. *Dispatches, New Series,* I, 116–21.   15. *Ibid.,* I, 304.

16. *Ibid.,* I, 344, 559.   17. *Ibid.,* I, 541.

18. *Ibid.,* I, 460.   19. *Ibid.,* I, 290.

20. LIEVEN, PRINCESS: *op. cit.,* 111.

21. NEUMANN, P. v.: *op. cit.,* I, 30.

22. CREEVEY, I.: *op. cit.,* 406.

23. TEMPERLEY, H. W. V.: *op. cit.,* 483–6.

24. *Dispatches, New Series,* I, 384–5.

25. *Ibid.,* I, 516–7.   26. *Ibid.,* I, 621.

27. STANHOPE, EARL: *op. cit.,* 232–3.

28. TEMPERLEY, H. W. V.: *Foreign Policy of Canning in Cambridge History of British Foreign Policy,* II, 60.

29. *Dispatches, New Series,* I, 626, 638–9, 649, 654, 671.

30. SHELLEY, FRANCES LADY: *op. cit.,* II, 114–15.

31. NEUMANN, P. v.: *op. cit.,* I, 113.

32. *Dispatches, New Series,* I, 657.   33. *Ibid.,* II, 34.

34. *Parliamentary Debates,* April 24, 1823.

35. *Dispatches, New Series,* II, 79.

36. *Ibid.,* II, 64.   37. *Ibid.,* 74.

38. TEMPERLEY, H. W. V.: *op. cit.,* 90.

39. METTERNICH, PRINCE DE: *op. cit.,* IV, 8.

40. SHELLEY, FRANCES LADY: *op. cit.,* II, 119.

41. *Dispatches, New Series,* II, 179.   42. *Ibid.,* II, 221.

43. *Ibid.,* II, 228–9.   44. *Ibid.,* II, 222.

45. PHILLIPS, W. ALISON: *George Canning,* 122.

46. SHELLEY, FRANCES LADY: *op. cit.,* II, 146–7.

47. TEMPERLEY, H. W. V.: *op. cit.,* 240–7; LIEVEN, PRINCESS: *op. cit.,* 61–74.

48. *Dispatches, New Series,* II, 317–25.   49. *Ibid.,* II, 277.

50. *Ibid.,* II, 385.   51. *Ibid.,* II, 364–6.

52. TEMPERLEY, H. W. V.: *op. cit.,* 147; *Cambridge History of British Foreign Policy,* II, 74.

53. LIEVEN, PRINCESS: *Letters during her Residence in London* (ed. Robinson), 1902, 71.

54. SHELLEY, FRANCES LADY: *op. cit.,* II, 122.

55. *Dispatches, New Series,* II, 382.

56. DISRAELI, B.: *Coningsby*, II, i.

57. *Despatches, New Series*, II, 570–1.

58. *Parliamentary Debates*, March 7, 1825.

59. SHELLEY, FRANCES LADY: *op. cit.*, II, 128.

60. *Ibid.*, II, 124–5; HAYDON, B. R.: *op. cit.*, I, 375.

61. *Dispatches, New Series*, III, 53–6.

62. LIEVEN, PRINCESS: *Diary*, 110–11; TEMPERLEY, H. W. V., *op. cit.*, 352;
CRAWLEY, C. W.: *Greek Independence*, 1930, 54–5.

63. *Dispatches, New Series*, III, 113.

64. GREVILLE, C. C. F.: *op. cit.*, I, 79.

65. SHELLEY, FRANCES LADY: *op. cit.*, II, 143.

66. ELLESMERE, EARL OF: *op. cit.*, 77; FRASER, SIR W.: *op. cit.*, 34.

67. *Dispatches, New Series*, III, 113–38.

68. *Ibid.*, III, 142–50, 222; BUCHAN, S.: *The Sound of State: Wellington after
Waterloo*, 1928, 90.

69. *Ibid.*, III, 159.   70. *Ibid.*, III, 220.

71. LIEVEN, PRINCESS: *Diary*, 112–13.

72. *Dispatches, New Series*, III, 145.   73. *Ibid.*, III, 302.

74. CROKER, J. W.: *op. cit.*, I, 321.

75. *Dispatches, New Series*, III, 314, 343.

76. CROKER, J. W.: *op. cit.*, I, 330, 332–45.

77. TEMPERLEY, H. W. V.: *op. cit.*, 415–16.

78. *Dispatches, New Series*, III, 417–18.   79. *Ibid.*, III, 376.

80. *Ibid.*, III, 491–5.   81. *Ibid.*, III, 500.

82. *Ibid.*, III, 531–2.   83. *Ibid.*, III, 566.

84. CROKER, J. W.: *op. cit.*, I, 363.

85. PARKER, C. S., *op. cit.*, I, 452–3.

86. GREVILLE, C. C. F., *op. cit.*, I, 91–2.

87. WELLESLEY PAPERS: I, 164–5; *Dispatches, New Series*, III, 611.

88. *Ibid.*, I, 156–7.

89. TEMPERLEY, H. W. V.: *op. cit.*, 418–29.

90. *Dispatches, New Series*, III, 628–31.

III

1. *Dispatches, New Series*, III, 631.

2. *Ibid.*, IV, 34.   3. *Ibid.*, IV, 10.

4. TEMPERLEY, H. W. V.: *op. cit.*, 431–2.

5. *Dispatches, New Series*, III, 655.

6. SHELLEY, FRANCES LADY: *op. cit.*, II, 166.

7. *Parliamentary Debates*, May 2, 1827; *Dispatches, New Series*, IV, 16.

8. *Dispatches, New Series*, IV, 35–7.   9. *Ibid.*, IV, 63–70.

10. CREEVEY, T.: *op. cit.*, 463–4.

11. GALLATIN, J.: *op. cit.,* 269.

12. *Parliamentary Debates,* June 1, 12, 25, 1827.

13. *Dispatches, New Series,* III, 574.   14. *Ibid.,* IV, 76.

15. GREVILLE, C. C. F., *op. cit.,* I, 107–8.

16. DISRAELI, B.: *Endymion,* III.

17. *Dispatches, New Series,* IV, 97; *Letter to Lord Westmorland,* Aug. 17, 1827. In the author's possession.   18. *Ibid.,* IV, 102.

19. HAYDON, B. R.: *op. cit.,* I, 413–14.

20. SHELLEY, FRANCES LADY: *op. cit.,* II, 159, 166; LIEVEN, PRINCESS: *Correspondence with Earl Grey,* I, 61.

21. SHELLEY, FRANCES LADY, *op. cit.,* II, 167–9.

22. BURGHERSH, LADY: *op. cit.,* 39–41.

23. SHELLEY, FRANCES LADY: *op. cit.,* II, 171–2.

24. *Dispatches, New Series,* IV, 162–4, 167.

25. GREVILLE, C. C. F.: *op. cit.,* I, 116; *Dispatches, New Series,* IV, 169; CROKER, J. W.: *op. cit.,* I, 399, 401.

26. RAIKES, T.: *Journal,* 1858, II, 371.

27. *Dispatches, New Series,* IV, 183–4.

28. PARKER, C. S.: *op. cit.,* II, 28, 30.

29. *Dispatches, New Series,* IV, 20.

PRIME MINISTER

I

1. DISRAELI, B.: *Endymion,* III.

2. ID.: *Sybil,* I, iii.

3. WELLINGTON: *Letter to Colonel Stanhope,* Dec. 10, 1819. In the author's possession.

4. LOCKHART, J.: *op. cit.,* VII, 182.

5. MAXWELL, SIR H.: *op. cit.,* II, 194.   6. *Ibid.,* II, 240.

7. *Dispatches, New Series,* I, 195.

8. CROKER, J. W., *op. cit.,* I, 363.

9. FRASER, S. W.: *op. cit.,* 35.

II

1. *Dispatches, New Series,* IV, 201.

2. CROKER, J. W.: *op. cit.,* I, 404.

3. BULWER, SIR H.: *Life of Lord Palmerston,* 1870, I, 215–20.

4. *Dispatches, New Series,* IV, 209.   5. *Ibid.,* IV, 221.

6. CROKER, J. W.: *op. cit.,* I, 397.

7. *Dispatches, New Series*, IV, 253.

8. *Ibid.*, IV, 321.   9. *Ibid.*, IV, 268–9.

10. CREEVEY, T.: *op. cit.*, 498.

11. *Dispatches, New Series*, IV, 335.

12. *Parliamentary Debates*, Feb. 25, June 6, 1828.

13. BULWER, SIR H.: *op. cit.*, I, 226, 249.   14. *Ibid.*, I, 246, 250.

15. ELLENBOROUGH, LORD: *Political Diary*, 1828–1830, 1881, I, 98, 104.

16. *Ibid.*, I, 107.

17. BULWER, SIR H.: *op. cit.*, I, 253–8.

18. *Dispatches, New Series*, IV, 449.

19. BULWER, SIR H.: *op. cit.*, I, 259–66.

20. *Dispatches, New Series*, I, 450.

21. CROKER, J. W.: *op. cit.*, I, 423.

22. *Dispatches, New Series*, IV, 453.

23. ELLENBOROUGH, LORD: *op. cit.*, I, 112.   24. *Ibid.*, I, 116.

25. DISRAELI, B.: *Endymion*, V.

III

1. BUCHAN, S.: *op. cit.*, 130; BULWER, SIR H.: *op. cit.*, I, 286.

2. LIEVEN, PRINCESS: *Letters from London*, 157, 163.

3. *Dispatches, New Series*, IV, 499.

4. GREVILLE, C. C. F.: *op. cit.*, I, 135.

5. CRAWLEY, C. W.: *op. cit.*, 109.

6. ELLENBOROUGH, LORD: *op. cit.*, I, 167.

7. SHELLEY, FRANCES LADY: *op. cit.*, II, 177.

8. WELLESLEY, LORD G.: *Cheltenham Spa in Country Life*, Jan. 16, 1926.

9. SHELLEY, FRANCES LADY: *op. cit.*, II, 180; NEUMANN, P. v.: *op. cit.*,
I, 192.

10. *Dispatches, New Series*, IV, 683.

11. LIEVEN, PRINCESS: *Letters from London*, 146.

12. *Dispatches, New Series*, V, 70, 117–19, 153, 184–5; HAYDON, B. R.:
Autobiography, II, 453–7.

13. BURGHERSH, LADY: *op. cit.*, 44.

14. *Dispatches, New Series*, V, 244.

15. CREEVEY, T.: *op. cit.*, 494.

16. GREVILLE, C. C. F.: *op. cit.*, I, 142, 148, 156.

17. *Dispatches, New Series*, IV, 194.

18. OMAN, C. W. C.: *Wellington's Army*, 326.

19. *Parliamentary Debates*, April 28, 1828.

20. *Ibid.*, June 10, 1828.

21. *Dispatches, New Series*, IV, 564–70.

22. PARKER, C. S.: *op. cit.*, II, 56.

23. *Dispatches, New Series,* V, 44–5.

24. *Ibid.,* V, 133–6, 252–68.   25. *Ibid.,* V, 326.

26. *Parliamentary Debates,* Feb. 10, 1829.

27. GREVILLE, C. C. F.: *op. cit.,* I, 217.

28. ELLENBOROUGH, LORD: *op. cit.,* I, 325.   29. *Ibid.,* I, 337.

30. MAXWELL, SIR H.: *op. cit.,* II, 230–1.

31. GREVILLE, C. C. F.: *op. cit.,* I, 171.   32. *Ibid.,* I, 188.

33. ELLENBOROUGH, LORD: *op. cit.,* I, 368.

34. *Ibid.,* I, 376–7.   35. *Ibid.,* I, 374.

36. *Dispatches, New Series,* V, 518.   37. *Ibid.,* V, 585–6.

38. GREVILLE, C. C. F., *op. cit.,* I, 198.

39. *Dispatches, New Series,* V, 527, 531, 533–8.

40. *Ibid.,* V, 539–45; ELLENBOROUGH, LORD: *op. cit.,* I, 403; GREVILLE, C. C. F.: *op. cit.,* I, 192–3; MAXWELL, SIR H.: *op. cit.,* II, 234.

41. ELLENBOROUGH, LORD: *op. cit.,* I, 404; CREEVEY, T., *op. cit.,* 542; GREVILLE, C. C. F.: *op. cit.,* I, 195; SHELLEY, FRANCES LADY: *op. cit.,* II, 188.

42. *Dispatches, New Series,* V, 546–7, 554–5.

43. *Parliamentary Debates,* April 2, 1829.

44. *Ibid.,* April 10, 1829.

45. CROKER, J. W.: *op. cit.,* II, 11.

IV

1. CROKER, J. W.: *op. cit.,* II, 4.

2. LIEVEN, PRINCESS: *Letters from London,* 187.

3. GREVILLE, C. C. F.: *op. cit.,* I, 222.

4. CROKER, J. W.: *op. cit.,* II, 15.

5. *MS. Proceedings of the Wellington Testimonial Committee,* April, 1829. In the possession of Lord Gerald Wellesley.

6. HALÉVY, E.: *op. cit.,* I, 276.

7. ELLENBOROUGH, LORD: *op. cit.,* II, 14.

8. *Dispatches, New Series,* V, 592–7.   9. *Ibid.,* VI, 248.

10. GREVILLE, C. C. F.: *op. cit.,* I, 209; CREEVEY, T.: *op. cit.,* 543.

11. *Hamwood Papers,* 381.

12. GREVILLE, C. C. F.: *op. cit.,* I, 253.   13. *Ibid.,* I, 238.

14. *Dispatches, New Series,* VI, 198–9.   15. *Ibid.,* VI, 20.

16. GREVILLE, C. C. F.: *op. cit.,* I, 250.   17. *Ibid.,* I, 252.

18. *Dispatches, New Series,* VI, 294.

19. NEUMANN, P. v.: *op. cit.,* I, 200.

20. *Dispatches, New Series,* VI, 34.

21. CRAWLEY, C. W.: *op. cit.,* 165–73.

22. *Dispatches, New Series,* VI, 28.

23. BEALES, A. C. F.: *Foreign Policy of Wellington,* 1828–30 (unpublished thesis, University of London, 1927).

24. RAIKES, T.: *op. cit.,* I, 64.

25. GREVILLE, C. C. F.: *op. cit.,* I, 262, 266.

26. *Dispatches, New Series,* VI, 527.

27. *Ibid.,* VI, 529.   28. *Ibid.,* VI, 533.

29. GREVILLE, C. C. F.: *op. cit.,* I, 275; HALÉVY, E.: *op. cit.,* II, 300.

30. PARKER, S. C.: *op. cit.,* II, 154–6.

31. *Dispatches, New Series,* VII, 106–8.

32. CREEVEY, T.: *op. cit.,* 553; BRETT, O.: *op. cit.,* 228.

33. CREEVEY, T.: *op. cit.,* 554.

34. ELLENBOROUGH, LORD: *op. cit.,* II, 280.

35. GREVILLE, C. C. F.: *op. cit.,* II, 3.   36. *Ibid.,* II, 13–16.

37. BULWER, SIR H.: *op. cit.,* I, 361.

38. GREVILLE, C. C. F.: *op. cit.,* II, 42.

39. *Dispatches, New Series,* VII, 153.

40. GREVILLE, C. C. F.: *op. cit.,* II, 21.

41. *Dispatches, New Series,* VII, 157.   42. *Ibid.,* VII, 165.

43. HALÉVY, É.: *op. cit.,* III, 5; GUEDALLA, P.: *Palmerston,* 1926, 145.

44. GREVILLE, C. C. F.: *op. cit.,* II, 94–5; LIEVEN, PRINCESS: *Correspondence with Earl Grey,* I, 257–8, 261, 274.

45. *Dispatches, New Series,* VII, 12. ("As to my nomination of the Polignac ministry, I think there is no public man in Europe who has less to say to this event than I. Polignac never spoke to me of his intentions. I have never written to him, nor to the King, since the birth of the Duc de Bordeaux, nor to the Duc d'Angoulême; nor have I communicated with anyone in France upon internal affairs.") Cf. *Parliamentary Debates,* March 28, 1831.

46. BUTLER, J. R. M.: *Passing of the Great Reform Bill,* 1914, 85–9.

47. *Ibid.,* 90.

48. *Dispatches, New Series,* I, 207.   49. *Ibid.,* VII, 226.

50. GREVILLE, C. C. F.: *op. cit.,* II, 94; RAMSAY, A. A. W.: *Sir Robert Peel,* 1928, 134.

51. *Dispatches, New Series,* VII, 352–3.

52. *Dispatches, New Series,* VII, 300–1, 322.

53. ELLESMERE, EARL OF: *op. cit.,* 62; ELLENBOROUGH, LORD: *op. cit.,* II, 417.

54. RAMSAY, A. A. W.: *op. cit.,* 135.

55. *The Times,* Sept. 13, 1930; SHELLEY, FRANCES LADY: *op. cit.,* II, 202; ELLENBOROUGH, LORD: *op. cit.,* II, 370.

56. *Dispatches, New Series,* VII, 281, 328; MAXWELL, SIR H.: *op. cit.,* II, 252–3; BULWER, SIR H.: *op. cit.,* II, 362–4; LIEVEN, PRINCESS: *Letters from London,* 262.

521

57. *Dispatches, New Series*, VII, 307–9; HAYDON, B. R.: *Autobiography*, II, 496–7.

58. *Parliamentary Debates*, Nov. 2, 1830.

59. RAMSAY, A. A. W.: *op. cit.*, 136.

60. ELLENBOROUGH, LORD: *op. cit.*, II, 417; GREVILLE, C. C. F.: *op. cit.*, II, 54–5.

61. *Dispatches, New Series*, VII, 354–5.

62. ELLENBOROUGH, LORD: *op. cit.*, II, 418–22.

63. BUTLER, J. R. N.: *op. cit.*, 102.

64. ELLENBOROUGH, LORD: *op. cit.*, II, 423.

65. LIEVEN, PRINCESS: *Letters from London*, 277; GREVILLE, C. C. F.: *op. cit.*, II, 61; LADY DOVER: *Letter to Lady C. Lascelles*, Nov. 18, 1830. In the possession of Mrs. Lascelles, Woolbeding; DUCHESS OF SUTHERLAND: *Letter to Lady C. Lascelles*, Nov. 18, 1830. *Ibid.*

66. *Dispatches, New Series*, VII, 361.

REARGUARD ACTION

I

1. ROGERS, S.: *op. cit.*, 220.

2. *Dispatches, New Series*, VII, 368.

3. LIEVEN, PRINCESS: *Letters from London*, 277.

4. GREVILLE, C. C. F.: *op. cit.*, II, 63.

5. *Dispatches, New Series*, VII, 373–5.

6. *Ibid.*, VII, 382–5; GLEIG, G. R.: *op. cit.*, 50–3.

7. LIEVEN, PRINCESS: *Letters from London*, 82.

8. CROKER, J. W.: *op. cit.*, II, 80–1; GREVILLE, C. C. F.: *op. cit.*, II, 80.

9. *Dispatches, New Series*, VII, 387.

10. CROKER, J. W.: *op. cit.*, II, 104; *Dispatches, New Series*, VII, 399–400.

11. *Dispatches, New Series*, VII, 409–10.

12. BURGHERSH, LADY: *op. cit.*, 51.

13. MAXWELL, SIR H.: *op. cit.*, II, 257.

14. *Observer*, Feb. 20, 1831.

15. *Parliamentary Debates*, March 24, 28, 1831.

16. *Dispatches, New Series*, VII, 425–8.

17. EDGEWORTH, M.: *op. cit.*, II, 174–6.

18. Information supplied by Georgiana, Viscountess Gough.

19. *Dispatches, New Series*, VII, 432.

20. ARBUTHNOT, P.: *Memories of the Arbuthnots*, 1920, 224.

21. *Dispatches, New Series*, VII, 557–8.

22. STANHOPE, EARL: *op. cit.*, 13.

23. *Dispatches, New Series*, VII, 470, 530.

24. GLEIG, G. R.: *op. cit.*, 59.   25. *Ibid.*, 68–82.

26. GREVILLE, C. C. F.: *op. cit.*, II, 153–4.

27. *Dispatches, New Series*, VII, 436; GREVILLE, C. C. F.: *op. cit.*, II, 159, 185.

28. *Dispatches, New Series*, VII, 493.

29. GREVILLE, C. C. F.: *op. cit.*, II, 189–92.   30. *Ibid.*, II, 197–9.

31. *Parliamentary Debates*, Oct. 4, 1831.

32. MORLEY, J.: *Life of Gladstone*, 1903, I, 75.

33. *Dispatches, New Series*, VII, 561; GLEIG, G. R.: *op. cit.*, 102–3.

34. STANHOPE, EARL: *op. cit.*, 32.

35. *Dispatches, New Series*, VIII, 30–4.   36. *Ibid.*, VIII, 143–5.

37. *Ibid.*, VIII, 71.   38. *Ibid.*, VIII, 98–9.

39. *Ibid.*, VIII, 147, 213; NEUMANN, P. v.: *op. cit.*, I, 263, 268–9.

40. *Ibid.*, VIII, 157–8.   41. *Ibid.*, VIII, 155.

42. *Ibid.*, VIII, 153.   43. *Ibid.*, VIII, 169.

44. GREVILLE, C. C. F.: *op. cit.*, II, 272.

45. *Parliamentary Debates*, April 10, 1832.

46. *Dispatches, New Series*, VIII, 280.

47. CROKER, J. W.: *op. cit.*, II, 150.

48. RAIKES, T.: *op. cit.*, 16–17.

49. *Dispatches, New Series*, VIII, 289.

50. DISRAELI, B.: *Endymion*, viii.

51. *Dispatches, New Series*, VIII, 340.

52. CROKER, J. W.: *op. cit.*, II, 154–69; GREVILLE, C. C. F.: *op. cit.*, II, 294–304, 340–1; DISRAELI, B.: *Coningsby*, I, vii, *Endymion*, viii.

53. *Dispatches, New Series*, VIII, 304.

54. BUTLER, J. R. M.: *op. cit.*, 396–7.

55. RAIKES, T.: *op. cit.*, I, 19.

56. *Dispatches, New Series*, VIII, 322.

57. STANHOPE, EARL: *op. cit.*, 176; SWINTON, J. R.: *op. cit.*, 166–8; FRASER, SIR W.: *op. cit.*, 21–3, 206; RAIKES, T.: *op. cit.*, I, 33; TUPPER, M.: *My Life as an Author*, 1886, 66; FROUDE, J. R.: *Carlyle's Early Life* (ed. 1896), II, 305; MAXWELL, SIR H.: *op. cit.*, II, 271; *Dispatches, New Series*, VIII; ROGERS, S.: *op. cit.*, 224–5.

II

1. MAXWELL, SIR H.: *op. cit.*, II, 270–1, 273; *Dispatches, New Series*, VIII, 380–1.

2. *Dispatches, New Series*, VIII, 361, 367–8.

3. *Ibid.*, VIII, 492.   4. *Ibid.*, VIII, 435.

5. *Ibid.,* VIII, 472–3. 6. *Ibid.,* VIII, 357.

7. CROKER, J. W.: *op. cit.,* II, 224.

8. FRASER, SIR W.: *op. cit.,* 11.

9. GREVILLE, C. C. F.: *op. cit.,* II, 363; MAXWELL, SIR H.: *op. cit.,* II, 274.

10. MAXWELL, SIR H.: *op. cit.,* II, 276. 11. *Ibid.,* 275, 277.

12. HAYDON, B. R.: *Autobiography,* II, 560.

13. GREVILLE, C. C. F.: *op. cit.,* II, 372.

14. RAIKES, T.: *op. cit.,* I, 104.

15. GREVILLE, C. C. F.: *op. cit.,* II, 380.

16. STANHOPE, EARL: *op. cit.,* 36. 17. *Ibid.,* 48.

18. MAXWELL, SIR H.: *op. cit.,* II, 289; SHELLEY, FRANCES LADY: *op. cit.,* II, 231.

19. SHELLEY, FRANCES LADY: *op. cit.,* II, 253; ELLESMERE, EARL OF: *op. cit.,* 46; FRASER, SIR W.: *op. cit.,* 159–61; CROKER, J. W.: *op. cit.,* II, 227–8; RAIKES, T., *op. cit.,* II, 373.

20. CREEVEY, T.: *op. cit.,* 628; MAXWELL, SIR H.: *op. cit.,* II, 296; GREVILLE, C. C. F.: *op. cit.,* III, 116; SHELLEY, FRANCES LADY: *op. cit.,* II, 252–7; LIEVEN, PRINCESS: *Correspondence with Earl Grey,* III, 2.

21. *Dispatches, New Series,* VIII, 147–9.

22. *Letters of the Duke of Wellington to Miss J.* (ed. C. T. Herrick), 1924, 39, 41; cf. MOORE, GEORGE: *Le Revers d'un Grand Homme* in *Impressions and Opinions* (ed. 1913).

23. MAXWELL, SIR H.: *op. cit.,* II, 210–11.

24. *Letters to Miss J.,* 42. 25. *Ibid.,* 43–7.

26. *Ibid.,* 49 27. *Ibid.,* 51–2. 28. *Ibid.,* 53.

29. *Ibid.,* 59–60. 30. *Ibid.,* 44, 63. 31. *Ibid.,* 65–90.

32. *Ibid.,* 91, 95, 103. 33. *Ibid.,* 105–6.

34. *Ibid.,* 118, 120, 122, 129–32. 35. *Ibid.,* 134–6.

36. *Ibid.,* 141–2. 37. *Ibid.,* 164. 38. *Ibid.,* 168.

39. *Ibid.,* 171. 40. *Ibid.,* 173. 41. *Ibid.,* 182–4.

42. *Ibid.,* 194–207. 43. *Ibid.,* 214. 44. *Ibid.,* 215–16.

III

1. DISRAELI, B.: *Coningsby,* II, iii.

2. STANHOPE, EARL.: *op. cit.,* 230.

3. PARKER, C. S.: *op. cit.,* 252.

4. STANHOPE, EARL: *op. cit.,* 62.

5. GREVILLE, C. C. F.: *op. cit.,* III, 149. 6. *Ibid.,* III, 155.

7. DISRAELI, B.: *Coningsby,* II, iv.

8. MAXWELL, SIR H.: *op. cit.,* II, 303.

9. RAIKES, T.: *op. cit.,* I, 235–6.

10. WELLINGTON: *Letter to B. Disraeli*, Jan. 3, 1835, *Apsley House Papers*; MONYPENNY, W. F.: *Life of Disraeli*, 1910, I, 246–7, 275.

11. WELLINGTON: *Letter to Fellows*, March 23, 1835, *Apsley House Papers*.

12. MAXWELL, SIR H.: *op. cit.*, II, 306.

IV

1. RAIKES, T.: *op. cit.*, I, 294–5.
2. GREVILLE, C. C. F.: *op. cit.*, III, 216.
3. DISRAELI, B.: *The Young Duke*, V, vi.
4. GREVILLE, C. C. F.: *op. cit.*, III, 232.
5. MONYPENNY, W. F.: *op. cit.*, I, 335.
6. *Gladstone Papers*, 1930, 23.
7. HAYDON, B. R.: *Autobiography* (ed. Davies), II, 579–84.
8. SWINTON, J. R.: *op. cit.*, 157–8.
9. PARKER, C. S.: *op. cit.*, II, 321.
10. BURGHERSH, LADY: *op. cit.*, 73.
11. GREVILLE, C. C. F.: *op. cit.*, III, 403.
12. *Ibid.*, III, 396; CREEVEY, T.: *op. cit.*, 662; BRETT, O.: *op. cit.*, 250.

APOTHEOSIS

I

1. ELLESMERE, EARL OF: *op. cit.*, 177.
2. RAIKES, T.: *op. cit.*, II, 378.
3. GLEIG, G. R.: *op. cit.*, 285–7.
4. SWINTON, J. R.: *op. cit.*, 146; RAIKES, T.: *op. cit.*, I, 455.
5. GRANT DUFF, SIR M. E.: *A Victorian Vintage: Selections from Diaries* (ed. A. Tilney Bassett), 1930, 103.
6. FRASER, SIR W.: *op. cit.*, 203; SWINTON, J. R.: *op. cit.*, 147.
7. RAIKES, T.: *op. cit.*, II, 373–4, 380–6.   8. *Ibid.*, II, 369.
9. *Ibid.*, II, 386–7; CONWAY, SIR M.: *Walmer Castle in Country Life*, Nov. 1, 8, 1919.
10. CURZON, MARQUESS: *Personal History of Walmer Castle and its Lords Warden*, 1927, 181, 256–7.
11. WELLINGTON: *Letter to Townshend*, Dec. 29, 1848. In the author's possession; *Letter to S. S. Curling*, April 24, 1844. *Ibid.*; CURZON, MARQUESS: *op. cit.*, 177.
12. WELLINGTON: *Memoranda to Capt. Watts*, Nov. 1838, *Walmer MSS.*; *Letter to Miss Edwards*, Aug. 11, 1847. *Ibid.*
13. CURZON, MARQUESS: *op. cit.*, 253.

14. *Ibid.*, 173.   15. *Ibid.*, 227.   16. *Ibid.*, 188.
17. MAYDON, B. R.: *Autobiography*, II, 644–65.
18. WELLINGTON, EVELYN DUCHESS OF: *Catalogue of Pictures and Sculpture at Apsley House*, 1901, II, 376.
19. BRIALMONT AND GLEIG: *op. cit.*, IV, 148.
20. CURZON, MARQUESS: *op. cit.*, 214–19.
21. WELLINGTON: *Memorandum*, Nov. 19, 1842; *Walmer MSS*.
22. CURZON, MARQUESS: *op. cit.*, 195.
23. BRIALMONT AND GLEIG: *op. cit.*, IV, 162–3, 166–7.
24. FORSTER, J.: *Life of Charles Dickens* (ed. Everyman's Library), II, 81.
25. KERR, MARK: *Land, Sea, and Air*, 1927, 345.
26. CURZON, MARQUESS: *op. cit.*, 176.
27. STANHOPE, EARL: *op. cit.*, 107–8.
28. WELLINGTON: *Letter to Lady Robert Grosvenor*, Walmer, Sept. 19, 1839. In the possession of Hon. Mrs. Maurice Glyn.
29. WELLINGTON: *Latter to Lady Robert Grosvenor*, Dec. 30, 1839. *Ibid.*
30. SWINTON, J. R.: *op. cit.*, 153.
31. CURZON, MARQUESS: *op. cit.*, 177; GRANT DUFF, SIR M. E.: *op. cit.*, 58.
32. FORSTER, J.: *op. cit.*, I, 409.
33. MAXWELL, SIR H.: *op. cit.*, II, 374; FRASER, SIR W.: *op. cit.*, 34; ELLESMERE, EARL OF: *op. cit.*, 77–8.
34. ELLESMERE, EARL OF: *op. cit.*, 174.
35. BURGHERSH, LADY: *op. cit.*, 83, 113.   36. *Ibid.*, 131.
37. WARD, D.: *A Romance of the Nineteenth Century*, 77–183; *cf.* GLEIG, G. R.: *op. cit.*, 290–3.

II

1. DISRAELI, B.: *Whigs and Whiggism* (ed. Hutcheon), 379.
2. BORROW, G.: *The Romany Rye*, 1857, Ap., chap. x.
3. WILSON, D. A.: *Carlyle at his Zenith*, 1927, 286.
4. FROUDE, J. A.: *Carlyle's Life in London* (ed. Silver Library), II, 413.
5. *Ibid.*, II, 48–9.
6. GREVILLE, C. C. F.: *op. cit.*, III, 408.
7. MAXWELL, SIR H.: *op. cit.*, II, 312.   8. *Ibid.*, II, 316.
9. *Ibid.*, II, 315.   10. *Ibid.*, II, 313.   11. *Ibid.*, II, 332.
12. VICTORIA, QUEEN: *Girlhood*, 1912, II, 163–75.
13. DISRAELI, B.: *Sybil*, IV, xiv; STANHOPE, EARL: *op. cit.*, 140.
14. WELLINGTON: *Letters to Lady Shelley and others*, May 10, 1839, *Apsley House Papers*.
15. STANHOPE, EARL: *op. cit.*, 194.
16. BURGHERSH, LADY: *op. cit.*, 139.
17. STANHOPE, EARL: *op. cit.*, 133.

18. WELLINGTON: *Letter to Miss C. . . .* May 2, 1846. In the author's possession.

19. STANHOPE, EARL: *op. cit.*, 296.

20. BURGHERSH, LADY: *op. cit.*, 143.

21. STANHOPE, EARL: *op. cit.*, 197–213.

22. CROKER, J. W.: *op. cit.*, II, 358–9; GREVILLE, C. C. F.: *op. cit.*, 267–9, 271.

23. *Ibid.*, 236–7, 264, 283.

24. *Punch*, IX (1845), quoted in MAXWELL, SIR H.: *op. cit.*, II, 335; information supplied by Miss Redgrave.

25. ABERDEEN, EARL OF: *Letter to Wellington*, Oct. 26, 1841, *Raikes Papers, Pierpoint Morgan Library, New York*; GREVILLE, C. C. F.: *op. cit.*, II, 59.

26. RAIKES, T.: *Private Correspondence with the Duke of Wellington*, 1861, 161, 196–7, 262–3.

27. *Parliamentary Debates*, April 6, 1840.   28. *Ibid.*, 62, 375.

29. STANHOPE, EARL: *op. cit.*, 195.

30. RAIKES, T.: *op. cit.*, 384–5.

31. PARKER, C. S.: *op. cit.*, II, 461.

32. GREVILLE, C. C. F.: *op. cit.*, II, 34.

33. VICTORIA, QUEEN: *Letters*, I, 389.

34. GREVILLE, C. C. F.: *op. cit.*, II, 58–9.

35. *Ibid.*, II, 77, 243; VICTORIA, QUEEN: *Letters*, I, 472.

36. GREVILLE, C. C. F.: *op. cit.*, II, 145.   37. *Ibid.*, II, 139.

38. *Ibid.*, II, 223.

39. VICTORIA, QUEEN: *Letters*, II, 130–5.

40. GREVILLE, C. C. F.: *op. cit.*, II, 351.

41. MAXWELL, SIR H.: *op. cit.*, II, 341.

42. CROKER, J. W.: *op. cit.*, III, 39.

43. *Ibid.*, III, 113.

44. VICTORIA, QUEEN: *Letters*, II, 74.

45. CROKER, J. W.: *op. cit.*, III, 52–5.

46. MAXWELL, SIR H.: *op. cit.*, II, 351.   47. *Ibid.*, II, 352.

48. *Ibid.*, II, 355.

49. GREVILLE, C. C. F.: *op. cit.*, II, 417.

50. WELLINGTON: *Letters to Lord John Russell*, 1846–50, *Pierpoint Morgan Library, New York; Russell Papers, Public Record Office.*

51. BURGHERSH, LADY: *op. cit.*, 197–8.

52. GREVILLE, C. C. F.: *op. cit.*, III, 75–6.

53. SHELLEY, FRANCES LADY: *op. cit.*, II, 272–89, 410–11.

54. HAYDON, B. R.: *Letter to Kendall* (undated). In the author's possession; *Autobiography*, II, 777.

55. HAYDON, B. R.: *op. cit.*, II, 684.

527

56. *Ibid.*, II, 642; CROKER, J. W.: *op. cit.*, III, 124.

57. ARBUTHNOT, C.: *Letter to Wellington*, Sept. 24, 1846. In the author's possession.

58. CROKER, J. W.: *op. cit.*, III, 126.

59. GREVILLE, C. C. F.: *op. cit.*, III, 91.

60. CROKER, J. W.: *op. cit.*, III, 128.

61. WELLINGTON: *Letter to Lord J. Russell*, July 10, 1847. In the possession of the Marquess of Lansdowne.

62. VICTORIA, QUEEN: *Letters*, II, 145–6.

63. MAXWELL, SIR H.: *op. cit.*, II, 368–70.

64. METTERNICH, PRINCE DE: *Mémoires*, VIII, 16–19, 24, 33, 51.

III

1. PARKER, C. S.: *op. cit.*, III, 546.

2. FRASER, SIR W.: *op. cit.*, 6.

3. BRIALMONT AND GLEIG: *op. cit.*, IV, 151–2.

4. BURGHCLERE, LADY: *A Great Man's Friendship: Letters of the Duke of Wellington to Mary, Marchioness of Salisbury, 1850–1852*, 1927, 73; BURGHERSH, LADY: *op. cit.*, 193.

5. SHELLEY, FRANCES, LADY: *op. cit.*, II, 312–13.

6. BURGHCLERE, LADY: *op. cit.*, 6.   7. *Ibid.*, vii.

8. *Ibid.*, 131.   9. *Ibid.*, 76, 80, 122, 321.

10. *Ibid.*, 86–7, 226–8.   11. *Ibid.*, 93, 112, 127.

12. *Ibid.*, 68–9, 208, 228.   13. *Ibid.*, 111.

14. MARTIN, SIR T.: *Life of the Prince Consort*, 1876, II, 253–62.

15. THACKERAY, W. M.: *Lines on a Late Hospicious Ewent*, 1850.

16. MARTIN, SIR T.: *op. cit.*, II, 265.

17. BURGHCLERE, LADY: *op. cit.*, 130–3, 135–7, 150.

18. *Ibid.*, 181.   19. *Ibid.*, 200.   20. *Ibid.*, 194.

21. GREVILLE, C. C. F.: *op. cit.*, III, 389; VICTORIA, QUEEN: *Letters*, II, 371–3; MONYPENNY, W. F., AND BUCKLE, G. E.: *op. cit.*, III, 295–6.

22. MONYPENNY, W. F., AND BUCKLE, G. E.: *op. cit.*, III, 348.

23. *Parliamentary Debates*, June 15, 1852.

24. BURGHCLERE, LADY: *op. cit.*, 270.

25. *Parliamentary Debates*, June 22, 1852.

26. CURZON, MARQUESS: *op. cit.*, 255.

27. BURGHCLERE, LADY: *op. cit.*, 311.

28. *Ibid.*, 312–15.

29. *Ibid.*, 318–20; CROKER, J. W.: *op. cit.*, III, 272–80.

30. *Ibid.*, 325–6; 329–30.

31. *Ibid.*, 331; BURGHERSH, LADY: *op. cit.*, 201–2.

32. MAXWELL, SIR H.: *op. cit.*, II, 386.

IV

Official Programme of the Public Funeral of the late Field-Marshal, Arthur Duke of Wellington, K.G., as issued by the authority of the Earl-Marshal, 1852; *Order of Proceedings and Ceremonies observed in the Public Funeral of the late Field-Marshal, Arthur Duke of Wellington, K.G.,* 1852; *The Times,* Nov. 11–19, 1852; *Illustrated London News,* Nov. 20, 1852; FROUDE, J. A.: *op. cit.,* II, 135–6; HODDER, E.: *Life of Lord Shaftesbury,* 1886, II, 337–8; MALMESBURY, EARL OF: *Memoirs of an Ex-Minister* (ed. in 1 vol.), 1885, 278–9; MARTIN, SIR T.: *op. cit.,* II, 464–72; MONYPENNY, W. F., AND BUCKLE, G. E.: *op. cit.,* III, 393–4, 578–80; REDGRAVE, F. M.: *Richard Redgrave,* 1891, 100–4; STANLEY, LADY AUGUSTA: *Letters, 1849–1863* (ed. Baillie and Bolitho), 1927, 46; TENNYSON, A.: *Ode on the Death of the Duke of Wellington,* 1852; TENNYSON, H.: *Alfred Lord Tennyson* (ed. in 1 vol.), 1905, 302; VICTORIA, QUEEN: *Letters,* II, 478–9, 487.

INDEX

531